YOUR MOTHER'S NOT A VIRGIN!

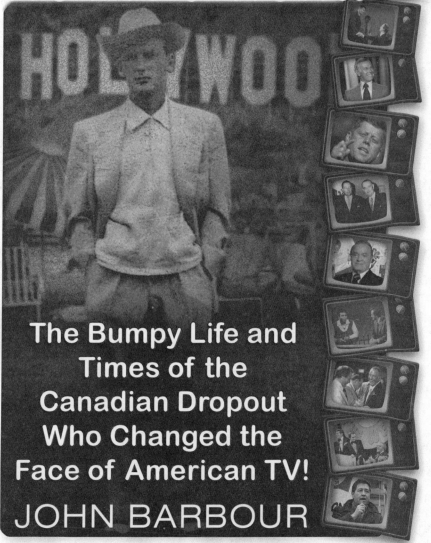

The Bumpy Life and Times of the Canadian Dropout Who Changed the Face of American TV!

JOHN BARBOUR

Your Mother's Not a Virgin: The Bumpy Life & Times of the Canadian Dropout Who Changed the Face of American TV

Published by:
Trine Day LLC
PO Box 577
Walterville, OR 97489
1-800-556-2012
www.TrineDay.com
trineday@icloud.com

Library of Congress Control Number: 2019931485

Barbour, John.
Inheritance – 1st ed.
p. cm.
Epub (ISBN-13) 978-1-63424-247-9
Kindle (ISBN-13) 978-1-63424-248-6
Print (ISBN-13) 978-1-63424-246-2
1. Barbour, John, 1933 -- . 2. Television personalities -- United States -- Autobiography. 3. Kennedy, John F. -- (John Fitzgerald), -- 1917-1963 -- Assassination.. 4. Garrison, Jim, -- 1921-1992. 5. Conspiracies -- United States -- History -- 20th century. I. Title

Original cover design by David Lispi

First Edition
10 9 8 7 6 5 4 3 2 1

Printed in the USA

Distribution to the Trade by:
Independent Publishers Group (IPG)
814 North Franklin Street
Chicago, Illinois 60610
312.337.0747
www.ipgbook.com

All the world's a stage,
And all the men and women merely players;
They have their exits and their entrances,
And one man in his time plays many parts,
His acts being seven ages. At first, the infant,
Mewling and puking in the nurse's arms.
Then the whining schoolboy, with his satchel
And shining morning face, creeping like snail
Unwillingly to school. And then the lover,
Sighing like furnace, with a woeful ballad
Made to his mistress' eyebrow. Then a soldier,
Full of strange oaths and bearded like the pard,
Jealous in honor, sudden and quick in quarrel,
Seeking the bubble reputation
Even in the cannon's mouth. And then the justice,
In fair round belly with good capon lined,
With eyes severe and beard of formal cut,
Full of wise saws and modern instances;
And so he plays his part. The sixth age shifts
Into the lean and slippered pantaloon,
With spectacles on nose and pouch on side;
His youthful hose, well saved, a world too wide
For his shrunk shank, and his big manly voice,
Turning again toward childish treble, pipes
And whistles in his sound. Last scene of all,
That ends this strange eventful history,
Is second childishness and mere oblivion,
Sans teeth, sans eyes, sans taste, sans everything.

– William Shakspeare,
As You Like It, Act II, Scene VII

Introduction

By Donald Jefferies

Like most people, I knew the name John Barbour primarily from the hit television program *Real People,* which he co-hosted. I didn't realize at the time that he'd also created it, and had such an extensive background in show business, or that he was the only individual to ever win Emmys for both news and entertainment. It wasn't until I watched the excellent documentary *The Jim Garrison Tapes* that I really took notice of John Barbour. I knew from researching the JFK assassination for many years just how unusual it was for someone in the entertainment world to publicly dispute the findings of the Warren Commission.

When I linked up with John Barbour on Facebook, I was pleasantly surprised at how friendly and responsive he was. I thought it was me; as it turned out, I wasn't anything special. After talking with him on the phone and then meeting him, I can tell you that John Barbour treats everyone that way. He has a respect for people that is rare in celebrities with one tenth of his resume. From his down-to-earth demeanor, you'd never know that he was Frank Sinatra's personal writer for several years, until their friendship ended over Barbour's defense of the embattled Thomas Noguchi, "the coroner to the stars." Or Lucille Ball's favorite writer. Or friends with the likes of Lenny Bruce, Neil Simon, Tim Conway and Tom Brokaw. Or Jim Garrison's Boswell, as the controversial New Orleans District Attorney talked only to him in the ten years following the Clay Shaw trial. You'd think he was just a pleasant, gregarious guy who cracks jokes and has a lot of interesting stories. He is all that, but he's also brilliant, and those jokes are the kind you might have heard on classic sitcoms like *Gomer Pyle USMC* and those stories are often personal anecdotes about some of the most famous people of the twentieth century.

Your Mother's Not a Virgin! is not your typical celebrity memoir. John Barbour recounts all the ups and downs of a fascinating show business career that has been an emotional roller coaster of thrills and disappointments. But he doesn't do so as an aging celebrity anxious to cash in one last time, hoping to bask in the figurative cheers of book sales. Barbour constantly fought the powers that be, at every level, and unapologetically still fights them. He lost at least as much as he won, but he never abandoned his convictions.

The cast of characters here is immense; everyone from top television network executives to the most powerful agents in the business, to screen legends like Cary Grant make an appearance in these pages. There is a memorable midnight dinner with George Burns among the recollections. There are fascinating behind-the-scenes anecdotes from Dean Martin's celebrity roasts, a slew of talk shows, and game shows. The list of those Barbour interviewed alone is mightily impressive; Muhammad Ali, Ronald Reagan, Jane Fonda, legendary mobster Mickey Cohen, and Cesar Chavez, to name just a few. He also dodged retaliation from powerful figures like Sam Peckinpah, Johnny Carson, Jerry Lewis, and Bob Hope. He worked alongside Tom Brokaw, Tom Snyder, a young Bryant Gumbel and a younger Robin Williams. His pride in the number one television show *Real People* is justified; as the father and instrumental mover behind it, Barbour's affinity for and interest in ordinary people with unusual abilities, hobbies, or interests sprung from the same populist instinct that inspired Frank Capra's films. Many of the stories he told on that program were socially important, and all of them moved audiences emotionally. Barbour's real life drama associated with this series, which included the murder of the attorney representing him during a powerful industry mogul's blatant attempt to steal credit for *Real People*, would make for a riveting film. In fact, Barbour comes off in this book as very much like a Jimmy Stewart or Gary Cooper character in a Capra movie, albeit one who sprinkles his conversation with the word "fuck."

John Barbour is eighty five years old, but he has lived a life full enough for someone twice as old. From his Dickensian childhood in Canada, to the London stage, to Hollywood, and finally working with Jim Garrison on exposing the killers of John F. Kennedy, John Barbour has displayed determination and unfailing courage. And he's managed to do it all with an old- fashioned, unique kind of civility. Having lost his faith in God during his miserable childhood, Barbour nevertheless navigated through the vipers and parasites of show business for decades, with a morality and set of principles that would put most devout believers to shame. Whether it's his own harrowing treatment at the hands of his flawed parents, or the most outrageous corruption on the part of our government, Barbour describes it all with an upbeat, never failing sense of humor. The reader can see the smile on his face, hear the soft chuckle, and feel the immense love and pride he has for Sarita, his wife of many years, and Christopher, his prodigal son turned very successful producer and screenwriter. John Barbour's life story would be fascinating, even if he hadn't succeeded in Hollywood. I was even a bit reminded of *David Copperfield* as I made my way through this book, which is nearly as long. Like many critics, I consider *David Copperfield* to be the greatest novel ever written in the English language, so that is no small compliment, and this book is no small achievement.

Your Mother's Not a Virgin! is a celebration of an extraordinary life, told by a man of immense talent who almost certainly would blanch at being called extraordinary. Barbour remains the critic he was for most of his career, as he assesses everyone and everything with a finely honed skill. I was honored just to read this book, let alone be asked to write an Introduction for it, and I'm even prouder to call John Barbour my friend. He is fond of not only attributing much of his success to luck, which very few people in life are wont to do, but of saying all the good things that happened to him happened accidentally. With all due respect, this astounding book was no accident; it was the culmination of over fifty years of struggle in one of the world's most difficult fields. Barbour's controversial reputation was hard earned; he bluntly confronted authorities of all stripes over their lack of integrity. His work, from the short-lived talk shows to *Real People* to his outstanding documentary on Ernie Kovacs to his recent, groundbreaking film *The American Media and the Second Assassination of President John F. Kennedy*, has produced a legacy anyone would be proud of. This book is the extra thick, delicious icing on the cake.

At forty six years of age, and unemployed, John told Morrie Gelman of *Daily Variety* that one day this Canadian dropout would change the face of American TV with what he called the "Entertainment of Reality." One year later, naturally by accident, he did just that. Now Barbour has been just as emphatic in declaring that this is absolutely the best autobiography ever written. Somehow, he can sound modest while making such a claim. After reading this thoroughly engrossing and captivating book, few readers will disagree with him.

Table of Contents

Foreword

This is the place where most authors/writers list the countless folks who have had something positive to do with either the writing of the book or the living of their lives. Not me. I am only going to thank two people. First, of course, my wife Sarita. If I didn't thank her for being my first biggest fan and best friend before I even had a real fan or a real job, I would feel guilty, and she might be so pissed I would not even be able to finish this paragraph, let alone the book. But this is no obligatory mentioning of a spouse. For years, every morning when I woke up, I was surprised she was still there. Living with a comic is like living with an emotional wife beater. As you read about her along the way, you will discover one of the most amazing humans ever encountered, as I did; the only human I ever met who envied no one. The only human I ever met, so at peace with herself that just getting up every morning at five, which she did every single day, ill or otherwise, for nearly fifty years, was a joy.

The other person I need to thank is James Griffith. I know very little about James. I've never been to his office. All I know is that he is about my son's age, nearly six feet tall, a full head of wavy hair, and a perfect smile, and is the enthusiastic president of a boutique publishing enterprise called Wordsmith Media. A nice name. I cannot even recall when I met him. But I do recall a phone call from him over five years ago. It was just after I had done my first interview with George Knapp, the Sunday night host, and best host of *Coast to Coast,* right here in Las Vegas. This led to my becoming a monthly regular on the controversial, but soft-spoken Jeff Rense internet show.

Evidently James had heard me a number of times. In his unexpected call, he told me he had been a huge fan of *Real People* as a kid and had only tuned in out of curiosity to see whatever happened to me. He said that no matter how much he loved me on *Real People,* though, the show I created, as well as co-hosted, he loved me telling those stories on the radio, and that he wanted more of them, especially in book form. I put him off, and found countless reasons to put off even starting: It was too hot. There's a mosquito in the room. Need to hit golf balls first. There's a weird noise outside. I have a stomach ache. Those pictures on the wall are crooked. But the morning after every show he would call again. He became a very pleasant pest. Who wouldn't like to hear how wonderful they were?

So, haltingly, five years ago I began. When I write, I write very quickly; that is when I write. To that end I feel exactly like Dorothy Parker did. Dorothy Parker was a brilliant writer/poet, one of the great wits who used to assemble at the famous Algonquin Round Table in New York, along with Robert Benchley and Alexander Woolcott, and half a dozen other quotable long-forgotten scribes. But she was the most quoted. One of my favorites of her's applies to me. She said: "I hate writing, but I love having written." That indeed was me. To be truthful, though, and in this book you will find a tsunami of truth-telling, I would have begun it without James badgering. Why? Because I always wanted to write a book about my life. We all do. But I am certain I had this self-centered thought long before any other human. The first time I thought that my life would make an interesting story I was eight.

It was January 1941 in Toronto. I was standing in my front yard not too warmly dressed in twenty-degree windy weather watching hints of snowflakes trying to avoid hitting the ground. I was fiddling with my battered hockey stick. Occasionally, I looked up at the bare branches of the lone maple tree in our front yard, and down to my moccasins filled with newspapers to help keep out the chill and hide the holes. I was waiting for my buddies to play street hockey. I was also waiting for my mother to come home from Buffalo where she had gone with one of my new "uncles." I daydreamed of the days before my father had gone off to the peace and quiet of World War II.

True, it was cold and I was alone. But I didn't feel alone and felt no chill. I was warmed with the expectations of again being Wally Stanowski of the Toronto Maple Leafs. It wasn't that I would soon have my teammates and enemies joining me to battle for The Stanley Cup, it was because I had myself for company. For reasons beyond my understanding or analyzing, I have always enjoyed my own company, and the images and thoughts that were always rolling around in my head. The deeper mystery was that I never had a negative thought. Anger, yes. Rage, yes. Disgust, yes. Love and laughter, yes, And often. But negativity was to me as absent as the leaves from the tree over my head. It was there that I first thought that my little life would make one hell of a story. Better than Tom Sawyer.

Every year, for over seventy years, I swear on the memory of Steve Jobs, who gave us this computer, that I have had the same thought that my life would make a hell of a story! I never got around to it, though, because I was trying too hard to live it. Very hard. James' verbal bludgeoning, especially his unsubtle reminders of my birthdate, nudged me to stop living my life for a while, and start writing about it. While doing so, I thought frequently about Mark Twain. He was born when Halley's Comet flamed through the atmosphere. And Twain's life flamed out seventy-five years later with Halley's Comet once again a witness. Since I had thought so long about my book, I figured when I finally get around to typing "The End," I will keel over.

I am, and always have been a loner. But not by choice. No one wants or chooses to be a loner. It is thrust upon us, but I was lucky to have a brain that kept me company. I was also lucky because along the bumpy byways I ran into scores and scores of people, mostly by accident, who smoothed the roads for me. Living is a team sport. You cannot play it well alone. In this book, you, too, will run across those team players. Their acquaintance is as distant as that January day, but their help, memory and stories are still at my fingertips as I type. Along the way, you will also meet some jerks and geniuses, me being the principal one. Like everyone, it is impossible to survive and live any kind of life without being both. You will also find some who were, and probably still are, just jerks. Real jerks. The kind that burn your bridges before you come to them or while you're on them or after you've crossed them.

Financially, the most successful years of my life in showbiz were the years on television when I told other people's stories. I have never worked deliberately for money. It came as a byproduct of work I would have done for nothing. And often did. From the time I was a six-year old kid reading to our first-grade class and listening to the short stories of Canada's Gordon Sinclair, and the magnificent Orson Welles-sounding voice of Lorne Greene on the CBC, or reading Guy de Maupassant, Somerset Maugham or the Tarzan books of Edgar Rice Burroughs, or Mark Twain, I have loved stories and good storytellers. Now it is my turn.

If, like me, you love a really good story, filled with other really good stories, this book is for you. And I promise, you will never read a book remotely comparable to this about anyone else who was ever in show business. Because that story, and that magical mysterious eventful life, only happened to me.

P.S. If, at the end, you feel otherwise, call James!

IN AMERICA: Standing Alone

See that black and white picture of me? That was taken near the pool at the old Flamingo Hotel in Las Vegas. I was sixteen or seventeen years old. Sometime around 1950. I can't quite remember. I can remember why I had a Stetson on, though. I thought it'd make me look like a big shot. I was a gambler – albeit, a small-time one. The same with those two-tone shoes. Where did they come from? And where did they go? Maybe I thought they'd look good when I ran away from Toronto and got to kick the world in the ass. Of course, the ass-kicking capital of the world was America. I have no idea who took the picture, or even what the occasion was. Or why I still have it. What I do know is that it's the only photo of me under the age of seventeen. Maybe that's why I hung onto it. There was certainly nothing else in my life I wanted to hang onto. Especially the memories. Perhaps I was just trying to hang onto me.

Everybody I know has childhood pictures; certainly, baby pictures. Even if they had lousy parents, or divorced parents, or were being put up for adoption, there was someone who cared enough to welcome them into the world with just a snapshot. Even if it wasn't going to be a welcoming world, there was this photographic proof that they existed. Or even mattered.

The only other pictures of me under the age of twenty are in someone else's possession. The first, if it still exists, would probably be gathering dust somewhere in the archives of Adam Beck Public School in Toronto's east end, which I haphazardly attended for seven shaky years, (having skipped a grade) under the non-birth name of MacLaren. One or two more photos would be headshots taken by the Toronto Police Department on Main Street. Later versions of those two same poses would be in the possession of US Immigration at Terminal Island, San Diego, long after leaving Las Vegas. I do remember the suit, though. It was soft blue; the only one I had. I should have been smiling because, by God, I was so happy to be away from a home that would have to be seriously mended just to be called broken. I was also happy to be out of the reach of some angry cash-short card players who didn't believe a teenage kid could fleece them fair and square.

My hands were in my pockets; one of which had a serious hole in it. The other had the six hundred dollars left of my winnings, after buying the train ticket and the used wardrobe, except for the kick-ass shoes, which were new. I look like I was wondering how long that money would last. Or how long the two-tones would last before they got holes in them. But the holes in my wardrobe were nonexistent compared to the hole in my soul.

I planned on going to Vegas because, to the addicted gambler that I'd been for two years, Vegas was the Vatican. My habit was so emotionally hopeless, even as a kid, I'd have to cut down just to be a junkie. I once stood under the maple tree in our front yard in autumn and bet my favorite and only hockey stick against my neighbor-buddy-adversary, Mel Nixon, on which leaf would fall first. I lost. Of course. Gamblers always do. But I didn't know that then. Vegas was where I wanted my financial prayers to be answered.

If I didn't have to stay there to make the easy money I envisioned, I might have gone to Hollywood. After Canadian winters, I loved the thought of picking an orange off a tree in December. And, in Los Angeles, with mostly sunny days, my blue suit wouldn't have to go to the dry cleaners so often. Those thoughts about the Golden State came to me around the age of six. In Toronto, with little to go home to, from that age on, when not at a rink, I would spend a nickel and hours sitting through two double-features at the Manor Theater on Kingston Road. The end of every film, of course, said, "Made in Hollywood." That's the place where the movies told me the rainbow ends and dreams really do come true. But I had to earn a living; so, Las Vegas was it. At least I thought it was, especially after learning how to gamble properly.

For the two years prior to boarding that train, the first time I'd ever paid to ride one, every cent earned working as a coal-shoveling fireman on the Canadian National Railway or bussing dishes at Kresge's or delivering mail at the Parliament buildings downtown, or borrowed, begged, or stolen, all four of which I was very adept at, I lost in marathon midnight-till-morn gambling orgies. I was the youngest loser in a group of usually eight. The two oldest were in their forties. One was a soldier; the other a truck driver. If I ever won, I stayed until I lost it. I had nowhere to go, so I figured what the hell, it was as good a place to be as any. It was usually poker, but sometimes it was craps. I was always the first to lose, and the last to leave.

I couldn't understand why I didn't do better because unlike those guys, I wasn't distracted by drinking and smoking. I was a clear-headed and clear-eyed loser! They didn't have any trouble getting my money, so when they were pushing drinks and cigarettes at me it was because they wanted me to be more like one of the boys.

One night they pushed me to the point of rudeness for my disinterest in imbibing or inhaling, asking if I was some kind of religious nut; I told them there was a reason I didn't smoke or drink. In one of the convenience stores I had worked part-time, I once stole a carton of cigarettes. I was so afraid of getting caught I tried to smoke them all, one after the other, and got sick. So, I never smoked again. Then another time, I confessed, I stole a carton of beer. And again, to hide the evidence, I drank them all and got even sicker. Then I pulled out a large pack of condoms and put them next to the chips, and said, "A year ago I stole a carton of condoms. I still have six left!" They laughed and never again offered me a beer or smoke. Thereafter, they started every session asking how many condoms I still had.

Hearing them laugh got my mind separated from the game; it was then I realized I wasn't really there to make money; I was there to make friends. But in reality, these guys were not friends; just acquaintances. My needs weren't monetary; they were emotional. So, I thought, if I'm going to gamble, which I did enjoy, obviously too much, then I'd better learn how to do it properly. I got two books from the library. One was called, *Scarne on Dice*, the other was called *Scarne on Cards*. Here was an expert who laid out all the mathematical odds on all the possible combinations and permutations of every bet on any pull of any card or roll of a die. When to press or when to back off. When to double; when to fold. What games offered the greatest odds of winning, and why. In two weeks I memorized nearly every page. If I'd been Kenny Rogers, I would have written a song about it.

I started my next midnight session with under forty dollars and played every night for a week. I found myself no longer needing to be in every hand. I no longer had to stay until dawn. At the end of the week, I had over seven hundred dollars, and seven very leery, unfriendly acquaintances. When l got up to leave, again before the sun, they asked if I'd be back Sunday to give them a chance to get their money back.

I said, "Of course. I may want more." I lied.

Sunday morning, I was on a train to Las Vegas, Nevada with over six hundred bucks. I had informed US Immigration authorities I'd only be in Buffalo for two days. Somehow or another on the way to Las Vegas the train had to stop. There had been a wreck a mile in front of us. For over an hour we were not informed that a wreck was the purpose of the delay, just that it would be long. Of course, as an almost ex-convict, I was convinced immigration had wired ahead and had them halt the train so they could haul me off. So, I scurried off. At the tiny depot where we were delayed, a nice man informed me that the nearest bigger locale was a place called Lake Tahoe, a three or four-hour bus ride away. I was on that next bus, smiling, thinking about how the law would find an empty seat on the train they stopped.

Lake Tahoe was stunning. It reminded me of a smaller version of pictures and movies I'd seen of Lake Louise and Banff National Park in Alberta; nature's perfect rendering of conifer trees, shapely mountains, and blue water. It was late afternoon when the bus stopped, not far from a gambling chalet called the Cal-Neva Lodge. Thrilled by the newness and elegance of it, not wanting to waste my time or talents, I rushed inside.

I had only seen luxury and sets like those in the movies. A Technicolor casino abuzz with smartly attired adults crowded happily and noisily around crap tables, blackjack tables and a lush bar. Surprisingly, I felt at home. After half an hour of wandering around, savoring every sight and sound, I ended up at the end of a crap table, my back to the entrance. I was five years too young to be doing that legally. But this was Nevada. This was gambling. Who cares? In that Texas outfit, no one questioned my age. For over an hour I held my own, and even some of the House's. The stick boss and a couple of fellows across from me began to eye me like they thought I knew what I was doing. Proudly, I did. After about half an hour, the guys across from me, who seemed to be matching my bets, stopped betting. They were looking behind me. Others also stopped, even dealers. They, too, were looking behind me. It was like a wave at a sporting event. Then all activity ceased entirely. I turned to see what had brought everything to a halt.

Strutting halfway across the casino, having just entered through the huge front glass doors, was a sight that was impossibly unreal to me. I literally had to shake my head so my eyes and mind could refocus. It was Frank Sinatra, a long black overcoat draped over his shoulders like an Italian Superman; he was arm in arm with a face I'd just read about and seen in the newspapers, Sam Giancana, Chicago's crime boss. Close behind them, their praetorian guard; three dark, tough-looking Italians. Just a few months earlier I had seen Sinatra in a movie at the Manor Theater. He was in a white tuxedo standing on a tall white pedestal singing beautifully, *Old Man River*. Now, he was walking right past me. Who could imagine? Certainly not me, that a fabulous celluloid star would be walking out of my recent past right into my present. All because of an accident. What sixteen-year-old runaway gambler could possibly dream other accidents would make Sinatra, this icon, a significant part of my later life? Right then, though, daydreams of movie stars were not for me. Dreams of being rich were. Lake Tahoe was not the place I saw that dream coming true. Las Vegas was.

The first month in Las Vegas saw me realizing the image of easy riches. I still had my six hundred and a few hundred more. Of course, I couldn't sit at the tables all day. There were only a couple of movie theaters, so I found myself going to the live shows. I did not see one that was not more thrilling than the best movie. At the Sahara, France's tiny Edith Piaf in a plain black dress standing in front of a red curtain filled the showroom with people and a huge voice that made it feel like a religious experience. At the Desert Inn, England's Noel Coward exquisitely performing his *Mad Dogs and Englishmen*. My favorite, though, that I saw often at The El Rancho, was comedian Joe E. Lewis with the greatest opening I'd ever seen. He was the opening act for famed stripper, Lily St. Cyr. She concluded her act by hopping into a curtained four-poster bed where she removed all her clothes. When the lights came back up, an announcer said, "Ladies and gentlemen, directly from the bar, Joe E. Lewis." There was loud applause and laughter, but no Joe E. Lewis. After about thirty seconds of silence he emerged from under the bed covers. There was an ovation. Seeing all this, and with a wallet that was growing slowly, I thought I was happy.

In one fateful night, though, it suddenly was lost. Not the money. The happiness. The dream. It came to this unexpected weird end at a blackjack table. My favorite game. Especially with one deck. It was at the Flamingo Hotel. I was at a table with a two-dollar minimum. I was not superstitious, but I kept sitting at the same table in the same chair. If it wasn't vacant, I wouldn't play. This particular night, I sat for three hours. Other gamblers had come and gone. Nearly all had lost. I wasn't up, but I wasn't down. I was holding my own. However, I wasn't smiling. Something had turned off inside me. I didn't know what was wrong with me. My mind went blank. The joy was gone. The challenge was gone. The rushes were gone. The dealer had a face card; I had a six, so I had to pull. The dealer had a three showing; I had twelve. I had to stand. The dealer had an eight. I had two tens. I couldn't split. I had to stay. I was no longer emotionally involved in what I was doing. I had become a disconnected mathematician. I had no emotional attachment to money. So, winning became meaningless. It was almost like an out of body experience. It wasn't me at the table. It was a stranger in a blue suit and Stetson. I had no interest in him. Or what he was doing. Or what I was doing. I was not engaged. Feeling as empty as my pockets used to be, I picked up my chips, walked away from the table, and cashed them in.

Watching my money being counted out, I panicked. What was I going to do? I had to find something, anything that would engage me. Mean something to me. But what? All I could think of, was how much fun it was watching the live shows. I have not gambled since, except on golf courses. So, there you see me standing alone in front of the Flamingo Hotel feeling that one hole in my pocket, with a much, much bigger one in my life.

Six decades later, at this typewriter, I'm happily sitting alone, recalling all the wonders that did engage me. However, before we pack up again and I take you to California where I did pick oranges for a while, I'm going to pause this picture. And put our story in flashback like the movie *Citizen Kane*. Only ours is called, *Not Yet Citizen Barbour*.

IN CANADA: We'll Meet A Stranger

There's someone I'd like you to meet. I'm introducing him to you very reluctantly because I have no real desire to meet him again. I haven't seen or thought about him for over sixty years. Even when I knew him well, I couldn't wait to get away from him. Because right now he is somewhere I never want to be. That is the past.

It is me. As a boy.

To me, revisiting a childhood is as useless as trying to taste a meal that's already been consumed and eliminated. Who would want to taste a meal again that was bitter to begin with? You can't truly recapture the taste, and in the end it all turned to shit anyway.

When I was a kid listening to adults, I was always given the advice and impression that if one was good and worked hard that cream would rise to the top. But in the world I was experiencing, I noticed that maybe cream did rise to the top, but so did shit. For cream to rise it must be stirred. Not shit. Shit floats up all by itself. When cream gets to the top and stays, it doesn't get creamier. It turns to shit. Even though it was all around me, I was surprised when people were evil or cruel. Now that I'm no longer that boy, I am surprised when people are good.

A few years before Dean Martin died, I was playing golf with him at the Riviera Country Club in Los Angeles. Just before we teed off, a fellow about Dean's age came up to him, extended his hand, and said, "Dean, you'll never believe this, but I saw you in a club in Steubenville when you were just starting."

Dean declined the handshake, walked away ignoring the fellow, and teed up his ball, saying to me, "Let's play."

I was embarrassed for the stranger, but said nothing. Dean noticed I was very quiet, which was not like me on a golf course. He said, "I hate the past, it means absolutely nothing. I never want to hear about it. There are only two things in my past that ever cross my mind. They were the two best things that ever happened to me." He stopped his swing, and looked directly at me. "That was meeting Jerry Lewis … and leaving Jerry Lewis." Then he hit his shot. "Life's like golf. You can never re-hit a bad shot, or any shot, or even think about it. It'll only get in the way of the most important shot, the one right in front of you!"

Nearly everyone I met who is screwed up, (and that could fill a football field) can't seem to live his or her life happily; they're too busy trying to psychoanalyze their unchangeable past. Driving forward is hazardous staring into the rearview mirror. It is true that when you're too young to understand or play in the game of life that the bad shots, and if there any good shots, they are all hit for you or at you by others, a parent, a guardian, whoever, but, like in golf, as Dean said, there comes a time when you have to take those shots where they lay, and continue the game on your own. Fortunately for me, that awareness came early.

There's an ancient Persian proverb that says, "If you're going to tell the truth, you'd better always have one foot in the stirrup." I like the truth of that saying. History is full of folks killing the bad-news messengers. I've been fortunate over the years earning a living telling truths as I saw them, and oftentimes not being able to earn a living for the same affliction. Writing this book, that homily does not apply to me. Telling the truth here, again as I see and experienced it, I do so with both feet on the ground and take what's coming – reward or remand.

So, now, I tell you a little about this boy who used to be me, a boy I barely recognize anymore. The telling is almost biographical rather than autobiographical because there is no longer any emotional attachment to this Dickensian Artful Dodger. Thus, it becomes easier … and more honest. We are like a reporter at the scene of an accident where there is a survivor – me. And as Jack Webb always said in *Dragnet*: "Just the facts, ma'am!"

On The Street Where I Live

The multitude of long-deleted miserable images and memories of me as a child, boy, and young teenager surprisingly come to me crystal clear. Totally free of hurt. I read recently in a medical journal about a number of American soldiers and Vietnamese civilians who had been so traumatized by the sight of the brutalities and horrors of that War, they went blind. Most of the time I felt so emotionally waterboarded by life, I deleted my emotions. Then later deleted my family. Somehow, though, I viewed my little life as if it were a brand-new bike, even though I never had anything brand new. I had to learn to ride it. The road was bumpy and potholed. It never seemed to be my fault that I kept crashing. I had been placed on a shitty road. In spite of this, I would get back up and try it again. Hundreds of times. I believed, maybe because of those movies, somewhere there were roads that were repaired. I liked that quality about myself. I still do. I have no idea where it comes from. It certainly didn't come from anyone in my family. Or my friends. It just seemed to be there. Like being right-handed or blue-eyed, I was happy-headed!

No one in my family had a sense of joy, or even a sense of humor. My feeling then of somehow being different, special, in psychiatric retrospect, may have just been a contrary survival mechanism; a way to keep me peddling and pushing forward. I was purposely programming myself to become the opposite of what my parents and my siblings were. Even if this feeling of individual specialness was artificially induced, it kept me company; it kept me alive. Kept me dreaming! It felt real, and eventually became so.

On the negative side, however, having a feeling of specialness, which no one around you seems to share or recognize, makes you feel alone. That feeling of separateness for social creatures such as us weakens us. It makes us sometimes question ourselves and wish we weren't special or different because we would so much love to fit in, to be one of them, to be liked, and like the others. The agony of those feelings, and it is an agony, believe me is harder, much harder for children because as crawling creatures we begin to feel immediately, but we don't learn to think or reason until we walk alone. For many, many adults I've known, even the famous, the latter has yet to occur.

For me, the aloneness, and the ride, began on April 24, 1933. That's the day some good Samaritans and surgeons at the charity ward of The Salvation Army Hospital in Toronto, Canada, helped a drunk give birth to a six pound, nine-ounce accident.

Two Houses Don't Make a Home

Up until the time I boarded the train from Toronto, I lived in two houses. Both of them on Lawlor Avenue, about five blocks from Scarborough Road, the city's eastern boundary. The first was a tiny, brick, attached single-story. It was so small we and our neighbors could have had little signs on our doors that said "Ladies" and "Gentlemen." We lived there until I was five. I only have two memories of it. I don't recall much about my younger sister, Margaret, or my older half-brother, Raymond, whom I called "Ronnie," and, as hard as I try, I can't recall anything good about my mother. I can recall my father. Not what he looked like, or even smelled like, because even in that small abode nobody ever got close enough to smell anybody.

He taught me the alphabet and to count to a hundred. He spent hours and days doing this. His pride and pleasure at listening to me haltingly getting to "z" and "100" filled me with the desire to keep going. When he was long gone from my life, I still loved to learn. I was four, about to turn five, at which time I would be enrolled in kindergarten at Adam Beck Public School. He was preparing me. He wanted to show them that his kid was too smart to be playing in sandboxes.

On the day of enrollment, he took me by the hand, walked the short block to the school and led me to class. He introduced himself and me to the teacher who now took my hand and led me to a seat. As l sat looking around at a bunch of strangers my size, my father and the teacher left the room. They returned shortly accompanied by an older man. After chatting a bit, the teacher motioned for me. "Your father tells me that you can count to a hundred. And that you can recite the alphabet."

"Yes, ma'am!"

"Come with me." She took my hand again and led me to the front of the class. "Children," she announced, "this is John. I want you to pay attention." She then turned to me and said, "Okay. Go ahead."

I was stuck. I didn't know where to start, with counting or the alphabet. I looked at my father and with a slight nod he indicated I should do it in the same order I did it at home. When l was finished, the kids just stared at me. They probably thought, *what was that all about*? But the teacher and my father were applauding as though I'd made a major contribution to the science of learning.

The older man, who turned out to be the principal, raised his hand, calling me over. "Come with me, son!" As I followed beside him, he kept patting me on the head. He opened the door to a classroom next door and motioned me in. The kids there looked a little bigger. "Miss Black," he said. "this is John. He's a new student."

So, I skipped kindergarten. And one more grade after that. I was to skip classes a lot at Adam Beck – by not even showing up.

1939

They say, the experts and all those that do the saying for us, that 1939 was the creative highpoint for Hollywood and the movies, including *Gone with the Wind, Dark Victory* with Bette Davis, Charles Laughton in *The Hunchback of Notre Dame, The Wizard of Oz* (The trees frightened me so much as a six year-old that I had to duck under the seat in front of me and close my eyes.) *Mr. Smith Goes to Washington, Stagecoach, Wuthering Heights, Young Mr. Lincoln,* and scores more. My favorite was *Goodbye Mr. Chips* with Robert Donat, a movie that made me do something that real life never made me do at that point, and that was cry. Whenever it airs today, I take the time to sit by myself and watch it. The blubbering has subsided, but the tears are still there.

It wasn't such a great year for me, though, or the world. That was the year we moved into the bigger house, and Germany moved into Poland. It would be the last year I would see my father. That was the year he enlisted in the Canadian Army to go off to fight strangers in the peace and quiet of World War II. I didn't cry then, or over twenty years later when I went to England and Scotland and tracked him down.

We moved into a bigger house on Lawlor Avenue because, evidently, my father's life and career, and his name, were expanding. My last name was Barbour. At least it was for the first five years. The car we rode around in then was bright red with "Coca Cola" written on it; so, I presumed that's where he worked. Like most immigrants, (He was from Glasgow, Scotland) he wanted to be somebody in his new adopted country. Most immigrants would do it by working and studying harder. Not him. He was smarter. He did it by lying. The *somebody* he wanted to be was somebody else. That somebody else was a famous Scottish writer named MacLaren. In 1939, he added the name MacLaren to his, and became Angus Barbour MacLaren, the brother, he said, of the well-known Scottish scribe. Everybody believed him, including *The Toronto Star* that hired him. Investigative journalism probably wasn't one of their strong suits at the time. So, I became "John MacLaren" for the next ten years, until my dash to America.

My father must have been athletic; you may be able to fake family lineage, but you can't fake ability. On our living room wall was a plaque that said he was in the finals, or the winner, of the 1939 Ontario amateur tennis championship.

There were only two other pictures on the living room wall, the only two in the entire house. One was of him. Alone. Looking a little like Errol Flynn. The other is that omnipresent painting of Jesus kneeling at a rock with his hands folded, looking wistfully up at some heavenly lights. I couldn't understand why that picture of Jesus was there. Nobody went to church. Nobody ever said grace. Religion was absent from that abode, as was affection. Maybe Jesus was praying to get out of that place. Soon, I would join him.

Unframed Photos

I only have a few mental images of my father; each is unframed, as though I had no desire or place in my heart to hang them; unrelated fragments of memory tossed in the attic trunk portion of the mind that is forced to store such stuff, never to be looked on again. Like scraps of a torn, faded road map that lead nowhere. To even think about them is a waste of time. But, for the purpose of trying to tell this tale as honestly and completely as possible, and out of curiosity as to why even these incidents, which aren't as important or as influential as others, still linger, I'm going to rummage around in the dustbin.

Living in a bigger home, having a second floor with three bedrooms and a bathroom, and being able to run up and down the stairs that had a landing was, for the first couple of weeks, a huge adventure for six-year-old me; even leaving or entering the house was fun. There was a large veranda with wooden railings to leap over and walk on. And stairs to jump off or skip up. And a maple tree in the front yard for me to swing on and yodel as I would later rehearse and prepare myself for my move to Africa after I devoured all of Edgar Rice Burroughs' books about Tarzan.

It was around the third week after we moved in. I had just finished playing, at what I don't know. I skipped up the stairs. I was always glad to come home. I ran across the veranda to the door and tried to open it, but it was locked. In those days, (The past, when you're talking about something that is supposed to be positive, is always referred to as "those days.") doors were never locked. Front or back. Night or day. But mine was locked. I tried it again. It was still locked. I tried it two or three more times. It didn't budge. I hollered, "Dad! Mom!" Most kids would have instinctively hollered for their moms first. In times of need or nurturing, it's always the mother's magical presence that springs to mind. Not for me. It was my dad I wanted. She was just an afterthought. Soon the narrow letterbox halfway up the door opened and my dad said, "Who's there?"

"Dad. It's me!"

"Who's me?" he asked.

"Me. Me."

"Me who?"

"Me!" I said louder.

"What's your name?"

"John!"

"John who?"

"John ... John MacLaren!" There was a pause.

"Oh. You don't live here anymore!"

Now I was scared. "Dad, let me in! Please."

The door didn't open for what seemed a while, but when it did, and I rushed in, and past my father. After that, the house never felt the same.

There were never moments of intimacy or affection between my parents. If there had been, I probably would have referred to them as my "mother" and "father" instead of the indifferent noun "parents." And there was never one expression of affection from my mother toward me. There was also no expression of hostility or abuse toward me from my mother – until my father left, and a parade of 'uncles" came into our house and our lives.

Aside from prepping me for entrance into kindergarten, I only remember one semi-close moment with my father. We were listening to the radio, which we did often at night. We spent more time lounging around the front living room doing that when in the house. Not once do I recall ever having a meal at our dining room table. It was always at the kitchen table with the stained oilcloth. The shows we listened to were Bob Hope, Jack Benny, and Fred Allen, *Fibber McGee and Molly, The Shadow. The Hermits Cave,* or Lorne Green or Gordon Sinclair telling stories and *Hockey Night in Canada,* with Foster Hewitt shouting, "He shoots, he scores!" To this day, I remember a line from one of Bob Hope's broadcasts that got him censored and kicked off the air. He said, "Did you hear about the young girl who was sewing and accidentally swallowed a pin ... and didn't feel the prick 'til she was sixteen!"

When he heard it, my father howled. At the time he was sewing. It was his way of relaxing. It was also his way of repairing tears or buttons; his wife did none of that. He was sitting in a deep lounging chair; I was on the floor at his feet. When he'd finished chuckling, he continued with his mending. I noticed the needle was exceptionally fine, that the point was really tiny and easily penetrated the fabric. After watching for a few moments, I said, "Does that thing hurt?"

"What do you mean, does it hurt?"

"Well, it's so small, if you stuck it in someone, would they feel it?"

"Do you want to find out?" he asked.

"No."

"Then why did you ask?"

"I was just curious. It looks so small."

"Well, let's find out. Gimme your arm."

"No, that's okay."

"Well, now *I'm* curious. Gimme." He grabbed my arm and raised his hand with the needle and made the sound of a dive bomber descending on its target as he moved it toward my flesh.

I hollered, "No, Dad. No!"

As he was about to strike, he suddenly stopped at the surface of the skin and began to laugh, louder than he did at Bob Hope.

He never spanked me; perhaps because I never really did anything to be spanked for. I didn't do those things until after he left home. But he did reprimand me once. It was at the kitchen table. For some reason known only to my taste buds, I hated asparagus. He loved it. This one night I would not touch them on my plate. They smelled like dirty socks, a close cousin to cooked cabbage. Not only does it smell awful, it looks awful. Like tiny seaweed spears.

"Finish your asparagus," he said.

"Dad, I can't finish it. I can't even start it. I hate it!"

"Eat it. It's good for you!"

"I can't stand the taste … or the smell. How can something so awful be good for you?"

"You'll eat it … or else!"

I said, "What does 'else' taste like?" I started to laugh at my little joke, and waited for my little sister and big brother to join in; but they didn't. They got real quiet. As did my dad.

He got up from the table and grabbed me by the bicep. I wasn't afraid of him hitting me, but I was scared of the unknown consequences of eating interuptus.

With a firm grip on my arm, he led me to the basement door. "You have a choice. You can either come back to the table now and finish your asparagus, or you can go down in the cellar until you get your appetite back!"

I just stared at him. "Dad, I'm not hungry anymore."

With that, he opened the door and pushed his six-and-a-half-year-old food critic down the stairs and locked the door. I heard it click and tried to open it, whining, "Daddy, Daddy!"

I heard a muffled voice. "Are you ready to finish it?"

I stopped whining and sat on the top step. It was pitch black. I didn't like the basement; it was always cold and dark and always half filled with coal for the furnace. A small front window of the basement was always left unlocked. This made it more convenient for the delivery men to push it open so they could open their sacks of anthracite and dump them. The mounds of dark, dusty coal rose all the way to that window, making it easier I thought for any creep to crawl through. The cellar always spooked me. I was terrified of being there. But asparagus scared me more.

I don't recall how this standoff ended. But I do know my stomach won, and to this day continues to win.

The Big Parade to World War II

1939 may have been a great year for Hollywood films, all of which I saw at the Manor Theater on Kingston Road for a nickel, but it was a lousy year for the world, especially my little world. A few times my parents had their beer-drinking friends over. I don't remember any of them because whenever they came over, I was told to leave the room; it was time for the adults to be alone. These adults behaved more noisily, sloppily and raunchier than any of us. Like bigger kids – who could drink and fornicate.

Whenever I was told to leave, I never felt rejected or upset; I would quietly but gleefully run three doors up the street to Mel Nixon's house. But first, I'd go up to the bathroom. Here, I'd open the window curtains and raise the blind; a preview of coming attractions for us.

If Neil Simon had ever written a "Junior Sunshine Boys" or "Junior Odd Couple," it would have been based on me and Mel. For nine years, from the time I moved in until the day I hopped a train, Mel and I were the best and worst of buddies. He was a beautiful, dark-haired kid who grew up looking like Tyrone Power. His sister, Margaret, a year younger, was even prettier, and smarter. She liked books and when she became a Jennifer Jones lookalike young teen, she took me to her bedroom one night to read me passages from *Forever Amber* she'd underlined while her parents were at one of those good movies. Afterwards, she used my young body and her hands to translate those passages into Braille. No book ever touched me so much. Mel and I played ice and street hockey under sunlight and lamplight; we got into enormous amounts of trouble, got arrested, and fought physically all the time. Only once can I recall a reason.

I was a better hockey player than Mel. But he was stronger. When we were on the ice, he could never catch me. I would outscore him in minutes, ten to nothing. When we were on the street, though, when I wasn't dodging cars I had to dodge his brutal body checks. Despite getting knocked flying into trees, curbs, and parked fenders, I would still manage to outscore him. This really irritated him. What irritated him more, though, was that after scoring I'd compliment my stick, which I called "the scoring machine," announcing like a gunslinger that I'm going to have to put another notch in it!

One night, as I was walking away when it was over, I noticed him looking not at me, but at my amazing scoring machine.

"G'night. See you tomorrow!"

"Yeah," he said quietly.

Even though our hockey sticks were our major possessions, we never took them into the house. We had elevated front porches with slats of wood like a small fence running from the stairs to the alley. There was nothing under the porch but darkness and dirt. This is where we hid our sticks when we went to bed.

One night I watched Mel watching me as I slid mine into its usual spot next to the stairs. Something about the way he was watching me made me feel uneasy. Three hours later, near midnight, this unease persisted. I got out of bed, got dressed, went downstairs and outside. Very quietly, I reached in and was relieved to find the scoring machine still there. I pulled it out and walked to Mel's front porch where I reached in and retrieved his stick, took it out and replaced it with mine. I then put his in my spot and went up to bed proud and smiling, knowing I had done something really Sherlock Holmes clever.

The next morning, without waiting for breakfast, I rushed outside. Mel's family was almost as dysfunctional as mine. He never slept well, and was usually standing in front of the house waiting for me. This morning, however, he wasn't there. I descended the stairs and bent over to retrieve the hockey stick. I grabbed the handle with its lump of electric tape at the end and pulled it out. But only the handle came out. A foot long, I reached in again and grabbed another portion of the stick. This piece was also only a foot long, as were the four other pieces I retrieved. He had cut it into pieces in the middle of the night. Suddenly there was this loud howling laughter, like when Richard Widmark as Tommy Udo in *Kiss of Death* pushes this old lady in a wheelchair down the stairs. Mel came from behind a car screaming with glee, "Now you've got six scoring machines!"

I was as calm as a fire hydrant. I just stood there. After a moment I strolled over to his house, up to the porch stairs, bent over and pulled out my hockey stick. He watched, confused. Sauntering back to him on the sidewalk, I handed him his six pieces of a CCM hockey stick. "This is yours," I said calmly, holding mine up triumphantly. "The hockey machine lives to score again!" He realized what he'd done. He quickly punched out the smirk on my face and the gleam in my eyes. I crawled into the house, taking the scoring machine with me. My mother looked at my bloody lips and blackened eyes and dismissed it by saying, 'You'd better give up that stupid game!"

Now back to the raised bathroom blind. Mel and I were just six. Margaret was five. Like monkeys, we would clamber up the back-pantry roof of the house next door, all the way to the roof. Once up there, we crawled very carefully across the peak to peek from the edge. The upstairs bathroom, still in the condition I had left it, was just fifteen feet or so from where we would lie trying not to giggle, let alone roll around and fall off. From experience, we knew after a few drinks the adults never noticed the shades were up. Sometimes they didn't even notice the toilet seat was down. For hours we'd lie there, watching and learning. My God, watching real life with no story, just action, was a whole lot more stimulating and fun than watching even the best of those 1939 flicks. We saw ladies raising their skirts and pulling down their panties to go potty or pulling down their panties so that a man she didn't come to the party with could grope her. Or she would fondle him. Or a woman bending over and another man with his pants down bumping against her backside. My parents were among the group-gropers, bumpers and bumpees. I didn't chuckle when they did it, but Mel was quick to remind me, "Hey, Johnny, look at your momma!" or "Geez, Johnny, look what your dad's doin'!"

These friends of my parents always ended up in huge arguments. Some outraged spouse always found out a lot of people up there were not going to the toilet. With it getting late, I wanted to get back in the house. Hating the growing loud confrontations and brawls, I would intercede the only way I knew how.

One of my dad's favorite scenes from a movie was a musical where some drunk danced while singing a dopey ditty. I knew it by heart. So, with raucous, rude, belligerent voices coming from the front room, I made my way back down from the roof and pushed the door open. The adults got immediately quiet, stunned by this loud little intrusion. I staggered in like a drunk singing and dancing my dad's favorite stupid song. It always worked. He would raise his glass and holler, "My boy!" The others cheered loudly. As only drunks do. I loved the sound of it. The applause.

My mother would tell me quickly it was bedtime in a voice I could not stand. It was not her voice. Not the voice she used to talk to my father or her friends. It was that weak insipid octave-higher voice that most mother's employ when talking to their child; unnatural squeaky baby talk. I hated it when I was four, let alone six. Hearing it made me feel she thought I was stupid. But worse, it made me feel like I was a stranger, different from bigger people.

One day, when my mother was quiet and sober, I got up the courage to ask her if in the future, when their friends were over, would she talk to me the same way she talked to Dad and them, in the same voice.

"What the hell are you talking about? I only have one voice; it's the same voice, stupid!"

Months later, when my father left us, she learned quickly how to yell. That experience of quieting a potential adult Armageddon with play-acting as a drunk stayed with me for a long, long time. It undoubtedly played a part in what I ended up doing. At the time, I only wanted to be a hockey player. For a few brief months, though, after reading every one of Edgar Rice Burroughs' Tarzan books, I put my hockey stick on hold.

For weeks I was climbing trees, foraging through bushes practicing my Johnny Weissmuller yodel, perfecting my swinging skills and gymnastics, all in preparation for my move to Africa when I turned sixteen. I gave this all up as quickly as a slap shot one afternoon after seeing a *National Geographic* documentary in the theater. There were never any flies or bugs in those Tarzan movies. And never in the books. So, there couldn't be any bugs in Africa. In the film that's all I saw. Elephants swatting them with ears and trunks. Lions shaking their manes and blinking their eyes. There were more bugs than animals. And worse, women had to swat them off their breasts while nursing babies.

I loved knowing that in Africa I could see endless bare breasts, but I hated flies more! So, it was back to hockey and movies. When not on skates, I was usually sitting in a theater seat, escaping into those engaging stories that contributed mightily, as Ben Hecht said about movies, scores of which he wrote, in his autobiography, *A Child of the Century,* to the dumbing down of Western Civilization. But not me. I learned from them. Gary Cooper taught me to whistle without using my fingers. For weeks I practiced curling my tongue behind my upper teeth and blowing. Till it came out. I whistled everywhere.

Mickey Rooney and Judy Garland taught me to sing and dance. I did that well enough to break up fights, and sing Christmas Carols door to door. I loved it till my father left; then the minor ability to do it left. I learned quickly that movies were the make-believe opposite of real life. In movies the bad guys always got caught and prayers were always answered. Not in my life. Movies were talking to me in the same unreal voice my mother spoke in. Still I loved them.

The last time I saw my father on Canadian soil was at the Exhibition Grounds just west of downtown Toronto, two years before America entered the war. I was standing on the sidewalk watching this massive parade of soldiers in dark-brown rough khaki uniforms marching off to glory, like Christians in those hymns. My mother must have been with me because I don't think I got there by myself, but she's nowhere to be found in the memory bin. There was my father, marching at the front in the column closest to me. He was not just marching, he was strutting, proud and confident, as Mark Twain said, "As a preacher holding four aces." He was the best marcher of the bunch, as far as I was concerned. He had to keep his eyes forward, on the flag, but did manage to look over at me and wink. That made me truly happy. He was the only one I cared about. I thought a lot about that wink for months and years to come. He was leaving home and marching off to battle for a better world. On Lawlor Avenue, all previous peace treaties were broken, and my battles were just beginning.

A Growing Boy's Menu

I've already identified asparagus as a tummy terrorist posing as a vegetable, but there were a few foods I did love to eat. Four, actually, if you could call them food. And I ate at least one of them every day for ten years. My favorite was fish and chips. Never on a plate, though, and never with a knife and fork. Two or three times a week during the summer, but two or three times a day in winter, especially after every hockey game. My hockey haunt was a boy's reformatory eight blocks from the house with two outdoor rinks. I was there nearly every night, mostly by myself, getting into pick-up games with the residents. I always played center and my favorite winger was a tall, engaging black kid, Ernie, who could really skate. Many weekdays, when the residents were in class, and I was not, having played hooky, I played by myself, imagining the cheers I would one day get at Maple Leaf Gardens.

Walking home, still with my skates on, I always stopped at a small hole-in-the-wall fish and chip store and got them wrapped in newspapers. I'd tear the end off and pelt the contents with vinegar and salt. There was something about these seasonings coupled with newspaper ink that always made this makeshift meal irresistible. And on a chilly day or night, the contents warmed the fingers. As they were plucked out, dripping with juices and raised to the mouth, the aroma of salty leather on my hands from the inside of a hockey glove mingled with that on the fish always turned this little boy's taste buds into an erogenous zone. I ate them every day, sometimes twice a day. My appetite for it never diminished, not just because it tasted so good, but because it made me feel so good. I still love them, even though maturing as a diner, I've been forced to put them on a plate, wash my hands, and stick a fork in them!

The other meal was something I have never been able to find on two continents outside of Toronto. They were the meat pies I found in one little pastry shop on Kingston Road. They were about the size of two hockey pucks, so immediately I liked the shape. The bottom half was filled with some kind of ground meat and small amounts of unidentified ingredients. The top half had nothing in it but air. Now, that may sound like a waste of space, but the moment you sank your teeth into that crust, coated with grease, you were a fish on a hook. When the baker reeled you into the mystery meat, your mouth wished it had more teeth. They were my main courses for ten years. I can remember eating nothing else. Not a salad. Not an apple. Not an orange. Certainly not a steak. Nothing nutritious. But, my two desserts were fantastic. One was an ice cream waffle sandwich, which could only be found in the basement leading from Eaton's Department Store under Queen Street to Simpson's Department store. Whenever I went to Young Street to see a movie or to Maple Leaf Gardens ten big blocks away for a fifty-cent standing room only hockey game, I always made my way there. When it came to these, I didn't just have a sweet tooth; it was a feeding frenzy.

Pathetically, the other staple on my menu was a crunchy chocolate-covered wafer and fudge bar that came wrapped in shiny yellow paper called Coffee Crisp. Because it was everywhere, closer than Eaton's, it was always a Coffee Crisp and Coca Cola that washed down those fish and chips and meat pies. I ate them even unaccompanied by my real food. I ate them like peanuts, until one day they began to eat back.

One evening, while brushing my teeth, I noticed a dark little hole had suddenly appeared on the upper left side of my upper front tooth near the gum line. I couldn't imagine where it came from. It wasn't there that morning. It wasn't painful; just ugly. I took a toothpick and poked at it. It went right through the hole. *Oh, God,* I thought. *What now?* If I told my mother, it'd just be more proof of what trouble I was for her. Hearing this high-decibel constant negative review of my character would only contribute more to my now constant bed wetting. What made my urinal wet dreams worse was that my bed was not level. There were broken springs on one side. When I tried to sleep on the other side, in the middle of the night I'd somehow roll over into this ditch-filled puddle of pee. But I had no choice. I had to tell her. I never saw any actors with holes in their teeth.

The following morning, I washed the smell off me, and went downstairs to show my mother my tooth.

"Did you piss the bed again?" she asked.

"I couldn't help it!" I said honestly.

"Jesus Christ, what's the matter with you?"

"Mom, I don't know." I pointed at my mouth. "Look."

"At what?"

"I have a cavity, I think."

"Jesus Christ Almighty!" Things were getting worse because Jesus, whom she didn't believe in, was now becoming "Almighty."

"What'll I do?"

"Christ knows I don't have any money for that!" Now, the Christ she didn't believe in was aware of her financial condition.

"The father of one of the kids I play hockey with is a dentist. He's just down at the corner," I said.

"Oh, Christ! I have no choice, I guess. Goddamn it, you are so much trouble. Why can't you be like your sister? I don't have the money. See if he'll take a few dollars a week. You're gonna be the goddamn death of me."

But I wasn't. I heard decades after her death it was anemia that killed her. And that she'd been sober for ten years.

The dentist was in an upstairs corner office with a full view of the street. He looked at the hole and said, "Johnny, we can fix that easily."

"My mom doesn't have any money and she wants to know if maybe you could fix it and she could pay you so much a week." I felt bad telling him we were broke. I also felt bad that he was in an awkward spot, being my friend's father, if he had to refuse me. He was not fazed and even cheerful.

"Well, you certainly can't go around looking like that. My son says you're the best hockey player he knows, and, if so, you'll probably get it knocked out one day, but 'til then, you should look good." He chuckled at his own joke. "I'll tell you what," he added, "this is going to cost you twelve dollars. You don't have to give me anything now, but do you think your mom could pay three dollars a week for four weeks?"

"Yes," I said, knowing it was iffy.

Every week for three weeks, I had to find a time when she was sober and alone to remind her of her obligations to the dentist. She would fish for her coin change in her purse, again asking the Lord where he had put it. The money was never placed in my hand; it was always thrust.

"Make sure he gets it, for Christ's sake!"

"I will," I always said. When the month was up and she thrust the final payment at me, I said, "I will" again. But this time I lied. I was beginning to have ever-increasing difficulties just being near her. I wanted to be out of the house, away from her … go to the movies, go to Maple Leaf Gardens on the street car, get fish and chips. Go to Eaton's. To do that I needed some money. So, I kept the final three dollars.

Even though this very decent dentist never saw me again, if there's a God for dentists, he helped extract, excuse the expression, revenge for him, even though it took Him a long, long time. Twenty-six years to be exact.

It was 1970. I was the original host of AM Los Angeles on KABC. The show was doing great and I was doing great. Except I did have a lot of pain in my knees and legs and sometimes my wrists, I attributed this to being body-checked a few too many times playing hockey, or being kicked in the legs playing soccer. Too many pains, I thought, for a thirty-seven-year-old in pretty good shape.

One Friday morning before the show, which was a live ninety-minute call-in show, I was combing my hair and taking a last look to see that nothing was stuck in my teeth. I noticed a huge, yellowish swelling in my upper gums, just above where that twelve-dollar filling was.

In five minutes I'd be on the air, and whatever I did, I shouldn't smile. Everyone would see what looked like a small boil! I called a dentist on Beverly Boulevard named Nathan Sperling. He was a fan of the show who had called and introduced himself. He was the dentist who capped all the stars' teeth. Even though I was on TV, he never suggested I get caps. He never solicited anyone for business. His clientele was all word-of-mouth. The great smiles he gave to an endless line of movie stars were his business cards.

"Come see me when you get off," he said matter-of-factly.

He took x-rays of my entire mouth, and brought me in to look at them. "That is one of the worst abscesses I've ever seen. You're lucky you came in today. It's starting to spread through your upper jaw."

"What would you suggest?"

"You need a lot of work."

"How many weeks would it take?"

"Do you want my suggestion?" he asked. "Let me put you in the hospital tomorrow. I'll clean that out, and prepare your uppers for caps."

"But I have to go on the air Monday!"

"You'll be able to. You'll have great temporaries, and in ten days we'll put in the permanent ones."

"How much is this going cost?"

"About three thousand."

"I don't make too much on the show and--"

"John, don't worry about the money, you can pay me over time," he said.

"No," I said quickly. "Whatever it is, I'll pay you in full immediately."

"You don't have to."

"Yes, I do," I said emphatically. Then added, "I should have paid the last three dollars."

"What?" he said.

I told him about the nice dentist I'd stiffed twenty-six years earlier and how that three dollars had turned into three thousand dollars and that if I didn't pay Nate, it might turn into thirty thousand.

I was out cold when he worked on me over the weekend. Monday morning, I was on the air. I obviously don't have the show anymore. I also no longer have any pain whatsoever in any bone or joint in my body. But I still do have Nate's beautiful teeth.

A Mental Multiplex

As I re-enter the theater of my memory, I feel as though I'm in a mental multiplex. There are twelve different movies running. It's difficult to pick out which one to watch, which scenes to replay, which characters to focus on. And is any of this going to be X-rated or just PG? Since I'm the only one in this busy theater, I'll have to be my own projectionist, as I've always been, and pick which films to run. I am uncomfortable with X-ratings, so I'll just stick with PG. Or at least try to.

Although Mel was nearly always my constant companion and co-combatant, there were four other boys who completed this roster of roustabouts. We were the dirty half-dozen. To us the three r's were rebellion, raunch, and risk. One of those moments of risk almost cost me my life or at least a leg.

Mel and I recruited the four others, not to form a gang, but to form a league. This league we created involved the only recreation we undertook that was either creative or clean. The reason there had to be six of us is because at that time there were only six teams in The National Hockey League.

Mel and I, hockey junkies that we were, had devised an ingenious and cost-free way to play hockey indoors, in any weather at any time. I am surprised that it didn't sweep through Canada as the number one pastime. Maybe nothing happened to it because no one could ever make any money from it. It was free, if you weren't too lazy. We called it flick hockey. Around a smooth piece of wood about two-and-a-half feet wide and three and a half or four feet long, we'd place the boards, about five inches in height, made out of cardboard, just like any professional arena. This was our rink. We then painted blue lines, red lines, face-off circles and all the markings that made it official. The players were also made out of very stiff cardboard. A picture of a famous player would be cut out of a newspaper or magazine and glued onto this piece of cardboard. On the back was glued a much smaller strip of cardboard so that your player could stand. Of course, there was a height restriction; they had to be shorter than seven inches and no wider than three and a half. Goalies were also glued together, but had to be in crouching positions with three or four small one-inch gaps or holes under their arms or through their legs where the pucks could fly. They had little clips attached to the back of their necks that enabled them to stick in the four-inch by six-inch nets without constantly falling down when struck. The puck itself, a quarter of an inch thick, was cut by razor blades off the end of crayons. At the start of the game, the puck would be placed between the two center-men, and a coin would be tossed to see who would "flick" the puck first. To "flick" the puck, you held your player by the head and shoulders, placed the puck at his feet, and snapped it forward. Elaborate statistics were kept in a giant journal on every game and every goal and every assist.

This was extremely serious business. Sometimes these cardboard pros would get into fights that resulted in body parts being torn off, which in turn would result in the owners leaping across the rink to bash one another, while the other four owners cheered them on. In the many years we played this wonderful game, I can only recall one or two that finished in regulation time. Or finished at all. Our problem was finding a clean basement and tolerant parents to turn it into Maple Leaf Gardens, and then referee without calling off the games.

My basement certainly didn't qualify. It was filled with coal and empty beer bottles. The same with Mel. Jerry Tomassini's basement was in use as a still. Jerry's mother was a tough, enterprising, young old-country Italian who loved to make wine and money. Both of which she did out of her basement. Years later, she opened a dump of a restaurant in the industrial part of town and at fifteen, when I had to leave home, she invited me to move in. It was here I had my first and last bout with hard liquor and a nude woman. Well, my last bout with hard liquor.

Bobby Osborne had the perfect basement, and was conveniently right across the street near the leagues' founders, but we never got to use it. The morning of the night we were to make our debut there, he found his mother on her knees in the kitchen with her head in the oven; the first suicide I ever heard of. It wouldn't be the last. We cursed our bad luck. Not only had we lost a venue, but now we had to find another owner for the Detroit Red Wings. His name was Don Lee. He lived on Scarborough Road at Kingston Road, a few blocks away. He was one of the sweetest people I'd ever met. There was always a gentleness about him that put me at ease. He never raised his voice and never cursed. Neither did his parents. If there's such a thing as a functional family, this was it; the only one I ever encountered. Even when we weren't playing flick hockey, I found myself wandering over to their house. I nearly always showed up unannounced, because I was afraid if I did announce it ahead of time, they might say they were busy. But they always welcomed me. I'd be led to the dining room, not the kitchen, and fed and talked to. At first, I did this once or twice a week; then it was three or four times a week, and then, almost every day, always without warning.

One day, while eating a grilled cheese, a new favorite, I said, "Mrs. Lee, do you mind if I ask you a question?"

She said, "Of course not, John."

"Why is Donny an only child? Why doesn't he have a brother or sister?"

"I couldn't have any more," she said, sweetly.

"Did you want one?"

"Yes. But I guess it wasn't in God's plan," she said.

In the months I'd known and visited them, even though they went to church every Sunday, they never once mentioned God or religion. Not only were they nice people, they were comfortable enough in their own faith that they didn't have to try to convert anyone, especially a kid.

For some reason my eyes started to tear up.

Suddenly I blurted out, 'Would you adopt me?"

She smiled slightly. "We couldn't. You already have a mother and father."

"My father's in England or Europe, or somewhere," I answered.

"He's in the War, in the army, isn't he?"

"Yes"

"Well, it's not as though he's left you. And where's your mother? Donald says she works in town here.

"Right now, she's in Buffalo," I said quietly.

"Buffalo?"

"She's with my sister … and … .and … some uncle I've never met."

"For how long? Are you alone?"

"She'll be back Monday, she said."

"Two more days? You're by yourself?"

"Yes."

"Would you like to stay here 'til then?"

"No, no, I'm okay," I lied

"Would you like to come to church with us Sunday, the Baptist Church across the street? It's real close by."

I wanted to be with them, so I said, "Yes, thank you." I had never been inside a church. I was curious to see if there might be something I could find in their church that could make me nice like them.

When I showed up the next morning, Donald's mother handed me a book. "What's this?" I asked.

"The Bible," she said. "Do you have one?"

"No. Is this for today?"

"It's yours. To keep."

"Thank you. Thank you." I tried to sound as grateful as I felt.

I thought the church's closeness might have been the reason the Lees lived where they did. I followed them self-consciously through the doors, relieved when they sat in a back pew. I felt if I sat anywhere else people would know I was a first-timer. I didn't want strangers staring at me.

The preacher was as pleasant as the Lees, delivering his sermon without pounding the pulpit. He then asked us to bow our heads while he said a prayer. He thanked God for all the blessings He'd bestowed upon us, and asked Him nicely to continue bestowing. He asked us to keep our heads bowed, telling us that the Lord was listening and that we should say a short silent prayer for ourselves.

Beginning to feel a surge of spirituality slowly rising in me, my silent short prayer was a no-brainer. The words to God echoed loudly in my head as I asked him simply to let me go home after the service to find my father there. He had been gone for nearly five years. I told God, as if He didn't know, that that's how long the war had been going on, and if my father came home just for a day or two and wanted to go back to it, it would still be there.

"Amen," the preacher said, his way of saying time was up. He stepped back from the pulpit and a blue-robed younger man from the choir stepped forward. He began to sing *The Lord's Prayer*. He was a bass-baritone. It was the most beautiful sound emanating from the human throat that I have ever heard. Not Pavarotti, not Mario Lanza, not Billy Eckstine, not even Frank Sinatra ever stirred me like that unknown choir member. The architecture of this little church amplified the magnificence of his voice. The stained-glass windows and wooden walls echoed the hypnotic, calming vibrato. If you didn't see a man in front of you opening and closing his mouth, you wouldn't know where the sound was coming from. Listening to him, my newfound spirituality wanted to burst from my body, but it had to settle for just being goosebumps. When he finished hitting the high, long sustaining final "Amen," I burst into applause. It was a few moments before I noticed I was the only one doing so. Everyone turned and looked at me. My God, I thought, now they know I've never been in a church. I looked up at Mrs. Lee. She was grinning.

"Oh, I'm sorry," I whispered.

She patted my shoulder. "That's all right," she said, also in a whisper. "I guess this is your first time in a church?"

"The second," I answered quickly and quietly. She looked curious.

"When was the first?"

"I don't remember."

"How can you not remember?"

"Well, I was told I'd been in one once to be baptized or circumcised or something," I stammered.

The congregation around us started to chuckle, then quickly got quiet again.

When we left, I tried to walk behind Mrs. Lee to hide from the preacher shaking hands, but the man of God spotted me. Smiling and clasping my hands in both of his, he said, "First time in a church young man?"

Before I could answer, Mrs. Lee said, "Yes!" Looking at me with eyes that told me I need not speak.

"Well, that's nice. And I'm sure Mr. Decker was pleased that you liked his performance. Will we be seeing you again?"

I didn't know what to say. I looked up at Mrs. Lee, wondering if she would want me to come with them again.

She smiled at me broadly. "Yes, we'll see you next Sunday."

As we were crossing the street back to their house, she said, "He does have the most beautiful voice. It's a shame more people can't hear him."

That made me feel as though someone had just put their arms around me. "Would you like some lunch now?" she asked.

"Yeah, Johnny," Don chimed in, "let's eat."

"Oh, no thanks," I said. "I have to get home."

"Is your mother back?" Mrs. Lee asked.

"No, but there's stuff I have to do," I lied.

"Will we see you next Sunday?" she asked.

I held up the Bible. "You bet and I'm going to read it between now and then!" This time I wasn't lying.

"Wonderful," she said. "On both counts. We'll see you next Sunday. And maybe he'll sing a different hymn. This was the third week in a row for *The Lord's Prayer*!" Now she chuckled.

God, I loved her and her family.

I really did want to stay. I was hungry, but I had a more urgent reason to get home. I had prayed. In a church. For the first time. With all my heart and soul. I prayed it would even be answered as I rushed home. For months, before this sudden burst of biblical belief, there were dozens of times I'd lie in the dark, alone, on a concave mattress that smelled worse than the bathroom, asking my father to come home. I knew those unspoken yearnings didn't really qualify as a prayer because I was addressing them to my dad. But today I did it properly. I asked God directly, almost in person. At His place.

When I ran up the stairs, I knew he would be there as sure as the door I was opening. I hollered, "Dad! Dad!" No answer. I stood a moment listening. I ran through every room in the house, upstairs and down. No one was home. I looked in the basement. I couldn't believe it. I knew I had done it the way you're supposed to. Maybe I screwed it up and it went undelivered because I applauded. There had to be a reason. My mind ached as I searched and searched for one. Until I got tired. Soon I was as quiet and as empty as my home. And hungry. I did what I always did when my mother was out of town for a few days with another "uncle." I poured a bowl of corn flakes.

I didn't quite know what to do with the rest of the day. I thought about running up to see if Mel was home, but realized I didn't feel like doing anything. Then I spotted Mrs. Lee's gift next to the empty bowl. The Bible. It made me feel better. Now I had something to do. I placed the dirty bowl in the sink with all the other dirty bowls, sat down at the kitchen table and began to read. I didn't get undressed. I didn't go to bed. I didn't even brush my teeth. I was close to the end when it was time to go to school the next morning. I was unfazed by the fact my mother and sister had not come home. I had become very proficient at forging my mother's name to those reason-for-John's-absence notes, so, I skipped class again. This time for something other than hockey, and dove into Leviticus and Revelations.

The Last Two Arenas

I only went to church twice again with the Lees. I again asked God to bring my dad home. I wanted to get it really right this time, so I wasn't too pushy. I told Him He didn't have to get him there that afternoon. Sometime that week would be fine. Wednesday would be perfect. Right after school. I was careful not to clap again for Mr. Decker, even though he deserved an ovation.

His voice was the only truly heavenly or spiritual thing in the building. Except for Mrs. Lee. As she had said, he sang a different hymn from *The Lord's Prayer*, which moved me even more. Especially the lyrics. I do not recall the title; just a few of the words: 'I wonder as I wander out under the sky, 'bout a poor little shepherd who came for to die.' God, it was beautiful.

Wednesday showed up, but not my father. Sunday my prayers stopped, along with church-going. In the middle of the sermon, I just stood up and started to walk out.

"Johnny, what's wrong?" Mrs. Lee asked.

"I don't feel well," I whispered. 'I'll wait outside."

Outside, I stopped, took a deep breath, then let the air surge out of me. It was such a relief, a sudden cleansed feeling of getting this heavy heavenly distracting stuff out of my system. I sat on the cement stairs to wait.

The minister had seen me leave. He was the first to greet me with the Lees, all asking if I was all right.

"I'm fine," I said.

The minister put his hand on my shoulder. "Are you sure?"

My eyes suddenly started to tear up. Not because his question was so penetrating, but because he was touching me. I could not recall ever being touched. To break the spell, and to be honest, I said softly, "This just isn't working for me. Praying." I looked away, not wanting to make eye contact with Mrs. Lee.

The minister patted my shoulder. "John, you just have to accept God's will."

Not knowing where it came from, I blurted, "I don't think I'm in it!"

Don chuckled. As did his father. The minister smiled, removing his hand. There was an awkward silence.

Mrs. Lee took my arm. "Let's get something to eat, shall we."

Later, Mrs. Lee said, "You know, John, you and your friends are more than welcome to come here and play your games a couple times a week,"

"Yes, John," the father added. "I'd love to see how you play it."

Don's father, always with a slight smile, almost never talked. His interest in our enterprise added to my affection for this family. It also added to the unease I was beginning to feel when with them. I was looking at them sitting next to me, and yet felt they were drifting away – like Dorothy in *The Wizard of Oz* when the Weather Channel lifted her out of Kansas. I realized I would never be part of this happy family. They could be no part of my life, nor I a part of theirs.

"That's nice," I said, "but we already have good setups in Smitty's and Franky's basements."

"We don't have much space in our basement, but you could use the dining room table. Wouldn't that be nicer?" Mrs. Lee asked.

Not knowing quite how to politely decline, I said, "We get awfully noisy sometimes!"

"That's what we'd expect from boys." She smiled.

If she knew what we did at Smitty's and Frank's, she would have thought we'd all gone to hell. I thanked her and her husband sincerely for all they had done for me, and that I'd come by to see them often. But I never did. Thirty-five years later, though, I saw Don in the audience for *Real People;* while I was doing the warm-up for my show I was walking up the aisles with a microphone searching out *Real People* announcers who would say before and after the commercial breaks, "We'll be right back with more *Real People,*" or "Welcome back to *Real People.*" The face of the first person I looked at seemed familiar. It was a round warm face of a man in his late forties. He was with his wife and son. It wasn't the face so much that was familiar; it was the gentleness of its glow. In an instant, I said, "Don. Don Lee!"

He smiled that still tolerant smile and said, "Johnny MacLaren!"

"I used to be," I whispered, then introduced him to the audience, telling them when I was a kid I wanted his parents to adopt me so I could be his brother.

Don said softly, "If you had been, you'd be sitting here like me. In the audience. Instead of there. On stage and a TV star."

All those years earlier, though, when I left their house filled with love, it was the first time I ever felt happy going home to my house deprived of it. I had this feeling of freedom. Freedom from the brief burden of belief in an unseen Almighty who never answered my prayers. I was also suddenly free of the belief that my mother and father would answer my needs for them. It was an epiphany. I realized I was alone in an unknown universe. I did not know how an acorn becomes an oak tree; how could I possibly understand how a bang or spark could create a universe? I'd read that it's an electric universe, and that sparks in water created life. That is chemistry at work; not the hand of God. Pursuing the how of that chemistry leads to knowledge. Pursuing an unknowable God leads to mythology. Nature gave us a life; however, only we can give it purpose. Heady stuff for a twelve-year-old.

Since that day I have never met a devotedly religious person who was not prejudiced; or a spiritual person who was. I had firmly believed I had given up prayer. But not quite. Since we're talking truth, twenty years later I was alone, broke, sitting in the small chapel of a Salvation Army Hostel on College St. in Toronto. The only thing religious about the dimly lit room was the statue of Christ on the cross. I didn't ask for money. I had long ago stopped asking about my mother and father. They along with any family had been deleted completely, along with the memory of the Baptist Church on Scarborough Road.

What I prayed for, by myself, was just to have more emotional and mental strength to continue my hopeless Don Quixote quest. There was nothing I ever wanted more than to go to America. Legally. But the US Immigration Service had said forcefully no. Twice. I prayed they would change their laws or I could change their minds. This one was answered!

Playoffs and Gas-offs

The two places where we held our games and our Stanley Cup Playoffs were at Larry Smith's and Frank Motley's. Larry, of course, was called "Smitty," which was later lengthened to "Shitty

Smitty" because of this weird, kind of crude entertainment that he prided himself on. His basement wasn't always available for our games because this is where "Smith Enterprises" was located. What this family enterprise was making or manufacturing was electric cords. It had started during the war as a way for the family to make a few extra dollars, but soon became so successful Smitty's father quit his job to work full time with his two brothers and his mother. This brought the family closer. Which was unfortunate, especially for the neighbors because families who work with one another eventually, no matter how much money they make, yell at one another. To Smitty's family, screaming was their means of communicating. That might have been okay had it been their own business; but it became the neighbors, always hollering for them to shut the windows and shut up. And, of course, the police came often to show them how the windows worked. None of which reduced the decibel level.

Smitty's arena was half a block down from my house on the other side of the street. Frank Motley's was a few blocks east of that just outside the city limits at the time. Frank's nickname was "BB," short for Beaky Buzzard. Frank's family was second generation English, but looked first generation in-bred. The father was the spitting image of Basil Rathbone, and young Frank was the spitting image of his father, which wasn't too attractive on a twelve-year-old. His appearance was also hampered by slightly bucked upper teeth. But that's not how he got his nickname. He got it because in profile, his Adams apple was in competition to be as long and pointed as his nose. It was bigger than Ann Coulter's. The only attractive one of the four was his eighteen-year-older sister, Dell.

Frank's father loved billiards, beer, and family time. To accommodate all three, he converted the downstairs basement into two large, separate, beautiful playrooms and lounging areas. At one end was a table for Frank's "rink," and at the other end, a pool table, a refrigerator, and cushioned sofas and chair. There wasn't one lump of coal. Often important playoff games were left unfinished. They were frequently interrupted by the upstairs sounds of love songs. This meant Dell was upstairs with her boyfriend. We never did get to see his face, just his backside. As soon as we heard The Ink Spots singing *You Always Hurt the One You Love,* Frank would put his finger to his lips and motion us to follow. We'd creep quickly up the stairs, down the hall to the back bedroom with its slightly open door, and peak in. Clothes were on the floor. Naked bodies on the bed. The familiar backside was on Dell. The Ink spots were now competing with the sounds of love-making. We always finished watching before they finished performing, and scurried back down to our game, which we never resumed. We'd giggle and sing *the Farmer's in the Dell*! I never questioned it, but I could never understand why Frank would want us to watch his sister. I also wondered about Dell, why her door was always ajar.

There were also similar distractions at Smitty's place. A film in French. It was black and white and grainy and about six minutes long. No matter where we were in our games, even the Stanley Cup Playoffs, the minute Smitty's parents were out the door and off to see a war movie, (a war they hoped would never end) we were off to see Smitty's movie. It was just a French maid in front of a full-length mirror removing all her clothes to try on lacy undergarments. Before she had the second one on, we all had ours off. We'd be lying on the floor, pants around our ankles, our backs propped up against the wall to watch the film, and each other to see who was the most man. It was Smitty. I said, "Of course it would be. He watches it more than us."

Once in a while, with trousers off we engaged in another embarrassing contest, one I have since learned is more common than when we did it exclusively. For some reason known only to Nature, when Smitty was excited, he did not produce sperm. He produced gas. He could burp on demand. And did often. More than that, he could fart forever, much to his own delight. He considered it an Art to fart. His solitary talent. None of us was his equal. To demonstrate his superior skills, he would bend over, asking one of us to get close and light a match. No one volunteered. Proudly he would light his own, and poof; in one short blast it was out.

"You guys try that!" I am ashamed to say we all did. Some of us were gasless.

"Jesus," Mel said, watching Smitty once again produce another instantaneous flame extinguishing fart, "do you think you could blow out a candle?" We all laughed. But not Smitty. His eyes lit up at the challenge. "Wait a minute." And he rushed off while we quickly pulled up our pants.

Momentarily, he returned with a large purple, scented candle that had been lit often. Evidently Smitty's parents watched that movie by candlelight. He lit it, handed it to Mel, then crouched. It gave off a lilac aroma. Smitty looked back at Mel confidently. "Hold it a little closer." Mel bent over to get it into Smitty's firing distance.

"Thank God." Mel bent over to hold it close to Smitty's firing distance. "This at least smells nice."

After a few more intakes of oxygen, Smitty announced, "Here it comes!" He let it fly.

The sound of flatulence was short-lived, drowned out by the huge explosion and fireball that followed. It was Krakatoa. Evidently Smitty had taken in too much oxygen. He fell over, rolling around screaming. So were we. In laughter.

"I'm burning. I'm burning!" he howled as he tried to leap up and run to the bathroom, his ankles shackled by his trousers. From the bathroom we heard the sound of water running and his imploring the Almighty or us to help him.

"God. God. Help me. Help me, please. I'm burned!"

No one could get up. We kept rolling around with laughter.

"I'm all red. I'm all red. It's blistering. Come and look!"

This invitation to view the changing of his skin color went unheeded. It only fueled our fits of stomach-hurting laughter.

"Oh, God. God!" he implored now in a maniacal falsetto. "My balls are turning black!"

"Stop it. Stop it," we were squeaking at him so we could suck in some air.

In time, his howling turned into whimpering. "Come and look. Come and look."

Curious as to what damage had been inflicted, but not too anxious to look, Mel said, "Who wants to see Black Balls?" That did it! We started guffawing again.

Sitting in the tub half filled with water with a tinge of red and black in it, and with his pants on and soaked, sat the most pathetic sight I'd ever seen in my life. I started to laugh against my will.

Don opened the medicine cabinet, found a jar of Vaseline and handed it to Smitty. "Here," he said. "This'll help."

I thought about how calm Don was, and recalled that over at Frank's house, he hadn't even come up the stairs to watch the floor show. While the French film was on, so were his pants. Also, while we had been rolling around on the floor laughing, he just sat to the side smiling. Never a participant. Always a spectator. He was never judgmental, or offended by what we did. He didn't need to engage in shenanigans like that to enjoy life more or to escape from it. He also never called any of us by our nicknames. Only our real names. Naturally, Mel insisted on nicknaming Smitty "NiggerNuts" from here on, but out of deference to my right-winger, Ernie, at the orphanage, we called him 'CC.' Short for Crispy Crotch!

In our boredom, thinking of things to kill time, we once thought of something that almost killed *us*. The Main Street railyard was one of the largest in the city, just a few blocks from us, on the other side of Gerard Street. Six major lines passed through the center to accommodate all the passenger and freight traffic. On either side were scores of other tracks where empty passenger cars and boxcars were constantly being stored or shunted around.

Climbing all over and hiding in these was something we did often. What we loved to do more, was to do that when they were in motion. When a line of empty boxcars was being assembled to be pulled off somewhere, we would wait until they began to pick up speed, then we'd run alongside and leap up, grab the steel ladders and pull ourselves up. Sometimes we'd just hang on; other times we'd climb to the top and walk shakily along the narrow walkways, the breeze blowing in our faces. We made a game of this: the last one to jump aboard the accelerating car was always declared the winner. One time, Mel and I tried clambering aboard at the same time, and by the time we'd gotten ourselves up, the train was moving so fast we were unable to jump off. We laughed all the way to Hamilton, about fifty miles away. We were able to secure our transportation home in the same manner the following day. Our families didn't even know we were gone.

One week, a story filled the newspapers and radio for days. It was about a young man who had been run over by a train and lived. He claimed he fell crossing the tracks and could not get up as a train approached, so he lay down between the ties as close to the ground as possible, and it passed over him without a scratch. We heard and read about it and thought we could do that. So off went four of us to the railyards we knew as well as anyone who worked there.

Bragging about this easy undertaking, which might get us in the news, we quickly crossed the first dozen or so storage tracks, climbing over or under where the boxcars were coupled together. We didn't waste time climbing over the tops and down the ladders. We stopped by the main center lines, watching and waving at a couple of passenger trains thundering by. We edged closer and closer to them, feeling the earth rumble and the wind blow, showing off our bravery.

When they passed, Mel was declared the bravest. Then we spotted the perfect place. A line of empty boxes so long we only knew there was an engine from the distant smoke. We hurried to get into position, lying down between the wheels near the coupling, giggling with excitement. The bottom of the cars was a couple of feet above the ground, but the railroad ties weren't really pushed down into the ground. They protruded about four inches. There were weeds, rocks and trash.

Mel said, "I wonder if this was the spot where the guy was."

"I'd lie right there, the way that guy did," Frank piped up.

"Yeah," Smitty agreed.

"Yeah," I said, not wanting to be left out. "I think I could do that, too!"

We were soon in position. And quiet. Staring at one another.

"We'd better put our heads down," Mel said. "Or one of us'll lose it."

We did so and got even quieter. It was really uncomfortable. All we could see was the close bottom of the boxcar above us. Suddenly we heard a distant rumble. Our heads popped up.

"What was that?" we blurted in unison.

"Nothing," Mel said, unconvincingly.

Then more rumbling. We sat up, more alert, listening intently. It was getting like a wave. Suddenly, the couplings over our heads jerked violently forward. The wheels on either side spun quickly, setting off sparks and smoke. Struggling for traction. It was moving! We were screaming and trying to escape, flailing our legs and feet.

"Jesus Christ! Jesus Christ!" we cried and yelled. Frank, whose face was frozen white, screamed that we were all going to die.

"Oh, God! God. God." We were crying and whimpering.

With only a few feet between the cars under the couplings, there was little time or space for all four of us to scramble through, but we all lunged unthinkingly in that same direction. Smitty and Frank were seated closest; they scrambled out first, the wheels barely missing cutting off their kicking legs. Mel and me were left underneath.

We crawled like mindless scared rats. The couplings jerked slowly, disappearing over our heads. There was a space for us to roll over the track before the next coupling was upon us. We were hollering incoherently now, screaming in tongues. Mel was first over the rails. To propel himself faster, he began kicking at me. I couldn't move. I was stuck, pushing him off with my hands and trying to push the wheels away with my feet. I was halfway out now; just my upper body. I could see the next set of wheels. I curled my legs up as far as I could and began kicking and thrashing, at the track, at the ground, then a wheel. I was almost out; I felt my right foot under the rolling wheel, this enormous pressure against my heel. I lashed at it with my left foot, screaming. And suddenly, I was out. I lay on the ground gasping and gulping. I grabbed my right leg to look down at my foot. The entire heel of my shoe had been severed. Even a piece of the sock was missing.

"Jesus Christ!" I kept repeating. Then, uncontrollably, I began to giggle. And giggle. I couldn't stop. I turned and looked to my left, and about twenty feet away, lying on his back staring at the sky was Mel. He was giggling, too.

We got up laughing like hyenas. But why? It wasn't funny. Fifty yards away, we caught up to Smitty and Frank, who were sitting at the top of the gully, safely away from the tracks. They also were rolling around giggling.

No one said a word. Not even months later. To speak of it would be a reminder of how our proud predictions about how heroically we would perform in a disaster morphed into real cowardice. Crises do not create character, they reveal it. As Redd Foxx said: "Heroes ain't born; they're cornered!"

Adam Beck School Daze

I was not a good student at Adam Beck public school, which was just two blocks down from where I lived. But I was a successful one; that is, if success is determined solely by grades. I never studied. Never did homework. At home, I was too busy dodging blows to be worried about books. School books anyway. But Tarzan and Huckleberry Finn, and short stories by Gordon Sinclair and O. Henry and even Somerset Maugham, I devoured. I didn't have to learn or memorize anything in those books. I just had to climb in and go on a journey. On tests, I never got below a seventy-five out of a hundred or below a B-plus. I was an honor student. In class. Outside the class, I was like the old joke: Yes, your Honor. No, your Honor!

For seven years, I attended fairly often, mostly when I felt like it. I took a few days off a month to play hockey or see a movie matinee. My grades allowed me to legitimately skip a year. My first attempts at successful writing were the excuse notes signed by "John's mother." My excuses were right out of Heinz: I had fifty-seven varieties!

Miss Britton, our very pretty, early twenties sixth grade teacher once remarked that I was a surprisingly good athlete for someone so sickly all the time. I got some of my best grades in her class, and some of my worst corporal punishment. She also singlehandedly ended my desire to play for the Toronto Maple Leafs. In a survey, she asked her students what they wanted to be when they grew up. Those who said doctor or nurse, or policeman or fireman or scientist were loudly applauded by her and the class. When I said hockey player, she immediately said, "No one plays hockey for a real living. Instantly, I began reeling off the names of the entire team before she hissed, "Sit down!" The class booed.

I still played, mostly because it was something I could enjoy alone, but the passion to be a pro melted like the August ice.

In her class, she liked to have the smartest kids seated closest to her desk. She could talk to them and call on them without having to stand up or raise her voice. As only a B-plus student, I was seated about a third of the way down from her in the middle aisle, until I inadvertently noticed something or rather a lack of something. Her class was on the second floor, near the stairs. One day when the bell rang, dismissing us from her class, I was out the door quickly, as I usually was, and in my haste to fly down the stairs, I dropped my books. The other kids pushed past me as I tried to retrieve them. Miss Britton usually came to the top of the stairs to watch her wards go to their other classes, recess or lunch. This time she leaned against the railing with her arms folded, and her legs slightly apart.

"Are you all right, Johnny?"

I scrambled to recover my books directly below her. When I looked up to answer her, I couldn't see her face. What I *could* see was she wore no panties!

"I'm fine," I said, lowering my head quickly, fumbling with my books. It was the first time I ever took them home to study.

In short order, my newfound scholarship found me in the front seat in the middle row, directly in front of her desk. Not ten feet away. A whole lot nearer than a stair landing. When she moved me there, she announced proudly to the class that "our little hockey player, Johnny MacLaren, was indeed learning something." I was now the top graded student in her class. Like the movies, I always liked those close-ups. I only had a vague idea of what sex was, but for some reason I was overcome with this need to see more of what I saw on the stairs.

The first week or two of sitting there, I rehearsed my moves. Cautiously, I would 'accidentally' drop a pencil or two, bend over, take a quick look, and retrieve it. I saw her knees, smooth and white. Always apart. No stockings. With this growing addiction, my clumsiness grew. I soon was agile and quick enough to linger longer in my search. The last one resulted in a few seconds' view of her thighs. The tunnel of love. Oh, God, what was wrong with me? That was all I could think about. Nothing in life existed, but getting to the light at the end of that tunnel. Fearing she might be getting suspicious, I desisted for three weeks. I waited until she was deeply engrossed in marking exam papers, an exam I mastered immediately.

With her head down and totally preoccupied, I dropped an eraser. Unlike a pencil or ruler, it made no sound. I got a lucky bounce. It ended up almost directly under her desk. Rather than bend over to pick it up and peek, I got out of my seat, down on my knees, and crawled forward. I was almost head first under her desk, in a perfect position for birdwatching, when her legs suddenly snapped shut and she stood. "Mr. MacLaren!"

Scrambling backwards on all fours as quickly as I could, I banged my head on her desk. It was nothing compared to the pounding on my head from the long pointer she bashed me with, screaming with each blow, "Never mind, Mr. MacLaren! They're white!"

The class was shocked into frozen silence. All I could think of was, she's a liar. She wasn't wearing anything. She never did. She threw down the pointer, lunged at me, yanking my ear, lifting me right out of my chair. She never let go of it till we got to the principal's office. I was used to this mode of involuntary transportation. The ear is the first thing angry mothers and female teachers grab. The principal was used to seeing me. And I him. He must have been close to sixty and 200 pounds. Clothes must have been hard to find for larger people then because he always wore the same ill-fitting brown pin-stripe suit. He seemed like a giant with a wide pasty face framed by extremely large flat pancake-shaped ears. His popular nickname was 'Uncle Jemima.' He had lashed my hands so often with his rubber metal-lined strap soaked in lemon water that they bled easily this time. I winced, but never made a sound. The first time he lashed me that hard was when he heard I was the author of his nickname. Each blow turned my mind into anger. If this were a court, I could prove Miss Britton had corrupted me and lied. Make her lift her skirt! I grew to hate authority. You can never reason with them because they are bigger and never wrong. And have no sense of humor. I also grew leery of men in suits. I still am.

A Midnight Enterprise

My dream of lifting the Stanley Cup at Maple Leaf Gardens may have been severely damaged by that classroom experience, but I never lost my physical passion for playing hockey. In the early 1970's, I got to do it again. John Perry, Matthew Perry's talented father, Bo Swenson, the huge Swedish star of *Walking Tall* fame, and I formed The Hollywood Celebrity Hockey Team, which I believe is still there.

In Toronto, hockey was the major pastime that kept me out of life's penalty boxes. After that career-day class ended my dream career, I still played hookie to play hockey down at St. John's. By myself, I still took the ten-mile trip at night on the streetcar to the Gardens on Carlton and Young Streets, and paid the fifty cents for standing room.

What was difficult to come by, though, was the fifty cents. I never got an allowance. Neither did Mel. Smitty "Crispy Crotch" got a few dollars a month for helping with the manufacture of his family's electrical cords. Jerry Tomassini got a quarter for every bottle of his mother's wine he'd sell. Beaky Buzzard got paid a pittance for the constant chores assigned him by his father. None of their income was shared with me and Mel.

Often at night, I'd lie in my sinkhole of a bed, imagining ways of making easy money. I even wrote them out efficiently. I needed at least \$3.50 a week. There was seventy-five cents for hockey and carfare. Fifty cents for movies and Coffee Crisps. A dollar for fish and chips. And a dollar and a quarter for the poker games I was starting to get into. That's \$3.50. No matter how hard I tried to conjure up an enterprise where I could make this prodigious sum every week, nothing came to mind. Be a paper boy. Are you kidding? In the winter, get up at 4:30 AM? I could think of more ways to steal it than earn it. I could begin with my mother. I saw her purse lying around as much as I saw her lying around. That became my *Treasure of Sierra Madre*. Of course, I had to be subtle and not steal all her change. It only led to \$1.25 a week. This was enough for standing room at the Garden, or to treat Mel to a movie and fish and chips. It wasn't that I liked his company. I liked the fact that when I treated him he wasn't punching me.

Early one nice warm evening, we were on the swings at the end of Adam Beck's cindered playground finishing our fish and chips, when through the front gate came the silhouetted figure of a woman moving very quickly toward us. I recognized my mother's walk from three hundred yards. Even if she was sober. But this wasn't just a walk. This was a jog.

She called out to me, "You little bastard!" her voice echoing through the playground.

"Jesus, it's my mother," I whispered hoarsely to Mel. But I was speaking to myself. Mel was gone. Along with our fish and chips.

My mother lunged at me; her half-closed fist plowed into my cheek. Chewed fish splattered out all over us. "You little bastard, you've been stealing from me. How long? How much?" She whacked me with each question.

With my head ducked in my arms, I said, "Just a couple of quarters, Mom. That's all."

"How long, goddamn it?"

"Just a couple of weeks." I answered truthfully but plaintively.

"Get home right now. Goddamn you. You selfish little bugger!"

"I'm sorry," I said, more in self-defense than honesty.

"You're just like your goddamned father! You little bastard!"

Somehow, having her compare me to my father made me feel, strangely, a little better about myself. Then she grabbed me violently by the ear, still raw from recent tugging. I never once saw her tugging my sister Maggie's ear.

At home in the kitchen, I thought I was safe, but I wasn't. She grabbed a broom, something she never used for sweeping, and began bashing me. With each blow she was informing me at the top of her shrill voice of my inadequacies, that I came from unmarried parents. That I was a worthless piece of crap who has come to no good end! I ducked, sheltering my head with my forearms, but kept an eye on her to see where she'd strike next. In doing so, this madwoman suddenly became the Wicked Witch of the North. A total stranger. Within a few years, she soon would be. Forever.

With my mother's source of trickledown economics denied me, I decided to go to my financial plan B. In those days, people didn't buy milk at the market. They had it delivered. At night. Late at night. By a milkman. Often just before the newspaper. And the milkman delivered it in bottles. The empties he would pick up. Each containing a minimum of eleven cents to a quarter to pay for the new delivery. These empties with their coins were usually placed late after dinner at the very top of the veranda stairs next to the railing to make it easier for the milkman, and us, to reach. I couldn't believe someone hadn't thought of it before. "What about it?" I said to Mel after explaining my brainstorm.

"Geez, that's terrific. That'd be easy! When would we start?"

"Right away. Tonight," I replied, anxious to get started before somebody else got the idea.

"Wouldn't you want to wait a few weeks?" he said. "Until March when it warms up a bit?"

"If it is warmer, there might be people out. This way there'll be nobody around."

"We'll freeze!"

"No, we won't," I insisted.

"Okay. Tonight then. After midnight meet me in front of my house. My mom usually puts a quarter in the bottle." Mel smiled.

"You're not gonna steal from your mom, are you?" I asked.

"You did!" he pointed out. We both giggled with excitement.

Waiting for the cover of darkness, I put on an extra sweater under a heavy jacket, and long underwear torn in a couple of places. After wrapping my feet in my usual newspaper, I put on a pair of big galoshes. I had only one pair of what passed for shoes. I then grabbed a pair of bulky mittens. Mel was dressed almost identically.

"Okay. Let's go," Mel said. "Where do you wanna start?"

We decided we'd better start much farther away from home. I immediately discarded the mittens. We scampered down the street on a wintery night under a full moon, a little nervous, and lucky that God was shining a spotlight on us.

We worked seven entire streets, starting on Main Street, which was right next to the police department and jail. The proximity of this ultimate symbol of authority made starting here more challenging and exciting. We cleaned out five blocks east of Lawlor Avenue in less than an hour. Like true thieves, we'd cuss the homeowners who left nothing in their bottles to steal. I began to imagine how much we could make over the next few years doing that just once a week. In a new location every time. Until we'd cleaned out Toronto. The whole city. Before l could calculate that, though, I needed to know exactly what our take was.

Back on Lawlor Avenue, half a block from home, I said, "Let's stop and count it."

"Not yet," Mel said. "Let's do one more street! It's early."

"Okay," I agreed. "Just Scarborough Road. Down to Kingston Road. And that's it!"

"Great," Mel said.

We emptied every available milk bottle on Scarborough Road of its contents in forty-five minutes, stopping just short of Kingston Road. The one house we didn't touch was Don Lee's. With so many coins in our pockets when we walked we sounded like a chain gang. Looking for a spot to stop to sit and count our earnings, we decided not to get too close to Kingston Road. As a major thoroughfare with streetcars and traffic there were too many lights. We were right in front of the Baptist Church. I'll be damned, I thought, this must have been a good omen. We had our own overflowing collection plate.

Warmed by the weight in our pockets, we sat on the curb. I emptied my bulging pockets onto the sidewalk. In the dim moonlight, the silver twinkled like stars; I counted and giggled. I was so lost in the luxury of all this wealth, I couldn't hear Mel. So absorbed was I, I hadn't noticed he was no longer seated next me. I was up to nearly fifteen dollars, and hadn't even finished. I turned excitedly to ask him how much he had. He was not there. I turned to my left, away from Kingston road. He was running back up the street into the darkness, being chased by someone in a uniform. Both were illuminated by a floodlight from the top of a police car that came screeching to a halt right next to me. A cop the size of King Kong leaped out of the driver's side, leaving the door open, and rushed at me. I didn't even try to move. The cop chasing Mel caught him quickly. As Mel's hands were clasped harshly behind his back, he started yelling at the cop, pleading, pointing in my direction. "He's got it all, it was his idea!" Sitting cuffed in the back seat of this caged car, all the way to the Main Street, my best friend kept announcing his innocence and my guilt. I couldn't look at him. He was Benedict Arnold. I stared out the window seeing homes we'd just robbed, wondering if I'd ever see them again, and wondering what they'd put in their cereal and coffee in the morning.

The car pulled into the back well-lit parking lot behind the corner station. King Kong opened my door, grabbed me by the left bicep and lifted me out, as easily as I had just lifted quarters, dragged me up the stairs and into the booking area. I was relieved. I wasn't being dragged by the ear.

Mel's captor ordered Mel to empty his pockets. All that came out was a flimsy, worn wallet, some chewing gum, and house keys.

Jesus, I thought, *where's the money*? *His pockets were as full as mine.*

King Kong ordered me to do the same. Out poured my fifteen dollars in quarters and nickels and dimes. And my flimsy wallet and a half-eaten Coffee Crisp.

"What's this, young man?" the beast of authority asked in a voice that was surprisingly casual and nonthreatening.

"Money," I said just as casually.

He stared at me, as if to say, don't be a smartass. "Where'd you get it?"

"Some ... some of it ... out of my mother's purse."

"Is your mother's purse shaped like a milk bottle?"

"No, sir."

"Come over here. Both of you!"

They led us to a desk that towered over us. There we stood while another officer went through the Dragnet routine of asking us our names, ages, addresses, and phone numbers. Finished, he pointed to a huge cell with thick metal bars. "Do you two want to wait in there for a couple of years, or would you rather sit there, while we call your parents?" He began dialing, his voice low and matter-of-fact. We couldn't hear what he was saying or to whom he was saying it. Nervousness suddenly overtook me. Thinking it might be my mother, I wanted to throw up.

He hung up, made his way around the desk, and walked over to us. I noticed that he'd only made one call.

"Do you know, if you two had stolen much more, you could be sent to a juvenile facility for two years."

We were as frozen and as silent as empty milk bottles.

"Right now, you're on our record books. If you do any of this sort of thing again, you will be in a larger cell than that." I was surprised when he added, "John, your mother is on her way. She did not sound too pleased to hear from us."

Oh my God. I felt better in handcuffs.

In a tone that seemed almost friendly, he said, "John, was this all your idea?"

"Yes," I said, feebly. Because it was my idea.

"We called Mel's mother. Since it's so late, we told her he was out a little too late, that there was nothing to worry about, and we'd see to it he got home all right."

Inside I was screaming. I only heard one call. When did he call Mel's mother? And what's this crap about a police escort home for a lying co-conspirator and partner in crime just because he turned State's evidence

The booking sergeant said to Mel, pointing to the officers who'd arrested us, "Go with them, young man. They'll take you home."

Jesus Christ! A liar's reward! It was a stomach turning, tormenting eternity until my mother showed up. Her eyes were slits, the kind of intense focus I'd seen in dozens of war movies when a sniper was about to pick off a Kraut or Jap. With a fake smile, she thanked the officer in charge, apologizing for her son's behavior, promising that nothing like that would ever happen again over her dead body, when what she actually meant, was my dead body! I'd heard it 100 times.

Without a word I followed her out the door into what was at that time the coldest, cruelest night of my life. We hadn't gone very far, me walking very slowly behind her, when she hissed, "I should've let them lock you up and throw away the key. You worthless bugger. Wait till you get home."

I picked up my pace, walking around her at a distance till I was about ten paces in front. I could hear her clicking heels and cussing. I felt I was being stalked. And I was. Her rage was so suppressed I knew she could not wait till we got home. Then she sprang, in a rage, just a block away from the station. Her fists hammered the back of my head wildly, each whack punctuated with profanity.

I could have outrun her easily. But I didn't. I would just be postponing the inevitable. So I stopped. I turned to face her. To look at her. This sometimes very pretty face was unrecognizable with hate. I knew I did deserve some kind of discipline. So, I thought I'd just get it over with, there after midnight, in the dead of winter on a moonlit deserted street. What hurt more than the blows, which I no longer ducked from, was the look on the face of someone I no longer recognized. Or knew. She had tiny tear in her eye.

"I'm sorry," I said in a whisper, and turned and ran, leaving her there.

Her curses echoed through the night. I raced through the front door and leaped two by two up the stairs into my room. It had no key, so I couldn't lock it. Instead I moved the bed, with its huge metal frame, behind the door and waited. I was The Hunchback of Notre Dame waiting in the cathedral while the enraged citizenry, in the person of my mother, would try to batter it down. I heard the front door open and close. My mother, ascended the stairs, grumbling. The grumble of an alcoholic. When she found the door wouldn't budge, she became more unhinged. "You're finally gonna get what you have coming to you. I'm going to tell Garth!"

Hearing that name brought me to a standstill. It terrified me. Garth was one of the more than half a dozen "uncles" my mother had brought home from her pub crawling. By far the worst. He was a sergeant in the Army, always in uniform, except in the house when he was in his underwear. He was the spitting image of a successful Hollywood actor named Dennis O'Keefe. Except bigger. He was what was called a terrible drunk. I wouldn't know the other side of him because I never saw him sober. He was often gone two or three weeks at a time, training recruits how to kill with their bare hands. Even during these Garth-free sabbaticals, I, and even little Maggie, were still tense with fear, knowing he would eventually show up. In the 1950's, I saw his exact likeness in *From Here to Eternity.* It was Ernest Borgnine sadistically and happily killing Montgomery Clift with his fists. I felt like Monty.

It was during one of these sabbaticals that Mel and I had embarked on our easy money escapade. For the few days after my arrest and beating, my mother made a point of avoiding me. I moved about the house, when I was home, quietly and cautiously, not on the lookout for my mother, but for Garth. The only time I saw someone I was remotely interested in seeing was when I brushed my teeth staring into the mirror. I was all I had.

I was my own best friend. But from what I was doing with myself, I was not a very good one. The only one I even thought of talking to was Mel. But what could I say to such a vile turncoat? I tried to rehearse what I'd call him, but all I wanted to do was punch him. Kill him.

As casual as you please, though, he just came and knocked on the door. When I opened it, the Tyrone Power smile was so surprising it drained the speeches and punches right out of me,

"Hey," he said, as though nothing had happened. "Wanna go to a movie?"

I was stunned., I couldn't answer.

"Come on, let's go. Gary Cooper's playin."

"I ... I ... don't have any money," I stammered.

"Don't worry. I got plenty," he said, almost laughing. "Let's go."

I didn't say anything. I closed the door and followed him down the stairs. He stopped for a moment. Reaching into his pockets without taking his eyes off me, he pulled his fists out and unfolded them like blossoming flowers. They were full of coins!

"Look!" he exclaimed.

"Where'd you get that?" I gasped.

"When I saw the cop car coming down the street, I dumped it under some garbage in the curb, and ran the other way, away from it." He was so pleased and proud of his deception. "He just chased me. Never even bothered looking. Dumb shit. After they dropped me off in front of the house, I waited until they left, then ran back and got it!" He was bursting with achievement. Now I wanted to punch that smirk off his face. "So, let's go to the movies and get something to eat. And of course, half of it is yours."

"What?" I asked, taken aback.

"Certainly, partner. We were partners."

I was not only surprised, I was moved. Holy smoke, I did have a best friend. His handful of coins, over seven dollars, may have enriched my purse, but his unnecessary generosity of sharing enriched my soul. It was nice to have such a friend, especially one I had often considered an enemy. I learned two valuable lessons that day: the value of friendship, and how to whistle like Gary Cooper.

A few years later, my friend and I were arrested almost at the same spot at the same time. This time for Grand Larceny. Again, on a cold winter night with nothing to do, we wandered down to Adam Beck to a dance. Mel wore a nice warm jacket. I only had a sweater. Neither of us intended to dance; just look around. The romantically lit room with filled with boys and girls, snuggled close, slow dancing to the Ink Spots singing *If I Didn't Care*. Mel was watching them. I was watching Bill Pugsley. He was checking a beautiful overcoat. I was checking it out.

When he and his date moved to the dance floor, and with the teacher checking the coats preoccupied, I grabbed the coat, grabbed Mel, and said, "Let's beat it." An hour and a half later we were sitting on Scarborough Road again, this time counting major spoils. On impulse, we had just looted a small confectionery store on Kingston Road, one which we had frequented often. With the new topcoat's sleeve protecting my hand, I bashed it through the glass by the handle. The pockets we filled with candy, pens, lighters, souvenirs, knickknacks, everything that would fit. When two police cars showed up this time, there was no running. Not even for Mel. We were locked up for nearly a week in the Don River jail. My mother, standing rigid and silent in the back of the courtroom, saw me sentenced to two years' probation on two counts of theft, then turned and left. Mel left with his mother. I certainly did not want to go home, so I walked to Jerry Tomassini's house.

A Woman Named Peggy

My mother's name was Margaret; her maiden name, MacDonald. Before I was born, she worked in some kind of line of chorus girls at the Loews Theater on Bay Street. Someone nicknamed her Peggy. The name stuck. But not her gig in showbiz.

I didn't like the fact people called her Peggy. My favorite singer was a balding, ex-law student named Buddy Clark. He had a hauntingly sweet lyric baritone voice, smoother than either Sinatra or Crosby; aside from his major hit, *Linda*, my favorite was *Peg O' My Heart*. When he sang it, images of my mother flowed into my head and ruined the song. I didn't like my mother. There was nothing to like about her. I never saw her read. Or sew. Or cook. Or clean. I never saw her take the initiative to do anything. Perhaps because she was so beautiful, even when drunk, guys did most of those things for her.

She had the face and soft blue eyes of Lana Turner, and the lush full lips of a Viveca Lindford or an Angelina Jolie. She had been a natural auburn brunette most of her life. Before running away to America, I heard from her mother the story of a horrifying encounter at the hidden hands of a jealous suitor-stalker that changed her face and hair and life. Walking home from a streetcar stop after her shift as a saleslady at Simpsons, she was greeted by an ex-lover standing on the stairs. When she looked up to ask him what he was doing there, he said, "This," and threw a bottle of acid in her face. She tried to duck, but it hit the left side, melting her ear into her neck, and scarring her cheek. Months later, when she recovered, she bleached her hair blonde and curled it down over her left eye like Veronica Lake. This made her look even more teasing and seductive.

Hearing this horror story in detail, for the first time, in no way altered my dislike of my mother. It was too late. She had already shaped and misshaped my feelings for her. I only heard the story because I had just gotten my passport and went to say goodbye to the only person I would remotely miss. My grandmother. I saw her seldom. But she was always sweet, making sure I always had tea and scones, some kind of Scottish pastry. She knew what her daughter had become. She also knew she was the reason I was leaving. I think she told me the story because she wanted me to have less hatred in my heart, or at least more tolerance. She told it matter-of-factly, without sadness, in her soft lilting brogue. All I could say when she was done was, "Oh, God. How horrible."

"Life can be horrible son. My mother used tuh say that tuh us wee ones in Dundee, then say, 'After that it just gits hard!'" I almost smiled. She paused. Her voice got stronger. "Ah hope yuh know what yer a doin."

"I do, Grammy. Honestly."

Hearing that terrible tale, I marveled a little at my mother's desire to still look attractive. Her resilience. Maybe that's where I got my genes. To keep going. What it did for me more than anything, though, was answer the question I was always afraid to ask, knowing from experience, anything personal about her was answered instantly with physical retaliation. I had seen the scars a number of times, mostly in the morning, when she hadn't quite finished her makeup. They were ugly. But the night I had to drag her up the stairs I was forced to look at them, and her, more closely.

My grandmother and her husband lived in a small two-story duplex a few blocks from Maple Leaf Gardens. Her husband, a baker at Brown's Bread, hardly spoke, especially to his wife. He had converted the basement into an alternate living room with tables, chairs, sofas, lamps, and radio, and linoleum for carpeting. This is where grandma would always lead me when I took the streetcar journey occasionally to visit.

I was the only one my grandmother ever smiled at. I reminded her of her only son, Buddy, my mom's brother. He, from what they said of him, was evidently a full-throated, full of life, lusty young man who worked on a construction gang. One Sunday morning he was preparing to make repairs to a railing on a bridge over the railroad tracks. He knew there was a truck backing up to unload the wet cement, but paid no attention as it approached, too busy with his task. The driver, however, did not see my uncle, the only real uncle I had. When braking, with his head turned, he pressed the accelerator instead, cutting Buddy in half. It was the first and last funeral I ever attended. There wasn't any wailing, screaming or crying to depress me. All those people filing past an open casket, and not a word. Not a sound. The silence hurt my head. That's why I love those funeral scenes in Italian, Spanish and Latin movies. They wail and scream and thrash the air as if they really missed the dead, even if the corpse is a stranger.

Emotion in my grandmother's house was like the carpeting in the basement. Nonexistent. What really existed was strained silence. After his shocking death, I found out the reason my grandfather built this comfortable underground living room was that he was forbidden to go into the actual upstairs living room. That had to be kept immaculate for company, company that never came. I also discovered that for those thirty years they didn't speak one word to each other. I noticed it during my brief visits, but always thought she talked to him through me because he was deaf. It was weird. "Son," she'd say to me, "tell yerr grandfather tuh git yuh sum napkins." In a flash the napkins would be there.

At sixty-five, when he was forced to take mandatory retirement, the thought of being almost alone in that house in that basement must have felt like being among the living dead. For the first time in his life he was going to ask someone a favor; it crushed his Scot's pride because the *someone* he was asking was his daughter.

My mother, for years, worked her way up at Woolworth's; first as a lunch counter waitress, then as a saleslady, to her final position as assistant store manager. She was doing inventory near the back when she heard a familiar voice say, "Maggie!" Her father never called her Peggy. Neither did her mother.

She turned. "Dad, what are you doing here?"

"I need to talk to you," he said quietly.

"Well, I'm busy right now. Can we do it later?"

"It won't take long," he said.

"I really don't have the time, but–"

"It'll only take a minute, please? Please?"

"Okay," she said. She led him over to the counter, sat him down, went behind it and poured him a cup of tea. Placing it in front of him, she poured in the touch of milk that he liked. "What is it?"

"I need a job."

"What do you mean, you need a job? You're retired. I know they paid you enough to take care of you."

"I don't need the money. I need the job. Any job," he said urgently.

"What on earth for?" my mother asked in a huff.

"I've got to have something to do. I … I just can't sit around the house." He refrained from saying a word about his wife, her mother. He didn't need to. My mother lived it.

"Can't you go back to Brown's?"

"No. I've already tried. I told them I'd work half price and teach the younger bakers, but they said no."

"How about other bakeries? Even some of these smaller shops? Have you tried them?"

"They told me I was too old." After a long pause he said, "There must be something I can do here?"

"Dad, there's nothing you can do here," she stated firmly.

"I could sweep the floors. I don't care, Maggie. Anything. I need to be doing something. Out of the house."

"I don't want people to see my father sweeping floors here, for God's sake."

They looked at each other for a long while. He paused. "They don't have to know I'm your father."

"I'll know you're my father. You go home," my mother said. "Let me think about it. Now, I've got to get back to work."

My grandfather sat for a while after my mother returned to her chores. That night, after his wife had gone to sleep in her small bed in her own room, my grandfather went into the garage, gathered up a large piece of rope, re-entered the house, and climbed the stairs. The next morning my grandmother found him hanging from the chandelier in the front room where he had been forbidden to enter for thirty years. He left no note. He didn't even want to talk to her in death.

An Uncle Named Garth

During the War years, 1939 through 1945, "uncles" around my house were like grapes. They came in bunches! There was "Uncle Ray," a cook from one of the major hotels who chuckled and belched whenever he had more than three beers, which meant he was constantly chuckling and belching. "Uncle Ralph" was a salesman from Hamilton who fancied himself the reincarnation of Rudolph Valentino, even though somehow in the recycling of souls process, Rudy's Latin looks had morphed into freckles and thinning red hairs. There was also "Uncle Bill," a professional boxer from Buffalo. He was my favorite because he was an American, and he asked me once if I'd like to come and live with him in Buffalo. I told him I'd like that, which pleased him, but not my mother.

While each was different, each had the same personality flaw that my mother's equally flawed emotional radar homed in on like a heat-seeking missile. After they had banged her, never in the bed upstairs, always on the floor in the front room or on the sofa, they banged her around. They beat her with their fists. "Uncle Bill," though, never did. He just slapped her, telling her to shape up. As an ex-boxer, fists would have been considered lethal weapons.

In the kitchen we had a gas stove with long, arched steel legs. On the left side were four burners; on the right a large elevated oven. Next to the oven, a wooden chair. One morning, following another sleepless, terrifying night filled with crying, screaming and bashing, I found little me standing on the chair watching my mother. Her back was to me. She was leaning over the sink, running cold water, wiping the blood from her nose and eyes, not appearing upset in the least. But I was. I could not understand how she could see these men who abused her. That thought was as clear and as adult to me then as it is now. I couldn't hold back asking her, "Mom, why do you always go out with men who hit you?"

She didn't even turn off the water. She whirled and sprang across the floor in one bound, smashing me in the face so hard I tumbled over the oven and onto the floor. Each blow was accompanied with her screaming, "They don't hit me. They don't hit me! How dare you, you little bastard! They don't hit me!"

I rolled across the kitchen floor as quickly as I could into the hallway and ran for the front door. She didn't bother chasing me. Before I flew out the door onto the street, I could not fathom how she could lie about something we saw all the time. I learned years later that not only do some people lie about and deny obvious evils, so do some societies.

It was 'Uncle Garth,' though, who scared me and my sister to death because he was the one who would almost beat my mother to death. If we knew he was coming, Maggie would be out the door to her friends, afraid of being assaulted. I was afraid to leave, for fear of what I'd find when I got home. I hid in my room, listening to the fights, imagining myself taking a baseball bat, creeping up to him when he would finally pass out on my mother or the sofa, and crushing his skull. Those nights I hated my mother.

But one night was the worst. It was the night I saw my mother's brutal scars up close. For over an hour I once again stood frozen in fear behind my bedroom door listening to the thuds and screams and curses and crashing from below, echoing through the darkness. It was the most horrifying I'd ever heard. I started to shake. God, I loathed my cowardice. Maybe if I opened the window, jumped into the yard, and ran to the police station, I could get them to help. But, by the time I got back, my mother could be dead. I started whimpering like an abused puppy. Their sounds and my stomach were killing me. I had no choice. I finally opened the door. The screaming and punching were clearer. Almost against my will, I crept down the stairs as slowly as I could, one forever step at a time, not even knowing what I was going to do. With the last step, I was in the darkened hallway, a foot from the closed frosted glass living room door.

The ten panels of glass had clear edges about an inch wide. I peeked in and could see a shirtless Garth on top of my mother. Her clothes looked torn. He was pounding his right fist into her motionless face. I held the doorknob in my hand, paralyzed. Perhaps there is something so deep in our genetic DNA that impels a child, a child who hates his mother, still to do something to protect her. Whatever it was, it compelled me to push the door open. I stepped in, stopped, and out of my mouth came a loud, plaintive, "Stop it, please. Please, stop it, Garth!"

"Get out of here," a voice said. It wasn't Garth's. It was my mother's. I couldn't believe it.

Garth's head whipped around. "Come here, you little bastard. You want some of this?" He pushed and rolled off my mother.

I did not see any more. I turned and leaped up the stairs into the bedroom. Shaking so badly me teeth clattered, I pushed my bed against the closed door just in time. It was giving way.

"You little bastard. You shit. I'll fix your ass."

I relived that scene when I saw Jack Nicholson crashing through his terrified wife's bedroom door in *The Shining*. In a matter of seconds, he would be inside my room. Like Nicholson's wife, I went out the window.

I scrambled out, hanging from the sill with my hands. It was twenty feet to the ground. But only ten feet to the roof of our attached neighbor's pantry, hard to see in the darkness. I rocked desperately from side to side until I had enough momentum to hurl myself toward it. The impact caused me to fall and roll. My hands filled with slivers as I clutched the slanted roof. I landed backwards, falling again. Looking up, I could see Garth staring down at me. Feeling no pain, I got up and ran. And ran, gulping breaths burning my chest. I didn't stop for the nearly twenty blocks until I ran through the front door of the police station I knew well.

"Please, help, please," I hollered. "My mother is being beaten. My mother is being beaten!"

One of the two officers moved quickly to calm me down. "It's all right, son. It's all right. Tell us what's going on and where."

I gasped out the story. They called in two other officers. The one asking the questions placed his arm around my shoulder. "Let's go, son."

They placed me alone in the back seat. They raced down the street, all the time telling me not to worry, that everything would be fine. My mother would be okay. They were comforting.

We reached 192 Lawlor Avenue in minutes. They opened the back door, asking me to come with them.

"I can't. I can't. Could I stay here, please?" In my mind I could only see an even more deranged Garth, lunging through the door at me.

"You'll be fine, son. Come with us." They placed me between them and walked briskly and business-like up the walk to the front door. One had a hand on his holster as the other knocked. There was no answer. My heart was pounding. They knocked again. The door opened easily. Standing there were my mother and Garth. They were dressed. My mother's hair was brushed; she had makeup on. Bruises or cuts on her were hard to discern in the dim light. I stared in disbelief.

Garth said, "Oh, there you are, Johnny. We wondered where you went."

My mother asked the officers, "A problem? Thank you for bringing him home."

"Your son says there has been some kind of altercation here."

"No," they said in unison. "We were having a misunderstanding; maybe a little spat and a little loud, but nothing serious. Nothing to bother the police about!"

The officer with his hand on his hip thankfully wasn't giving up. He must've had a lot of experience with domestic violence. "Your boy jumped out the upstairs back window and ran twenty blocks to get us. He wouldn't have done that if it had just been a misunderstanding." He stared at them, waiting for a response.

Mother answered, "Officer, I'm sorry if we caused you any trouble and I'm sorry if my son misunderstood what … what … we were doing. But everything is fine now."

The officer then shone his light in my mother's face. We could now plainly see there was smudged mascara and considerable bruising under the makeup. She raised her hand, shielding her face from the light. They then shone the light in Garth's face. He didn't blink; he stared back. And smiled.

"It won't happen again. We're sorry," Garth said in flat voice.

The officer was quiet, then turned to me. "You'll be all right, son. You can go in now."

I didn't move.

He repeated, "You'll be all right. Go on."

I still didn't move. He leaned closer. "Johnny, you won't have to run to get us next time; we'll be parked out here for a while. Go on in."

I almost cried at his thoughtfulness. And wisdom. I entered, moving quickly past my mother and up the stairs. I heard the officer say, "You two have a better night, okay? We'll be outside for a while."

"We will," my mother said. "We're sorry."

By the time the door closed I was barricaded back in my room. I listened for a long quiet time to what was going on downstairs, not by my door, but next to the open window. For the first time in my life I thought sometimes maybe authority was not too bad. I stood listening for an hour. Fully clothed. To the sound of silence. Soon I heard two muffled voices and the front door opening and closing. There was no sound from below. For ten minutes, I stood listening for something. Anything, Feeling the quiet was eerie, I opened the door and again made my way slowly down the stairs.

The living room door was closed, but I couldn't see my mother or Garth inside. I grabbed the handle to push it open. It didn't budge. Something was pressed against it. Peering through the edge of the frosted glass, I could see a body slumped on the floor. I hurried down the hall, through the kitchen, into and through the dining room, and circled back to the front room. It was my mother. Unconscious. I shook her shoulder softly, saying nothing. I thought Garth might still be somewhere.

Getting more concerned, I said, "Mom, Mom, are you okay?" There was no response. Scared, I shook her a little harder. "Mom, Mom, are you all right? Answer me!"

She was breathing. When I shook her again, she made this strange gurgling, wheezing sound. I wasn't strong enough to pick her up. As gently as I could, I pulled her along the floor, turning up the rug so that

I could open the door. I turned her on her back, placed my hands under her armpits and began to pull her up the stairs. To do that, I had to sit on the step, lean back, and pull her on top of me. It was a long, emotionally agonizing, unpleasant process. I had no choice. She was my mother. It took forever just to get her to the landing, with five more steps to go. I was drained. I had to rest with her on top of me. How was I going to get her to bed? Do I undress my own mother? Suddenly she started to groan, but it wasn't the groan of someone who is hurting; it was the groan of someone who is defecating. She relieved herself all over me and herself. And the landing. The stench was like a vicious punch to the nose. I never ever hated this disgusting woman more than at that moment. The hate was so overpowering, my mind and body could not contain it anymore. It gushed out of me. And vanished. It was gone. Totally. Along with any emotion or caring that I might have had for her. In that moment, lying on my back covered in her fecal matter, I had a crystal clear, almost out of body epiphany. I was staring down at a woman, a stranger now, whom I knew I soon would never see again. Or be like. Liquor would never ever do that to me. (I didn't have a glass of wine until I was thirty-five.)

Feeling physically and emotionally refreshed, I left her on the landing, lying in her feces. I ran a tub and cleaned myself. I ran another for her. I returned and dragged her into the bathroom. Not wanting to undress her, or to see her naked, I lifted her into the tub fully clothed. I didn't want to clean or touch her. I sat on the toilet seat watching her, waiting for her to come to. Her hair was all askew and matted. It was then I saw closeup those disgusting scars. She looked like the phantom from *The Phantom of The Opera*. How sad. Gone also was any curiosity I had about how she got them. When she eventually opened her eyes, she squinted at me, and said nothing. Neither did I. I got up and went to my room. I lay on the bed reliving the night. I was at ease, thankful that I no longer wanted to kill Garth. I never wetted the bed again.

I'm Dreaming of a White-Knuckled Christmas

I never believed in Santa Claus. Not even as a toddler. As long as I can remember, I felt he was some hired guy who dressed up in a red suit, put a pillow over his stomach, a white beard on his face and got a job for a week in both Eaton's and Simpson's department stores. Maybe this disbelief occurred to me the December day when I got to see two of them.

Like every other kid, I sat on their laps. They asked me what I wanted for Christmas. What I wanted I had already seen my mother place behind one of the large stuffed chairs in the living room: CCM skates. So, not embarrass him, I said, "Skates!"

I could see this guy in the red outfit with the big bag of goodies and toys could only fit enough stuff in that burlap bag for a few houses on one block; never enough for an entire country, or the whole world. Reindeer don't have wings. They have antlers. They don't flap. If reindeer were flying, they'd have to fan like hell to be propelled like rockets. Any six-year-old can see that. But, I was the only six-year-old who said it out loud. All my buddies, except for Mel, were believers, and grew up like most believing in stuff just as nonsensical. For a fleeting moment I had an urge to believe in the Tooth Fairy. When a tooth fell out, I placed it under my pillow; in the morning I awoke to find a nickel in its place. I thought, how wonderful; if only this was true. But I knew it wasn't. I had smelled my father's arms and hands as he gently slid it in there.

The last Christmas I celebrated on Lawlor Avenue, I was twelve. I had all the hockey equipment I needed, so when my mother asked what I wanted that year, I had no answer. She told me in that case, Santa would surprise me. She never really took any interest in what I might actually want or need. She would just get something from where she worked, and a few days before Christmas dump it behind a large corner stuffed chair, usually unwrapped, with a small white card with green holly on it that read "John."

This particular Christmas the unexpected gift was too cumbersome to wrap. It was a bow and arrow set. Not a kid's bow and arrow set. A real bow and arrow set. A long, powerful bow with half a dozen polished arrows with perfect feathering and shiny steel tips. You could kill a deer with it – or a person. She knew I loved Robin Hood with Errol Flynn; giving her the benefit of the doubt, maybe she did give this gift a little thought. Garth had been relatively calm since the visit from the law. There had been no fights for a few weeks. But, I was always edgy and leery when he was around. Instinct told me not to pull my present out, just leave it hidden.

My older brother Ronnie left earlier with a buddy. My younger sister, Maggie, had been dropped off at our grandmother's. There were just the three of us. My mother, Garth, and me. They were sitting next to each other on the sofa by the large front window. They were unwrapping a few small gifts, sipping beer, looking slightly sober. I was about to leave when Garth said, "Kid, go see what your mother got you."

I stopped, not sure what to do or say.

"Go on," he pressed.

I strolled to the corner stuffed chair, kneeled on it and looked over. This exquisite bow and arrow set no longer looked like a gift. It looked like a weapon.

"What is it?" he asked. The tone of his voice indicated he knew exactly what it was.

"A bow and arrow set," I said.

"Well, let's see it."

"Oh, that's okay. I'll look at it later," I said.

"Whadda ya mean, you'll look at it later? Goddamn it, it's Christmas. You're supposed to look at it now."

"I saw it," I muttered.

He tried to stand, but with some difficulty, which irritated him. "Your mother gave you a Christmas gift, goddamn it. Show her you appreciate it!"

"I do appreciate it."

"Well, goddamn it, get it and let's see it!" He wobbled toward me. "Let's see how this thing works!"

I moved in front of him, quickly pulling up the bow and arrows. "I've got it," I said nervously.

He stopped and looked at me, putting his hands on his hips. "Okay, let's see how it works."

"Let's ... let's go out in the yard."

"Whadda yah mean, the yard? In here's good enough! Go on, load it up. We'll play William Tell." He chuckled.

"Mom," was all I could get out, urging her to intercede.

"What are yah talking to your mom for? She's not playing with us!"

I turned to my mother. She, too, looked glazed.

"Garth! Leave 'im be."

That was all she had time to say. He whirled around and heaved the half empty beer bottle at her. It barely missed her head. Beer splattered all over the ceiling and wall as the bottle crashed against edge of the window. Then he lunged at me. "Gimme that goddamn thing! I'll show you how it works." He jerked the bow out of my hand. I pulled away and ran into the dining room, ducking under the table.

"No, no, I'll do it," I yelled, hoping he'd give it back. "It's my present."

With his free hand, he lifted the table as though it was made of foam, and smashed it against a corner cabinet, shattering it and the chinaware inside."Give 'em to me. You cowardly little shit." He grabbed and twisted my wrist. The arrows dropped to the floor. "Now, gimme one, and I'll show you how it works!"

I couldn't move

He growled, "Gimme one, goddamn it!"

I crawled over to the arrows, picked one up and raised it toward him. Tearing it out of my hand, he began to fumble with trying to place the arrow in the string of the bow. I was still on my hands and knees where the dining room table used to be. Fully exposed. I watched, horrified, as he tried to pull it back. Aiming at me. Doing so it began to wave uncontrollably. He was staggering and laughing. Planting his feet, he now held it motionless. He pulled the string effortlessly till the steel tipped arrow touched the bow.

"Okay, kid. What do we test your little present on first? We gotta see that it works all right, right? The chair!" he said triumphantly. "That'd be a good target, right? Right?"

"No, please. Please, don't," I begged "Garth, stop it." My mother whispered to herself. "Watch this!" With that, he let it fly, yelping like an Indian in a Western. The arrow hissed through the air through the stuffed chair. He cackled with glee. "Jesus Christ, did you see that? Well, gimme another one."

"Please. Please, Garth!" I cried. "Don't. Stop, please! *Mom*," l hollered again.

She was now rocking back and forth as if in a trance, moaning, making a sound to drown out the sounds she was hearing.

I rushed along the floor to try to grab the remaining arrows. He grabbed my arm, lifting me like a rag doll, and tossed me against the wall. I fell onto broken glass and wood. He snatched up a second arrow, fumbling again to place it in the string. His voice was louder. And sicker.

"We're gonna play William Tell. We're playing William Tell, aren't we kid?" He was ten feet from me. Sweat pouring out of me, I stared up at him. Terrified. The bow was fully extended. Again, he was a little shaky as he tried to aim and maintain his balance.

"Where's your apple, kid?" he cackled. "Where's your apple? You lost your apple!" He was in his full sadistic military glory.

My throat was as tight as that bowstring. I tried to yell, to speak. Fear and desperation kept me mute.

"I guess we won't need an apple, kid, will we?"

Hearing that, I knew he was about to let go. I rolled desperately across the floor, over the broken glass and wood toward the kitchen. I wanted him to think I was trying to escape, which I was. But not through the kitchen. It was a deke, like in hockey. Rising to my feet, I feinted a sharp move to my left, took a few steps, then suddenly turned back to the right toward him. It was the last thing he expected. No sooner had I recoiled from this move when an arrow hissed by my left ear, embedding in the wall near the kitchen entrance.

"You little son of a bitch. You little bastard!" He was now fully enraged and challenged. With one hand he grabbed for another arrow and with the other hand extended, holding the bow, he tripped me up as I tried to leap by him.

"Mom, Mom!" I screamed, my voice coming back. "Stop him! Stop him!"

"Stop it! Stop it!" she shrieked, not raising her head, her hands clamped over her ears.

I rolled back onto my feet. He was scrambling for a third arrow. "I'll kill you, you worthless son of a bitch. This is your last goddamned Christmas!"

I darted back and forth across the room. I grabbed a broken leg from the table. I hurled it at him just as he released the next arrow. This one whooshed by my right ear, smashing into the curtains and window. The table leg bounced off his arm like it was made of cardboard.

This act of defiance by a kid unhinged him. Out of arrows, he hurled the bow at me. Seemingly now sober and focused, he bent to retrieve the table leg. As he did so, I raced past him, through the living room, through the glass paneled door, slamming it behind me. It was instantly shattered by the wooden leg that zipped through it, grazing my left arm. I opened the front door, and as hard as I could, I stood still and slammed it shut. This was going to be another deke. Instead of running out, I leaped up the stairs into my room. I heard Garth throw open the broken living room door, and rush to open the front door. He stood there yelling to the world, "Come back here, you little bastard. Come back here. I'll kill you. I'll kill you!"

Once again, I was out the window, but not to the police. Instead, I ran to the railway tracks, and the safety of an empty box car. I knew if I went to the police, I would not come out of their next visit alive. Without food or water or much sleep, I stayed three days in a dusty empty boxcar. They were the most peaceful three days I'd ever had in my life.

Years later, I laughed really loud when I saw Mel Brooks doing his 2,000-year-old man routine on television. His partner, Carl Reiner, asked him what the happiest day in his life was.

Mel said, "In an empty rowboat in the middle of the ocean." Carl asked, "Why's that?" Mel said, "Because a minute before, I was in shark infested water!"

The following summer, I was on a train again, a passenger train. My mother was getting rid of me for three months. She was sending me to a boarding farm in Northern Ontario, in a place called Burke's Falls, not far from Sudbury, Ontario. It was a boarding farm cut right out of the middle of a forest. Here I would meet a girl, get lost, and learn to kill.

A Summer Short Cut

"You're just too bloody much to handle!" my mother said through gritted teeth as she alighted from the streetcar into the clear, crisp morning sunlight, my small suitcase in her hand. "This will be good for you. Here, carry this and follow me."

I took the suitcase she thrust at me, and followed her through Toronto's main downtown train depot. I would get to know it well a few years later when I worked the midnight to dawn shift as a fireman shoveling coal on a steam engine. Right then, though, it was strange and foreboding, like a setting in a foreign espionage film. There were half a dozen passenger trains with hundreds of well-dressed people shuttling about; a new sight to me. I was used to tracks full of boxcars with a hobo or two. I was looking at what I guessed was the other side of the tracks.

She had made arrangements for me to spend a quarter of the year at a boarding farm in Northern Ontario run by a couple. One morning, she just told me to pack my stuff, stuff that would barely last three weeks, let alone three months. Aside from the worn loafers, what I wore mostly was rubber boots; I wore those often, especially to school, so the kids and teachers wouldn't see I had no socks. I had two pairs of thinning trousers, a few tee shirts, a hockey sweater, and two pairs of jockey shorts that I'd always washed in the sink myself. It's a habit I occasionally have to this day. This shortage of a semi-decent wardrobe for a twelve-year-old who was about to be dropped into the wilds of Northern Canada was of absolutely no concern to my mother.

I walked wordlessly behind her, carrying my bag. This was probably the fastest I'd ever seen her move; certainly, the straightest. We didn't stop at the ticket counter. She had already done that. She led me straight to the train, directing me to climb the stairs. Before I did, I turned to look at her. I thought maybe she'd hug me, say goodbye. She made no motion to do so. As I ascended, she said casually, "They're expecting you. Someone will be at the train station to meet you when you get there."

"Okay." I shrugged. "Who's meeting me? What's their name?"

"Uncle Bob," she said flatly." His name is Bob Jurow, but he says the kids call him Uncle Bob."

Jesus Christ. I almost choked.

She hollered, "And don't cause any trouble!" Without waiting to hear the "all aboard," she turned and walked away.

I sat in the first seat, too self-conscious carrying the ragged suitcase to walk past the other passengers. I watched my mother moving briskly back toward the exit. I noticed how well she was dressed. And moved. She held her hand up to her hair to keep it from blowing in the breeze, exposing her scars. Sadly, she looked beautiful. Silhouetted in the large, arched exit doorway, she stopped, looking from side to side. Moving toward her was a man, a man I'd never seen before. When they met, they embraced; he put his arm around her waist, leading her away. She was still holding her hand on her hair.

It was a day-long train ride. The views must have been beautiful, but even with my head pressed against the cool glass I could see nothing but the jumbled images inside my head: a moment with my father, a moment on the ice, fish and chips, an arrow whizzing by my head, a movie. Scores of muted memories zipped by. Nothing stuck. They were still running when I fell asleep. I was awakened by the sounds and lurching of the train pulling to a stop. I was relieved to look out the window, especially relieved to stop thinking. The train station could have been built by a set designer for John Wayne's *Stagecoach*. It was made of wood. Of course. Unpainted. Atop it was a faded, dusty one foot by six-foot sign in black and white that read: Burke's Falls. The structure itself was about the size of a dozen outhouses.

There's always a water tower in those westerns. But not there. There were a few patches of dirt on either side of the station that served as a parking lot, yet I could see no road that led up to them. Just trees; nothing but trees. Pine and conifers on steroids. When I alighted, suitcase in hand, I couldn't help staring at the endless, dark green, real forest that looked as ominous and strange as the one that scared me in *The Wizard of Oz*.

"John. Johnny MacLaren?" It was a gentle voice.

I turned. Walking toward me with coveralls on and an attempt at a white shirt, was a nice looking, open-faced man in his early thirties. And the nicest teeth I'd ever seen in someone not on the screen. He was the only one on the platform. I was the only one to get off the train. "How was your trip?" he asked

"Fine," I said.

He extended his hand and shook mine firmly. "Welcome to Burke's Falls. My name's Bob. Bob Jurow. I hope you like it here. I think you will. Here, gimme that." He took the suitcase from my hand. "The kids call me Uncle Bob."

I hated hearing that, but I liked him immediately.

"You'll find it's all very informal up here. Very casual." I followed him to the parking area. "Of course, a farm is informal, so I don't want you to have to say Mr. Jurow. That would be too formal. I'm not that old anyway. And you're too young to call me Bob. So, it's Uncle Bob. Is that okay?"

"Yes, sir."

"Good. And, no *sir* stuff either," he added, as he stopped by our transportation. It was a tractor or some kind of farm machinery. It was as clean as his shirt. I looked for the words Ford or Chevrolet, but saw instead Massey Harris. It was right out of Ma and Pa Kettle.

"Climb aboard," he said, pulling himself up easily.

"All set?" he asked.

"Yes, sir."

"No *sir* stuff. Here we go." We were on a few miles of a very narrow, rutted, one lane, bumpy dirt road. Trees on either side were so close, dense, and tall, it felt like a tunnel. The midday sunlight barely filtered through. I was mesmerized. It was spellbinding. Over the chugging of the motor, I could hear the eerie, echoing sounds, all kinds of birdcalls. I got goosebumps. One cry stood out above the rest. It sounded like a bird, a very big bird. Its scream was almost musical, made up of three distinct notes. Whoop do whee! Whoop do whee!

"What is that?" I was wide-eyed.

"A whippoorwill. You hear them more at night."

"Are there bears?"

"Tons of them. Mostly Black bears," he said matter-of-factly.

"Do you see them often?" I gulped.

"Quite often. They sometimes wander onto the north field where the cows are, but they don't bother you. We might even see a couple on the way home."

"Will they attack?"

"No. They're just as afraid of you. Except if their young are around."

"And … and then what happens?"

He smiled. "Just be glad you're on a tractor."

We came to and drove through an open gate that said, "The Jurows." It was still a hundred more yards to go to the farmhouse. Standing in the distance were half a dozen people waving and yelling at us.

"Hi, Uncle Bob. Hi, Johnny!" they shouted, as we dismounted. I was startled they even greeted me.

Mr. Jurow, holding my suitcase, began the introductions. "Johnny, this is Aunt Jean." His wife was a very pretty, well-fed shapely woman with a smile and teeth as good as her husband's.

We exchanged 'hi's', but were not close enough to shake hands. Down the row we went. Their seven-year-old daughter, Jane, prettier than her mother. An eight-year-old boy, Jeffrey, and his six-year-old brother, Chuck, and their two-year-old cocker spaniel, Chuckie Jr.

"And this is Ben." Uncle Bob pointed toward the ground to someone I hadn't even noticed. No wonder. And what a wonder! Ben was fourteen, but only about two feet tall. He wasn't a dwarf. He had a normal size head. And a normal size chest, but he had no hips or legs. Just feet. Normal sized. They grew right out of where his hips should have been. And he had arms the size of my legs. Those, and massive hands, are what propelled him. In a carnival, he would have been considered a freak. Like the wall of trees, I couldn't take my eyes off him.

"Hi, Johnny," Ben said in a growly but full voice. "Welcome." As he said this, he leaned forward placing his fists on the ground, like a gorilla, moving himself forward with his Popeye arms. He shook my hand, crushing it. Doing so, he announced loudly to me, so everyone could hear, "My name's Benjamin, but they call me Ben for short." And he howled. The others laughed, also probably having heard it a dozen times.

"Hi, Ben. Hi." I repeated, still stunned.

"I'm Ann."

I looked up from Ben. If Ben was an unattractive freak, nature was making up for it with Ann. She was beyond stunning. Brunette. She was thirteen. Becoming a woman. If you placed her next to Elizabeth Taylor in *National Velvet*, you'd be looking at Ann.

"Ann Taylor," she said. Jesus Christ. Her last name was even Taylor! "Welcome.

You're going to enjoy it here."

My eyes locked on her face. Gone instantly were the endless thoughts that almost kept me awake on the train. No mother. No Garth. No hockey. Nothing. Unbelievable. Just that face. My head and heart had been immediately emptied of any emotional luggage. My God, what was a girl like that doing on a boarding farm? I knew why I was there. I was a troublemaker. But why was she there?

The Little Outhouse on the Prairie

The Jurow farmhouse was wide, solid single story, and beautifully built, mostly out of wood. The large area in front had no grass. Just dirt. Grass couldn't survive there; chickens, goats, pigs, and the occasional sheep were allowed to wander wherever they wanted. I learned quickly, if you got too close to a piglet, the mother would appear from nowhere and charge! I got knocked on my ass a couple of times. The back of the house had a huge veranda running the entire width of it. It had been converted into a barracks with bunkbeds. The back wall was a screen that made you feel as though you were sleeping outside. It let in the rain, the sun, and the night sounds that never stopped. A wooden partition separated the boys' quarters from the girls'. Each had room for eight boys and eight girls. I chose the upper bunk closest to the wall near the girls. On the lower bunk was Ben; next to us, the two brothers, and Chuckie Jr. Bob's daughter had a bedroom of her own in the house, but she chose to sleep in the girls' section to keep Ann company. Fifty yards outside was the outhouse. My using an outhouse for the first time was not a pleasant experience. Using it for three months was more unpleasant. The stench burns the inside of your nostrils up to your skull. I never got used to it. Toilet paper was always in short supply.

Sometimes Uncle Bob left his newspaper there, the stories put to better use. To drop it properly, you had to look where it was going, otherwise it might end up on the seat beside you. Looking down, about ten feet, you couldn't help seeing days of recycled meals. It made your eyes water.

I endured this for a few weeks, and gave up. I decided I'd rather go into the fields where the air was fresh. Answering Mother Nature's call in Mother Nature though, came to an abrupt halt one day. So rushed, I forgot paper. I decided the large single leaf on the ground would have to do; when I lifted it, a huge snake sprang at my buttocks, and I discovered

I had not totally emptied my bowels. They, and I, moved instantly. I was yelling and releasing. I had literally shit my pants on the run. I returned to the outhouse. I have never squatted in a grassy field since. Not even on a golf course.

A hundred yards west of the house was the main barn the size of small airplane hangar. On one side were the horses' stalls; on the other side, the milking area for the cows. Above that, accessible only by the ladder, was a hay loft with an open door that allowed for the pitchforking of hay to the ground outside. Our outside shower shed was between the sleeping quarters and the outhouse. It was all dark wood, and dimly lit. A rope attached to the end of a bent rusty pipe supplied the always cool water. Against two walls, around the center drain, were wooden benches. There was no lock on the door. You just had to pull it shut and hope it stayed. Ben liked to hang out in there, even when he wasn't taking a shower. Often, he and I would just sit in there and talk.

At first, I thought it odd that I felt comfortable with him. Was I some kind of freak lover? Was it because he was an outsider? No. It was because he was amazingly comfortable with himself. He didn't mind in the least that he was physically different. He almost seemed to enjoy it. Proud of what he could do with what he was given made him the center of attention. No matter where he went. He certainly attracted the attention of Chuck, the six-year-old. Often, when Ben and I were in there, little Chuck would push open the door and run right over to him, standing in front of him, eye to eye.

"Do that again, Ben," Chuck would say.

Immediately, Ben would roll himself off the bench onto the floor, and proceed to stand on one hand, and then the other, and then walk a circle around the little boy. "Like this?" Ben said, upside down.

"Yeah. Yeah." Chuck giggled.

Ben would then swing himself down on his tiny feet, and flex a muscle, like Charles Atlas. Chuck would reach over and feel that incredible bicep.

"Wow," he said. "That's great!" And he'd skip out the door. "See yah later, Ben!" It was a ritual all summer.

There were two main meals, breakfast and dinner, with snacking on sandwiches, fruit and vegetables all day. I'd never seen or tasted such food. It was the first time I ever ate a salad. The meals were at six in the morning and six at night. I was never a morning person even when playing hockey, so getting up for food was difficult. It got more difficult when I found out that I'd have to work for it.

Once we were seated around a long table that accommodated all of us, the meals would start with Uncle Bob or Aunt Jean, saying, "Enjoy!" I thought, *Thank God they don't make us say grace.* This was more than home cooking. This was farm cooking. Stuff we were eating had been growing or walking around outside just that morning. I discovered tastes and taste buds I never knew existed. Mashed potatoes with homemade butter, string beans just harvested, tomatoes off the vine, tasted as though they belonged in your mouth. I savoured the saliva-pumping fried chicken in my mouth, from chickens that I'd seen leaping on the tree stump in the front yard. Chickens I was soon asked to kill and pluck. The tree stump was the guillotine.

After dinner, a week into my stay, we were sitting on the front porch watching the zoo scurrying about. "How do you like it so far?" Uncle Bob asked.

"It's nice," I said. "Different. I could never imagine being here."

"It's the best place for you to be. A farm. You know why? You'll know where you come from. What keeps you alive." He looked at me. I looked back at him. He seemed an out-of-place philosopher, but a right-place farmer.

"The dirt," he said. "The earth." He could see I was listening. "The world went crazy for half a dozen years," he continued. I presumed he was talking about the war. "One of the reasons for that is that people, especially people in the cities, have lost contact with the dirt, the earth that provides their food. That's where it all comes from. They think it comes from supermarkets in cans or packages. Their chickens are already plucked, cleaned or cooked. So are their steaks. Albert Schweitzer talked about the reverence for life. ("*Who the hell is Albert Schweitzer*?" I thought.) "There can be no reverence for life without first reverence for the land that produces life. And sustains it. Most people give that no thought at all now. They're not a part of what the Indians call The Circle of Life."

He was deep into what he was saying. So was I. What is The Circle of Life? I never heard anyone talk like him. Not in school. Not on the radio. Not even in Mrs. Lee's church.

"Do you know that Indians never owned land? They thought the ground was sacred, owned only by Mother Nature." He looked at me, smiling now. "You'll have lots of time to play and explore and do whatever you want to do, but for a few hours a day I need you to help us with some chores. Gathering eggs, checking the salt blocks for the cows, milking them, feeding the pigs, haying the horses, and feeding the chickens. Okay?" he asked pleasantly.

"Okay," I replied.

"And killing them and plucking them occasionally." He pointed toward the executioner's block. "And we'll start tomorrow."

A Couple of Killings

The following morning after breakfast, Uncle Bob took me on the rounds of what I'd be doing one way or another for the next two and a half months. Every morning. First, there was the feeding of the chickens. That was easy; I'd just grab a sack full of seed and throw it all over the place because that's where the chickens were – all over the place.Then I'd have to take a basket into a hen house that was an animal madhouse. Doors were never closed. There were no cages, just a bunch of cubicles where the hens would sit and lay. My assignment was to reach under the hens and retrieve their unborn children. They didn't like that. Neither did I. They lunged at me, pecking at my arms and hands. Sometimes they'd even strike at my head, much to the amusement of Ben, who sometimes carried the basket for me. The offspring of these angry mothers turned into uncooked omelets on the ground. At breakfast, I found myself eating them more slowly, looking at them while I ate.

Next was feeding the pigs; dumping big buckets of some kind of slop into large wooden troughs, and trying to get out of their way as they trampled and squealed and bit and tumbled over one another to get to their grub. On the way to the barn, we'd stop in the fields to check large one-foot cubes of salt blocks with ruts cut out of the tops from the cows licking them. How would anyone know to feed cows salt? When I asked Uncle Bob about this, he said, "All mammals need salt. You'd die without it."

"Really?" I asked unbelievingly.

"That's where the word salary comes from," he said.

What has that got to do with anything?

He continued, "That's how the ancient Roman Emperors paid their troops. With salt. Thus, the word salary."

This farmer, in his thirties, in overalls in a field in the middle of nowhere, was suddenly the most interesting person I'd ever met.

Then it was off to the barn and the haying of the horses, and an attempt to milk a cow. I was too emotionally and physically ill-equipped to remove milk from an unwilling mother. All I got from the cow when I inadequately squeezed her teets was kicking and mooing. Getting under that huge animal terrified me. To hide my fear, I'd turn it into a comedy routine, falling back on the stool, or telling the animal if she didn't help, the kids would starve and die. The kids watching me howled. Especially Ann. I loved her laughter. The first week I was assigned my chores, the others knew it was the first time this city boy had done such a thing, so they hurried to be a witness to it. I did them all, happily, showing off for Ann to whom I had barely spoken. Thereafter, when my audience was gone, I did my chores not so happily. But what pleased me the most about doing them were the smells. The hay, the grass, the horses, the cows, the trees, but, most of all, the air. It made one involuntarily breathe deeper to savor it.

Uncle Bob relieved me of my cow-milking duties. He had another in mind.

"Are you a vegetarian?" he asked

"A what?"

"A vegetarian. Someone who mainly eats vegetables and fruits."

"No."

"Well, you pick tomatoes and pull up potatoes, right? You know, they're living entities until you pick, pull and cook them. A chicken is a slightly higher form of living entity. It lives off the ground, but it's not attached to it."

Jesus, this man's not a farmer; he's a bloody philosopher, and he's going to make me kill a chicken.

"Tomorrow for dinner we're having chicken, potatoes and tomatoes. We already have the potatoes and tomatoes. Which you helped pick. Would you help pick the chicken?"

"Just... just... help... pick it?" I stammered, afraid of his answer.

He laughed. "No. Kill it."

"Oh, God, Uncle Bob, I don't think I could. I don't. Honestly."

"It's smaller than a cow." He smiled. "It'd help if you would try."

"Okay," I whispered.

"You'll be fine."

Minutes later we were in front of the house watching scores of chickens rushing around, pecking at the ground searching for food. I swear they started moving faster when they saw us, knowing we were also searching for food.

"I'm not going to demonstrate how to do it, John," he began, "Because then it would be done. You're going to have to do it. Grab him with both hands around the wings so he can't fly. Put him on the block face down. Keep your left hand firmly on his back and wings. Then take the ax I've sharpened and put it on the stump. And chop its head off. Even though it's sharp, you have to hit hard. And don't let go of the chicken. They've been known to jump up headless and run around for half an hour."

I was getting sick, but having failed at milking a standing cow I did not want to feel more like a chicken in front of him than the scurrying ones in front of me. I stood slowly. And in a deliberately whiney voice said, "I don't wanna be chicken!" He chuckled.

His further instructions followed me as I followed my prey. "After you've cut off the head, lift him up by the feet and hold him upside down till all the blood drains out."

"My blood is draining out!" There were no giggles this time. I didn't want to do it. I'd never killed anything. The only blood I'd ever seen up close was mine, on hockey rinks; my mother's, on date night!

I walked slowly toward my target, hunched, my arms hanging down to grab him. Like the cow, he sensed I was a nervous novice. He must have remembered a few of his siblings disappearing after being around humans who walked like that. He darted off.

"He's getting away!" It was the sound of laughter coming from everyone now assembled on the porch, like a crowd in an ancient Roman arena. Then I saw Ann, smiling like an empress.

I chased that little bugger around the yard faster than any Centurion ever chased a Christian, running, tumbling, grabbing and missing while it leaped, flew and ran helter skelter, clucking and screaming. Suddenly, I had him by one leg, and just as suddenly he turned and dug his beak into my arms. Goddamn him. I grabbed his throat, squeezing it hard. I had it. I clutched his wings against his body. He squawked, his feet insanely thrashing. I struggled to hold him.

There was light applause and soft cheering from the crowd. I wondered what do I do now? I didn't want to kill him. I didn't like him. He had bit me. But I did not want to kill him! They all knew what I was about to do. What I had to do. Everyone got quiet. Except the chicken. We were both afraid.

I carried him to the tree stump, holding him above it for a moment as I looked for the ax. I pushed him onto the stump, face down, applying all pressure to hold his flailing body down. His screaming literally hurt my ears. Keeping my eyes on the back of his twisted neck, I picked up the ax. The dog started to bark and jump crazily. My sweating right hand raised the ax shoulder height and stopped. I looked at the target. My left hand was just inches from his neck, the only part of him not moving. Christ, if I missed, I could chop off my hand. I pumped the ax up and down slowly, rehearsing, then crashed down through the chicken's neck, stopped only by the wood. The chicken's head flew to the ground. The dog growled, racing around and barking at it. The blood didn't just flow out of the chicken's body, it squirted out like a monstrous water pistol. Ten feet at least. The crowd cheered.

"Pick it up by the feet," Uncle Bob called.

I did. It was still thrashing, wanting to run away. Headless!

The kids moved closer to get a look. Ben was the fastest, propelled by those arms. Ann stared at the draining twitching creature, then looked at me. Even in that horrible moment, covered with blood, I thought, *How beautiful she is*!

"You did good, Johnny," Uncle Bob announced to more applause. "Now let's see how well you pluck it."

After Uncle Bob's brief demonstration with a few feathers, covered in more blood than the corpse, I sat on the front steps and began tugging and tearing feathers out of that pink, goosebumped skin. The real show over, everybody scattered. Ann looked down at me, the last to leave. "Good luck!"

Her voice and smile went right through me.

Aunt Jean came out, saying, "Now we have to clean him."

I whined, "Do I have to do that, too?"

"No, I'll do that." She chuckled, taking the chicken from me. "Good job!"

My catch was devoured the next night at dinner. But not by me. I barely nibbled a small piece of breast. I could still see it pecking its own dinner.

Farmer John

I killed and plucked my second chicken the following week. I hadn't been there two weeks and I turned into a serial killer! A one-man Colonel Sanders. In the ten weeks I did it, I never got used to it. I was always apprehensive, even sad. I am almost ashamed to say that the taste of each kill, though, got more and more delicious. To this day, I've yet to find anything comparable.

Then one morning, Uncle Bob asked if I liked pork chops and bacon.

"I love them," I said too quickly, suddenly aware of why he was asking that question.

"I kill only one pig a year. There's more than enough meat to last. Would you mind helping?"

"I don't know what I could do. I couldn't catch one."

"No, I'll do that." He smiled. "I'll let you know."

Awaiting that call to pig killing, I went about my days feeling happier with each sunrise. Not once was there a memory of Lawlor Ave. or Kingston Road or Maple Leaf Gardens. I missed nothing. There was nothing I wanted to return to. Or anyone. I certainly didn't want to be a farmer, but I was strongly content there. Maybe it was the Taurus in me. In reality, it was the intense crush I had on Ann Taylor. I wanted to learn all about her; and soon I would. I was also intensely curious about Ben, my buddy. This unshakable curiosity about different or unusual people, which lasts to this day, and became my career, began on a wooden bench in a shabby makeshift shower.

"What is it like?" Ben asked. It was noon. The chores were over. He was standing on the bench a few feet from where I was sitting.

"What is what like?"

"Killing the chicken and watching all that blood?"

"I don't like it," I said. "I have a hard time squashing bugs. Except flies."

"My brother killed a cat once."

"How?"

"He shot it. With a BB gun. It didn't die right away so he clubbed it with the butt end."

"That's awful," I said.

"Yah, he's kind of cruel. We don't get along too well."

"Do you have other brothers or sisters?" I asked.

"A sister; she's a couple of years older. Sixteen. She's okay," he replied.

"Why aren't they here?"

"They didn't want to come. Just me."

"Your parents sent just you?"

"No. They're paying for it and all, but when they told us about it, I said I wanted to come. I thought it'd be fun. Something different!"

I couldn't believe anyone would volunteer to be there. "How could your family let you travel so far alone? Don't you miss your friends?"

He laughed, a full laugh. He spoke without a trace of pity. "People like me don't have friends, Johnny. We just have people we hang with. For a while."

"But wouldn't your folks, your brother and sister worry … worry … about … about you … alone? Up here by yourself?"

"I'm tougher than all of them," he said. "My folks are fine, and my sister wouldn't care; she's always off chasin' guys anyway. I seldom see her."

There are thousands or millions of people born with deformities, but not one of those I ever saw looked like Ben. The most curious question I had, I couldn't hold back. "Have … have you … uh … or … do you … have you … ?"

"A girlfriend?" He laughed. *Christ, how did he know what I was thinking*? "I'm working on that." He laughed again. "How about you?"

I didn't answer for a long while. I was thinking about the few girls I liked, even had crushes on: Vivian Consitt, ten houses up from mine, Joan LaFevre, two blocks over, girls I had little luck with. "No," I said honestly. "I have better luck killing chickens."

He howled. He was becoming friends with someone who had other kinds of limitations.

"What's so funny?" It was Ann. She had pushed the door open and was smiling at us. Ben and I were both startled. "Nothing!" we mumbled.

"Aunt Jean sent me. She's going to take us all swimming. Wanna come?"

"That's great." Ben lowered himself to the floor and, chimpanzee-like, shuffled out the door. "I'll get my trunks!"

I just stared at Ann, unable to say anything. I felt if I started, I couldn't stop. I wanted to go with her badly. I was embarrassed to tell her I had no swimming trunks. "No," I finally said, "that's okay. Thanks. Uh … uh … I got things to do. I can't."

I was hoping she'd try to talk me into it. Anything to have her stay a little longer. "Okay," she said. "See you later." She closed the door and left.

I sat there thinking maybe I could wear my underwear. God, no. That would look tacky. Or maybe I could just go and watch them. Sit on the sand. While I was debating with myself, the door opened again. This time it was Aunt Jean.

"Johnny, you have no chores to do, so grab your swimsuit, you're coming with us!" She was so sweet I couldn't lie to her.

"I … I have no swimsuit. I didn't bring one."

"Well, we'll fix that!" Shortly, she returned with a pair of blue and white flecked trunks that tied at the top and had a pocket that buttoned. "These should do for today. If not, I'll alter them for you."

"Whose are they?" I asked.

Straight-faced, she said, "A boy who was here last year. He drowned."

My eyes popped open.

She laughed a pleasurable laugh, her eyes twinkling. "I'm just kidding."

The trek to the pathway on the road that led down to the lake was a mile from the house. The narrow trail from the road to the water was another half mile. Had Aunt Jean not been with us, we would have never found the pathway or the lake. The narrow trail was so thick with foliage, you could barely discern the person in front. You could only hear them. They were giggling with excitement. Not me. I was just thinking 'bears.' No one was more relieved than I when we finally emerged onto a small beach. There was a rickety short wharf. Tethered to it was an old community rowboat with two oars. Jeff and Chuck rushed to it, telling Aunt Jean they wanted to go for a ride. She obliged, joining them, along with their cocker spaniel puppy. She left the picnic basket with her daughter and Ann, saying, "Keep it closer to the water. It's safer."

Then she and the boys and yapping dog were soon out to sea.

All I could see was Ann. She was wearing a skintight full-bodied red bathing suit. And what a body. She and Jane rushed quickly into the water and began playfully squealing and splashing each other. Ann was in profile. With each move, her developing breasts jiggled. Oh, my God. My eyes wished they were hands. It was the first time I was ever interested in women's breasts. Not once had I looked at Miss Britton's. That wasn't my target. My eyes would not let go of Ann's. Looking at them made me tingle. I was a pretty good swimmer. I had spent many summer days in Toronto's Kew Gardens swimming in Lake Ontario. It was time to show off. I dove into the water to join them. It was crystal clear and cool. I could see Ann's creamy shapely legs moving slowly. I also saw sticks floating underwater surrounded by small pieces of dark wood. I hadn't noticed them floating toward me. When I emerged quickly next to her, I hollered "Surprise!"

Ann smiled broadly, splashing me playfully. "Hi, Johnny."

I never got to reply since some of those little black pieces of wood were stuck on my forearms. I shook them, but they never fell off. I plunged my arms in the water, but they didn't come off. Looking down, I saw black bits all over my legs. I began thrashing and kicking. They stayed stuck. I raised my arms in panic. "What is this? What is this?" I shouted.

Jane looked at my arms. "Oh, just leeches," she said casually.

"Leeches? Leeches?" I blurted. "Are they poisonous?"

"No. They're harmless. They'll drop off when they're full. Just bloodsuckers."

"Jesus Christ. What!" I tried to run back through the water, shaking every part of my body, but they didn't move. They were still dining. Ben watched me explode out of the water, brushing my arms violently. He luckily had never left the sand and was now rolling around in it in hysterics. Feeling the sliminess of their un-budging, bulging little bodies kept me crying a stream of "Oh, God!" Jumping up and down didn't help. Then I felt a hand on my shoulder.

"Johnny, stand still. They're harmless." It was Jane. She was plucking them off with her thumb and forefinger as casually as she would pluck cherries. Ann had a big smile. It meant nothing to me. Neither did her breasts. "Why aren't they on you? Why? Why?" I asked concerned.

"Maybe you taste better," Ann said. Ben howled louder. The girls giggled. It wasn't funny.

Worse than the leeches was the sickening embarrassment of my uncontrollable cowardice in front of Ann. It made me sick thinking it could never be undone. I got still, amazed by the ease and calmness at which Jane removed the critters. I was even more amazed when Ann got on her knees and began to pinch them off. Her right hand did the pinching while she pressed her left hand around my calf for leverage. With her hand touching me it was all I could feel. It felt so good; looking down, I noticed her breasts again.

Nearly ten years later I went to see *The African Queen.* When Humphrey Bogart emerged from that swampy water yelling in fear, batting at the leeches all over him, I groaned and started squirming. I didn't realize what I was doing until I noticed almost as many people looking at me as at Bogart. The story of my being the only buffet for the bloodsuckers provided days of mealtime amusement – until it was pork chop and bacon time.

The Slaughterhouse

When Uncle Bob informed me of his annual pig kill, the other boys begged to watch. It'd be much more exciting than my headless chicken act. Bloodier and more fun. "No, boys. It's not for you," he said. "Just Johnny."

Why he thought I should see it, let alone participate, I had no idea. I was afraid to ask him, why me? Mercifully, my assistance was almost nonexistent. Unmercifully, the film in my head has refused to fade. At the moment of the kill, he did stop and tell me, thoughtfully, that I could leave. I didn't leave. And didn't answer. I just stood there. Why I wanted to continue watching the most gruesome part of this already brutal unbearable experience, I don't know. It was about killing. About ending a life. I could not do it. Not to something that big; I doubt even if I were starving. Watching that animal's death, necessary to feed us, has forever baffled me how it is so much easier for humans to do it to one another. By the millions. For profit.

The slaughterhouse was twice the size of the shower, located over 200 yards from the barn and henhouses, on the opposite side of the house. You would know why if you were in the barn or henhouse when the screaming of the dying creature filled the air. Every animal got skittish and noisy. Somehow, they knew. There was an eight-foot square cement floor that angled slightly from all sides down to a large grate and drain. Against three of the walls were waist-high built-in benches covered with saws, hatchets, crowbars, hammers, huge pliers, and all kinds of knives; all of them spotless and glistening. Above the drain, ten feet off the ground, ran a huge beam. From it hung chains with hooks and a pulley. This is where the animal was hanging, the hook dug into its neck. Even with severed vocal chords, the screaming exploded in my ears.

I had done almost nothing to get into that position. I just watched earlier while Uncle Bob lassoed it. A dozen pigs had been jostling one another, greedily slopping up the food in their twelve-foot long trough near the front of the house. Close to the chickens. Even though there was plenty to eat, it seems pigs could not just do that without fighting and biting one another. Uncle Bob approached them holding a hollow six-foot-long pole in his right hand. A looped rope hung from the end of it. A few of the pigs lifted their heads and stopped eating. They had seen this pole before. They backed off snorting. The one Uncle Bob picked was the biggest, about 200 pounds and thigh high, its head buried in the slop. Standing a short safe distance, Uncle Bob nudged its side with his left foot. Irritated, the animal lifted its head to look. Instantly, the rope was around its neck. It was being tugged and tightened as the animal thrashed about screaming. The others deserted the trough grunting, then stopped to watch. The chickens were also long gone. When the lassoed pig saw its captor, it made no effort to run; it attacked, lunging and snorting. Uncle Bob didn't move. He raised it off the ground. It was unbelievable. He couldn't have been more than 185 pounds himself. He dragged and lifted the pig like this all the way, even though the animal's squirming and screaming increased with every step closer to the slaughterhouse. Inside, Uncle Bob stopped over the drain, lifting the animal till it was erect. It was there he asked me to do the only thing I did.

"Johnny, 'he said, calmly, "undo that latch on the bench that lowers the chain with the hook."

Shaking and gulping, I did so. The chain rattled down quickly, the huge steel hook at the end stopping near the pig's chest. Transferring the pole to his left hand, Uncle Bob grabbed the hook quickly, and with his right hand plunged it under the animal's neck. He dropped the pole, grabbed the chain, then secured it on a pulley; he tugged on this briefly until the pig's hind legs were a foot above the drain. The desperately screaming, crying, bellowing sounds shook the room and pounded my ears. The sight pounded my eyes, which were never averted. Uncle Bob walked unhurriedly to a bench where he retrieved the largest knife I had ever seen. About half the size of a sword. He walked back, stood a safe distance from the legs clawing the air, then with the handle in both hands plunged it as hard and fast as he could into its chest. Blood erupted and gushed out. From its throat came the scream of an animal who knew it was about to die. It was still whimpering and gurgling and bleeding when Uncle Bob again put two hands on the handle. With a slight grunt, he pulled downward violently, slicing it open from chest to crotch. I gasped. Jesus, what was I watching that I couldn't move? And it got worse. The slit from which only more blood was oozing was only a couple of inches wide. Uncle Bob, obviously having done it often, pulled the belly skin fully apart. Some of the pinkish insides began to seep out. He then stuck both hands deep inside the belly and pulled, stepping back as he did so. Now everything tumbled out, a mountain of guts splashing endlessly onto the drain. The screaming had stopped. The only sound was me breathing and blood draining.

Uncle Bob turned to me. "Thank you, Johny. You can go."

But I hadn't done anything really. Just watched. He didn't need me. Why was I there? I said nothing. I couldn't speak. I wanted to stay. It was not the sight that made me leave. It was the smell. The smell of death.

For two weeks, pork chops and bacon were no longer a part of my diet. I had become a short-term vegetarian. But you can't sink your teeth into lettuce. Only meat. So, my newly avowed principles of abstinence from flesh-eating vanished like New Year's resolutions. Now, though, meat had more taste because it had more meaning. I was also introduced to the taste of homemade ice-cream.

In the three months I was there, not one day did the Jurows venture to Burkes Falls for supplies, tools or food. Everything was homemade. Even ice cream. When I heard one warm day we were going to have ice cream for dessert, I of course thought they had stored a bunch in a fridge, the way they stored parts of the pig. But it came from a small wooden bucket. I was amazed at the taste of it, almost as much as by the making of it, all of which we participated in. A small bucket with a crank was filled with cream, ice, and topped with mountains of salt. Each of us, on the porch, took turns turning this crank endlessly, like an old model T that wouldn't start. The ice cream that magically emerged from this worn bucket was more delicious and addictive than any ice cream that ever came out of a Baskin-Robbins, or Häagen-Dazs, or Ben & Jerry's beautiful tubs.

Hay Fever

I do not like talking about sex, except maybe with my partner at the time. If I had one. This discomfort in sharing intimacies made me a misfit with my buddies. Be they juvenile or adult, well-known or unknown, that's almost all they talked about. Had they wanted to talk about politics, religion or whatever, they would have had a hard time shutting me up. On this subject, I am as quiet as an untouched keyboard. However, if one is going to tell true tales of one's life, the subject is unavoidable; sex is life. It is the prime force of nature, which is only interested in the three F's: fornicating, food, and fighting. The fighting and the food is to permit the fornicating.

You've all heard sex sometimes referred to as a roll in the hay. The truth is, there is something about the touch and texture of this horse food that transforms it into an aphrodisiac. At least it was for me as a twelve-year-old. There's much about the farm that I don't recall, but the smell and touch of that hay are still with me. Gone, though, are the touch and smell of Ann who inspired it. We only had a few encounters in the hayloft. The first was accidental; the others were secretly and sweetly planned.

We had all gathered in a field just outside the barn, uninvited. All except Aunt Jean. We had heard Uncle Bob talking at breakfast about a mare being in heat. When he left quickly, we knew something important was up, so we followed. When we got to the pasture, what we saw that was up was the stallion's penis. Not up, actually, but down. And about two feet long. But it didn't look like a penis. It looked like a slender cone in reverse, the small end being the tip. Uncle Bob patted the rump of the mare as it lifted its tail and backed nervously toward the stallion. The stallion whinnied as he lifted his front legs onto his mate's back, trying to thrust his hips. His huge penis just waved back and forth. With his left hand still on the mare's left quarters, Uncle Bob grabbed the penis in his right hand, lifted and inserted it, much to the pleasure of the horses and us. Up until now none of us uttered a sound. We were too lost in this new wonder of nature. The biggest wonder to me was why did the stallion need help. Hadn't horses done this by themselves forever? I was too embarrassed to even ask. I was also surprised at how short the thrusting was.

"Okay, gang, that's it. Chore time," Uncle Bob announced. During the coupling, I had glanced at Ann. She was staring intently at reproduction. At meals we seldom talked; sometimes, though, I caught her looking at me. When I did, she always smiled. I thought she liked me, but I had no idea how to start talking to her, when all I wanted to do was just grab and kiss her. It was a lifetime inability with females that I never could quite overcome. Everyone disbanded, off to do their chores. Mine was to the barn to pitch hay, as I did every morning, from the loft to the horses outside. From the loft window, I noticed Ann trying to pet a frisky colt. Behind her, a concerned mare. I hollered. "Ann. watch out! Behind you!"

She turned, spotted the irritated mare, and quickly backed away.

"Thanks," she said. "What are you doing?"

"Playing farmer John!" I said. "Watch out again!" I tossed another forkful of hay to the ground.

She watched it land, looking up again. "It looks like fun."

"Sort of!" I shrugged

"Can I help?"

I was stunned. The only time she invited me to do anything was swim, which turned into a disaster. "I guess so. Sure. Come on up." I waded through the sea of hay to the narrow wooden ladder. "Be careful," I called down.

"I've never been up here before," she exclaimed. Reaching the top, she held out her hand. "Help me," she said. "This is a little scary!"

I took hold of her hand, remembering the soft feel of it on my leg. I got goosebumps. Holding it tightly, I led her through the soft mounds of hay as she struggled to get a footing.

"Oh, my God." She giggled. When we came to the opening, I let go of her hand. "Thanks," she whispered, out of breath. She then shuffled to the edge and peered down.

"Be careful," I said.

"Wow. Kind of scary! But maybe if you fell, it wouldn't be too bad cuz you'd land in all that hay."

"Or on a horn!" I said.

She giggled. "Yeah, just like in those stupid westerns when a guy leaps off the building and into the saddle."

At that time, to me, no movie was ever stupid. "You'd better move back," I said.

"Are you finished?"

"No. Just a little more to do. Then I have to put some in the inside stalls." I reached for the pitchfork.

"Can I do it?" She reached for the pitchfork.

"Sure, but be careful." I pointed to a pile behind me. "Take it from there so you won't be so near the edge."

She plunged the pitchfork into the pile. She looked at the few strands on the prongs and laughed. She plunged it in again. Harder. And as she pulled it out with a yanking motion she stumbled and screamed, dropping the pitchfork as she hit the floor.

I rushed over. "Are you okay?"

She scrambled to her feet. "That was smooth." She giggled.

"There's really enough down there now," I said. "I'll wait a bit, then I'll go down and put some in the stalls."

She stood, looking at me. I didn't know what to do. Or say. She broke the awkwardness. "How often do you have to do this?"

"Every day."

"Do you come up here even when you don't have to work?" Her deep brown eyes were looking right at me. About two feet away.

"Once in a while," I said.

"I thought so," she said.

"Why?"

"Because a couple of times I wondered where you were."

The tingling that was just in my hand was spreading through my entire body. I couldn't believe she just said she'd been thinking about me.

She continued. "It's nice up here. What do you do by yourself?"

"I've only been up here a few times by myself. I don't do much of anything. Just daydream."

She stared at me for a long time. Without blinking. "Where do you sit? Here?" She indicated a spot near the door. A solitary bale of hay.

"Sometimes."

"Can I join you?" she asked, her head slightly tilted.

"When? The next time?" I stammered.

"No, silly. Now!" She laughed

"Well ... well..." I fumbled for words. "I've got to put the hay in the barn and–"

She interrupted me. "The horses are still there, and you said you were going to wait a bit."

She reached out quickly, took my hand in hers, and led me to a bale of hay. "Is this your spot?" Before I could answer, she pulled me down next to her, and let go. "There," she said, pleased.

Strangely enough, the silence for a minute or so was not awkward. It was actually comfortable. Almost like we'd sat like that before. She spoke first.

"Johnny..." She stopped.

"What?" I asked.

"What did you think when you saw the horses?"

Oh, my God, how do I answer that? Jesus. I wanted to show her how smart I was by telling her what I was afraid to say to Uncle Bob, about why did the stallion need help. That's not what came out.

"Amazing... amazing," I stammered.

"It was wonderful," she said dreamily. "Wonderful. In a few months there'll be a baby."

"Yeah, maybe."

She turned to me. No makeup. No lipstick. Nothing but beyond hypnotically beautiful. "Would you like children?" she asked.

I chuckled. "I'm barely one myself."

She laughed.

We sat side by side for close to an hour. She asked where I was from, about my family, what I liked to do for fun, and what I wanted to do when I was older. I told her I had a full sister and half-brother whom I seldom saw, a father who was overseas in the army, and a mother who was always away at work. My fun was hockey and movies, but since hockey no longer seemed a credible career, I told her I might become a lawyer because all lawyers had to do was talk ... and I could do that. I loved to see her smile. My questions to her were the same.

She lived in a nice area in York, north of Toronto. She had, she said, two neat parents. Her father was a lawyer and, smiling, she said he did a little more than just talk. Her fun she said was music and dancing. "Do you like to dance?" she asked.

"No," I said. "I'm not really very good at it. I move better in skates than shoes."

She laughed. "Do you have a girlfriend back home you dance with?"

"No, on both counts," I replied.

"What do you mean?"

"Well, I don't have a girlfriend. The couple of times I tried to dance with any girl, might be the reason I don't have one. It's awkward for me." I started to get fidgety. My eyes were crazy-glued to her face. I wanted to kiss her so badly I ached; it was an effort to keep from trembling.

"Were they a good dancer?" she asked.

"Uh ... uh ... I guess so, but not with me." I stammered, my eyes now locked on her mouth.

"Were any a good kisser?"

Oh, my God. She's reading my mind. Am I that obvious? "Oh ... oh ... uh ... I guess so," I muttered.

"Are you a better kisser than dancer?"

The question went to the pit of my stomach. And lower. "Well ... well ..." I was struggling to be cute or calm or clever. "It's easier than dancing ... your ... your ... lips don't have to move to the music."

Her low laugh thrilled me. "How about you?" I asked

"How about me, what?" she replied

"Are you a better kisser than dancer?" I lifted my eyes from her lips to her eyes. She was looking at my lips. Is she thinking what I'm thinking? The silence was painful. Goddamn it, John, do something. Say something.

But mercifully, she did. In a deep whisper, she said, "Would you like to kiss me?"

Oh, God help me. I froze, forcing myself to calm down; otherwise, I'd jump all over her.

"Would you?" she repeated

"Yes," I said, almost choking. To relieve the tension strangling my body and mind, I said, "As long as we don't have to dance!" I laughed, pleased with myself for being so glib. She ignored it. Her lips started to part. I leaned toward her. As I did so, she reached out with her left hand and placed it on the back of my neck, pulling me toward her. Like they do in the movies. Then her lips met mine. Mine exploded with pleasure. But her lips were not together like the girls' lips I had been fleetingly used to. Her lips were apart, literally covering mine. Then her tongue moved slowly forward, searching for mine. Jesus Christ, I thought my body would explode. She was so grown up. She knew stuff I didn't. When we parted, her face was just inches from mine.

"You haven't kissed a lot of girls, have you?" she asked matter-of-factly.

Damn it, is it that obvious?

"Have you?" she asked again.

"I … I guess not."

"Do you like it?" she asked

"Like what?"

"Kissing. Kissing me?" She was whispering.

"Yes … but … but … "

"But what?"

"But … but if … if you could tell, I … I hadn't kissed too many girls … maybe … " I interrupted myself. "Did you like it?"

She looked into my eyes, her lids almost half closed. "Yes." she said. "I like you."

"That's not what I asked," I said.

"Open your lips a little." She sighed, pulling my face toward hers again, this time with her hands on my cheeks. I did as instructed. Her tongue again slithered slowly toward mine, this time a little harder. Mine searched back. We were literally licking each other's tongue and mouth. I suddenly had this urge to bite her, to sink my teeth into her. I began to sweat. My heart pounded and my crotch began to ache. And then, for the first time I heard one of the most erotic sounds one could ever hear: the low moan of a woman luxuriating in being loved. Pain and pleasure flooded my being.

When we parted again, mostly to catch our breaths, her eyes were misty. "Johnny," she whispered, (I loved to hear her say my name.) "that was nice. Very nice!"

I stared at her. I had never felt so full of myself. So alive. I got glib again. "Will you teach me to dance, too?" I whispered back.

"Yes," she said, as she leaned forward with another lesson.

We were engaged like this so deeply and for so long, we didn't hear Uncle Bob calling us right away.

"Johnny! Johnny!" Uncle Bob called from down below.

Oh, my God! I brushed myself off, wiping my lips, even though she didn't wear lipstick. Anyone could see how swollen they were, though.

"Yes, Uncle Bob, here I am!"

"Have you seen Ann?" he asked in a way that indicated he knew the answer.

"Yeah. She's… she's up here. She's been helping me for a couple of minutes!"

By that time, Ann had made her way to the edge. "Here I am, Uncle Bob. What is it?"

"You've got a call. Long distance. Your mother."

"Oh, thanks. I'll be right down."

With that, Ann turned and scrambled down the ladder without even looking at me. Not one backward glance. Halfway down the ladder, she hollered as casually as you please, "Johnny, I'll see you later."

On the ground, Uncle Bob just glanced at me. He knew I was pitching more than hay up there. From that point on, the work assignments became more like work and more time-consuming for both of us. But where there's hay there's a way. Being illicit made them all the more alluring!

Ann

Because of management's awareness of our interest in one another, getting to the barn became more difficult. Seeing Ann became my only reason for being. It was impossible to think of anything else. The week apart, except staring at each other at meals, killed me and my appetite.

One afternoon, Uncle Bob was at the farthest end of the pasture, near the forest. He was retrieving some wandering cows. Aunt Jean was sewing. I found Ann by the henhouse, whispering that our watchdogs were busy. She giggled, quickly put down the basket of eggs and took off toward the barn. I chased her, feeling like that stallion.

She was the first one on the ladder. I was below her, looking up at her as she ascended. She was wearing a checked skirt that fluttered wide as she climbed. Her legs were shapely and cream white. As were her panties. I felt embarrassed for staring so I stopped, till she got to the top.

"What's wrong?" she asked

"Nothing".

"Well, come on!" she said, as she scampered away, and sat in our spot. I was barely seated when she clutched my hand and kissed me. Hard. We kissed and kissed until our lips were sore. Fighting the urge to maul her, I started to get fatigued. And an awful pain surged through my crotch. It hurt so much I had to lean back and lie down.

"Are you all right?"

"Yeah. I just gotta catch my breath. Kissing you is more exhausting than playing hockey."

"You're so cute," she said, crawling on her hands and knees to me. She put her head on my shoulder and her hand on my stomach. I wanted her to move her hand toward my pain, but I said nothing. We lay like that for a long time, saying little, watching the sun descending into the treetops. Suddenly she rolled on top of me, her breasts pressed against my sides, and kissed me. The urge and the energy to touch them just as suddenly surged through my whole being again. But then she said, "Oh, Johnny, it's getting late."

"Oh, God, yes," I stammered. "Let's go!"

We rose quickly, brushing ourselves off. I stared at her hands flicking the hay off her breasts, wanting to help. She stopped, looking deep into my eyes. She knew what I was thinking. Should I, I debated. Instead, I said, "I love you, Ann."

"I love you, too, Johnny." Then she was gone. Down the ladder.

I just stood there, both elated and depressed. I couldn't understand why I didn't touch her breasts or explore her body. She seemed more than receptive. I mean, she initiated the kissing. She ran here first. Maybe it wasn't me I didn't understand, maybe it was women! We never had a long enough session after that to find out.

The Long Shortcut

It was a perfect early morning late in August. No clouds and no wind, a soft gray mist hovered a few feet above the lake. We had all once again pushed our way through the tangled thick shrubbery to the beach. I was not about to go swimming. I was only there because Ann was. We could not keep our eyes off one another. Out there in the open, though, when we met, we smiled broadly because we had a sweet secret. I bravely announced that I'd love to take the boat out with her alone, staying above the water. Aunt Jean smiled. "You two can do that when we get back. The girls promised Ben first."

"Aunt Jean, I could fit in there."

"Who'd look after the boys? There's not enough room," she answered.

I looked at Ann, who smiled to see I was disappointed. "We won't be long, Johnny." She climbed into the boat alongside Aunt Jean and Jane. "Come on, Ben," they shouted.

His leg-sized arms propelled his weird small body down the wharf. He slung himself into the boat, grabbed by the girls. Happily aboard, he looked back at me waving with the biggest smile I ever saw on him.

"Ship ahoy, sailor boy." I watched them untether the boat and begin rowing, and giggling.

Aunt Jean hollered back, 'If you have something to eat, be sure and cover it."

I was left with Jeff and Chuck and the little cocker spaniel, Chuckie, who was having a lot more fun than I was. The boat and the sounds faded in the distance. I had spent very little time with the brothers over the weeks, so I didn't want to be there. Bored, I got up and looked for some flat stones that I tried skipping across the water. Jeff and Chuck joined me in our stone-tossing contest. With each toss, the dog plunged excitedly into the water, trying unsuccessfully to fetch them. Feeling bad for the dog, I found a few small sticks and began tossing them, just a few feet in, though, so he wouldn't come out with leeches instead of lumber. He brought them back to us, yelping happily.

The boat was gone. Out of sight. Jesus, it'd be forever before it got back. Then I began to realize that Uncle Bob and Aunt Jean were well aware of mine and Ann's interest in each other. There's no way she would let me go out on that boat with her alone. So, why should I even stick around.

I turned to Jeffrey, the older brother. "I don't wanna stay here. We can't even swim. What do you think?"

"You mean, just leave?"

"Yeah. We'll meet them at home."

"Yeah, okay." Jeffrey shrugged. We started toward the overgrown pathway. "What about the picnic basket?" Jeffrey asked.

"Oh, just leave it. They'll be hungry when they get back."

"Shouldn't we take a sandwich or something?"

"No. It won't take us long anyway. As a matter of fact, we could get there quicker."

"How?'

"Through the forest," I said, as though it was obvious. "A shortcut!"

"Do you know one?"

"Well, it's simple," I said, pointing. "The path is up this way. And the road goes that way. And the farm is there. We'll just cut right through. It'll be fun," I chirped.

"Yeah," Chuck said, now eager for the adventure.

To the right of the path, we began walking into the pines trees, which seemed to have less underbrush than the trail down. The little dog, Chuckie, dashed in and out of them with more glee than when he was plunging into the water to grab a stick. It never entered my mind that I might be making a mistake. The once-frequent thought about bears was gone.

It was about 10:30 in the morning when we started out. The sun was still well above us, rising in the clear sky. But very little sunlight hit the ground. Everything was in the shade. Only by looking straight up, which I did often, could we see it and bits of a sharp, blue sky. Within minutes, it was so thick it was impossible to move in a straight line for more than a few feet. Our arms were never at our sides, but in front of our faces to push bushes and branches aside. Chuck was right behind me, because he was the smallest and youngest, followed by Jeff. For a little while Chuckie scampered in front of us, barking in delight, running back to us to make sure we were still there, then off again. Soon though, he got tired. He moved next to Chuck, staying so close to his little master's feet that twice Chuck tripped over him. The last time, rising to his feet, brushing himself off, he said, "Johnny, are we there yet?"

I was surprised at how calm he sounded; looking at him in his tiny, baggy bathing suit, I realized how young he was. "We're okay," I said. When I said that, I wasn't really looking ahead, but behind us, in the direction from which we'd come to see if it might be easier to go back. I couldn't even make out one footprint or pathway we'd taken. I felt a tinge of regret but said, "We just have to keep going."

I was certain, though, I was moving in the right direction, that soon we'd emerge onto the dirt road right in front of the farm. We barely spoke as we pushed ahead. My demeanor kept them calm, including Chuckie. Inside, though, I was becoming a little apprehensive, in spite of my growing restlessness; however, I loved being there, in the impenetrable forest. The newness of it. The feel of the dirt on my bare feet. The massive pines. The colors of the flowers and berries everywhere. The songs and squawks of birds, never seen, but always heard. The adventure of it. But most of all, the smell. The deep, rich scent of fresh pine and whatever else made up nature's perfume. Every breath in nature's oxygen tent pumped me up. But reality brought me back.

About twenty-five minutes in, the part of the shaded forest we had trekked, ended. We stepped out into the bright sunlight for the first time and gasped. In front of us was a circular area the size of two football fields in which not one blade of grass grew. It was entirely desolate and grey. There were grey boulders the size of small houses everywhere. Only a few grey dead trees were standing. The rest were bent and broken. There were small patches of shallow water everywhere. It was a dead zone. Totally lifeless. Right there in the middle of nowhere. It looked like a meteor had crashed into it.

As the three of us stared at it, Chuckie started barking, and backed away from it. We were looking at a scene from a science fiction horror movie. In unison, we all whispered, "Wow."

"What could have caused that?" Jeff asked quietly.

For minutes, we just stood motionless, surveying this otherworldly sight. "Is this the shortcut?" Chuck asked.

"No," I whispered, suddenly aware of the fact that in the time we'd spent penetrating this shortcut, we'd have been on the road had we just gone back up the trail. "We'll have to go around it," I said a little louder, trying to buoy my own confidence. "Let's go!"

We moved again to our right, skirting the edge of the desolation. Ten feet into the trees, we could no longer see it. Fifty yards in we came out onto another open patch, half the size of an ice rink. It was a patch of brown earth covered with pine needles and yellow flowers. Three sides were surrounded by towering trees. The remaining side was walled in by massive boulders that framed a cave big enough to drive a car into. At first, I had this intense feeling of curiosity, to creep over and peek in. Then fear informed me, what if we find a bear? It was the first time that thought hit me. And it hit me hard. I was suddenly scared. And keeping quiet, not to frighten the boys, made it more intense.

"Let's keep going," I said, moving quickly in the direction we'd been going.

The dog was now silent, but the brothers started to whine. "Johnny, why aren't we there yet?"

"Don't worry. We'll be there soon. We're fine." But I wasn't. Had I made a dreadful mistake? I stared up through the trees, searching for the sun; it was now past being directly overhead. This meant it was past noon. We had been moving for three hours. Surely, we must be getting to the road soon. Shortly, we came upon a cluster of bushes covered with thick red berries.

"I'm hungry," Chuck said, reaching for them.

Jeff joined him. "Me, too."

Anxiety had drained my appetite. "Jeff, Chuck, I wouldn't take a chance on eating those."

Chuck already had a fistful in his hand. "But I'm hungry. They're berries."

"Yeah, but they could be poisonous," I said. "I wouldn't."

The boys evaluated them, then dropped them to the ground.

"We'll be eating soon," I said. "Come on."

As I started to move, out of nowhere, I began to sing *Onward Christian Soldiers.* I couldn't believe what was coming out of my mouth. And stuck inside were prayers I had to keep to myself. The boys chuckled, relieving my stress. Chuckie was barking again.

My solo stopped when we came upon another open patch. This was also the size of an ice rink, bordered on three sides by forest... with brownish pine needles and yellow flowers. The other end walled by massive boulders above a cave. It was the same place we'd stumbled on an hour earlier! *How could that be?* A bolt of fear shot right through my chest and throat.

"What!" I gasped. I couldn't understand what had just happened. How did we get there? We were lost. But we couldn't be. We'd been moving in the right direction. In a straight line. I just knew we were. (I learned later this is a very common phenomenon encountered by those who brave walking through forests and jungles caused by the rotation of the earth.)

"Is this where we were before?" Jeffrey asked, totally frightened.

"I think so." I could barely speak.

"How?" Jeff asked, incredulous

"I don't know. We were moving in the right direction," I exclaimed.

"Johnny," Chuck said, "I'm scared. Are we lost?"

"No. We're not lost," I lied loudly. "Somehow, we just got turned around. Let's go. Come on."

We started back, on the same trail we'd taken earlier. I stopped. Having seen this in a movie, with Indians, I said, "Every little bit, let's bend a branch or something so we can mark our way so we don't do this again." We started to move quickly. Every ten or fifteen steps, Jeffrey and I were snapping branches. The thought I was finally doing something smart calmed me down.

Shortly, our scratched blistering hands and arms were beginning to ache. "Hold it," I said, looking skyward. The sun was now in front of us, to the left. We had been out almost six hours. It was impossible for us to be out that long and not come out somewhere. It was now late afternoon; the shadows were deepening. The air was getting cooler.

We started again and, in just a few steps, stopped. I wanted to scream. It was that same cave clearing! Again. It couldn't be. We would have seen bent branches. "Jesus Christ!" I cried out loud.

Jeffrey panicked. "Johnny, why do you keep bringing us back here? Why?" he yelled. "Where are we?"

His brother grabbed him, crying, "Jeffrey, I wanna go home. Please. I'm cold." The dog was running in circles. As we had.

We were hopelessly lost. I wanted to scream for help. But what if just the bears heard us? Or wolves crossed my mind. But if I started to panic or holler, the boys would totally lose it. They might even run off and make it worse. I had to hold myself together. But I didn't know what to do. Going to the right just led us back to that terrifying place. Twice.

I looked skyward again, for some kind of divine intervention. Something. Anything. I didn't know what. There must be some way to move in a straight line and not keep going around in circles! The sun was on its way down. Soon we would be stuck out there in the dark. There'd be no moonlight; even if there was, it'd never reach us. I had to get a look at the sun. Suddenly, I wasn't standing next to Jeff and Chuck, I was sitting in the hayloft. With Ann. Watching the sun say goodnight. That was it! It's setting in the west. To our left. Not to our right.

I literally yelled, "The sun. The sun sets in the west. We've been going the wrong way. All we have to do is follow the sun. That'll keep us from going in circles. Come on!" I was ecstatic.

"No." Chuck was still crying. "I want to go home!"

"This is the way. Believe me," I implored. "Sometimes when Ann and I were in the barn we'd watch the sun go down. It's going down that way." I pointed to the left. "All we have to do is follow it. Honestly. It goes down right behind the barn."

They had no choice but to follow me. We moved, more quickly now, with a purpose, breathing heavily. Our gasping and thrashing were the only sounds we heard, along with the whippoorwills. For quiet minutes, we trudged and plodded, and pushed and scrambled. Soon the sun was no longer visible behind the trees. I motioned the boys to stop. I picked the tallest tree with the lowest hanging branches and began to climb. All that experience I had playing Tarzan finally came in handy. I ascended about eighty feet. The top half of the sun was taking its last peek at us above the sea of treetops. To the west.

"There it is," I hollered, descending quickly, pleased with myself. "This way," I said. We rushed toward the vague last light, for maybe 100 yards, until it vanished. We had to stop.

Chuck started crying. Out loud. His brother, surprisingly, was comforting him. "Don't cry, Chuck. Please."

The forest was getting dark, too dark to move. It was also too dark to stay put. And too cold. We couldn't just stop there. Where would we rest? Or sleep? We talked about climbing a tree, but Chuck was too small for that. Then there was the dog. We moved so slowly we could barely see one another. We kept asking if we were still all there.

In the darkness, we soon came upon what looked like the widest tree stump I'd ever seen. It was in a slight clearing. As we edged closer to it, we could see in what moonlight there was, that it wasn't a tree stump at all. It was some sort of small log cabin. We touched it like we were blind. The wood crumbled in our hands. It was about twelve feet square and twelve feet tall. "We'll stay here," I whispered, relieved.

We found two small openings for windows; a little too high for us to reach. There had to be a door somewhere. And there was. A narrow crumbling wooden door that was ajar only about eight inches or so. When I tried to open it, it wouldn't budge. It was embedded in two feet of dirt and growth that accumulated around its base

"Let's stay here tonight," I said, struggling to open the door wider.

"I don't wanna stay here. I'm scared," Jeff said, plaintively.

"Jeff, it's too dark to move. We'll be all right. Come on. Help me." Even with the extra hands, the door wouldn't move

"Well," I said, "let's see if we can squeeze in there. Chuck, you go first."

"Why?" he asked, shaking with fear.

"Because you're the smallest. You should go first. It's safer."

"Safer from what?"

I didn't want to say it, but I did. "Bears."

He started to sniffle. "Are there bears?"

"You know there are," I said as calmly as I could.

Chuck put his little chest against the door and wedged his way in. Jeff followed. It was a little tougher for him. And even tougher for me. The door tore against my chest, gashing it as I slid in. From what little we could see, there was nothing on the ground but mounds of dirt. The roof angled from the middle down to the sides. Feeling around, in the darkness, we bumped into a couple of wide, worn wooden posts about seven feet tall. They supported a shaky wooden platform above us that was missing a few of its boards. If this had been a hunter's cabin, this platform must have been where they hung their furs. Pointing to it, I said. "We'll have to sleep up there."

"Why?" Jeffrey whispered. "A bear can't get in."

"Snakes," I whispered back.

Jeff looked up at it. "It's too high. We can't reach it."

"Yes, we can. Put your back against this, cup your hands. I'll climb up, then pull you guys up."

Jeff leaned against the pole, cupped his hands in front of his thighs. I placed a foot in, reached over his head, grabbed a plank, and pulled myself up. There wasn't much room. As I had guessed, some of the boards were missing. Chuck put his foot into his brother's hands and was up easily. The dog began whining. Jeffrey lifted him with his right hand. I grabbed him by the scruff of the neck. He was shaking uncontrollably. Getting Jefferey up was tougher. To keep from falling, and to get anchored, so I could pull him, I had to straddle a loose board, and let my legs hang down. With his hand locked in mine, and my chest pressed against the board, I tugged and gasped. The board creaked and bent. His free hand finally grabbed the edge and he rolled on top of me.

We lay in this awkward position for a few minutes, fearful of moving or falling through an opening. Chuck was clutching his dog. Both were whimpering. When I reached to pat him, the structure shook. I froze. "Chuck, you're okay. We're okay. We're safe. We've got a place to rest.

They'll be looking for us."

"They'll never find us." Jeffrey was close to tears. "God. God. God!"

I was thinking what Jeffrey was crying, but I couldn't pray. Even though I wanted to. Worse than feeling lost and frightened, I felt stupid and alone. I thought I'd given up on God, yet found myself stifling praying because if I did so, I would be showing the boys my confidence was gone. It was. But it'd only frighten them more to know that. The frailty of the platform made it impossible to lie down. We could just curl up on our sides on the spots where we sat. It was impossible for me to imagine we could even think of closing our eyes in such conditions. But we did. I fought it to see that Chuck and Jeffrey would fall asleep before I did. They did. Chuck first, then his brother. Even the dog was out. Then I nodded off.

I was awakened by Jeff's hand digging hard and deep into my arm. "Listen, listen," he whispered.

Chuckie was yelping and growling below us.

"Jesus, did he fall?" I gasped.

"I dunno," Jeffrey said. "Listen. Listen. At the door."

We couldn't quite see him, but that is what he was barking at.

"Chuckie," I yelled. Be quiet. The barking became more frantic. Then we could hear it: a low, grunting and snorting that sounded like it was just inside the door. Chuck awoke, and started screaming, "Chuckie. Chuckie!"

"Be quiet, Chuck. Be quiet. Listen." I grabbed his arm to keep him from moving.

Then a louder grunt, followed immediately by the sound of a large body pushing angrily at the door. It was a bear. It had to be. If it was as big as the sound it was making, it was the size of a bull.

"It's a bear," I whispered. "Stay still."

Jeffrey's grip tightened on my arm. My heart pounded in my chest and in my throat, gasping for air. The fear was so intense, it hurt. Not even Garth at his most vicious made me feel that terrified. After a minute, the banging stopped. We could hear the bear shuffling outside, snorting. Instantly, there was another harder lunge and louder growl as it plowed into the door. His head had gotten further in. The door was creaking. But it stuck. We could hear the scraping and roaring as he rocked his body back and forth in a rage. The dog retreated to a corner, cowering and crying. Pee was trickling down my legs.

The more the door held, the more the bear thrust himself at it. He may have started out hungry. Now he was pissed. There were a few more brief pauses for breath and a regathering of strength. It was as though it would never end. In an hour, it did. We hadn't moved. We waited and listened. It was over. Soon, so was the night. We did not dare go back to sleep. Or talk. The early morning sun began to trickle through the little windows into our abode. Our fear had made us forget how cold it was.

Rescued and Rebuked

In spite of the flickering morning sun, the cabin was still in dark shade. We were still where we'd spent the night. "What'll we do?" Jeffrey asked, surprisingly calm.

I didn't hesitate. "You guys stay here and let me go look outside.to see if that bear's still around."

"You won't go far?" he asked, nervously.

"No. Just to look around." I lowered myself to the floor. Happy to see me, the puppy followed me to the door. "Stay here, Chuckie. Stay."

Barely sticking out my head, I saw no bear. We were in a small, thick, grassy knee-high clearing. Still shaking, I squeezed slowly out, scraping my chest again. Everything glistened with dew. It was sunny, and cold, the forest a cacophony of bird calls.

Keeping the cabin in view, I edged further away. I was about to take a few more steps when there was a sudden roar above me. It was a helicopter, swooping overhead.

I screamed, "Here! Here! Down here!" But just as quickly, it was gone. Then there was another roar. This from on the ground. Just in front of me. About twenty feet away. A bear was making a weird motion, bobbing its head up and down, then rising to its hind legs, then down again, as it stared at me. I ran like a madman through the cutting bushes, racing for the cabin, whimpering because I was too terrified to scream. I went head first through the cramped door, tearing my skin. Inside I grabbed Chuckie. "Jeff. Jeff. Catch!" I tossed him up, and shinnied up the pole, slivers penetrating every part of me.

The bear was now at the door. We could see his snout as he pushed it in and sniffed the air. He was not as angry as before, but still started thrusting his shoulders at the opening. We could see the door bending and crackling. He suddenly stopped, and backed away. I figured he was repeating the same routine from the night before. But he stopped.

Trying to reassure Jeffrey, I whispered, "Did you hear the helicopter?"

"Yes. Yes," he said. "Did they see you?"

"I'm not sure, but they're looking for us. They're getting close!"

"What should we do?" he asked

"Wait here a minute," I said. With that I crawled carefully over the loose boards to one of the small windows. On my hands and knees, I peered out. There was no bear on that side. No sound of him either. I looked skyward. There was no helicopter, but I could see the accessible roof. Excitedly, I crawled out and pulled myself up and onto it, laying on my stomach to survey it. It was in the same shape as the platform we had spent the horrible night on with loose boards and holes everywhere. Steadying myself, I rose slowly to my feet. We were surrounded by a fortress of trees. I was sick. I knew we could not get through them. And in what direction. We could not leave this place. We had to stay until somebody found us. I wanted to scream, but if I did, the boys would know I had given up. I screamed anyway. "Help! Help! Help!" I stopped, straining for a response. What came echoing back was me shrieking. I yelled again, hurting my throat. "We're over here. We're here! Help. Help!"

I was suddenly stopped by an explosion. It sounded like gunshots. I started frantically waving my arms, almost losing my balance. "Over here. Over here!" They weren't shrieks now. They were cries of joy! Then more gunshots. Closer. And a few more, as if in response.

Then a man's voice, surprisingly close, hollering, "Over here. They're over here!" More shots echoed for miles through the forest. Within moments, a man I'd never seen pushed through the trees and bushes, his rifle held high. He saw me immediately.

"Are you okay? he yelled.

"Yes! Yes," I gushed.

"Are there three of you?" he yelled again, getting closer.

"Yeah!" I hollered back.

"Are they okay?"

"Yes. They're inside."

Another man, carrying a shotgun, emerged from another angle. He asked the same thing.

We were rescued. Not being able to open the door themselves, they waited outside for us as we squeezed back out. The men had canteens and blankets with them. We all took sips, not realizing how thirsty we were; the men put the blankets around our shoulders. One of them took a towel, dampened it, and gently rubbed the blood off my body.

"You guys had the whole country looking for you! You don't know how lucky you are." With that, he raised his rifle in the air and fired three quick victory shots.

With their hands around our shoulders, they led us away. We hadn't gone thirty or forty feet when we spotted it. The road. The dirt road. We had stopped this close to the road and couldn't see it. We emerged onto it half a mile from the farm. It was swarming with people to greet us. Army personnel, mounted police. Farmers with shotguns. Women I'd never seen.

As we approached the gate, a woman was already running toward us, screaming, "Chuck, Chuck! Jeff! My boys. My boys! Thank God. Thank God." Crying, she clutched them to her body.

"Mommy. Mommy. Mommy." The boys were crying in relief.

I looked around for my mother. She wasn't there. The ones who greeted me were Uncle Bob and Aunt Jean. She caressed my cheek, and patted my head, smiling. Uncle Bob just looked at me, as if studying me. It was a look that said he was glad to see me.

"What happened to you?" he asked.

"We tried to take a shortcut," I said softly.

"We'd better wash you down. And get you something to eat. Did you eat anything out there?" he asked

"No," I answered.

"Smart boy."

With that, Aunt Jean put her arm around my shoulder, took me into the shower and scrubbed me with my trunks on. One by one, she pulled the slivers from my punctured body.

"Get into some clean shorts and get to bed. I'll bring you some soup." She led me to the back porch with the cots, opened the door, and motioned me in. "Leave the wet trunks on the end of the bed."

The soup she brought, I could not eat. My mind was on my mother, wondering why she wasn't there. I had visions of her crying and hugging me like Jeff's mom. I couldn't wait for her embrace, her tears of gratitude, showing how much she missed me. My daydream was interrupted by Ann and Ben. They were at the foot of the bed, looking as though they shouldn't be there.

"How was it?" Ann asked.

"Scary," was all I could say.

"Did you see any bears?" Ben asked with glee.

I didn't want to recall it. "Almost."

"Wow," he responded.

"We're glad you're okay." Ann smiled.

They stared for a moment, uneasily, then left. I fell asleep. One of the few times I did so without dreaming.

I was awakened by Jeff and Chuck being tucked in and tended to by their mother and father. The mother was still crying, but more quietly now. "You're safe, my darlings. You're safe. You're going home tomorrow. Mommy's prayers were answered."

I closed my eyes, wanting them to think I was asleep, not wanting to intrude. But the mother had seen me. Suddenly, she lunged at me; an animal sound erupted from her – part scream, part howl. "You son of a bitch. You little bastard!" She began battering me. "You little bastard. It was your fault. You could have killed my babies. Goddamn you!" She yanked at the blanket I tried to pull over my head. I couldn't tell her to stop. She was right. It was my fault. Her husband watched.

"Mrs. Butler! Mrs. Butler!" Uncle Bob rushed in. "That's enough. Your boys are okay. We've had enough anguish!" He grabbed her by the shoulders and pulled her off. He handed her to her husband. "Make her rest!" Wordlessly, her husband led her away.

Uncle Bob stood next to the boys' bunks. "Are you guys all right?"

"Yes." They could barely be heard

"You're mother's upset. She loves you. And she was concerned. She'll be fine, though. Go to sleep." He patted them, then turned to me. "Are you all right?" I could only shake my head.

He put his hand on my shoulder and just stared for the longest time. He often looked like he was studying me. "You were lucky, you know."

"Yeah," I whispered.

"I hear it was a big one. That's why Mrs. Butler is so upset. You can't blame her, can you?"

"I know. I'm sorry."

Uncle Bob looked at me long and hard. "Do you mind if I tell you something?" He cocked his head a little.

"No," I said.

"I never give advice. Never. Not even when I'm asked. Even by my wife or daughter. I just tell them their nature will tell them what they need to do. So, this is in no way advice. It's an observation. About nature. About the way it is."

I was too tired to sit up, but I was listening closely.

"You know, when a mother bear has cubs, she tends to them very carefully for a couple of years. She teaches them how to hunt and climb, the things that they need to learn to survive. If they goof up, as kids do, she whacks them. And sometimes real hard. Then you know what she does?"

"What?"

"After two years, she drives the cubs up a tree. And leaves them there. If they try to get down to follow her, she whacks them and sends them back up. Then she runs off. Never to see them again. When that cub descends, of course it cries and whimpers and looks for its mother. But she's gone. And you know what?"

"What?"

"Realizing it can't and won't ever find its mother, that cub then has to fend for itself. It is forced to become its own adult." Uncle Bob's face was soft, his gaze warm. "Johnny," he said, patting my shoulder, "You may have just been chased up the tree of life. I'll see you in the morning. Get some rest." He left.

I did not close my eyes right away. I was thinking hard about what he'd just said.

The Spell Broken

No one was allowed to wake me the next morning. I didn't see or hear Jeff and Chuck leave. All I saw was their made beds. I was never a morning person. My body chemistry is somehow programmed to tell me that the crack of dawn is ten a.m. So, at ten I dressed and walked to the kitchen. Aunt Jean and Jane were doing dishes and preparing lunch. They greeted me warmly.

"Morning. You slept well. Would you like something to eat?" Aunt Jean asked.

"No, thanks," I said, still not hungry. "Is my mother coming?" I blurted.

Aunt Jean looked at me. "I don't know. We contacted her."

I walked to the front door and gazed out at the road. That was where she would be coming from. I pushed open the door, descended the stairs, walked past the blood-stained chopping block, and off in to the fields and pastures. I wasn't going anywhere in particular. I didn't want to see anyone. Or talk to anyone. I just walked. Past the cows. Past the horses. All the way to the back pasture. I found a small fence, climbed up on it, and sat facing the farmhouse in the distance. Whatever fun I had had there, whatever pleasures, were over. The spell had been broken. I didn't belong there. Or anywhere. Surprisingly, that sudden awareness did not depress me. I was too busy wondering what I was going to be doing next. When I got home. Not home actually, but to Lawlor Avenue, wondering what would happen between me and my mother now.

"Johnny! Johnny!" It was Ann, running toward me waving her arms.

"I think it's your mother," she shouted.

In the distance, I could see dust and a car coming through the gate. I leapt to the ground and ran as fast as could, all the time feeling how wonderful it was going to be when she grabbed me to her bosom. Adrenaline pumped into my leaping legs. Running and running, reality popped into my head for a millisecond. My mother was not like Jeffrey's and Chuck's. It didn't matter. My flooding emotions knew this time she'd be different.

Others had seen the car. They ran to the front of the house where it would stop. Aunt Jean saw me rushing toward them. "It's your mother." She smiled. I stopped in front of them, gasping.

The car stopped twenty feet in front of me. I did not move toward it. I could make out the figure of a woman on the passenger side, not moving. It could only be my mother. I stayed this distance because when she got out of the car I wanted to see her running toward me, sweeping me up in tears.

A man emerged from the driver's side, walked quickly around the front of the car, and opened the door. My mother emerged slowly, stockinged leg first. She was dressed in a dark brown suit and wearing a small hat with a veil. She looked beautiful. She stopped, looking at everyone, saying nothing. Neither did they. She stared at me, still wordless. And motionless.

I was suddenly overwhelmed by embarrassment. So, I rushed to her, my arms outstretched.

I was stopped by a hard smack to the face with her almost closed fists.

"You had to get into trouble, didn't you?" she hissed.

I didn't know what to do. Neither did anyone else. It looked and felt like a freeze-frame in an ugly black and white movie. My mother turned briskly to get back into the car, stopping briefly to look at Uncle Bob. "He's paid up until Sunday, then send him home!"

The driver closed the door behind her, got behind the wheel, turned the car around, and drove away, faster than he'd driven in. The sight of it was soon lost in the trailing dust. No one had moved. I could not look at anyone, I was choking with shame. Why did she even bother coming? She could have phoned those instructions. But she had to tell the world I was a worthless troublemaker. I wanted to run back to the field, but I didn't. I walked back to my bunk, climbed up and lay down, wide-eyed, wondering what it all meant. If anything.

For the few eventless remaining days, no one said anything to me about the incident. I stayed to myself, continuing my few chores alone, chores Uncle Bob said I did not have to do. At meals, Ann and I barely chatted or looked at one another. On the Saturday she left, I stood my distance and just waved. She waved back.

Ben was still there when I left on Sunday. I had the feeling he would never be leaving, that his parents would pay to keep him there forever. We shook hands, mine lost in the hugeness of his. "Good luck, Johnny!" he said.

Aunt Jean hugged and kissed me on the cheek. So did Jane. Uncle Bob asked if I wanted to ride to the station on the tractor or the truck. I was through with the farm, so I said the truck. The bumpy ride to the depot was without a word. When we got there, he handed me my flimsy suitcase, shook my hand firmly, then reached over and opened the door for me. As I got out, he said, "Johnny."

I stopped. "Yes?"

"Good luck, son. You, my boy, are going to do really well."

"Thank you, Uncle Bob. Thank you for everything. I did like it here. I am sorry I caused you so much trouble."

He laughed. "That's what farms are. But, remember one thing…"

"What's that?"

"You just got down from a tree you were forced to climb."

I turned and walked away, my battered suitcase in my hand, my battered life in my head, and tears rolling down my face.

Back in Toronto, at 192 Lawlor Avenue, I spent more time by myself. I avoided my friends, even Mel. My new friends were books. I joined the library for their company. I loved getting lost in them. My mother was seldom around. Neither was Maggie. My brother, Ronnie, was making plans to leave the country to join the US Air force.

Often, though, I found myself thinking about Ann. How beautiful she was. How she said she loved me. I missed that more than kissing her. I wanted to hear it again. I had this need to see her. Her smudged address was still in my wallet. She was up in York. The third week home, I decided to visit her on a Saturday to make sure she was home. I walked the ten blocks to Main Street where I got on a streetcar to Young Street, and transferred to the one that took me North, the long ride to York. It was a two-hour trek. The walk to her house was another ten blocks. It was a beautiful two-story atop its own little hill. Lush landscaped steps led up to the big black double front doors adorned with a brass lion's head door knocker. I was hopeful and very happy, albeit a bit nervous. I lifted the lion's head carefully, banging it softly on the black wood. It thundered through the house. Nobody answered. I was reluctant to pound again. Maybe they were out. I didn't know whether to knock again or leave.

Then it opened. But not all the way. Just a crack. It was Ann. God, she was even more beautiful with a hint of lipstick and eyeliner now.

"Hi," I said hopefully. "How are you?" I had imagined her sudden smile and giggle of glee when she saw me. I wasn't even sure of what I would say to her. Nature would take its course. She didn't even have to tell me she loved me again. Just that she was happy to see me.

Her greeting was as sudden and as short as my mother's had been a month earlier.

"I'm sorry, I can't talk to you," she said bluntly, closing the door.

What was this? A couple months ago she was all over me in a hayloft. Why was she so upset with me? How could she fall out of love so quickly? Was she angry because our story had been in the news? Or was it because maybe I had been too clumsy, or in my mind, too gentlemanly, to not have touched her more when I knew she wanted me to? I had gone there wanting to see her, talk to her. Now I just wanted to ask one question: Why? Why, the change? I'd never know the answer. It was a warm Saturday. There was time to go to a movie. Or the library. None of which could ever explained women to me.

The New Boarder, New Visitor and Drop Out

This was a day where events beyond your control change your life. It was the end of my first year at Malvern Collegiate High School, the day of our final exams, which I was looking forward to. I had no friends at Malvern, and I saw my buddies, including Mel, seldom. I didn't miss or need them. I loved being there. I was an A-plus student who had started doing homework.

Algebra, trigonometry, beginning calculus, history, literature, French, German, Latin, social studies; mind food that I gorged on. I wasn't looking for grades, just more knowledge. My father had watered my mind, teaching me the alphabet and counting before I was three. Even though he wasn't home, he was ever-present every time I got an A.

With books in hand, I walked down the stairs to the sidewalk. My mother followed me out the door, and hollered from the veranda, "John. John." I stopped. She held up a letter. "You think that deadbeat of a father of yours is coming home. Well, think again. He is not. The bloody war's been over for months. This letter says that useless bastard is staying in England. He got some Goddamned Order of The British Empire. You'll never see him again!" She slammed the door, still cursing. At first a tinge of pride surged through me. He'd gotten some kind of honor. A medal. Maybe for bravery. Then it hit me. The sick feeling that I would never see him again. I wanted to go back in the house. Just give up. But I couldn't be inside with her. I continued slowly to school.

I had the middle front-row seat, for the brightest kid in the class. Sitting down, I noticed a small package and note. It was a bar of soap. The note said, "Please use it. No directions necessary." First my father's note. Then that note. God, could the day get any worse? They say bad things happen in threes. There would be a third.

I wasn't shocked. Or hurt. What could hurt me more? I half expected it. Not having real shoes to wear to school, I often wore rubber boots. Even on clear days. But I had no socks. Putting the boots on in the morning, the smell often bothered me. I raised the soap and note over my head. "I will."

The class cheered. The teacher, with a pained look on her face, handed out the dozen or so exam papers. "You have all day," she said. It took me five minutes. On each paper for every subject, I just wrote a huge zero, which my life had suddenly become. I placed them on the teacher's desk, walked out of Malvern Collegiate and, later that day walked out of 192 Lawlor Avenue. I couldn't even refer to it as home.

My little suitcase again in hand, I took the Kingston Road and Queen Street streetcars to Mrs. Tomassini's new restaurant. It wasn't new, actually, but it was to Jerry's mother. Having made and sold homemade wine in the basement of her house on Gerrard Street, it was her dream to have such a place, no matter how run down. Her two-story eatery with the white painted menu scrawled on the large front glass windows was in the heart of the industrial district, a block from Toronto's train terminal. It looked perfect for me.

There were three customers when I entered, one at the counter, and two at one of the half-dozen booths. All looked like railroad workers. Mrs. Tomassini did most of the cooking, but had an aging chef in the kitchen. She was the only waitress and cashier in the afternoon, a no-nonsense, blue-eyed, brown-haired widow approaching forty. Her attractiveness was diminished slightly by the sharpness of her tongue. She was the Italian version of *The Golden Girls'* Bea Arthur.

She looked up from pouring coffee when I rattled through the door. "Chonny. You a goin' someplace or you a sellin' somethin?" she said, straight faced.

"Uh ... uh ... Mrs. Tomassini, could ... could I talk to you for a minute?"

"You must be a sellin' somethin!" She motioned me toward the kitchen. We stopped at the bottom of the stairs. "What ees it, Chonny?"

"Mrs. Tomassini." I was barely audible. "Could I stay here with Jerry for a couple of days until I find a job and a place to stay?"

"Whatta you mean, a job? You in a school," she said forcefully.

"I quit school."

"When?"

"Today. I can't go back."

"Why not? You in trouble?"

"No. I just can't go back. I don't want to."

Her voice softened. "What your mother a say?"

"Nothing."

"Wadda you mean, nothin? She noa angry?"

"She ... she wasn't home to say anything. I just left."

She took her hands from her hips and folded them in front of her chest. "You meana she don't aknow you gone?"

"No," I said.

She knew about my mother. Everyone in the neighborhood did.

Her silence made me nervous. "Mrs. Tomaasini, I can't go back home again, either. I can't. Just for a couple of days. Please!"

"Ona one aconditon, OK?' She said sternly.

"Yes. Anything,' I blurted.

"You tell your momma."

"I will."

"OK. You can stay long asa your need..but work."

"Oh, thank you. Thank you," I gushed, wanting to hug her.. "Is Jerry here?"

"No. He play baseball."

"Thank you. Thank you." I rushed out the door leaving my suitcase on the floor.

St. John's Reformatory was where we played hockey in winter and baseball in summer.

Families of those sentenced there, sat in the left bleachers. Spectators and friends sat in the right bleachers. I stood by the right bleachers, too excited to sit. Jerry spotted me and waved. With his team coming up to hit, he grabbed a bat and rushed over to me. "How yah doin, buddy?"

"Great. Guess what?" I asked, beaming.

"What?"

"Your mother's letting me stay at your place for a while."

He grinned. "You're kidding! How come? What about school?"

"I quit. I'm gonna get a job!"

"What'd your mother say?" he asked.

"Good riddance."

He laughed. "Well, good news. Your brother was here."

"What?" I shouted. "My brother?"

"Yeah. In a US Air Force uniform. He was looking for you. He was with your sister. He looked great."

I was on my feet. "Are you sure?"

"Yeah!"

"Where'd he go?"

"He said he was gonna get something to eat."

"Oh, my God, Wow! Thanks!" I jumped up.

"Ronnie doesn't drink, does he?" Jerry asked.

"No," I said with certainty. "Why?'

"He had a bottle of beer in his hand."

He could only be one place. A small coffee shop at Lawlor and Kingston Road. We went there often for grilled cheese, cokes, and milkshakes. As I started to leave, someone touched my arm. It was Ernie. In my excitement I hadn't noticed my right-winger.

"Johnny, do yah mind if I join you? I'd love to meet your brother."

"Not at all. Come on."

There was only bus service from St. John's, but I was too pumped to stand and wait, so we ran. It'd been almost two and a half years since I'd seen him. He must look fabulous. A pilot in the US Air Force. He already had a resemblance to actor Richard Widmark; in uniform, he must look like a movie star. And he lived in America.

I ran through the coffee shop door and spotted my sister, Maggie, facing me. Sitting across from her, with his back to me, was this broad-shouldered man in a beautiful, blue-green uniform. When my sister smiled, he turned. It was Ronnie. My God he looked fantastic!

I rushed to him and placed my hand carefully on his shoulder. I wanted to grab him, but I didn't want to mess up his uniform. "Ronnie! Ronnie! You look great!" I yammered.

"Hi, y'all, little brother?" he said, smiling.

The sound of his voice made me stop. It wasn't quite the voice I remembered. There was no Canadian "eh" anywhere. He sounded like he'd just stepped out of *Gone with the Wind*. From the Confederate side. And there was a slight slur. In his hand was an almost empty bottle of beer. The sight of that stunned me. He never drank. He hated it. The rare times we had conversations, he was vehement about his disdain for beer and liquor and what it had done to our mother. He couldn't wait until he was eighteen to get away from all that. As far away as possible. Even up into the sky, he once said.

He slid over and tapped the seat with the bottom of the beer bottled. "C'mon, little buddy, have a seat an' tell me what's been goin' on."

I sat next to him. I was happy to see him, but more curious about his transformation. I didn't want to tell him I'd just quit school and moved out that very day. I didn't want Maggie to hear it. either. It would change the subject away from Ronnie. I had almost forgotten Ernie.

"Ernie, grab a seat."

"Hi, Maggie," he said, sitting next to her where he often had. He extended his hand to my brother. "Hi, I'm Ernie. Pleased to meet you. Heard tons about you." His hand was suspended in air when the room was suddenly rocked with a vocal and physical explosion. Jabbing me in the ribs, my brother threw me onto the floor. He jumped to his feet, erupting in rage. "JESUS CHRIST," he bellowed in that horrible *Deliverance* accent. He smashed his beer bottle against the corner of the table, and lunged at Ernie.

"You brought a fuckin' nigger in here. Tuh sit next mah sister!" He reached over, trying to grab him by the face so he could cut it.

"Ronnie, Ronnie, stop it," Maggie screamed, putting her hands in front of Ernie.

Ronnie slashed, barely missing his face as he ducked under the table. I leaped up, grabbing my brother's arm. He lifted me off the ground. People watched in horror, too frightened to move. Ronnie clawed at Ernie's back as he tried to crawl away, screaming, "Help."

"You fuckin nigger. Sit next to my sister. My white sister. I'll fuckin' kill yah!"

"Ronnie! Ronnie!" I screamed. "Stop it! Stop it! He's our friend!" That comment was like a booster rocket to his rage. "You fuckin' niggah lovers," he shrieked. He started bashing me in the face with his forearm trying to make me let go.

"Get out the way. Outa the way, you goddamn kid, lettin' him sit with yer sister. Are you fuckin' nuts, boy?"

I was no match for him. I tumbled backwards over Ernie. As I did so, I grabbed the lapels of my brother's uniform, that gorgeous US Air Force uniform, and hung on. He tumbled over me, the bottle slipping out of his hands. The three of us were on the floor flailing around, my sister crying and shouting, "Stop it! Stop it! Please."

"I'll kill 'im with my own fuckin' hands!"

Ernie was on his feet now, near the exit. I jumped up, kicking my brother. I ran past Ernie, pulling him by the arm, screaming, "Run, run!" We lunged through the door, onto the street and ran like hell. That could not have been my brother. It just couldn't have been. What had happened to him? I had heard people putting down Jews and Italians and Catholics and blacks and whatever, but it sounded more like gossip than prejudice. Never anything vicious. Ever. Not even in movies. The worst I'd ever seen was in the first grade. Our teacher asked us all to stand and tell the class what religion we were. Most, of course, said, Christian, to which she added, "Very good." When I stood and said, "I'm not sure," she and the kids laughed. But when a lovely dark-haired girl named René said, "Jewish," they booed. We never saw her again.

I did not know what to say to my friend. All I could manage was, "I am so sorry." He did not respond. I never saw him again.

Mrs. Tomassini let me stay for nearly two years. During that time, I worked at a number of different jobs, including the restaurant and Eatons. I also lost my virginity to a woman five years older than me, and lost my first and last bout with real booze. I felt I wasn't fully present at those events. My mind was elsewhere.

Mrs. Tomassini liked her booze, the stuff she made and the stuff she bought. She kept half-filled bottles everywhere, so she didn't have to look for one when she wanted a taste. She wasn't an alcoholic like my mother, just a recreational sipper. Saturday was her night out. Jerry was at a poker game I was too broke to attend. Alone, on the radio, Frank Sinatra seemed to be singing to me: *Saturday Night is the Loneliest Night of The Week.* Indeed, it was.

Laying on the bed listening, I spotted an almost full bottle on the hall table. Suddenly, I was curious. What was it about liquor that made people drink it? Was it the taste? And what was it about drinking that makes people behave differently? Did it really make them forget bad stuff? Did it free them to do stuff they wouldn't do drinking milk? Curiosity only had me retrieve the bottle and bring it back to bed. Like Mrs. Tomassini, I didn't need a glass. I would just take a sip and put it back.

I could barely get the bottle to my lips. It smelled God awful. My eyes watered. Challenged now, I sucked a few drops. The taste was even worse. I shuddered at its bitterness. It has to improve, I thought. So, I sipped again. There was no improvement. Maybe it was like hot peppers; you have to get used to it. I was determined to see if I could. By the time I realized the taste would never improve to my satisfaction, the bottle was empty.

When I got up to return the empty to the table, my knees had developed hinges. They were bending in every direction. I placed one foot in front of the other as purposely as I had following the sun through the forest, until I had returned the empty to its proper spot. I was giggling at my athletic accomplishments.

Leaning on the table, my stomach churned and gurgled. I had to go to the bathroom. The hallway looked like an underground subway station. The toilet was at the end of the line. Trying to walk, my legs were rubbery. I placed my hands on each wall, and moved, rocking from side to side, ever so slowly down the tracks, all the time pleased at my awareness. I reached the bathroom just as my bowels reached their limit. I undid my belt, unzipped my trousers, pulled down my pants, and bent over. That's all I remember.

I was awakened hours later by Mrs. Tomassini's horrifying screaming. She was standing over a body with the head resting against the bottom of the tub, pants down to the ankles, with a soiled backside staring her in the face, having missed its target.

"Avwvwh. Awww. Goddamn it," she screamed.

That's when I stirred. I twisted my head to look up at her.

"Oh, my God! Jesus. Jesus a Christ. What you do? You a okay?" She pulled me out, laid me on the floor, ran the tub, undressed me, helped me crawl back in, washed me, and the next day washed my clothes. Half the time she kept mumbling, "Just like a mya goddamn husband." It was the only time she mentioned her dead husband.

My curiosity about booze ended forever that night. So did my belief when drunks or addicts I knew did something cruel or stupid, claimed they could remember nothing. Though smashed, I remembered every wobbly detail. Those who claim otherwise are full of what I remember missing the toilet with.

Whistle While You Work

In spite of being a dropout, I had no trouble finding jobs. I could have stayed at any of them, but I didn't. Boredom forced me out of the first three, fear for my life forced me out of the most interesting one, and fear of unplanned parenthood propelled me out of the last. Having spent a summer at a boarding farm, and almost my entire life on the streets made me want to be outside, in the sunlight. And fresh air.

Mrs. Tomassini's restaurant was adjacent to the city's largest railway yard. It had the only factory in Ontario that actually repaired damaged locomotives. Engineers and firemen came often to the restaurant. So, one day, I crossed the tracks and applied for a job on the Canadian National Railway as a fireman. And, happily, got it. However, there was to be no sunshine for me. I was assigned the midnight shift, twelve till eight in the morning.

In those days, the engines were steam driven, fueled by coal and water. I sat on the left side of the cabin; the engineer sat on the right. His job was to do all the driving and whistle blowing; my job was to keep an eye on the glass tube in front of us; this indicated the water level in the boiler. When that level got down to three quarters empty, I was to pull a lever that refilled the boiler. My other job was to make sure the fire never got so low it couldn't boil the water. To refuel that fire, I had to shovel the coal carried in the car immediately behind us, coal that often spilled out onto the platform. It often reminded me of our basement.

My engineer's name was Victor. He had been with the railroad for over thirty years. As a senior engineer he could have requested a daytime shift, which I encouraged him to do so he could take me with him. He preferred the darkness. He once had daytime shifts. He asked for the midnight shift after his wife committed suicide. He was slender, not much taller than I was, with lines in his face that made him look older than fifty-two. In the darkness, he talked frequently about his wife and the books they used to read. Sometimes he'd recite poetry. I was astonished to find someone so bright and well-read sitting across from me. He never once raised his voice. Not even when I put us in danger by falling asleep. When I did wake up, I could not see any water in the gauge. I panicked. I didn't know whether or not to pull the lever. If there was no water in the boiler and you suddenly pumped it in, the entire engine could blow sky high.

Terrified by my stupidity, I yelled at Victor that I didn't see any water in the gauge. He looked at the gauge and calmly said, "You're all right. Put some in." I hesitated. He repeated, "You're okay. Nothing's going to happen. Go ahead." He said it in a faraway, peaceful tone that gave me the impression he did not mind if he met his wife. My hand trembled as I pulled the lever to let in as little water as possible; there was a loud hissing sound, and it flowed without incident.

Almost every other night, Victor had a story about another person he'd read about or had heard about who committed suicide. He asked me if I knew anyone who killed themselves. I told him just one. A young Mrs. Osbome, my friend Bobby's mother, directly across the street from us who stuck her head in the oven. I purposely did not mention my grandfather hanging himself. I did not want to encourage him to talk even more about the very unsettling subject. But he was obsessed with it. Ad nauseam, he catalogued all the ways people do away with themselves: hangings, shootings, jumping off buildings, jumping into rivers, onto railway tracks, (He'd seen some of those) pills, and the slitting of wrists, which is what his wife did. He was a Wikipedia of ways to end your life.

"Have you ever thought of it?" he asked me one night.

"Gosh. No," I said forcefully. "I'm only sixteen!"

"You know," he said, "teenage suicide is a fast-growing phenomenon in this country and especially in Sweden."

Trying to change the subject, I said, "I'd be more inclined to kill someone else before I'd kill myself."

Not missing a beat, he said, "Like who?"

"My father." I was shocked at my quick response. I was even more surprised that after saying it, I may have meant it.

"How would you do it?"

Jesus Christ, he was relentless! "I don't know. Actually, as much as I dislike him, I never, ever thought of such a thing. It just popped out."

He paused for a long time. "Life is funny," he said wistfully. "And… and… mostly meaningless."

Listening to this night after night was getting tougher than shoveling the coals. I was getting blisters in my eardrums.

That was the last conversation I had with that very learned, very sad man. A week later, on one of my nights off, they said a fireman had neglected to properly monitor a water gauge. A locomotive blew up in the main terminal, blowing a hole in the ground big enough to bury the engine, and the crew. I was afraid to call in to find out who it was. I was more afraid to go back to work. I didn't call to tell them I was quitting. I just stopped showing up.

Buffalo Bound

I did not want to end up like my brother. But I did want to end up where he was – in America. I had heard news about a possible American war with Korea, and I thought I might help them win the battle by becoming a pilot. And then a citizen.

The U.S. Air Force recruiting station was in the heart of downtown Buffalo, a short cab ride from the terminal. For a kid who had spent his life in the east end of Toronto, called at the time "Hog Town," where the nearest tallest building was a reformatory, the buildings in Buffalo were neck-bending. I'd only seen buildings like those in the movies, mostly New York. In spite of the uniqueness of their design, architecture, and colors, they looked dirty. The building housing the recruiting station was a hotel. The recruiting office was to the right side of the lobby. There was a dullness to the place that bordered on being seedy. Not nearly the kind I'd seen in those endless war movies. The entire wall was glass. I could see what was going on inside. It was packed. There were three desks; at each, sat a recruiter. In front of him a line of ten to twelve young men, mostly white, with half a dozen blacks. I went to the end of the middle line behind a black man who was the size of three of me. I wondered why there were so many waiting to enlist on a weekday. I mean, these guys were already citizens. Were there that many crappy jobs in America? Or that many crappy parents?

I was prepared for the question about my age. "You're kind of young. How old are you?" the recruiter asked, staring hard at me.

"Eighteen, sir." I figured he'd like the "sir" stuff.

"Do you have some identification?"

I produced my Canadian National Railroad I.D. card where I'd turned the six into an eight on Mrs. Tomassini's typewriter. I handed it to him proudly. "They say I look young for my age."

"That you do," he replied, examining the card. "Canadian, eh? *Eh*?" He repeated the "eh," trying to be cute.

"Yes, eh," I answered.

"Why do you want to be in the Air force? Why not the Navy where there are more fellows your size?"

"My brother's in the Air Force. Keesler Air Force Base, Mississippi," I said, trying to impress him.

He handed me a form."Fill this out, then wait over there. You'll be going inside to take some tests."

"What kind of tests?" I asked.

"General knowledge and information." He pointed to a small auditorium filled with school desks. Sitting or standing by them were all the other potential enlistees, filled form in hand. I joined them, the smallest of the bunch.

An hour into the test, an officer rang a bell. "That's it!" He lifted his hand dramatically. A recruiter quickly picked up our papers and pens. "Take a forty-five-minute break. Go out and get a cup of coffee or something, and come back. We'll take a quick look at these and inform you who'll be staying for tomorrow's physicals."

Did that mean we'd have to stay over? I was too nervous to eat or drink anything. To kill time, I walked back out to the street to let my eyes and mind digest the skyscrapers. I could imagine King Kong on any one of them. What an amazing, strong place America is! We were all back in our seats in just over thirty minutes.

"Gentlemen," the officer started, "I'm going to call some names. When you hear yours, stand. You men will be staying in this hotel at the government's expense. We will feed you tonight and tomorrow morning. If your name is not called, you may become a Marine or a sailor."

My name wasn't called. I couldn't understand it. I was certain I'd done well. About fourteen of us were left sitting. The officer held up an exam paper. "I held this test till last." He looked at again. "If this is not your name, the Navy is down the street. "Mr. MacLaren," he said, louder than the others.

"Yes, sir," I said, jumping up.

"Young man, no need to jump, standing will suffice. Gentlemen, the reason I'm holding this test up is because this young man, who claims to be eighteen, from Toronto, got nearly every one of these questions correct. In ten years, I've not seen anyone else do that. Congratulations, young man. Now let's see how you do with the physical."

He had singled me out. Me! I was staying over. For the physical. I was going to get into the American Air Force! Even if they found out later I was sixteen and had been arrested, it would be too late. And if they find out beforehand I was only sixteen, I'd get my mother to sign for me. I was sure she would. I could get killed and she'd get the insurance.

They fed us the biggest and best meal I'd had since the farm: sirloin steak, potatoes, vegetables, bread rolls and dessert. Following this, we were led up to the fourteenth floor, filled with cots for sleeping. I was pleased. It was like a real barracks. Passing time till the ten p.m. curfew, some read, some played cards, some chatted, or just lay on theirs beds like me, daydreaming. I reveled in mine, daydreaming about swooping down in a jet over Adam Beck and Malvern Collegiate.

"Okay, that's it," a voice barked by the door. "You'll rise and shine and run like hell at six!" The lights went out. I peered out at the lights across the street and above me. What a wonderful new sight. And what a wonderful new feeling of hope, and a dream coming true. In a moment I was out. Rocking woke me up. *Where was I*? I was airborne, my cot three feet off the ground. Six strangers, three on each side were lifting it. Another next to my head was opening the window. The one lifting the end of the bed higher, growled, "So, the little, smart son of a bitch wants to fly! We'll see the little asshole fly!"

"What are you doing? What's going on? This isn't funny," I screamed.

"You think you're smarter than anybody else. Let's see you if you fly better than anyone else."

Some cheered. They had turned on the lights to watch. My bed was being tilted toward the open window.

"I didn't say I was smarter than anyone else. I didn't say a thing. It wasn't me. Please." For a flash I felt they didn't mean it. They were just teasing. Joking. But the looks on their now ugly faces looked like those on the face of my brother going after Ernie with a broken beer bottle. I was almost at a forty-five-degree angle. My eyes darted around the room.

"Help me. Help me. Please." I was crying and begging. No one moved. Jesus Christ, they couldn't be watching and not do something. Say something.

The guy at the end was laughing at my pathetic plight. "Let's see how well these fucking Canadians can fly! On the count of three!"

They began to rock the cot back and forth, chanting, "One, two, three!" With that they heaved the cot against the wall next to the window with a loud thud. "Crash landing. Crash landing." One hollered. The room exploded in laughter. They had deliberately scared me, bashing the cot against the wall. "Okay. One more time. One ... two ... "

As they drew it back again, the rest of the room started to cheer. I flipped myself as hard and fast as I could off the cot, tumbling to the floor. Some applauded. Some booed. I didn't move. They might have just done this as a sick joke. I didn't want to stay to find out. They didn't look like they were about to do it again. They began to drift away, satisfied. I wanted to run, but thought if I did, though, they'd chase me.

With forced casualness, I gathered up my clothes and shoes. A million thoughts flashed through my head. I truly hated them. If I'd had a baseball bat, I would have taken it to that last guy's face. I wanted to tell them they should join the Nazi Airforce, where they belonged. Who wants to be associated with those kinds of people?

"Where you off to now, flyboy?"

I was clutching my clothes to my chest. How I wish I had the courage to say calmly to what was exploding in my head to him: *I am going someplace where I'll never see your face again. A library. I'm off to fuck your mother. If the line isn't too long!* All that came out was, "l think I'll sleep in the hallway."

I walked to the door in my underwear, holding my clothes and shoes, knowing my adventure there was over. Being in the Air Force with people like this was not for me. But being in America was. Trying to dress in the hallway, I began shaking, just as I had when I lost half my shoe almost being run over by a train.

I walked to the elevator and pressed the button. Anxiety overtook me. I looked for the exit. Suddenly, I was racing down the stairs. Fourteen flights through the deserted lobby into the lamp-lit night. If running was a part of the Air Force's physical, I would've come first in that, too. Walking to the train station in the dark, I felt safe. In replaying what had just terrified me, it occurred to me, not one of my tormenters was black. Those guys were not even in the Air Force, yet. They hadn't been turned into someone cruel like my brother had. They were already that way. Was it something about America that made them like that?

From Mail Boy to Male Man

This is the short story of the last job I had in Toronto before leaving for America. I was a mail boy in the Province of Ontario Government Building on University Avenue in Toronto. (I pause a moment to ponder how much of this tale to tell, because as I mentioned earlier, I do not like to talk about sex. However, since it was engaging in my first full body contact with a woman that propelled me to procure my passport, and since I am trying to be truthful, I will try to relate this other life-changing experience as briefly and as tastefully as possible.)

As I squirrel about in my mind, trying to figure out what to leave in or leave out of a sixteen-year-old boy's first encounter with carnal knowledge, and the months' long struggle with it that almost killed me, I am reminded of Mark Twain's comments about sex, comments he didn't want published until after his death. Sadly, society has since become shockproof to such openness. I am of an older generation, though, where modesty is still intact. To paraphrase Twain, he said the problem with religion or Christianity was that they deprive mankind after they die of Earth's greatest pleasure: sex. Instead of that, he wrote, when you got to Heaven, they give you a harp. Instead of fornicating, you play it and sing. The girl I met could sing.

She wasn't a girl exactly; she was twenty-one, five years older than I was. And she could sing. Beautifully. As a matter of fact, here's something rather odd and interesting, to me at least: over a lifetime, I've been with surprisingly few women; you could count them on the fingers of both hands and cut off a thumb. But, just like I have known more people who died by their own hand than by disease, old age, accident or war, every woman I was with could all sing; some magnificently. As for my own abilities, after my father left at the age of six, I shut down and became tone deaf.

This young lady's name was Beverly Macdonald, the same as my mother's maiden name. About five feet four inches, she had stunning Maureen O'Hara red hair and blue eyes that highlighted her freckles; a perfect smile, and a perfect full figure. She was the assistant to a minor Provincial Government Minister whose office was on the third floor. I saw her two or three times a day when I delivered his mail to her.

While working there, I accidentally discovered through the records division that I had two legal names, and two different legal birth certificates. I would later use the name I was born with to leave Canada … and my first love affair.

Beverly sat at the first desk to the right of the entrance to the Minister's corner office – the first inviting sight I'd see when I opened the door pushing my cart. Every day she greeted me with a perky smile and hello. While I liked looking at her a lot, I paid little attention to her because she was obviously older.

One day, three weeks into rounds, as I pushed my cart up to the front of her desk, she said, "Hi, Johnny! How are you today?"

I was stunned. I had never told her my name.

"That is your name, isn't it?"

"Yes." I gulped

"Well, after three weeks, I think you should know my name's Beverly, and that's Shirley." Shirley, who was about the same age, giggled. She also said hi. Beverly leaned forward and said, "Well."

I said, "Well, what?"

They both laughed out loud at my awkwardness. "Aren't you going to say hello, Beverly?"

"Hello. Beverly," I stammered.

"That's better," she said. "I want to hear that every day from now on. Okay?"

"Okay," I answered, turning to get out of there. When I got to the door, they shouted, "See you tomorrow, Johnny!" And laughed.

I don't recall much about the first date, if you can call eating in the cafeteria a date. She initiated almost everything we did. Until testosterone kicked in, leaving me no choice. I felt awkward sitting opposite her. She was not a girl like Ann. She was a woman, a very well-developed woman. There was nothing youthful in her manner or talk. She smiled, laughed, conversed and ate with ease. I could barely nibble. Or mumble. At one point, during our second luncheon, she casually reached over with a napkin and wiped crumbs from my mouth. The touch sent an electrical charge right through me.

"You don't eat much, do you?" She smiled. "Maybe that's why you're so slender!"

"When I'm with you, I think I'm too nervous to eat," I said.

She was pleased with that, tilting her head, smiling even more broadly. "Why are you nervous?"

"I've ... I've never been ... been out with ... with a girl like you."

"We're not really out! We're just having lunch," she said

"It's ... it's out to me," I mumbled.

"And what kind of girl am I?"

I thought for a moment. "Older."

She laughed. "Well, I've never been with a sixteen-year-old boy before." She looked straight at me. "As a matter-of-fact, I don't go out much with boys of any age."

"Well, I guess, all this is sort of new for both of us."

"And for you, so will your next meal be. That is if you like," she said.

"Like what?"

"How would you like to have dinner at my house? My mom's a great cook. I'd like you to meet her and my younger brother. He's eighteen."

"That'd be nice," was all that came out.

"I'll check with my mom tonight. We'll see if we can make it for Friday or Saturday. That's the night my folks like to go to the movies. Is that okay?"

I could only nod.

"Is there anything you don't like to eat?"

"No. Anything is fine."

She smiled and got up. "Good. I'll see you later."

Saturday night came quickly. Beverly's mother and father were terrific. They welcomed me as if they'd known me for years. Their conversation was comfortable and unforced. Not once did they ask the usual about my family, school, or my age. They just accepted me. Her brother and I got along great. We talked hockey the whole meal, which made me relaxed enough to eat. He chowed down with gusto, excused himself and left. The team he was on was playing that night. It was a great meal. I thanked Beverly's mother profusely.

Beverly looked at me, smiling, "You must have liked it. You got it all in your mouth again."

"Beverly, what's that supposed to mean?" her mother asked.

"Nothing, Mother, just a private joke. If you and Dad are going to the movies tonight, Johnny and I will do the dishes."

Her father kissed her on the forehead. "Thanks, love. We won't be late." He shook my hand. Firmly. "Johnny, nice to have met you. Come as often as you want."

"Thank you, sir," I said.

Soon they were gone. Beverly stacked the dishes in the sink, turned on the water, and handed me a towel. I didn't know what to say. Thank God, she began to sing, handing me dishes to dry as she did so. My insides melted. When the dishes and the song were done, she turned to take the towel from my hand.

"That was beautiful," I whispered. Then, "So are you" tumbled out. Her singing made her even prettier.

"Let's go in the front room," she said. I followed her. She turned on the large four-foot-high radio and moved to the sofa. "Come here," she said, patting the cushion next to her. I did as I was told. "Do you like singing?" she asked.

"I love it."

"Sing something for me."

"I can't."

"Anything."

"I can't sing."

"Sure you can. Everyone can. How about *Oh, Canada*?"

"Not even that." I shrugged.

"Come on. Sing *Day After Day* with me. Come on." I tried it. "You're right," she said quickly. "But if you'd like, I'd like to teach you. It'd be fun, wouldn't it? Would you like that?" Her face was inches from mine.

I could barely get the words out. "I'd like that, but I'm tone deaf."

"Then I'll just have to be a good teacher. And it all starts with the mouth. The lips." With that she leaned forward and kissed me right on the lips. Then she put her hands on my cheeks, pulling me closer, and kissed me again. Harder. They were also much fuller, and warmer than Ann's. I didn't sing that night, but I hummed a lot. They were so delicious. The hard kissing and gentle pawing and humming went on for a dozen love songs from the radio. Her actions were also more deliberate than Ann's. She leaned back, pulling me almost on top of her. Through her clothes I could feel her thighs, her, tummy, and most of all, her breasts. I started to get intense pains in my crotch. I tried to sit up, but couldn't. I bent forward clutching my stomach with both hands. "Ooooh," I groaned.

"Are you all right?"

"Yeah," I gasped. "It must have been something I ate."

"Would you like some Alka-Seltzer or water or something?"

"No, thanks," I said. "I'd better go." I could barely stand. "It was a wonderful night. Thank your folks."

"Johnny, they won't be long. You can stay until they get here."

"No. I'd better go." I hobbled to the door, opened it, and when I turned to say goodnight, her face was next to mine. She kissed me again.

"I'll see you Monday," she said softly. I looked at her and, through my pain, said, "I can't wait for the next lesson." She laughed. I closed the door and hobbled down the steps. In the streetcar, my groin hurt so much I stood clutching a pole, ignoring the empty seats and the curious passengers.

The restaurant was about to close. Mrs. Tomassini was sharing a drink with the last two men at the counter. She said, "You okay?"

"I'm fine."

She walked toward me and threw a hanky at me, pointing to her mouth as she did so. "Wipe a you face," she said loudly.

I wiped my mouth, noticing the hanky was now covered with lipstick. I hadn't even noticed it or thought of it. Maybe that's why the people on the streetcar were staring at me.

"You a in a pain?"

"A little, my stomach,' I whispered.

"Stomach uh my ass. Nuts. Lovers Nuts." The guys at the counter bellowed.

"What?" I groaned. "I had this pain before."

"Lover's nuts. You with girl all kissy face, an do nothin, so you a nuts fill up with juice. Lovers nuts!"

How to Spell Real Relief

The next few Saturday nights Beverly's parents were at the movies. Beverly and I rolled around on the sofa. Fully clothed. Those Saturday nights I went home, doubled over in total agony. Every time Mrs. Tomassini saw me, she laughed. "Jesus Christ, you'd a better get yourself another a girl. An easy one. Or a you gonna turn into hunchaback."

She was right. I just could not do it anymore. Then came a breakthrough. Or at least I thought so. We were in our usual spot, thrashing around. By this time, with my lips and tongue exploring her mouth, my hands had begun exploring her body. Under her skirt my hand squeezed her warm thighs, but no higher. They also squeezed her ample breasts outside her blouse. Then I stopped.

"Johnny, is something wrong?" she asked

"Beverly," I said, staring right at her, "every night when I leave you ... and ... and go home ... I can barely walk. The pain down here," I pointed to my groin, which was pointing back, "is ... is unbearable. Sometimes it lasts for hours. I just ... just can't take it anymore. I can't do this anymore!"

"Can't do what?"

"It's a thing guys get. I don't know what it's like for you, but if ... if there's no release ... it builds up, causing awful pain." She looked at me as if she were studying me. I stammered on, "I love to kiss you ... and ... everything, but if ... if it's going to turn me into a pained pretzel, I just can't do it anymore." I leaned back.

"I'm a virgin," she said, gazing into my eyes.

"Oh, my God," I blurted, "that makes two of us!"

"I'm also twenty-one. Five years older than you. I've had other boyfriends my age who wanted to go all the way, because they had with other girls, but I didn't. I couldn't!" Her eyes were almost closed. "But I like you more." I remained still, listening. "I wanted to wait until I was married." She paused for a long time. "I still do! But ... but ... I ... I don't want you to be in pain. I love you too much."

It was the tenth time she'd said she loved me. Ann had said it in the hayloft and I lost her. *What do I do now*?

"Would you like to take me on the sofa?" she whispered, leaving me dumbfounded. She took my hand. "I can't take my clothes off. We'll just have to do it with them on." She laid back, spreading her legs slightly. I cannot go into details about how I went from a mail boy to a male man this night; it was all very odd and awkward, but when she lifted her skirt, I was expecting to encounter panties. Panties made of lace. Or cotton. Or silk. But hers weren't. They were made of rubber. Not the thin rubber of surgical gloves. The rubber they make inner tubes out of. They fit tight around her thighs. She could have had Goodyear printed on them. I could barely pull them back from her leg; sometimes they slipped from my fingers and snapped back against her skin with a clicking sound.

"Geez, if I can barely get my fingers in there, how will I get anything else in there?"

"I'm sorry. I can't take them off," she whispered. "I love you, Johnny."

"That's okay," I lied, somehow managing to get in and ease the pain. The inner pain was over, but an outer one would soon erupt.

"Thank you, Beverly," I said, lifting myself up and seeing blood.

"Oh, God, Beverly, I'm sorry! Are you all right?'

Her face was flushed. She smiled. "I'm fine!" And she was. "Kiss me!"

I leaned forward and did so.

"I'd better clean this up," she said.

I didn't know whether to be proud of myself for having accomplished such a manly thing, or to feel guilty because she was no longer a virgin. But when I looked down, I could see I was bleeding too. Her Goodyear had almost circumcised me. For weeks thereafter, we copulated everywhere as often as we kissed, but what could have been a rubber chastity belt remained glued to her. I often limped into her office. She and her friend would howl with laughter, thinking Don Juan was faking fatigue, but if I was to avoid the pain, she would have to leave her Goodyear in the hangar. It was just a matter of telling her. It took place in the cafeteria and I was more forthright than my rehearsals.

"Beverly, you know how much I love being with you."

"Just *with* me? Not in love with me?" She looked hurt.

"Yes. Yes, I am. And I'm glad I was your first but–"

"So am I," she interrupted.

"But I can't see you for a bit."

"Why? What are you talking about?"

"I have to get cured."

"Cured of what?"

"Your Fruit of The Loom fortress!"

"What on earth are you talking about?"

"Those rubber pants you wear. They cut me so bad, I look like raw sausage."

She laughed.

"Bev, it's not funny. If I keep seeing you and doing it, it'll fall off."

She kept giggling.

"Bev, you're not a virgin, right?"

She blushed. "True."

"So why do you insist on still wearing those things?"

"I don't know. Maybe scared a little. Maybe it makes me feel like I'm still ... still ... a good girl."

"Look, let's just take a week off. Let me heal a little and–"

"Johnny, I can't be a week away from you."

"Bev, me neither, but I've got to."

"I'll take them off," she blurted.

I was stunned. "Thank you. Thank you. But I still need a few days. It's raw."

"I promise," she said, leaning into me.

"Thank you, and I'd feel more comfortable if you'd come to my place."

"Oh, I'd love that. I'd love to see where you live. And, Johnny..." She hesitated.

"Yes?" I asked.

"I may take more than that off."

"Oh, Jesus," I gasped.

And she did.

T.G.I.F.

I was embarrassed and awkward asking Mrs. Tomassini about having my girlfriend over, but she was amazingly and liberally maternal. "Jus' donna make a much noise. I have customers."

"We won't," I promised.

"And donna drink. I donna wanna finda two of you in a the tub," she said straight-faced.

"She doesn't drink," I said quickly.

"And a most important, Chonny…"

I interrupted her. "Wear something?"

"No," she said firmly. "Wash!"

It was an amazing and wondrous Friday night. I remember every detail about it. Beverly was even more beautiful without clothes. Lying next to me in the dark, the touch of her skin on mine, transformed my entire body into an erogenous zone. This 'skin time' as I called it, was often as comforting as the sex itself. From then on, we copulated like monkeys, everywhere, in all kinds of positions. Delivering mail to her, knowing she wore no panties, was an aphrodisiac. At lunch, we often found relief in the coat room. Then one day, back on her sofa, she said something that made me want to give up sex forever.

"Johnny, I think I'm pregnant."

"Are you sure?" I stammered

"I think so. It's been nearly six weeks since my period."

"What … what do we do?"

"Well, I've tried really hot baths, but nothing seems to bring it on," she said.

"Oh, God," was all I could manage.

"We might have to get married," she said.

Jesus Christ, I thought, *I am only sixteen*. I don't want to get married. To anyone. Ever. "Married?" I gulped out loud.

"I'm having a baby," she said.

"Jesus Christ," I exclaimed. "I'm barely a baby myself!"

"We have no choice."

"Beverly, Jesus, I'm a mail boy. I couldn't support a baby, let alone a wife. Don't women get rid of these things? How far along are you?"

"I don't know and I've tried to get rid of it."

"Oh, God." I was sick to my stomach. "Beverly, I'm of no help to you. I don't know what to do. I've got to think about all this. I'll see you tomorrow." I rose deliberately.

She followed me to the door, then leaned against it, not letting me open it. "Please don't go. I have this feeling you're not coming back."

"I'll see you tomorrow, I promise. I just have to think about all this."

"Johnny, if you don't marry me, I'll kill myself." Tears were rolling down her freckled face.

Shamefully, sympathy for her plight was not on my mind. I was terrified and felt trapped, more so by her threat. I pushed her aside and opened the door. "I promise, I'll talk to you tomorrow."

I was too frightened to undress or sleep. I was too bloody young to be married. Even if I wasn't, I had no desire to ever have a child. Who knows what kind of father I'd be. At any age. What tortured me more than anything was the thought that if I didn't marry her she really might kill herself. The only out I could see was to run away; otherwise, my life would be over.

The next day, as promised, I saw Beverly at work. Handing her the morning mail, I asked if she had a moment to talk privately. We stepped into the hall. Staring at each other we both knew it was over. We were almost strangers. It was impossible to recall or feel that just a few short days earlier there was this intense lust for each other. Now nothing! Absolutely nothing. How weird.

"Beverly," l said softly, "I can't marry you. I'm nearly a kid myself. You're a woman.

And from what I've been through, I'd probably be a horrible father. "Besides, you might not be pregnant."

"I meant what I said," she interrupted. "What are you going to do about this?"

The cold bossiness of her question made it easier for me. "There's nothing I can do. I have no choice but to leave."

"Leave me?" she hissed.

"Leave Toronto. I'm sorry, Beverly. Honestly. I am." I turned to leave.

"You will be sorry," she called after me. "Very sorry, you'll see!"

It was the last time I heard her voice. A few years later, I did hear her mother's.

I left the building. I didn't even go back for my paycheck. A week later, following a round of card games, I left Toronto for Las Vegas with seven hundred dollars in my pocket.

BACK IN AMERICA

Lost and Found In Las Vegas

The flashback is over. As was my desire to stay in Vegas. The performers I had seen, a second and third time during my short stay, were the only things that brought me real pleasure; as a kid, aside from hockey, it was the movies, and later, books. Winning money never did. The actors in the movies and the characters in the books were as real and more comforting to me than anyone I'd encountered in real life. Errol Flynn, Jimmy Stewart, Cary Grant, Bette Davis, Barbara Stanwyck, Judy Garland, Mickey Rooney, Humphrey Bogart, Robert Donat, Laurel and Hardy, Abbot and Costello, Bob Hope, Bing Crosby, scores more, including character actors by the dozens whose names I still know, made up for the people I knew. I had to follow my joy, as Joseph Campbell said, to the place where these people came to life, and into mine: Hollywood.

A discounted ticket and seven hundred dollars had brought me to Las Vegas, but I wasn't sure it was enough to get me to Los Angeles. In Las Vegas I'd earned a little by gambling. That would not be an option in Hollywood. There I'd have to work. So, I thought I'd better get used to it. The manager at Union Pacific liked my application, with its neatness and correct spelling, and hired me as a clerk. Except for a few movies and shows, I saved every nickel. I moved to an inexpensive motel room on the edge of the desert where I was the only non-hourly tenant. For every grain of sand that blew into the room, there was a cockroach to keep it company. Having been on a farm for three months, they didn't bother me in the least. They were tiny compared to the two-legged ones I found years later in Hollywood. With close to fifteen hundred dollars, a newer suitcase, and a discounted ticket, that's where I was off to.

A House Not on Elm Street

There could have been no more enjoyable way to arrive in Los Angeles than into the main, sprawling, downtown Spanish art deco train terminal right out of an MGM musical. The architect must have been a Busby Berkeley fan. The walls and tiles were bright oranges, yellows, and maroons. The same with the multicolored tile floor, a delight to the eye and the feet. I was so happy I almost skipped on them. I felt like Ray Bolger on the yellow brick road on my way to Oz!

Emerging onto the sunlit street under a cloudless sky was even more of a delight. Not just the sights, but the sounds. I was on Olvera Street being serenaded by a trio of magnificently dressed strolling mariachi musicians. I had seen it before in *Anchors Aweigh* with Frank Sinatra, Gene Kelly and Katherine Grayson. Many of the shoppers and tourists looked like extras who'd been dressed by Salvador Dali; it was magical.

Holding my suitcase, I must have looked like I was waiting for a cab. One stopped right in front of me. A yellow cab, again just like the ones I'd seen a hundred times in films. Geez, I felt like I was in my own movie.

"Waiting for someone?" the driver asked.

"No." I answered, not even looking at him, just at the sign.

"Can I take you somewhere?" he asked, without sounding pushy.

I had no idea where I was going, but I said, "Yeah, okay."

"Put your bag in the back seat, and you can sit in the front."

I did as he instructed. When I got inside I was still gawking and listening out the open window.

"Where to?" he asked.

"Hollywood!"

"Where in Hollywood?" The only address I'd ever heard of was Hollywood and Vine, so that's what I said.

"Where you from?"

"Toronto."

"You're a long way from home!"

I wanted to tell him there was no home. I'd been there five minutes and felt more at home in the Technicolor town. He asked me if I knew anybody, if I had a place to stay. Was I vacationing, or was I planning on moving there?

I answered "yes" to the last question.

"You know," he said, "I can drop you off at Hollywood and Vine, but if you're looking for a nice inexpensive place to stay, with two meals a day, breakfast and dinner, there are a couple of nice boarding houses on LaBrea just off Hollywood Boulevard."

"Is it far from Hollywood and Vine?" (Which is what I really wanted to see.)

"Not at all. You could walk it. Or better yet, take the electric car. It's real cheap."

"Thanks. Take me to LaBrea then."

If Olvera Street was such a delight, I could not wait to see the elegance and glamor of Hollywood and Vine with maybe a movie star or two on the sidewalk. Seeing it was like being punched in the eyes. Hollywood just could not be that ugly. An unexpected drab office building on one corner, a five- or six-story dull brown Broadway department store on another, all next to trashy looking souvenir shops, all of which were not as clean as Mrs. Tomassini's restaurant.

Blocks and blocks of cheap inelegant bargain price stores from Vine to La Brea looked like Tijuana. The pedestrians looked no better. My disappointment and shock were palpable. This could not be the world-famous street of the stars!

I perked up a little when the driver pointed out the beautiful Egyptian Theater on our left, then got genuinely excited further down when he parked for a moment in front of Grauman's Chinese Theater on our right. That was the Hollywood I expected. I stared at the crowds of people with cameras taking pictures, comparing handprints and footprints in the cement, and made an excited note to do the same.

A couple of blocks past Grauman's he turned right on La Brea, slowed down and pointed out the few boarding houses on the right. The last one was on the corner of Delongpre. That was the one I picked. It was two stories, the largest and the whitest. I had never lived in a corner house. I thanked, paid, and over-tipped him, something I still do. (I had learned tipping in Las Vegas where folks expect one even before saying "Hello." I thought it was a generous American custom I'd never heard of. Wanting to be American, more American than others, I adopted it.)

I retrieved my suitcase and walked to the front door.

To this day, it remains one of the most interesting, fascinating, bewildering, and entertaining places I would ever live in. The unbelievable people who lived there were as different as snowflakes; a couple were just flakes. An unpleasant encounter with one, melted the hopes of my American Dream.

The New House I Live In

An ample-bodied lady in her late forties was the pleasant owner and gourmet cook. There were never any leftovers. Her size may have been the reason. She was the only woman in the house. All her tenants were men, with the occasional female guest for dinner. The oldest, who'd been there the longest, over five years, was a tall elegant former star of silent films. He had a wonderful full head of long grey hair, a low rumbling voice that should have made him successful in talkies. But didn't. His last name was Kirkwood. I never tired of asking him about those days and those movies and those stars. And he never tired of telling me. He lived in one of the back rooms so he wouldn't have to climb stairs.

Next to him was a part-time radio announcer in his early forties who was also a part-time teacher in a boys' school. He also had a deep rich speaking voice, which he loved to listen to. It sounded not unlike that of Orson Welles or Lorne Green, a Canadian story-telling radio star who later moved to America to become Ben Cartwright on *Bonanza*. Our announcer had a tape recorder in his room into which he constantly read copy and commercials. Often, he would invite me in to join him. I was thrilled when he would ask me to do the same. I only listened once. Next to his, my voice sounded high and thin, but, no matter, I was delighted to be around people who were in show business, even if just on the fringes. I didn't get to do it again anyway. One day the police showed up and hauled his tape recorder and him away for child molestation.

The saddest, most interesting of the half-dozen residents was a jeweler in his mid-forties. He had dark wavy hair, wire-rimmed glasses, with a right eye wider than the left. This was from the years of inserting a magnifying glass into the socket and bending over to repair fine watches or examine diamonds. His black mustache made him look a little like Groucho Marx. He also had a slight hump near the top of his back, again from all that slouching. His name was Leonard. He moved in eight months prior to me, after his wife committed suicide.

Lenny, as he preferred to be called, took a special liking to me; maybe because he saw I was out in the world by myself. He was a decent man who could discourse with clarity about anything and everything, unlike Victor, my engineer, with never a touch of self-pity. He was truthfully much more interesting than the actors. He had an upstairs room as did I. Mine was the front corner with huge windows on the front and right, with wonderful views of both tree-lined streets. In a back room was a light chocolate-skinned Egyptian salesman in his early forties, with hair and eyes as black and dark as I'd ever seen. He wore the same smart dark brown suit every day, and spoke with a decidedly soft thick lyrical Middle-Eastern accent. Often, 'Omar Sharif" would saunter into my room and start talking to me. It wasn't talk so much as constantly asking me questions about myself, about girlfriends I never had. It got creepy. He was not nearly as creepy, though, as the clean-cut good looking smartly dressed young American accountant.

He was twenty-eight; the oldest young man I'd ever met. And the most uncomfortable to be around. Everything about him was rigid, including his posture and ideas. His life was lived by rules and numbers. The rules were anything that came out of the Bible or Republicans. He was the only one I met in person who wore a 'Better Dead than Red' button on his lapel. When I first saw it on his coat at dinner, I said, "Why don't you put a flower there like most people?" I thought I was being cute. So did everyone else who chuckled. He did not. For the nearly twelve months of those interesting, lively dinners, I said a number of things that did get laughs, but not once from him. But he did get the last one.

The first two jobs I got had nothing to do with showbiz. It was to earn money and save what I had. The first was as a dishwasher at Dupar's restaurant at Farmers Market at Fairfax and Beverly. Between the boarding house and there, I ate really well, but had very few clothes, and my blue blackjack suit was wearing thin, so I got an additional job as an assistant salesman, or assistant to a salesman, in the young men's section of May's Department Store at LaBrea and Wilshire. Getting the jobs was easy. I needed a Social Security card. Not knowing what one was, I asked Lenny one evening at dinner.

"John, it's a retirement savings protection plan set up during the Depression by Roosevelt to save the workers and capitalism."

"Bloody, crippled commie," the accountant hissed. I had no clue what a commie was. I did not want to ask and show my ignorance, so I said, "Why do you say cripple?"

The accountant snorted. "Because he was. Legs crippled by polio. Mind crippled by Marx!" I didn't know what or who Marx was. I would make it a point to ask Lenny later in private.

At the Social Security office, the only identification I showed was my Union Pacific card. When asked where I was born, I said the same place as my brother, Holyoake, Mass. Despite the years and years of upcoming trauma with the Immigration Department and their laws, I still have that card and number.

At the May Company a lot of the help was very pretty. It was the first time since leaving Beverly I began to think about girls again. One afternoon I casually pointed out some of the pretty help to my only friend there. He was eighteen and a full-fledged salesman in the men's department.

He said, "They are nothing. You should see Jack Owens' daughter."

"Who's Jack Owens?" I asked

He looked at me like I was stupid.

"He's a famous singer. He wrote *Hi Neighbor.* He's got a radio show every week at CBS Radio on Sunset. He invited me to come and see it when he was in here a few weeks ago with his daughter. You should see her. Wow. Sixteen, but looks like a woman. Wanna come?"

The thought of girls vanished. But the thought of seeing a real star, in a real studio in showbiz thrilled me. "Yeah. Okay," I said.

"Great," my friend said. "I'll pick you up."

The Jack Owens' show was a fifteen-minute radio broadcast live every Sunday from the CBS studios at Sunset and Gower. The studio was small, perhaps a hundred seats, all but two filled by women older than my landlady. Those two were reserved for us. The announcer came out and gave us instructions as he pointed to the applause sign. My head was on a swivel, taking in everything; God it was exciting!

The show began with the loudest applause being provided by the two of us. I even whistled. Jack had a pleasant Irish face and a light ordinary voice to match. For an encore, he sang his only hit, *Hi, Neighbor,* much to the delight of the ladies. When it was over, I just wanted to sit and savor it, but my friend rushed me backstage.

"Come on. We've been invited."

Speechless, I was introduced to a real star, and his daughter who should have been. My friend was right. Sixteen and five-feet six, almost eye to eye. The most stunning, shapeliest, brunette or woman I had ever seen.

Jack smiled. "Were you whistling at the show or my daughter?"

"The show, sir," I said.

"And where did you learn to whistle like that?" he asked.

"A Gary Cooper movie."

"Well, we're off to the house for some snacks and you're both welcome to join us."

The entourage started to leave. She had her arm tucked warmly under her father's. My buddy grabbed me by the arm, leering. "C'mon. C'mon. I'll get the car."

Their house was not what people call a house. It was a mansion. In Pacific Palisades. It fronted directly onto Sunset Boulevard, not far from the ocean. It looked like a replica of the Palace of Versailles. I thought, *one song can do that?* A dozen happy guests gathered there every week after the show. There were trays with mountains of small triangular gourmet sandwiches, desserts and drinks of all sorts. Those who didn't help themselves were waited on by Mrs. Owens, as pleasant and comfortable as her husband and daughter. I ate nothing, but drank in everything. The opulence. The people. Some played tennis or swam. I wandered around with an unfinished Coke in my hand, and ended up on a balcony overlooking the pool. Some of the women in bikinis were almost as beautiful as Jack Owens' daughter. But I was looking at real mountains with large mansions, some on stilts perched atop them; and in the distance, the pale blue Pacific Ocean. I fell asleep and was awakened by someone shaking my shoulder. My eyes opened to a late sundown, and that beautiful face.

"Oh, there you are. Are we Americans that boring?"

"Oh, no, no," I stammered. "I've got two jobs, and I was a little tired."

She took my hand, and stuffed a piece of paper in it. "That's my number, if you'd like to call."

Why was she doing this? I barely spoke to her. Or anyone.

My friend appeared. "Let's go, Johnny. Everybody's gone." I followed them inside and down the wide winding staircase. She opened the huge door. She thanked my friend for coming.

"I'll see you next week," he gushed, leaning forward. She gave him her cheek, which he kissed.

"Wonderful," she said, unconvincingly.

"Thank you, ma'am," I said, following him. But suddenly her arm stopped me.

"I will drive Johnny home. I have something I need him to help me with. I'll see you next week."

"Oh. Okay," he said.

I was shaking, unable to fathom what was happening. She closed the door firmly, led me back into the house, into the living room, asking if I wanted anything else to drink or eat.

"No, I'm fine. Thank you," I said

She sat on the edge of a huge sofa. There was plenty of room next to her. She smiled at me, seemingly entertained by my dilemma. Nervously, I sat opposite about ten feet away in a very large stuffed chair. She watched me fussing in it. When I get nervous or frightened or angry, I tend to get flippant or glib to relieve the stress.

I said, "Do you name your furniture?"

"What?" She laughed.

"This one should be named Jonah. It almost swallowed me."

She laughed. Geez, pretty women are even sexier when they laugh.

Clumsily I asked. "What…what is it…you wanted me to help you with?"

She smiled. Not a teenager's smile. A woman's smile. A smart woman's smile. "To help me with getting to know you better!" It came right out of her spontaneously. And warmly.

"What … what would you like to know?" I whispered.

"Everything. Your family, friends, Canada. Why you're here. Your girlfriends."

Being in that inexplicable accidental situation, that sumptuous setting, looking at the beautiful daughter of a star, I was not about to utter one negative word and break the spell, so I said, "My experience with girls is a little like my experience with mansions like this … I've only been in one."

She howled, falling back on the sofa. "Oh, God, Johnny, that's so cute!" She remained there, reclining, with only her head on the arm, smiling at me. "I like you," she said, staring at me. Wordless, I stared back. She had that look of 'wanting' that I'd seen on Ann and Beverly. I did want to kiss her, but there's no way a dishwasher or clothing clerk could date such a stunning creature. I was also incapable of a quickie one-night stand. Sometimes I hated my mind. That was one of them.

I jumped up. "Thank you. Thank you so much for the wonderful day. I really enjoyed it. And thank your parents."

"Are you leaving?" She sat up, shocked. "Why?"

"I…I…just have to go."

She was in disbelief. "How will you get home? Do you want me to drive you?"

I felt heroic, like in those movies. "No," I said. "I'll walk."

"Are you sure? It's a very long way."

"I'll be fine. Thank you again. And your family. It was a great day."

She stood at the open door watching me till I got to the sidewalk.

It took two hours to walk from Brentwood to LaBrea. With each step I fingered the piece of paper in my pocket, hating myself. Leo Durocher, the famed, trouble-making outspoken coach of the Brooklyn Dodgers once announced to the world that "Nice guys finished last." The truth is, sometimes nice guys don't finish at all.

And Shakespeare said: "There's a tide in the affairs of men, which taken at the flood, leads on to fortune, omitted, all the voyage of their life is bound in shallows and in miseries!" Missing that easy, wanted affair was not because I did not understand women. It was because I did not understand myself when around them.

The Lady in Black

During the day, once or twice a week, when I had time, I would stroll down Hollywood Boulevard past Grauman's, stop to look around in Edmund's legendary used bookstore, then visit Lenny in the jewelry shop. His workbench was close to the front window and entrance where passersby would stop to watch him buried in his craft, hunched over a small piece of jewelry or a watch, wearing that ever-present eyeglass. He would always take a break to talk to me, mostly about American history and movies, never about himself, always about how I was doing. But not that day.

He was waiting on an unusual, looking lady in her forties, slender and shapely. She was dressed entirely in black, wearing a broad-brimmed black hat. She looked like a silent movie star. My entrance interrupted their conversation.

"Johnny, I was just telling this beautiful young woman about the loss of one of our fellow boarders, the announcer-teacher hauled off by the law."

"That was terrible, Len. It's hard to believe," I said.

"Evidently, he was on probation. He violated his by violating one of his A students. Or his student's A!" Lenny chuckled.

The lady giggled. "Oh, my God!" Her voice was the deepest woman's voice I'd ever heard. It had a rumble to it, like actress Tallulah Bankhead. Or Patricia Neal.

"Len, that kind of stuff is just too hard to imagine. A grown man and a boy."

"Johnny's just down here from Canada. He's got a lot to learn about life," Lenny said, returning the item to the lady.

"It doesn't sound as though you've been out in the world much, young man," the lady in black said.

"Guess not." I smiled. It was nice to see Lenny chatting with the woman. Maybe he'd date her. To give them some space, I strolled to the back of the store, admiring the content of the counters. Lenny called to me.

"Johnny, where are you off to when you leave here?"

"I don't know. Maybe back to Edmund's. Then home."

"Laura wants to buy you a late lunch."

"Young man, have you ever been to the Roosevelt Hotel?"

"No. I pass it often, but have never been inside."

"Oh, you must see it. Old fashioned Hollywood. Would you like that?"

I looked at Lenny who gave me a thumbs up. "There you go, Johnny," he said.

"Oh, wait a minute," the lady in black said excitedly. "I have a better idea. You need to meet people. We can do the Roosevelt another day. I am having a few people over tonight. Here's my card." She pulled a card from her small purse and handed it to me. It was beautifully embossed. Black on gold. Obviously very expensive.

"You call me and I'll come and pick you up. You too, Leonard."

"Oh, no, no. thank you," Lenny said. "I need my beauty sleep."

"Miss–" I started to say.

"Laura, young man. *Laura*. And I'll call you John."

"Laura, is this address on Highland your home? Is it near the Hollywood Bowl?"

"Yes. Just a block down."

"You don't have to drive me. I can walk it easily. I enjoy walking."

"That's wonderful then. Around seven. Casual." She turned and left.

"Good for you, Johnny," Lenny said. "You'll have a terrific time and meet some new people. Laura knows everyone in the town."

Back home I laid out a nice pair of trousers and a clean dress shirt, then took a nap. I awoke around four thirty and took a quick shower in our community bathroom across the hall. I had left my door open as I always did, except for when I slept. Standing in the middle of the room when I entered, wearing only jockey shorts, was the Egyptian in his brown suit. He often just strolled in to chat, so I was not surprised.

"Oh, hi," I said. "What's up?"

"Lenny says you have a hot date tonight."

"No, no. It's not a date. Just dinner. I'm too young for her anyway." I reached for my trousers.

He laughed. "Men built like you never too young for the ladies. The younger the juicier. Where you get legs like that?"

I paid little attention to his moving closer. "Hockey. Playing a lot of hockey," I said, zipping my pants.

"You must have lots of girlfriends?"

I was only half listening. My mind was on the upcoming dinner, and who might be there.

"Actually no. I am not very good with girls. This is just dinner with a friend of Lenny's and some new people.' I reached down for my shirt.

"I don't believe that," he said standing behind me "You're pretty yourself. How do you take care of your needs?"

What did he just say? I turned to look at him. I had barely one arm in the right sleeve when he lunged at me. His fingers clutched my shoulders, his nails dug into the skin. With a violent yank, he pulled me off my feet toward him. As he did so, he threw his head downward, pushing his face into my chest, and with a low throaty growl sank his teeth hard above the right nipple. I grabbed at his hair, pushing him back as hard as I could, but he was pushing me back toward the bed. I bashed my open hands into his nose and eyes, yelling, "Jesus Christ, what are you doing? What are you doing?"

He let go, and didn't move. His face was flushed; his eyes watery and bloodshot.

I stepped back, staring at him, bewildered. In a weird way I felt sorry for him. I had been more frightened by the bloodsuckers than that desperately sad-looking man.

"I'm not into that."

Without a word, he left. I wiped the blood off my shoulders and chest, and finished dressing. I stayed longer in my room than I should have, giving him time to vacate the premises, which he did. Soon Lenny was in the room, having heard the commotion. I told him briefly, without too much detail.

"Johnny," he said, "you'll find Ernest Hemingway was right when he said, most people live lives of quiet desperation."

The next day at dinner when the landlady and other tenants wondered aloud about the sudden disappearance of the stranger from the Middle East, Lenny said, "Only Isis knows."

"Who?" I asked.

Before Lenny could answer, Mr. Kirkwood did. "The Egyptian Goddess of Fertility."

God, some people are smart, I thought.

"He was interesting, though," I said, and, as an afterthought, added, "Florence of Arabia!"

Lenny howled; he was the only one who got it. Almost every time he saw me after that, he would mutter, "Florence Of Arabia."

Walking up Highland to Laura's house, it was impossible not to think of what had just happened. The months I knew the Egyptian and the announcer, there was never ever any sign of homosexuality or pedophilia. They had deep masculine voices, especially the announcer. Laura also had a beautiful deep voice. Holding her card in my hand, looking at the address on it, and on the door in front of me, I thought, *Jesus, what if Laura is really Larry!* I debated whether or not to keep going. *Laura is a woman. She has to be. I felt her arm. I stood next to her. I smelled her perfume.*

I was still carrying on this monologue when I rang the doorbell. The house, as were many in Hollywood, was totally unique. Near the bottom of the hill, but up three long flights of tiled stairs lined with flowers pots, was a small castle, complete with turrets. The bell didn't ring. It gonged. The huge thick black door opened immediately. There was Laura, minus her hat. The blackness of her hair made her pale white skin look almost ghostly. She was very petite and pretty. And all smiles.

"Oh, there you are. Come on in. You're late. I thought you changed your mind."

Late? I didn't think I was late.

As she took my arm and led me in, I looked at her more closely. Yes, she was indeed a woman.

The interior was all blacks, browns and reds, with matching furnishings that hinted of the Orient. And money. The living and dining rooms had vaulted ceilings and chandeliers. The outside gave no hint at how expansive the inside was. She led me directly into the large kitchen. Sitting, or almost sitting, on one of the stools around the island was a nice-looking young man in his early twenties. He was fussing with his chair and giggling.

"Laura, these damn things are too high," he muttered.

"And so are you, my dear!" Laura said, without missing a beat. "I'd like you to meet my new friend, Johnny. I invited him to dinner."

The young man got his feet onto the floor, steadying himself with one hand on the island. "Johnny. You're a little late. The food's almost gone, but there's still plenty of booze, so you'd better get crackin'. I'll be in the front room."

"Come on. Let me introduce you to everyone," Laura said, her hand still warmly on my arm.

The guy was right. Scraps of small sandwiches and deviled eggs were evidence there had been food, and a half-dozen liquor and wine bottles, some still with something in them. I thought that I'd be introduced to a crowd, but there were only three people in the magnificent room with wall-to-wall Persian carpeting and a wall-sized window overlooking the houses and the street below. There were also open bottles on the large oriental coffee table.

"You two have already met," Laura said, pointing to the young drunk who was now sprawled out on the arm of a large leather chair. Seated in the chair was a very pretty blonde, also holding a drink. She couldn't have been more than nineteen or twenty.

"Johnny, this is ..." Laura hesitated, apparently not knowing the young girl's name.

"I'm Ashley." She saluted me with a wave of her drink.

Laura led me across the room. Sitting with his back to the window, with his arms stretched out, resting them on the cushions, a drink also in his hand, was a handsome man in his forties. He looked like someone I'd seen or met before, but I was too absorbed in why this wasn't the dinner I expected.

"Johnny, this is my best friend and companion, Richard. Richard this is Johnny." She sounded like she, too, had had a few.

I extended my hand, but Richard did not extend his. "That's ... that's my drinking hand, as you can see. Here." With that, he extended the back of his left hand, which I could only shake with a few fingers of my right hand.

"Come on now, let me feed you." Laura led me back into the kitchen.

"Here, you sit there, and I'll sit opposite you so I can look at you."

I had not eaten since morning, but wasn't hungry. I lose my appetite around drunks. I politely picked up a small sandwich as a prop, trying to think of an excuse to leave.

"Would you like something to drink?'

"I don't drink," I said quickly.

"You must drink water or milk?" She smiled.

"Water'll be fine."

She poured me a glass of water and placed it in my hand "There. That's a good boy." She returned to her seat "You drink."

Laura and I exchanged chit chat, strained on my part. Soon the noise and laughter from the front room got louder. Laura glanced a few times in that direction, then returned her attention to me. Finally, she said, "Would you like to go in and see what they're up to?"

"In a minute. I just enjoy talking to you," I lied. There was a strangeness in the air. An uneasiness. The darkening sky through the kitchen window only added to it.

There was a banging or thumping in the other room. Followed by laughter and curses. The lights went out, and the giggling and swearing got louder. Suddenly, a single light went on. A moving light, like a large flashlight. It was tumbling all over the place, accompanied by more giggles and grunts! Then a man's drunken voice hollered, "Goddamn it, Laura.

Get in here and help us with this. I can't also be my goddamned lighting director!"

Laura looked at me with a knowing smile. "Come on, Johnny. Come with me!"

I didn't move

"Nobody's going to bite you," she said sweetly. "Come on." She held out her hand. I didn't take it, but I followed her, but only to the archway.

"Goddamn it, Laura. Get the fuck in here," a man's voice bellowed. "I can't do all this by myself."

I was stopped dead by what I saw.

Richard was standing in the middle of this partially lit room, clutching the middle of a tall floor lamp, moving it around like a dowsing rod over silhouetted figures on the floor. Seeing Laura, he thrust it toward her.

"Here, goddamn it. Take this, and hold it properly so I can instruct this young man on what to do!"

Laura took the light stand, and casually walked to the middle of the room, maneuvering the light right over the bodies on the rug. The sight did not phase her.

"That a girl," Richard said. "Now, goddamn it, kid, get your face down in there." He reached over and placed his hand on the back of the younger drunk, and pushed.

Now fully lit, from the waist down, were Ashley and the young man. Her dress was pulled up over her chest, her panties were off, hanging on the top of the lamp. Her legs were spread-eagled. She was mumbling, "Come on. Come on. Do it!"

The young man was naked from the waist down. His pants on the coffee table. He was obviously not aroused, but trying to be co-operative. "I'm trying. I'm trying," he gasped

With that, Richard shoved his head right into her crotch. "Goddamn it, if you don't do it right, I will!"

What little sandwich I had in my stomach was coming up. As slowly as possible, I backed out of the room, keeping my eye only on Laura so she wouldn't see me. They were too engaged to notice or care. I backed into the foyer, took a huge breath, and quickly and quietly opened and closed the door. I almost leaped down the three flights into the night. Jesus Christ. What weird people in this town! The Egyptian gay Dracula! The Announcer boy banger! A female filth facilitator! They had perfect facades that belied their reality. Just like most of the movies the town made.

When Lenny asked how my evening went, if I met any interesting new people, I told him they were indeed new to me and very interesting. I said nothing more, in case Laura was a friend.

I couldn't get the porn movie sight out of my head. It kept rerunning. My God, that young girl. Where did they find her? How could she do that? What replayed the most, though, was the face of Richard, the director; what an arrogant, unpleasant jerk, yelling at Laura to help. And cursing the young man. Then it came to me. I recognized it. I knew I knew that face. I had seen it many times in the movies. In *Gone with the Wind*. He was a movie star. I'd seen him often. It was Richard Carlson, the actor! In a couple of years, he would star in the TV series, *I Led Three Lives.*" Wow, did he ever.

That I never said to Lenny, either. Or anyone. Who would believe it? When I recognized him again on his TV show, I watched every episode with glee. It was subtitled, *I Was a Communist for the FBI*. Every time he snatched a commie, I giggled, knowing better than the FBI what he really loved to snatch was snatch. And that he'd rather be a director!

Another Familiar Face

I loved Los Angeles. It was almost always sunny and clear, meaning my clothes didn't have to go to the dry cleaners all the time. The homes, buildings and people were unique and colorful, the electric cars a joy to ride. I took them everywhere, from The San Fernando Valley to the Pacific Ocean. There was Griffith Park, probably the largest city park in the world, with its golf courses, zoo, horseback riding, and magnificent observatory; the pier at Santa Monica with its permanent carnival and roller coaster. When I wasn't on an electric car or bus, I hitchhiked everywhere. And never failed to get an immediate ride. Time off was tourist time for me. I was two low-paying jobs away from being a bum, but it didn't frighten me in the least. A desire to be somebody, a star, was as foreign to me as my desire to gamble. Nothing kills ambition like contentment.

For wonderful conversations and giggles there was Lenny. He was a Wikipedia of wisdom, knowledge and experience. I learned more from him in just a few sittings than I ever did in school. Everything he talked about always came out positive. Even when he talked about the pogroms suffered by his Jewish grandparents in Russia that led them eventually to Europe. Or when he explained how Jews became moneylenders in Europe because Jews were not allowed to own land to grow a potato, so they became bankers and bought them. And sold them. For a profit. He loved his people, his heritage, even though he stopped going to synagogue after his wife's suicide. He especially loved America where his grandparents eventually bought land. I had not one thing to contribute to those conversations other than an eager ear. He almost treated me like the son he never had.

This particular Sunday, I went to one of the films and lectures at the observatory. While watching it, I couldn't wait to see Lenny afterwards and tell him about what I'd learned about the universe. When I walked into the boarding house, the landlady was screaming at two expressionless men in suits. Two of the boarders were standing frozen by the dining room table.

"Oh, my God! Oh, my God," she was almost crying.

"What's wrong? What happened?" I shouted.

"Oh, Johnny, Johnny. It's terrible."

Before she could answer, one of the men touched her gently on the arm. "Which room?" he said softly.

The landlady pointed at the stairs. "The…the second one…on the right…at the top."

"Thank you. We won't be long." They ascended the stairs.

Nobody spoke. The landlady was clutching her face, whimpering.

Finally, Mr. Kirkwood spoke. "What happened?"

The landlady barely whispered, "Lenny killed himself."

"It can't be," I gasped. "I just saw him." I felt the blood drain from my body.

The men descended the stairs, thanking the landlady who was sobbing uncontrollably.

"Excuse me, excuse me," I said to the men, my voice cracking. They stopped by the open door. "What happened to Lenny?"

The older man didn't miss a beat. "He shot himself."

"Where? When?" I blurted.

"This afternoon. In his shop."

"Did he leave a note?"

"It may have been a note. We don't know exactly. All that was written on it was, 'I miss you.'"

I imagined Lenny slumped over on his workbench, his eyepiece next to him. It had to have been a last note to his wife: *I miss you.* My throat burned. Tears felt hot on my cheeks. God, Jesus, Abraham and Moses, I would miss him. What also brought tears to my eyes was the thought of how it must feel to be so in love with another human that you'd give your life for them; I was suicide proof.

Hours later, unfed, still fully dressed, lying sleepless all night on the bed thinking about Lenny, I thought I had to get back to paying attention to what I was going to do. Surely, I wasn't meant to spend my time as a permanent tourist in Los Angeles. I couldn't just drift in the choppy ocean called life. I had to start rowing in some direction. I could not spend my time doing nothing. Or working two jobs. The next day I quit both.

Movie studios and theatrical agents were open during the day; live theater and acting classes did business in the evening. If I was going to pursue my affection for show business properly, I'd better find some kind of job with a midnight shift. And I did, almost immediately at a place called Bireley's Orange just east of LaBrea and south of Santa Monica Blvd. Bireley's was a large, well-known company that made orange soft drinks, juice and concentrate in a building that took up almost half a block. It was about twenty blocks from the boarding house so I walked there every night just before midnight, and home every morning, just after eight. During my shift, dozens of trucks would line the street and take turns dumping tons of oranges onto a massive complex of conveyor belts. My job, sitting almost side-saddle on a little wooden seat or slab that folded out from a beam, twenty feet above the floor, was to pick out what looked like damaged or rotten oranges as they tumbled by, and toss them into another conveyor belt that led to the machinery that would turn them into pulp and concentrate. It was dummy robot work. It is impossible to work a mechanical, receptive job like that midnight till dawn without having your mind wander. Mine did a lot. Yet, I felt strangely free, like I was being paid to daydream.

With one of my days off, I enrolled in an acting class at Hollywood High School on Highland. There were about twenty of us in the class, of varying ages, including one fellow about my age with sharp eyes and nose and a kind of interesting, nasally twang to his voice. The teacher's name was Strickland, once a very successful radio actress. She was in her late forties, with perfect posture, an ample bosom, red hair and a voice as interesting as any I'd ever heard. She really knew her stuff and I loved her class. I made sure I did some new speech or scene for her every week.

The young man with the nasally twang, though, did nothing. Ever. He sat in the same seat for three or four weeks in a row, a seat on the aisle, three rows back from the stage, and just watched. And listened. Miss Strickland finally noticed his lack of participation, and one night from the stage, said, "Jack, would you like to come up here and read something?"

"No, thanks, Miss Strickland."

"When would you like to?"

The young man just stared at her, and got up. "As a matter of fact, Miss Strickland, no offense, but I don't think this is for me." He got up casually and left.

It put a damper on the class, especially me. How could anybody just walk out? A number of years later, I saw this young man in a meaningless Roger Corman film. The voice was unmistakable. His name was Jack Nicholson.

One Sunday morning walking home from work, I would hear another familiar voice. It was a bright, clear usual LA morning. It was always a pleasant walk up LaBrea. I was thirty or forty yards short of the walkway to the door when I noticed a shiny convertible heading in my direction, but on the other side of the street. It looked like a Cadillac. A new shiny one. The only yellowish-looking car I'd ever seen, except for a cab. The driver, a nice-looking deeply tanned man, perhaps fifty, noticed me watching, and smiled. He must have thought I was staring at him. Just after it passed me, it stopped. He backed up, across the street, stopping right next to me. Having reached my walkway, I stopped, looking at the lush leather seats and the driver.

"Hi, there," he said in a pleasant accented voice

I was just a few feet from him, looking down at him. He had a warm easy smile, revealing the most perfect teeth I ever saw, even in movies. He had dark, almost black, eyes. His fully wavy black hair, sprinkled with grey, was parted on the right. He was wearing an expensive looking casual, yellow silk shirt.

"Where you off to?' he asked.

"Home."

"Need a lift?"

"I'm here," I said pointing to the building.

"Lucky you." He smiled. "Been a long night?"

"Eight hours," I said, not knowing whether I should continue the conversation.

"That sounds more like a job than a party."

"Yes, my job."

"Well, that's no fun!" He smiled again. "What'll you do now?"

I thought that an odd question. "Have some breakfast, I guess."

"How would you like to have breakfast with me?"

There was no doubt I was going to say "No, thank you," but nothing came out right away. In my head I was looking at pictures of the Egyptian and Laura.

"You'll be back home in an hour," he offered, cheerily.

"No. No, thanks. That's very nice of you," I finally said. And nodded. He was so pleasant.

He waved the back of his left hand. "Well, have a good day." He pulled away, still smiling. Like my struggle to recall Richard Carlson's face, I struggled with that one also. I knew I had seen it. But more than the face was that voice. It was so familiar. I knew I had heard it a million times, with that hint of an English accent. It came to me as I opened the door. It must have reminded me of the opening scene in *The Philadelphia Story*, one of the greatest opening scenes in movie history. Cary Grant! It was Cary Grant. That's where I've heard that voice. The greatest male movie star ever! How unbelievable. Cary Grant. Talking to me! I mentioned it to no one, but that amazing Sunday morning moment entertained me often and sparked my limited ambitions. I was more determined than ever to study and work harder at acting with Miss Strickland, or whoever. If a poor kid like Archie Leach could become Cary Grant, maybe John Barbour could become somebody, too! What I became eventually was a mailboy at Paramount Pictures, where I saw him again.

A Jewish Superstition

Aside from Miss Strickland's class, I joined a theater group half a block from the house, the Music Box Theater at the corner of LaBrea and Hollywood Blvd, a spacious professional live-performance theater. We did workshops and a new thing I'd never heard of called improvisations. Most important, though, we put on real plays that real people paid real money to see. And they came. Not a lot, but they came. The initial season's most successful production was *Bus Stop*, which somehow, I ended up directing, but not acting in. I had never directed anything. This just grew out of what I had been doing in the workshop. I had no idea what a director was supposed to do. I never liked giving orders, but in putting scenes together with other actors, I knew as a viewer what I would like to see. So that's what I did, and that's what they liked. I was totally confident in what I liked to see on stage. This confidence rubbed off on the actors, and for mostly insecure actors, there's nothing they need more than someone in charge who is confident. I may not have been confident in many areas, but there I was. One of the liveliest performers in the troupe was an extremely personable, attractive girl with a big bosom and mouth to match. She was funny. Years later I was delighted, but not surprised, to see Joanne Worley on *Laugh-In*.

I wasn't making much money, but nothing beat the joy of it. Not even hockey. I loved theater people. Everything about them was right on the surface. Their emotions, ambitions, venalities, egos, and insecurities were as easy to see as their eyes. Most performers are kids. "Hey, Ma, look at me!" Self-centered, spoiled and reeking of jealousy, many will stab you in the back, while others with open-hearted generosity will share their spoils with you. I encountered this often in the years that followed. Sometimes it hurt my career, sometimes it saved it. But it never hurt my feelings.

I can recall vividly three times in my life when I said out loud to myself, "Boy, I'm so happy doing this. And so lucky!" And the happiness and source of it disappeared immediately. As if by black magic. Or a curse. Being at The Music Box Theater was the first time. It wasn't the money or the thought of fame. It was the wonderful camaraderie of playing make-believe with others. It was being absorbed in something outside yourself that paradoxically made you feel more yourself. I was successfully working toward my dream. This was the first time in my life I was happy. So thrilled with the depth of the emotion, I verbalized it out loud, as though to a God I did not believe in. But some other Gods who were not too fond of me must have been listening and it was gone in a week. This happened twice more years later when I achieved my dream. When it happened the last time, the greatest loss, it made me recall a brief convocation I'd had with Lenny years earlier.

"How many Jews have you known, Johnny?" he asked out of nowhere.

"Just one, I think. When I was five."

He smiled. I recounted the incident in the first grade, when the teacher asked us all to stand and tell the class what religion they were. All the kids but me and one girl said Christian, and got applause. I said I didn't have one that I knew of, and got laughs. But one pretty young dark-haired girl, said, Jewish and got booed. She never came back to class. I told Lenny I was so shocked at her being booed, I could still recall her name: Renee.

"Lenny, I just don't understand why some people are prejudiced," I said.

"Johnny, people just do not like differences. Religion. Color. Nationality. They won't look beyond that at their common humanity. In *The Merchant of Venice*, Shylock says, 'If you prick us do we not bleed?' They blame us for killing Christ. We did not. The Romans did. Certainly some of us helped." He smiled again.

"Especially the moneylenders he kicked out of the temple."

"Johnny, you can learn a lot from Jews. Especially how to laugh. The best defense and offense against bigotry. Even how to eat. From observation over 5,000 years ago in Leviticus they learned a lot about food. No meat with dairy products."

He stopped to see if I was absorbing this. Indeed, I was. He was so smart. About everything. So, I asked the inevitable question.

"Lenny, do you believe in God?"

He smiled broadly. "Johnny, that question is unanswerable because it is unknowable. To ponder the Universe is interesting. To ponder a Creator is a waste of thought." Then he started to laugh.

"What's so funny?" I asked.

"Me." He chuckled. "Just like a Jew. I don't ever think about God, but I believe in something sillier. A Jewish superstition. And we have tons of them."

"What's that?"

"Johnny, if you ask a rich Jew how he is doing, if he is rich he will never say terrific. Fantastic. If he does say that, he's lying!" He laughed out loud.

"What do you mean? I… I… don't get it," I said.

"Because if he says fantastic, he is convinced the gods will punish his arrogance and take it away. What he will only say is: 'It could be better.' So, remember, if you say fantastic, not only will you piss God off, but a lot of very jealous people!"

Of course, I did not remember. It was silly nonsense. I did not remember until it happened. Three times.

Who's That Knocking on My Door?

I've never had much luck with men in suits. To me they represented authority, or worse, somebody who wanted to be in authority. A man in a tailored suit, except in the movies, always looked threatening. It was the uniform of the Establishment. This discomfort was a simple conclusion drawn from experience. When not in a military uniform, the men who mistreated my mother wore suits. One even wore a red carnation in his lapel. The principal who delighted in bloodying my hands with a leather-wire strap soaked in lemon water wore nice suits. The male teachers who judged and graded me, the detectives who questioned me, and the employers who interviewed me, all wore suits. It got so just the sight of an adult male in a suit made me shiver at the possibility of some unknown calamity.

The young accountant at the boarding house was always in a suit. He had weekends off, but his suits didn't; even then he wore one. I cannot remember his name, only the dark blue suit he wore constantly, the one he wore at the breakfast table the last Sunday I ate there, the Sunday men in suits came to the door.

At breakfast or dinner, the two talking the most were usually me and "Better Red Than Dead," or Lenny when he was alive. Our lively disagreements were a constant source of entertainment for our fellow diners. The discussions were always politics, about which I, of course, knew almost nothing. I didn't dislike him. I was just bewildered by the rigidness and the superiority of his convictions. Basically, I had none. So, he was an easy target to tease. To him a conservative Republican Party and a vengeful God not only went hand in hand, but fist in fist. His beliefs were as unshakable as a fire hydrant. He never talked about his family or school, and I never saw him with a girl. It was impossible to know if he was shaped by society or genes. His main pride was being an active Young Republican. The first time he told the table this, I said with a straight face, "That's the first time I've heard young and Republican in the same sentence." The table roared. His hatred was instantaneous. I was the "Young Canadian commie!"

Sometimes our exchanges got heated, but he was the only one raising his voice. I just sat back. It was like shooting a dart at a huge balloon, and watching the hot air swoosh out. At one point in this last meal, and last exchange, I complimented him on his dedication, and added, "If the Young Republicans begin training suicide bombers, I presume you'll be the first to volunteer."

His witless rejoinder was the standard, "Why don't you just go back where you came from?"

So, I continued, "No. On the other hand, being a real Republican, you would not volunteer. You'd find others to do the fighting for you." The giggles turned to 'oohs' and 'aahs.' It was turning into a food fight.

"It was commies like you and Roosevelt who crippled this country. That's why God crippled him. And gave him that wife." This he said often.

Sensing it was getting out of hand, I thought I'd ease up. But I just had to have the last word. "God crippled him long before the depression. The one caused by an old Republican, Hoover. After whom they named a vacuum cleaner." Once again, there were muffled giggles from the ringsiders.

He looked as though he wanted to stab me with his fork. "How do you foreigners get so stupid?" he hissed.

"Watching American newsreels," popped out. As did more laughs.

"Made by Liberals and Jews," he barked. "I read books. Books by businessmen who show how they destroyed Capitalism. And support Russia."

"The stuff I read said Roosevelt saved Capitalism." (But I hadn't read anything. I was just repeating stuff I'd heard from Lenny. I started to feel smart.) With Federal Works Programs–"

"Socialist programs," he barked.

"And Social Security. Without that, the twelve million unemployed would have taken to the streets like they did in Russia. Only the Second World War put those people back to work."

"We should have let the Germans finish off the Russians."

"They almost did. They killed twenty-five million Russians." I paused. "Do your grandparents collect Social Security?"

"What has that got to do with anything?" he snapped.

"Well, if they do, they can thank Roosevelt, and if they're thanking Roosevelt, they should thank Norman Thomas because as the Presidential candidate for the Socialist Party in the late teens, Social Security was part of his platform."

Mr. Kirkwood, old enough to remember, applauded.

It was getting out of hand, but I couldn't stop myself. I really knew none of this. I was just showing off. I was on a roll. Vanity was triumphing over common sense.

It ended when he tossed his napkin, jerked back the chair and left. Everyone nodded at my victory speech. Usually when someone unpleasant leaves a room, the room lights up a little. Not in this case. The room felt dark. I got a very uneasy feeling. Without finishing, I excused myself and went upstairs to brush my teeth. I tried to think about grabbing my bathing suit and going to Santa Monica, but the sick feeling of anger at myself for my inability to shut up at times, got in the way. That's when the knock on the door came. I sat up immediately.

I heard the landlady's voice, then a man's voice. I just knew it had something to do with me. I rushed to my door, edged to the landing and peeked down. Two men in expensive suits were showing the landlady identification.

"Yes, he's upstairs." She gestured. I rushed back into my room straight to the window facing De Longpre, and yanked it open. I scrambled onto the shingled, slanted roof, and slid on my backside down to the rain trough. I braced my feet against the curved metal, surveyed the sidewalk below, preparing to jump. As I stood, the front doors of the black car parked below burst open. Two more men in suits leaped out. "That's far enough!"

Sheepishly, I crawled back up. The first two suits were standing in the room watching me crawl back in. All I could say was, "Are you looking for me?"

"Are you John Barbour?" one suit asked.

"Yes."

"Could you show us your visa or green card, please?"

I was surprised by his politeness. "Who are you?"

"FBI." He dutifully held up his badge. "Your visa?"

I had no choice but to be honest. "I don't have one. A green card neither. I just came as a visitor."

"Visitors, are only allowed two weeks. How long ago did you visit?"

"Fifty-two weeks ago."

He didn't smile. "You'd better come along with us."

"Why?" I asked. "I didn't do anything."

"We need to talk to you. Then you'll need to talk to INS."

"What's INS?"

"Immigration and Naturalization Service."

I started toward the door.

"You'd better pack your stuff."

They stood next to me as I packed. They escorted me down the stairs. One in front. One in back. Everyone was crowded around at the foot of the stairs. I was comforted by the obvious sympathy on their faces; all except the accountant. He was standing tall, having saved America from another Soviet subversive, but I had brought that upon myself. As writer Ben Hecht said, "Revenge is sweeter when you can see the victim."

The agents did not handcuff me until we got to the car. I was placed in back. On the way downtown, they said not a word to me. Or each other. Finally, nervously, to break the scary silence, I asked, "How did you know where I was?" They did not answer, but they did not have to. I knew before they even showed up. The rest of the ride, the only thing I thought of was that I'd miss The Music Box Theater. That hurt.

In the upstairs office of the FBI headquarters downtown, still with handcuffs on, they had me sit, and began asking me a bunch of questions. The first one, was I a Communist?

I said, "No." Trying to relax myself, and let them know I was no threat to the U.S. government, I added, "Not even a Junior commie." They were not amused. They then asked if I had a job and a Social Security card. I told them I had both, and showed them. They were quick to ask how as an illegal was I able to get one. Or was it fake. I said I just went to the Social Security and asked for one. And they gave it to me. They asked if I lied about where I was born to get it. I answered immediately, "Of course I lied. How else could I get it?" This forthright honesty did not impress or amuse them either.

I was fingerprinted. Knowing what their search would reveal when asked if I'd ever been arrested or convicted of any crimes or felonies, I answered honestly. "Yes. It was stealing an overcoat and later breaking and entering a convenience store where I had worked. I broke in with a friend of mine, Mel Nixon, one night when I was around sixteen."

Satisfied I was not a threat to national security, or a commie, they turned me over to the Immigration and Naturalization Service. Only one suit from INS was required to transport me to their prison compound at Terminal Island, San Pedro. I was taken downstairs and placed in a dirty blue bus. Every seat was taken, loaded with mostly Mexicans, Latin Americans, a Frenchman, and an Englishman. As a suspected commie, I was treated better, forced into a front seat.

Terminal Island in the 1950's was not exactly Ellis Island in the 1890's. Ellis Island in New York was where America welcomed its immigrants. Terminal Island is where they said goodbye to them. The one on the East was coming, the one on the West was going. If Terminal Island in San Pedro hadn't had twelve-foot fences, barbed wire, and a couple of gun turrets, it would have been the ideal spot for a luxury vacation hotel; it looked directly out onto the harbor and ocean. On the landlocked side, it was surrounded by palm trees and acres of green grass.

For the first two weeks I was in limbo. I had not been charged with anything. I was just locked up. During that time, I did nothing but stare at the ocean, watching the scores of large boats and tankers sailing in and out, already wondering and planning how I could swim to one of them. I couldn't make it in the Air Force; maybe I could make it in the Navy. Even if it was just the merchant navy.

In the third week, I was called in for what they call a preliminary hearing. It was quick. I was informed that while I had been convicted of two felonies, they were not deemed crimes of moral turpitude, so I would not be deported. I was thrilled. The agent continued, "You will be allowed voluntary departure."

"What's that?"

"You will be given a few days to leave the country voluntarily once you show us proof that you have a way to depart."

"Would I be able to come back?" I asked eagerly.

"You'd have to apply at the Consulate in Toronto or your hometown."

"Would they let me back?"

"It is up to them. Not us. But if you come back again illegally, you will be deported and have no chance of ever staying. So, Mr. Barbour, would you like the voluntary departure?"

"How do I do that?"

"You buy a ticket and get on the bus or plane and leave. It's that simple."

I was stuck. "I don't have any money."

"What about friends or family? I think the last boy who went from here to Ontario paid around $38.00."

I was touched by his sincere delivery of this information. Where could I get $38.00? That was a lot of money. I could ask the landlady. Or Mr. Kirkwood. Maybe even Joanne Worley, or one of the actors. I was sure they might help me, but I was just too embarrassed. It wasn't up to them to help bail me out. That only left one person, my mother. I hadn't spoken to her in over a year.

"Could I phone my mother?" I asked.

"Certainly!" the agent said

"But…but I don't even have money for that."

"Call her collect. Do you have her number?"

"Somewhere," I said.

"Okay, then we'll do that in the morning. I'll come and get you around ten o'clock."

Our sleeping quarters were the size of an ice rink. Rows and rows of metal cots with brown blankets. That night, I had less sleep than money.

Last Call

At ten the next morning the Immigration Officer came to get me. "Use the phone on the end," he said, pointing to a small bank of phones on a narrow shelf. Each phone was partitioned by a short piece of wood that gave them the meaningless hint of privacy.

My mother's phone number, like the addresses, was always in my head, impossible to erase. I did not want to call. Hearing her voice and the obvious litany of my deficiencies made me ill. To call collect made it worse. But I had no choice. What if she refused the charges? My stomach churned as I lifted the receiver and dialed.

"Operator."

I gave my mother's name and number, my name, then the dreaded word, collect. I could hear the operator dialing then the ringing, a long ringing. I started to hope that she wouldn't answer. But she did. The operator asked if she was Margaret MacLaren and would she accept a long distance collect call from John Barbour.

"Calling from where?" she asked with an edge.

"Los Angeles, California," the operator said. There was a long, long pause. "Ma'am?" the operator asked.

"Okay, I guess so," she said.

"You will accept the charges?" the operator asked for clarification.

"Yes!"

"Thank you. Go ahead, Mr. Barbour."

"Mom," I whispered.

"Where are you?"

"I'm at a place called Terminal Island in Los Angeles."

"What are you doing there and why are you calling?"

"It's ... it's sort of a prison for people they're going to deport."

"You're in jail again? You've been arrested? Jesus, you'll be the goddamned death of me yet!'

She hadn't learned any new ways to denigrate me. "No, Mom. I didn't steal anything or do anything wrong. I just don't have a visa to be here, and they want to deport me. But they said if I get a $38.00 bus ticket, I can leave on my own and it won't be on my record if I want to come back." I blurted it out as quickly and as quietly as I could.

The long silence was cruel. "You want $38.00 from me? Do you think money grows on trees? (Another of her catalogue of old country phrases.) Where do you think I'm gonna get $38.00? And if I had $38.00, do you think I'd give $38.00 goddamn dollars to you?"

She was turning me down. Probably the only reason she took the call was to again tell me what a piece of crap I was, and how I caused her nothing but grief. I could have told her it was nothing compared to the grief she caused me. This time I remained silent. So anguished, I didn't even hear her hang up. Then something weird happened. I was not upset not getting the $38.00. I was strangely relieved at the loss of my mother. As quickly as her voice had suddenly disappeared, so did the ever-present pain of her existence. It was gone. As was she. I never saw or talked to her or thought about her ever, until this book. It was such a feeling of freedom. Yet, I still had to figure a way to find freedom from Terminal Island.

The Great Escape

I was in Terminal Island for six months. Half a year. That's a long time. It was longer with nothing to read, and nothing to listen to but mariachi music. I spent most of my time staring out the windows at the boats, the sea, the families coming to visit. I didn't realize it at the time, but I was casing the place. I was told they only send violent offenders back one at a time. Other than that, they wait for a few more going in the same direction to save the government money.

Carlos, in the bunk next to me, was in charge of the laundry collection and distribution on our floor. Once in a while, just for something to do, I'd help him. We'd gather up all the sheets and towels in a giant hamper with wheels, push it to the chute in the hallway next to the secured elevator, and dump it down the three stories to the basement below. He did not speak much English, and I spoke no Spanish, but we got along really well.

My thoughts about swimming out and boarding one of the tankers were replaced by thoughts of Carlos's hamper and the laundry chute; and how deep that pile of laundry was on the basement floor. It became an obsession. Even without his assistance, I felt it would be easy for me to just slip in and cover myself when no one was looking. I now volunteered to help him every day. And every day we got to the chute, with the guard paying little attention, I could see myself doing it. Before, when I sat at the windows watching the family and friends as they walked to and from the buildings, it was just passing the time. Then it was a blossoming plan; I made note of everything. What time they came and went. What time gates and doors were locked or unlocked. There was a long seventy-five-yard walk from the front gate to the main entrance. The one guard atop a tower at that gate asked for no identification from anyone coming or going. He was a human scarecrow. That was done when you entered the building. From eight AM to five PM every Monday through Friday the gate was open with a short walk beyond to a bus stop.

I could walk up easily from the basement to the first floor and out, or bypass it altogether.

I would do it on a Wednesday, midweek. It was a slam-dunk.

The two weeks I rehearsed it, though, I got nervous. There always seemed to be too much activity in the hallway. I did not think I could do it alone. If I wanted to do it, I had to ask Carlos for help. It was not easy. It was like pantomiming a comedy routine on the Sid Caesar Show. Something about his friendliness told me if he said "No," he would not turn me in.

In our rounds, we had stopped at a bunk and began to pull the sheets off. I began whispering and pantomiming my diving into the hamper. "Carlos, Carlos, me amigo, por favor. I want to..to..vaminos!" He stared at me, smiling. "Si!"

I pantomimed another dive into the hamper and repeated, "Comprende?"

He chuckled. "You…you like a towel?"

I wasn't sure what he meant. That I liked towels, or I would act like a towel. "Carlos, me, Juan, Vaminos," I whispered, accompanied by a running with my index and middle finger.

"Si si." He nodded. "You…towel…dirty blanket. Si. Vaminos. Comprendo. Bye, bye."

He got it.

"Que dias? Que dias?" he asked.

I wasn't sure how to say Wednesday, so I pointed it out on a calendar. He nodded again and said nothing.

"Gracias, gracias," I gushed, grabbing his hand.

I had to wait five days till Wednesday. No matter what the conditions were or how much was going on in the hallway, I was going to do it. I just had to. I could not be locked up anymore. The wait was killing me. Each day I folded and refolded my escape wardrobe. I gave no thought whatsoever as to what I'd do or where I'd go once I was out. That would take care of itself. Just getting out was everything. What made me feel uneasy, though, was that every day a few more Mexicans were smiling at me. Did they know? Did Carlos say something? I was afraid to ask him. First off, I couldn't say it in Spanish or pantomime it, and if I could, it might insult him. I felt everyone in this huge barracks was looking at me.

Wednesday morning came. At breakfast, I couldn't eat, a fellow with an English accent whom I'd never spoken to walked by patted me on the shoulder, bent over and said, "Good luck, mate."

Oh, God, I thought. *I can't do this now. It's become a Mexican spectator sport. The guards must know.* I was sick. Then I thought, "So what if I get caught. It's not a crime like a prison break where they give you a few more years. They're sending me back anyway. If they catch me, maybe they'll send me back sooner."

Carlos and I made our rounds picking up the sheets and towels in silence. We were watched by grinning faces and a few subtle thumbs up. I felt doomed, but determined. When we exited to the hallway, a stranger joined us. He and Carlos chatted amiably. Obviously, a friend of his. As we neared the chute, the stranger walked off and just past the guard. He then started coughing like he was sick. The guard walked toward him. Carlos quickly lifted some laundry and pointed. Without thinking, I dove in, and he tossed it on top of me. I heard the chute door creak open, and the hamper being lifted and tilted. I began tumbling and falling in the darkness. I could hear myself whining. In an instant I plowed into a pile of laundry with more following on top of me. My heart was banging against my ribs.

I lay there for a long time. Listening. Nothing but the sound of me gasping for air. The stench from the foul laundry did not bother me. It was the smell of freedom. The basement was empty, lit only by a few overhead bare bulbs. I stood confident and relieved, straightened my clothes and walked directly toward to the east door, which led to the long walkway. The walkway that would lead me to the gate, then to the bus stop.

My soft footsteps made a slight echo. As I approached the door I was certain was the right one, I thought I'd open it really slowly, and just peek out to evaluate my next move, in case it was busy. The knob felt cool and smooth when I gripped it. But it didn't turn. I tried it again. It didn't move. I yanked at it. Back and forth. It didn't budge. What was wrong? I'm on the inside. It should unlock from the inside. I panicked and ran quickly to a middle door that must lead to the harbor. That was locked, too. Jesus Christ! What happened? In desperation, I ran to the last door on my right. I had no idea where it might lead. I just wanted a door that would open. It didn't budge. Like a trapped rat, I scurried back and forth repeating my useless actions. I wanted to cry. I stood motionless, breathing deeply for what seemed forever. Exhausted and trying to think, I sank into the pile of laundry to rest.

Then the last door I had tried opened. I looked up at a guard. He glanced over at me, stunned.

"What the hell have we got here? Dirty laundry with a body in it!"

"Hello," I mumbled.

"Get up."

I did.

"What the hell are you doin' here?"

I shook my head forlornly. "Trying to escape!'"

My honesty did not amuse him. Like the King Kong cop in Toronto, he almost crushed my left bicep as he pulled me up and through the open door, all the way to the office. Had I opened that last door, I would have run into the main office. Two other officers perked up at the sight.

"Geez, Jeff, what yah got there?" one said, grinning.

"Dirty laundry with a body in it." Jeff repeated, ordering me to sit.

He explained to the two officers where he'd found me and how I got there. They thought it was funny, and began questioning me. They were more concerned about my accomplices than my failed escape. They didn't believe I'd done it all on my own.

"I can show you how easy it was."

"That's not necessary," they said. "Just sit still."

After confirming my identity and looking up my records, I was told my voluntary departure was being revoked. I would be there another three to six months, until they had a quota going back to Canada. I stared into empty space, the empty space that was my future.

"Let's go," the guard who found me said. "Upstairs!"

I got up slowly. Then just had to ask: "I thought during the week that everything was unlocked between eight and five. It's Wednesday. Why is it so quiet? Why is everything locked?"

They stared at me like I was an idiot, looking at each other with growing grins. The superior officer said, "It's July 4th, a big holiday in this country!" They laughed.

It was a tale they'd tell for years. Almost thirty years. When *Real People* became the number one show in the country, I got a note from Jeff. He said every week he told someone the story, which he says they don't believe. Then he asked me how I spent my Fourth of July's.

When I was returned to my cot, Carlos, to my surprise, was even friendlier to me. He knew I did not snitch. I then had a nickname. He and his friends referred to me from then on as Julio Quatro. I felt my life was over. I could see no future. no life for me in this country at least. But something kept nagging at me. Even if I had no road map to a real life, I still felt If I just keep moving something good might happen. I would begin this next trip by learning more about American History.

IN CANADA AGAIN

Boomerang Boy and Unfinished Business

Much to my surprise, in just a few weeks, I was on my way back to Toronto. I was not part of a quota of cooked Canadian geese being flown North. I was alone, handcuffed to an INS officer on a commercial airliner. Walking in front of him, making my way down the aisle to our seats, a few of the women passengers smiled sweetly. When they saw the handcuffs, though, attached to the giant suit behind me, I went from Huck Finn to Charlie Manson. The plane had a layover in Chicago. For some reason they would not explain to me, I had a ten-day layover in Cook County Jail, and found out why they called it America's Devil's Island. Two Chicago uniformed police officers were waiting for us at the bottom of the stairs. With almost no words, they waited as my escort removed the cuffs, and handed over the paperwork. With a hand on my head I was shoved into the back of their car. They placed my suitcase in the front where the passenger opened it, looking inside. They did not answer when I asked plaintively where we were going, and why? They led me to a room where I and my suitcase were handed over to a detective who told me to sit. I wasn't being fingerprinted or photographed or even questioned. He, too, ignored my inquiries, just fingering the papers indifferently.

I finally blurted, "How long will I be here?"

Before he could answer, if he was ever going to, the door burst open. Two white detectives were dragging in a black man who was crying, "I didn't do it. I done nothin." He looked to be about forty. His face and torn shirt were slightly bloody. His hands were handcuffed behind his back. The detectives did not sit him down. With the suspect still protesting, they led him across the room to a wall. They got behind him, each grabbing a cuffed wrist and started lifting him. He began to scream. Then, like a sack, they picked him up and hung him by the cuffs on a large hook. His shrieks were unearthly.

"We know you did it," one said casually. They walked back to their desks, and sat down, oblivious to the thrashing, kicking, and screaming. It was like an everyday occurrence. Hanging from the hook, flailing about, the prisoner looked and sounded like Uncle Bob's pig. I bowed my head, groaning involuntarily. My detective seemed more bugged by my sounds.

"Come with me." He stood up and led me out to the rows and rows of jail cells. The ten terrifying nights I spent in that cell, not knowing when and where I was going, the sounds of anguish and loneliness lasted for hours. The pained voices of men praying, crying for their mothers, protesting their innocence, all at the same time, in the dark murdered sleep. I was also wondering what the cops stole from my suitcase. A couple of nights, though, the mutterings and moans and out-loud talking to God were silenced by the sweet soft deep haunting sound of a voice singing Negro spirituals to himself.

Just as surprisingly and as suddenly as I had ended up there, I was awakened the morning of the eleventh day.

"Let's go, kid," the guard said. I followed him into the detectives' room. The same two detectives were there. The hook was empty. I was handed to the two uniformed officers who had brought me. Thankfully, they had my small suitcase. This time it accompanied me in the back seat to O'Hare where I was handed over to a new INS suit and handcuffed.

It was cold when we deplaned at Malton airport north of Toronto; a cold I enjoyed as a kid, but no longer. I was seventeen, jobless, homeless, and just under two dollars from being broke. As I write this, I find myself laughing in amazement and wonder. Was that really me shivering at the bus stop waiting to take a bus then a streetcar to Yonge and Carlton Streets?

I got off at the YMCA, a block from Maple Leaf Gardens. I had seen the building dozens of times going to standing-room only at the games, but could never imagine living there. With only one question or prying as to why I was there, a smiling man in his sixties led me to my own little room. It was a comforting feeling to be in a place without bars. And a solo shower. The one question he asked was if I had a family they could contact. I told them no.

At the end of the week I had a job, sorting boxes in a warehouse. The second week, I moved to a very small room with a small black and white TV set two blocks away. After a couple of months, I had a second job as a busboy at the restaurant on Eaton's Department store ground floor, not far from the tunnel below with those luscious ice cream waffles.

I spent almost nothing. I walked nearly everywhere. I ate at the restaurants and bought no clothes. Not even in winter. I seldom went to a movie. The thought of no longer being in the town that made them saddened me. In six months, I had saved a remarkable $500.00. There was no purpose for the savings. I wasn't saving for anything in particular. My little bankbook was like my little friend. One weekend, though, I went to the Loew's on Yonge Street. It was a film called *My Friend Irma*. I loved comedy teams, especially Laurel and Hardy and Abbott and Costello. I was curious to see this new comedy team, Dean Martin and Jerry Lewis, making their debut. I loved them. They were something I'd never seen on screen, a riot of undisciplined mayhem with out of control actions from Jerry Lewis that looked so spontaneous they could not be rehearsed. For months thereafter, I did this exaggerated warped impression of him for crew and customers when bussing my dishes. I'd walk like a spastic, legs and arms all bent, sometimes with my eyes crossed, screeching in that high nasally voice, "Hey, Dean. Dean, look at me!"

One of the customers who came in regularly for coffee, and who laughed heartily, finally introduced himself. His name was Louie, a Greek immigrant. In his mid-forties, always in a suit, I failed to notice that it was always the same suit. He was immensely charming. He said he left his successful restaurant business to come to Canada, where next spring he was going to start something revolutionary, a restaurant on wheels, a catering truck to go to all the new construction sites and office buildings.

"Maybe you'd like to work for me," he said. "One day get your own truck. Make a lot of money."

"I don't have a driver's license," I said.

A couple of times a week he came in and sat in the same spot. One day he showed me pictures of his family in front a small restaurant in Athens. "You know," he said, "I'm a gonna start my business sooner. No waste so much opportunity. You could still work with me. I drive, you sell"

"I can't sell," I said.

"Yessa, you can. You clean cut nice boy. People like you. I like you. We have a Woolworths on wheels. You don't a wanna be stuck in here forever, do you?"

"No," I answered, not really knowing where I'd want to be stuck.

"We get to know each other better. Sunday you come with me."

"Where to?" I asked.

"You see. I pick you up you place."

Sunday, I met him outside of my place. He was in his grey pinstriped, wrinkled suit. We boarded a streetcar, which he paid for. We got off at a crowded Greek church. Everyone knew him. Even the priest. They all flocked to him, chatting happily and loudly in Greek. He introduced me to everyone as his friend. We even attended the service. It was an extremely pleasant experience.

We did this every Sunday for a month, Louie telling me how rich he was going to get, adding a new truck to his fleet each week. He never mentioned money. I began to think he might be right. I began to think about it all the time. What if, in a couple of years, I was associated with a rich businessman. Maybe had my own truck or two. Surely, they would let a successful businessman back into America. This was the first time in almost a year that America crossed my mind.

The last Sunday, he did not take me to church. He took me to a used car dealer. The salesman greeted him by name, and led us to a used catering truck.

"This is a gonna be my first one, Chonny," he said confidently.

"Louie," I said, (I did not like calling him 'Louie' because he was so much older, but he insisted.) "Louie, if the catering business is so good, why is this here?"

The salesman answered for him. "The guy was doin' so good he traded this in for a new one."

"Chonny, come here." He put his arm on my shoulder and led me aside. "Chonny, I don't wanna you just work with me. I wanna you be my partner."

"How?" I asked.

"I have a thousand dollars. You get a thousand from you family, and we get rich. We have fun."

"Louie, I don't have a family."

"Everybody have a family!"

"No, Louie, not me. Sorry!"

He looked at me briefly, smiled, and patted my arm. "That's a okay. We get one soon." He walked back to shake hands with the salesman.

Like an idiot, I hollered out, "I have five hundred."

His eyes lit up. He raised his hands. "Stay there."

I didn't move. He chatted quickly with the salesman then rushed to me, grinning. "Youa bring you five hundred tomorrow, and we a gotta our first truck." He grabbed my hand. "Partner."

I took the next day off from sorting boxes, and withdrew my $500.00. The weird thing was I did not feel comfortable about it. It was like someone jumping out of a window, and halfway down changing their minds. But I couldn't stop myself. Because I was underage, Louie signed all the papers. In his name. He also did not have his thousand dollars. He said he had to send an emergency eight hundrend to his family in Greece. The two hundred he had left would go to painting the truck and a sign that said: "Louie and John's Fine Catering.' He had gotten the truck for just a $500.00 deposit. My five hundred. He promised to pay off his half of $250.00 weekly out of the profits.

The truck did look great. I quit both jobs. And Louie worked like a happy madman. With the enthusiastic help of half the lady parishioners, we were stockpiled immediately with the greatest sandwiches and goodies and drinks. I never saw Louie pay for any of it. They loved him. The first place he wanted to drive were the construction sites around Exhibition Park. He was right. We were swarmed. At the end of the first week we had made over $200.00 profit. He counted the coins like a gleeful Fagin in *Oliver Twist*, but did not offer me any of my $250.00. It was just our first week. I could wait.

The second week was different. We went to the same sites. The same workers taking their lunch breaks were there, but so was another catering truck, one a whole lot bigger and fancier. Everywhere we stopped, it stopped. No matter how many times we moved, so did it. Five straight days. We were being stalked by the motorized mafia. Our profits were almost cut in half. Louie said it was no problem. There were bigger construction sites in the West End. We'd drive there the next week. But there was no next week. At night, the truck was parked outside Louie's rooming house. Monday morning it would not start. A quick call to one of Louie's mechanic friends discovered someone had put sugar in the gas tank.

I had been in business for fifteen days and lost everything. I was unable to get my job back sorting boxes, but I got my busboy job back. I stopped doing my Jerry Lewis impression. And Louie stopped coming in for coffee. I tried to figure out what made me do something that I really didn't feel comfortable doing. Something so foolish. But I am worse at self-analysis than I am as a businessman. The truth is, I was more inclined to be superstitious about it. Losing the $500.00 might have been payback, as had my being caught and deported; Karmic payback for what I had done to Beverly.

In LA, I had made no effort to enquire about what might have happened to her, even though I thought of it often. When led off the plane at Malton Airport, the chill of the air was made colder with the realization I was back in the place where I might bump into her. If she were alive. I felt sick. I had run away. What if I had become my father? My thoughts were not about love. They were mostly about relieving the guilt.

I began saving money again. Every penny. This time with a purpose. I was going to go back to Los Angeles. I'd rather be hunted there, than haunted in Toronto. For weeks and months of going nowhere but to work, afraid of bumping into someone, I stayed home, watched TV, and pondered my problem. Dean Martin and Jerry Lewis were now on *The Colgate Comedy Hour,* but I found myself unable to laugh. I had to get that growing cowardly cancer out of my system. It was consuming me. I thought of "screwing my courage to the sticking place," as Lady MacBeth said, and just going and knocking on Beverly's front door. But what if she had killed herself and the father answered? He'd kill me. I phoned instead, from a payphone next to Maple Leaf Gardens, half a block away.

I fumbled the coin into the slot and, with my hand shaking, dialed. I counted to five rings, hoping they'd never stop. They did.

"Hello," a soft, warm woman's voice said.

"Hell… hello. .uh… is… is Beverly there?"

"Johnny? Johnny MacLaren?" the voice asked.

"Ye..ye..yes," I stammered in fear.

"No. She's not. She doesn't live here anymore."

Oh, God. Thank God! Hearing that I thought, *she's alive*. "Do you think I could talk to her?" I mumbled.

"I don't think that would be wise. She's married."

"How long?" I asked.

"Over a year."

This announcement startled me a bit. I gathered my breath before asking, "Does… does she have any children?"

"No. Not yet, but she's expecting."

Oh, God. Yippee. That horrible anguish poured out of me.

"But I don't think this conversation should be going any further, Johnny, so I'll be saying goodbye."

"Please tell her I called."

"I don't think that's a good idea."

"I'm glad she's doing well."

"So are we! Goodbye!" She hung up.

I did not place the phone in its cradle right away. I was looking at it in disbelief! You mean to tell me I suffered all this agony for all this time. For nothing? She lied. She lied. Goddamn it. She could live without me! I almost floated back to my room I was so relieved. I could walk to work or go to a movie or whatever, feeling liberated, thinking only about the day a few months off when I could sneak back into America without the heaviest weight in the world, emotional luggage.

IN AMERICA AGAIN

A Good Fit for A Misfit

Some people are just meant to be someplace where they were not born. Or where they grew up. For all of us I'm sure there's a spot somewhere on the planet where all the forces of nature and the universe somehow magically come together to embrace you, to welcome you. To make you more at peace. Lawrence became himself when he left the sceptered isle of England to roam the sands of Arabia; Gaugin put down his stockbroker's pen and departed to Tahiti to paint. Los Angeles was it for me. My geographical G-spot. I was back again, this time with less than the first time. No small suitcase, and less money. And, worse, back in the same streets where the FBI had scooped me up. I was attracted to it like a moth to flame.

Once again, I had gotten off at Union Station, hopped on an electric car, and made my way back to Hollywood. I got off fifteen blocks short of La Brea and the boarding house and the accountant, if he still lived there. I exited at Wilcox in front of the Warner's Theater, and a huge clock on the corner. With a twenty-dollar bill in each shoe, in case of emergency traveling money, I walked a block up to Yucca Street. There was a solid red brick six- or seven-story apartment building on the corner. I rented a room for a month. I would find out years later that this was the same building Carol Burnett and her mother lived in when they first came to LA. Probably at the same time. (It is still there.)

I started my new job. I was a chalkboard marker at E. F. Hutton's at Hollywood and Vine. Whenever a broker bellowed out a stock price change, I was the one marking it on a huge blackboard. I had no interest whatsoever in money or the markets, but I loved the noise and the energy, and watching the people, nearly all men. One of the things I learned soon was that 'experts' is a misnomer. Especially in finance. One morning the glass door was flung open, and a huge man, about six feet five, dressed casually, but wearing a huge cowboy hat, and carrying a black satchel, bellowed out in a country voice, "Bahy me fifty thousand shares uf Virgina Irion 'n' Coal." Everyone stopped, watching him plow his way through the crowd to his broker, twirling the bag over his head like a helicopter blade

I turned to my boss. "Who is that?"

"It's some rich kook from Pasadena who can never just phone in an order. He has to make an appearance, like Patton or MacArthur.

"Is he serious? Virginia Iron and Coal?"

"Oh, yes. He'll buy it!" he answered

I looked at the board. Virginia Iron and Coal was a dollar and an eighth. That meant the cowboy from Pasadena was going to plunk down nearly sixty thousand dollars, which he proceeded to do. He dumped stacks of money onto his broker's desk, some wrapped, some unwrapped, some falling to the floor, quickly retrieved by his broker. I had been there a few months and had nearly $500.00. I had never invested a nickel in the stock market, but if Virginia Iron and coal was good enough for this man, it was certainly good enough for me. I told my boss to buy me some.

"Don't be silly, John. Save your money. He's crazy!"

"He's also rich. He must know something."

"Who knows where he got his money! Probably inherited it. You can see he's a loon. Save it."

So I did. Two days later the stock was up to $2.50. I snuck over to another broker and bought 200 shares. At the end of the week, it was just over $4.00. That morning when the hat walked back in shouting, "Sell mah fifty thousand shares uh Vuginia Iron n Coal," I sold mine.

I had nearly doubled my money, but as with blackjack in Vegas, it gave me absolutely no satisfaction or sense of accomplishment. It was just a few extra dollars to pay more rent.

My apartment was on the third floor. I had two interesting neighbors. To my right was a handsome, stocky dark-skinned Cuban opera singer, a tenor, in his late thirties. His name was Manola Mera. We almost never spoke because I couldn't understand him, nor he me. I also could not understand what he sang when practicing a cappella, but whenever he did, which was often, I stopped everything to listen to a lyrical man's voice like none I'd ever heard. Whenever I bumped into him in the hall, I'd say, "Bueno voce. Bueno." He'd smile. "Gracias, amigo."

The elderly man on my left reminded me of an older Lenny. He became a bit of a mentor also. He, too, was Jewish. In his late 70's and not in good health, he shuffled rather than walked. So, he seldom left the room. He often left the door open, in case someone walked by he might want to say hello to. That was often me.

"Kid, c'mon in,' is how he invited me in every time he wanted to talk. And he loved to talk. There was nothing wrong with his voice. He never ran out of stories to tell about the absence of God in his life. They were never sad. Actually, they were often humorous, even when he told of his wife dying in her sleep.

"No one would have known it. In bed she was like that for years." He said it with a straight face. I fought chuckling. He looked at me, and added, "I found out when I tried to change the sheets."

I burst out laughing. "That is not true."

He raised his hand, pointing to the sky. "We Jews do not lie. We only exaggerate!"

Like Lenny, I loved listening to him. To save him a slow painful weekly trip, I began going to the corner market for him. His favorite was a pastrami on rye. I invited him a couple of times into my room. He always declined. When he felt the urge to talk, he'd knock on my door, and motion me to follow him. I always did. After a couple of weeks, he began talking about his son, an only child in his fifties. There was no sense of pride when he spoke of him, so I was stunned when he said, "He owns this Hamm's Brewery."

"You mean the one they advertise on TV?"

"Yeah. So, I get free beer and this apartment."

Hamm's was an extremely popular local beer, made more popular by its ditties sung by Lou Rawls.

"That's terrific," I said. "You must be very proud of him. Couldn't you be living with him?"

He pointed to the sky again, as if poking the God he didn't believe in. "If we lived in the same house in the same room with cots, he'd never visit me." He sounded like a great comic I got to see and work with years later, Jackie Mason. Even sad stuff sounded funny. "In two years he's never visited me once here. It's better to not talk to him here, than not talk to him there."

"That's kinda sad," I said.

"Here I can do what I want."

"That's true."

"He does send over a couple of people every month to look in on me, though."

Thinking he was talking about nurses or doctors, I said. "Oh, that's nice."

"Or I look in on them!" He chuckled, a huge sheepish grin on his face. I did not understand what he meant by that.

"Okay, kid. That's it. See yah tomorrow. On the 21st maybe you could meet my visitors."

I did not meet them nor did I want to when he gleefully offered to introduce me. I had forgotten it was the 21st. He had not. There was knock on my door. When I opened it, he said, quietly, "Kid, take a look." He scurried the few feet to his door and opened it. What I saw made me step back into my room, and just peek. Two of the most beautiful young women, in their early twenties, dressed to kill, or rather dressed to undress, were sauntering down the hall. There was nothing trashy about them. Separately you would not think they were hookers. They giggled as they approached him, calling his name. He said nothing. He opened the door wider for them, then closed it, singing the Hamms' commercial.

The noise of ladies' laughter lasted a long time. My God, I thought. He's almost eighty. He cannot be having sex with those girls. Or can he?

Our conversations became different. They were no longer about a mean nonexistent God or about life. They were about a sex life. Mostly his, and a little bit of mine, which I told him was nonexistent. He didn't believe me.

"Such a good lookin' young man. That's like eating soup with no matzo. You sure you don't want to meet my girls?" He was serious.

"No, no thank you. I am fine."

"Anybody without a little shtupin'is not fine … "

We both got quiet. I was uncomfortable. When we talked of other things, it was like we had something in common. Even through the age difference. However, talking about sex, we had nothing in common. I was too embarrassed to tell him I had not had one date in all this time.

"Kid, I don't do anything to these girls. They do it to each other. I just watch." He started to tell me what he watched, but I stopped him.

"Can I get you something from the market?"

He laughed. He knew I was changing the subject.

"You're a nice kid. A goyish mench."

In the months to come, he never mentioned his son again. Our conversations were less frequent. I did not have time for them. I was involved in a project that would make me rich and famous. The few times we did talk, it was again about the absence of God and the importance of kosher foods. Six months later, he died. I was told they found him on the floor, an unfinished pastrami sandwich in his hand. I wondered if the hirelings and his son showed up at the funeral. Or if God did.

The $64,000 Question

It was the mid-fifties. I was around twenty, and had avoided being caught for a few years. Loving it more and more in America, I was consumed with how to become legal. The only possible option was to marry someone. Being a recluse, my only entertainment being TV, made meeting girls impossible. There had to be another way. And there it was. Right in front of me. On television: *The $64,000.00 Question*.

Some guy won $64,000.00 for cooking knowledge. Are you kidding? Dr. Joyce Brothers, a psychologist, gained fame and first prize for knowing boxers. All they had to be were experts on one subject. The same was true for the other show I became addicted to, *Twenty-One*, hosted by Jack Barry, and created by Dan Enright, a man I would share an office with decades later. The guests on this show were as bright and appealing as the ones on the show hosted by Hal March. More than that, though, you could win fifteen times the money. A guy named Oberholzter won a million dollars. In those days, a million dollars was even big money at The Pentagon. If Oberholtzer, with a name that didn't sound American, had been illegal, with that fortune and fame he would be given a passport. That would be my passport. The *$64,000 Question*. All I had to do was figure out a subject and learn it. My first discarded choice was Edgar Rice Burroughs and his Tarzan books. I didn't think that was quite intellectual enough. Then Mark Twain, America's greatest writer, author of *Tom Sawyer, Huckleberry Finn,* and published after his death, *Letters to the Earth*. Perfect. Beginning my research, I discovered someone had already flunked that category.

I elevated my choice to the greatest writer in history, William Shakespeare. I saw Lawrence Olivier's *Hamlet* when I was fifteen. Of course, I didn't understand all the language, but I loved the theatricality of it. I did not fully appreciate it until I read it. *To be or not to be*. My God, I thought, how brilliant. How moving. A prince talking about suicide in six short words. Indeed, "Brevity is the soul of wit!" At the library, Shakespeare soon took the place of Burroughs. I loved the theater. Showbiz. This was a subject I could master.

I bought two large loose-leaf binders. I joined the public library five blocks down on Wilcox. Thankfully no ID was required. Lies sufficed. There were shelves and shelves of him. Two loose-leaf folders were not enough. I bought two more, and wrote small.

Day and night for two months I began my cataloguing, reading and making notes during my lunch breaks. Going nowhere. Only watching that show. Thirty-seven plays and 154 sonnets. The plays were broken down into categories, comedies, tragedies, and histories, then into one-line scene descriptions and characters. Hundreds of pages cluttered my kitchen table. Before I would put them in the binder, I'd test myself by picking up one at random. That endeavor was the only well-organized thing I ever did in my life, and it wasn't a chore. More than that, though, I was seeing myself on television, showing off my applause-getting knowledge. I was growing more and more confident.

I went to one of those arcades with a photo booth, had my picture taken for a quarter, and wrote a letter to the producers asking to be a contestant. To insure they'd pick me, I sent a carbon copy letter to Charles Revson, the president of their main sponsor, Revlon, in New York, and another to the president of Geritol, just in case I didn't qualify for *The $64,000 Question,* I'd end up on *Twenty-One.*

Walking to work or the library or to the market, I was quoting scenes from *Romeo and Juliet,* tirades from *Macbeth,* Marc Antony's funeral speech, and my favorite, *Richard the Third's* opening soliloquy, "Now is the winter of our discontent, made glorious summer by this sun of York." I talked to no one. Only myself. I was thinking in old English. Every day after mailing my letters, I rushed to the mailbox awaiting my invite. I hated Saturdays and Sundays. They just got in the way of Monday. I became more excited about my appearance and possible fame, and passport, because of the monstrous national media attention being paid to the handsome young potential big winner, Charles Van Doren. He was becoming bigger in America than Marlon Brando. He was becoming a cultural superstar. His name and face were everywhere.

He had a Jimmy Stewart appeal about him; a round affable face topped by curly dark hair. The son of a Pulitzer Prize winning poet, the most admired intellectual in the country since Einstein. I wanted him to win. Because the one thing that could top the wealthy son of a famous father winning $64,000 he didn't need was a poor kid with no parents. Me!

The whole country was waiting to watch and cheer this big winner. Instead, the nation got to watch the biggest losers in television history: Game shows.

My breakfast was interrupted by the news: the number one game show, *The $64,000 Question* was rigged. Charles Van Doren was a fraud. He had been given the answers. Sponsors pulled out immediately. My scrambled eggs came up immediately. The show was canceled immediately. The two other networks followed suit by canceling every quiz show. It was the domino effect of game show destruction. So much outrage from pulpit to press flooded Congress. Hearings were immediately set up to delve into what became known as "The Quiz Show Scandals."

Years later, there wasn't that much outrage or curiosity from Congress about the murder of President Kennedy. No such moral outrage exists in America today. No shows would be canceled. No one fired. They'd be reassigned to a different show. And Charles Van Doren would be given his own reality show to compete with the Kardashians.

I had literally puked my dreams and my guts out. With an empty stomach, and empty head, I had to face the fact that movie-induced daydreams were not for people like me. Magic does not happen. But luck does. And it soon happened to me when I got a job at Deluxe Film Labs as an IBM keyboard operator. But first, this Shakespearean aside.

I thought the quiz show incident was entirely out of my mind and forgotten like the four lost binders and a thousand other slings and arrows of outrageous fortune; evidently it wasn't. In 1994, Robert Redford directed a movie about that scandal, called *Quiz Show*. After ten years as a film critic, I had to quit to pursue my own shows. After doing so, I seldom went to the movies. But I did have this curious urge to see that one. One afternoon by myself, with popcorn and Coke in hand, I took an aisle seat in the very back corner at the Regal Theater. The theater was relatively full for a weekday screening. Ralph Fiennes played Charles Van Doren. Ralph is a very convincing actor, but I did not like him in this. Maybe because he became Charles Van Doren. When he got inside that glass cage to answer the questions he'd been given, I said out loud, "You asshole!" It was the only big laugh in the film. People turned to me, chuckling.

"Sorry," I whispered. I got up, leaving my popcorn and Coke.

Take Me Out to the Ballgame

I was as unlucky in trying to find a girlfriend, as I was inept. After looking at her smudged phone number for months, I even called Jack Owens' daughter. Her mother answered. Her daughter was on a date. A cute waitress at Tiny Naylor's was uninterested. Neither was one of the very pretty tellers at my bank. All I got out of her was a laugh when I said, "Oh, I guess with you I will just be depositing money." But unlike girls, finding jobs was easy. The one that unknowingly began to shape and change my life was at Deluxe Film Laboratories, a film processing plant for all the major studios.

My job was typing and sorting IBM cards. I did this standing. It was another mindless job. To keep mine from wandering, I would sometimes talk to myself. Once in a while, it was some low mumbling from Shakespeare, but I had heard and memorized a really funny comedy routine that had become number one on the radio. It was called, *What It Was, Was Football.*

This hick from the South had gone up North and was describing this new game he saw to his kinfolk in the Ozarks. The comic was Andy Griffith. During our coffee breaks, I was often asked to perform it, which I did. A black co-worker, a little older than me, would sing. He was so good a few of the guys put some money together, to which I contributed, so he could record a song. Sadly, nothing happened to it or him. But the breaks were wonderful. All my co-workers were men of all ages; our boss, with a really sharp, cutting wit, was from England. He was our resident critic. The only things talked about were movies, plays and performers. It was fun.

The standing, though, did get tedious. I loved and missed the physical activity of hockey, soccer, football, lacrosse, basketball. I only got to Santa Monica beach about once a month. Of course, I could have exercised, but I hated it. That required discipline, a good habit I never developed. In sports, everything is instinctive and reactive, and mostly competitive. And winning is such fun.

My boss, Al, was my size, but much better built and in his early thirties. During a break, he asked "Johnny, in Canada, do they do something other than hockey?" Everyone chuckled.

"Every summer," I said. "Hardball."

"Our team is softball. Really soft." He smiled. "What position?"

"Mostly second, sometimes catcher."

"Are you any good?"

"Better behind the plate," I said. "I like to be active all the time, and I get to talk to the batter."

"Can you hit?"

"Switch-hitter actually. About .250 from either side."

"Good enough."

"But I bat a thousand with my mouth!"

He smiled. "How'd you like to play on our team?" A few of the guys cheered. "We have a studio league and play every week over on Gardner.

Would you like to join us?" It was an answered prayer that turned out to be a scarier one.

"We're playing Fox. Our catcher's on location. How's your arm?"

"Not as good as my mouth."

He laughed. "You really can hit?"

"I can strike out from either side."

They were all smiling, giving me a thumbs up. It was nice to be liked.

He continued, "I'll call Ray. See you Wednesday?"

I arrived at the field early; not because I was anxious, which I was, but because I am always early. For everything. One of my few good habits. The games were scheduled late, close to 9 p.m. because of the long hours of players working at the studios.

My new glove in hand, I sat in the bleachers waiting for my supervisor, watching the players warming up. There were only a couple my age. Most were in their thirties or forties, even a couple in their sixties.

"Ray, this is Johnny. Our catcher tonight."

It was Al, with two smiling men; a slender pale-skinned man, probably in his late forties, and a fellow a couple of years older than I was who could have been an actor with dark wavy hair; dark eyes, and a constant grin.

"Johnny, this is Ray Livingston, our captain, and this is Billy, his assistant. Billy Howard. Fellas this is Johnny Barbour."

Once introduced to everyone, I was anxious to play to show a bunch of old guys how well I could really play that game. I got to catch, but not very often. The ball was lobbed so softly it seldom got past the plate. Nearly everybody got a hit. There was a lot of whooping and hollering and some toasting. Our team, from Paramount, I was informed, was drubbed seventeen to twelve.

"Johnny, you got two hits. That's great." Ray was patting me on the back. "Welcome to the team. They outscored us, but we'll outdrink them. Are you coming?'

"Oh, no thanks, sir. I don't drink."

"Neither do I. But join us anyways." I was surprised at how softspoken, almost gentle, he was.

I felt a little out of place. "No, thanks very much. I have stuff to do."

"We'll see you next week, then."

I watched them all strut happily and noisily to their cars.

I stayed up late, so delighted I had something athletic to do, to look forward to every week with a bunch of nice guys. Our team had been called Paramount, but I did not think it was Paramount Pictures, not the movie studio. Just a company called Paramount. At work, Al, in a voice that had a happy hangover edge to it, told me how well I had done, and how much Ray liked me. How could he like me? We barely talked.

"Al," I asked, "your team…uh…our team is called Paramount, but since we don't work at Paramount, is it Paramount Pictures?"

He laughed. "Yeah. Most of the teams have ringers. Warners, Republic, Universal, last night Fox. but they have to be employees!"

"Is Ray an employee?"

He laughed louder.

"Ray's a star. He and his partner, Jay Evans, are two of the best songwriters in the business. Livingston and Evans, *Buttons and Bows,* the Bob Hope movie."

"You're kidding," I gasped. And I mean, I gasped.

Al was delighted at my naivety.

"Does Billy work there, too?"

"Billy Howard? He's assistant head of the mailroom there."

"Wow." I said. "He looks like he could be an actor."

Al smiled. "He's just the son of one. Dorothy Lamour's son."

"Are you kidding?" l said even louder.

I had shaken hands and played ball with Dorothy Lamour's son, the gorgeous brunette in the sarong in those "Road" pictures with Hope and Crosby. How exciting. And I'd get to do it every week.

An Offer I Couldn't Refuse

The night of the games, I never thought about hitting, catching, running or the score. What my buddies liked and encouraged was my running Don Rickles-like commentary about the opposition. Our last game was with Universal; their last batter was a leading production executive. He came to the plate with men on base and two out. And us with just a one-run lead. I welcomed him loudly: "Here's the only guy on your team that's had fewer hits than your studio." Howls. He would have missed a beach ball. Three straight whiffs! Our sudsy celebration was a joy. I had begun to join them at the late-night bar on Formosa, and was always invited to sit next to Ray. We both drank Cokes. The season was over.

"See ya next year, Johnny. You were great. It was a ball havin' you." Ray patted me on the back.

"You're fun," Billy said. "Can't wait till next season."

"Thanks," was all I could manage. I exited with them. They were walking to the parking lot, and I, as always, was walking home.

Suddenly, Billy said, "Hey, Johnny, how'd you like to work with me in the mailroom?"

I was staggered. Over the weeks, I couldn't even allow myself to daydream about such a wonderful job. Once they ran the background check, I'd even be off the team, and running. I would have embarrassed everyone.

"You could start a week from Monday." Billy got right in front of me. Ray watched us, smiling.

"Well?" Billy asked.

I thought maybe I should just say no thanks. I like where I am, but nothing came out.

"You'd love it and I'd love to have you." Billy couldn't have been nicer. Except for the game, I didn't know him. Or Ray.

"Well, Johnny?" Ray asked.

"I'd…love it, but…but…when…they run a background check, uh, they'll find that I didn't finish high school." That was as close as I could come to the truth.

Ray laughed. "You don't need a master's in mailing to work for Billy. Christ. For him it was a demotion being in the mailroom. He went to UCLA for God's sake. For you it's a promotion."

I blurted, "I'd love that!"

They shook my hand. "Wonderful," Billy said. "I'll talk to my boss. He loves smart-mouths, and Ray'll talk to personnel."

Frozen to that spot, watching them walking and chatting to their cars, I was much more frightened than excited. Had I made another mistake with my mouth?

Billy turned and shouted, "A week from Monday, eight o'clock, the Marathon main gate. There'll be a pass for you. I'll meet you."

And they were gone.

The following day I felt really sheepish and terrible telling Al about what had been offered to me. I apologized, assuring him I had in no way solicited Billy's offer. He put his arm around my shoulder. "Are you kidding, kid? That's terrific. You'll do great there. As a matter of fact, that's always where I thought you'd end up."

"In a studio?" I asked with disbelief.

"No, a mailroom!" He howled at his joke. "I'll still see you next year."

I had no idea of what was going to happen to me when I showed up at The Paramount gate. I was uneasy, but curious. Also, even under the worst pressures or conditions, it always felt nice when people were nice to me. It always came as a surprise. The biggest surprise, though, was that they hired me on the spot. The only background check was my previous pleased employers.

Some Say Cheese Better Than Others

The mailroom at Paramount was right in the middle of the lot on the west side of the ground floor of a production building. The writers' offices were upstairs, which shows you what Hollywood really thinks about writers; just a few steps above mail boys. In front was a bike rack that I never used. I preferred to walk, or even to run. The oldest mail boy was a balding German immigrant in his late thirties. One lived in the exclusive Hancock Park area nearby. He was the six-foot two-inch son of the president of a large retail chain who wanted to do nothing on his days off, except fish and hunt, and avoid his father. And Billy, my boss. I was the youngest and the most eager.

Stars I'd seen a few years earlier in the Manor Theater in Toronto were on the streets, in the cafeteria, on the stage, in the elevator: Spencer Tracy and Robert Wagner making *The Mountain.* Humphrey Bogart, William Holden and Audrey Hepburn making *Sabrina.* (I once wandered through the open door of Holden's dressing room when he failed to answer the knock, and found him making real love to a woman who was not his co-star. They didn't stop when they looked up and saw me. He just told me to leave the mail and close the door. There was also Clark Gable making *Teacher's Pet*; Fred Astaire and Audrey Hepburn making a musical, Chuck Heston making a western and then *The Ten Commandments.* Frank Sinatra, whom I'd seen in Lake Tahoe, was making *The Joker is Wild*; Kirk Douglas making a western, Tony Perkins sitting in the middle of the street, barefoot, in ragged jeans reading poetry, making all the traffic go around him. This was prior to *Psycho*, a part for which he was perfectly cast. The movie he was making then was with Sophia Loren. It was a screen version of an Eugene O'Neill play. Perkins was the love interest to Sophia in the film. Only in Hollywood could they create such make-believe. Tony Perkins making love to Sophia Loren would be like trying to irrigate the Sahara with an eye-dropper!

One afternoon, months after that film had wrapped, I was about to get in the elevator to take mail to Paramount's brilliant glamor photographer, Bud Fraker, when a woman's foreign voice said, "Coulda you hold ona please?" As I stepped in and turned, moving in right next to me was Sophia Loren. She had a big smile and a big "thanka you!" And big breasts. She was my height, looking at me deliberately, eye to eye. Her presence literally gave me the shakes. She was going to Bud's studio for a glamor shot, already dressed for it. Or, undressed for it.

"Going to see Bud?" she asked.

I could barely nod. The elevator stopped. She exited first and I watched her walk away. She looked just as good from the back. I ran past her, dropped Bud's mail in his basket, retreating as quickly as I could. She chuckled, watching me scurry about. As I passed her on the way back to the elevator, she said, "Tomorrow, I'ma ona stage 5."

Why would one of the world's most famous sex symbols be saying such a thing to such a clumsy kid? I certainly wouldn't have anything to say to her, but the next day on my lunch break I was on stage 5. The sign on the door said: "Houseboat."

I walked in slowly, staying close to the back wall. The crew was making preparations to shoot a scene aboard the deck of this houseboat. The Director was talking to Sophia and her co-star, Cary Grant. *Jesus Christ.* I thought, *that's the guy in the convertible who tried to pick me up*. It was all too weird.

Sophia spotted me and waved. She was so natural and appealing, it was difficult not to gawk. During filming, it seemed almost as though Cary Grant wasn't even in it. His performance looked like a casual rehearsal. He was so low key he didn't appear anything like that amazing classy one-of-a-kind sparkling talent that filled the screen. Sophia filled the stage.

One of the wonderful perks of a mail boy was the freedom to wander anywhere on the lot at almost any time. Every day at ten a.m. they screened the dailies. And every day at ten, I'd clamber into the projectionist booth to watch the actors, directors, and producers below, watching the previous day's shoots. Once I was almost caught. The daily was a scene from *Sabrina* with Humphrey Bogart and William Holden. Aside from women, Holden had an affection for booze. In this scene, he had blown a line, or knocked something off a table as he turned to Bogart. I could not hear his line. I guess Bogey couldn't either. He said straight faced to his co-star in that beautiful sharp-edged voice, "What the fuck was that?" I blurted from above, "Wow!" *Oh my God. Oh my God. Did you hear that? Humphrey Bogart uses the F word.* I retired quickly down the back stairs.

Soon, I was watching the previous day's shoot from the scene with Sophia Loren and Cary Grant, but I barely saw or heard Sophia at all. She was not filling the screen, even though she was filling that blouse. It was Cary Grant. Something weird had happened. I couldn't help it. I found myself drawn to him. On the set he had been less, on the screen he was more. How did he do that? He didn't. The camera did. The camera loved him and you could tell, he loved the camera. I went back to stage 5 whenever I could to watch the finish of the film. Sophia waved to me often, but it was Cary Grant I came to watch, a consummate artist at work. Only once after that, years later, did I run across that kind of camera charisma in an actor, when a seeming nothingness in person was transformed into stardust when filtered through a lens. That actor-turned-governor was Ronald Reagan. That time it was a television camera. And I was interviewing him.

Extras, Extras!

Nobody could quite figure out why a middle-aged, highly educated balding German was delivering mail. He knew everyone it seemed; stars, writers, directors, producers, executives; some, even from other studios, would call him periodically. And often he was off to lunch with them, or at their places over a weekend. His elite connections were a mystery, and a lively source for rumour and innuendo. He didn't seem in the least demeaned by hopping on a bike to peddle around a basket of mail. Actually, he seemed relaxed doing it. Other than to say 'good morning' or 'hello,' we never spoke, even when we sat next to one another waiting our turn. One noon hour it surprised me when he said, "You vonted like to be un aktor, Ja?"

It took me a moment to answer. I nodded reluctantly. I had never mentioned this to anyone. I figured that's the last thing anyone would want to hear around a studio from some kid delivering mail. It would be an easy way to get yourself fired.

"How vould you like to do a little extra verk?'

"They'd probably can me," I said.

"No, not here. On your days off. Nobody vould know. I vouldn't say nussing."

Somehow, through this enigma sitting next to me, I ended up with a day's extra work in two films. When I showed up as instructed and introduced myself to the first assistant director, I was treated like minor royalty. (What was this Kraut selling or doing for these people?) I was crowd background in *Love Me or Leave Me* at MGM with Jimmy Cagney and Doris Day. When the camera was on, my job was to watch with admiration, which was easy. I did that when the camera was off.

During downtime, Cagney would retreat behind the sets and take up his place at a makeshift poker table stuck in the middle of a pile of sets. His five opponents were the electricians and prop men working on the film. I stood fifteen feet to Cagney's left. He nodded and smiled once. Amazing. They played for quarters and dollars. I never saw a more congenial, joyful poker game in my life. Over the years, I ran into very few major stars as gracious as Jimmy Cagney. Onscreen, he had often terrorized me as the essence of evil, especially in *White Heat* standing atop that burning water tower screaming, "Look, ma, look at me!" and cackling with sociopathic glee as he burns to death. It was impossible to imagine that that person could ever exist, even in make-believe, in that sweet man who was so much more at home with the other men who make the movies.

In my other film as an extra, I got to holler, not just watch. And once or twice I hollered when I wasn't supposed to. The movie was *Trial,* starring Glenn Ford. It was one of those many predictable, cumbersome, preachy anti-communist clunkers that Hollywood pounded Americans over the head with in the Joe McCarthy fifties. I didn't know that until I saw it. It wouldn't have made any difference anyway. I loved doing it.

The all-day outdoor shoot was on the campus of a Santa Monica High School. In the film, some Mexican kid had raped a white girl. The culprit was inside the locked school being shielded and protected by a teacher from an irate mob of real Americans. I was one of them. We were trying to batter our way through the door using a telephone pole. When instructed to yell that the teacher was a commie, I screamed for blood. Glenn Ford was the kid's lawyer from the ACLU. He was just an observer of the fracas, awaiting his moment to be the star and save the kid and the day for law and order and the American way. For four hours of takes and retakes and different angles, the battering and hollering continued until hundreds of extras and their stomachs began to growl. We were getting hungry. And tired. So, when the second assistant ordered a stop and a setup for a new angle, I spoke up loud enough to be heard. "Sir, when do we eat?"

The mob that was screaming just seconds before, then grumbling, was instantly silent. And still.

"Who said that?" the second assistant demanded.

Not thinking I'd done anything wrong, I raised my hand. All you could hear was the mob's breathing while the stocky assistant walked purposefully toward me.

"What's your name?" He stood at the edge of the crowd.

"John," I said, fearing I was about to be dismissed in front of what had just been my battering buddies.

"John what?" he hissed.

"John Barbour."

"Well, John Barbour, my name's Earl, and you know what I can do? I can tell you when you are hungry. Do you understand that?"

"Yes, sir," I stammered.

"And you're not hungry, are you?" he declared

"No, sir."

"And you're ready to get back into position for the new setup, aren't you?"

"Yes, sir," I said, thankful I wasn't drummed out of mob service.

"Okay, then, let's go. Crew, onto the roof!" He looked at me. "Everyone here hold your positions. Exactly. Don't move. We're matching from above."

With that, scores of technicians and camera people made their way through the school hallways up to the roof, and began their new setup. We had to stand in our positions, or close to them, while all this was going on. To relight with reflectors and to set the cameras took almost another hour. When the setup was complete, Earl stood three stories up on the roof and hollered through a megaphone, looking like a young Cecil B. DeMille, "Extras resume position." We did, and while I was picking up the front of the telephone pole, I thought he didn't have to call us extras. What a jerk!

"Action!" finally came the director's call from the roof. We pounded and hollered and screamed for Mexican blood, exclaiming that we were honest taxpayers and had the constitutional right to kill the little wetback. We had to repeat it again. And again. Why? It was always the same! My stomach was killing me. It must have been six hours since breakfast. The scores of extras around me were morphing into a real mob. I couldn't take it. I let go of the pole, made my way down the concrete stairs through the crowd, and out into open space. I stopped and looked to the roof.

"Hey, Earle!" I hollered. I expected my grandstanding boldness would get a supportive cheer from my famished compatriots. Instead, it got deathly quiet. Even on the roof. Everyone stopped and looked down at me, then at Earl. Even the director stopped and looked. I felt alone, scared, and soon to be unemployed. I wanted to say, *Oops. I'm sorry.* Instead, I stepped forward and hollered Earle's name again. I didn't give him a chance to answer. I screamed at the top of my lungs, louder than I had screamed for Mexican blood. "Am I hungry yet?"

The director, Mark Robson, moved to the edge of the roof and yelled down, "Lunch!" He laughed amidst the mob's cheers. As we hurried to the truck, I saw Glenn Ford and Dorothy Malone eating a sandwich and chuckling at me. I thought, *God, I just love showbiz*!

Another Greek with Another Idea

Directly across from the mailroom was the studio's Still Department; this is where they filed and mailed the thousands of eight-by-ten glossies to fans and the media. The fellow who ran it was a nervous fellow named Angelo. I won't mention his last name because I'm sure some of his relatives are still in Chicago selling their famous buns.

Angelo was thirty-two, but looked fifty-two. His hair was prematurely grey; his shoulders were slightly hunched like he was carrying a load. He was awash with more tics and twitches than any human I'd ever seen. His body language was a recently caught fish out of water. He could not sit still without his right leg pumping up and down like it was attached to a runaway sewing machine. If he tried to sit still for more than twenty minutes, he would reach his right hand behind his head, turn his head slightly to the left, then grab his left cheek and yank his head forcefully further back, producing a loud cracking sound from his neck and a sigh from his lips. When I asked him if he learned that from a chiropractor, he said he hadn't, stating proudly that he'd discovered the maneuver himself.

He took an immediate liking to me. I think one of the reasons for that was he seemed pleased to hear I had no father. So, when we talked he knew he didn't have to hear about mine. Just his. His father, an old-country Greek, had built an extremely successful bakery in Chicago, which he expected and trained Angelo, his only son, to take over. But Angelo loved the movies. As a kid after school or after making bread and buns, he'd sneak off to the nearest theater. On his thirtieth birthday, he was to be made a full partner. Instead, Angelo boarded a plane to Los Angeles and Hollywood. When he arrived, he called his father to apologize, to tell him he really wanted to be in show business. His father couldn't hear him through his own screaming. The next day Poppa was on a plane to drag his grown son back.

Good for Angelo, he wouldn't budge. His father wasn't in town two hours. Every week for two years Angelo got a call from his father. Each started with soft begging and ended with loud ancient Greek curses. His father screamed he had no talent to make movies, that he was lucky he had talent to make buns, and that's only because his father had taught him.

To prove to himself and his family he was there to stay, he bought a bungalow. It was on Gower Street between Hollywood and Sunset. And to prove to them all how much he loved showbiz, and to enrage them further, he married a Jewish girl. The wedding was unattended by anyone from the family. The calls and curses stopped.

I wanted to see Angelo succeed almost as much as he did. He loved being at Paramount. He had no interest in acting. Just the production end of it. His idol was Spiro Skouras, who became the Greek head of 20th Century Fox. Angelo wanted to be a producer, the man in charge and the house on Gower Street, he told me, was where he'd begin his climb to Hollywood fame and a bun-free life. For months that little bungalow became our artistic and creative center. Acting classes were held here. Little theater productions were rehearsed there. Workshops with guest speakers were held there. And sometimes, unapproved couplings took place in the back rooms. The place was alive with talent and testosterone.

One day, Angelo was sitting in his huge sofa chair next to the front door. He looked a little more forlorn than usual. His head was lower and his leg pumping fast. "Do you know who Andy Fennady is?" he asked.

"No, who's that?"

"He's at Paramount now. He's a Greek. About my age. He wrote a low-budget script that he made a movie out of on his own. Got another guy to direct it. Irv Kirshner. And Paramount signed him to a deal." He stared into some far-off place.

"That's terrific. Good for him," I said.

After a hushed moment, Angelo said, "I can't write."

"Angie, you don't know unless you try."

"If you were going to write a low budget film, how would you do it?" he asked.

"Well, obviously, I'd have it all take place outside and in one day. That way there'd be no sets or lighting and little cost. And make it a western."

"Johnny, I have ten thousand dollars. If you could do something like that, maybe we could shoot it in 16mm! We know a bunch of good actors and you could be in it. Get some real film on yourself."

"Angie, I can't write. You could do it better than me. I don't know the first thing about this stuff."

"l could pay you. How about five hundred dollars?"' He sat up and stopped twitching.

"Angie, I wouldn't want your money for something I've never done."

"Would you try it? Please?"

"I don't know that I could make anything up."

"Sure, you could. And I *will* pay you!"

"No, I don't want anything. Give me a couple of weeks and let's see what I come up with."

He jumped up, embracing me "That's great. That's great."

"Can I borrow your typewriter?" I asked

Two weeks later, I returned his typewriter, along with a script. It was called *The Sun Sets in Hell*. All the action took place in one day. Four bank robbers bungle a job, kill a clerk, two are wounded, and while escaping through desert and mountains chased by an unseen posse, they begin to unravel emotionally and as friends. At the end, we discover one of the thieves was not such a bungler. Angelo loved it. He would have loved the Yellow Pages. Two days later he came bounding into the mailroom and pulled me outside. He could barely contain himself.

"Johnny, Johnny. Tomorrow I'm delivering the script in person to Lindsay Parsons. He's the biggest producer for Allied Artists. Andy set it up. We're on our way. I'll let you know what happens."

For three long days, Angelo developed new twitches. His wife was certain that any moment his excitement would give him a heart attack. The fourth day, while reading actors for our script, the phone rang. Angelo leapt like a cat catching a fly.

"Yes. Yes, sir. Yes, sir. Thank you. Thank you. We'll be there." Angelo cradled down the receiver gently, saying in awe, "That was Lindsay Parsons. Johnny, we have a meeting at his office on Cahuenga on Friday."

We all whooped while his wife hugged and kissed him.

"Unbelievable," I said.

"Johnny, what you won't believe is that Barry Sullivan will be there, too. He wants to direct it." The whooping and hollering lasted the rest of the night. No one could concentrate on anything, except making a movie.

The Meeting

Lindsay Parsons' small office building was on a side street just off Cahuenga Boulevard, a quarter mile from Universal Studios. It was the best looking building on the short block, nestled up against a hill coated in concrete. It had a massive, ornate, polished wood door, the kind that should belong to a producer who made Westerns. We had wisely parked a block away, and walked. It was the prudent place to park Angelo's unwashed ten year-old Dodge.

Angelo whispered urgently, "Johnny, just watch what you say, you know. You tend to wise-off."

I said, "I'll watch my mouth, if you watch your leg."

"What's my leg got to do with anything?"

"Just keep it still." I smiled.

Angelo opened the door nervously. The interior was even more ornate and polished than the door. The receptionist was on her feet and smiling. She led us straight into Mr. Parsons' office. Already sitting there were four men, laughing and chatting. Mr. Parsons got up from a desk three times the size of his front door. He was about Angelo's size, a little thick of body and thin of hair, with a warm smile and voice. He introduced us to the other three men who also rose to greet us: Haskell Wexler, totally unknown to us at the time, but a brilliant cinematographer who years later did *Medium Cool, Who's Afraid of Virginia Wolf*, and won an Oscar for *Bound for Glory*; Barry Sullivan and his agent were also there. It was all so Hollywood, like a scene out of a movie. Our movie! I was directed to sit next to Mr. Sullivan. I was ten when I saw him in his first film, a musical with Ginger Rogers called *Lady in The Dark*, and there I was shaking his hand. My stomach began to feel like Angelo's leg.

All three complimented me on the script. Barry Sullivan said he had wanted to become a director for a long time, but found nothing that impressed him until *this script*. Haskell told us he was having membership issues with the Guild of Cinematographers, that he'd get them resolved, that he loved the script's grittiness, and would do it cheap if he had to. Everyone laughed except Angelo and me. We were stupefied with disbelief.

Finally, Mr. Parsons stood up to shake hands and say goodbye. "Boys, congratulations. You're going to make your first movie."

Angelo and I walked casually to the door. Outside, we ran and skipped to his hidden dirty Dodge. We were wordless, afraid to break the spell. Did what just happened really happen?

Angelo turned the key, gunned the accelerator and headed to the freeway. We were on it for five full minutes, still silent. As we passed the Hollywood Bowl on our right, we looked at each other and, as if on cue, rolled down our windows, stuck our heads out, screaming, "We're gonna make a movie! We're gonna make a movie! We're gonna make a fucking movie! Hollywood here we come."

When we got to Angelo's, his wife said there was a message from Mr. Parsons' office that they were preparing papers to be signed in a few days and that we'd be notified when we'd start and how much we'd make. We talked and giggled for hours. Not one word was said about the money we'd make; only the movie we'd make.

In a few days, though, we'd found out what every veteran writer, director and producer already knows: making a movie in Hollywood is like making love; the couplings are pleasant, but seldom lead to a birth.

The Waiting Game

For three days it was impossible to eat or sleep. We talked *ad nauseam* about the phone call. When would it come? What would he say? We paced like caged animals. Angelo's wife, Molly, snapped, "Jesus Christ, would you guys calm down or go in the back room?"

I had my own place, but Angelo insisted I stay with him and Molly, just in case the call came. I slept in the back room on top of the covers; who knew what kind of condition the sheets were in from all the rehearsals? I stared into the quiet darkness, trying to fight the happy visions popping up before me. But what if it didn't come true? How would I cope with it? I would soon find out.

The morning of the fourth day while Molly was at work, Angelo leaped over furniture to grab the ringing phone. His eyes lit up. "Yes. Yes, Mr. Parsons. I'm fine, sir. How are you?"

As he listened, the sparkle in his eyes went out, the color drained from his face. It was an open book I did not want to read. "Thank you, sir. Thank you. It was really nice of you to call. It was also a real pleasure meeting you. Yes. Yes, I hope there will be another time."

The call over, he held the phone in the air. To cradle it meant the call was over. Ended. As was his dream. I did not take it nearly as hard. Making a movie was not my dream. I was just back where I was a few weeks earlier. I felt horrible for Angelo.

"What'd he say?" I asked.

Angelo was fumbling with the phone and receiver, shaking. "He... said...that...that even though everybody liked the script, Allied Artists doesn't want to be in the business of making any more Westerns."

"Jesus," I mumbled.

"He thought the plot might lend itself to being a gangster film. And if we rewrite it, to bring it back." He paused, studying me. "Do...do you think you could?"

I had no desire to rewrite the first thing I'd ever written. "It wouldn't work as a gangster film. It's a Western," I said flatly. "But maybe you can find someone to try it. It's all yours." Angelo's heartbreak had been too difficult to watch. I stayed away from his house for weeks. I avoided him at work. Not even a call. It was just too painful. Then my phone rang. It was Haskell Wexler.

"Johnny," Haskell said in his happy, high-pitched voice, "sorry about Allied, but that shit happens all the time in this business."

"Angelo hasn't given up on it. He's still pursuing it," I lied.

"Could you set it aside for a bit? I have something better for you. An adaptation. Could you write an adaptation?"

"You mean like from a book?"

"A very big book, soon to be a very big book."

"Haskell, I've never done anything like that. This was my first attempt at writing."

"I know you could. You're a natural. I gotta go now, but I'll call you and you'll come up to my place. You'll meet the family and I'll give you a copy, tell you about it. Why it's gonna be big, and we'll get started. And you'll get paid. Okay?"

"Yeah, yeah," I muttered. Surprisingly, I was not excited after what I'd just been through. Of course, I wondered what the book could be. I also wondered if I should call Angelo. Maybe he could be a part of it. I decided against it. What if it led to another disappointment? I couldn't even call to ask how he was holding up.

A couple of days later, Molly called. She was leaving Angelo, and Angelo was leaving LA. He was going back to Chicago to the bakery business. His father had won, Angelo had lost.

"When's he leaving?"

"Tomorrow," she replied.

"And you're not going?"

"Fuck no. I filed for divorce weeks ago."

"Wow, that's too bad, Molly. I'm sorry. If you do talk to him, please wish him well for me."

"Aren't you gonna call him?"

"I think he'd be too embarrassed to talk to me. He'll call if he wants to."

"Well, Johnny, I'm in town. I got a job at The Directors' Guild. We could have lunch one day."

"That'd be nice. Talk soon." I hung up. I never did see her again. Unattended lunches in Hollywood are more frequent than unmade promised movies.

I imagined Angelo with his father, sitting next to each other on the plane in first class. Was having a father like that better or worse than having no father? Long ago images of my father, images that should have been blurred by then, were somehow becoming increasingly sharper. I knew one day I'd pursue him the way Angelo's father had pursued his son.

Haskell's call came the day Angelo left. His happy, welcoming voice cheered me up. He gave me the address to his home in the Hollywood Hills. The book he wanted me to look at was titled *A Long Day in A Short Life* written by Albert Maltz, a writer who was currently blacklisted. I had only a fleeting notion of what he was talking about. All the constantly blasting blacklisting news almost daily in the media, and all the House Un-American Activities stuff, was just background noise to me. Whenever that mean-looking Senator named McCarthy popped up calling everyone commies, I turned off the set or the radio. He sounded like the accountant who got me deported. What did I know? I cared even less. Instead, I was waiting to read Maltz's book. And cash Haskell's checks.

What's A Blacklist?

Haskell's house was a mile up in the Hollywood hills not far from Laurel Canyon, just below Mulholland. It was the kind of home or villa you'd see in an Italian movie, perched on the side of a hill overlooking the Mediterranean. The Mediterranean, in this case, was a panoramic view of Los Angeles and Hollywood below. This awesome sight over forty yards of luscious gardens was totally unobstructed. The front entrance was surprisingly close to the sidewalk, and, of course, like a lot of mansions, was white stucco.

I had barely touched the doorbell chime when I heard horrific barking. Haskell, two books in hand, opened the door, smiling and restraining a very aggressive German shepherd. "Blackie, say 'hello.' This is Johnny. Come on in." When I hesitated, he led the dog to another room and then hollered for me to come in.

The interior was right out of *The Great Gatsby*. The first room I stepped into was an auditorium-sized dining room with no separation from the equally large living room. There were floor-to-ceiling windows. The wall separating the dining room from the kitchen was a library-sized bookcase with not one space for another book.

Standing to greet me were Haskell's wife, Marion, and their young son, Mark. If Quakers held beauty contests, Marion could have been a contestant. She wore no makeup, had a striking face and smooth creamy skin. She never spoke above a whisper. The son seemed like any other kid of that age. I found out later while house-sitting that Blackie was more housebroken and potty-trained than the boy. A child psychiatrist was summoned to the house almost as often as the cleaning lady.

Over the months I got to know them, they made no secret of their son's only act of inexplicable rebellion, something he never did around me. When the shrink showed up, I always retreated. I didn't want to be near or hear anything about another family that might in some way be dysfunctional, no matter how minor. It was none of my business. For inviting me into their home and lives, I developed a deep fondness for them. Especially Haskell. He was in his late thirties, thin and tall with a voice that always seemed to be smiling. He turned out to be the brightest, most articulate, intelligent, and passionate person I'd ever met at that point. His passion was for justice. And equality. It was the first time I'd heard such talk from anyone.

With that first visit, he led me to the living room, two books still in hand, directing me to sit. He sat opposite me on the sofa, leaning forward. "Have you heard of Maltz?" he asked.

I didn't want to be frivolous, but when I get nervous I am inclined to be. "The only malts I've heard of are chocolate and vanilla."

He did not smile. "Albert Maltz is one of the blacklisted writers who refused to testify before HUAC and was–"

"What's HUAC? Sorry, I don't know. I hope that doesn't bother you."

"Not at all. It may be an asset because you can come to this book unprejudiced. The House UnAmerican Activities Committee. He refused to testify and was sentenced to a year for not answering their questions, admitting to whether or not he was a commie, and for refusing to name names."

"I don't quite understand something. Remember, I'm Canadian. I don't know much about what goes on down here other than movies, but don't you guys have what they call a Constitution?"

His head flew back. He howled with laughter. "Oh, my God, that is so perfect. Wait until I tell my brother."

"Anyway, while Maltz was in prison, actually county jail, he wrote this book." Haskell handed one of the books to me. I looked at the cover. There was a picture of a jail cell and the title: *A Long Day in A Short Life.*

I looked up at Haskell. "What's the other book?"

Haskell held it up. "A great book by William Bradford Huie. *The Execution of Private Slovik.* About the only soldier, the only American soldier, ever executed for desertion. The book in your hand is going to be in demand soon. I own it. I bought the rights to it the other day. That's why I didn't call you right away until I heard I had them."

He let this all sink in, but I wasn't sure what was sinking in. It sounded all so important and urgent, but Greek to me.

Haskell stood, jabbing the air with the book. "Frank Sinatra bought the rights to the Huie book. He's made a deal at Columbia to make it. And to top it off, Sinatra has hired Albert to do the screenplay. He had the balls to hire Albert who'll now come off that fucking un-American blacklist and his books will be hot properties." He handed me the other book. "I want you to read both. Then I want you to do a screenplay of Albert's. Do you think you can?"

I was flabbergasted. I felt like a hungry derelict, suddenly placed in front of an endless buffet who doesn't know where to start. This could not really be happening. Good things just do not happen this quickly; they have to be earned. I put up my hand as if I were stopping a speeding car.

"Haskell, I really appreciate that. But why me? You must know dozens of writers, good writers, established, who could do this easily. Why me?"

"I do know some good writers, but frankly some of them wouldn't touch it. The others would want too much money. Besides, I loved your script, especially the dialogue. Dialogue, even with a lousy plot, can make a movie. Also, the similarity between the setting in Albert's book is sort of similar to your script. The setting here is confined to a jail. Yours was confined to one day, outdoors. No plot really, but great dialogue. Also, I never announce what I am doing. I just do it. It speaks for itself. So, I'd like you to keep this to yourself. Okay?" He gazed at me intently.

"Yes, but while I absorb all this, could I ask you a few questions?"

"Of course," he said.

"This may sound stupid. Like I'm auditioning you, but other than that short meeting and being here for a few minutes, I know nothing about you other than that you're a cameraman with a wife and son and mean dog and a house that's a small hotel. How did you get into this business?"

Haskell told me, in shorthand, that he and his brother were raised in Chicago. His dad was very successful, building a huge company called

Allied Radio. His younger brother, Yale, wanted to be an actor, so Haskell financed a small film called *Stakeout On Dope Street,* and had a friend, Irv Kirshner, direct it. (Irv became a major Hollywood director for the next three decades.) He said because he was not in the cinematographer's union at the time he made *Stakeout* the Guild was giving him grief, but that'd he'd prevailed in the end and he was doing a film at MGM.

"Is your brother an actor now?'

Haskell laughed. "Right now, he's using the Pacific as a water bed. He's living in a small yacht in the Marina and fucking his limited brains out. He says women go crazy when they fuck on water." He laughed as my eyes got wider and wider. I had never heard anyone ever talk like that. The blacklist stuff was quickly forgotten.

"How long will it take?' Haskell asked.

"To read them *and* write the script?"

Haskell leaned forward. "How's $600 a week? Does that sound fair?"

"For ... for...how many weeks?" I didn't mean to say that. It just popped out.

"Could you do it in six to eight weeks? *Slovik* goes into pre-production shortly, so that timing would be perfect."

"I think I could do it in six weeks," I said with a mild amount of confidence.

"Great." Haskell patted me briskly on the arm. "That's $3,000.00. No problem. I'll drop off a check to you every week or you can come by and pick it up, and you don't have to show me pages till you're done."

I hadn't made that much money in two years! Suddenly having so much money scared me. What if the script wasn't any good?

"Haskell, Haskell,' I said. "I don't want any money up front."

"What? Don't be silly. What are ya gonna live on? You'll earn it."

"To me, it's not the money you're giving me. It's the opportunity. I prefer the opportunity."

"You're gonna have the money," he insisted. "And there'll be more, a lot more in the budget when we go into production."

"If you like what I do, you can give it to me at the end. Okay?"

He looked at me a little befuddled. "Okay, but I know it'll be terrific. In the meantime, I'm shooting at MGM for a couple of weeks. I want you to get used to coming up here. Marion will be here. And Mark. I want you to get to know them."

"And Blackie?"

He smiled. "That's the one you really have to get to know."

I left the house, the books tucked firmly under my arm. I was confident and relaxed. They had welcomed me as an absolute equal. No questions about anything. Background. Parents. Work. School. Nothing. Who does that? They were making me a part of their amazing interesting lives, the famous people they knew. For me, lucky to be a mail boy, that was payment enough. I was going to be taking my first real steps down the Yellow Brick Road.

So That's What Blacklist Means

I read the Maltz book in one day. I don't remember enjoying it, but I wasn't reading it for enjoyment; I was reading it for information. It was a character study of miscellaneous criminals and ethnicities confined to the LA County jail, with language and behavior not seen in films. I saw it as a black and white movie, and happily pounded away for five weeks until it was finished. I was surprised at the ease I was able to do something I'd had absolutely no training for or interest in. Yet it just flowed. What I was doing, it seemed, was just functioning as a stenographer, transcribing the movie playing in my head. I called Haskell to tell him I was finished.

"Wow, that's terrific. A week ahead of schedule. Can you drop it off at the house in the morning so I can take it to the studio with me?"

The following day the phone rang in the mailroom. It was Haskell. His voice was a little higher than usual. "Johnny, this is absolutely terrific. That scene where he's talking to the black kid. Wow. I'm about halfway through and couldn't wait to tell you how terrific it is."

He said, 'terrific' a lot. I was really pleased. He said nothing about the money I said I didn't want till I was finished; and neither did I. Talk of money always sounded like an intrusion.

Haskell continued, "I'll finish it tonight. I've got a couple of ideas. When I get them worked out, I'll call you, but what I'm hoping to pull off is a reading at my place with actors."

Actors? "Yale?" I enquired.

"No, actors!" Haskell said loudly, laughing. "But he'll be there. I'll call you." The call came three days later. "Are you free next Thursday night?' he said.

"No," I said, "but I'm reasonable." I said this in the hope he'd make me feel a little more terrific by mentioning money. It didn't work.

"We're having a reading at my place. I've got a couple of actors lined up. Karl Malden, and I'm waiting to hear about Widmark."

"Richard Widmark?" I almost shouted.

"Yeah," Haskell said, sounding pleased that I was so excited. "I may not have time to call you, but be there before seven, okay?"

"I'll be there Wednesday."

He chuckled. "Thursday's fine! See yah!"

When he hung up, I ran around my room cackling like of one of Widmark's most infamous characters, Tommy Udo. At quarter to seven that Thursday night, when Haskell opened the door, he did not have that usual happy smile on his face.

"Hi, Blackie's in the back. Come on in." He turned toward the living room. "Marion, Johnny's here." She greeted me warmly, asking if I'd like a drink or anything. I declined.

Yale was sitting on the sofa. There were just three people there. I was the fourth. After a very awkward silence, Haskell sat on the sofa between Marion and Yale. He said, "It was all set until about four this afternoon. Everybody was coming."

"What happened at four?" I asked.

"Columbia scrapped the project," Haskell said flatly.

"Whadda yah mean?" I asked.

"They're not doing it. Columbia changed its mind."

Trying to sound like I knew something about that business, I blurted, "Well, couldn't Sinatra do it someplace else?"

"It's Sinatra who doesn't want to do it now," Haskell said. "From what I could find out, Sinatra is close to the Kennedys through Peter Lawford. John Kennedy has presidential aspirations. The world knows Kennedy is close to Sinatra. What they don't know is that Sinatra was close to hiring a commie. He got word to Sinatra through Lawford that hiring a blacklisted writer at this time was not the prudent thing to do, that Sinatra's association with Maltz would reflect badly on his association with the Kennedy family. So, Sinatra backed down."

"Couldn't he just hire another writer?" I asked. "It's still a great story."

"Nah," Yale piped in. "Now he thinks the project itself is too controversial."

After another long silence, I said, "How well is Maltz known? I mean outside of this town?"

"Not much at all," Haskell answered.

"Was his book a best seller?"

"No, not at all."

I became quieter in my questions and as diplomatic as possible. "Haskell, could I ask you a question?" He nodded. "You like the script, don't you? I mean my script."

"I love it,' he said.

"It stands by itself, you think?"

"Absolutely."

Yale interjected, "It's terrific. That's all he's talked about."

I started to say, "Dalton Trumbo is a blacklisted writer–" when Haskell interrupted me.

"You've been doing your homework."

"Trumbo earns a living writing under an assumed name and they still make his scripts into movies. Haskell … then … then Maltz's name doesn't have to be on this script. Just mine. A nobody. We don't even have to say it's an adaptation." I paused.

Haskell was thinking. "I don't know," he whispered.

"Haskell, you say it stands alone. You could do it yourself. Like you did *Stakeout* with Yale." I began to push. "You shoot it in black and white in any jail in the country. You probably know people in Chicago. They've got a lot of jails there. It wouldn't cost much."

Haskell said, "Let me think about that for a while." He rose and moved toward me. "Don't worry, Johnny, we're gonna do something together. Your stuff is terrific."

The instant he said that I knew we wouldn't be doing that script together. I didn't feel as down as I thought I might be. I felt I had held my own with one of the brightest people in Hollywood, and had asked common sense questions, and made good suggestions. I almost talked like his equal.

"I'm sorry, Johnny. I'll call you in a couple of days. I'd like you to do a favor for me and Marion, and you're the only we could trust to do it. Okay?" Putting his arm around my shoulder, he led me through the dining room past the library of books. It was a comforting feeling. Marion had gone to the back door to let Blackie in. He came rushing through the kitchen straight at me growling. Haskell said nothing as the dog's nose touched my thighs; when he did, the barking stopped.

Haskell laughed. "See. He likes you already. I'm glad because I want you two to be friends." As the front door closed behind me, he said, "We'll see you in a few weeks."

The favor he wanted was for me to be his house sitter, something I'd never heard of, but common among the rich. Haskell was on his way to someplace called Recife in Northern Brazil to film a documentary about underprivileged natives and farmers. In less than two months I had gone from an unpaid terrific screenwriter to a terrific house-sitter for room and board. I was thankful to be able to do it, that someone so successful and rich thought enough of me, a stranger, to stay in their home was a warm encouraging feeling. My only company was Blackie and the books. For twenty-one days, I hung around the house, the backyard with the dog, and the bookcase. I had no desire or interest to go anywhere, just an intense curiosity to read as many of Haskell's books as possible. If America was changing my unsettled life, Haskell's massive library was about to change my politically empty head.

Here Comes the Son

Ronnie, my brother, was the only one in my family I saw reading a book. But only in the library when we would go together. He never took one home. Only I did. I have no idea where my love for books came from. Even though they took longer to get through than movies, I preferred them to films. You could hold them in your hands, take them to bed, cuddle with them. Their words created pictures in your head more elaborate than anything you could ever see on a screen.

I was a junkie for the Tarzan books of Edgar Rice Burroughs, the short clever stories of Canadian writer Gordon Sinclair and France's Guy de Maupassant. I never looked for subjects; I'd look for authors. Dickens, Somerset Maugham, O.Henry. As much as the reading, I loved the learning. Haskell's enormous wall of books provided me with a learning experience I could not have had anyplace else. Except Russia.

Beautifully bound books on world history, American history, biographies and autobiographies, mostly of politicians, three books each on Jefferson and Thomas Paine, at least three dozen on economics and communism, everything from Karl Marx's *Das Kapital* to an analysis of *Dialectical Materialism*. And not so surprisingly, because who needs them when you're rich, not one book on self-help.

I began with Karl Marx, because if Albert Maltz had been a communist, and there was such a fuss in America about this Cold War thing, I wanted to know what it was about. I ended with a biography of Thomas Paine, the intellectual voice behind the American Revolution. His earnings from his treatise, *Common Sense*, all 50,000 sold, he gave to George Washington. Because of this, this son of an English shoemaker was made an honorary America citizen. But later, after a trip to France, he wrote a book questioning organized religion, and when he went to DC to cast his first vote, he was chased away. When he died, his body was refused burial on or in American soil. Instead, the body was shipped back to England. While en route, though, some Christian sailors took it upon themselves to throw his body into the Atlantic. (The Bin Laden of his day.)

In what school in America, or Canada, I thought, could anyone read or hear this stuff? Not knowing or even caring if all I was reading was true, it was still thrilling, mind-expanding material. Haskell had it at his fingertips all the time. I had it for three wonderful weeks that are still with me.

I was proud of Haskell. Although his father was a generous mega-millionaire, Haskell made his own way and spent his own money on what he believed in. How different from Angelo and his father, or me and my absentee father.

I tried to tell myself how lucky I was to not have a father. But I did have one. The thought of him abandoning me, in spite of efforts to block it, were becoming an emotional distraction sitting in that big house. I remembered how smart he seemed to me. Haskell's books were the reminder. I had just written two screenplays, something I'd never done, that people liked.

Maybe I could write something else I'd never done, a letter to my father.

I wrote two letters to the Canadian consulate in London seeking information about his whereabouts. With the 'Hollywood' postmark, I thought I'd get an immediate reply. One came back undelivered. The other was forwarded to the Canadian Army Headquarters in London. It informed me that any enquiries about Lt. Colonel Angus Barbour MacLaren would have to be made in person, but even then, if there was information as to his whereabouts, any enquiries I did have would be forwarded if the party was not deceased. Whether or not the informed party responded would be entirely up to him. I found this letter when I returned to my apartment. I hung on to it.

Haskell and Marion returned and thanked me for taking care of the house and Blackie. I thanked them for the privilege, and especially for the chance to read all those fabulous books.

With two failed movie possibilities, the mailroom became a discouraging dead end for me. I called to tell Haskell I was quitting. He invited me to a Sunday brunch. He, Marion, and Mark were like family. They could not have been sweeter.

"What are your plans?" I showed him the letter. "You're kidding," he said. "That's terrific. Do you need some help?"

"No, I'm fine."

He knew a lot about me. He especially loved the story of when we were all lost. I told them objectively, not as though I'd lived them, but as though I'd seen them in a movie. I told them with the joy of a survivor. At the door they all hugged me. When Haskell shook my hand, he stuffed some bills into it.

"Be sure and write me. What a great story."

"I will. You'll be the only one."

"And let us know where you're stayin.'"

The door closed. I counted the money. Over $600.

I really wanted to stay in Los Angeles. Being illegal, though, I was always unsettled. Having my father on my mind all the time now, was even more unsettling. I had to get it out of my system.

The other thing that prompted me to go on such a wild goose chase, as they call it, was, like Haskell, I could have an inheritance somewhere. After my mother stood on the veranda, yelling at me on my way to school that my father was not coming home, she said in a tirade weeks later that he might have stayed there because he took the inheritance that might have been left for me and Maggie when his parents died. I recalled that his parents always sent me and Maggie nice birthday and Christmas gifts. I went to London, and the address on the letter.

IN ENGLAND

London Bridge Is Falling Down

Fortunately, when I left Toronto, I had secured two passports: John MacLaren and John Barbour. Just in case. So far I hadn't used either. Now I would have to. But which one? It would have to be John Barbour. That's what I was known as here and with immigration. It was my birth name. I liked it. I liked me. I did not like my father, so, the MacLaren passport was out.

I had more than I'd ever had, over fifteen-hundred dollars. I booked the cheapest one-way flight from LA to New York, then overnight to London. I did not sleep the entire trip. I kept admonishing myself for what I was doing. What a dreadful waste of time. For what? To try to see someone who doesn't want to see me? I never felt as lost or useless. My life, mind and future looked darker than the endless black sky I kept staring at. We landed at Heathrow around nine a.m. I wasted no time. I took a cab to The Canadian Department of Veterans' Affairs.

Letter in hand, I introduced myself to the information officer, explaining that I had just arrived all the way from California. He was unimpressed, polite, and totally non-committal. He repeated the information already in the letter, then instructed me to leave my name and a contact phone number and address, which, of course, I couldn't do.

"When you have that information, John, come back," he said.

"Then what?" I asked

"You leave it with us."

"I mean, and then what?"

"And then you'll leave it with us. That's all I can tell you. I'm sorry. I can't tell you more. But when you have a place to stay and a number, come back."

I thought he wouldn't have me come back for nothing. So, I hurried to find a place.

That afternoon I had a bed and breakfast just a couple of blocks from Piccadilly Circus, the Times Square of London. It was almost a replica of the boarding house I'd stayed at on LaBrea. The landlady was almost the same age and build, except with a different accent. It was weird, but oddly comforting, as though I'd been there before. That done, I hurried back in time to leave the required information.

"We'll be in touch, son," the officer said.

My concern was, in touch when? I had enough money for maybe eight to ten weeks. Then what? I couldn't get a job. And how would I pass the time? Oh, God, what a screw-up! I went to my room at the top of the stairs, and fell asleep with my clothes on. Something I did often as a kid.

Breakfast was delicious; a large serving of eggs, ham, bacon, sausage, toast, tea, a thing called a crumpet, and the tastiest marmalade I ever ate. Knowing the reason for my visit, my new landlady was especially sympathetic and nice to me. There were always extra portions on my plate and offers to do my laundry, which I declined. When she heard me say one of my favorite dishes was fish and chips, she directed me to a small shop a few blocks away. Being from America, she thought I might also miss a good hamburger, which I did, so she directed me to another place in Piccadilly Circus called Wimpy's. It was one of a chain of hamburger franchises in England named after an American comic book character.

Movies were her love. Knowing I was from Hollywood thrilled her. We chatted for hours about actors and actresses, and scenes in movies. She pleased me no end telling me constantly I should be in movies or on stage. She also repeated it to the other diners. Her favorite actor ever, she said, was Charlie Chaplin. "Do ya like 'im?" she asked.

"Actually, I've never seen him in anything."

"What?" she almost screamed. "The greatest genius evah, and you've nevah seen 'im? And you wantin' tuh be in showbiz!"

"Well, in America, it's hard to find a Chaplin film. I think the government's banned him," I said.

"A pretty sad state of affairs when a government's afraid of an artist! Well, they're havin' a Chaplin festival at the corner Piccadilly Theater. You get down there an see it. Even if you don't wanna be in showbiz or whatever, he is a must see. The one they're playin' now is *Gold Rush*. You get down there, lad, and see it. Even if I have tuh take ya myself!"

She was right. I just couldn't sit around. I was in England, 'this sceptered isle,' once the centerpiece of the planet's biggest empire, and in London, heralded as the most cultured, civilized city in the world. And I had never seen Charlie Chaplin. Actually, I had never wanted to. He didn't talk. I loved the dialogue, the wisecracks in movies. It was curiosity, rather than laughs I had in mind when I found myself at the box office of the three-story-high theater mid-afternoon. The spacious, ornate theater was packed on a weekday. I'd never seen a silent film. There was a silent film theater on Fairfax in Los Angeles, but I never went to it. I knew I would be watching make-believe because the world isn't silent. Only language could transform and take you on a journey. I discovered that afternoon genius could also do that. Chaplin's inventiveness went immediately from the screen right into my funny bone. When he got to the scene where he was trying to elegantly eat his shoe, I was howling. How could anything be that original and funny, and why hadn't I seen it before? His talent was inspiring and intimidating. Who could match that, let alone top it? I gushed out my review to a very happy landlady, suggesting Chaplin may have discouraged as many from getting into films as he did those he intimidated to stay out of them. I mean, who could equal *Gold Rush* or the others? Why had America banned such an obvious, world-renowned talent?

Coming from a modestly educated landlady, this floored me: "John, lad, remember this: nobody ever remembers a politician, even the good ones, but everybody remembers the artists because they feed your soul. Nobody can be Charlie Chaplin. And nobody can be Johnny Barbour.

So, you be the best you can." My first ten afternoons were spent watching Charlie.

Two weeks brought no response from the Army Office. I had enough money still. Maybe I should just go back to California.

Thinking about LA also made me think about hamburgers. So, one afternoon, following *Limelight,* I went to the highly recommended Wimpy's just down the street. I sat at the counter near the door. Business was light. Only two booths were occupied. I was the only one at the counter. The small burger was surprisingly good. Halfway through it, daydreaming and thinking negative thoughts as usual, I was suddenly aware that someone was sitting next to me.

It was unsettling because there were lots of empty stools. I turned to see who it was. I was greeted with a soft smile from an older woman. She was beautifully dressed in a suit, with dark hair, dark eyes, probably in her late thirties or early forties.

"Hello," she said in a thick accent that wasn't English. "I always come here for de hambairgers. Do you mind I sit here?"

"Not at all. Happy to have someone to chat with."

"Me, too. I'm on my way to de museum. My name's Agdas."

Agdas

"I'm John." I extended my hand. Her handshake was firm and delicate. "You like their burgers?"

"Yes. De closest ting I get to America. You from 'merica?"

"California, sort of. I was born in Canada. Toronto."

"Why you here?"

"I wanted to try their hamburgers."

She laughed, a warm, deep, throaty laugh. "No, why London?"

I didn't want to tell her, but it just started pouring out of me. I couldn't stop myself. I had no idea why I was so vulnerable. Out of control. I mentioned my daily trips to the Canadian Department of Veterans Affairs, that my dad had retired with the rank of Lieutenant Colonel and had gotten something called the Order of the British Empire, that he certainly wasn't lauded as Father-of-the-Year, and that even if he was dead, they wouldn't tell me even where his grave was. I was careful to sound casual, even glib, so as not to give the impression I was feeling sorry for myself.

"What you do eef you find heem?"

I paused. "I don't know," I said dishonestly, because a part of me did know. I presumed the bastard had stolen our inheritance. I pictured myself tracking the son of a bitch down and fighting the urge to crush his skull, just like Cagney.

I turned fully to look at her. "Agdas, why are you in London? And where from?"

She told me she was from Iran, here with two children, a boy, thirteen, and a girl, twelve.

That she'd been sent here by her husband while he was negotiating something with his second wife. She said that like a lot of successful men in her country, he wanted more wives, which he could well afford. She didn't know how long she'd stay. Her children were in a school they liked. She concluded by saying she enjoyed it so much here she might not ever go back.

She said this all without rancor or remorse, in the same calm voice she'd ordered her hamburger.

I studied her face, everything about her, wondering what it must be like to grow up in a country and culture like that.

"I'm going to de museum after. Would you like to go?" she asked

I thought it might be nice, even without her something else to do to kill time. "I hate to ask this," I said, "but is it expensive?"

She laughed. "It's a museum. It's free. We go by bus." She reached for my check. "I don't want go alone."

I took the check from her. "I'll buy the burgers. You buy the bus tickets."

The, like she'd done it many times before, she slipped her arm through mine and led me out the door.

I could see why she would want to go to the museum, and back again. It was bigger than three football fields, every foot stuffed with objects that demanded attention. There weren't enough hours in the day to absorb just one room. Or a dozen. In one area alone, they had re-erected a portion of a thousand-year-old Greek city. We spent the afternoon covering just a very small area, ending up in Babylon. She was amazing, explaining, like a tour guide. She delighted in informing a very wide-eyed interested me.

Her arm once again under mine as we left, she said, "Where you go now, Chonny?"

I liked the way she couldn't pronounce my name. "You like to come to my place, meet my children? Have dinner. I very good cook, especially lamb and rice."

"Lamb, for God's sake," I blurted. "The animal they make sweaters out of. That sounds barbaric. I've never eaten lamb. And the only time I ever had rice was in rice pudding or Rice Krispies."

"You never eat lamb? My God, how you grow up? Maybe that's why you not so big. It's better than pig or cow."

"I dunno." I shrugged

"You come. Meet my children. I feed you lamb and rice. You love it. Come." This time she gripped my arm tighter, and led me down the wide, long concrete stairs.

Instead of the bus, though, she hailed a taxi. I was overwhelmed by both where she lived and her children. She lived on the top floor of a very luxurious apartment building. She had a corner two-bedroom complex with a great view of the streets and the city. The place was immaculate. Not a speck of dust, not even on the windows. It was furnished beautifully with unique colorful accessories, indicating the occupants were not British or Christian, but Muslims from the Mediterranean.

Before she opened the door, I heard giggling and voices on the TV, or telly as they called it. Her two children were watching a show called *Hancock's Half Hour.* Seeing their mother, they immediately jumped up and rushed to greet and hug her; something I didn't see many American kids do. They were physically the most beautiful children I'd ever seen, with olive skin, jet black hair, and eyes so dark you couldn't distinguish a pupil. Their manners were flawless and unforced. Their graciousness and politeness were as natural to them as their tanned skin. I was surprised to find myself so comfortable with them, more surprised when they turned off the telly to talk.

Agdas instructed us to stay in the living room while she prepared dinner. Not knowing quite what to say to these kids, especially knowing the circumstances as to why they were in England, I asked them what they had been watching. Enthusiastically, they told me it was a comedian named Tony Hancock, that he was hilarious. They stood up, acting out some of the bits, totally natural and at ease. Like they knew me. I told them I loved comics, and would they mind turning him back on. I told them I'd never heard of him. I also told them I'd just seen my first Charlie Chaplin film. They rushed to the TV and up came the tail end of *Hancock's Half Hour*. In a matter of minutes, we were best buddies. And I wasn't that much older than them.

In the months I remained in London, I visited as often as possible. To see Agdas. To see the kids. And to see Tony Hancock. And other comedians. One was the new *Goon Show* with a young Peter Sellers.

Hancock's half-hour, though, was a different show or format every week. He was verbally what Chaplin was visually. Next to Peter Sellers, Jonathan Winters, Ernie Kovacs, and Robin Williams, Tony Hancock was the funniest, most inventive TV comic I'd ever seen. Years later, long after I'd left, I was deeply saddened and disturbed when I read that he had committed suicide.

That night, though, it was my first taste of Tony Hancock, and lamb and rice, which has since become one of my favorite dishes, but only if cooked by a Middle Easterner. I helped Agdas with the dishes while the children retreated to their shared big bedroom to read and finish homework. Agdas washed while I dried. It was almost like the first time I was alone in the house with Beverly.

"You like?" she asked, as she handed me a dish, her arm barely touching mine each time.

"Yes," I said. "Absolutely delicious. I couldn't believe how good it tasted. And your children are wonderful, too. Are they getting by? Do they miss their dad?"

"They talk to him every day! They okay. They have each other." She got quiet and stared off as she finished the last of the dishes.

"Do you miss your husband?" I said barely above a whisper.

She thought for a moment. "No. I no miss him." She paused before adding, "I miss a man, though." Her look and words went right through me. *My God.*

I said, "Aren't ... well. Aren't there ... clubs, uh. Iranian clubs where you could meet someone? Like we have the YMCA?" *Jesus, what a dumb thing to say.*

"No, one Iranian man enough for me, but one Iranian woman not enough for him." Her eyes glistened with a hint of tears. "Thank you for coming," she said. "Thank you for going museum with me. My children like you."

"I like them, too. They're terrific kids!"

"You come again? Huh?"

"That'd be nice. I'd have to figure out the buses."

"We go to movies sometime? You like that?"

I didn't really know what to say, thinking about the cost. She picked up on it immediately.

"You no worry. I pay for movie. Then we take taxi, you no worry about bus."

"Agdas, I can't be letting you spend any money on me. I'll be fine."

"What I gonna spend it on? Huh? It please me spend on you."

"You don't even know me. I don't even know how long I'll be here, and even if you just bought a movie ticket, I don't know when I'd ever be able to pay it back."

She took my hand and pulled it to her chest. "Chonny, I no spend on you. I spend on me. I no want to see movie by self. Lots men talk me. I be here four months. I no talk to them. You first man I talk to. I no spend on you. I spend on me."

I took her extended hand in both of mine, something I'd never done before. I felt sorry for her. I also liked her. Here was a very attractive woman, twenty years older than me, an adult, with children, and yet she seemed needier than me. It made me sad."I know how you feel, I'm almost a kid."

"You no a kid. Now you eat lamb, you a man!"

I burst out laughing. "God, that's funny."

She pulled me toward her and kissed me. To my surprise, even though I was nervous and uncomfortable, I kissed back. "You like to stay tonight?" she asked in a whisper.

"I can't. No." I was thinking of her children in the other room. I didn't want them to wake up to 'Uncle John.'

"You can sleep on couch," she said

"Agdas, I can't. I have things to do tomorrow–"

"I fix you good breakfast and take you home."

"I have to leave town for a couple of days," I blurted.

"Where you go?"

"Aberdeen." It had just been a passing thought while I'd been in London, the business of checking out my father's parents' will, but it popped out.

"What? Why you go Aberdeen?" she asked, like she thought I was lying.

I told her that if it turned out there was an inheritance there for me, I could pay her way to the movies. She laughed and kissed me again. This time harder.

"You wait here," she said, as she turned and walked back to the living room. She returned, handing me a piece of paper. "This my phone number. When you come back, you call. Okay?"

"I will," I said.

"And you a take this." She gave me a handful of bills. "You a need this." I refused, pushing it back to her. She grabbed my hand harder, folding my fingers over the notes. "You need it go Aberdeen. Okay?"

"Agdas–"

"Chonny, I got lots money. Do me no good. Little bit for you. Do good. Okay?"

Now my eyes were misty, feeling sad for her, moved also by someone, a total stranger hours earlier, being so nice to me. "Thank you." I gave her a tight hug.

She kissed me gently on the forehead. "You call me when come back?" She sounded like a hopeful child.

"I won't be long. A couple of days at most." I did want to see her again, the wonderful lonely woman with two kids in a foreign land not of their choosing. But, thanks to her, I was off to Aberdeen. I would pay her back. The way she wanted.

Where There's a Will

The thought of being in London to find out if I was in my grandparents' will was never ever a priority or purpose. It was an occasional uninvited daydream. Daydreaming was my mental oxygen. Good or bad. At times, both. With still no word from The Department of Veterans' Affairs, I had more time to kill. It was something to do. Probably nothing would come of it. That was one of my few correct predictions.

Getting off the train in Aberdeen, I went directly to the Hall of Records. As everywhere, wills are part of the Public Record. I was the only one there, except for the nice slender middle-aged lady who happily helped me. She had a sweet low brogue, which was very difficult to understand. Often, I had to repeat stuff. I did not know the first names of my father's parents, when they died, or where they're buried. Nothing. I just had my father's information.

"Well, young man, let's see what we can come up with for ye!" She disappeared behind a smoked-glass door that said Records.

I paced the floor. When I wasn't pacing, I was leaning on the counter rocking back and forth. I couldn't stand still. Neither could my thoughts. What was I about to discover? That I truly was rich? That I was the abandoned heir to Scottish nobility? How much would it be? Could I change it into dollars? Did I have to live the rest of my life in the British Isles to cash in on it? What if it was gone? Vanished? Stolen by my father? That greedy, thoughtless bastard. Then I thought, maybe my father was just like me. An unhappy kid who had to get to Canada. I was sorry I was there. Only politeness, waiting for the nice lady, kept me from walking out, going back to London, to see Agdas, to watch the telly with her kids, to repay her, the way she wanted. I was lonely. The more I thought, the lonelier I got.

Those mixed musings came to a halt when the door opened twenty minutes later. In a pleased proud brogue, holding two papers aloft, she said, "Ah think we may have found what you were lookin' fer, young man!"

Curiosity was killing me. "How much will it cost?"

She pulled the pages back as I reached for them. "Oh, Laddie, it does nay cost yah a thing. It's public. Yah cannay buy it, but yew can look at it." She laid the pages on the counter for me to see.

My eyes darted to their names and the scroll on top that said, Last Will and Testament. Not even bothering to look for the beneficiary, I looked for the amount of money, the estate and its valuables that had been bequeathed. I scoured the document. There was no money amount. There was no estate. I looked again. There was nothing. Helpless, I turned to the lady. "Where ma'am… where's the part … that says how much they left?"

She pointed to the middle of the page. "Here, lad is what they left."

I followed her finger. It led me to the valuables. A few pieces of furniture. A bed. A sofa. Rugs. Knick-knacks, and three wooden chairs. Jesus Christ. Three wooden chairs? I had been bashed in the belly. But what was I expecting? What did I ever get from my daydreams? Nothing. Absolutely nothing. Was this my life? My destiny? To be endlessly disappointed?

I couldn't look into that helpful lady's eyes. She'd see how greedy I was. Why else would I come all the way from California to look at some will?

"Thank you very much," I said mostly to my shoes as I turned and left. It was almost like the universe was having some kind of sick joke on Johnny, fucking with me. An empty will. An empty life. The surprising thing, though, also emptied from me, was malice. No anger. No vindictiveness. No rage at my father. I began to call him Dad. Not the more distant Father. Maybe I was my father's son. In that case I should cheer up. He made it. So could I.

I arrived at the boarding house too late to call Agdas. I called the following morning. She was surprised and very pleased to hear my voice.

"There's something I hate to have to tell you…" I paused, trying to frame the words.

"What you hate say?"

"Agdas, if we're going to go to a movie, you'll have to pay."

She burst into laughter. "We go movie today." Her voice up. "Okay?"

"Okay. We'll meet at Wimpy's, and I'll pretend to pick you up."

She laughed even harder. "Chonny, you so funny. I like you!"

She took me to a movie that afternoon, then took me home. I told her as much as I wanted to be with her, I would not do anything if the children were home. Afternoons the children were in school. We were in bed. Wow. And another wow. She was nearly twice my age, but twice as needy. She indeed needed a man. Almost as much as I needed a woman. And a lot of lamb.

Being with her and her children calmed me down.

I was questioning how much longer I would stay in London. I had already been to the Department of Veterans' Affairs three times, and nothing. But it no longer seemed as important to me.

That's when the phone rang, and I missed another afternoon with Agdas.

The Call

"Johnny…Johnny, a call fer you!" the landlady called up the stairs.

I stopped cleaning up, preparing to see Agdas, and rushed to the top of the stairs.

She whispered hoarsely, "It's a man."

Thinking it could only be my father, knowing it could only be my father, or then again the fellow from the Department of Veterans' Affairs, I broke out in a cold sweat.

"He's on his way, sir," she said into the phone, then turned to me. "C'mon lad."

Taking the steps two and three at a time, I reached the bottom and took the phone from her. She patted me on the shoulder.

"Hello," I said tentatively.

There was a pause. "Hello, son?" There was almost a question in the soft, rich voice.

"Dad?" I questioned. I couldn't imagine it could be true. Not after all the years.

"I got your note. What brings you here?"

"You."

"I'd like to see you," he said.

My heart pounded. "That's why… why I'm here."

There was another pause, then: "How about I pick you up tomorrow morning around eight-thirty. Would that be okay?"

"That'd be terrific."

"I'd like to take you to my home in Scotland, to meet my wife, so bring some extra things. Would that be okay?"

It was more than I ever could have imagined. I gripped the receiver as tight as I could, trying to stay calm. "That'd be even more terrific!"

"Great, then, son. Tomorrow at eight-thirty it is. I can't wait to see you."

"Me, too."

The rest of the day and night were spent in a fog, a torrent of blurry images, a few from the past, but most from what I imagined then next day would bring. A father that may really want me. A home in Scotland. And his wife. Would she want me, too? Would I enjoy living in Scotland? I Immediately dismissed the fact that he had never divorced my mother. Who cares? I was going to see him. All's well that ends well. I was beginning to identify with him. At my age, he left Scotland for Canada to live his dreams and lies. Just like I had left Canada, living lies.

Agdas was thrilled for me. I told her I'd be totally lousy company at the movies or for dinner. I just wanted to stay home and fidget, fuss and think. To work off some of my intense nervousness and shout my joy to the world, I wrote Haskell a long letter. After sealing it, I packed and paced.

The only time that time doesn't fly, is when you want it to. I paced so long, I could have walked to Scotland. The next morning, I was standing by my door with my bag. Occasionally, I ran to the window to look out at passing cars. At eight-thirty sharp one pulled up in front. It looked like a limousine. I pulled the curtain back to get a better look. A man in a uniform got out. Not a military uniform, a chauffeur's uniform. I wondered if this was my dad. Then the uniformed man opened the back door. One of the best-dressed men I had ever seen, outside of Cary Grant, emerged. The dark suit, white shirt and conservative tie were creaseless. That was my dad. My father!

From atop the stairs, bag in hand, I could barely hear the soft ringing of the doorbell over the thumping in my throat. The land lady, bless her heart, knew he was coming at eighty-thirty. She had been at the door for twenty minutes, waiting. "Gud mornin', sir!"

"Good morning, ma'am. Is John in?"

She scurried to the bottom of the stairs. "Johnny," she called. "Yer father's here!"

I descended the stairs as calmly as I could. There he was. Finally. My mind took an instant Polaroid. It has never faded. It is as bright and in focus as the day I took it. My father was three feet in front of me. He was even more handsome than the Errol Flynn look-alike photograph in the front room. The mustache was gone. The face was a little fuller, but the sky-blue eyes brighter. He was about three inches taller than me, and more solid. In an obviously very expensive suit tailored to that body, he looked like an extremely successful executive, or owner of something, which I later found out he was. On his left wrist was a solid gold watch; below that, on his finger, a wedding band with a square diamond. He stood as still as I did, examining me the way I was examining him. He had a slight smile. I was so overwhelmed at the sudden reality, I could barely breathe. He was, in a word, beautiful. Literally, a dream come true. As thrilled and stunned as I was, though, I made no move to hug him. Neither did he. He finally extended his hand. It was a warm firm handshake, but brief, business-like.

"Son," he said in a surprisingly sweet voice, "I am so glad to see you. You look wonderful."

What do you say after twenty years? A thousand words and phrases poured through my mind, but none found a voice. As usual, when I'm nervous, my first words were a little flippant. "I think you're just saying that because I look like you."

"Are you ready for the road?"

"Have bag will travel."

He turned to his uniformed chauffeur who had been standing dutifully by the car, holding the rear door open. "Malcolm," my dad said.

Without further instruction this taller, older man walked quickly over and reached for my bag. I had never had anyone carry my bag. It made me uneasy to think of an older man carrying it. So, I held on to it.

My father turned, saw this, and pointed his finger at me like it was toy gun, from the hip. It was body language to let him do his job. Malcolm placed the bag in the front seat, then moved to attend the rear door.

"Son, you and I will sit back here. Where we can chat."

I climbed in. My father followed. When he sat, I could feel the warmth of his body. My God, this was all so amazing. Who could be happier?

"To the office first, Malcolm," he said, before turning to me. "Afterwards, we'll meet my wife and you'll stay with us."

The car, which looked like a Bentley, moved noiselessly through traffic and onto the highway. My father said we'd chat, but we didn't. We were silent for so long, I thought I'd better say something. "Where's your office?"

"Glasgow. Scotland. It's a long drive.'"

"I was just there. Scotland."

"What for?'

Oh, Jesus Christ. I shouldn't have said that. What am I going to do, tell him I went looking for his parents' will?

I said, "I didn't think I'd ever hear from you, so aside from wanting to see Shakespeare's Stratford On Avon, I figured I'd just take a quick tour of my background."

He looked impressed. "That's quite nice!"

My tension dissolved. I thanked whomever for giving me the talent to lie. And what a whopper. It was brilliant. It suddenly opened up a dialogue between us.

He didn't volunteer any information about himself. And I didn't pursue it. He asked about what I'd been doing, where I'd been, but not one question about my little sister, my older half-brother, or especially my mother. Since I perceived him as being a snob, I was surprised when he made no comment when I told him I had to drop out of school in the ninth grade to go to work shoveling coal. He perked up when I mentioned my experiences as a mail boy at Paramount Studios and the closeness I came to making a movie.

"That sounds like fun. I was writer for a while. *The Toronto Star*."

"I know," I said.

"I still do a bit. Is that what you'd like to do?" he asked.

"I am not sure."

"For someone who's been around a lot, you seem to have survived and done pretty well for yourself."

"Not as well as you."

"You're going to do fine." He then hesitated, before saying, "Do you mind if I close my eyes a little? I'd like to be sharp when we get to the office."

I told him I didn't mind. He patted my leg and closed his eyes.

I wondered about his wife. Did she have children? Did *they*? I wondered about his work, his obvious success. Where we were going? Where was I going? Every question was a happy one.

Birth of a Salesman

It was shortly after mid-day when Malcolm parked the car and woke my father. We had stopped in front of a three-story smart, solid looking reddish brick building. A large bronze plaque to the right of a polished solid wooden door said Angus Barbour MacLaren Advertising Agency. It was in the heart of Glasgow's main business thoroughfare, Sauchiehall Street. My father looked at me looking at the sign. "Our office."

Malcolm opened our doors, my father's first.

"Come back in an hour or so, Malcolm. We should be ready then." I followed my father inside where three employees were quick to greet him, a middle-aged woman, a younger woman and man.

My father pointed to me. "This is John." To the young man, he said, "Martin, everything on time?"

"Yes, sir."

Without stopping, my father motioned for me to follow. This beautiful, ornate, shiny staircase, with thick handrails on both sides, was in the center of the building. Small offices at the bottom were on either side. At the top, in front of us, was a very spacious, colorful production office. In the middle was the requisite long, narrow table with a dozen or so chairs. On it were neat stacks of scripts or memos, glass jugs of water, and tea cups. The walls were covered with movie posters, beer, golf, other product posters, graffiti, and photographs. It looked like a fun room.

Two young women, both very attractive, emerged to greet him. This time my father didn't bother with introductions. He pointed at the room. "This is where all the brainstorming is done."

I muttered in amazement, "How and why did you ever get into advertising?"

"Something I've always been interested in."

He hadn't mentioned I was his son. I was cautious not to preface my questions by calling him 'Dad.' So, I just said, "Aside from some of your *Toronto Star* articles, I once found a wonderful drawing you'd made of a building."

He smiled. "Selling is the highest art in the world. I've always said, gravity is the force that keeps us down to Earth, but selling is the force that keeps the Earth spinning."

"Writing your column or even designing a building, that's creative."

"Believe me, you will learn there is nothing, absolutely nothing, more important to you or the planet than selling. The ability to sell. Whether it's an idea, or a talent, or yourself, or a product. It is everything. Great artists and politicians don't always survive. Great salesmen do."

I was surprised at how talkative he now was. And impressed by what he said. As was his audience of employees. Then came the kicker I was sure he had said a hundred times. "Popes and preachers are the world's greatest salesmen. They've got people putting money into a collection plate for something or someone they can't even see."

He again motioned me to follow him. We entered a smaller room that was as high tech as any I'd ever seen. Editing machines and monitors covered one wall, with cushy black leather chairs to work and watch. A large screen was dropping down from the ceiling as we entered.

"All set?" my dad said to a youthful female employee.

"Yes, sir." She clicked on a projector.

On a screen appeared the roll-down numbers, which I'd seen often at Deluxe Film Laboratories, and then a color film. It was a commercial. It was silent. Out of a box on a kitchen counter popped what looked like the Pillsbury Doughboy. My father was staring intently at the screen, holding a microphone. The assistant counted down and he began to sing. I was stunned. I had never heard anyone in my family sing. Ever. But my father had a beautiful lyrical baritone. It was the sweet soothing sound of a good pop singer. The timbre moved me. The lyrics, though, for this small pile of dough made me giggle.

"Oh, that's perfect, Angus," the young lady said. "You got it in one take!"

My father handed her the microphone and looked at me. "What'd you think?"

"Amazing. A real surprise!"

"Surprising… the business I'm in, or the singing?"

"Both, actually."

"Okay, let's wrap for now. We'll finish up tomorrow," he said to his staff. They busied themselves gathering up the storyboard, tape and a few other items, and exited the room. He turned to me. "Wait here. I'll be right back and then we'll leave."

Alone in that impressive environment I never could have imagined, I tried to tune into what I was feeling, where I was and what was happening. Or about to happen. After all those years, did I just win the father-son lottery? As the song says, was I about to take the high road to Scotland? Or the low road? I began to feel depressed. How could I? But for reasons beyond reason, I felt suddenly out of place. I did not belong there. What was wrong with me? I could not suddenly have a father after twenty years; I didn't even know him. He didn't know me. And what about his wife? She could not suddenly have a stranger in her house and call him son. His money, his business, I had done nothing to earn it. He earned it. He had built his new life without us. Without me. I might have felt I deserved to cash in on his success, if indeed he had stolen my inheritance, but all he got were three wooden chairs. I was an interloper. He never came looking for me. And never would have. I found him. That was enough. I should get back to my own life, whatever that was going to be.

"Son," my father said, pulling me from my thoughts, "you've come a long way, and I'm glad you did. You'll meet my wife in a while; she's looking forward to it. I just called her, and tomorrow we'll have breakfast. And if you like, we'll have Malcolm go with you to pick up the rest of your things. You can stay with us for as long as you like while you decide what you'd like to do. How's that?"

He had called me son with no one around. My eyes started to burn and my throat constricted. I braced myself not to cry. I wanted to accept his offer; it was so generous and life changing. In days and years to come when things got even tougher, I often wished I had done so.

"Dad, can I talk to you for a minute?"

"We can talk lat–"

"Please, for just a moment. I don't know what kind of relationship you had with my mother–"

"Son, I don't wish to talk about her."

"Neither do I. It's about you."

His face got flush.

"If I could have left home earlier, I would have. Even at seven or eight she wasn't the kind of person I'd want to know, but you must have at least liked her once. You had three children with–"

"Two," he snapped. "Raymond was from someone else. An American."

"But you still married her, then had two of your own. And even though I was five or six when you left, I had nothing but fond memories of you, sitting with me listening to the radio, teaching me to count and recite the alphabet. You must have liked us. Maybe I can see you leaving my mother. But … but why us?"

His face tightened. "You have a right to be angry."

"I'm not angry. Honestly. I am really happy you came to see me. Really. I'm just thinking, it's all so weird. Thinking about all the things that you must have gone through. You were born here, then moved to

Canada when you were about my age. Then for some reason added the name MacLaren. Did well. I was so proud of the stuff you wrote in the paper. I reread it all the time. Married a woman with a child, had two of your own, then joined the army and went to war and became a Lt. Colonel and got the Order of the British Empire. I was so proud when I heard that. But then you never came home."

There was a tense pause. He was expressionless.

"You know, I even went to check on your parents' will because I was told that they had left an estate to me and my sister. And I thought you'd stolen it. I'm glad you didn't. And I'm really glad you're doing well."

He turned toward the window, then turned back. "It sounds like you don't want to stay. Or you don't like what I do."

"What do you mean?"

"My work."

"Whatever gave you that idea?"

After a moment, he said, "Would you like Malcolm to drive you back to London in the morning?" He was saying goodbye. It was in the tone of his voice, his body language.

"No, that's okay. If he could drive me to the train depot, that'd be fine."

"Do you have any money?"

I had the equivalent of thirty American dollars. He pulled a hundred pound note from a stack in his pocket and handed it to me. I stared at it, not wanting to take it.

"Here. You'll need it." He extended it to me, his hand careful not to touch mine. It was an obvious gesture that I caught immediately. But I was unhurt by it.

"Thank you," I said.

"I'll have Malcolm take you to the station." He started walking toward the top of the stairs. "You know where I am now. You can be in touch anytime." It was a tone that was clearly not an invitation to take him up on it.

"Thanks. I'm glad you came for me." I descended the stairs looking back up at him.

Malcolm drove me to the station, the suitcase beside me. I felt light. The lightest and loosest I'd felt since finding Beverly alive and married. Two decades of much more emotional baggage had just been left in an ad agency in Glasgow. I also felt a slight touch of pride. When I was questioning my father and unburdening myself, I was proud of the fact that while two thoughts crossed my mind incessantly, I exercised enough self-control to keep my mouth shut, a talent often lacking in years to come. I wanted to tell him he never once called me by my name or told his staff I was his son. Then I wanted to say to him, you mean you gave up three children and one wife and went through a horrible war just so you could end up singing to a donut. It was cruel. And funny. But I didn't have the heart to hurt him.

A Foggy Year in London Town

On the train back to London, I happily wrote a full accounting of my encounter with my father to Haskell and mailed it upon arrival. The landlady asked me anxiously how it went. I told her it was wonderful, which brought a huge smile to her face. I was more honest with Agdas. I told her I was thrilled and relieved to see my father, relieved that any need and curiosity about him was out of my system, and that there was little need to stay in England. The first week back, I spent the afternoons with her, and evenings watching the telly with her and her children. An unbelievably remarkable live performance by a young Richard Burton as a stuttering Martin Luther prompted us the next day to go to a play instead of a film. We saw Laurence Olivier in Ionesco's *Rhinoceros,* and giggled all the way home, having not understood a word of it.

My interest in live theater, though, was again piqued. And I was living in a country that subsidized it. An aspiring actor wouldn't have to be sorting oranges at midnight. I had even visited Shakespeare's birthplace, astonished at how small it was to have created such a giant.

Then Agdas showed me a small ad in the *Times*. A place called The Castle Theater in Surrey, just north of London was auditioning actors of any age or origin for the new season of repertory.

"What do you think?" I asked her.

"You like. Is not far. And you stay England." She shrugged with a smile.

I had the money, the time, and no plans. And nothing to lose. The following day, ad in hand, I was at The Castle Theater.

There were quite a few people there. All types. I looked like the only foreigner. When it came my turn, the director handed me a scene from *The Grass Is Greener,* later a movie with Cary Grant. They also handed me the opening soliloquy from Richard the Third. I was thrilled, couldn't wait to do it from memory from my quiz show notebook.

In the middle of my *Grass Is Greener* scene, the director stopped me. "John, what brings you to England?"

"Personal matters," I answered quickly.

"'Do you plan on staying long?"

"It depends, I guess."

"Well, could you stay at least six months and would you mind living in Farnham? We've got lots of good bed and board."

"That's almost all I've ever lived in. You mean, you're hiring me?"

"You're good, and we need someone with a trans-Atlantic accent."

"You…you mean I won't be doing *Richard the Third*? I know it."

"Maybe later in the season. Maybe he'd sound more villainous as an American."

The handful of people in the audience chuckled and applauded. It was that simple. Just like that I had a job as an actor, in England; home of Robert Donat, Laurence Olivier, Alec Guinness, Richard Burton and William Shakespeare. Wow, I would actually be paid for something I loved! Things that are meant to be, do happen that easily.

Agdas was pleased, even though I'd only get to see her a few times a month. We did a new play every two weeks while at the same time rehearsing the next one. I kept my room in London and got a bed and board a block from the theater.

"Youa work with a pretty younga ladies?" she asked, trying to sound casual.

"Agdas, they are my work, you are my pleasure." I was embarrassed, realizing I'd just said it in front of the kids. But they applauded.

She pulled me to her, hugging me, saying loudly, "I ah better be!" Then whispered hoarsely in my ear, 'Or I ah keel you … .in bed."

She came with the kids to see me in *The Grass Is Greener*, and gave me an ovation. They and the local press and townspeople treated me like a star. It was all very flattering. A number of young female fans graciously offered their company to a young man away from home, but I liked Agdas. A lot. And was always a one-woman man.

English actors, even the enormously successful ones, have a reputation as incorrigible drinkers. It was a habit that didn't elude a few of the members of The Castle Theater. In long pub sessions, where I nursed a soft drink, I expressed my incredulity at such a self-destructive habit for people who are working at what they love subsidized by the government. I said I could understand it if they were in America and had to work as cab drivers or waiters, orange pickers or gas station attendants, to earn enough to support their dreams. And added, American actors didn't take to drink and drugs until they became successful and saw what they had to read. This always evoked a laugh, but they were never quite able to explain the English actor's proclivity to drink, unless maybe it was just living in England, which eventually got to me.

An Untossed Coin

My six months at The Castle Theater were up. I was given a couple of choices that would have allowed me to continue my craft. I was offered another six months with the company; the other, which was much more meaningful and probably more important, was the invitation extended by the director who hired me. He had been offered the position as Director of The Bristol Old Vic, which, next to London's Old Vic, was England's most prestigious theater company. This I thought long and hard about. I knew I did not want to continue at The Castle Theater. It would lead nowhere. The Bristol Old Vic could. We never got to do a Shakespeare play, but I was forever strolling around reciting endless monologues. I loved it. As did some of my fellow actors. Hearing me was why the director had invited me, but, I was becoming much more interested in television. Not movies. Not live theater. However, before I get back to The Castle Theater, and my decision to leave it and London, a few observations on why, in the beginning, television was so often literate, informative, and truly funny. And no longer is.

In the late forties and early fifties, the makers of TV sets had this box. In it was a tube that could broadcast pictures. In order to sell this box, the manufacturers had to have pictures that would compel people to watch. And buy. In the beginning, these boxes were placed in department store windows. People would gather on the street to look at them. The box builders knew people loved to be entertained and informed. So, they hired and gobbled up all the proven entertainers and public speakers around; they came from Broadway, burlesque, radio and later movies and newspapers, and were given shows. Milton Berle, aka Uncle Milty, became Mr. Television. People wanted to get off the sidewalk and sit in their own living rooms, so they began to buy the boxes, even though they were just black and white pictures.

In a couple of years, Uncle Milty was bumped out of first place by an articulate cleric, Bishop Sheen. Discovering talkers also sold boxes, they put on the boxes the best journalists and talkers the boxes would have with the likes of Edward R. Murrow, Charles Collingwood and Alistair Cooke, along with a host of other dedicated truth tellers.

Then came color, and Ed Sullivan and Lucille Ball, and a dozen wonderfully written and performed sitcoms. And on daring live television, the brilliant plays of Rod Serling and Paddy Chayefsky, never to be equaled again with gems like *The Twilight Zone* or *Star Trek.* The makers were now selling their boxes like M&M's by the millions. Families did not have just one box; they had two, three or four, with kids watching their own. Around the dinner table, if they ever gathered anymore, the conversation only came from the box.

Then the advertisers, the snake oil salesmen of our nation, moved in. At first, the makers of cars, which were unsafe, and sellers of cigarettes that killed you, or pharmaceuticals that drugged and addicted you, just bought a few minutes of commercials. They began selling products by the millions. To insure this profit-making would continue, they decided they wanted to have more control over what went into those boxes, so advertisers began to produce their own shows.

Then came reality television; my participation in the birth of it with *Real People* unfolds in detail down the line. With this, writers, performers and talent were no longer needed to fill these boxes. All that was needed for this genre was for the participants to have no sense of embarrassment or shame. With so many millions of boxes being sold with their technological improvements, there was no need for them to have any meaningful content. So, for the most part, they are back to where they started: empty boxes.

In the fifties, there were only three networks. Today there are hundreds. More straws in the same septic tank. Gary Deeb, probably the brightest critic of American television during the seventies and early eighties, syndicated by *The Chicago Tribune,* had the very best line about the boxes I ever read. He said, "Television is the only business in America where competition does not improve the product."

Shakespeare might have called what I have written above an 'aside;' but it is not. It is a preface to more interesting tales to come, tales nonexistent to me at the time.

I was torn between going to The Bristol Old Vic, and staying with Agdas, or going back to Los Angeles, or at least try to sneak back to Los Angeles. I took a shilling out of my pocket, thinking I'd toss it like Cary Grant in *Mr. Lucky.* The thing that kept crossing my mind as I stared at it, was that it was

English. I was American, or at least felt like one. Being an actor is playing make-believe. An escape from reality. I did not want to escape from reality. I wanted to live it. Enjoy it. The landlady interrupted my debating.

"Johnny," she hollered. "There's a phone call for you. From California," she said, handing me the receiver.

It was Haskell. He had loved my letters, and was anxious to tell me how happy he was for me, thrilled to hear I had been an actor, wanting to know if I was staying or ever coming back to LA, and if so, no matter when, to call him.

After hanging up, I pocketed the coin, and made a reservation to fly to New York.

IN AMERICA . . . AGAIN

A Goodbye Burger

Agdas and I said goodbye where we'd said hello: at Wimpy's over a hamburger. Neither of us ate, or even talked much. We knew this day was coming eventually, so it was surprisingly stress free. She was staying in England, fighting her husband's requests to send the children to him for two weeks. She felt he'd never return them. I felt bad for her. She was a decent, warm, generous woman, but I was too preoccupied with my own uncertainties. We did not kiss. We hugged, and shook hands. And that was it. Feelings for someone who'd been so intimately close and encouraging for over half a year were as absent in me as my appetite for the burger. I felt there was something wrong with me. Maybe there was, because I never had deep feelings for anyone. Sometimes, not even for myself.

Eight hours later, I was a basket case getting off the plane at LaGuardia. I had to go through immigration and customs. It wasn't going to be as simple as walking across the bridge at Niagara Falls. Anything could happen. The worst, which is what I expected, was that I'd be detained and sent to Toronto. I handed my passport to the large Immigration Officer, and said, "Wow, it's great to be home."

"Where's home?" he asked.

"Toronto," I said cheerily.

He looked at my passport, then me. "Why didn't you fly straight there?"

Just as cheerily, I blurted, "Two reasons: this is the quickest flight I could get out of London. And Toronto has no Stage Deli!"

He chuckled, handing me back my passport. "Enjoy your sandwich!"

Till now, this was one of the proudest moments in my life.

I had my sandwich at Grand Central, eating it while boarding a train to Los Angeles. I could have flown, but once past immigration, I was in no hurry. I would save money and have a lot of time to think. I had brought with me a half dozen rave reviews from the Castle Theater, which I read over and over. I could continue to pursue acting. I had impressive clippings to show agents. I had read somewhere that famous actor Robert Cummings had no theater background at all. He paid someone to put his name on a theater marquee, took a picture of it, and was signed by the first agent he showed it to. This time, though, I would not live in Hollywood. I would get a place just over the Hollywood Hills on the edge of the San Fernando Valley. It was a short electric car ride up the Cahuenga pass.

For the third time, I disembarked at Union Station across from Olvera Street. This time it had absolutely no fascination for me. I'd seen and heard it all. I picked up a newspaper, grabbed the first yellow cab, and got off at Cahuenga. Here I boarded an electric trolley. Ordinarily, I loved this ride, looking at the homes on the hills, the Hollywood Bowl on one side, the Pilgrimage Theater on the other. This time I was looking at furnished apartments for rent. I found one half a block from the stop on Bluffside Drive. It was a two-story brown stucco building below street level, with parking in the rear, and no swimming pool. There were about twenty furnished apartments, the largest being two bedrooms. I got the smallest and cheapest; second floor rear, over the garage. And loved it. The Valley was so much cleaner; so much more like California. It was head-shaking to imagine that a few days earlier I was living in a room in London.

Finding a place to live in the Valley was no big deal; there were thousands of apartments available. Finding a place to live, though, accidentally, that absolutely and totally changes and improves your life is more than a big deal. It is a big mystery. And maybe no accident. Maybe it is divine intervention. My luck was changing.

Having written this, I feel conflicted. You already know that I do not believe in this stuff. But what happened to me, and the people I met, I could never have met anywhere else. Some of Hollywood's most successful movies have been about haunted houses. If some homes are haunted, some may be blessed. For me, Bluffside Drive was blessed.

Friends and Neighbors

One of those blessings was Mort Lachman. He was in the two-bedroom, almost directly below me. It was not his residence. He had a huge house. This was his office. Every day of the week and often on weekends, at all hours, he and his partner, Bill Larkin, got together to pace and pound away on typewriters, writing jokes for Bob Hope. Mort had been Hope's head writer for years. He was in his mid-forties with dark hair, dark eyes, with an extremely low-key, devastating sense of humor. When Jackie Kennedy's daughter died right after birth, Mort said, "I wonder how much she left."

For me, there was no star bigger than Bob Hope. Mort and Bill always worked with the front door open. Often, when they'd see me, they'd call me in to chat. Why, I don't know. Even though I wanted to, not once did I ever ask about Bob Hope. I only asked about them and how they ended up doing what they do. When they asked me what I wanted to do, I said I wasn't sure. Maybe acting.

One day, Mort asked me if I'd been up for any parts recently. I told him I was up for a part as a waiter.

"In a film?" he asked.

"No, in a restaurant!" He and Bill howled. I continued. "It's an Indonesian restaurant on Lankershim. It's free food."

"Good for you." Then after a moment, Bill said, "Are you interested in writing?"

"Truthfully, I'm more interested in reading. I don't even know if I could write. Certainly not jokes."

"You'd be surprised at what you can do if you have to; like eating Indonesian food," Mort said with his usual straight face.

"You know," I said, almost apologetically, "Lucille Ball is the only comedienne I've ever heard compliment or mention her writers. Mr. Hope refers to you as 'the boys.' Doesn't that bother you?"

Mort didn't miss a beat. "That's not how he writes the checks. We refer to him as Piggy."

"Piggy? Why?"

Bill chimed in, "He can't go to a restaurant, meet some official or change planes without calling at all hours of the night or day and asking us for restaurant jokes, official jokes or changing plane jokes. Thus Piggy!"

I never mentioned that I had written two almost-produced screenplays, or that one was for Haskell Wexler. Every waiter and cabdriver and barber in town had a screenplay. I also put off calling Haskell to tell him I was back. I didn't want to appear as though I might need a job. Or sympathy. I'd wait a while.

In the apartment directly below me was another blessing, a tall, gangly bachelor in his late thirties who resembled Gary Cooper. He was always sitting on the steps holding a guitar that he seldom played. His name was Wes Butler. He was the director of a local morning childrens' show on KABC TV called *Chucko the Clown*. He had a lot of time on his hands after nine a.m. I didn't have to go into the restaurant until late afternoon, so we spent a lot of time just sitting and talking. What we talked about mostly was the sad state of TV, especially *Chucko the Clown*.

In the two-bedroom apartment to my right was a successful liquor ad salesman, Robert Klein. He was tall, had a pleasant pale face because he never came outdoors, about forty, and had the worst toupee I ever saw. Indoors he was always on the phone. Lying down. Toupee askew. He was not soliciting business; he was soliciting women. Every single day. And almost every single day, one would show up. He introduced himself to me, which I thought was thoughtful. A few times he invited me into his apartment for a drink or chat. But the chatting was him on the phone and me watching in amazement. He was soft spoken and chuckling, never once uttering anything remotely salacious or sexy. Just chit chat. And not long after he'd hang up, there'd be a knock on the door. And I would leave. Only Errol Flynn or Warren Beatty could have had as many women as Robert. He was a woman whisperer.

A very attractive friendly couple in their late twenties lived on the second floor of the apartment building directly across the driveway. Both accountants and Republican. Their proximity led to a lot of very lively discussions about Castro, Cuba, the Cold War, nuclear war, and fallout shelters.

Every one of these neighbors changed my life. The one who changed it the most, though, was not a neighbor. He was a customer in the Indonesian restaurant: Abe Pelter. He was in his late forties, the father of three bright, lively, sweet children, two boys and a younger girl. His wife had the kind of warmth you'd want to see in a woman of her position: a head nurse at Cedars Sinai Hospital where her brother, Dr. Kleeman, another gentle soul, was head of surgery.

They were totally unlike Abe, the patriarch, as was I. He was a tough, angry, opinionated Jewish private investigator with a perpetual five o'clock shadow, which made him look meaner. He had a sack of chips on his shoulder, one for all the enemies of Israel and for every American politician and reporter, except for I. F. Stone. How and why he took a sudden liking to me, I have no idea.

He and his family came in early one evening and sat at my table. Before handing the menu to the customers, I had to recite a small story about the origins of the food, their Indonesian names, and how they were prepared. Seeing everyone was seated and comfortable, I approached the table, afraid to begin my story. Abe, in a very loud voice, was regaling his family with the tale of some politician's latest skullduggery. His family looked at me, obviously waiting for him to finish.

Following their gaze, he turned to me. "Whatta you want?" he growled.

"Excuse me, sir," I stammered. "Before I hand you the menus, I'm supposed to tell you a story about the food, but I like your story better."

"That's funny," one of his kids said.

Abe glowered at me. "Go ahead, tell it. It's our first time here. And it may be our last."

I told my story and handed them menus.

"What does all that Indonesian gibberish mean?" he grunted.

"Sir, honestly, I haven't the foggiest idea. But I think it means yummy."

The kids laughed; so did his wife.

"Do you eat this stuff?" he asked

"Twice a day."

"What do you suggest?"

"Dupars," I said with a straight face, referring to another restaurant.

He didn't crack a smile, just stared at me, but his family roared.

They eventually ordered the lamb and peanut butter sauce, which I said was really their best dish. And it was.

During the meal, he called me over, asking where I'd come from, what I wanted to do, did I have family? I kept my answers short to not intrude on them. When he paid the bill, he handed me a twenty-dollar bill as a tip

"Sir," I said, as I said to everyone who overtipped me, "that's too much. It's more than twenty percent."

"Kid, that's not for the service or food, that's for the story," he said with a hint of a smile. "And we won't be coming back."

"Oh, I'm sorry. You didn't like it?"

"It was fine, but not for us, but we'll be seeing you again."

I looked at him, bewildered.

"No family, eh?" The 'eh' was his humorous attempt at making fun of Canadians. "Well, next Saturday, the Sabbath, you're coming over to our house for lunch." Whereupon he thrust a note with their name, address and phone number on it. I hadn't heard him ask his wife or children if they thought it was all right. As he walked away, he turned and growled, "You be there."

His wife, Ruth said, "Please, come." She smiled. The kids waved.

That Saturday was the first of dozens of lunches, dinners, and gatherings I had with this unique, argumentative, loving family to whom I would become sort of a surrogate son and brother. At the head of the table sat this always hard-as-nails, no-nonsense pit bull of a man with this inexplicable, unlikely soft spot for me. His toughness and loud prejudices and opinions were expressed at every gathering. One day, to my total shock, it manifested itself physically to a family member.

A Goodbye Gathering

As radically pro-Israel as Abe was, the family's observances of Jewish Holidays were rather casual or almost nonexistent. They were more an excuse to a have a large gathering of relatives and friends over. Most of the friends and family had larger homes or positions in life, especially his younger brother, Lenny, who had become a millionaire selling real estate in the Valley, but it was always Abe's abode to which they came.

One gathering I was invited to attend was especially large and important; it was Rosh Hashanah. It wasn't so much to welcome in the New Year, but to say goodbye to Lenny.

Lenny was six years younger than Abe, and six inches taller. They had the same intense blue eyes, the same voice, and the same angry way of expressing even the mildest of opinions, except that Lenny didn't seem to have any soft side. And Lenny drank. A lot.

As the evening wore on, people gathered around the two brothers. Usually it would be Abe holding court, but now it was Lenny, with a wobbly glass held high.

"Little, big brother," came the loud slurp, "I beat you to it! Monday I leave for New York then Tel Aviv. El Al. Best goddamn airline in the world!"

Everyone cheered and raised a toast, "L 'Chaim!"

"Twenty-five years," Lenny went on, "selling real estate in this goddamn valley to all kinds of fucking goyim, and a few Jews, and saved all my money, just bought beer."

They all laughed.

"You know how I said goodbye to this fucking job and this fucking valley?" He paused, savoring what he was about to say. "Last night I took out my ladder, climbed on my roof, took out my dick, and pissed on San Fernando Valley."

The awkward silence was broken by his wife. "He actually peed all over his deck chairs." There was loud laughter of relief.

Abe hugged his brother. "I'll miss you," he said. "But, I'll be joining you."

Knowing what the occasion was going to be, and out of my affection for Abe, I had asked Bob Klein how to say something nice in Hebrew or whatever. I didn't like him, but I said, "Lenny, la shona tova teka tavul." Yiddish for *May you be written in the book of Life,* one of the nicest blessings Bob said that you could bestow upon a Jew at this time of year. Everyone stopped, as in a freeze frame, then applauded and cheered.

Abe raised his arms and rushed over. "My goyisha," he exclaimed loudly, as he put his arm tightly around my shoulder.

"Where'd you learn that?" he asked with a proud smile

"My next door neighbor."

"Good for you," he said. "Oh, by the way, I've got something for you. Come 'ere!" He led me into the living room and handed me a copy of I. F. Stone's *Weekly*. "I got you a subscription. Six months. If you like it, after that, you're on your own."

I got I.F. Stone's incredible newsletter for over twenty years, until the day he retired. The *I* stood for Izzy. I never found out what the *F* stood for, unless it was fuck the establishment. There was absolutely no one like him on TV or in print. At the time, there were a few effective journalists: Ed Murrow and Charles Collingwood on television; in the newspapers, Drew Pearson and Jack Anderson, and earlier, H.L. Mencken, the savage sage of Baltimore, but Stone was better than all of them, offering his literate insights and revelations in a tiny paper never more than four to six pages in length. At the height of The Cold War with the Evil Russian Empire, he uncovered illegal war profiteering by corrupt military contractors and congressmen, exposed the racism of Southern senators and politicians long before the Civil Rights Sixties, detailed unconstitutional rulings by the Supreme Court, and prophetically catalogued the machinations of the moneymen whose maneuverings were leading America inexorably into a land war in southeast Asia. He did it in a language and style that was like music for the eyes.

As much as I wanted to be a citizen, I loved reading about the shenanigans of our rulers and wreckers. The high and mighty lowlifes. For reading, it was Stone; for listening, it was Abe. Even more so than Haskell. I had told Abe of my failed screenwriting adventure with Haskell. He asked if I'd called him since returning from England. I told him no.

"Why not?" he asked gruffly.

"Mr. Pelter–"

"Abe," he corrected.

"He … he is very rich and famous. I feel a little out of place."

"What are you gonna do? Just call poor people? He likes you. He can help you. Call him."

"Yes, sir." I nodded.

Lenny and the others were still in the dining room. Abe and I were interrupted by a high-pitched voice yelping, "Whee! Whee!" We turned. Jumping up and down on the large sofa by the back window was a seven or eight-year-old boy.

Abe said sternly, "Hey, Albert. That's enough."

Unperturbed, Albert continued his bouncing. "Whee! Whee!"

Slowly and deliberately, Abe rose, crossed to the boy and stopped. He watched calmly for a moment, like a spectator. When young Albert was mid-air, Abe grabbed him by the waist, pulled him forward and placed his feet on the carpeted floor.

"That's not a trampoline, young man. That's a couch, and that's what it's to be used for."

He returned to his seat and, as though he had put the recorder on pause, we continued our conversation exactly where we had left off. In less than a minute we heard the thumping and a much quieter "Whee."

This time Abe whirled from his seat, raced across the short space, waiting for the boy to be airborne. The boy was smiling at Abe as he bounced. When the kid reached his joyous apex, Abe smacked him hard right across the face. The boy somersaulted through the air, landing near the dining room. There was a loud thump and an even louder scream.

"Albert! Albert!" the mother screamed, rushing to her son. Everyone froze, watching in shock. She shrieked at Abe. "My baby. My baby! What did you do to my baby? You're insane! Horrible!"

Abe stared at the mother for a moment, letting her scream, then said calmly, "No, Milly, what's horrible is how you're raising your son. I've seen it too often. I don't care how he behaves or misbehaves in your house, but not in mine."

The mother grabbed the boy, pulling him to her chest, yelling, "What do you know? You don't know anything?"

Abe was calm. "What I know, Milly, is that you have a dog that you have taught to sit, and you can't train your kid to do the same."

"We're outa here. Outa here," she bellowed. She carried the boy through the kitchen to the front door. "We never want to see you again. Ever!" She jerked the door open, child in tow, followed by her wordless, but well-trained husband, then slammed it shut.

The tension was broken by Lenny. "Jesus Christ, Abe, that was terrific. You know how many times I've wanted to punch that snotty little bastard! That calls for another beer!"

I was stunned by what I had just witnessed in a family. For an instant, it brought back unwanted memories. But I saw no viciousness in Abe's actions. He was calculated and casual. The more I knew him, the more I could see his ever-present aura of toughness was a shield to a soft, concerned heart that had a gravitational pull to all who came in contact with him.

Two months later, at another large gathering, even larger than the goodbye get-together for Lenny, there was another one. As if nothing had ever happened, there were the parents and Albert. The occasion for this hastily called affair was to welcome Lenny home. The Lenny I saw that evening was not the Lenny I had seen a mere eight weeks earlier. It was as though he was a soldier returning from the carnage of war. He was quiet. And sober. When he had left for Israel, he sold everything. He was going to live the dream he and his younger brother had dreamed for years: to live in a country that was theirs, where they belonged, free of prejudice and pogroms. He wanted to live in a kibbutz, to sing, *This Land is My Land*. But here he was, sitting at the end of the dining room table, next to Abe.

Many had come sixty days earlier to witness his departure; more were in attendance to witness his return. There was lots of food and plenty to drink as usual, but few were eating or drinking. Even the kids were quiet. Everyone gathered around the long table, sitting and standing, craning to hear the two brothers talking. Finally, Abe patted his brother on the shoulder. "Okay, Lenny, get up and tell everyone why you're back." Lenny didn't move or look up. "Come on, Lenny." Abe patted him again.

Lenny rose slowly, glancing at the faces locked on him. After a thoughtful pause, he said flatly, "Too many fucking Jews like me. The rudest, meanest, toughest bastards I ever met. I couldn't stand it." Then he sat, as though defeated.

It was the first time I'd heard Abe chuckle since trying to serve him at the restaurant. Soon everyone was laughing. Someone I couldn't see said, "Lenny, are you kidding?"

Lenny replied, "No. Goddamn it, I can barely stand myself. I don't need to be around a bunch of me's!"

I didn't know whether to laugh or feel sorry for him. The months I was invited to be with this colorful, cultured, involved family made to feel like one of them, whatever ambitions I had, expanded. I wanted to be able to keep up with them. More than that, I wanted to accomplish something so that I might be able to share something with them. To repay them. To make them proud they had befriended me. To them, I was never a waiter. I was what was inside me. The more they liked me, the more I liked myself. So, I called "the rich famous guy," Haskell. He was thrilled to hear from me, scolding me for not having called sooner, inviting me over right away because he had a terrific idea for me. An idea for a script. No one was happier for me than Abe.

Another Script

Marion and Haskell's greeting was warmer than ever. As was Blackie's; he, too, was glad to see me. Haskell admonished me again for not calling sooner, asking why.

"I just wanted to get settled. Get a place and a job."

"How long you been back?" Hsskell asked.

"Six months."

"Jesus Christ, you should have called. You have a job?"

"A waiter. At an Indonesian restaurant on Lankershim."

He chuckled. "You definitely should've called. Makin' any money? Good tips?"

"The best tip I got was from a William Morris agent. He told me to leave town."

Haskell howled. He loved Hollywood putdowns. Didn't everyone?

"Johnny, Marion and I reread your letters a dozen times. They are beautiful." He was leaning forward. "I have a terrific idea."

Inside I smiled. There was 'terrific' again. It was as common in his dialogue as 'You know,' to some people, and 'eh' to Canadians, but this 'terrific' was more up than usual.

"Your story," he said emphatically. "You'll do a script about your story." He smiled at me, letting the good news sink in.

"What story?" I asked. I couldn't be telling him and the world I was an illegal, and may always be. "Finding my father. That's just an incident. Not a story."

He got really animated. "No. No. No. Your story. That summer lost in the woods. The farm. The girlfriend. And that freak, your friend with no legs but feet. And why you were there. That Uncle." He was now standing. "Johnny, it's a killer. An original. How often do you ever see a sexy real love story between young kids? Kids younger than Romeo and Juliet? And domestic violence. It is an epidemic in this country. Never mentioned. Never really shown. This is the perfect black and white movie. And you can write it."

"Wow," was all I could manage. I was overwhelmed.

"Movies like this only come out of Europe. Sexual awakenings. Real life. We could shoot it in Canada. You're Canadian. Canadian content. They'd help fund it. Johnny, I have the money. There's no one to say no. No Sinatra, no Columbia. No politicians."

He was trying to sell me, as though I was important.

"What do think? I have an office and secretary at Metromedia. You use her and the typewriter during the day, and keep your night job, if you like. What yah think?"

It was a surprising joy for me to look and listen to him. Probably the most intellectual man I knew; the only multimillionaire I knew, acting as excited as a kid getting a new toy.

"It sounds interesting."

"Hell, it's more than interesting," he exclaimed. "It's terrific. You write fast. How long could it take?"

"I think I could do it in less than six weeks."

"Great I'm going to South America again. I'll be back in about five weeks. Marion and Mark will be here, but you can come up anytime."

Marion who had been watching and smiling all the time said, "John, consider this a second home. You come anytime, and don't have to call."

"And," Haskell added emphatically. "this time you will get $600 a week, and take it. When we start it and finish it, there'll be a couple larger paychecks." He had the warmest, most satisfied smile ever directed at me. "How do you feel? Your third script is the charm." He patted me firmly on the back, like a buddy.

"Great," I said. "Really great. Thank you." What I really wanted to tell him, though, was how I really felt: that I belonged.

Endless Summer

That's what I would call it: Endless Summer. I couldn't wait to call Abe with the news.

"Are you getting paid?" he asked.

"Six hundred a week."

"I didn't ask you how much, just as long as you're getting paid."

"For five or six weeks."

"Be sure and save it. If you need anything, holler. And don't be a Hollywood stranger. We're here."

"You know I'll be there." I chuckled.

"Good for you, son, and good luck." He hung up. His "son" went right through me, to my heart. My God, I was happy to be able to share good news with him and his family. Misery and bad news I had always kept to myself. Regardless of how miserable or bad, people don't want yours heaped on top of theirs. But the pleasure of good news is often doubled when shared with those you care about. The reason I write "often" though, is because when I got to be 'rich and famous' some folks absolutely hated to hear my good news!

Haskell's spacious, sparsely furnished office was at the Channel 11 Studios, KTTV on Sunset near the freeway. I sat down at my own desk in the back room, clicked on the new electric typewriter and inserted the first blank page. I was what they call in Hollywood, a 'hyphenate.' I was a writer-waiter, seven exciting days a week, from eight a.m. to four p.m., writing my Canadian story, then off to Lankershim Boulevard to write Indonesian food orders. My energy was limitless. As was my happiness. The summer I was writing about was not that far away, but it flowed easily and painlessly. I had a permanent smile on my face. My life had a purpose. For five weeks, anyway.

Having a deadline always makes writing easier; time is standing over you with a whip. Haskell's secretary, in the front office, retyped mine into proper script form. She was slender, tall, and as verbal and smart as she was attractive. If she was any barometer of how I was doing, I was doing really well. Every day at four, I'd give my finished pages to her. And every day she would comment, "Oh, Johnny, this is really, really wonderful." A couple of times she had tears in her eyes. Seeing that coming from her meant more than the $600.00 coming from Haskell.

With the immediate captive audience in front of me, the pages flew off the typewriter. During that time, I never spoke to Haskell. A week before his return he called from Brazil to talk with his secretary. I heard her say softly to him, "Haskell, it's wonderful." My last day, I handed her the final pages and thanked her for her help, and said I hoped to see her again soon.

"Are you kidding? We'll be working together a long time. I can't wait to read the ending. It's wonderful!"

That was a Friday. It was weird not having anything to type over the weekend. At the restaurant, as busy as I was, I had a post-birth empty feeling. The script was done, but I had no idea just how *done* it was.

A Pink Slip of the Tongue

Sunday, Haskell's secretary called from the office, saying Haskell wanted the script delivered to his house Monday morning, and would I be in the office by nine so he could talk to me? As she hung up, she said, "It really is wonderful, Johnny. I loved the ending. Made me cry. Good luck!"

The ending was a kid boarding a train to America, Haskell's camera staying on it till it disappeared over the horizon. Fade to black.

On the way to KTTV early Monday, I did what I often did when I am nervous about whether I was going to get good or bad news on an important day; I looked for omens from the universe; just little hints about what may lie ahead. Green lights, parking spaces, beams of sunlight. Stuff I knew was stupid, but could not help. There were no such signs until I got to the office, a half hour early. The door was locked. My stomach tightened. Was this an omen?

Haskell's secretary arrived, smiling brightly as she opened the door and apologized for the delay. She had just come from Haskell's. I waited for another compliment from her. It never came.

"I'll wait in my office," I said.

"He'll be calling shortly, John. I'm sure."

Too pumped and too nervous, I couldn't sit. I just paced. She thoughtfully brought *The Reporter* and *Daily Variety,* as she did every day. I couldn't even glance at them.

The phone rang, and my insides jumped. The calls weren't from Haskell. Then the first one came. About nine-thirty.

"Kid, this is terrific stuff," he said in a high voice.

I was immediately relieved. What a great omen!

"How far in are you?" I asked, nervously.

"About twenty-five pages. Just terrific!"

"How did your shoot go?" I didn't care. I was just trying to make conversation I knew he liked.

"Fine. Let me finish this, and I'll get right back to you!" He hung up.

Waiting, I thought about his comment about my third script being the one. That made me feel better. Then I began to think about the other two that went nowhere, but how much he said he loved them; how he would call me from the studio so excited. That made me feel worse. Hamlet was absolutely right: Too much thinking is not a good thing. At times like that, my mind is not good company.

The phone rang. His secretary called out, "Johnny, Haskell!"

"Kid, (the first time he ever called me that) "the Christmas scene with you dodging that bow and arrow, unbelievable stuff. Absolutely terrifying. Just terrific. Gimme an hour. Let me finish it, then we'll meet and get down to some serious business. Good for you." He hung up again.

I was euphoric. How lucky am I? I lived that. And there I was, illegally, about to make a movie about it. More than having a movie, I would have a passport. It was difficult not to cry.

The secretary made me even happier. She peeked in with a big smile. "He seems to like it. A lot. Good for you." Then closed the door.

When Haskel called the third time and, as it turned out, the last time, he didn't sound quite as enthusiastic. "There's a lot of good stuff here, really good stuff, Johnny." He wasn't calling me, kid now. Just Johnny. "But I don't like the ending. We've got to fix it."

"What's wrong with the ending? Your secretary loved it. She said she cried." I felt stupid saying that. What does he care what his secretary thinks?

"That may be it," he said. "It's a little sappy and upbeat."

"What do you mean?" I asked, firmly. "Where?"

"The ending. I mean, you're telling this heavy story about this poor kid, a neglectful, battered alcoholic mother, and her thug lover, and it's a great touch of irony, he's in the military, then the ending, this young teenager hopping a train to America. A little corny."

I was stunned. And edgy. "But that's how it happened, Haskell. It's true. That's why you liked it. The kid had hopes, and so will the audience."

"It doesn't work for me. It's almost Disney. We can rework it."

"How?"

"The whole story is dark. That's what makes it interesting. The ending has to reflect that. It just looks Disney to me."

"Haskell, it is not dark. It's about surviving the dark. Disney? You're kidding!" My voice was louder than I wanted it. "Disney never came close to making a film where a drunken soldier tries to murder a child with a bow and arrow, and beats the shit out of the kid's drunken mother, so much so that the kid has to clean the shit off the stair landing. That's nonsense." I stopped. I didn't mean to say 'nonsense' to that very successful cameraman. And he didn't like hearing it from a kid. His silence said it. For him. I tried to continue softly. "What do you suggest I do to fix it?"

He did not answer. I did not speak to break the long silence, afraid I might offend him again. After all, who was I? I could sense he was drifting away. It was verified with the flat distant tone in his voice.

"I'm, I'm not sure." He paused again. "It has to be made darker, especially the end. We'll have to talk about it. Let me think about it."

The tone, not at all like the way he talked, told me there'd be no thinking or talking about it. What could I say to win his enthusiasm back? Nothing. I wasn't going to suck up and beg, no matter how rich and famous. And no matter how much I wanted it.

I was seething. For him to compare it to Disney was ridiculous. "Haskell," I said calmly, "maybe you just solved the problem on how to make it darker."

"What do you mean?'" he asked with an edge

"We'll make the kid black!"

I wasn't sure where it came from. I was not even happy I said it. I was pissed. He was even less happy. He banged down the phone immediately. We never talked again. I had struck a nerve.

He had loved hearing the story about my brother Ronnie, spending two years at Keesler Air Base in Biloxi, and coming out a raving murderous Southern redneck killer. And how my sister and I had to keep him from murdering my black friend in a Toronto diner. He talked passionately and often about civil rights in his living room. But when the doors opened, I never saw him walk the talk. His documentary about poor peasant farmers in Brazil went nowhere. I loved his work, though. He was a brilliant cameraman. I loved his family, and especially his library. I would happily suffer that major disappointment again for the experience of knowing him again.

Showbiz and Other Odd Jobs

I phoned Abe and told the story. He laughed, as though he knew the outcome. And laughed even louder, unusual for him, when he heard what I had said to end my screenwriting career.

"Ya know, son," he said, "when negotiating or arguing with people, there are only two categories of words: One, what I wish I'd said, and two, what I'm sorry I said. It sounds like you did the impossible and employed both at the same time!"

"Well, I guess it's back to Indonesian food," I said.

"Don't worry, son. You're gonna do fine. And you know there's always a different menu and friends here. And we expect to see you a lot.

"Thanks, Mr. Pelter."

"Son, it's Abe. From what I know of rich limousine liberals like your friend, they never go beyond lip service. What you said to your friend in defense of your work, hit him where he wished he lived ... in his heart and not his mouth."

"Sir, I just hope it is not a bad habit I have."

"Don't you ever hold back your truths. It cleans you out. Now get some rest. We'll see you soon."

But I didn't see them soon. Or often. I was totally committed to becoming an actor, a working actor.

There are no proven blueprints to follow in establishing a theatrical career, so I just scrambled around. I was like an isolated sperm pushing my way up the fallopian tube of fame, looking to latch on to a life in showbiz, looking for an agent. Let alone a job. I had quit my real one to pursue in Hollywood what they call making the rounds. That is the perfect word for it. 'Rounds.' You go in endless circles. It is also a boxing term. Boxers only get punched for fifteen rounds maximum. In Hollywood, actors get punched hundreds of rounds. Without an agent, there's no one in your corner to pull you up to continue the fight. You're on your own. It is brutal.

The dozens of agents, those who would even see me, said I was no different from thousands of other struggling young men in Hollywood, and that my reviews from a small English repertory theater were worthless. The agents interested in me, and there were a lot, were not interested in me as an actor, but as a young man. One of the town's most successful agents to two of film's most successful 'heartthrobs,' came right to the point. In rebutting this one, I said, "Are there any lady agents in this town you could recommend?"

Not even the two female agents I saw wanted me, not even as a young man. So, I stopped wanting an agent. But I wasn't giving up on theater where hopefully I'd get reviews that mattered.

I joined a workshop at a theater called The Player's Ring on Santa Monica. I did a few scenes attended by agents with a nice fellow about my size named Robert Vaughn. He was gobbled up immediately, off to make movies, and years later to star in TV's *The Man from Uncle*. After a few months of not even a nibble, I gave up on being in workshops. Instead, I would build one. And a small theater. The town was crawling with people like myself, paying to get into workshops, and paying more to get into one with a theater, which was not that common. After weeks of scouting, I found the perfect spot. It was on Ventura Boulevard in Studio City, upstairs over a Russian restaurant. It had a perfect, low proscenium stage, but no chairs. These were surprisingly easy to get. Small theaters were closing down almost as fast as people were leaving town, giving up to go home. We got forty-five fairly decent ones. Perfect. Fifteen against each wall facing the stage, making it almost like theater in the round. When word got out, half a dozen fellow thespians and strangers showed up to help. We lined the stairway leading up with movie and theater posters. It looked fabulous. We called it The Studio City Playhouse. Ads in the trades and Valley Papers brought dozens of calls. I canvassed shops on Ventura about buying a five-dollar ad in our programs. The first buyer was the owner of a hole-in-the-wall deli with no tables and only six stools. His name was Art, close to my age, with the slight belly of one who enjoyed his own sandwiches, which he wrote in his ad 'Each sandwich a work of Art.' Years later, he catered nearly every show I did. The theater, even the building is long gone. Sadly, so is Art. But his meticulous, large deli on Ventura has grown into one of the very best in the country.

When Bob Klein saw out first show with the ad-filled program, he told me I could make more money part-time selling liquor ads for him, saying people prefer booze to corned beef. I declined because in the beginning, everything was coming up roses. The thorns came later. Over the six months or so that we had our cabin in the sky, as one actress called it, there were always about twenty of us, all shapes, sizes, and sexual orientations. One of the surprising things I learned early as the director was that women of all ages, married or otherwise, would offer, and sometimes beg, to do anything for just a small part in a small production, even if there was no money. Some even offered that. Many of those women came from what appeared to be good families or relationships. What possibly could be forcing them to demean themselves just to be seen? And not seen by too many people at that. Maybe it was just a way for them to say they matter. But regardless of the attractiveness of some of the offers, I always declined. It had nothing to do with morality, which in a different setting I might have lacked; and it had nothing to do with lusting, which I didn't lack. It simply had to do with control. You cannot control those you roll. Politics may be best when it's democratic; Ironically Art is best when it's fascist.

The other thing I learned was how godawful hard it was to make any money at this. The workshops were always full, kept at twenty, to make it sound elite, so there were always folks clambering to get in. Our first production was *The Tender Trap*. (The film starred Frank Sinatra, Debbie Reynolds, and David Wayne.) We ran Fridays and Saturdays, a different play every month. Although almost always well reviewed, and sold out, some weeks I barely broke even. After half a year, my emotional bank was also draining.

Abe had brought his relatives and friends a couple of times, which thrilled me, but theater-going was not his thing. He always complimented me, yet I could see he was there more for moral and financial support, rather than artistic nurturing. With a few free days and nights, I figured I'd take Bob up on his offer.

Two Deaths of a Salesman

The part-time job Bob offered me was simple: Walk into liquor stores in Orange County without an appointment, talk to the owner or manager, show him a fancy catalogue, which went free to thousands of potential customers, and tell him his ad would only cost a hundred bucks. To get to Orange County, Bob lent me his car. I hated it. And the managers seemed to hate me. Often, I had to just stand by while he was dealing with a customer. And he could sense why I was hanging around. Not only was it a pain in the ass, it was a pain in my arm. The fourth day I got such a severe pain in my left arm, I could not lift it. I could barely drive back to Bluffside Drive to quit. (Ten years later, while getting an insurance physical exam for a show, the doctor asked if I'd ever had a heart attack.)

"That's okay, kiddo," Bob said. "Not everybody's cut out for it. Maybe you'd be better at selling if you didn't have to look at people." He chuckled.

"What do you mean?"

"I have a friend, Sy, who's really successful. He runs a boiler room in Hollywood. A big one. He makes a fortune."

"What's a boiler room?"

"People sit at phone banks and make calls to homeowners to make appointments for the sales guys to go out and sell siding."

"Siding?'

"Aluminum siding. It's an aluminum wrapping or coating that goes on the outside of a house to make it look nicer and protect it from wear and weather. And maybe increases its value. At least that's what they tell the buyers."

"Does it?"

"I dunno. It's an easy sell. You love to talk to people. Do you want me to talk to him?"

"I guess it couldn't hurt. Thanks"

Sy's boiler room was two blocks from Melrose and Santa Monica in Hollywood. Sy, a handsome man in his late thirties, dressed in a smart shirt and slacks, led me down the basement stairs from his comfortable office, and introduced me to his manager, Lenny. Lenny had tired skin and tired eyes, and with his grey unkempt hair, looked older than he was.

They pointed proudly to their operation. It was a long room. All the way down one side were about eighteen cubbyholes or cubicles, each one occupied by a man talking on a phone. All men. Not one woman. The low rumbling and soft chatter sounded like a nest of angry hornets.

Lenny handed me a piece of paper. "Take a look at this. Memorize it. And don't try to improvise. This is tested. And proven." It was a typed sales pitch.

Sy patted me on the shoulder. "Take it home. And if it's for you, you can start tomorrow. Any hours you want. Four dollars an hour, plus five percent commission."

I started working just Monday through Wednesday, then Sunday, four hours a night, leaving plenty of time for my Studio City Playhouse. That little theater was my whole life; making those phone calls to strangers was a way to help keep it going.

To make the calls easy, each of us was given a reverse phone directory. This is a phone book sold by the phone company to telemarketers. It lists addresses, then the names. This way we know who is answering the phone, so we can address them warmly by name. My area was central Los Angeles. The black area. From the first call, what was surprising to me was it was never a man who answered, but always a woman. If the woman wasn't interested in what we were selling, she was often happy just to be talking to someone. Being me, once engaged in some of those conversations, I lost all interest in selling. I just enjoyed talking to them, listening to their stories. It was a revelation. Some I'd talk to for over an hour. On a few occasions, I was invited to the house and told not to bring aluminum. I always warmly declined, saying it would cost me my job.

Strangely, just talking to and not selling, those ladies led to a lot of leads, which led to a number of sales. Before the month was out, I earned more in commission than Sy's top callers. Sy came to me, a big smile on his face. "Kid, how'd you like to make ten times what you're makin'?"

"How?" I asked.

"Lenny says you are a natural. He'd like to go with you as his partner. We have two-man teams. Your commission would be a chunk of the sale. Wanna try it?"

I shrugged. "Sure." I wasn't thinking of the money so much. I was intensely curious about meeting the people I was talking to, where they lived.

Having been the voice on the phone, I would be the opener; the closer. Lenny, the pro. Lenny explained how it all worked, as though he was teaching me how to hunt. The average cost to the homeowner for the siding was between $1500.00 and $2000.00. Sometimes more. Almost none of the buyers had a nickel to deposit. That didn't matter. The contracts were always approved and carried by the Bank of America, who would give us the money upon closing.

He smiled. "A piece of cake, kid. Chocolate cake."

We were on our way in Lenny's Cadillac. My first customer sounded like a very nice lonely woman with one boy, and no husband; the good news, she owned the house outright, inherited from her folks, and could well afford the siding. Lenny was pumped.

We took the Harbor Freeway to the exit nearest her street and address in the heart of Watts. When we turned off, it was like turning into another country. I'd never seen anything like it. Certainly not in movies. Not even in newsreels. Or even TV. Not in America. There were rows of shabby untended homes, trash and junk all over the front yards. The early evening made it all look darker. Even ominous. Especially with folks stopping and staring at the Cadillac. Not to Lenny, though, who was humming to himself. He was very familiar with the neighborhood.

We passed one or two homes where the tenants had tried to create a nice front yard, or grow a little garden, or even paint and clean the house. It was commendable. And sad.

"That's one of our jobs," he said, pointing through a haze of his cigar smoke at a home covered with pink aluminum siding. "Twenty-three hundred bucks," he said. "Here it is. Let's go make some money!"

He stopped in front of a two-story, rust-brown small frame house with a bicycle and a few toys scattered around the front lawn. After ascending the short flight of wooden stairs, we crossed to the front door. The screen door was locked. The lady was expecting us. She said she would be glad to see us at the appointed time. I was curious to see the owner of that nice voice, who I was certain would greet us with a smile. I was also curious to see how I would do in such strange surroundings.

There was no response to my knock. I knocked again. Harder. Again, no response. I listened and said, "The TV's on. Do you think she hears us? Think she's in? She said she'd be waiting for us."

"She's in. They're always late." He flicked his cigar butt onto the narrow driveway.

I heard a lock being clicked back. "Here she is," I said.

The door opened slowly. When it was halfway opened, I looked into the darkness, expecting to see a woman. Then a small indifferent voice said, "Whatcha want?"

I looked down. Looking up at us expressionless was her boy, about eight with dark brown skin and even darker eyes and tight curly hair.

"Hi, is your mother home?" I asked politely.

"Whatcha want?" he repeated, motionless.

"Your Mom's expecting us," I said.

"Whatcha want?" His tone was unwelcoming.

The boy's tone irritated me, but I remained gracious. "My name is John Barbour. I spoke to your mother the other night about something that might benefit her, and she invited my associate here, Lenny, and me to come by at seven this evening to sit with her to talk about it. Is she in?"

"Whaddya want?" he repeated.

It was obvious he wasn't going to budge. I was in a standoff with this kid. "What's your name, young man?" I asked, as sincerely as I could fake it.

He didn't miss a beat or change his script. "Whaddya want?"

I was really irritated. I thought, *I'll show this little bugger*! "Young man," I began matter- of-factly, "we are duly authorized representatives of a national and global manufacturing consortium, which is currently engaged in a major advertising campaign that is seeking in specific geographical areas a number of domiciles most suitable to showcase and exploit a remarkable new colorful alloy that would not only enhance the aesthetics and functionality of the selected domicile, but would also enhance substantially the revenue of what might be an even impecunious owner of such domicile and would therefore–"

I was suddenly cut off in mid-sentence by a woman's loud voice calling from the back in the house. "Henry, who dat?"

Henry shouted, "It's da aluminum man agin, ma. Wan any?"

There was a brief pause, then Lenny whirled around and started howling. I was dumbstruck. I stared at the kid who just stared back. Lenny was doubled over, clutching his stomach, almost stumbling back down the stairs.

I said nothing to the kid. What was there to say? I walked back to the car, which Lenny was already in, still howling. I never felt so useless in my life. Or so used. I waited for Lenny to light another cigar, which he had a hard time doing between chuckles, then handed him my pad.

"I'm done. Take me back. This is not for me!" I said.

On the freeway, he kept laughing. "Done in by an eight-year-old."

I was also done with my Studio City Playhouse.

Mirror, Mirror on the Wall

The world was changing. America was changing. I was changing. Castro had taken over in Cuba and had gone in a matter of months from democracy's saviour to Russia's Satan. News was awash with the twenty-four-hour warnings of 'Duck and Cover' from the imminent nuclear war, causing people to dig holes in the ground for survival. None of this interested me, though; I was too busy trying to dig myself out of a hole of depression.

I had lost my theater, and any hope of having a career in it. I had fleetingly become more enamored of television; I didn't have to leave the house to enjoy it. My affinity for it was due to one man, Jack Paar, the absolute best, most unique, wittiest, and truly curious person to ever host *The Tonight Show*. He introduced intellectuals like Gore Vidal and William Buckley, Alexander King, a once junkie artist, Oscar Levant, an insanely funny and insane pianist, Elsa Maxwell, an unattractive fat, rich celebrity party-giver and hilarious story-teller; politicians like John F. Kennedy and Fidel Castro, and often talented performers no one ever heard of. I saw the night he introduced a young offbeat comedy team from Chicago's Second City, Mike Nichols and Elaine May, and they bombed. He walked to the edge of the stage, stared at the audience, then scolding them, saying, "These two are funny and I will keep bringing them back till you discover it." And he did. I saw him almost every night for five glorious golden-age years. What captured me the most was that he talked to those people. He had conversations with them. In real life, real conversations were a rarity. He had them every night about real stuff. And was making a superstar living at it. I thought, *God, how I'd love to do that.*

The one other person I admired was newsman Ed Murrow. He talked about and exposed even truer, tougher stuff, news no one else would touch. Not even President Eisenhower. His one-man TV assault on Senator Joe McCarthy, who had terrified America, silenced Hollywood with its blacklist and destroyed the First Amendment, gripped the country by the throat and eyes for days. The commie-under-every-bed Senator found himself, like the hundreds he once attacked, destroyed. Ed Murrow's *Harvest of Shame* documentary about the exploitation of migrant workers in the South, showed what Murrow always said TV could do: sell ideas and change, not just products. The shame was that products won. Coca Cola, who owned the land, stopped buying ads. CBS stopped Murrow from doing any more news. He became what TV would soon become, a celebrity pusher. He ended up hosting *Person to Person.*

But, if I could not get into movies or theater with a halfway decent resumé, how could I ever imagine getting into TV? I couldn't. I stayed home and stewed. If I had not become depressed, which was really rare for me, I would have felt nothing. No country. No dreams. I had nothing, nothing to look forward to. I found myself not getting dressed, not going out, and staring into the mirror longer than I should have. I wasn't looking at me. I was looking *for* me. And couldn't find me. It was inevitable that suicide crept into my empty dark head. I recalled the suicides I knew. More had died of their own hand than disease, or what they call natural causes. If I did it, how would I do it? Not hanging like my grandfather. Not a bullet to the brain like Lenny. Not sticking my head in an oven. Or slashing my wrists. Or jumping out of a window, or under a train. Why should I hurt myself? I was trying to stop being hurt. Life had done enough of that. Maybe just pills, and go to sleep. But, as Hamlet said, "What dreams may come when we have shuffled off this mortal coil."

Thinking of that, and the scores and scores of Shakespeare lines I had stupidly memorized in the hopes of becoming famous on a top quiz show, made me suddenly smile. I smiled at my pathetic weakness. What a mess I was. Then I got upset at the truth. If I did myself in, the truth was, no one would miss me. Maybe just the Pelters. The thought of Abe stopped me. I closed the mirror. Everybody has it tough. And, indeed, it did get tougher. Many times. But this time it got tougher right away. Philosophers and Dr. Phil say, "You attract what you think." Negative thoughts bring negative results. Since that was all that was in my head at the time, that's what showed up at my door.

A Closed Mouth Goes Farther than an Opened Mind

I started to go out again, to lunch, dinner or a movie by myself. I got a newspaper every day to look for a job. I avoided reading or watching the news. I knew, good or bad, politicians are the playwrights of real life, but I was only interested in getting mine back together. I made an effort to visit and chat with Bob and Wes, and Mort and Bill, but never for long. Mort was delighted when I told him I thought his joke about the Cold War was the best I ever heard. "The Russians getting sputniks up in space before us proves the Russian German scientists are better than our German scientists!"

Late one afternoon, after an unsuccessful day of job hunting, I was stopped by my neighbor, Eric, who lived across the driveway. He and his wife could have been the models for Ken and Barbie, both very attractive. Their apartment, to which they invited me twice for coffee and conversation, was spotless. They were better to look at than listen to. If they weren't talking about the joys of Rome and the Church, it was about Moscow and the Commie Menace.

As I was starting up the stairs, he said, "What do you think of this Cuban thing?"

"What Cuban thing?"

"Castro. Coming to this country. To New York."

"What about it?" I asked.

"He's a commie, for God's sake. Whatta ya think?"

I stared at him for a moment. "Eric, I don't know what you mean."

"It's a disgrace. Letting this commie bastard into our country. Whatta ya think?" he pressed.

He obviously was not interested in my opinion; just voicing his own. I tried to be casual, and smiled. "He didn't just row a boat here like he did to Cuba. He was invited."

"That's what I mean. A goddamn disgrace. Some of those commies in the State Department."

"Eric, that would have to be approved by the President. Paar had him on. So did Ed Sullivan. The *New York times* raved about him. A modern Zapata."

"You like him?" he blurted.

"Eric, I don't even know him. Like Will Rogers said, I only know what I read in the papers."

"He's a commie dictator, don't you know that?"

It seemed I had conversations like this on LaBrea. I thought of stopping. But I was comfortable, feeling we were just having a short chat. "He may be a dictator, but right now he is not one of ours."

"What in God's name are you talking about? We just fought a World War against fascists and turned them into democracies."

I retorted, "And I read we turned democracies into *our* fascists. In Iran. Even Guatemala." I was showing off what I'd learned from Haskell's library and Abe's I. F. Stone.

Eric was livid. "Where'd you read that shit?"

"I.F. Stone's *Weekly*," I said proudly.

"What is that? A commie rag?"

I felt he could not be upset if I was just talking reasonably about facts. "Let me ask you a question, Eric. How do you feel about the Mafia, about corruption, gambling, prostitution, illiteracy, poverty, sickness?" He didn't answer. Just stared in disbelief. I kept going. "I'm sure you're opposed to them. Castro said he was too. He says he wants to eliminate all that. We'll see! Then we can judge."

"John, he is an enemy. You'll see. A commie, and a threat. There's no question."

"A threat? Militarily? That is nonsense. That's like being afraid of Catalina."

"John, you must be kidding."

"Eric, you're an accountant. Just follow the money, they say. Aren't all wars about money?"

"No, John. They're about truth. And freedom."

"Mark my words, in the next few months, we'll all know if he's a commie or not."

"How? I mean, he is already!"

"No, right now he's a successful revolutionary. Watch to see what he does with the King Brothers Ranch, or the casinos, or the refineries."

"I don't follow. What's the King Brothers Ranch? And what's it got to do with anything?"

Indeed, he had relaxed. As did I. Like telling a child what he should know about the facts of life, financial life, real life, I continued, showing off stuff I was glad I knew, or at least thought I knew. In a few words, which he listened to intently, I told him how I. F. Stone and Drew Pearson reported The King Brothers holdings were so vast, Cubans had to get permission to grow a potato. That America might refuse to refine Russian oil that Castro was buying at less than half-price. And if so, Castro may have to confiscate their holdings, if he wished to continue his revolution. Spouting all this, I felt alive again. Then I asked Eric, "And how do you think Castro will repay them?"

"He won't repay anybody. Commies only steal."

I ignored his ignorance. "He'll repay them by the value they say the property is worth on their U.S. tax returns!"

"You've got to be kidding, John."

I repeated, "Just like Will Rogers, I only know what I read."

"Boy, you read some wrong shit." He turned, leaving me standing at the bottom of the stairs.

I watched, then hollered, "I read the Bible, too!"

He did not stop, but my gut told me I should have. Long ago.

History later proved me, and those I read, right. The next day proved me right about thinking I should have kept my mouth shut!

Knock, Knock ... and it's No Joke

It was no surprise the next morning when there was a knock at the door and I opened it, looking at two tall clean-cut looking men in their early forties in uniforms of dark suits, starched white collars and grey ties, holding up folders identified themselves as FBI.

"John Barbour?" the taller one queried politely.

"Yes." I opened the door wider. "Come in."

They surveyed the room as they entered. I pointed to the sofa. "Would you like a seat?"

"No, thanks. We won't be long."

I was surprised to hear them say that. They certainly didn't act as though they were going to rush to arrest me like the first time when the building was surrounded.

"Do you have permission to be in the United States?" The tall one did all the talking.

I noticed neither one had a notepad to refer to. "Yes."

"Could we see it please? A green card, visa, or passport."

"I don't have those," I said, standing a few feet from them. The door was still open. They were silhouetted by the daylight outside, making them look like the Men in Black.

"Then how do you have permission to be here?"

"I just got off the plane in New York. Actually, they didn't say anything."

"Did you tell them you had been deported?"

"They never asked."

"How long did you tell them you'd be in the United States?"

"They never asked that either. I just told them long enough to get a sandwich."

They did not smile. "How long ago was that?"

"Two or three years ago." They looked at me, satisfied that I'd responded honestly.

I had surrendered to the inevitable. I was almost relieved. It was over. All that anguish. All that struggle. All that planning. I was tired. I was not even upset at Eric. I had brought it on myself.

"Are you going to arrest me?"

"Mr. Barbour, we are not arresting you, but we're sure you don't wish to be deported again. We will be turning your information over to the INS. They may or may not offer you a voluntary departure again. That's up to them. If you have the means to leave the United States on your own, and early, we suggest you do it."

"Thank you," I said, impressed at how gracious they were.

"Good luck," they said, without shaking hands and left.

I closed the door, thinking I needed to call Abe. He would be the only one who'd care. I'd miss my neighbors. They were fun. But Abe and his family were the only ones I'd truly miss. The closest I'd ever felt to family. The hard part about telling them, though, was that I'd have to tell them the truth about this troublemaking stranger they'd brought into their home. I did not want to disappoint them more. I certainly had enough for bus fare. I could leave then send a letter. I owed it to him, though. His unquestioning generosity to a kid not even Jewish was as astonishing as it was rare.

I picked up the phone and called him at work, telling him the FBI had just left.

"Get over to our place tonight at seven. Don't be late," he said harshly, and hung up.

The Last Supper

The nearly ten hours I had to wait were a lifetime. All I remember doing was packing. What I could have done in minutes, took forever.

Abe, knowing it was me buzzing, opened the door. I'm glad it was him. "Follow me," he ordered. We went to the dining room, the table packed with food. He pointed to a chair at one end. "Sit down."

He sat at the other end, his back to the open kitchen. His wife and young daughter were seated to his right; the two boys to his left. Usually they always greeted me with a big "Hi." This time they just stared wide-eyed.

His daughter blurted, "You got busted by the FBl?" The others tried not to smile, admonishing her for being impolite.

"Yes," I said barely above a whisper. "Twice."

"Twice?"

Pointing a fork at me, Abe said, "Son, start eating or talking."

"Mr. Pelter–"

"Goddamn it, son. It's Abe. How many times have I told you? You're like one of my own. Never listen."

"I'm not hungry, Abe. My … my stomach is full, full of pain. I have such affection for you all, I wouldn't want you to feel as though I'd somehow let you all down–"

"Then if you're not gonna eat, just tell us the goddamn story!" he said. He was gruff. The same as when he sat at my table in the restaurant.

I started from the beginning. Everything, as matter-of-factly as possible. Abe only knew about my being lost in the woods, only because of my script for Haskell. Other than that, he knew nothing else. He never asked, and I certainly never offered. They stared at me their mouths dropped open. When I got to the part about leaving for America, his wife said, "John, your life would make a terrific movie."

Abe raised his hand for her to be quiet. "He tried that. It didn't work. Go on. The FBI, the first time?"

I recounted my arguments with the young accountant, the sudden appearance of the FBI, and me trying to jump out of the upstairs window. The corners of their mouths now turned upwards into smiles.

"You putz," Abe said softly. They all giggled.

I had a difficult time telling them my laundry-chore escape story, they were laughing so hard. Tales I thought were going to generate sympathy instead were getting huge laughs. I started laughing myself.

"What about this morning?" Abe asked.

I relived the brief encounter with Eric and then the appearance of two FBI agents.

"You putz," Abe repeated. "Don't you know when to keep your mouth shut?"

The younger boy turned to his father, "Do you, Dad?" Abe looked at his son; his smile indicated pride more than pleasure.

"So, what's your plan now?" Abe asked.

"I'm all packed. And I guess in the next couple of days, I'll catch a Greyhound and go back to Toronto."

"Aren't you gonna see a lawyer?"

"What for?"

"Whadda ya mean, what for. You wanna come back, don't you?"

"Yes, of course, but I don't know any law–"

"I do," Abe interrupted. "And here's his card. Sydney Kaplan. Used to be with INS. A great lawyer and a nice man. You call him tomorrow."

"But, sir," I stammered, "from what little I know about the law, with my background, I don't think I'm eligible."

"That's what lawyers are for. How are you fixed for money?"

"I have enough for the bus ticket and a little more."

"You are not taking the bus. And you're gonna see Kaplan tomorrow. You have an eleven AM appointment." He rose from his end of the table and walked toward me, patting me on the shoulder, a touch that almost brought me to tears, and placed his other hand in mine. "Take this for now." He forced something into my hand and returned to his seat. When I glanced down at it, I could see it was tightly folded hundred-dollar bills.

"Mr. Pelter, I may never see you all again … and … and I don't know how I could repay you or when." I was choking as I spoke.

"You'll see us again. The rest isn't important. Now, you can start to eat, but first, a toast."

Everyone raised their glasses of Manischewitz and held them high, except for me. Abe said, "La tina shova tika tayvu. Son, may you be written in the Book of Life." They all clinked glasses. I was too absorbed watching that amazing family. Then Abe added, as he waved his glass in the air again, "To our Johnny Barbour. Canada's leading putz!" They all followed suit. "L'chaim. To Canada's leading putz!"

At eleven the next morning, as instructed, I was in Sydney Kaplan's office.

Sidney Kaplan

Sidney Kaplan's office was on the eighth floor of an old twenty-story, large grey-brick building in the heart of downtown Los Angeles, a part of the city that looked as rundown as Hollywood Boulevard. The door was right out of one of those Humphrey Bogart Sam Spade movies, frosted glass in the upper half with the name, Sidney Kaplan:

Attorney-at-Law Immigration. The office itself was much smaller than I imagined, and a little messier, file folders everywhere. He was in his late forties, had slightly grey hair around the temples and wore a wrinkled dark suit and shirt and tie.

"Hello, young man," he said in a comforting baritone voice. "Abe has told me a little about your situation. Why don't you fill me in on the details?" He motioned for me to sit and leaned back to listen.

"Sir, I don't quite know where to start."

"Well, Abe tells me this is your second encounter with the FBI, that you were deported a few years ago, and that as a youngster you had some run-ins with the law, in Toronto, was it?'

"Yes, sir."

"Well, then, begin with those, the nature of them, and bring me up to date."

Everything I had told Abe and his family, I now told a total stranger. He never took his eyes off me. Never moved. And didn't even smile at the dumb parts that Abe's family laughed at. When I was through, after an uncomfortable silence, I asked weakly, "What do you think?"

He leaned forward. "Quite honestly, young man, it doesn't look good."

"You mean, they'll never let me back in?"

"In order to get permission to get back, you first have to get permission to even ask permission."

"I don't understand. What does that mean?"

"People who've been deported just can't apply for permission to re-enter the country. They first have to go through a screening process, and if they get through that successfully then, and only then, can they apply for permission to re-enter."

"What if they don't survive this screening process?"

"Then they can't even apply to re-enter."

I was trying not to get sick. "Do you think I could get through this screening process?"

"I doubt it. It's not so much that you've already been deported once. Lots of people get to come back even after that. Your problem is that you have two separate felony convictions at sixteen. The law does make allowances for minors, but that allowance is for only one felony conviction, and none for moral turpitude. Unfortunately, you've had two."

My mind went into fast-forward. "What if I marry a US citizen?"

He smiled for the first time. "You have someone in mind?"

"No."

"Well, even if you did, with your background, it'd be very iffy."

I had nothing more to say. I was out of hopeful things to ask, so I just lowered my head and stared vacantly at the floor. Finally, I asked, "Is it over?"

"Well, John, it's never really over until the process has run its course."

"Will I just be wasting my time and yours?"

"My mother used to say in her Yiddish accent, 'Son, if it weren't for the dark, you couldn't see the stars!' If you want my help, I won't be wasting my time. I'll be getting paid. Hopefully. And you won't be wasting your time. No matter what happens in the next months, and it'll take months. You'll probably end up knowing as much about immigration law as I do, and more importantly, you'll learn a lot more about yourself."

"What do I do now?"

"The first thing I want you to do is gather up as many character reference letters as you can. From Abe, his family. His brother-in-law, Dr. Kleeman, head of surgery at Mt Sinai, people you've worked for and with. Friends. As many as you can. And get them to me as soon as possible. When I get them, I'll notify INS that within the year we'll be applying for permission. So, let's get started." He rose to lead me to the door.

"How much do I owe you?"

"Right now, nothing."

"Mr. Kaplan, right now is the only time I might have anything. I've got seven hundred and something dollars minus a plane fare."

"You'll need it. Keep it. We'll talk about this later," He opened the door.

"But, you can't be doing this for nothing. What would your mother think?"

He laughed. "She thinks I'm terrific no matter what. Right now, please don't worry about it. I owe Abe a lot of favors."

"So do I. It's his seven hundred dollars."

He smiled. "Get those letters to me ASAP, and let me know where you're staying. We'll be in touch. Let's get started." As I stepped into the hallway, Mr. Kaplan's voice rose. "John!"

I turned. "Yes?"

"Leave the country!"

"I will. Right away."

"And don't stop to get married!"

Where to Start?

If I never had a real purpose or direction in my life, I certainly did now, which was to go through the legal process as instructed by Mr. Kaplan. It became my be-all and end-all. To go through it for the long year ahead I only needed a small room and a mindless job. I was good at getting both. My job was something I had mastered. Many times. Bussing and washing dishes. My room, once again, was in a small rooming house. This one was purposely within walking distance of The University of Toronto's Law Library, and just two long blocks from the YMCA. I went there twice a week to work off excessive anxiety and energy. And once to the chapel. Mr. Kaplan had phoned to inform me that the letters of reference I had requested from everyone were now in his possession. The Pelter clan. Mort Lachman, Bill Larkin, every employer, landlords, actors and actresses I'd worked with. Guys I played baseball with. Even one from Haskell Wexler, whom I didn't remember asking. And many more. Mr. Kaplan said he was stunned by their content. I didn't know how to thank them. So, I ended up in this little chapel, thanking the universe. It was a place to go after a workout to sit alone in the semi-dark to just clear my head.

It was this uncluttered head I took to the University of Toronto's Law Library. Not being a student or lawyer, I was not allowed to take books out. I had to read them there. Almost every available hour, three, four and five hours a day, for days and weeks on end, I plowed through everything they had on US Immigration Law. I learned even being convicted as a youth of two felonies, or major felonies, or even being a Nazi war criminal, I could become a citizen. If I could make a contribution to America's culture, a member of Congress could sponsor me. If I could contribute to America's rocket program or military, I didn't even need Congress.

The books cited hundreds of precedents, but not one close to mine. I had an impossible battle on my hands. Why even go on?

Every day and night I replayed my arrest with Mel; the stealing of Bill Pugsley's overcoat at the dance, the breaking into the store, the cops arresting us, and the two convictions with two years' probation. A couple of times I phoned Mr. Kaplan, repeating desperately and *ad nauseam* the details of that night. He would always listen sympathetically, saying, "John, it doesn't alter the fact that the two convictions are separate. The law is very specific." I knew I was boring him, because I was boring myself. But I kept blurting ideas out.

"What if I could get one of those small convictions expunged?" I didn't really know what I was talking about. I'd just seen that word a number of times in the books.

"That is unlikely, but even it were possible, the INS already has the original records. I'm sorry I don't sound more hopeful. And another letter came in for you today. Wes Butler, your director friend."

"Mr. Kaplan, thank you. I'm sorry I'm such a pest."

"John, you are not a pest. I know what you are going through. I've seen people going through it from both sides for years. You have to do what you have to do. We're not done yet."

It's true, we were not done. It had just been a few months. What was done was my going to the law library. I'd been over it all, to the point I had memorized more than I wanted or needed. For weeks, I went to work, stayed in my room, watched TV, gave up reading anything, worked out, ending up strangely one night back in the chapel for the last time.

Sitting in the back in the dim light, looking at Christ up front crucified, probably feeling as bad as I did about some stuff he said, I got a quick jolt. A thought. It was the kind of thought smart lawyers might get fighting a tough case. It excited me so much, I had to calm down. I dared not bug Mr. Kaplan again. He might inadvertently shoot it down. I did not know how I could 'expunge' one of those two small crimes. If it were possible, Mr. Kaplan would certainly know how. But ... but ... what if I could prove those two small crimes were part of just one bigger crime?

How could I do that? I had no idea. The American Consul could not or would not just take my word for it. Even if it had happened on one night. Maybe they'd take Mel's word! Mel Nixon! My partner. What if he said it was all part of one big robbery plan. Eureka! I had to find Mel.

Finding Mel

Where on earth would I start? I hadn't seen or heard of him in over a dozen years. Today, I could just Google 'Mel Nixon' and everything would pop up. Even arrest records. The only thing I could look into then was the phone book. I rushed to a phone booth. And there it was: Nixon, Margaret, 196 Lawlor Avenue. Jesus Christ, this was impossible. Margaret Nixon. She was Mel's beautiful brunette, becoming-a-woman younger sister, when I knew her. She seemed to like me as a kid. We played spin the bottle a couple of times; once she showed me underlined passages in her favorite book, *Forever Amber*. And if I hadn't had to jump out of her bedroom window one night, I might have learned what those passages meant. Memories, smiles and nervousness rushed at me as I picked up the phone.

"Hello," an edgy female voice said.

"Hello. Uh, is Mel there?"

"No. Who's this?"

"John, John Barbour."

"We don't know any John Barbour."

"Oh, I'm sorry," I said quickly. "I'm John MacLaren. I used to live just--"

"Johnny MacLaren! Johnny MacLaren! I'll be damned. Johnny, this is Margaret. How are you?"

"Fine, I guess. How are you?"

"Pregnant." She giggled. "Not married, though."

"You're still living there?"

"That's why I answered." She giggled again. "Johnny MacLaren. Jesus Christ and Mother Mary. Where have you been? Somebody told me you were in California."

"I was. Up until a little while ago, but I had a little trouble with their immigration."

"God." She laughed. "The more it changes, the more it's the same thing. You and Mel were always in trouble."

"That's sort of what I want to talk to him about, Margaret. I don't know if he really can help in any way, but the main thing keeping me from going back to the States is when we were caught by the–"

She laughed again. "Yeah, the cops busting you on Kingston Road. What a couple of dummies. What on earth has talking to him now got to do with immigration or whatever? But I doubt he could help you. He's in prison," she said flatly. "Maximum security."

"What?" I shouted.

"Armed robbery. A bank."

"A bank! Oh, my God, are you serious?" It was impossible to imagine.

"A few years ago. Would you believe this, he came back from Asia a war hero, medals and all. They gave him a fucking parade. A few months later he walks into a bank with a machine gun. Now he's got numbers on his chest."

"Oh, God, Margaret. It's unbelievable. How long is he in for?"

"Twenty years."

I began to feel sick, opening the phone booth door to breathe. "I'm ... I'm so sorry. Where is he?"

"Sudbury."

"Way up there?"

"Yeah. Just to be in Sudbury is like being in prison."

"Do you think if I went up there he'd see me?"

"I dunno. I don't think he ever has visitors. We talk about once a month, but usually only if he calls."

"That's sad. Do you think he'd talk to me?"

"Oh, shit. For sure. He'd probably love to. Are you kidding?"

"Margaret, I am so sorry. And ... and sorry about your not being married."

"I'm not. And I'm sort of looking forward to having a baby. I'll call him tomorrow for you. On one condition, if he agrees to see you, regardless of what happens, you have to promise to come by and see me. I'd just love to see you."

"Even if he doesn't want to see me, I'll come by to see you."

What I just heard was incomprehensible. How could that happen? His problems were really problems. It was the first time in a while I was not thinking of myself.

I called the following day at noon. Margaret answered immediately. "He was as surprised to hear you're here as I was," she said. "He said he'd see you."

"Does he know why I want to see him?"

"Oh, yeah. His visiting hours are between ten and two, weekdays."

"You mean, I just show up and ask for him?"

"Yeah. He said he'd inform them, that he presumed you wanted to go up this week."

"Oh, yeah. Yeah! Margaret, again, thank you very much."

"Never mind that. I want to hear a thank you in person.

"I will. I promise. No matter what happens."

With only a toothbrush, a comb, and a warm jacket, I was on the night train to Sudbury. I was early and nervous. Any images in my head about entering that alien grey fortress, having to show my identification, and to whom, being led to the interview area are gone and never recorded. My head was too filled with the fog of the Mel I was about to see, and the memories of our endless inseparable days and nights together. In spite of our endless fights, which he won, all I could see was the fun.

I sat, as instructed by a guard, in the wall of cubicles staring through a wired glass partition, a wall phone on either side; exactly like the ones I'd seen in every gangster movie. I was the only visitor. Shortly, a door on the other side opened. Another guard held it open, motioning someone to enter. It was Mel. Unmistakably Mel. Not even the drab, blue-grey prison garb could take away from that still-handsome face and sheepish movie star grin. And hair. It was still a glistening jet black, unparted and combed back with that sharp crow's foot slanting onto his forehead. Jesus, he looked more than ever like Tyrone Power. He grabbed his phone

"Jesus, Johnny, what a surprise! How are you?"

I didn't know what to say. How to start. "I'm not sure. Stunned more than anything seeing you here."

"Not as stunned as I am, seeing you out there. How the hell are you? What have you been doing?" He smiled.

"Getting into trouble." I smiled back.

He laughed out loud. "Where I am is troubled, man. This is trouble."

He in no way felt sorry for himself. His genuine pleasure at seeing me put me at ease.

"Geez, Mel, how did you ever end up here?"

"Margaret said she told you. By the way, she was thrilled to talk to you."

"I was stunned I just found her in the phone book, but shocked to find you here. What happened?"

"I tried to rob a bank." He shrugged.

"But why?"

"I needed the money. Why does anyone rob a bank?"

"But you were a war hero. Margaret said you got medals and a parade. Everything."

"Ya," he said in a faraway voice.

"Why'd you join the Army? And where were you fighting? Canada's not at war."

"I didn't like any of the jobs I had. Bored, I guess. Lookin' for a little adventure." He paused, nodding his head, smiling at the memories.

"But where?"

"Asia."

"Asia? Are you kidding? Canadians were fighting there?"

"Ya. They still are."

"What are Canadians doing there?"

He laughed. "What they're told., Johnny. We used to say, America is headquarters; Canada is just a branch office."

"Jesus, but with the stories Margaret told me, you were all over the papers and media about being a hero. You must have been able to get a job you liked."

"I didn't want one. I'm just not cut out for nine to five, I guess."

"Then why not another tour? The Army would've loved that. Why rob a bank?"

"They wanted me to go back. Badly. But, Johnny, it's all bullshit." He paused, staring at me, still with a slight smile.

"But why a bank?"

"Because I thought I could get away with it. I walked in with an automatic and announced that I was making a withdrawal."

"Are you kidding?"

"I didn't get a chance to say anything. They tackled me right away." He cleared his throat. "Okay, tell me why you're here. Margaret says you're having some kind of trouble with U.S. Immigration. What has that got to do with me?"

I told my tale to him, the same stories I recounted to the Pelters and Mr. Kaplan. I was tired of telling it. Like the Pelters, Mel laughed.

"Jesus, Johnny, you're almost more of a fuckup than I am. But, you know what? You were the only one in our little group I was jealous of. That's why I always tried to beat the shit out of you."

"Jealous? Of me? Geez, what for? I didn't have anything."

"You were the smartest and funniest. Nothing ever bothered you, and you always had these great ideas. That flick hockey was genius."

Listening to Mel, the intense anxiety about the outcome was fading. Compared to him, my problem was not really a problem. If getting back to America didn't work out now, maybe it would later. Canada's entertainment community was small but growing; many moving to America. Maybe I could do that. I certainly had a background to draw on.

"Now how can I help you?" Mel asked.

I explained the reason Mr. Kaplan said I would probably be denied permission to even ask since we had been convicted of two felonies when we were sixteen. U.S. Immigration will only forgive one felony.

"We were dumb even then."

"I've been thinking my only remote hope is that since we stole Pugsley's overcoat at the dance and then broke into the store fifteen minutes later, and stashed the stuff in the coat, that maybe they'd consider this not two separate acts, but one."

"See, you are smart. You shoulda been a lawyer. So, what do you want me to do?"

"I could write this out for them, but coming from me, they'd think it was a lie. I was wondering if you'd mind saying something similar?"

Mel looked at me closely. Then he flashed that incredible grin. "I'll go you one better. I'll write up something that says it was all my idea, and I just dragged you into it."

"Mel, you can't do that."

"Sure I can. Why not?"

"First of all, it's not true. Second, they'll think that coming from you, you being in here for twenty years, they'll know it's bullshit. It has to be honest. It was both of us."

Mel bowed his head, thinking, rocked back and forth, then looked up. The smile was gone.

"I'll get a pad and pen and write it up the way it happened."

I hated to ask him, but I did. "When?"

"Right now. It'll take me about a half hour. Lousy writer. I'll ask the warden's office to notarize it." He then motioned for the guard. Before replacing the phone, he said, "Johnny, be sure and let me know if it works."

I didn't have a chance to thank him. He disappeared behind the door. It was the last time I saw him.

An hour later, my pacing around the circular marbled entrance was interrupted, not by a guard, but an older man in a dark brown suit who did not identify himself. He had a piece of paper in his hand. "John Barbour?"

"Yes, sir."

"I believe this is for you."

On the train back to Toronto, I reread Mel's scratchy scrawled notarized note, and relived that long-ago night at least a dozen times.

Woman in Blue

The next day in Toronto, Mel's paper clutched in my hand, I called Mr. Kaplan long distance. Excitedly I explained what I had and what I had done.

"John," he said with a strong ring of sympathy, "that is commendable. I don't know how else to describe it. I am not sure it will help in any way. It just does not alter the legal record. I hope you don't get your hopes too high."

"Mr. Kaplan, the truth is, I don't have any hopes anymore."

"John, it's not over till it's over. Send it to me registered mail if you can. I will put it in your file. By the way, you may not have to wait out the full year. Things are moving pretty quickly. Your interview may be just a matter of weeks. Not months."

"You really don't think it'll help?"

"It certainly can't hurt."

"I'll send it right away. Thank you again."

My next call was to Margaret, thanking her.

"When will you know?" she asked.

"I'm not sure. Three or four weeks A couple of months."

"Do ya think you'd have time to come by and see me?"

"Margaret, if it's negative, I don't know if I'd be able to do anything."

"It won't be negative. Believe me, you'll get it. But, no matter, please come by. Okay?"

"Okay," I said.

That was it. Now it was just wait and worry. But I just couldn't stew like that. I had to prepare in case it was a lengthy interview. So, back to the law library I went. This time to read up on everything they might ask me about the Constitution, Bill of Rights, how many members of Congress, the Senate, their names, the Supreme Court, the number of presidents, their names, the Civil War, the war of 1812, even the Mexican-American War, the number of States, their capitals. It was more of a grind than rereading and rereading immigration law, made more of a strain because I knew it just was not as important as the law. The law was what they would go by. Not by what I would have to say or know. But I stuck to it. There was nothing else to do.

Four weeks later, the call came from Mr. Kaplan. I had been gone just over half a year. "John, your appointment's Thursday ten a.m. The American Consulate on Spadina, with the Consul General. Good luck."

"Mr. Kaplan, sir, no matter what happens, I'll never be able to thank you enough. Or Abe. I'll call you right away."

"John, it's been our pleasure to help you. Good luck." He hung up.

I felt numb. Judgment day. Hearing Mr. Kaplan describing the Consul as 'General,' hurt my stomach. General! The ultimate authority figure. I rushed to Eaton's and bought a dark blue suit, white shirt, and tie. The tie was red, white, and blue. How corny. How obvious.

The American Embassy was on Spadina Avenue, on the west side of the street, in the middle of the block. It looked like The Ministry of Fear. Above it, fluttering aimlessly in the breeze, flew a beautiful large stars and stripes. Inside was not at all what I expected. There were no crowds of people, papers in hand, lining up to get out of Canada. And no uniformed Marines. It was eerily quiet. I walked to the one lady behind the large lobby desk.

"Hello. My name's John Barbour and I have a ten o'clock appointment."

She glanced at a calendar and said, "You're early."

"I'm always early. A bad habit."

"A bad habit more people should have. Just take a seat over there, Mr. Barbour. The Consul-General will see you in twenty minutes."

Being early is not always a good habit. It gives you too much time to fret. I could not sit. I did not want to crease my trousers. And I didn't want to be pacing up and down in front of the receptionist. I asked where the restroom was; she pointed down the hall.

The deodorant had done no good. Sweat was pouring down my sides. In spite of three or four efforts, I couldn't pee. I just paced, staring at myself in the wall-to-wall mirror. I did not look good. I felt even worse. Oh, God, just let's get this over with. I tried to go over questions that might be asked, but nothing stuck. There was a knock on the bathroom door. I rushed to it.

"Mr. Barbour, the Consul-General will see you now."

I followed her to two large, shiny, ornate doors. She motioned me inside. It was a beautiful, simple but imposing office. I looked immediately at a smart-looking woman in her early fifties, grayish white hair, sitting behind an exceptionally large desk. On either side of her were the Canadian and American flag. She wore a perfectly fitting blue suit, and did not rise when I entered.

"Mr. Barbour. Hello, I'm the Consul-General. Sit down."

"Miss ... uh ... Ma'am, do you mind if I stand? I'm obviously awfully nervous." I couldn't believe I had just said that.

"Mr. Barbour, there's nothing to be nervous about. Sit down."

I sat. She casually opened what could only be my file. I watched intently, looking for some kind of reading on her face. There was nothing. She closed it, again casually, and looked directly at me. I was awaiting her first question. What part of American history would it be about? I was prepared and anxious to show off what I knew. I was totally unprepared, though, for what she did ask. How could I not have thought of it?

"Mr. Barbour, why do you want to go to the United States?"

Oh, my God. What an obvious question. And I had not even thought about it. My life's film raced through my mind, trying to find a picture, a word, something so I could start to speak. I wanted to cry. I was stuck. I did not know what to say, but I had to say something.

"Ma'am, it's not that I want to go to your country. Want isn't a strong enough word. I *have* to go to your country. As you can see, I've already tried that twice. When I went a dozen years ago, I hadn't the foggiest idea how to go about it properly. In all of the books and biographies I've read, the famous or the ordinary folks who came to America came for one of two reasons, to achieve a better life or to escape a dreadful one. My mother and father came from Scotland. Both for a better life. After the war, my father deserted us and went back to Scotland for an even better life. My mother, left alone, looked for her better life in bars and in the arms of many men."

The woman in the blue suit was unmoved, but listening.

"My interest in your country began I guess much the same as it did for millions of others around the world, at the movies. From the time I was six, twice a week I'd go to The Manor Theater and for a nickel sit through a double feature. It was an escape. It was also home. It's not that I wanted to be in the movies, even though I was on the fringes of showbiz in California, I wanted to be where they were made. Hollywood. I know a lot of what I saw was, well, fairy tales about life and probably screwed a lot of people up, including me."

There was still no response from her.

"I got most excited about America when I saw Capra's movies with Jimmy Stewart or even the tougher ones like *All the King's Men*. That led me to the library where I read everything." I paused. She was still expressionless.

"As a matter of fact, ma'am, I thought your first question to me was going to be about the history of your country. Ask me whatever. I think I know it, but your country, America, is not just unique in its laws, but its people. Your country is the only one in the world made up of people from every other country in the world. Yours is the only country that didn't just happen; it was planned around a blueprint, the Constitution, the Bill of Rights, written primarily by the brightest and one of the richest men in America, Thomas Jefferson, with laws that protected ordinary people from folks like himself. Protected people like me. And he even called for periodic revolutionary bloodshed to nourish what he called the tree of liberty. Your intellectual founder was the poor son of an English bookmaker, Thomas Paine, whose pamphlet, *Common Sense,* sold fifty thousand copies and he gave every cent to Washington to pay for and feed his army. I identify more with him than Jefferson. In your national anthem, you don't sing it to an emperor or president even. You sing it to a flag, the country it represents. Like the one over your building. In school we have to sing to a queen. In your country, they say any boy can grow up to be president. How many Canadian boys grow up to be queen?" I paused. I knew I could add a punchline to make it a joke. Thank God, Abraham and Moses, I kept my mouth shut. It would have been inappropriate. And flippant.

"Ma'am, simply, in a few words, to every foreigner who goes there, your country is a country of second chances. But I don't want a second chance at life. I just want a first chance.

"I've never had one here. And I never will. I know lots of people have it worse than me, but for me, it's been a nightmare. On the other side of that border, you have what you call the American dream. For me, even unwanted and illegal, it wasn't and isn't a dream. It's a reality that I've already experienced and want to experience the rest of my life." I stopped, fighting back tears and an urge to beg.

She looked at me a long while still quiet and expressionless. I didn't know if she was evaluating me, or weighing the words she had to say to me. It was forever before she spoke. "Mr. Barbour, my granting you permission to apply to the Immigration Service for re-entry into the United States does in no way mean that they may grant it. The truth is, they may deny you. They've done it before."

I couldn't believe what I was hearing. Was she saying yes?

"But," she continued, "I would not want to be the one to stand in the way of your dream, or your reality. I am granting you permission to apply." She stood, still not extending her hand. "The papers will be ready in a few days. Just remember, my approval is absolutely no guarantee. INS might turn you down. I wish you good luck, Mr. Barbour, and a good life."

My mouth quivered against my will; tears gushed down my face. I couldn't stop crying. A lifetime of relief and gratitude poured out of me. I tried to thank her, but couldn't finish two simple, overwhelming words. She watched me while I turned and fumbled my way out the door. She had probably seen it a thousand times. Outside, I just started to run and run. It was impossible to stand still, or even sit on the street car. I just kept running. What miracle had just happened!

Bursting into the rooming house, totally breathless, I called Mr. Kaplan, screaming, "She said yes. She said yes!"

He chuckled softly, not sounding surprised. "That's really good, John. Now, I want you to get your birth certificate and passport. You'll need them when we apply to INS. which will be in three or four weeks. Okay?"

"Oh, wow, thank you. Thank you. Thank you." I then called Mr. Pelter. "Abe, Abe, Abe," I shouted, almost crying again, "they said yes. I don't know how I can ever repay you."

"Son, this call is payment enough. We'll see you when you get home."

Tears of happiness gushed out again. How could I be so lucky? I called Margaret.

"Oh. Johnny, I'm so, so happy for you."

I was sniffling. "Thank you, Margaret. And thank Mel for me. I'll send him a note.

And good luck with the baby."

"You know, if it's a boy, I may just call it Johnny. You will come by and see me before you go, won't you?"

"I'll try. Honestly." I put down the receiver and leaped up the stairs to my room. It was the middle of the day. I couldn't sit and watch TV, so I leaped on the bed and began jumping up and down as if on a trampoline, whooping and hollering. I was on my way to America. Legally. I had won the daydream lottery! The American Dream Lottery!

IN AMERICA, YET AGAIN

The Green Card

It was June 1962. Nearly a month after my meeting with the Consul-General. I was on the phone, long distance, with Mr. Kaplan, telling him I had my passport.

"Are you planning on flying, taking the train, or bus, or what?"

"Flying. I want to get there as fast as I can."

"Well, get your ticket then to LA. One way." It was the first time I'd heard him come close to a laugh.

"But don't I have to go to some immigration office or something?"

"That'll happen when you get to the airport in Toronto. You'll pass through immigration there. I believe it's called Malton Airport."

"Wouldn't it be easier going through some place like Niagara Falls?"

"It wouldn't matter. Every port of entry has your information."

"What if they deny me?" I was shaking.

"Unless something horrible has happened in the last forty-eight hours that only they know about, I think your chances are fairly good. Get your ticket."

Five days later, I took a taxi to Malton Airport where I had disembarked many months earlier in handcuffs wearing the same color suit I wore to the Consulate. At the counter, I was directed to a simple, mostly glass office not much larger than a cubicle. The sign above it said, 'United States Immigration and Customs.' There were three uniformed officials inside. The oldest, probably in his early fifties, extended his hand. "Your passport, please."

I handed it to him, trying not to shake. Scanning it in some machine, he looked back and forth from the screen to my passport. He then pushed a couple of buttons and returned, handing back the open passport. On it was a small green plastic card. "Welcome to the United States, Mr. Barbour."

I was physically jolted. "That's it?"

"What else did you want?" He smiled slightly.

"You mean, I don't have to answer any questions or take an exam or anything?"

"You do that when you become a citizen. Good luck here."

I tried to say one 'thank you,' but a bunch of them poured out of me. Clutching my passport and green card, I felt six feet taller. I couldn't believe it. It couldn't have been that easy. I had prepared for another brutal, painful encounter. I rushed into a small shop on the concourse and grabbed three postcards, all with the same skyline of Toronto. The first one I addressed to the gracious lady in the blue suit. I wrote that was the sight I'd see as my plane took off for California, that I would one day justify her generosity, closing by writing thank you numerous times.

The second card I sent to Margaret, apologizing for not coming by. I told her I had been too stressed and anxious to do anything but get to America. I thanked her, asked her to thank Mel again. The third I sent to Mel, thanking him for giving me the view of Toronto that I never wanted to see again. I then called Mr. Kaplan.

"I got it. I got it," Mr. Kaplan. "They gave it to me."

He chuckled. "That's wonderful. I'm happy for you. The truth is, John, I am surprised. Frankly, I wasn't very positive it would happen."

"I can't believe it, either. Oh, Mr. Kaplan, I don't know how to thank you. Or Abe. It wouldn't have happened without you."

"Thanks, but the biggest factor was you. I think had this happened to someone else, they'd still be in Canada. The difference with you is that you can talk!"

I laughed.

"As soon as you can, when you get here come by the office and we'll wrap things up."

I hung up and then called Abe. I gushed that the first thing I wanted to do when I got there was to show him my green card, thank him again in person, and pay off the seven hundred dollars as quickly as possible.

"Son," he said gently, "you forget about the money."

I liked when he called me son. I said, "Sir, this wouldn't have happened without you. If I paid you seven hundred dollars seven hundred times, it wouldn't be enough."

"Son, money has nothing to do with it. Besides, you might have to send it to Israel and it might not get there."

"Whadda you mean?"

"I'm moving there. This week."

"For how long?"

"I want to be buried there. Where I belong."

"Mr. Pelter, are you sick?"

"Just sick of being here."

"I'm trying to get in and you're trying to get out."

"If you were Jewish, my boy, you'd understand."

"But look what happened to your brother. He didn't last two weeks."

"Son, I'm just a poor private eye. And that's where I've always wanted to be." He paused. I had a feeling, a dark feeling, that there was more at work in his life prompting this decision. Maybe it was something personal. I was afraid to ask.

"Mr. Kaplan said one of the reasons he thought I got my green card was that I could talk. Now I just don't know what to say."

"Just say what I'm saying to you. Good luck. And I'm proud of you."

"Good … good luck, Mr. Pelter." I couldn't speak. Tears streamed out of my eyes again. Something was cut out of my insides. I stared at the receiver long after he hung up.

Mr. Pelter moved to Israel. Without his children. And died there. He was where he wanted to be. I was where I wanted to be. In America.

On the plane, I hurried to a seat next to the window. I wanted to see every bit of the topography, from Toronto to Los Angeles, but I saw almost none of it. All I did was stare at that green card. There was my picture, and my date of entry: June 22, 1962. It was more than a green card. It was a birth certificate, a rebirth certificate. I was twenty-nine years old. Once again, I had little money, no job, little wardrobe, and no family. And yet I had everything. I had a future. That green card was a clear, clean, free blank slate. On it I could write anything I wanted. Up till then that was the only completely happy moment in my life. I was now legally in Frank

Capra's and Jimmy Stewart's America, now being run by the youngest, brightest president since Lincoln and Jefferson, John F. Kennedy. My life would change in ways I never, ever could have dreamed or imagined. So would America.

Like a homing pigeon, I returned to the apartment complex on Bluffside Drive in Studio City. I got the same apartment. To my right, Bob Klein was still trafficking in female visitors. Mort Lachman and Bill Larkin were still conducting marathon writing sessions for Bob Hope, and immediately below was Wes Butler, still directing a children's show on KABC TV. It's as though nothing had changed. It was like a Rod Serling *Twilight Zone*. After the fade out and fade in, I had this magic Green Card.

Whatever forces were at work in the universe that conspired to assist or hinder one's way on this planet were now clearly working on my behalf. There is no other explanation for it. This was where I was meant to be. In America. In LA, and in that building. So caught up was I in the euphoria of being legal, for the first few days I never thought of what kind of job I'd get when a job popped up out of nowhere looking for me. It was a job I'd never sought, one that I'd never even thought about, and one for which I had absolutely no background. It was the job of producing the morning children's show that Wes was directing called, *Chuck the Clown*.

One lazy, warm, sunny afternoon, and that could be like almost any afternoon in LA, Wes and I were sitting on the concrete steps in front of his apartment chatting when he asked me if I'd ever seen the show he was directing.

"Wes, why would I watch a kid's show?"

"Well, you're not alone." He chuckled, then added. "Well, it's not doing too well, and Chuck Runyon asked me if I had any ideas on what to do to spruce it up a bit. I told him I didn't. Would you do me a favor and look at it and tell me what you think?"

"Sure."

"Thanks. Tomorrow's Monday. Watch it this week and Saturday I'll make a lunch date with Chuck and his wife Millie at their favorite restaurant on Los Feliz. You'll like her. She's very bright and very tough. Really runs the show."

"Wes, I don't know anything about kids' shows. Or kids, for that matter."

"It doesn't matter. I know you. You've got ideas about everything."

As promised, the following morning I was up early to watch it. Having never seen one, I didn't know what to expect, but I didn't expect to be so horrifyingly bored. Here was this guy in this dumb clown garb, painted face and spinning hat talking in a squeaky voice higher than the voices of the kids. Who talks like that? Ten minutes was all I could stand. I shut it off. Not for a moment did I entertain the thought of being involved in something like that, unemployed or not. I didn't have the heart to tell Wes I hadn't really watched it and didn't want to meet the Runyons. Every day I saw him, though, he'd give me a big smile and thumbs up, and say, "See you Saturday."

Saturday came. Wes drove me to this very large, beautiful blue and white building on a corner in the upscale Los Feliz district. Charles, or Chuck, and Millie were sitting in what they told me was their favorite booth. They appeared to be in their mid to late forties. Chuck had a warm face, and nice voice, which wasn't in evidence on his show. Millie was a handsome woman with a tougher voice and demeanor, which signaled immediately and correctly that she was the tougher of the two. Looking around, it was easy to see we were the youngest people in the restaurant. When I mentioned this casually, just trying to relax with small talk, Millie said, "It's a favorite for all the retirees around here. The food's good, cheap, and easy to chew."

I howled. "Mrs. Runyon, that's funny."

She was pleased at my comment. "Millie. Call me Millie."

"Maybe in the afternoon, your husband could do a show for these folks called, "Chucko, the Chiropractor."

They laughed out loud. I asked Millie, because she was obviously the one to talk to, how Chuck got started. She told me how they'd gotten together after the war in Long Beach, and she said that she thought if Easter has a bunny and Halloween a ghost, that birthdays should have a clown. So, it started at private parties, then supermarkets and malls.

Chuck then asked anxiously, "Did you see the show?" Wes looked at me, awaiting my answer.

I liked them, and I didn't want to hurt them, but said, "I only watched ten minutes on Monday morning and turned it off."

They were stunned, mouths agape Chuck stammered, "Uh … uh … why?"

"Honestly, it bored me," I said as gently as I could. To break the shock and deathly silence, I added, "Mr. Runyon, you have a very nice speaking voice, but I didn't know that until I sat down here. I told Wes that I knew nothing about kids, that I'd never had a childhood, but one thing I remember distinctly was that when my mother had friends over, they would talk to one another in normal voices, but when they saw me they put on this high-pitched kiddie voice, as though I was something other than a person. Kids aren't stupid.

"When you're meeting your young guests for the first time, even though you're in costume, and they know it's a costume, talk to them in your normal voice, so they can answer in theirs, then when you start playing they'll know you're playing, use your clown's voice. Also, every kid loves to compete, physically and mentally. You should design some simple games and quizzes for teams and individuals. They don't want to just sit and watch cartoons. Most of that should be eliminated."

"John," Millie said, "would you produce the show for us?"

Shocked, I said honestly, "Millie, I told you I know nothing about kids."

"You'd never know it from this brief conversation. Could you think of some stuff Chuck could do with the kids? You, Chuck and Wes could sit down for an hour and come up with a dozen things. We'd like you to do it!" she said, without glancing at or talking to her husband.

"I like your ideas, John," Chuck said. "Especially your honesty. I've been doin' this so long I lost track."

"I've never produced any kind of TV show before. Just plays. Theater stuff."

"Then this'll be your first one." Millie smiled.

And there it was. I'll be damned. Thank you, America!

Send in the Clown

The KABC TV studios were located just off Talmadge Street, the east end of Hollywood. I drove up to the gate, window down. When the guard asked me my name and destination, I felt like I was being greeted by St. Peter at the Pearly Gates. I couldn't get the smile off my face. It was all so unreal.

I was directed to the far end of the lot to a couple of adjoining offices marked, "Chucko the Clown". (Those same two offices would turn out to be mine in six years when I became the original host of *AM Los Angeles*, where my real career and confrontations began!) It was a Friday. As instructed by Millie, I arrived following the show. They greeted me enthusiastically.

"Here's our new boy producer," Millie exclaimed happily, arms aloft.

"Millie," I said, "who was your previous producer?"

"Chuck and me," she replied, straight faced.

"You mean you fired yourselves to hire me?"

"That's right, and we're gonna get along great."

And we did. For the six months KABC kept the show. Gone were the meaningless cartoons, and Chuck's squeaky voice, at least when he talked to the children. We divided the children into teams, a concept they loved and looked forward to. They competed in quizzes with questions that were sometimes challenging, and in playful, physical games. The most fun and entertaining, and sometimes show-stopping, was a game where an apple or some object was placed under a child's chin and he or she would have to pass it to the next child who could only retrieve it with his or her chin. The lines were all boy-girl boy-girl. It was often a riot, and as weeks passed, the game that all the kids requested to play.

Within just a few short weeks, the ratings were up a point and a half, which was considered significant for a throw-away morning show, as were requests by mothers to have their children on the program. Not all those requests came by mail. Some came by phone; some even insisted on coming down to the studio to plead in person to show me how anxious they were to have their children on such a wonderful TV show.

One lady, a beautiful young woman in her late twenties from Quebec found her way into my office. She was so desperate to get her son on TV, she offered in broken English to show me how he was conceived. It brought back recent memories of casting calls at my little Studio City Playhouse; women of all ages and sizes and backgrounds openly offering sex for even the smallest part in the smallest theater. But TV was bigger. So were the offers. I booked the French Canadian's boy on the show, but turned down her offer, and mentioned my shock to Millie.

"John" she said, "I'm proud of you, but get used to it. These broads throw themselves at Chuck all the time, even when he's wearing that clown suit."

The ratings continued a slow improvement. I spent most of my time thinking of additions or bits for the show, or reading mostly political books and articles. Lunch was a sandwich eaten on a bench while soaking up the sun. One day I was interrupted by a deep voice that said, "You're doin' a good job, young man."

I turned to see a strikingly well-dressed handsome man with a crewcut. He appeared over six-feet tall. If he hadn't been in an impeccable Brooks Brothers suit, he should have been in some kind of military uniform. I didn't know him.

He extended his hand. "I'm Elton. Elton Rule. The General Manager."

"Oh, Mr, Rule." I started to stand to shake his hand.

"Don't get up. I just wanted to tell you, like I told Millie, that Chuck's show is looking good and doing pretty good. She said it's mostly your doing. Is this what you've always wanted to do?"

I said thank you, adding, "What do you mean?"

"Producing a clown's show."

"No, sir. Do you think anyone dreams of producing a clown's show?"

He smiled. "I guess not."

"I actually never thought about it. It just happened by accident. For me all the good things seem to happen by accident, while all the bad things are really well planned."

He laughed. "That's so true. What is it you'd really like to do?"

"Mr. Rule, if I told you, I don't think you'd believe me."

"Try me."

"A documentary about Red China."

"What? Why that?"

"Well, we're in the middle of this Cold War, which is all over your six o'clock news. First with Russia, and now with this so-called new Red Menace, China. I'd bet my green card, not one in a million Americans, or most of those politicians, has the foggiest idea how China went from being controlled by the British with the introduction of opium and The Boxer rebellion, the genocidal invasions by the Japanese, to becoming our ally under Chiang Kai Chek, to a Russian ally under Mao Tse-tung." I was a little stunned that just poured out of me. It was the first time I ever felt comfortable talking politics.

He stared at me, even more stunned. "Isn't that rather an ambitious undertaking?"

"Not really. There's all kinds of free footage and photos around. All you'd have to do is write the script and add the pictures."

"Have you started?"

"Gosh, no. Actually, I just thought of it now."

He looked pleased. "Start on it. Let me know in a few weeks what you've done." Without shaking hands, he turned and left.

For the next three weeks, I devoted almost every moment to researching and writing the, hopefully, objective history of the political evolution of China. This was an undertaking that was well-planned. And, like I said, it didn't work out. Elton Rule never got to see my script. Within the month he was promoted from General Manager at that local station to president of the entire network. I didn't have the nerve to call someone in such a lofty position about my little project, so I tore it up.

The week he left we got word Chuck would be off the air in two months. I was almost back where I started from when I got off the plane. Except now I had a green card, and a bit of a TV resumé. But to do what? A kids' show? I hated it, but I loved TV. In the months I did Chucko, the most interesting five minutes I had spent was on a bench talking politics with Elton Rule. Could I ever earn a living on TV just talking to people like, Jack Paar? In researching Paar, I discovered he had been a comedian. He was discovered telling jokes in the army. That was why he still did those great monologues at the top of his show. Maybe I could do that!

My Kingdom for a Joke

There was never a talk-show host, day or night, as compelling, entertaining, or even as human as Jack Paar. Whether doing a monologue, which he did as well or better than anyone, or an interview, which he certainly did better than anyone, he had an impish, Huck Finn sincere curiosity about him that made me feel like he was an extension of me. He drew me in emotionally; Johnny Carson, Steve Allen, Leno, Letterman, Cavett, or Bishop couldn't do that. The closest any host ever came to make an emotional contact with on audience was Oprah. But what they all lacked that Jack Paar had in abundance, was courage, and that courage was not to do the show for an audience, but for himself. He believed that if he liked something or someone and found him or her interesting, his audience would too. And they did.

As a result, he booked onto his show an array of unknown original talents, intellectual artists, and verbal misfits, including William Buckley, CIA-funded conservative crossing left and right swords and words with free-thinking, Gore Vidal, one of the last American writer-historians to possess a real wit, Jonathan Winters, the funniest ad-lib comedian America ever produced until Robin Williams. On one show, Jack just handed him a two or three-foot stick, and Jonathan converted it into nine minutes of unmatched comic gold. There was also the Smothers Brothers, two misfits but loving, entertaining youngsters from San Francisco. Also from San Francisco, an almost middle-aged housewife who gave up a piano concert career for laughs: Phyllis Diller. And she got them first on Jack's show.

I saw them all. My contact with the real world, or the world I imagined, was watching Paar. What kept drawing me to him was the simple and surprising realization he talked to people. Really talked. And listened. While I loved and admired comics, especially Bob Hope, Henny Youngman, Alan King, Jackie Mason, Lenny Bruce and Mort Sahl, I had absolutely no aspiration to be one. But to be where Paar was, I had to become one. How does one do that? Where do you start?

I could see, to do stand-up comedy you have to have funny material and courage. The only thing harder to come by than funny material, is the courage to stand alone and do it. No artist or performer comes close to possessing the courage of a standup, stand-alone comic. An actor leans on a writer, and other actors. Singers and musicians have their instruments and music to lean on. Not a comic. His only defense is that he'd better be funny. If not, it can be soul-destroying rejection. When a comic doesn't do well, they say he bombed. When a comic does well, they say he killed. It's the joyful, revengeful pleasure of mowing down the enemy and turning them into a friend. Comics who've been in the army will tell you they felt safer facing an enemy with guns, because they had a gun and a bunch of buddies with guns. On stage a comic is unarmed, confronting strangers.

But where was I going to get good material? The obvious and easiest place, of course, was joke books. I headed back to my Shakespeare Hollywood Library on Wilcox and checked out half a dozen of the thickest. On the way home I stopped at Edmund's used books on Hollywood Boulevard and bought half a dozen of the thinnest. Then I bought the albums of the most successful comics at the time to listen to what they said and how they said it. Mort Sahl made caustic funny comments about America's politics. Bob Newhart, an accountant from Chicago, made gentle, funny, pretend phone calls. Shelly Berman did angry funny pretend phone calls. Lenny Bruce, probably the brightest and funniest of the lot, had savagely satirical observations of a sick society, earning him the title "sick comedian."

Scouring the dozen books over a two-week period looking to steal material was extremely unproductive, even discouraging. Most of the jokes were not funny. The few bits or lines that were, everyone knew. What I learned from the albums, though, was enlightening. Each performer had his own voice, style, and point of view. They did material that they liked, material that suited their personalities. Being themselves is what made them unique and successful. That was what I should do, but I realized I didn't know who the real me was. I had no style, no personality that I knew of and, definitely, no point of view.

Days and nights I paced or sat incubating on what my point of view should be. I don't know if I had a point of view about anything really. But I knew I had opinions. Lots of them. Most about politics and religion. But politics was already the bailiwick of Mort Sahl and Bob Hope. How could I approach it differently? Every day when they were on a break, I'd stick my head in Mort and Bill's always open door, asking if they had a minute. Not once did they say no.

I confided that I wanted to be a comic, and plagued them for hours asking questions about Hope and his start. They told me, like Sinatra, Hope briefly wanted to be a boxer. His name was Packy East. We talked endlessly about comics. Those who came from tough neighborhoods with miserable childhoods. The Jews and the Irish often wrote the funniest stuff about life, turning shitty backgrounds into funny fertilizer while Will Rogers, who came from a successful banking family, and Mark Twain, who came from a comfortable loving family, made the funniest observations about politics and people.

"John," Mort said one day, "I've been writing for Bob for over twenty years. Not once did I feel I had the courage to do what you're thinking of doing. It is tough. But remember this, the more often you bomb, the longer you bomb, the longer will be your success! Anytime you want to come by and run some of your stuff by us, Bill and I would be happy to listen. Not help. Just listen."

I was sky high with enthusiasm. The two best joke writers in the country encouraging and listening to me, but I did not want to talk about my childhood. I could find nothing funny in it. Besides I was just so happy to be in America, it no longer seemed that miserable. *Awww,* maybe that's it. Talk about America. My observations about the differences between Americans and Canadians. There really weren't that many; it was a stretch. But it was a start.

The first two jokes I wrote were: 'Hi, I'm appearing here tonight through the courtesy of the NAACP. The National Association for the Advancement of Canadian People. Just moving to Los Angeles, I'm having the hardest time finding the perfect California house. One that's fireproof and floats. You know, the largest selling magazine in Canada is *Time*. Down here you call it *Mad Magazine*."

It poured out of me as if coming from somewhere else. I felt I was just taking dictation. At one sitting, I painted a cutting word picture of the perfect American as revealed by the commercials on television. I had a routine about my first American car, a fifty-nine Chevy. That wasn't the year, that was the number of times it was in the shop. How any American boys can grow up to become a president, but how many Canadian boys grow up to become a queen? More than you know. Only we don't call them queens. We call them mounties. They always get their man.

In less than two hours I had my first five minutes. I was so excited, I took the yellow legal pad, held it before me and stood in front of the mirror to perform it. I sounded too much like Bob Hope. I would have to find the 'key' for me, something I struggled with through every performance for weeks. Even years. That key turned out to be deceptively simple. Since I am not a comic personality, someone people instinctively smile at when he walks on to the stage, I would not ever try to get laughs. I would just talk in a normal voice. This way the audience would know I'm not trying to be funny. Just talking. If it is funny, that's a bonus.

Not wanting to appear to the audience as a clone or poor man's version of Hope or Paar, and because I so admired Lenny Bruce's routines, I decided I'd augment my one-liners with some story or situation. I wrote a story about an unemployed Jewish carpenter who lost his job because he talked too much. He ends up at the unemployment office where the only job available is building wooden crucifixes for the Romans. At the end of the week, I didn't just poke my head in Mort's office, I burst in.

"Mort. Bill. I have something. I have something. Can I run it by you?"

They smiled. "Go ahead."

"I have it memorized, but I'm too nervous, so I'll just read it."

They began chuckling, then laughing. What a glorious feeling.

"Do you like it? Is it okay?"

"John," Mort said seriously, "it is funny. But that Jesus thing's gonna keep you in the unemployment line, too."

"What do I do now? How do I find someplace to try it?"

"The best place in town," Bill said.

"What's that?"

"The Horn," he said. "It's a club on Santa Monica Boulevard in Santa Monica. That's where everybody goes. They have some hillbilly kid there now who sings opera. The damnedest thing."

"If I go, would you guys come to see me? Give me a critique?"

"If we have time, and you get by the audition. Sure."

The Horn

The Horn, not too far from the Pacific Ocean, was the perfectly designed and managed nightclub for a beginning performer to start. On your left as you walked in, was the stage; an eight foot by eight-foot red-carpeted platform a foot high backed up against the wall.

Around and in front of it were tables that sat no more than four people on wooden chairs. Capacity was about sixty or seventy people. The bar with stools, was well to the rear where the clinking of glasses and opening of bottles could not be heard. Everything was designed to be focused on the performer. It could only have been designed by someone who had been a performer himself. And it was.

The owner/manager was a middle-aged, barrel chested, slightly grey-haired Italian named Ricardo, Rick to the regulars. He had been an opera singer, a basso who looked and sounded like Ezio Pinza. Monday through Thursday, during the day, he taught voice. At night he ran his club like a gulag. He was the one I was told to talk to.

I wanted to wait till after the show. What had just looked like customers, people would pop up from various tables singing, "It's Showtime." Rick possessed a powerful, beautiful voice, but never intruded himself into the proceedings, unless begged to do so. It was obvious his performers had learned to beg. This night I saw a very funny comedienne named Jeanine Bernier. She was quickly forgotten when this awkward goofy sounding, head bobbing hillbilly telling Ozark stories took the stage. He heed and hawed about his roots and his family, back in the hills. About ten minutes in, he asked the audience if they would mind if he sang a little ditty he'd learned. Regular customers who'd obviously seen him, hollered for him to do so. You could see and hear immediately why they were regulars, why they had asked him to sing. With the very first note, that rube from the hills transformed himself from Li'l Abner into Pavarotti. Out poured a perfect Nessun Dorma. His name was Jim Nabors. During the intermission, spotting Rick at the cash register, where he spent a lot of time, I introduced myself. "I understand, sir, you're the one I should talk to about auditioning."

He looked down at me, his appraisal making me feel even smaller, which I think he intended. He had an eye for talent and a knack for intimidation. He asked, "Whatta you do?"

"I want to be a comic."

"Whatta yah mean, 'wanna be?' You not done it before?"

"No, sir."

"What makes you think you're funny?"

"I don't know, but I was told by Bob Hope's writers that this was the best place to start. That's why I'm here."

He stared at me a moment. "Come here, kid."

I thought he was showing me the door and throwing me out. He pointed to a door next to the entrance. "See that door? That's the annex.

That's where I audition, and beginners perform. You go in there and watch the show. Then come back next Friday at seven and I'll see what you got."

"Yes. Yes, sir."

The Annex didn't even look like a room. It looked like a wide, long hallway with about ten narrow rows of chairs facing a very tiny stage with no musicians. It looked like a poor fundamentalist church. People came there to confess, not to perform. I watched a couple of fair singers, a guitar-playing poet who couldn't rhyme, and a comic who couldn't get laughs. My stomach began to hurt. I went home determined to come back the following week. I had to.

I got there at six p.m. Rick was in the main room setting up with his staff and some performers. No one got paid. Most of the performers, even the really popular ones like Jim, volunteered just for the opportunity to be seen. I didn't mind the thought of performing for nothing. It was a chance to develop an act and a style. He barked his instructions. When giving orders, he was incapable of anything but a bark, always from his perch next to the cash register. He noticed me and looked a little surprised to see me.

"You're early."

"I always am."

"Good. Go next door and wait. You'll go on around seven-thirty. I'll be in to see you."

He turned away, bellowing more instructions

The Annex was empty. Looking at the bareness of the room, feeling the silence, I began to wonder why I was there. I did my usual and paced, imagining no one showing up. Around six forty-five, though, they began to trickle in. They were the overflow from the sold-out main room.

By seven it was packed. One of the performers introduced himself to me, announcing that no sets were to be longer than twelve minutes. I would be on third. He walked onto this tiny stage, which now had an upright piano on it, welcomed the audience, and began to sing a Broadway medley to the accompaniment of a good piano player. He was all right. The audience liked him; a good thing. I was too self-involved and nervous to listen.

Finishing his set, he gave a nice introduction to the next act, a girl guitar-playing folk-singer, making her third appearance. She was not quite as good as Mr. Broadway. Her voice was too whispery; while I'm not musical, she also sounded a little flat. I wondered what Rick might think of her. I turned around looking for his reaction. He wasn't there. Now, I panicked. I'd be going on in a few minutes and he wasn't even there to see me. The young, want-to-be Joan Baez finished to applause that seemed to be more for her folk song topics than her talent.

Mr. Broadway then introduced me, saying it was my first time at The Horn, and added unnecessarily, I thought, that it was also my first time as a comic. The applause was polite. It wasn't the audience I was worried about. It was Rick's absence. The moment I took the mike, though, he appeared through the door, and stood watching, his arms folded.

I said, "Thank you, ladies and gentlemen, and those of you who are undecided."

I was shocked at the loudness of the laughter. I then did what I would later always do no matter where I appeared. I would make observations about where I was, maybe the people present, or something in the news that day. If I did that, the audience knew immediately I didn't have a canned act. In this case, I made a few observations about the room. I welcomed them to the annex, telling them that it's called the annex because it's from the Italian word, annexio, which in English means, not good enough for the main room. They applauded. I pointed to Rick at the back doorway, saying, "The owner, Rick, is standing back there watching and making an evaluation." They turned to look, and giggled. He didn't crack a smile. "He's not evaluating me. He's evaluating you. To see if you're good enough for the main room. He wants you to be comfortable. But not in these chairs." They cheered. I then made my observations about the place being more like a fundamentalist church, where people come to pray, not perform. They laughed. They pray for cushions. They applauded again. I segued into my Canadian stuff; I couldn't get over the exhilaration and warmth. I was being embraced by the sound of their laughter and applause. There is no feeling on earth like it. My stuff was all one-liners. Then it was time to do my unemployed carpenter bit. In isolated spots, it brought screams and applause. In other spots, huge gasps, and at the end, a full room ovation. But not from Rick; his arms were still crossed.

I stepped down. As I made my way toward Rick, as proud and pleased and as warm as I'd ever felt, some folks were still chuckling and clapping. Some patted me, wishing me luck. I was taken aback, though, by a still unsmiling Rick who motioned me out onto the street.

"You went over. You did fifteen minutes. Nobody does more than twelve."

"I didn't mean to, sir. When I rehearsed it, I thought I'd be lucky to have five minutes of stuff."

"Where'd you get that Jesus shit?"

"I wrote it."

"Well, tear it up."

"But they seemed to like it."

"They can like it someplace else. Not here. I don't want that shit here. You got nice stuff. And you look clean."

I wanted to argue with him, but it flashed through my head that Lenny Bruce, as brilliant, original and socially aware as he was, was never offered the shows that Jack Paar and Bob Hope got. I was certainly no revolutionary of any sort. I had no desire to be controversial. Just funny. And employed.

"I don't need to do that. I just thought it'd be different."

"Young man, you're already different enough." He patted me on the shoulder, a slight smile creased his tough face. This warmed me much more than the audience had. "You come every Friday and Saturday for a month to the Annex, to get comfortable. Then I'll put you in the main room."

Standing on the dimly lit sidewalk, I was in heaven, show business heaven. In the lamplight there were no sudden daydreams of instant success or a future 'John Barbour Show.' To me the successful future was coming back to The Horn Fridays and Saturdays, to experience the warmth, glow and thrill of getting laughs.

Advice from the Future Gomer Pyle

After a month, as promised, Rick put me in the main room, Fridays and Saturdays, along with Jim Nabors, a couple of other good singers, and a singing comedienne. The always packed audiences were unbelievably responsive. After all the music, it was a respite to sit for twelve minutes and listen to a stand-up.

It was a great time for news. John Kennedy was this intellectual, handsome refreshingly new president with a fairytale family and a fashion plate first lady who dominated the airwaves. They were made even more iconic with the largest-selling comedy album in history: Vaughn Meader's brilliant imitations of all the Kennedy clan called *The First Family*. Liz Taylor was making *Cleopatra* and making out with with Richard Burton whom her mother called her 'fun-in-law.' Conservatives were trying to get us into Southeast Asia. Blacks were trying to get into Woolworths.

The country was alive with vitality, energy and high expectations, or so it seemed. I made observations about it, commenting on all sides.

There was one joke I did in a routine that Rick absolutely hated, but he let me keep it in because it got the loudest sustained laughter and applause. It was a bit about a drill sergeant in Vietnam, who sounded a lot like Jim Nabors, yelling at his troops telling them they could not shoot at the Viet Cong until they saw the 'whites of thur eyes! One GI answering quietly says: 'Sarge, with them Asian Viet Cong, no matter how close we gits, their eyes are never wide enough to see the whites.' The biggest laugh always came from Jim.

One night, at closing, he motioned me to his table. I was surprised. Other than the casual "hello" or "good show," he never talked to me. He told me he was excited because he was about to make his first film appearance on a show with Andy Griffith.

"Geez, Jim, that's terrific. You'll be great.'"

"Aw hope so," he said.

"You're a natural. You can't miss."

"Thanks," he said, adding, "Yer a natural, too. But do yah mind if I tell ya somethin'? I'm a real fan. Like ah say, yer a natural funny man, a wit I guess they call it. And ah'm a big fan. You write some funny stuff. Original, too. That's a talent. Some of them jokes, a couple about Kennedy, and that one about the Viet Cong, they're funny, but some of them is a little tough."

"Yeah, I guess so. But they're not cruel."

"Oh, no," he was quick to say. "Just pretty tough. An ah love to listen to ya, but one thing ah've noticed since ah come to this town is that there's something more important than talent for the people who run this place."

"What's that?"

He looked right at me now. "Johnny, it's better to be liked than talented."

"Am ... am I not likable?"

"Yeah, yah got a nice face and a nice smile. Good teeth. Great blue eyes. But yah've got to be careful with some of those tough jokes, even if they are funny. It's not enough in this town that people admire that talent, which more than not they envy; they've just got to simply like you."

"Thank you, Jim. I appreciate that."

"Johnny, yer likable enough, and if you focus on that, yah cain't miss."

At that moment, a really nice-looking, tall, dark-haired, casually dressed young man approached Jim and patted him on the shoulder. "Okay, star, your ride's here."

Jim beamed, then put his hand on the hand on his shoulder. And left it there. Oops, I thought, this guy must be more than a ride for Jim in a car. I always made a conscious effort to never judge anyone on first impressions. To do so would mean you'd never know that some caterpillars become Monarch butterflies! But when the fluttering is obvious, you sometimes can't help it. I wondered why Jim had picked me out to give such sage advice, advice which I would soon discover was and still is right on.

The Hungry i

During the summer months of 1963, performing Fridays and Saturdays, but during the week I drove nearly every night to different clubs to try out the new material. I wrote five hours a day, slowly building a fairly successful act. I never thought about money, then or now. Sadly, I knew nothing about how to build or pursue a career. My future was always just the next night and the next club. From watching Mickey Rooney and Judy Garland movies as a kid, it was embedded in me that if you just keep doing a show and doing it well somebody would show up and make you a movie star. For me that someone approached me after my Saturday night set at The Horn.

He was my age, my height, had dark eyes and hair, and wore a tailored navy suit. He identified himself as an agent from The Agency for the Performing Arts. "APA," he said. "My name's Bill Donohue. You're very good. That's nice stuff you do. Do you write it yourself?"

"Yeah, thank you."

"Do you have any representation?"

"What do you mean?"

"An agent. Do you have an agent?"

"No. Not yet," I said. "Actually, I wouldn't quite know how to go about it. I'm sorta new at this!"

"Could we talk about it? I think we could help you. Here's my card. Could you come by the office Monday, say, around ten? We'll talk then, and I'll introduce you to some of the guys." He handed me his card, shook my hand firmly and left.

The following Monday, well before ten, I was at Bill's office. He introduced me to half a dozen well-scrubbed, well-dressed agents whose youthfulness and enthusiasm were surprising. The first thing Bill said when we were alone and seated in his office was "I've got a job for you."

"What kind of job?"

He laughed. "Stand-up. Your act!"

"You're kidding!"

"No. Saturday I had the booker from the Versaille Room in Pasadena come down to see you. He liked what he saw."

I'd heard of the place. Ronald Reagan's daughter had worked there recently with an act featuring other famous celebrity's kids. It was like a mini-Vegas main room. It had a reputation of being what they call a classy place. I was speechless.

"This'll be your first professional job, won't it?"

"Yeah," I mumbled.

"It'll be for a week. You'll get three hundred dollars. What do ya think?"

"I'm stunned."

"Have you got any glossies?"

"What's that?"

'Eight by tens. Pictures. We're gonna need some. And a bio."

"I don't have much of a bio. This is my first job as a professional."

"You have a great bio. Put down all that terrific theater stuff. You know, you do some really good topical, political stuff. Few people do that. Maybe Mort Saul. Ever heard of The Hungry i in San Francisco?'

"Who hasn't? I have Saul's albums from there. Johnny Winters. Lenny Bruce, a bunch."

"Good. That's where I think you should be. But let's see how it goes. You open next Saturday. I'll be there with some of the guys."

"What about The Horn and Rick?"

"You're a pro now. Getting paid. I'll talk to him."

"No, I better do that. If it weren't for him I wouldn't be here."

I performed the following Friday night at The Horn, then told Rick, rather cautiously, about my upcoming gig the next night in Pasadena.

"You know, young man," he said in a voice that was the quietest I'd ever heard from him, "you're the only one I've had in my room I let do the kind of news stuff you do. It always made me uncomfortable. I just want my customers to be entertained. Music and what have you. But they liked you. So do I. You'll do well, and you're welcome back here anytime." His handshake was as firm as it was sincere. I was touched. I never had the occasion or need to return.

For a hundred bucks, Bill's photographer took the necessary pictures. To my surprise and delight, in the lobby leading to The Versailles Room, there was a large four-foot by six-foot blowup of one. That quick. It made me look like a star. The bigger-than-life size of it made me nervous. I was hoping just to live up to the picture.

The room was full. Nearly 600 people. I had on my best, and only, dark blue suit and tie. Every man in the audience was dressed better than I was, their women too. That week the main news story was a massive sex scandal in England involving a couple of beautiful call girls. It looked like it would bring down the British government. I never used profanity in my act. It made me uncomfortable. That's not how to talk to strangers, but the story out of England was so huge, I couldn't resist. After my introduction, and the band playing *When Johnny Comes Marching Home,* I waited a while for the polite applause to end, looked out very slowly at almost every seat in the audience and said, "If you watched the news today, they said some male members of the British government are going down." I paused, feeling like Bob Hope. First there were chuckles, which built slowly, then huge raunchy guffaws, and then the place erupted into applause. "But it's just like our news not to finish the story." More loud chuckles "They didn't say on whom!" Roars and applause. My fifteen minutes had stretched to over twenty. Every night for the week, it was a full house.

After Bill's commission, the glossies, and the dry cleaning, I had just over a hundred and fifty dollars left. I never felt so rich, financially or spiritually. How wonderful to be paid for something I had enjoyed doing for nothing. The two very positive reviews made me feel even richer. After all the backslapping and congratulations, Bill told me he'd read the reviews to David Allen, the guy who books the Hungry i, who said, "They sound good, but we don't book anyone sight unseen."

The thought of my second professional job being at the 'i', as everyone called it, the Yankee Stadium of nightclubs, was a little scary. It intimidated me more than that four-by-six blowup.

"Bill, should I film my act so he can see it?"

"No, he said he'd have to see you, John, which means you'd have to audition for him. He said you could do it one of the next two Saturdays."

"I have to pay my way up there myself and audition to an empty house?"

Bill shrugged. "I guess so."

"I've got nothing to lose, I guess."

I had seen the City by the Bay and the Golden Gate Bridge a hundred times in films, so I was as excited about seeing it in person as I was auditioning.

The 'i' was located near the city's downtown business district on Broadway, in an area called North Beach, a predominantly Italian community. Like an old speakeasy, it was located downstairs in a corner building. What kind of comedy club could be in a basement? I was totally unprepared for what I saw. It was elegant. The polished flooring made up of large black and white squares, like an oversized chessboard. The almost wall-to-wall brightly polished wooden bar to the right was as sumptuous as any in an old MGM musical. Doors on either end of the bar led to the relatively small showroom, also like no other I'd ever seen, or would see. There were no tables. Just plush theater seats; on each armrest a place for a drink. The audience had to look at the performers. What a smart idea. The only ordinary thing about the decor and design was the stage, a carpeted twelve-foot by nine-foot riser about a foot and a half off the ground, Behind it a plain red brick wall.

A man in his late 40's in a rumpled blue suit and the bartender, who looked like Don Adams, (Maxwell Smart) the only two on the premises, were chatting by the bar. The man in the suit looked at me. He had the deepest bags under his eyes I'd ever seen, made deeper by the fact he never smiled.

"Hello, Mr. Allen?" I asked, extending my hand. "I'm John Barbour."

"Aww, right. Thanks for being on time. Come on in."

He opened the door to the showroom and sat in the very back corner aisle seat. Not an encouraging sight, seeing him right next to the exit.

"Let's see what you've got," he said, flatly, pointing to the stage where a mike stand had already been placed. My mouth and throat were dry and tight. *God, nobody can audition like this. Who's going to laugh?* I reached the stage, turning to look at him, not knowing what to say.

"Go ahead," he said off handedly. "The mike's live."

My voice echoed through the room. There was no laughter. It was dark in the back, so I saw no smile. I imagined myself just rehearsing in front of my bathroom mirror. The fifteen or twenty minutes I'd done in Pasadena shrank to ten minutes. Mr. Allen could only tell I was done when I said, "Thank you."

He rose, said "Thank you," and exited. I did not see him when I left. The flight back to LA was the bumpiest I'd ever experienced. We bounced up and down, and I could see the wings flapping. It felt like some kind of omen. For four days, I avoided calling Bill. I didn't want to hear how I'd bombed, or how his agency was having second thoughts about representing me. Curiosity was killing me, on the fifth day I reached for the phone. As I did, it rang. It was Bill.

"Hi, buddy, how ya doin? Sorry I didn't call. We've been swamped. You open in September," he said casually.

"I what?" I gasped.

"You open in September. Two-weeks gig."

"Where?"

"Where else? The Hungry i. Three-fifty a week."

"You mean…you mean he liked me?"

"I have no idea. He didn't say. He just asked if that Canadian kid would be available for two weeks in September, and I said yes."

"Oh, my God, I can't believe it."

"He's sending the contracts express mail. I'll call ya to come in and sign them. Congratulations." And he hung up.

My second professional job in the most revered comedy club in the country! Unbelievable!

I opened in the middle of September 1963. The first week, the headliner I opened for was a very successful, sort of a folk-singer named Glen Yarborough. His thin tenor voice was not unlike John Denver's. His act was pleasant; so was he. Offstage, we barely talked, as is often the case with opening acts and headliners, but he filled the house, which made it easier for me.

The audiences came for a fun night out on the town, dressed fashionably. They could not have been more receptive, so the real fun was mine. Every night someone rich or famous or infamous was sitting in front of me. Vivien Leigh was there shortly after her release from a mental ward with her blonde lover half her age. A regular was the Communist (so the conservatives said) leader of the Longshoreman's Union, tiny Harry Bridges with half a dozen bodyguards. The country was alive with news and nervousness. The Bay of Pigs disaster. Civil Rights. And rumblings of JFK's '64 campaign, probably against Barry Goldwater.

I opened with my very first impressions of this historic, romantic, one-of-a-kind city. Its population was fifty percent Catholic, and fifty percent homosexual, with the Catholics losing ground, in spite of the fact homosexuals practiced birth control. I had scores of topical jokes about the Kennedys, how the media lied about his getting his bad back during the war while aboard PT 109; he actually hurt it jumping out of Angie Dickenson's window. His story was being told in a film starring Cliff Robertson called *PT 109*, while Barry Goldwater's story was called "Putt Putt '64"… starring Sonny Tufts. Almost every joke, including this last rather silly one, got applause. It was a heady, joyous feeling. The second week, though, the mood abruptly changed. Replacing Yarborough as the starring act was a black singer I'd never heard of:

Amanda Ambrose.

Amanda was about my size, fairly attractive, naturally curly short hair, the first black female performer to wear an African native dress called a 'dashiki.' She was also the first to perform African folk songs. When she strode on stage, after the applause for me subsided, she looked quite regal. She had a full, warm voice, perfect for folk songs and southern jazz and blues. She looked and sounded ahead of her time. To my astonishment, many in the cultured, sophisticated audience were rude and cruel. Often, before she reached the microphone, there'd be shocking comments: "Why don't you dress like an American?" "Go back to Africa." "Get rid of that hair." It wasn't just one or two. It was often half a dozen. It was incomprehensible to me. These were educated, well-dressed, well-informed people. This was liberal San Francisco! On the news, I had seen the intense bigotry in the South, but not in that city, not in 1963, in one of America's most so-called progressive communities.

Occasionally there'd be a lonely voice coming to her defense. Not often, though. Her biggest defender was the owner himself, Enrico Banducci. He would move in quickly from the back of the room like the bouncer he looked like, and lift the offenders right out of their seats. If Enrico had been a wrestler, he would have been Hulk Hogan. He and his personality were oversized. He capped off his enormous charm with his beret that I never saw him without. It made him look like a French painter, rather than the best club owner in the country. He was the unelected mayor of the city, as well as The Godfather of North Beach where he owned the most famous pool hall diner in California called Enrico's. The audience's very warm and enthusiastic reception for me never changed. But I no longer had that heady feeling while the audience was laughing or applauding. I felt subdued. I knew what was about to happen to Amanda, and was powerless to prevent it. When Glen was performing, I always tried to get out to watch him. With Amanda, I went straight to the dressing room waiting to console her; every night she came in crying.

One night, midweek through our gig, she entered the dressing room a little later than usual. Tears were pouring down her face. She was almost sobbing, clutching something in her hands.

I rushed over to her. "Amanda, what is it? What did someone do to you?"

She gasped for breath, trying to talk and stop the tears. When she finally got control of herself, she said, "Look… look at this." She held out a ring.

"Why are you crying?"

She sniffed a couple of times, took a deep breath and spoke softly, "This lady called me aside after the show and said she wanted to talk to me. I didn't want to go with her. She said for me to come with her. It'd be all right. We went into the corner of the bar and she said she wanted me to know that not everybody was like those people who'd been rude to me. That a lot of people liked me, especially her. Then she handed me this ring. Johnny, it's real. It's an emerald."

"Wow that was nice of her. So, why are you crying?"

"God, who wouldn't cry. She was so kind! And beautiful. So beautiful."

"Is she still here?"

Amanda walked to the dressing room door and peeked out. I was right behind her. She pointed to a woman with brunette hair with her back to us, sitting at a far bar stool talking to Enrico.

"That's her," she whispered. "Isn't she beautiful? I think she said her name is Sarita. I'm not quite sure. I was so stunned."

"Would you introduce me? I'd like to also thank her on your behalf."

She giggled. "You're full of crap. Wait here."

Amanda walked across the checkered floor, toward the end of the bar and the mysterious, generous brunette next to Enrico. She stopped, saying something to the woman. She turned and looked toward me. She was the most beautiful, exotic creature I'd ever seen in person. She could have been Hedy Lamar or Jennifer Jones, but to me, in that instant, I could only see Liz Taylor in *A Place in The Sun*. And I was Monty Clift. In a flash that whole movie fast-forwarded through my mind. Here was this rich beautiful young heiress, and me, Monty, this young guy who only worked occasionally. I was pathetic. I never could have a daydream based in reality.

The brunette suddenly smiled at me and motioned for me to come over. My heart leapt so hard it caused my whole body to leap. Like some little kid playing hopscotch, I literally skipped across the checkered floor. Amanda and the brunette giggled at my gymnastic entrance. I felt like an idiot. Enrico must have thought I looked like one, too. He glanced at me with a straight face, saying he had some business to attend to, and walked off.

"Sarita, this is John. He wanted to meet you."

When she turned to extend her hand, her knee touched my leg and I almost buckled.

"Pleased to meet you, John. I've seen you almost every night."

Her handshake was firm with a warm softness I'd never felt before. I clutched her hand with my right hand, then grabbed her wrist with my left and started pumping like the water well had run dry. "Really, you have?"

"Yes," she said. "You're very good."

I released my grip on her arm, and apologized. "I really wanted to meet you because I thought what you did for Amanda was thoughtful and generous."

As soon as I said that, Amanda hugged her again, and a few more tears fell. While this young lady was holding Amanda, I noticed that the slightly tanned skin on her arms was totally devoid of hair. Every woman I had ever known well or casually always had some kind of body hair, sometimes a lot, sometimes a little. I would find out later that she could thank her Mexican Indian ancestry for that very attractive feature. The other feature, other than her face and skin, which was so compelling and unique, was her speaking voice. On the screen, the closest voice to it would have been Patricia Neal's, who starred with Gary Cooper in *The Fountainhead* and Andy Griffith in *A Face in the Crowd*. But Patricia's voice had an edge to it. Sarita's didn't. It was all deep, peaceful warmth.

I had the weirdest thought while I was looking at her. I didn't feel like Monty Clift, a man, gazing at a woman, Liz Taylor. I felt like John Wayne evaluating the perfect horse. What flashed quickly through my mind, was that if I ever became a star, this would be the perfect looking woman to have next to me. The perfect trophy.

"Amanda and I would like to take you to a late dinner."

"Oh, I can't," Amanda said. "I wish I could. I have an engagement I can't get out of. Sarita, thank you so much. I'll always treasure this" They hugged again. Amanda left us alone. I was furious. With her there, the brunette couldn't say 'no.' She'd have to go to dinner. She certainly wasn't going to go alone with a bumbling stranger like me. I shut down. I couldn't move or speak.

"Well," she said casually, "I guess that just leaves the two of us. Are you hungry?"

I tried to keep from hopping up and down again. "You mean, I can buy you dinner?"

"Yes. Enrico's," she said matter-of-factly, as she slipped off the seat. "It's just up the street. We can walk. You ready?"

"Oh, lemme get my coat. I'll be right back." Trying to be cool, and reserved deserted me.

I found myself skipping back to the dressing room. Amanda was just getting off the phone, checking her face in the mirror.

"Amanda," I blurted, "she's going to dinner with me!"

"I think Mr. Banducci has an interest in Sarita, Johnny. They're together talking every night at the bar. So just be careful what you're getting into. And who you're getting into."

Pat Morita

We walked the few blocks to Enrico's in the cold night air. Sarita's touch kept me warm. This generous, beautiful lady I'd just met casually put her right hand through my left arm as soon as we exited the club. It was as though she had walked with me often.

At the late hour, the place was full, but we had no problem getting the last empty booth. All the help greeted her with enthusiasm. Seeing this and remembering Amanda's warning led me to think Sarita may indeed be close to Enrico. I made it a point to sit opposite her, to keep my distance in case Enrico showed up. But mostly so I could just look at her. Afraid of any silence or lull in the conversation, I peppered her with questions. What did she do? Her family? Her politics? Her religion? And, finally, how close was she to Enrico?

She smiled, telling me she and Enrico had been friends for years and that he valued her opinion on the acts he hired. She said that she'd just retired from tap dancing at twenty-six after thirteen years as a professional. She did that so she could begin a new career singing at a famous Chinese club called Forbidden City, then later with jazz great Earl Hines' Orchestra.

"Enrico asked me if he should have you back. He thinks at times you're a little awkward on stage, but that you have great material. He admires that. You might hear tomorrow. He called your agent and booked you the last week in November."

"Thank you, Sarita. To me that's worth more than Amanda's ring."

She told me she was Mexican, but not Catholic. She had an older sister who was a teacher, had no real interest in politics, in spite of the fact she always seemed to end up at black political rallies where comedian activist Dick Gregory would try to recruit her. She said she had no plans to ever marry, and no immediate ambitions other than to see where some of the recordings with Earl Hines would take her. There was no hint of ambition when talking about her singing. She was absolutely the most peaceful person I had ever been around.

"Other than wanting to be famous and rich, what other ambitions do you have?" she asked.

"Well, it's not so much being famous, or even rich. I just love doing this, and hope I can earn a long living at it."

"But, other than that?"

"Other than that, my other ambition is to have a talk show. And not to have kids."

She smiled. "Why not?"

I certainly didn't want to talk about my stupid childhood. While trying to figure out what to say, I was interrupted.

"Excuse me, I don't mean to interrupt you, Mr. Barbour."

I looked up. Standing next to our table was a short Japanese fellow, a little younger than me, wearing a nice suit and tie.

"I've been to see you a couple of times at the club this week. My name's Pat Morita. I'm trying to be a comic."

"What can I do for you?" I said.

"I'd just like to ask you a few questions, if I could." He stood there awkwardly, looking from me to Sarita. Sarita slid over, motioning for him to sit next to her.

"Oh, thank you." Pat sat down. "Mr. Barbour, I really like what you do. It's funny and clever."

"Thanks," I said. "What is it you do?"

"During the day I punch and collate IBM cards, but if you mean my act, it's sort of a hodgepodge, and all this week I'm at a comedy club working it out."

"What kind of material do you do?' I asked.

"Jokes mostly.

"We all try to do jokes. What kind of jokes?"

"Some ethnic jokes. They're pretty funny. They get laughs, but they're ordinary."

"If you already know that, then make them extraordinary."

"I wish you could see me, to get your opinion. I ask every comic who comes to town, but they look at me like I'm the enemy."

I laughed. "Well, Pat, the war's long over. You don't have to worry about that here. You can ask all the questions you want in the next five minutes, and I'll answer them." Then I stopped myself. "Hold it, I can see some of your act. Do your first two minutes here."

"Here? Right now? Are you kidding?"

"Pat, I did my entire act for just one person two months ago, David Allen. And he booked me. You've got twice that audience. Sarita chuckled and turned to him, patting him on the arm.

Pat gulped, gathered his nerve, and started. "Good evening, ladies and gentlemen, this Irishman, this Catholic, and this Jew got on the bus–"

"Hold it," I interrupted him. "That's the extent of your ethnic jokes? When you said ethnic I thought you meant Japanese. Tell me those."

"I don't have any. I don't do them. Who wants to hear a Japanese comic?"

"I do, for Christ sake! There isn't one. Do you hear Dick Gregory and Godfrey Cambridge and Slappy White and Redd Foxx telling white jokes? Their acts are black."

"I'd be too nervous. I wouldn't know what to say."

"What it was like for you growing up in America. The cultural differences even between your parents' generation and yours. You'd be the first, the Jackie Robinson of Japanese."

"Oh, gosh, I don't know."

"Look, you could tell the audience even though you were born here, you had trouble assimilating into American culture. In America there are thirty-one days in December; in Japan there are only thirty. There's no December seventh."

He howled.

"You can tell them America had a big hit movie in the fifties with Susan Hayward playing a drunk singer called *I Want to Live*. When they released it in Japan they made her a kamikaze pilot and called it *I Want to Die*. Pat, you have a gold mine of material. Just go dig it up. And now, your five minutes are up." My look told him it was time to leave.

He rose, shaking my hand as vigorously as I'd shaken Sarita's. "Thank you, Mr. Barbour. Thank you so much."

Sarita said to him, "Pat, he's right. And you're in the right town for it."

After he left, she reached across the table and touched my hand. "That was very nice of you."

"You know, it's weird. I'm just a struggling comic like him. This is only my second paying job, and yet all kinds of comics come up and ask for advice. Like I know."

"Well, you do. Did any of them ever heed your advice?"

"Only one. A fellow named Johnny Dark. When we would go out for coffee, he was always the funniest one at the table. He was hilarious. He did the funniest impression of Johnny Mathis you ever heard. He never shut up. He was always on. But when he got on stage, he'd bomb."

"How did you help him? Because you can't just get over stage fright."

"I told him to shut up. For three weeks. I told him when we went for coffee, or when I was around him, I didn't want to hear a peep out of him for three weeks."

"Why?"

"Because he was burning up all his fabulous energy over coffee. If he would stifle it, it would just bubble out of him on stage. And it did. He's terrific and getting a lot of TV work now. He'll do well."

Johnny did not do as well as Pat, however. A few years later, Pat invited me to his new house in the Hollywood Hills to meet his wife. He was doing his Japanese act, and getting TV gigs and supporting roles in sitcoms. A few years later, he had a bigger house, a younger wife, and was co-staring in those *Karate Kid* movies.

The evening was late. I'd run out of questions. It was quiet. I reached for my wallet when the check came after midnight. It wasn't in my pocket.

"Sarita, I'm so embarrassed, I left my wallet in my room. I don't have any money."

She laughed, like I was some kind of clumsy kid, which around her I was.

"That's okay. I'll get it." She reached into her handbag and pulled out a stuffed wallet.

I don't know what comes over me sometimes around women, especially if it was one I was strongly attracted to. I was always too laid back, never forward or aggressive. Once in a while, though, out would pop something a little naughty or suggestive. It was a harmless, humorous way of relieving my tension. Sitting across from this beauty, I was extremely tense when out popped: "Well, Miss, since you've bought me a late dinner, you'll just have to stick around so I can buy you an early breakfast."

She kept fiddling with the money and the check as though she hadn't heard me, and placed it at the end of the table. She smiled slightly, and said, "Then we'll be even."

To my astonishment she got up from the table, and again slipped her hand under my arm. As promised, I bought her breakfast the next morning.

November 22, 1963

Each night, for my last three nights at the 'i', Sarita spent a few hours with me at the hotel before going home. In the quiet, dark hours around midnight, I'd accompany her to the parking garage, and watch her climb into her new red Thunderbird convertible, wrapping herself warmly in a knee-length mink coat. God, there was no question I was comedy's Montgomery Clift.

Bill called immediately, delighted to tell me I would be going back to the i the last week in November; and immediately after that I was booked into Fresno's largest nightclub for ten days with a well-known tall blonde entertainer.

Friday morning was the last day at the 'i,' and my stay at the hotel. Each morning was like each night; Sarita would be there to take me to an early breakfast. Then she'd be off after taking me back. Those breakfasts were at a restaurant called The Cliff House overlooking the Pacific. It was a sight that put every appetite into overdrive. This morning I was looking forward to the same routine, but when I opened the door, she just stood there with a wry smile.

"You know what?' she said. "I must like you. You know why?"

"Why?"

"Because I've been with you for three days now, and I'm not bored!"

My mind had barely gotten an opportunity to digest what I just heard. I absolutely exploded. It was the first time in thirty years I'd ever raised my voice in rage at anyone, and never at someone I liked. I was furious. How dare she say I didn't bore her. What am I, some rich girl's plaything? I could not help myself.

"You spoiled cunt! Fuck you and your goddamned Thunderbird. What do you think? That I'm some goddamned boy toy that you can just screw around with for a few days? Find somebody else to not bore you. I have no interest in entertaining you or seeing you again, so fuck off. And tell your old Italian friend he can cancel me if he wants." I slammed the door.

In one moment I'd gone from Monty Clift to Jimmy Cagney. Wow, how quickly things can change. I wondered if I should even show up for my last show. There was a knock on the door. I opened it. Sarita was standing there laughing.

"What's so funny?"

"No one has ever talked to me like that. It's the first time I've even heard some of those words."

"Well, somebody should have said them to you. You sound like a spoiled brat."

"I'm sorry," she said. "I meant it as a compliment." There was an awkward pause. "If you really don't want to see me again, I'd miss you," she finally said.

"I've never known anyone like you. I would obviously miss you, too, but tonight's my last night and I'll be gone."

"But you'll be back in a few weeks," she said.

"Don't you have a boyfriend? One that doesn't bore you?"

"No. You're the only one so far." She leaned in and kissed me on the cheek. "I have a bunch of stuff I have to do," she said, "so I can't have breakfast, but I'll see you later at the club, okay?"

"Sure."

"And tomorrow I'll drive you to the airport. On the way, if you like, I'd like you to meet my family."

I watched her walk down the hall like the smooth dancer she was, wondering what had just happened and what would become of all of it.

Late that afternoon, having only written a few jokes, unable to focus on anything but her, I decided to go to the club early, to hang around. And, truthfully, to gloat a little over my success with my act and this girl. If I thought I had gone overboard with raising my voice to Sarita, it was nothing compared to what I heard as I descended the stairs. It was Enrico, bellowing at someone about some "goddamned mealy-mouse puny unknown comic who would never see the inside of his club again, and that he'd fix it so the little shit would never work anywhere."

When I got to the bottom, I glanced over at the bartender who motioned me to quickly retreat up the stairs.

"What's going on?" I whispered across the room.

"He's talking to your girlfriend."

"I don't have a girlfriend."

"He thinks you do. His. You'd better beat it."

Taking a step backwards, I could see his office door was open. He was gesticulating and flailing his arms like a wounded matador, bashing and throwing items in his rage. Then I saw Sarita walk calmly over to him and place her hand on his waving arm. She started talking to him softly.

I went back to the hotel and my room, lying on my bed fully clothed. I accepted the fact I probably wouldn't be going back to San Francisco, and that it was unlikely Sarita would drive to Fresno. Like a lot of things I think too much about, I was wrong. As nervous and distracted as I was that night, the show went great. Enrico was restrained, but did acknowledge my presence. Once again, Sarita spent a few hours with me before going home. And, as promised, returned in the morning to drive me to the airport after a detour to her house and family.

Her home was a surprisingly simple, smart two-story on a street called Eucalyptus. It was a short walk across the bridge to Harding Park Golf Course. The inside was immaculate and tastefully furnished. It was not the mansion I expected, considering how expensively dressed and bejeweled Sarita was, but it was comforting and warm, like Sarita and her father. He was in his fifties, and could have been Anthony Quinn's stand-in. He had perfect natural teeth, black hair without a strand of gray, and dark eyes like his daughter. He was probably the sweetest, gentlest man I'd ever met. His name was Ernest. Her mother, on the other hand, made me nervous. She was only attractive because she was well-dressed. Like Angelo from Paramount, she couldn't stand or sit still. Frequently while the father and I were getting acquainted, she'd just wander off somewhere. There was little doubt that her polite avoidance of me meant I wasn't rich enough for her daughter. Her name was Sara. It was obvious Sarita's sweet disposition and beauty did not come from her, but Sarita must have gotten her, "you don't bore me yet," attitude from her mother. I also did not take to Sarita's sister, Ernestine, or her husband, Glen. Both were teachers; and both surprisingly standoffish for Mormons. Like the mother, it was obvious they did not wish to engage me in conversation. At the point when they abruptly decided to leave for unfinished business, the father followed them to the door. I overheard the conversation. It seems Glen was a car collector. And had three of them. I heard the father say that his car was in the shop, and could he borrow one. Glen said no.

I didn't even know him, but thought, *what an asshole.* For decades neither they nor the mother gave me an occasion to change my mind. It seems, with all the wealthy suitors of Sarita, including Enrico, I was the only one she had ever brought home to meet her folks.

When the father and I were alone for a moment, he asked, "What country club do you belong to?"

I thought, *Holy shit. Don't tell me I was wrong, that she got her snobbery from her father.*

I replied, "They don't have a golf course at The Salvation Army."

He smiled warmly. "Oh, I'm sorry, Johnny. Sarita says you are very good." He was the only one who called me Johnny.

Sarita interrupted us, informing her father it was time to take me to the airport. I told her parents how nice it was to meet them. Her father shook my hand and said, "Johnny, please come back again. Next time for dinner."

Sarita and I spoke little on the way. She eventually pulled up and stopped at Departing Flights. I turned toward her. "Do you mind if I ask you a question? Well, maybe a couple of questions."

She grinned. "Three to a customer."

"Do you think Enrico will cancel me?"

"That's just like a comic." She laughed. "No. You're coming back."

"That was the least important question. That's why I asked it first."

"Okay. Are you his girlfriend?"

"No. We've known each other for years."

"He acted like you were his wife for God's sake. Screaming like that."

"He's asked me a number of times to marry him. He gets upset when I keep turning him down."

"Because he's older?"

"No. Because I don't love him."

"Have you ever been in love?"

"That's more than three questions."

"You must have been in love. I mean, from what your sister and mother said, suitors were coming in limousines."

"Maybe once."

"What happened?"

"I caught him with someone else, but maybe it wasn't love. Because I didn't miss him the way I thought I might." She paused before saying, "You'd better catch your plane. I'm not driving to LA."

"Why did you take me to your home? It sounded like something you've never done before." She looked straight into my eyes and said, "Because you need me. Now get out. I'll see you in a few weeks, and you can call if you want."

We kissed sweetly, not passionately. I thought about her all the way to Burbank and beyond. I was back at Bluffside Drive daydreaming and writing. This time with a purpose. I saw my return to the 'i,' listening to the laughter and applause, taking the bows, and seeing Sarita. The new funny material about the Kennedys poured out of me. I was really happy.

On Friday, November 22nd, just before noon, I was standing with my neighbor, Bob Klein, by his friend's second story window looking down at the swimming pool. He was pointing at a very attractive buxom redhead in a tight swimsuit. "She'll be up soon," he said.

The pool was crowded, the sounds of laughter and music echoing through the complex. It was a beautiful day. The TV played quietly in the background.

Suddenly the soft voices coming from the TV abruptly stopped. We turned to look at the set blasting some kind of signal and a loud voice saying, "News Flash. News Flash. This just in."

Walter Cronkite appeared in shirtsleeves. He looked stoic, his voice cracking. Not like him. Not at all like he appeared a month earlier when he interviewed President Kennedy, when the president told him, and us, that Vietnam was not America's war to win.

"It seems," Cronkite said, trying to remain professional, "it seems President John F. Kennedy has been shot in Dallas. Three shots in Dallas."

It was unbelievable. It was unimaginable. It was impossible. Not in America. It was as though someone had punched me. I lost my breath.

"Holy shit," Bob barely whispered.

At that moment, Bob's girlfriend bounced into the room, aware we were glued to the TV.

For over an hour we couldn't move. Soon Cronkite removed his glasses, looked up at the clock, and informed us the exact time President John F. Kennedy was pronounced dead at Parkland Hospital.

"Jesus Christ. Jesus Christ." I shuffled out of the apartment in a daze. In my own room, I didn't turn the set on. I could not bear to hear it a second time. I could not sit. The reality of what had just happened would not sink in. My whole being rejected it. Curiosity and shock compelled me to turn the TV back on. How did it happen? Why did it happen? Who did it? Maybe Cronkite would tell us.

Walter said they'd arrested the killer, Lee Harvey Oswald. From Friday to Sunday, I watched and listened and wondered. For two and a half days, I didn't eat or drink, didn't wash or undress. And barely slept. I was unbelievably sad. I wasn't necessarily a fan of Kennedy's, politically at least. I couldn't vote for him. But I was a fan of him personally, or at least the image he projected. He was charming and bright, and probably the only witty intellectual to ever serve in that office since Jefferson. I recalled his comment when he had a dinner for over a dozen Nobel Prize winners at the White House: "There hasn't been this much brain power in this room since Thomas Jefferson dined alone." He and his family seemed to fill the country with hope and possibilities. And class.

My funk and gloom suddenly disappeared on Sunday when Lee Harvey Oswald, surrounded by an army of Dallas's finest, was shot dead by Jack Ruby on live television. *How is this possible*? I thought. *Hold it! There's something fishy here.*

Every clumsy explanation made by every official, newsman, politician, or talking head that cluttered the cameras only made me wonder more. To paraphrase Hamlet, something was rotten in Dallas. That uneasy feeling of suspicion and distrust, which I didn't want to inhabit my body or thoughts, was only made worse when the casket carrying the dead president's body was unloaded at night in the dark in Washington, and this tall Texan, the new president, in a hillbilly twang, reached into his inside pocket, extracting a piece of paper, and had to read from it how badly he felt for the nation and the family. He, or someone, had to write it. He was incapable of speaking his grief from the heart. Unless there was no grief.

The president was gone. As ashamed as I was to think about it, though, so was half my act. It was a very selfish, but practical and necessary thought. I had to go back to San Francisco in a week. Who can write jokes? Who'd want to? Who would go to listen to them? Then I thought of Vaughn Meader, the brilliant comic who recorded the best-selling comedy album in history, *The First Family*, remembering a casual remark I'd made earlier that year: that nothing better happen to Kennedy or Vaughn would be out of work. Sadly, he was. In the early seventies. Enrico tried to help him relaunch his career by booking him into the 'i'. Nobody came. It was like that for me a week later. San Francisco was a ghost town. Nothing moved. People were staying home to watch the post-death proceedings in the Capitol's rotunda. Little John standing to the right of his widowed mother, Jackie, saluting the procession. The few people who came to the show were primarily just trying to get away from the tsunami of heartbreaking news. They were polite and mildly responsive. My fragile ego, and new, no Kennedy joke's act, barely survived.

Surrounded by grief, Sarita and I spent a lot of quiet time together. It was difficult to talk about anything. I turned down her invitation to come again to the house for a family dinner. I told her I would not feel uncomfortable, that I was even more uncomfortable thinking in a few days I'd be opening at the biggest club in Fresno. It was ten times bigger than the 'i'. It was depressing enough half the 'i' was empty; how would that look when only a handful of people show up to a barn that holds 600?

Then Sarita said, "Would you like me to come with you? We could drive."

"For opening night?"

"No. For two weeks."

"You mean to stay with me for two weeks? What about your family?"

"I'm an adult and it looks like you might need the company of one."

"Thank vou. I think I need that."

Fresno

We arrived at noon on a Saturday. I don't remember the name of the place. My mind wasn't focused on anything. Everything was still a blur. I do remember it was a resort, a sprawling one-story stucco structure that covered an acre. In the lobby, just outside the showroom, was a billboard on a stand with a picture of the headliner,

Phyllis Inez, and below it, Canadian comic: John Barbour. I peeked in. It was huge, about half the size of a hockey rink. My stomach churned, certain it was going to be empty. I wanted to cancel.

The manager greeted us cheerily, as though they'd never heard the news, and led us to our sumptuous suite. He then led us to the dressing rooms, informing us Phyllis was already there. The adjoining dressing rooms were as smart as any in Las Vegas, each stocked with a bar, refrigerator, flowers, colorful plush furniture, and a TV set.

Phyllis was even happier to see us than the manager. She was seated, fiddling with her face, glancing up occasionally at her TV turned to the Kennedy funeral. "Oh, hi," she squealed, jumping up. "You're Johnny. I've heard so much about you. I'm so glad we'll be working together."

I said 'hello' and introduced Sarita.

"Oh my, Sarita. You're beautiful. Pleased to meet you. I used to look that good." She was still attractive, tall, shapely, but a shade too much makeup on her forty-year-old face. "My manager tells me, Johnny, that you do a lot of political stuff in your act."

"I don't think I'll be doing much of that for a while."

"Oh, isn't it terrible?" she said, in a tone that sounded as though she'd just lost a button off her blouse. "I don't know much of anything about politics. I have no interest in it. But I'm learning something this weekend. Ya know, if Kennedy hadn't been shot, I'd have never known what a rotunda was."

I couldn't believe what I'd just heard. Did she really say that? Jesus, it was right out of *Born Yesterday* with Judy Holiday. Sarita and I stared at each other dumbfounded.

"I guess I'll get back to our room and get some rest," was all I could manage to say.

Of course, I did not rest, just paced, wondering how I was going to handle an empty house; I was desperate to put together and remember material that was miles away from politics. Showtime was seven p.m. At six fifteen, I went to take a furtive look at the room, to see how empty it was. It was full. Not just full, but packed, with people waiting in line. Those seated were eating hearty meals, chatting happily, drinking and laughing. *How could this be possible*? The news was nothing but the funeral, assassination, the killing of Oswald, and rumors about Russia and Cuba being behind it. And these people were having a great time. Fresno is not far from San Francisco, which was still a ghost town. Who could believe these festive crowds during such a horrible time? Could those people not care that their president just had his head blown off?

Forty-five minutes later, literally shaking, I walked on stage. The bandleader gave me a nice introduction, mentioning my success at the' Hungry i,' and that I was from Canada. He then played *When Johnny comes Marching Home Again*. The applause was quite enthusiastic. They were out for a good time.

I stood looking at them, surveying the room till the giggles subsided, then said matter-of-factly, "Even in Canada, I was aware that Fresno was the agricultural capital of America." They nodded. "That your biggest crop is Armenians." They howled. "Not rhubarbs. Though some say it's the same thing." They howled again. "One of the main reasons I'm pleased to be here is educational. In Canada when we were kids we were told Santa Claus lived in the North Pole, that his true identity was unknown. Well, today, in the paper, I found out that was a lie. Santa lives right here in Fresno. And his name is Garabedian."

They cheered. There was an ovation. The paper I'd read that afternoon had pointed out that the very successful businessman, Garabedian, was indeed going to be playing Santa Claus in their Christmas parade. And he was in the room. Everything I said after that was a hit. For the entire week I wore a pained empty smile.

Phyllis asked if I'd like to work with her in Southern California. Since I had no other offers I said yes. Indeed, Phyllis was a star of sorts in California, which is the only place she seemed to get work. It was like Wayne Newton; big only in Vegas, the only town he could draw a crowd. Sarita flew to Los Angeles to join me again.

We spent a lot of time on the road with Phyllis, and at her house in the Los Feliz area of Hollywood. It was a mansion compared to our very cheap motel on Ventura Boulevard in Studio City. A real dump. To Sarita, it was an adventure, something she'd never seen or experienced. She came with her ankle-length mink coat, beautiful clothes, jewels, and a disposition that was brighter than her gold and diamond watch. Sometimes we just had one meal a day. It never phased her. She had this magical quality of someone who just seemed happy to be alive. I had never seen that peacefulness in another soul. She was free of envy, gossip, and even ambition; getting up at five a.m. every morning with the birds was success enough. In the months that we lived in that awful place, she never once asked when were we going to move, or if I was going to marry her. I kept reminding her not to get pregnant because I definitely wasn't going to have a child. She would just smile. She was the only person I ever envied. I told her, if I could have had anything, I would want her disposition, her personality. With that I could become a real star.

Her phone calls to her mother, thoughtfully, she kept at a minimum. Her mother hated me, reminding Sarita of all the successful men she'd walked out on, leaving town with a bum. Sarita never told me of her mother's comments. I could hear them. After hanging up, she always turned to me and say, "My father said, give my best to Johnny!"

Sarita had enormous talent as a dancer and singer. Occasionally, when I got up at a club to try new material, I'd ask her to sing. Once in a while, reluctantly, she would. She was the only person or performer who silenced an audience just by walking onstage. It was an aura of calm that immediately brought all eyes to her. She could get on an elevator with a stranger, and by the second floor that person was a stranger no longer. He or she would unburden themselves to her as they would a priest or psychiatrist. Because of those gifts, I encouraged her to pursue her talents professionally.

"Why do you keep pushing me to do that?"

"I'm not pushing you," I said. "I'm encouraging you. You have these terrific natural gifts. Me, I have to work at it. And I don't think anyone can be happy, if they're not doing something that is their own creatively."

"You know if I do that, I'm going to be around all kinds of men."

"So what? That doesn't mean anything."

"You're the only man I've known who isn't jealous. And, also the youngest."

"Sarita, you're either gonna like me or you're not. I can't make you do that. Keeping you away from other men won't make that happen. It's up to you. It's that simple. And, truthfully, your mother's right; I'm no prize."

"You are to me. Not just a prize, but a surprise. There'll be just one in showbiz in this family."

"We're not a family," I said.

She smiled. "In this twosome, there'll only be one in showbiz, and right now that's you. I used to work in an office and–"

"You did? You never told me that."

"There's lots I haven't told you. I'll get an office job, and if you like, we'll try to find an apartment instead of a room."

Within a week she had a job at one of the best literary agencies in the business, H.N. Swanson on Sunset Boulevard. Swanson handled almost every famous novelist in America for films, from John O'Hara to Hemingway. Sarita became the personal assistant to Swanson's personal assistant. Like everything in her lucky life, it all came to her without effort. She went to an employment agency. They did not even ask for a resumé.

They just said, "Oh, you'd be perfect for this agent." They sent her over for an interview. Sarita was given the job within five minutes.

We got a second floor, two-bedroom apartment at 12034 Kling Street in North Hollywood with a balcony overlooking Gelson's market. We weren't married, and never talked about it.

The Bottom of the Ladder

Comedian Phyllis Diller said early in her career, "It's easy climbing the ladder of success; what's tough, is getting around the crowd at the bottom."

I was part of that crowd for a number of years. I never missed a day when I didn't sit down for three or four hours and write material. When I didn't have a paying job, I would travel miles to various clubs to try it out. There were numerous freebies at The Ice House in Pasadena where I first saw an awkward Steve Martin or an ordinary New Yorker named Robert Klein. There were countless jazz clubs, folk clubs, and even a few makeshift comedy workshops that didn't last as long as some comics' acts.

I was booked at one of LA's best clubs on Sunset Strip, The Crescendo, a couple of times as the opening act for an outstanding singer named Sue Raney. It was a terrific gig; the only negative was that every night Sue's agent hit on Sarita. This was something that went on for years. The bigger they were, the harder they fell. Above The Crescendo was another club, The Interlude, which booked a lot of black acts. There I opened for a young, struggling Tina Turner shortly after she left Ike. In spite of her room-shaking brilliance, the room was never more than half full. The same with one of the best stand-up comics I had ever seen, Redd Foxx.

Initially, I had no interest in seeing Redd. I was familiar with, but not a fan of his party records. The recording qualities were poor, and while some of the material was funny, it was dirty. Strangely enough, it was Sarita who urged me to go and see him. When Sarita was singing with the Earl 'Fatha' Hines band in San Francisco, she met and befriended numerous black entertainers, including Dick Gregory and Redd Foxx. Of Redd she said, "He does a lot of off-color material, a lot of which I don't understand, but I think you should see him and meet him. He makes a better connection with audiences than anyone I've ever seen outside of Lenny Bruce."

So, off we went to The Interlude. We picked a Saturday night. It's best to see comics when there are lots of folks present so you can see the performer at his best. That night there were only about eighteen people. I told Sarita not to introduce me to Redd before the show. I didn't want to distract him. As usual, I sat at the back of the room. Looking at the empty seats, I felt bad for him.

After a rather ordinary introduction, to scattered applause, and a few loud hoots from a couple of fans, Redd walked onto the stage carrying a drink. He placed the drink on a stool, looked around at the few people with a wry smile, then took out a cigarette, placed it in his mouth, and casually pulled out a lighter and lit it.

"Nice ta see ya. Ah still have the talent to pack 'em out!" The audience laughed, as did I, at the honesty of it all. "Tomorrow there'll be more atheists attending Sunday school." They howled. I applauded. "I like ta smoke up here. Like the song says, smoke gets in my eyes. Ah don't mind, though, cause that way ah don't have ta look at some of ya cause some of ya is really ugly." They howled again. "The governments tryin' ta bus black kids 'n white kids ta schools all around town. They'd be better off if they just bussed ugly people out of town. Some of ya could git on board. Git a free ride. You all know who you are."

With each line, spoken as conversationally as he might be speaking to people in his living room, the laughter built with each pause. Then he said, "I don't know one white man who wouldn't prefer Lena Horne over Kate Smith ... even Governor Wallace!" They screamed and applauded. "Just leave me Ann Margaret over Ella!" More screams.

Before long he'd been up there for forty-five magnificently entertaining and enlightening minutes. I wouldn't see anyone hold an audience that raptly until years later when Hal Holbrook did his amazing *Mark Twain Tonight*. But look who Hal had writing for him.

When it was over, I had forgotten there'd been such a small crowd because the room was filled with joy. I turned to Sarita. "He's amazing."

"Come on," she said, "let's say hello."

Redd was pleased and surprised to see her. "You singin' down here?" he asked.

"No, but living here now. I wanted my boyfriend to see you. He's a comic, too, and he's very good. This is John Barbour."

I told him he was one of the best comedians I'd ever seen.

He said, "What you see, young man, is me and five other guys. I went through a lot of 'em before I found me."

He sounded almost like me, having gone through all those albums looking for a comedy key. I told him that even though I was doing pretty well, I wasn't sure if I was doing me.

"John, there are three ways to make it. Give the audience what they want to hear, like Bob Hope, Henny Youngman and Red Skelton, or give the audience what you want like Mort Sahl and Lenny Bruce. And the third thing, never give up," We shook hands and he added, "I'll be workin' around town a lot. I'd love to see y'all again. Even if I'm not workin'. I love this lady! You take care o' her."

Show business is a transient's profession; friendships frequently never outlast the job. For me, Redd's friendship and counsel lasted until the day he died. If I had one real friend and mentor in this business, Redd was it. I was thinking of making a list, a short list, of the friends I've kept over the bumpy or prosperous years in this industry. But there is no list. Just one name: Redd Foxx.

It's Tough to be White

When you're a novice performer, or even an established one, there are a lot of quiet anxious times waiting for a call. You fill this empty time with thinking, and those thoughts, nine out of ten, are going to be negative. You begin to feel like an unfunny Hamlet. To be a comedian, or not to be a comedian. Hamlet was luckier. There were no phones in his day, so he wasn't aware of how many people didn't want to be in touch with him. My down time was filled with much of this unwelcome negativity, watching TV, mostly variety shows to see the comics.

Every day Sarita would come home and tell me about the famous writers she'd spoken to, either on the phone or in person. She knew of my deep admiration for writers. What used to make me shake my head, though, was if she met one of those famous movie scribes in person, as happened often, invariably they would offer her a part in a film. Jesus, she was never interested, never looking for it. She just sat there and it walked in the goddamned door. That is not a talent. It's a destiny, and it certainly wasn't mine. Maybe as a consolation prize the Gods gave me a little talent instead. After all these years, I still envy that magical, rare karma, or whatever, that she was just born with. And never had to work for.

The only other TV shows I watched, besides the variety shows, or Jack Paar or Merv Griffin, were the smarter talk shows. The best of these, for me, was David Susskind. This one night I was watching David's show and heard an unintentional faux pas that everyone on the panel missed. It came from one of the guests in a voice that was cracking, not from anguish, but from alcohol. David's guests were two ex-convicts recently released from prison after serving years for homicides they did not commit. One, a Jew, had served twenty-seven years. The other, a black man, had served seventeen. Another guest was a well-known civil libertarian lawyer named Ehrlich from San Francisco. This night he had been drinking. Susskind leaned into him, ignoring the fact the Jew had served more time, and asked passionately, "As an attorney, how is it, in this country, a man with this dark skin could be so badly railroaded into prison for a crime he did not commit?"

His voice cracking, Ehrlich pronounced loudly, "David, David, look at this guy. Don't you know now that when they arrest a Negro in America, he doesn't stand a Chinaman's chance?"

It caused me to laugh hard and long. I only stopped because a thought popped into my head: starting with that story, then making observations about the twenty-four-hour a day newscast about the marching and protesting and civil rights stuff going on, I was going to do an album called, *It's Tough to Be White*.

I grabbed a pad and pencil and begin to write. My fingers barely kept up with the stuff that flooded full and funny onto my pages. Jokes flowed easily and within an hour and a half I'd written both sides of an album; on the flip side was the first material about cigarettes and cancer, and the Vietnam War. I was so proud of what I'd done. There was no question it would make me a success, put me right up there with the topical, edgy comedians. I couldn't wait for Sarita to get home.

"That is funny," she said.

"I didn't hear you laugh," I said, a little surprised.

"Well, it is funny, and it is true, but it'll probably upset a lot of people."

"Why?"

"You've got to be kidding. Because it's so sensitive."

"You mean blacks might get upset. I think they'd be the first to recognize the funny truth about it all."

"Whites might get more upset, especially liberals, because you're saying what they're probably thinking, and they'll resent you for bringing it out."

"Sarita, funny is funny. And this is funny." I wasn't as forceful, or as confident as I had been seconds earlier. "Do you think I should talk to Redd?"

"Yes. That's a good idea. Let's see what he thinks."

Ten o'clock on a warm spring Saturday night, Sarita and I were standing on the sidewalk with Redd just outside a club called The Slate Brothers on La Cienega Blvd. He had just finished killing another packed house. This was his favorite place to perform in Los Angeles. When he got to do *Sanford and Son,* he bought it.

Puffing on his ever-present cigarette, he said, "What's this ya wanted ta ask about?"

"I have an idea, a concept for an album, my first. It's about what's going on now, civil rights and all, and it's called *It's Tough to Be White.*"

He chuckled.

I told him a few of the jokes I'd written, that dumb comment made on Susskind's show, and waited for a reaction.

He was smiling and nodding. After a moment he said, "So?"

"Redd, I wouldn't want anyone to think I was a bigot."

Without missing a beat, he said loudly in his best ghetto accent, "Sheeeit, man! Make it fust, then explain. Funny is funny!"

"Thanks," was all I could manage, laughing inside at the wisdom and humor of his comment.

"Ah have some cats who do a lot of gigs on World Pacific, great jazz label. That's where ya should do it. Lemme check it out."

I was stunned. Not only did he like the idea, he wanted to help me get it done. That kind of encouragement and support amongst performers in those days was not uncommon. It was the norm. While there certainly were the jealousies and bad-mouthing, as in any endeavour involving humans, there were more helping with material or suggesting jobs. That has vanished in show business in America today ... along with politicians who run on a Peace Platform. Two days later, I was sitting in the office of Richard Bock, President of World Pacific Records.

"We did do a comedy album of sorts a while ago with Lord Buckley. We loved it, and were the only ones in the country who did." He laughed. "But yours could be a winner."

I couldn't believe it was all happening so fast.

"We won't record it in a club. We'll record it right here. We have plenty of room. We'll have more control, and we'll have an invited audience. How does that sound? About a hundred people, and I know them all. They'll love it. How soon can you do it?"

My stomach was churning. I had never performed the material. A bunch of strangers. Touchy jokes and subjects. In a studio setting. Not a club. What if they didn't like me? I wanted to say maybe I needed to rehearse at The Ice House or someplace. Instead, I said, "Whenever you want me to do it."

"Great. I'll set it up for a week from Saturday. In the afternoon so people can still do their Saturday night stuff." He stood, shook my hand firmly.

I was going to have a comedy album. Like Newhart and Berman. I could hardly eat. I had no idea my ambitions would be inflicting so much physical and psychological pain on me. My anxiety was made worse when Redd told me his father was ill, that he wouldn't be able to be there.

The sun was out that Saturday. As Sarita and I walked into the studio, I thought how out of place trying to do comedy was on such a perfect day. Richard greeted us with a huge smile.

"Would you believe this? We had to turn people down. Most of them never heard of you, but they love the idea. Look at them."

The studio was full, abuzz with chit chat. There were nearly a hundred people, a mixed audience of races seated on comfortable folding chairs. They were well-dressed, as though they were in an actual nightclub. There was a small riser about a foot high on which Richard and his technicians had placed the solitary mike.

"John, I want you to meet one of my best friends. This is Barry Sullivan, a neighbor."

Mr. Sullivan grabbed my hand. His smile, those teeth, and that voice were unmistakable.

"John, really pleased to meet you. I can't wait to hear what you have to say. Good luck."

I remembered him vividly, not just the smile and that interesting voice from films, but the handshake from years earlier when he greeted me and poor Angelo with the same anxious energy in Lindsay Parson's Production office. He was looking forward to directing his first film. Mine. Unbelievable. Here we were, nearly a decade later, and he was going to be in my audience. How weird life is. I knew him, but he hadn't the faintest idea who I was.

Richard introduced me to the audience. "Thank you all for being here. You are in for an original, a very original treat, that we are really proud to be a part of. Ladies and gentlemen, John Barbour."

I approached the mike, and began. I felt like a school kid being judged by a roomful of teachers. Knowing they were Richard's friends, I was more anxious about not wanting to let him down. But, I loved my material. I trusted it. When I spoke my first words, I could hear the tension had raised my voice half an octave. That would never do. I had to get it down to a conversational level, but I couldn't. It was stuck there, making me sound a little excited, which I certainly was. At the end of the first sentence, though, came that thrilling, relieving sound of laughter, and it continued for forty-five minutes. There were guffaws and applause, and at the end, a standing ovation. My God, I'd never had such a thing.

Afterwards, there was much backslapping, handshaking, and invitations to meals and parties and tennis matches and whatever. Richard and Mr. Sullivan were thrilled. Richard said, "John, come in Monday, and we'll go over the artwork for the cover, and liner notes. I've got an expert, award-winning artist."

That Monday, is when I first learned to never to listen to the experts.

"I really liked the material. This could be huge!"

"Thank you." The fellow I was thanking was Richard's graphics and arts designer, famous in the music business for what were classy, imaginative album covers. He was in his late thirties, had a goatee, wore jeans, and fiddled with a pencil. The three of us were in Richard's office.

"Did you have any thoughts on what your cover should look like?" he asked.

"Well, my favorite album covers are Lenny Bruce's, especially the one on *The Sick Humor of Lenny Bruce* ... where he's having a picnic in a graveyard!"

The artist smiled.

"It's sort of a rip off, I guess, but I'd like to show me in working clothes picking cotton in a field, and hovering over me on a white horse is a huge black wearing a tuxedo and carrying a whip and grinning."

Richard laughed. "That is funny!"

The artist shook his head. "I don't think that'd work. It's too strong. Racist. Maybe even a little childish."

I didn't want to appear in the least adversarial; after all, I was just a beginner, and he was a recognized expert.

He continued, "The title of the album is tough enough. I think the buyer should see what we saw in the studio, just you standing there and giving us your opinion and observations, funny opinions and observations."

There was silence. We looked at one another. Richard was nodding. "I like it. I'd be curious to see what this clean cut, nice looking young white man has to say."

The artist laughed. "So, we'll get Charlie and have him take some terrific simple pictures of John standing up there." Then he turned to me. "Whadda ya think?"

I didn't like it. It showed no imagination. Didn't even hint at humor, but I was afraid to say so. "Well, it's a comedy album and I don't think I look much like a comic; I look more like Billy Graham."

"Well, we can fix that easily," the artist said. "We'll put a cigarette in your hand, and not a Bible." Now he laughed louder. So did Richard.

"Very good," Richard said. "Oh, the other thing, John, do you know any comics who might want to give us an endorsement, other than Redd?"

"What's wrong with Redd?"

"Nothing. He's terrific, but he does party records. That's not your audience. You're not dirty. You're more like a Mort Sahl."

"I've met Mort a couple of times. I could talk to him," I said, thinking his helping an unknown wouldn't be likely. Then I had another thought. "My wife knows Dick Gregory really well. Perhaps I–"

"Wow, Dick Gregory! That'd be fantastic. Perfect. That'd take the edge off of it for everybody. Do you think he'll do it?" Richard was ebullient.

"I'll see."

We all shook hands and set a date for my album cover. I was off to try and get liner notes and endorsements from the two most famous topical comedians in America, Dick Gregory and Mort Sahl.

Dick Gregory And Mort Sahl

In the mid-sixties, there were only two new comedians more popular than Dick Gregory and Mort Sahl: Bob Newhart with his 'Button-down Mind' and Shelley Berman with his funny phone calls, but none as important as Dick Gregory and Mort Sahl.

Mort was President Kennedy's favorite topical comedian, often contributing material to his speeches and press conferences. He was razor sharp, talking about either the right or the left, making observations on things that mattered, unlike Bob Hope whose jokes were a triumph of engaging glibness. Watching Mort stand on stage or in front of a camera with that constant grin and giggles, fidgeting while clutching the daily paper and wearing his ever-present wool sweater was often unsettling. A year or so after the assassination, though, Mort's appearances were suddenly less frequent. He graciously invited me to his house in Beverly Hills to talk about my album.

Dick, though, was the breakout comic I would never miss. He stumbled onto the American cultural scene almost by accident, which is how most good things happen. He was hired to fill in for one night at Hefner's Playboy Club in Chicago. He got fifty dollars, a landfall for him and, again, quite by accident a reporter was there from *Time* magazine. He was stunned by the wit and sharpness of this elegant young black performer and mentioned it in a brief paragraph. That was all it took. The reporter's brief kudos to Dick changed his life overnight. He was soon everywhere, being billed as the black Bob Hope and the black Mort Sahl. He was changing the country, and his bank account, but it never changed him.

When Sarita introduced me to him at Banducci's Restaurant and Pool Hall in North Beach, where half a dozen of us sat around commenting on anything and everything, I couldn't believe he was a comic. His contributions to the conversation were infrequent, but softly right on. He was quiet and gracious, barely spoke above a whisper, and totally devoid of the egocentricity every comic is inflicted with. He was also devoid of the anger that churned in every comic I ever met. Like Mort, though, he was unbelievably smart and sharp.

A few days after recording my album, Sarita tracked Dick down in London where he was now heralded as America's King of Comedy. I had only met him that once, even though I'd seen him dozens of times, so I felt a little awkward when Sarita put me on the phone with him.

He said, "John, I would like to say your album is going to be dynamite, but I wouldn't want anybody to buy it and throw it in a church."

I didn't know whether to laugh or not, but couldn't help myself. "Dick, that's funny and kind of scary."

"From what Sarita tells me that sounds a little like your stuff, too. What can I do for you?"

"Well, the record company thinks that if you did the liner notes it would sort of take the edge off the title."

"John, I don't want to take the edge off anything. Everything's been too soft already." He paused. I was certain he was going to turn me down. "But I'll happily write something for you, and you'll get it immediately."

Within the week we had his liner notes, with the 'dynamite' line included. Richard was delighted. "You know, John, Dick's notes are priceless. They may be all we need."

I said, "But it would be kinda nice to have Mort and Dick side by side. And Mort's already invited me up to his house Saturday."

"Try him, but I think we're all set. The cover of you as a smoking Billy Graham looks terrific." He laughed. "Now we're trying to set up some promotion and reviews."

Mort's house was halfway up Beverly Glen in Beverly Hills on the west side of the street. A clean, rising walkway led up to a smaller house, but elegant and modern with bright pastel colors and lots of glass. He opened the door before I could ring, greeting me with a huge smile and a firm handshake.

"Nice ta see ya! C'mon and sit down. Ya want anything? Coke or liquid coke?" He chuckled. "Or wine or anything."

"No, thanks," I said, as he motioned me to a large pillow chair in his front room.

"So, you've done an album. Sounds funny. I love the premise. Can't wait to hear it."

I was trying to think of how to mention my desire to have him contribute to the liner notes when he took off on his views about comedy and comics. I had the immediate impression he was glad to have someone to talk to.

"Ya know, kid, I've seen you a few times, and what impressed me was not just some of the material, but you always had it in the same order. Not me. I'd get bored to death. I'm never sure what order I'm gonna say anything. If you've seen me up there, you see my hands and arms darting back and forth, like pigeons eating." He laughed. "What I'm doing is really pulling my stuff out of mental filing cabinets. It keeps me on edge, and gives me kind of a nervous anxiety, hoping I can remember what filing cabinet my stuff's in. How'd you do it?"

"Well, it's like a play. Neil Simon writes these funny plays, and the actors just can't come out every night and do the lines in some haphazard order. The lines have to be precise and properly delivered. What I do is sort of a short portion of a mini play with one line sort of leading to the next. If I had to try to do what you do, I'd get lost. I'm not as fast as you."

"Nobody is," he said without a smile.

I was a little surprised at this brief display of ego, but it may have also been the truth. His tone, though, was one of anger, an anger looking for an outlet, and a listener. And I was it.

I said, "I've missed seeing you as much as I used to, but delighted to see you doing colleges and universities. They must love you."

"That's about the only place I get gigs now."

"You're kidding. You were all over the place. You were John Kennedy's favorite comic."

He interrupted me. "That's right, and the old man ended it for me."

I didn't know whom he meant by the old man, but there was no mistaking his underlying rage. He continued without prompting from me.

"Even though my friend Kennedy was president, I still made jokes about him and he enjoyed them, used to call me and tell me so. They all enjoyed them, except the old man, Joe. He called me in the middle of May and asked if I'd stop doing some of those jokes about his son, that they'd hurt the chances of his re-election. He said that they'd only won the election by about a half of one percent and that that half percent represented the small progressive faction of the country, and they might lose them if I keep doing those jokes. I told him I had to earn a living. He suggested I take time off and do some movies. I told him I was no Jewish Cary Grant, and I wasn't sure I'd do that well in them. He assured me I'd do great, and would call some of his friends to help me get parts. Then he calls my manager and tells him the same. So, I got a couple of offers, did a movie or two, stopped performing for months and then they killed Kennedy."

All I could say was a weak, "Geez!" I felt like an illiterate idiot. Here was a man who'd travelled to the pinnacle of power in showbiz, been with presidents and world leaders, and there I was sitting at the bottom of the barrel while he got to scrape the top.

"Those school gigs are almost all I get now, and can never get those fucking Kennedys on the phone!"

I didn't know what to say. There was nothing I could say. He and his success were out of my league. I mean the cover of *Time*! It was obvious his insides had been churning for years to holler this to the Gods, to ease the rage of the feeling and knowledge that he'd been used. All he had to vent to now was a struggling comic looking for some liner notes.

"So, what did you want to talk to me about?"

"It doesn't seem at all important now. Especially to you after what you've gone through, but it does mean a lot to me. As you know I did this album for Pacific Jazz–"

"A great label. I got a lot of their stuff."

"It's called, *It's Tough to Be White*–"

"That's funny. And appropriate. Getting more appropriate every day. Wish I'd thought of it!"

"I'd love it if you could do a few liner notes. It would mean a lot."

"Sure, send it over. I'll listen to it right away."

Trying to soften him in case he had any reluctance to help, and let him know he was in good company, I told him about Dick, that we had terrific liner notes from him and that we'd place his next to Dick's, sort of an equality of liner notes. I thought he'd be impressed by that. I smiled, anticipating his reaction. How I could have misread him was astonishing. I had made a major blunder. He exploded. This time his rage was directed at me. He leapt up and leaned into me while I was still seated. I had never seen anyone that emotionally out of control anywhere.

"What? What?" he bellowed. "Dick Gregory. Dick fucking Gregory? You'd put me next to Dick fucking Gregory. Are you nuts? He thinks he's the black Mort Sahl. I've seen that horseshit. There's only one Mort Sahl. He's not on an equal plane with me. Nobody is or was!"

He continued screaming at me, and the world. I could no longer make out what he was saying. My fear morphed into sympathy. As the room echoed with his promethean diatribe, it was too palpable for me not to be moved by it. We've all felt this kind of pain and rage at one time or another. I held up my hand, motioning it slightly for him to calm down.

"Mort, Mort," I said as I stood. "I'm sorry I upset you. I didn't mean to. You were, and are, one of my inspirations, that someone could make it in America doing meaningful humor. Thank you for giving me your time. I'm sorry again. I'd better be going."

I followed him to the door. When he opened it, he stopped. He was breathing deeply. I thought he was about to have a heart attack. Then he said wistfully, "Good luck. It's a tough business."

I looked at him and said, "So is life."

Mort and I never spoke again. Years later, we were both involved in trying to tell the story of Jim Garrison, the New Orlean's DA who brought Clay Shaw to trial for conspiracy to murder President John Kennedy, and still he never spoke to me. Mort was seldom seen again on network TV; his major national exposure with Garrison's story was on The Steve Allen Show. For many weeks, he did a wonderful show locally on KTTV with Paul Williams as a frequent guest. Mort's weekly attempts to inform viewers about the assassination and The Warren Commission shortcomings led to its quick cancellation. In the ten years following the Clay Shaw trial, Jim Garrison only gave one interview about his case, and that was to me. In 1992, when I did *The Garrison Tapes,* I was certain Mort would contact me, and thank me for mentioning him very positively in the film. He did not, so I called him. He never answered. To this day Mort has never once mentioned that fabulous, historic documentary told by the man he was championing! As the French say, c'est la vie. As smarter people say, "That's showbiz!"

Catch a Falling Star

With the constant barrage of media coverage about the Civil Rights movement, the Black Power movement, and the FBI's and the Government's maligning of the Black Panthers, Richard and Pacific Jazz became more enthused about the release of the album while I became more nervous. I was nervous about having to perform the touchy material in front of paying audiences, nervous about the reviews and the media's reaction. After all, they were not kind to Lenny Bruce who, only slightly, touched on the subject. I was also nervous about success. How would I handle it if it came? Would I feel more secure if it came. In spite of these thoughts, I still rehearsed my Grammy acceptance speech.

There were dozens of well-wishers, calls telling me I'd soon be a meaningful Bob Newhart and the white Dick Gregory. God, it was nice to be liked. Half a dozen clubs had already booked me, including the Playboy Clubs in Atlanta, Miami, and Los Angeles, just on the album's title alone. Not one review. But one was coming. I paced our front room the entire morning awaiting the review from the *Los Angeles Times*. Richard told us it would be in the afternoon edition.

Come late afternoon, Sarita and I rushed to the newsstand and bought five papers.

There it was at the top in bold print, *It's Tough to Be White*. There was no preamble leading up to the review. The critic expressed utter contempt for what he described as the worst tasteless album recorded. I did not need to read anymore. I was so shaken, I checked another copy of the same paper to see if it was the same in that one. My head shook reading it, as though I was dodging blows. A few short sentences and my career had been knocked out.

Sarita said, "He doesn't know what he's talking about!"

"Honey, his readers don't know that!"

"Your album is wonderful, and the *Times* isn't the only newspaper."

"It is in this town!"

I sent a note to the critic: 'You were supposed to listen to it, not eat it!"

There was a disappointed, comforting call from Richard. Redd called congratulating me for pissing off Whitey! A few of the clubs that had booked me, cancelled. Except The Playboy Clubs. They told me I would still go to Atlanta, Miami, and Los Angeles, but they did not want me performing any of the material from the album. I needed the job as much as I needed to perform, so I agreed. I had bunches of other material to fall back on. I worked in Atlanta and Miami a week later with a fabulous singing-impressionist, Marilyn Michaels, who did Streisand as well as Streisand. The reception of my safe stuff made me feel better. I was looking forward to Los Angeles.

I had given up any hope of the album ever going anywhere. That was okay. I tried, and it didn't work. Besides, I'd gotten limited distance doing other jokes and routines. But the comedy gods, or just the gods themselves, weren't quite through with me and that subject. While I was in Florida, Los Angeles erupted in the worst race riots in the city's history

Smoke Gets in Your Eyes

The manager who booked me into the Playboy Clubs was a wiry, slender, solid, dark haired, dark-eyed, always angry fellow named Lee Wolfberg, the manager of the LA club. He never conversed, just gave orders. He seemed to like me, but it was hard to tell.

On my opening Saturday night, there was a surprisingly full house in spite of the fact the city was in a state of unease. There was no opening act. I was it. Lee patted me on the shoulder. He wasn't smiling. That's because he never did. "Good luck, and remember none of that shit from the album."

Trying to think of something to open with, I was distracted again by his repeated warnings about the album. I am not deaf. I got it. But once was enough. He didn't have to pound it in. I got irritated, and when this happens, I get a little rebellious. I do not like being ordered what to do when it comes to my work. And how can one avoid what is obviously the truth? Half the city was in ruins and under martial law.

The black room manager, Charles, gave me what I thought was a rather short tepid introduction. "Ladies and gentlemen, a very warm Playboy welcome to John Barbour." The applause was surprisingly full for an unknown. I surveyed the room a long time. Just stared. As I did in Fresno. A few chuckled nervously. I pointed at the huge dark room-length window to my right, the third-floor window that overlooked the city.

"You know," I began, "Jerome Kern must have been dreaming about a girlfriend in Compton when he wrote *Smoke Gets in Your Eyes*. More nervous giggles. "The rest of LA learned how little power it takes to really light up this city … .one Watts."

The room howled, and erupted into applause.

I saw Lee leap out of his office, halting in silhouette.

"Two weeks ago, Charlie was a busboy." More chuckles. "After the riots, they made him a manager. Now they don't trust him around the knives and forks."

They screamed, and applauded again. Charlie acknowledged me and gave the audience the Black Power fist and a triumphant smile. They cheered and applauded him even louder.

I did at least half of the album to a thrilling reception. I was so pleased and proud. The material did work. I left to one of the very few standing ovations I ever got.

Lee was waiting for me. "Get in here, goddamn it. What the fuck were you doing? What the fuck did I tell you, you little prick?"

I followed him into his office. He ran to his top desk drawer, yanked it open and pulled out a magnum revolver, waving it at me as he bellowed. "What the fuck were you doing? I told you none of that black shit. You could've started a fucking riot. You have no fucking idea how bad it is. Why do ya think I got this?"

'Lee, Lee, but you saw the reaction. It was terrific."

"You idiot. I thought I was going to have to shoot somebody."

"Lee, you were going to shoot some blacks, but you don't want me to make jokes about them? And it's not about them, it's about whites like us and how we are reacting. Don't you get it?'

"Well, get this. If you wanna finish the fucking week, you're not doing that shit again."

"But you heard them?"

'Fuck them. They're not paying you. I am. And I don't want any trouble."

"You heard them. They liked it."

"If ya wanna stay, kill it."

"What if I could prove to you that blacks like it?"

"I'm not interested."

Not knowing where it came from, I blurted, "What if I invite the staff of *Ebony* magazine down here on Monday, and do the same show for them?"

"What the fuck are you talking about? I don't care if Martin Luther fucking King is here, you're not doing that black shit in my club. If you wanna do it, go down there."

"Lee, you're right. I should go down there. What a great idea."

"You're nuts. You can go down there after you're done here, because you may never be coming back. And I mean that in more ways than one. So, what's it to be? There are a lot of hungry comics waiting to replace you."

"I'll do other stuff."

"Good. I like you. You got balls, but this place is only interested in showing tits 'n' ass!" I smiled. I thought what he said was funny. He didn't. He just knew it as a fact of doing business.

While Lee was waiting to see what my act would be on Monday, I spent the day tracking down the LA editor of *Ebony* Magazine.

"Are you sure you want to do this?" The question was posed by the West Coast editor for *Ebony* magazine. I sat opposite a bright, youngish looking middle-aged executive in his plush office. He was flanked by two aides who had quizzical smiles on their faces. I was alone.

When I finally got him on the phone after half a dozen calls, he told me he'd be happy to meet with me. He thought what I was proposing was something he'd be interested in.

"There is a lot of funny stuff there, John," he said, referring to my album. "True, too. But what do you hope to gain by doing it in our part of town?"

"It's been bombed by the *L.A. Times*, ignored by every other paper and radio station in the country, all white owned. Whenever I do the material, though, it gets a wonderful reception, especially by blacks. I just thought if I could prove that to everyone by performing it in a club in Watts or someplace, that would give it the Housekeeping Seal of Approval."

"You want us to endorse it?"

"No, not at all. Just witness it. Book me into one of those clubs, and just report on the reaction."

"You're that confident?"

"As Mark Twain said, 'As confident as a Christian holding four aces!'"

He laughed, as did his assistants. "I know the owner of the California Club. It is in the heart of Watts. I must tell you, or warn you, it is very black. The only time they see a white person in there is on TV. I'll see what I can do, and I'll call you."

"Could you make it a Saturday night? I'd like it to be full."

"Now you're making me more curious. I'll call you." That afternoon, late, he called me with the directions.

"Are you gonna drive down by yourself?" he asked.

"No, I'm bringing my wife."

There was a pause. "Are you sure about this?"

"Absolutely."

"There'll be three or four of my staff who are really curious about this, and a photographer. The more I think about this, the more I think it's a great story. No matter what happens, it'll be really interesting stuff."

With all the stars with whom I'd worked over the years, Sinatra, Martin, Hope, Goulet, Darin, never was I as excited and as enthused about a performance as I was that night in anticipation of verifying my belief in myself in the heart of Watts.

Sarita and I arrived while it was still light. I was due to go on at eight. The club was on a corner near Sixtieth and Central. Standing near the entrance as we pulled up was a small crowd, the editor and his assistants, a cameraman, a couple of other people, and a big, older man who turned out to be the owner. I was introduced to the owner who stepped forward to shake my hand. In a tone of disbelief, he said, "Our emcee usually introduces da acts, but to make sure yahs okay, I'll introduce ya myself. I gotta see this! Come on in."

The place was packed, probably four hundred people, including standing room. The audience area was dark, but the stage, on a small carpeted riser, was professionally well lit. We stood in the back against the wall in almost total darkness. The cameraman began taking pictures. Evidently it was some kind of talent night because the girl singer we walked in on was not very good; and, like the Apollo, they loudly let her know it. She let them know they were stupid. Suddenly there were two performances, one on stage, the other in the audience. I had never witnessed anything like it. It frightened me and struck me as rude, but then it struck me as uncomfortable honesty. I wondered what they were going to do to me.

The owner tapped my shoulder. "You'll go after Buzzy. He's up next. He wants ta be Jerry Lewis."

Buzzy did not receive a much better reception than the girl singer. He was slender, in his twenties. As the owner mentioned, Buzzy did want to be Jerry Lewis. He had that loud nasal squawk down, and that spastic distorted body language. The audience was not amused, and let him know it. He finished with a high wave and grin to a smattering of applause, and a chorus of, "Git uh job!"

The owner walked to the mike. "Ah'm gonna introduce a young man who asked to be here tonight. He just recorded an album that our brother Dick Gregory liked." At this the audience cheered. "But evidently the white crowds at The Playboy Club didn't wanna hear what he has ta say." There were boos. "Would you?" Cheers again. "Well, here he is, John Barboo!" He mispronounced my name and the audience applauded politely, a little less than I expected considering the introduction.

I took the mike and placed it back in the stand. Then, as usual, looked out at the darkness, barely able to distinguish anyone. While I was trying to adjust my eyes, and think of something to say, someone hollered out, "Scared, boy?" The audience chuckled loudly.

Instantly, I rose my voice in the direction of the heckler, "Hey, don't you ever call me scared!" They laughed, and a few applauded. "Although my underwear might agree!"

More nice laughs. Someone shouted out, "Sheeeeit!" The audience was getting more laughs than I was. I had to wait a long time for the laughs to die down.

I said, "I almost did. Wanna check?" They screamed. "One of the reasons I wanted to be here tonight was I've been told you don't have to wait until Monday to read what the *Sentinel* has to say about you. Saturday night is amateur night, and critics' night."

"That right, boy."

"I did think you were a little harsh on Buzzy."

"He ain't funny," came a shout.

"But," I continued, "he never lost that smile. As a matter-of-fact, I haven't seen Buzzy that happy since three weeks ago when a bullet almost hit Police Chief Parker." They cheered. (Chief Parker was to Watts what Governor Wallace was to Alabama.) "If you were gonna be critical of Buzzy, it's that he's a lousy shot!" A few stood and clapped. "Buzzy is a hard act to follow. The cops lost him."

I never knew laughter could sound like thunder. It was almost scary. When they quieted down, I did one of the opening lines from the album. "I want to thank you for letting me be here, and I hope you like me, but I don't want you to like me just because I'm white." There was silence. Then a few giggles. Then the laughter of disbelief.

I recounted opening night at the Playboy Club, why I was there, then went into the entire album. There was the laughter and applause, not of entertainment, but of appreciation and truth. And of hearing someone say it. They even guffawed at the simple, silly material.

"The main difference I've seen between whites in the south and blacks in LA is that when a white man signs his name with an 'x,' he's illiterate. When a black does it, he's a Muslim."

Hoots and hollers, raised fists and happy faces I could quickly distinguish as the cameraman moved about the room flashing pictures. It was thrilling. A feeling of power.

"And Muslims even have their own code names for their favorites. Dr. King is trying to clean up the dirt that is in the South, and his nickname is Kleenex." Knee slapping laughter.

"And Malcolm is always preaching loudly about the corruption that's in the entire system. Elijah Mohammed calls him Windex."

I touched on everything, even Vietnam, a subject nobody ever mentioned on a stage. I could do no wrong. It was an audience reaction and affection I'd never see again. It was the happiest moment in my life. Like getting the Green Card to comedy. I hadn't made a nickel from it; just proved my point, and trusted my instincts.

Outside with Sarita and the owner who kept shaking his head in wonderment, the editor said, "What an amazing story this is gonna be. You'd have thought at one point you were Ray Charles or James Brown!"

"Yah wanna come back?" the owner asked.

"Oh, no, thanks. I could never duplicate that. I was just trying to prove a point."

The editor said, "Well, you certainly did. We got some great pics. I'll be in touch, right away."

On the way home in the car, Sarita said, "They loved you. You know there are two kinds of people you can't lie to: blacks and musicians."

"Well," I said, "let's wait and see what happens."

We waited. And waited. And waited some more. Almost two weeks. During that time, I thought of how wonderful it would be to be discovered by a black audience, and made famous by a black magazine. *Ebony* was their *Life* magazine. It would make bigger news than Dick's short paragraph discovery in *Time*. There would be a whole article with pictures and quotes. I'd certainly get invites to entertain at the NAACP conventions, or even to the White House. When my daydreams started, which was often in those days, I could never curtail them, so I rode them, and enjoyed them. I was thankful I never had daydreams that were negative. Even when they turned out just to be daydreams. As this one did.

All the King's Horses' Asses

Waiting for the release of the *Ebony* article was made more unsettling by the long-distance harping of Sarita's mother. She let her daughter know frequently she'd have been better off in San Francisco with one of the many rich businessmen who pursued her rather than with some underemployed comic. She had a fit when she heard Sarita got a job. She didn't care that her daughter liked it. When Sarita told her *Ebony* was coming out with a great article about me, her mother screamed, "Who cares what they say?"

Not having heard from *Ebony* for two weeks, I finally called. When I got through to the editor, he said, "I was going to call you earlier, but we've been swamped here. We're not doing the story."

"What!" I hollered. "Why not?"

"We liked it. We all liked it, but when we ran it by the owner, he turned it down. He thought it was too controversial."

"How could it be controversial? The audience loved it. You were there. They loved it! Who would it upset?"

"Him, evidently."

"It's a natural. It's interesting. And it's certainly different." I was trying to think of all the things that would change his mind.

"It is all that. I've been spending days telling my friends about it. It was amazing, but I'm not the boss. I'm sorry."

"I'm stunned. I wasn't surprised by Playboy's reaction, but I never, ever expected the same from you guys. You're the editor, for God's sake."

"We've got some great pictures, though. Would you like them?"

I could see those smiling faces lit by the flash. Did I want to look at them again? "No. Why would I want a reminder of how cowardly even some rich blacks can be?" I slammed down the phone.

The doors that were opening for me were trapdoors. Maybe I was trying too hard to mount a horse that didn't want to ride in this race about Race. Maybe I should just stick to the Lee Wolfberg stuff. Then the phone rang. The first time in two weeks.

"John Barbour? This is the Bob Crane show."

"Who?"

"Bob Crane, CBS radio. KNX at Gower and Sunset. Bob would like to have you on his radio show."

Bob Crane was the most popular radio personality in Los Angeles. He had a lively, irreverent quality, with a show that had no format. He just did what he pleased, and evidently it pleased a lot of people. This was shortly before he became the star of *Hogan's Heroes,* and years before he was murdered in a bizarre sex scandal. I didn't realize it at the time, but something bizarre was happening for me. It seemed a number of people, some of them prominent, were intrigued by my album. One of them was Bob Crane. He was the only radio personality in town to not only book me, but to actually play cuts from it, and howled over my attempts to get *Ebony* to cover it. This didn't sell any copies, but it did sell a few other people on talking to me. One was Louis Lomax, the only black journalist in Los Angeles with his own television show, on KTTV. He spent an hour with me. Again, no record sales; then a call from the most successful TV host in town, and soon, in America: Joe Pyne.

Joe Pyne was the godfather of attack-talk television, an ex-Marine with a bad leg, a bad attitude, and a bad smoking habit, with the anger of an Irishman whose pub had run out of beer.

He was a monster hit on KABC Talk Radio. One day he picked up the phone and called Chuck Young, the General Manager of KTTV, channel 11 in Los Angeles, whom he didn't know, and hollered, "Hey, Chuck, I am the best fucking talk show host in radio; when are you gonna put me on the fucking air?"

Chuck said, "Joe, when can you get here!" That is how this genre started, birthed by Joe.

Joe was merciless with his guests, or victims, and more with his audience. He had what he called a 'Squawk Box,' placed in front of him. He would invite people to mount it and express their opinions. One of his kindest, most repeated, and most applauded pieces of advice he offered to those poor souls was, "Why don't you just go home and gargle with a mouthful of razor blades!" The country was shocked and outraged, and tuned in every show to let him know it.

The call I got was from his producer. "Joe would like to have you on the show."

"I'm not sure I'd like to do it."

"You'll do great. He loved the album, and he heard you with Bob and Louis."

"I don't think Joe likes anything, except beating up people."

He laughed. "Well, considering what you've been through lately, you don't look like the kind of guy who gets beat up easily. C'mon. You'll love it."

He was right. I had taken a bit of a beating, and was curious to see how I'd do. Also, I had nothing else to do. Joe's producer, Hal Parets, was a fiftyish, greying chain-smoker whose voice sounded as dark and scratchy as his lungs must have looked. He met me in front of the Capitol Records building on Vine Street.

Joe's studio was as big as Joe's mouth. It was huge. At one end of the large room, at a table that had to be thirty feet long, and six feet wide, was where Joe sat as I entered. It was almost the same table I saw years later in *Network* when Ned Beatty invited Peter Finch into his private dining area to regale him with the omnipotent financial facts of life.

Joe didn't rise. "Thanks for coming."

Hal sat me at the other end, near the exit. There was a table mike in front of me, and one in front of Joe. The show started. Not at all what I expected. Or what the audience must have expected. At least not from Joe. We were actually having a conversation, a meaningful conversation. It was exhilarating, sometimes a scary verbal ping pong match. His barbs weren't quite as harsh as I expected. He was pleased I handled them humorously and humanly. When the half hour was over, he said, "Wait a minute!" It was more an order than a request. He pushed himself up from the table, and limped toward me. "I'm sorry you had to sit so far away. I don't like to sit near people, just in case I might like them." He smiled and shook my hand. "I like you!"

As I was led to the exit, Hal, sounding stunned, said, "He must have really liked you. He's never said that to anyone."

More than a dozen years later, after Joe's death, Hal Parets was unemployable. The town said he was too old. I hired him.

Art Linkletter's Talent Scouts

I had no album sales or jobs to speak about, and no agent to speak for me. Still, every day I sat down to write jokes, and every night tried to find someplace to perform them. Then I got a call I never could have imagined. It was from the assistant to Perry Cross, the producer of Art Linkletter's *Hollywood Talent Scouts*. He asked me if I would mind coming over to CBS TV at Beverly and Fairfax to interview with Perry for the show. I was sure this was a sick joke from another warped comedian.

"What's your phone number?" I asked, suspiciously. "This has got to be some kind of joke."

The fellow, laughing, gave me a number. "I'll be right here." And hung up.

I dialed frantically.

Show business, all the way from radio to television, was never without some kind of amateur show. A young Sinatra was on *Major Bowes*. Vic Damone debuted his sweet voice on *Arthur Godfrey's Talent Scouts*, as did The McGuire Sisters and Julius La Rosa. There was *Ted Mack's Amateur*

Hour, and bandleader *Horace Heidt's The Youth Opportunity Program. Art Linkletter's Talent Scouts* was a revisit, as much is in television and films. It was huge, that day's *The X Factor* and *America's Got Talent*. And they wanted to talk to me.

The same voice answered the phone, chuckling. The appointment was made for eleven a.m. on a weekday, two days from the call. The stark CBS building at Beverly and Fairfax with that all-seeing eye made it look like some kind of government surveillance bureaucracy. Perry Cross's office was at the end of a very long basement corridor, not exactly where I thought a successful producer should be housed. It was also smaller than I expected. He rose, shaking my hand firmly.

"John, thanks for coming in. Sit down. This is my assistant, Greg." His assistant smiled, and said hello in the phone voice I recognized. Perry was smartly dressed, probably close to forty, and had the most beautiful black hair I'd ever seen outside of Sarita and Mel Nixon. He wasted little time.

"I loved your album."

I was surprised that he had heard it, startled that he might want me to do some of it on his show. He quickly set those thoughts aside.

"It has some really tough funny stuff on it. I think you deserve a break for just making it. Do you think you could do five minutes or so that's not on the album?"

"Mr. Cross, uh, you've just made it a little tougher for me to be white!" He and Greg chuckled warmly. "Yes," I continued. "I have lots of stuff that I did before the album, and lots since. When would you like me to do it?"

"Right now, if you don't mind."

"Right now? Here?"

"If that's okay! We're a good audience."

I stood shakily and started, looking right at Mr. Cross. "Well, it's true that in some of my more successful club bookings, I have appeared before smaller crowds." I did my safe five minutes. They were a receptive duo. As I finished, Perry nodded a few times, smiling.

"Young man, you're booked. You're funny!" He rose and shook my hand again, as did Greg.

Art Linkletter was one of television's most popular personalities who had made an even more successful transition from radio. His type of performer is called a personality because they have no evidence of any distinctive talent other than the ability to talk glibly; no one, not even Godfrey, was better at it than Art. His voice was rather high pitched, almost lyrical, very engaging, and always sounded like he was having fun. His first big radio, then TV hit, was the endearing *People Are Funny*, followed by the daytime blockbuster, *Kids Say the Darndest Things*.

Having heard him since I was a kid, I was in a state of head-shaking wonder that I was to be on his show, and actually meet him. Perry took me upstairs to the studio where the show was taped. People, cameras and lights were moving all over the place. As new as it was, it didn't feel strange. I felt at home, like that was where I belonged. The creative clutter of a studio, any kind of studio, always seemed to energize me. The only thing missing were Mickey and Judy.

"Art, this young man, John, is going to be on your next show," Perry said.

Art looked down at me. He was taller than I had imagined. And cooler. "That's nice," he said. "Looking forward to it." He turned and walked away.

Every day and sleepless night was filled with my mumbling five minutes of fame; in the car, in restaurants where I couldn't eat, I kept going over it. An hour or two every day, I was in the bathroom checking my facial expressions. I spoke to no one, except myself. I was sometimes terrified I'd walk out on that stage and forget my act.

The taping was in the late afternoon, just before dinner. I wore my only good suit and tie. Perry led Sarita to a front-row seat and me to makeup. Following this, an assistant led me to my dressing room. There was my name on the door. Above a star. The room was indeed furnished and decorated for a star with mirrored walls, baskets of flowers, a tableful of snacks, plush cushioned chairs. Really classy. It reeked of success.

Perry entered, accompanied by a face I recognized immediately. He was, outside of Bob Hope, my favorite comedian on television. I never missed the first two years of his show; I even saw him a few times at the showroom in the Ambassador Hotel on Wilshire. It was George Gobel. He was carrying a bottle of whiskey and two glasses. George had the kind of style, material, and demeanor that not only made you want to laugh, but also hug him. His soft-spoken country delivery with his mischievous, twinkling blue eyes topped by that boyish crewcut, made you believe elves were real. With this as his foundation, he built some very strong, funny material. I really liked him.

"John," Perry announced, "George is your sponsor. He's going to introduce you." In this new version of the show, the 'discoveries' were to be introduced by truly established stars. Mine was George.

I clutched his hand. "Mr. Gobel, thank you very much. I…I don't think I'll be able to follow you."

He held up the bottle and the two glasses. "I have an assistant here that will provide you with some courage."

Perry smiled. "I have to attend to showbiz now. You have about forty-five minutes." He left. George put down the bottle, turned the glasses upright, and shook my hand. 'You'll do great, kid. Perry's never wrong."

"Thank you."

"You're welcome. Aaand, (He had an endearing way of stretching words.) you'll give me another thank you right after I pour this." He filled both glasses. He offered me mine first. I didn't wish to be rude, so I said, "No, thank you very much. I don't drink."

His head bobbed back playfully. "You mean, you don't drink? How can you go out there alone?"

At the moment, I didn't realize how funny what he said was. I was too nervous about my act, and about not offending him. "But, sir, you did get another thank you. This time with a 'no' in front of it."

"I'll drink to that." He took a gulp. "And I'll drink your share, too." He took my glass. In one gulp it was gone.

It was evident he had started on the bottle on the way over, but like a lot of successful drunks I knew, if you could really call a heavy drinker a success, you couldn't tell if he'd had anything at all. His eyes were clear, as was his speech and mind.

"Why don't you drink, kid?"

"Why do you?"

"Bad memories!"

"Me too."

"I like you, kid. Here's to some good memories. Beginning tonight!" He downed another one. And began to chat. To me. A bit to himself. About his life. I totally forgot about my act. I was lost in and enamored of the unbelievable talent and star who was sharing stories with me as though I was his best friend. Next to the bottle, at the time, I probably was.

"Do you look at the audience?" he asked out of nowhere. "Me, I look over their heads, which is where most of my stuff goes. But come here, I wanna show you something. What you can look forward to when you're a hit." He led me out of the dressing room behind the stage to the closed curtain. He pulled it back an inch or two so we could see the audience. They were abuzz with anticipation.

"See that lady in the second row on the aisle with those fancy duds?"

I peeked out. "Yes.'

"That's Art's wife," he said.

"See the brunette sitting in front of her?" He was pointing to Sarita.

"Yes," I said. "That's my girlfriend."

"Good for you. Well... well ... uh... see that blonde sitting opposite on the aisle second row? That one's Art's mistress. She loves showbiz."

Suddenly Perry appeared. "There you are. George, five minutes."

"Okay, chief," George said, cheerily "We're informed and ready."

I can barely remember George's delightful introduction or the applause. If I didn't have a tape of my appearance, I doubt that I could remember any of the material. What I do remember is my affection for George.The reception was wonderful. The planned and rehearsed five minutes ran nearly ten.

Backstage, Perry gave me a huge hug. "Johnny, boy, that was fabulous!"

"Thank you. Is Mr. Gobel around? I'd like to thank him, too."

"He left. Upright!" Perry patted me on the shoulder. "Showbiz! Anyway, Art said he'd like to have you back. You'd be the second one ever to make a return appearance on the show. And Art wants to introduce you himself. How'd you like that?"

"I'd love it." Maybe it was good thing *Ebony* never published my story!

And Send Two Copies

The second appearance was even more successful than the first. That may be attributable to the fact that Art introduced me, giving me his Good Housekeeping Seal of Approval. (You can see it at youTube/johnbarboursworld.com.)

As always, after what I thought was a good show, I would wait for the showbiz world to come knocking on my door. But they never did. In every musical, big or small, that I saw, I can never recall one of those stars having an agent. So, I was indifferent to agents, and their importance, and even more indifferent to managers. If you have an agent, why on earth would you also need a manager? The only manager I ever heard of that I had a distinct admiration for was Jack Rollins, Woody Allen's manager, whom I'll get to shortly.

I always wondered why an obvious talent would need someone to sell him. Couldn't they sell themselves? Couldn't the producers, directors or buyers see for themselves this obvious talent? Because of my indifference and unawareness of the agent's position in the showbiz game, the few I had justifiably became indifferent to me. We drifted apart. There were never any acrimonious words. Usually no words at all. Just the silence of long inactivity.

Opportunity is not a door that someone knocks on and enters. It's a door that only opens out. And can only be opened by pushing it hard and often. Or as in many cases, is swung open by luck. The door to *Hollywood Talent Scouts* was opened by the 'luck' of Perry Cross hearing the album and calling me. The door to The Agency for The Performing Arts was closed months earlier because they, and the world, didn't want to hear about *It's Tough to Be White.*

Brooding over the fact that my ladder to success only had one rung on it, which was now broken, the few phone calls I did get after the airing came from just one source, a source I did not want to hear from – Sarita's mother.

Whenever I answered and it was her, there was never even cordial small talk. It was always, me saying "Hello," and her saying, "Is Sarita there?"

This particular time, since I only had a few complimentary calls, I was hoping for more from her. As usual, it was, "Is Sarita there?" And, as usual, when I handed the phone to her I left the room. Just listening to Sarita's side of the conversation was upsetting. When it was over, Sarita came into the bedroom. I was lying on the bed reading.

"Well," I said, "what'd she say?"

"She doesn't think you're funny."

I howled. "That's funny. What else?"

"That's it."

"You mean she just called to spend ten minutes saying how unfunny I was? Would she think I was funnier if we got married?"

"Probably. Then again, probably not! She's not much of a fan of showbiz, even when I was doing it."

I looked at her for what seemed forever. She was beautiful, movie-star beautiful, with the most peaceful, warm center I'd ever seen in a person. Here she was, in a strange city, with the most unsuccessful man she'd ever been with, not asking for anything, never complaining, but encouraging and contributing by working at Swanson's. I had nothing to offer her; absolutely nothing. I don't know why I said it, but I did.

"Would you marry me?"

"Are you being funny?"

"If I was, I'd expect a laugh. No. I'm serious."

Giving it almost no thought, she said, "Yes. Okay. That'd be nice. Yes." Her soft smile and deep voice, a voice deeper than mine, went right through me.

"Could I ask you a couple of questions?"

"Sure."

"You know I don't want any children. Does that bother you?'"

"No. I understand it. And I don't blame you."

"I'm not religious at all and you spent half your life in church."

"It's Episcopalian. That's a social pastime, not a religion. Catholicism, that's a religion."

I smiled. Seldom did she make comments like that. "Are you sure you don't mind? I mean, I really don't have much to offer."

"Yes, you do. What better offer is there than the future? And your future is going to be better than you know."

"Do you want to call your mother?"

"No. I already know what she's going to say."

"You don't mind what she thinks?"

"She has never done my thinking for me. If she did, I wouldn't be here." She stood by the doorway, and I lay in bed, the book resting on my chest.

"Well," I finally said, "I guess that's the easy part. Now how do we go about it? And when?"

"The sooner, and the simpler, the better. The two largest weddings I ever went to didn't last a year. Half their wedding gifts went back unopened. I want ours to last. I'm only doing this once."

I smiled. I'd never heard her sound almost forceful. "You want a city hall wedding?"

She shook her head. "No, too cold."

"How about that little brown church, I think on Coldwater near Riverside. You comment on it every time we pass it. I think Reagan and Nancy got married there in the fifties."

"That's very nice. Perfect."

I was in a strange untravelled land the next few weeks. Being a comedian, I barely spent a minute thinking of anything other than myself and my material. Now I had to think about a wife.

We got a license, the blood tests, and booked the church for late October, their first opening. With only fifty extra dollars to spend, we drove to Beverly Hills. We found a small corner jewelry store. The owner, who fell in love with Sarita, as everyone seemed to, showed us two plain gold bands. I pointed out quickly they were clearly beyond our budget.

"For fifty dollars," he said with a flair, 'it's my wedding gift to you both!"

We sent out no announcements. With casualness and an 'oh by the way' attitude, we mentioned it to a few friends. The reason for letting anyone know at all was, I needed a best man. He turned out to be another struggling comedian, Bill Morrison. Bill was a surprisingly handsome and likable man for someone wishing to be a comic. He had black wavy hair, solid black eyes, and the most bizarre sense of humor; he said he got it from his mother, a mortician, who loved to tell him funny stories about embalming people, especially the fat ones. Since he resisted telling jokes, I wrote him an act that didn't require any, but got huge laughs. He would have audience members, if any showed up, blow into different colored balloons, and then he would give them a reading, claiming he could read their futures by touching the skin of the balloons filled with their breathe and aura. His house, which was paid for, was one of the half-dozen places we used as an infrequent workshop. One frequent attendee, and close friend of Bill's, was another aspiring actor, Craig Nelson.

There were seven others at the wedding. Two were non-comedians, Sarita and the minister. The other four, whom we didn't know too well, three guys and a girl, heard about it at the workshop and had nothing to do that day so, out of curiosity, decided to attend. It was so informal and matter-of-fact that no one brought a camera. Or even thought of it. It was probably the least romantic wedding the minister ever witnessed. But it was probably the most down to earth and meaningful. I wore my second suit and Sarita wore a stunning blue chiffon dress. When it was over, we kissed casually. After all, we'd been kissing less casually for over two and a half years. We were being modest in front of the sparse crowd.

We walked out of the simple brown building the size of a one-car garage hand in hand into the afternoon sun.

"That was nice," Sarita said.

"Let's do it again. In ten years." And we did. In Las Vegas. Our honeymoon consisted of doing the same thing we had done every day: a glass of wine at Bill's.

Back at the apartment, I asked Sarita, "Do you feel any different?"

"No. Why should I feel different?"

"I feel the same as before," I said.

"Honey," she said, "you must've spent much too much time at the movies. It's only a piece of paper. It only means what you want it to mean."

"Do you think you should call your mother?"

"Yes. Let's get that over with."

"I'll wait in the bedroom."

I could not make out what she was saying, which was good because she wasn't raising her voice. Usually I heard her when she hung up; not this time. She returned to the bedroom, stopping in the doorway, looking exactly as she had when I asked her to marry me. Only more beautiful in that blue dress.

"She didn't believe me," Sarita said. "I tapped my ring into the phone and said, "Listen, do you hear that? She yelled, and swore and said she didn't believe me and that I'd better send two Xerox copies of that damn wedding certificate!"

"My god. Your mother's funny. She's funnier than I am!"

Whitey

"Mort Lachman gave me your number and suggested I call," the voice on the phone said. I lightened up as I always did when anybody mentioned Mort. "My name's Gordon Mitchell. Most people call me Whitey. I'm a musician. I play bass. Most recently with Benny Goodman, but my brother Red is the famous one in the family. Ella Fitzgerald's bass player. I don't really want to keep doing this. When I mentioned to Mort that I wanted to be a writer, he said to talk to you and gave me your number."

"Well, Mort's certainly a lot more successful than I am, and I'm not even a writer."

"You write funny stuff, though. Mort said I'd have a better chance of becoming aTV writer, if I had a partner. He said that although you do standup you had a lot of time on your hands."

I laughed. "That's true, but I have no interest in writing for someone else. Or TV, but since it's Mort, and I do have time on my hands, why don't you come by tomorrow afternoon?"

Gordon, or Whitey as he preferred, arrived early in the afternoon. He was a little taller than me; nearly everybody is, had thinning blonde hair for a man in his early thirties, an oval face, pale blue eyes, and a very strong voice. I told him again that I had no interest at all in writing sitcoms or anything for television, except my own jokes. I was just curious why a fairly successful, respected musician would want to change what he'd done his whole life. He told me he had three young children, a wife who didn't work, but while he was still able to support them living in a small house in the valley, he couldn't see himself still doing it at fifty.

Since Sarita had been a singer, I, of course, asked him about his experiences, especially with a legend like Benny Goodman, and some of the famous vocalists with whom he'd worked.

"Some were terrific, as people and singers. One of the nicest but most difficult was Eddie Fisher." At the time Eddie Fisher was one of the most famous names in showbiz, not only as a nice singer who had a string of hits like *I'm Walking Behind You,* and *Oh, My Papa,* but as the ex-husband of Debbie Reynolds who had been recently horsing around with Liz Taylor who was also horsing around with Richard Burton.

"How was he difficult?" I asked.

"He was a lousy musician. Absolutely no sense of rhythm."

"How's that? He had so many gold records."

"And I'm on some of them. We had to have a guy stand right next to him at the mike, and on every word or every phrase where the beat was, he'd have to wave his arm so Eddie would know when to change. It was awful."

"Unbelievable. So," I said, "how are you going to go about trying to be a writer?"

"Well, after I talked to Mort, I called the Writers Guild because I'd heard they are soon putting on their annual show. I asked if I could participate. They gave me the name of the guy who runs it, Hal Kanter. I asked him if I could contribute something. He said he'd be happy to meet with me. I don't want to do it alone. I'm not even sure I could. So, that's another reason I'm here."

"Whitey, I'm only interested in writing my own stuff."

"You still could. I mean, you said you have time on your hands. Look, we could have been writing something this afternoon. You don't have to commit forever. Just when you feel like it."

He looked pained. I felt bad for him. "Look," I said, "if you want to try it for a little bit, I'll give it a shot, but you're going to have to do the legwork and hustling and phone calls or whatever, because I have no interest in calling agents or producers or any of that stuff. But I will put in the time to help you write."

"How does one go about getting an assignment or doing a script?" he asked.

I laughed out loud. "Are you kidding? You're asking me? I haven't the foggiest idea. I imagine you don't get an assignment unless they know you can write, so you probably have to write a script on spec."

"For nothing?"

"Yes. I'm sure that's how most of them get started. What's your favorite show?"

"*Get Smart,*" he said.

"Well, that's what we should start on first. Since you like it and I like it, it'd probably be fun to do."

"That sounds great. Can we start after we meet with Hal Kanter?"

"Why would we meet with him?"

"He's producing The Writers Guild show. He's huge in the business. We could certainly learn something from him. We may even come up with some material or skits they'd use. I hear it's a really funny show. Better than the Oscars."

The Writers Guild was on Beverly Boulevard, a corner building that could have passed for a small complex of dentists' offices. The receptionist directed us to a first-floor conference room. Seated around a large rectangular table were a dozen writers, all men, and to our amazement, Groucho Marx. Wow, a legend of comedy. At the head of the table was Hal Kanter. He rose and greeted us. He was well over six feet tall, had wavy hair with a hint of grey, and eyes that always seemed to be smiling; no surprise considering there was always something funny swirling around in his head.

Hal gestured to the others. "This is Whitey and … ." He motioned to me and I introduced myself. He turned to the group at the table. "They are new and want to contribute to our little show." We were directed to the far end of the table.

Whitey and I sat quietly for half an hour while those very funny men batted around ideas and notions for the show. A skit had already been written by Neil Simon for Walter Matthau, who would be one of the stars. It was hilarious.

Soon Groucho spoke up. "Hal, how are we going to open this thing?"

Evidently, Hal was in charge of putting together Groucho's intro, and Groucho couldn't have been in funnier hands than this man. He had been writing the best material for the Oscars for years. He produced and wrote *The George Gobel Show,* and later produced and wrote the first sitcom for a black performer starring Dianne Carroll.

Hal started humming, *Thanks for The Memories,* Bob Hope's theme song, then said, "That's the music we hear, full orchestra, the curtain opens, there's no one there for a moment, then Groucho, you walk out, and say, "Isn't it great to hear that music and not have him show up?"

I laughed and said, "That's funny." Groucho said, "Naw, that's not for me."

Hal continued, as though he hadn't heard, and said. "Then you say, 'We're honored to have Lew Wasserman in the audience, but I'm not going to do any jokes about him. I never kick a dog when he's up.'"

I chuckled again.

Groucho glanced at me, then at Hal. "I'm not doin' that. Something else." Everyone got quiet. I finally broke the silence.

"Mr. Marx," I said cautiously, "excuse me, I'm new to this, but that's funny. Why wouldn't you do it?"

Groucho didn't miss a beat. "Bob Hope is a legend. I'm not doing anything to insult him. As for Wasserman, I like to work."

"But you're a legend, too!" I said.

He looked at me like I'd insulted him, then said to Hal. "You play my music, the curtain will open, and four beautiful harem girls will carry me out on a gondola … . like I've done before."

"Groucho," Hal said, "we're trying to get away from reruns."

"You never get away from what works," Groucho said sternly. "That's how I'm doing it." He got up and left.

Hal and the writers continued the conference, too busy to take notice of us. I turned to Whitey. "Geez, I can't believe it. Did you see that? Groucho Marx, a comic giant, afraid of Lew Wasserman's shadow. Like a beginner. I mean that was funny stuff."

"Evidently, John, you haven't been around many of these giants who are often emotional midgets, and cowards. Do you have any ideas you wanna kick around, maybe suggest to Hal?"

I thought for a moment, and remembered something I'd written years earlier but never got to use. "Actually, it's something I'll run by you. When I was starting out at The Horn a few years ago, I did this bit about an out of work carpenter in Jerusalem two thousand years ago, fired for talking too much, who goes to the employment office to pick up his shekels, and they say there's a job for him working for the Romans building crucifixes." Whitey laughed. I continued. "Even though it got big laughs, the owner wouldn't let me perform it again."

"That's funny," Whitey said with a big smile. "Let's turn it into a skit.

"Well," I said, "the problem is an actor to play Jesus."

"There are tons of them. Maybe we find a midget, Billy Barty."

"That's funny. Having someone play Jesus is a problem. In all those religious movies, like the one Jeffrey Hunter was in, he or any actor destroys the image of Jesus. Blue eyes? Come on. Maybe you're right. Billy Barty. You wouldn't have to lift him too high to put the nails in."

We howled and continued adlibbing, excited. "Instead of doing a skit, let's have an agent sell the idea to a studio. That way people can still imagine what Jesus looks like, and won't be distracted."

"Yeah. Sell it to Lew Wasserman," Whitey chirped.

"Terrific. The biggest agent in town is Swifty Lazar," I continued. "Billy Barty could play him."

Irving "Swifty" Lazar was indeed the most successful literary agent, and most notorious in the business. He rightly earned the moniker "Swifty." While some book was in galley at a publisher, he'd call the various studios informing them that he'd just bought the rights and that he was open for bids, and they'd start bidding. When he found and accepted a bid he liked, he'd call the publisher and author, and option the unpublished book at a fraction of what he was just offered. He then did the same with actors. While on a set, involved with a movie, he'd casually and off-handedly tell the star he wanted that he was already in negotiations with a bigger star for this just-optioned book. Whereupon his companion would beg for the part, often at a lower fee. Swifty was only five feet, two inches tall. Perfect for the only midget star in town.

"How'd we open the scene?" Whitey asked.

"Well, the set would be Wasserman's office. There'd be a sign, 'Universal Studios,' and a much bigger sign saying LEW WASSERMAN, and on his desk maybe a huge mirror that he always glances at, and … and he's sitting on a kind of throne. The intercom buzzes. He says, 'Yes, Doris', and she says, 'Mr. Wasserman. Mr. Lazar is downstairs on his way up.' And Wasserman says, 'When he gets here have him wait in the 'in' basket!' Whitey laughed out loud

"You, guys seem to be having fun," Hal said.

In our enthusiasm, we hadn't noticed the room had cleared.

Whitey said, "We were just kicking around a notion."

"What is it?" Hal asked. "I'd like to join the fun."

"Well, I'd better let John tell you. He's the performer and it's mostly his idea."

I told him guardedly what we'd conjured up. His smile grew. "What do you call it?"

"An Out of Work Carpenter on His Ass!" I blurted. Whitey laughed. Hal snorted.

"Have you typed it up?"

"No," Whitey said. "We were just adlibbing it now."

"Good. That's good. Type it up. Get it to me tomorrow. You're in the show. We'll put it in after Matthau." And he left.

That beautiful, intimidating conference room was now empty except for Whitey and me. We looked at each other and shook our heads. And hands. Who would have thought the day before that two unknown writers would be there, giving material to the best joke writer in the business, and being a part of the best show in town. And not even members of the guild.

"John," Whitey said, his face lighting up, "this might be easier than you think. You might like it."

On screen, no actor had the charisma of Cary Grant, but on stage, it was Walter Matthau. It was impossible to take our eyes off this giant lovable man with that distinctive, almost whiney deep voice. His appearance in the Writers Guild Show was, as always, a joy. His work and Neil Simon's words were a hard act to follow. Our little enterprise, though, which was unquestionably irreverent, got a surprisingly large and warm reaction. It launched Whitey and me as a neophyte writing team that night.

Whitey was determined to become a comedy writer. It was only his persistence and ambition that pushed us forward. I was lazy, and still not too enthusiastic. It indeed was rewarding to see and hear a roomful of professionals laughing and applauding our stuff, but in my mind, I was wishing I was on stage.

Whitey got us an agent I met with once, just so we'd know what each other looked like. I wanted my relationships with people to be friendships, not business. In business relationships I had the uneasy feeling people were just getting together to use one another. I knew it was an emotional shortcoming on my part, something I never got over, and something that cost me often in my career. But I admired Whitey's drive and resilience.

Shortly after he started making money, his wife ran off with the choir director with whom she had had a long affair, from the first time she sang *Jesus, I'm coming.* Whitey was left to raise the three children she gave up. He did the best he could.

We were still going to work on our spec script for *Get Smart*. In those days, we had something called Green Stamps. When you bought something, you'd receive a certain number of these stamps. After they accumulated, you could redeem them for gifts. Everyone knew what green stamps were. Our script simply revolved around Chaos, the villain in the show, counterfeiting these green stamps to bankrupt America. The producers of *Get Smart* didn't buy the script, but liked the writing. They asked to meet us. This meeting led to meetings with a few of real biggies in TV comedy: Sheldon Leonard, who had become one of the major forces in the business with T*he Dick Van Dyke Show*, Danny Thomas, and Andy

Griffith. And a meeting with Desi Arnaz. Desi was not the slim, handsome Cuban we'd seen trying to cope with Lucy. He was heavy, unkempt, with his tie askew. He was also not sober. Somehow, though, he liked us. They both did, which led to doing scripts for *Gomer Pyle, My Mother the Car,* and *The Tammy Grimes Show*.

Whitey and I were becoming a hit. We spent our afternoons at my apartment acting and hacking out scripts, and early evenings hitting golf balls at the Studio City driving range. Yet, writing came to an end abruptly one afternoon when I could just no longer do it. When we wrote, he'd sit on the couch while I walked around playing all the characters. This one afternoon we were working on another *Gomer Pyle* assignment. I was pacing and acting the part, imitating Gomer. Suddenly I stopped, realizing how stupid I sounded. "Whitey," I said, "I can't do this anymore. I can't go on writing this stuff anymore."

"You're kidding. You're terrific at it. We're doin' much better than I ever imagined."

"This is not what I want to do. I want to do standup."

"Maybe we could write something."

"No. No, Whitey. I just don't have the heart to do it anymore. I'm sorry."

Whitey bowed his head. I felt horrible when he found out he didn't have a good marriage partner; now he was losing his writing partner.

"That's all right, Johnny. I really understand. Look, I am a good bass player, but I couldn't do that anymore either. I understand. We'll still play golf together?"

"Oh, absolutely."

And we did. For years.

It wasn't long before Whitey had another writer to work with named Lloyd Turner, who only had one arm, but played golf. It also wasn't long before Whitey and Lloyd were staff writers on *Mork and Mindy* with Robin Williams. Whitey died in 2009. He was living in Palm Desert with his second wife, Marilyn. Every day he played golf … and his bass!

Manley and the Mob

Chris Hayward and Alan Burns had a small office in the Four Star Production building in Studio City where they were preparing to shoot a pilot called *Ace of the Mounties*. Chris was a former band singer who had come to Hollywood, enrolled in a writing night-class, and got his low pay, long hour start with Jay Ward making enormous contributions to *Rocky and Bullwinkle* and *Dudley Do-Right*. Chris and Alan later created a show called *The Munsters*. Their prominent agent sold it to Screen Gems, as his own creation. It became a monster hit, and a ten-year monster lawsuit until Chris and Alan finally got their rights and residuals back. Chris said, "Some agents just take ten percent. Our guy took a 100!"

When I entered their office, Chris was sitting behind the desk, while Alan leaned against the wall, evaluating everything.

"Have you ever done any acting?" Alan asked, as though he expected a negative.

"I was with a British rep company in Farnham, Surrey for nearly a year."

"England?" Alan was stunned.

"Yes. 1960."

"Well, we're doing a pilot for ABC called *Ace of the Mounties*. They want Bob Newhart, but Bob doesn't want them, so we're looking for sort of a Bob Newhart look alike and you're the closest we've come. Would you like to test?"

"I'd love it!"

"Terrific," Chris said. "We'll set it up for tomorrow or the next day." After shaking hands, I left feeling sky high. I didn't have to do anything. I didn't even have to read in their office. The night was, of course, sleepless and anxious. I was testing for a lead in a show. The morning brought a phone call that was more than a little deflating.

"John, Chris. We sent your tape to ABC. They said they liked it, but would rather go another way. They say they have an actor in mind, but won't tell us. Evidently, he's unsigned. Alan and I think you'd be perfect for this, and you're Canadian besides. So, to get you on camera, we've asked to audition dogs. Every Mountie has a German shepherd, so would you mind coming in and walking the dogs for us?"

I laughed. "Sure. It'd be fun. And thanks for still being interested."

"We'll get back to you this afternoon."

That afternoon the phone call came, more deflating than the first. Now ABC didn't even want a dog. When Chris told me, I laughed.

"Geez, what a business. I'd just better stick to standup, but, thanks anyway for considering me."

So, I started to think of clubs I could get into, or even variety shows. After all, I had two pretty good pieces of film. Maybe I needed a manager instead of an agent. Two days later, Chris Hayward was on the phone again.

"John, I don't know if this is much of a lead for you, but do you know Freddie de Cordova?"

"No. Never heard of him."

"He's a friend of ours, casting for a pilot called *Manley and The Mob*, about a bumbling detective. He's already tested three or four leads, and they all bombed. Alan and I told him about you, and he agreed to meet you. Could you do that?"

"Sure. When?"

"Here's his phone number. Call him right now. He's expecting it, and we'll see what happens."

I called immediately. A deep friendly voice answered the phone. "Johnny?"

I laughed. "Yes."

"Chris said you'd call. Can you come by this afternoon?"

His office was in the same building as Chris and Alan's, on the first floor, and a lot larger. It was his office until he moved to NBC a few years later to become Johnny Carson's producer. He was over six feet two inches, wore dark horn-rimmed glasses that couldn't hide the constant twinkle in his eyes, plus he had the deep friendly voice of an announcer who enjoyed selling anything.

"Thanks for coming in." He stood and motioned me to sit. "Chris speaks very highly of you. How long have you known him?"

"About twenty minutes," I answered. "Wait till he knows me half an hour and see what he says!"

Fred laughed a hearty welcoming laugh. "Johnny, I don't know if this will lead to anything, and I certainly can't promise you anything, but we're testing a bunch of folks for the lead in a show that ABC is excited about. I see nothing wrong with putting you on the list. Is that okay?"

"The front or back?"

He laughed again. "Unfortunately, at the end, to which we might not even get. You'd be number thirty-two."

"Sure. Put me down. I'm honored."

"Here's the pilot script, with the two test pages marked in pink. Take it with you. Keep it to yourself. If we get to you, I'll give you a day's notice. We'll be shooting tests for nearly a week."

"Who are some of the people on the list?"

"Well, since you're a comic, you might know George Carlin and Streisand's husband, Elliot Gould."

"They must be near the head of your list."

He smiled. "Actually, they're numbers thirty and thirty-one."

"Whoa. You must be testing some good people."

"I hope so."

I glanced down at the script. The writers were Gerry Gardner and Dee Caruso. "Are these two writers who used to write one-liners for President Kennedy?"

He looked impressed. "How did you know?"

"I might have heard it from Mort Sahl or read it somewhere."

"Well, it's pretty good. I think you'll like it. About a bumbling private eye."

"Sort of an American version of Peter Seller's Inspector Clouseau?"

"That's it. An original rip-off!" He laughed.

I left, the script clutched in my hand. During the next week, I got a call from Chris almost every three hours for five days filling me in on the results of the disastrous tests made by some well-known actors. He was positively gleeful recounting every one. I don't know if it's because he resented ABC, or because he was hoping I'd finally get to test for something, which was weird because he had no idea if I'd be any good. Neither did I.

Friday morning he called to let me know they were down to George Carlin and Elliot Gould; they'd test before noon. There was no call from Chris late that afternoon, so I figured either George or Elliot had been successful. Over the weekend, I sat down to write some jokes, trying to figure out what my next step might be for my standup. There was no possibility of going back to the Hungry i. First, Banducci's favorite female had run off with me, then married me. So, I figured I should try the East Coast.

Monday morning Chris called. "They bombed. ABC hated them! Freddie'll be calling you soon."

"How could they bomb? George is funny, and Elliot's a pretty good actor."

"Who knows? You're the end of the list. Good luck!"

As soon as I hung up, the phone rang. It was Freddie. "Did Chris call you?"

"Yes."

"That guy should be your goddamned agent. Anyway, can you come by this afternoon? One o'clock for makeup, and test at two."

I was at the studio at twelve-thirty. Freddie said, "I hope you're as good as you are punctual."

"Do you mind if I say something about the script?"

"What you say can't be worse than what ABC is saying. Now they hate it. Don't think it's funny. A month ago they were hysterical."

"This... Manley... he is supposed to be a bumbler, a sort of Inspector Clouseau, right?"

"That was the idea."

"In the test scene there is no indication that he's a bumbler. He's just sitting at his desk. The phone rings and he starts to talk. So before I answer the phone, do you mind if I invent a little bumbling business, so people will know I'm a klutz?"

"Johnny, you do whatever you want because, truthfully, I'm worn out and ABC wants out."

Instead of makeup, I headed straight to the stage. In the tiny office setting they'd built, a gaffer was moving some lights and talking to the cameraman. I introduced myself. They were professionally pleasant but indifferent. I went to the desk where I'd be sitting prior to answering the intercom where my secretary would inform me of an incoming call. There was some mail on the desk, a mail opener, and the usual stuff you'd find on a desk. I looked at it all, imagining what Peter Sellers would do with all the ordinary stuff. Picturing it in my head, I was off to makeup. A few minutes before two everyone was on the set, about fifteen people; not one looked happy, especially Freddie.

"Are you okay?"

"I hope so. I've put together just a few seconds of business before the intercom buzzes so the cue for that will be the drawer falling on the floor."

"The what?" Freddie asked in disbelief.

"The drawer. You'll see."

He shook his head, as he addressed the crew. "Okay, everyone, Johnny's gonna do a little business before we cue the intercom, but start shooting as soon as he sits."

Freddie called, "Action." The cameras rolled.

I sat at the desk sort of fluttering my hands in frustration at all the mail in front of me. I discarded a couple of pieces then picked up a big brown envelope. I couldn't open it. I couldn't tear it. I turned it upside down and tried the same without success. I moved stuff on the desk looking for the letter opener. It was stuck in an apple. There were chuckles from the crew. I pulled it out, and tried to insert it in the top of the envelope. I pushed once, twice, then shoved it a third time right into the palm of my hand. But I didn't scream. I just opened my mouth wide. There were louder laughs. In frustration, I gathered the mail in my left hand, looked around at where to put it, looked down at the drawer to my right, and tried to pull it. It wouldn't open. I yanked harder and it came out and fell to the floor. More laughs.

Then the intercom buzzed. Instead of clicking the intercom button, I picked up the phone.

"Yes, Mabel. Mabel?" The intercom kept buzzing. I spotted my mistake, got mad at the phone, smashed it down and clicked the intercom.

"A call for you."

I picked up the phone. "Hello. I know you're not Mabel." I continued with the brief dialogue. When I was finished the crew applauded.

Freddie clutched my shoulders. "Johnny, that was terrific. You were perfect. You may just have yourself a TV show!"

"Wow. That'd be fantastic. I'll call Chris."

"So will I," Freddie said happily. "I'll be talking to you within hours. Go home and celebrate."

By the time I got home, Chris had already called, telling Sarita the good news. Sarita was the best female tap dancer I'd ever seen, on or off the screen. The only time she'd ever danced now, though, was when I'd come home from a week's gig or a short trip somewhere. She'd open the door and do a welcoming tap and song. It was always a delight to see and hear. That is how she greeted me after getting Chris's call.

We were too excited to eat, so we just talked about how nice it'd be to have a show with a nice income. How much fun it'd be to make a few plans with a little money in the bank. Even in my enthusiasm, however, one of those plans would not include having a child. I was going to avoid having a child the way I was going to avoid liquor. I didn't mind maybe a small house, or a dog or cat, but no child. Sarita had no problem with that. She said she just wanted to see me happy, and she said this was the happiest she'd ever seen me. She added, "That includes at the little brown church!"

The call from Freddie did come within hours, almost eighteen hours to be exact. "Johnny, they loved the test, but, there's a little problem. They knew the script was funny, but they want the lead to go to Paul Lynde."

"Paul Lynde!" I screamed. "Are they kidding? They'd be better off with Carlin or Gould or anyone but Paul Lynde. He's funny, but America is not ready for gay funny. He's better as a sidekick."

"Johnny, I agree with you. I made all those points. I pointed out to them that it was you that made the script funny, not the other way around. So, they want you to be the sidekick."

I was silent for a long time.

"Would you do it? I'm sorry to ask, but if you're still connected with it maybe they'll change their minds."

"Freddie, I'm heartbroken." I sighed in resignation. "But I'd be happy to do it."

"Great. We shoot in two weeks."

I didn't end up being Paul's sidekick. I ended up being the heavy's sidekick. I got third billing. But as I predicted, and expected, ABC was unhappy with Lynde. When Freddie suggested they redo it with me back in the lead, ABC said no. Freddie called me into his office to give me the news, and apologize for the disappointment.

I said, "I was number thirty-two on that list. Why on earth would ABC keep me on it, if they were never going to use me?"

"Because," Freddie said matter-of-factly, "nobody knew you, so they had nothing against you. Now they do. You're a heterosexual."

Jack Rollins

Acting was not a profession over which I would have much control. Decisions on whether or not I'd work would never be mine; they'd always be somebody else's. The somebody else's that I kept running into were usually incompetent. The one thing I felt I had control over was writing and telling jokes, but not how to get a job doing so. I needed help; not just an agent's help to get a job. A manager's help to teach me how to think and plan. Agent's don't do that. That's why they only get ten percent and why managers like Elvis's Colonel Parker got fifty percent.

I had read an article about Harry Belfonte, the most famous singer in America, and how he was dumping his New York manager, a guy name Jack Rollins. The article applauded the star, and wondered in print if Jack Rollins would soon be out of the business. The story had this brief background:

Jack worked out of a small office in New York with a partner named Charles Jaffe. He had discovered a young Harry Belafonte singing jazz in a club in New York. That's what Harry wanted to be, a famous jazz singer. Somehow Jack convinced this ex-Navy man not to sing jazz, but to sing calypso, something that Belafonte knew nothing about. So, Jack took him to the New York Central Library where they researched calypso music from Trinidad and the Caribbean.

Shortly after, Harry recorded *The Banana Boat Song,* which became a huge hit. Harry was on his way to becoming a major star on TV and in films. With this success secured, he felt he no longer needed Jack, so he dumped him. The industry was shocked. Some were outraged at the ingratitude of Belafonte, but not Jack. He said he was pleased at Harry's success, that his talent deserved to be seen; with that talent, he would have succeeded even without him. Now, he said, he would continue to try to help others with talent.

I was always a fan of underdogs. And a hater of ingratitude. Just reading that, I was an instant fan of someone I did not know. So, I researched to see if he'd found any other talent. He had – and what talents. And to my joy, they were comics. One was Woody Allen. The other two were Mike Nichols and Elaine May. Woody's primary interest was in just being a writer, a comedy writer, and perhaps someday to make films. He hated doing standup. He told Jack it made him uncomfortable. Jack convinced Woody that the quickest way to becoming a filmmaker would be to become famous doing standup, something that Woody could write easily. This made him someone Jack could book on the multitude of variety shows at the time. So, Woody listened.

Mike Nichols and Elaine May came out of The Second City in Chicago. They were extremely cerebral, low key, and very, very funny. Because they mostly did situations and not jokes, most critics and club owners didn't understand them. Work was tough to get. So, they sought out Jack. Jack met them for lunch at The Russian Tea Room. During the meal he had them do a routine. Before dessert, they had a handshake. Here, for Nichols and May, is where luck plays an important part in one's life and career, often the most important part. In this case, it was Jack getting them booked on the Jack Paar show who kept bringing them back until they got laughs!

I love original talent and I loved the insights and talents of Jack Rollins. I was happy he became even more successful after Belafonte. It was probably too much for me to expect he would be interested in an ordinary comic like me, but I wouldn't know unless I tried. So, excited, I called him.

There was no secretary. He answered the phone himself with a gruff hello. He sounded like a New York bookie, which he could have been. I discovered later his hobby was showbiz; his real passion was horses and cigars. I introduced myself and the reason for wanting to meet him. He surprised me by knowing who I was, but had never seen me, saying quite accurately, "The smallest world is the world of comics." He grunted a low, short chuckle when I mentioned the failed album, *It's Tough to Be White*. "Send it to me and we'll meet."

"Thank you, sir. I'd be happy to have someone other than me and my wife listen to it." I waited for another chuckle, but it never came. "I hope you like it," I added.

"Even if I don't, we'll meet anyway. Send it today. When will you be in New York?"

"I'll come next week."

"You're coming in just to meet with me? You don't have a gig?"

"No gig. Just to talk to you."

"You're taking a chance. You might be disappointed."

"Mr. Rollins, it's not a chance. It's an opportunity meeting and learning something from you, even if it is a no. I can't be disappointed. Poorer in pocket, richer in mind."

"What could you learn from me?"

"How to sing Calypso!"

A chuckle. "Call me tomorrow around noon."

"But you won't have the album."

"Just call me." And he hung up.

As instructed, I called him. He answered on the first ring, and got right to the point. "A week from Wednesday at eight-thirty. You'll have about a ten-minute spot at The Bitter End. Meet me outside around eight. You know where it is?"

"I'll find it."

"And send the album."

A week from Wednesday he was where he said he'd be, standing in front of The Bitter End. He looked to be close to fifty, slightly grayish hair, a pumpkin face, large lips wrapped around a cigar, a brownish topcoat not unlike the one worn by Peter Falk in *Columbo*. His nod as I neared indicated he knew me. He had been chatting amiably with a tall, barrel-chested man who seemed to always chuckle when he talked. Jack introduced me.

"John, this is Fred Weintraub, the owner, who set this up for us."

"Can't wait to hear you," Fred said. "You did the *Talent Scouts* a couple of times?"

"Yes."

Jack and Fred continued their conversation, which I could barely hear, primarily because I was listening to what was going on in my own head. Before long, Fred said, "C'mon. Let's go inside. It's almost time."

Physically, the place was not impressive in the least. Just ten or fifteen feet inside the door we almost bumped into the small, but elevated wooden stage on which a folk singer was performing. It wasn't nearly as clean or as classy and as upscale as the 'i,' but its reputation was much higher. This was the pinnacle of the creative counterculture movement; to make it there, as the Sinatra lyrics go, was to make it anywhere. Knowing that made me nervous. My throat and lips were dry because I still hadn't worked out the material for my set. I had a bunch of it, but wasn't sure what to use. Jack sensed it immediately. How did he know?

"Come here." He pulled me off to the side.

"Look, I don't care what this audience thinks. They may love you, but I may not. They may hate you, but I may not. I just want to see you in front of people. And, I liked a lot of your album. A lot. Go ahead."

Fred lumbered onto the stage; at six-foot two or three he looked like a giant. The audience loved him. And he loved them. There was that ever-present giggle in the very nice introduction he gave me, saying I was a very bright new comic, a Canadian with a keen eye for America, and a sharp mind for comedy. I stepped up, smiling, took the mike from him, and scanned the audience. The brief thought I had of doing something from the album, even though Jack liked it, disappeared. I wanted to feel safe. I did the proven stuff from TV and clubs that always worked. I got a warm round of applause and left the stage, feeling I'd missed something, the sense of daring, the sense of something new. I felt ordinary, like I'd just done something routine; maybe that's why comics call it a routine.

Freddy patted me hard on the back. "Terrific!" But I was looking at Jack. After a moment, he said, "Why didn't you do the *Tough to Be White* stuff?"

"I had thought about it, but when I got up there, frankly I got scared. This crowd probably fancies themselves progressives, which maybe they are, but I had the weird feeling some would think maybe I sounded racist so I backed off."

I waited for the thanks for coming. Have a safe trip home, instead he said, "I like you. A lot. Even though I was hoping to hear the album. We'll talk about that in my office tomorrow. I'd be proud to manage you."

"Honestly? Really?"

He smiled, handing me his card. "Eleven o'clock tomorrow. The contract'll be ready."

I stared at the card all night after calling Sarita. "My God, honey. Jack Rollins. Jack Rollins. Woody Allen. Nichols and May. John Barbour. Jesus Christ, I can't believe it."

Jack's office was like his wardrobe, a little unkempt and mildly cluttered. Files and notes everywhere, along with a couple of racing forms. There were a couple of large stuffed chairs more suitable to a dining room than an office; they and the entire decor were a musty dark brown. He was at his desk when I walked in past a front desk with no secretary. He rose and greeted me warmly. He motioned me to the stuffed chair in front of his desk. I sat, but he stayed standing.

"You know," he started, almost dreamily, "you wait a long time to find what you believe could be a unique talent. That's the exciting part about what I do. Finding it, that's the hard part. Developing it, that's the easy part."

My stomach was beginning to sense something my heart did not want to hear.

"Young man, I think you are a unique talent because you are absolutely you. You are the closest thing I've seen to what could be this generation's Jack Paar." Hearing that made my heart leap.

He continued graciously. "I stayed up all night thinking about that. In a heartbeat, we could have you hosting a network talk show, but I have a conflict ... " He stopped for what seemed forever, then explained why. "The conflict is I represent a young man we're already grooming for a talk show, and it wouldn't be fair to either of you."

I looked at him when he paused. I knew my moment as a client was gone. He obviously liked me, though. I'd have to settle for that.

"His name is Dick Cavett. Know him?"

"I've seen him a couple of times. He used to write for Paar, didn't he?"

"Yes. All we have to do is get him a few more good exposures, and we'll have the networks begging him to do a talk show. Especially ABC. They're the most desperate. Those would be the same spots we'd have to groom you for, so you can see why the conflict, and why it'd be unfair to Dick since we had him before you."

I nodded.

"The truth is, I think you're better. You're softer. But I gave my word, and my allegiance is to Dick."

I stood. "That's all right, Mr. Rollins. It was a privilege to have met you, and an enormous compliment to me that you even spent this much time on me. Thank you." I extended my hand to shake his.

"Before you go, though, you should know that in two weeks you open at Mr. Kelly's in Chicago. You'll be Dionne Warwick's opening act."

"I'm doing what?"

"Just like I said. I called George Marienthal and told him about you and he said yes. Woody appeared there, and I think you'll do every bit as well. Or better."

I was in a fog when I thanked him. I didn't feel as bad as I thought I might. I knew he knew I was good enough. It didn't matter that no one else knew it. If I had not taken the chance of flying to New York, I would never be comforted by what he had said, and I would not be flying to Chicago.

Mister Kelly's And Ms. Warwick

What the Hungry i was to San Francisco, The Bitter End was to New York; Mister Kelly's was to Chicago, even more so than Second City. Shecky Greene, the most powerful, dominating, and funniest performer I'd ever seen on stage, told me Mister Kelly's was his very favorite club, even more so than any in Vegas where, for a few years, he became the town's highest paid entertainer.

I was exhilarated to be in Chicago, not just at Mister Kelly's, or opening for Dionne Warwick, one of the most famous singers in the country, but because it was where my second favorite American writer got his start as a cub reporter to later become the most famous columnist in the city, Ben Hecht. Hecht's autobiography, *A Child of The Century*, was the best ever about anyone in showbiz. I reread it a dozen times.

More than any city I could think of, Chicago's history could have been the history of America. It admired intellectuals with the same zeal it admired workers. And crooks. During the day, Sarita and I explored every part of it like kids in a human, concrete zoo. The newspapers were filled with the daily mayhem abounding in the city. The residents, though, found those corruptions and carnage more entertaining than threatening. Finding and writing a few minutes of opening material every night was easy. All I had to do was reference the news. As was the case in the headlines about a prominent citizen, do-gooder, and fire inspector who was arrested for shaking down shop owners for a hundred dollars a pop for a positive inspection. The mayor announced that henceforth, to cut down on that kind of corruption, the inspectors would go out in pairs. I said this prompted one shop owner to complain that the inspection would now cost him two hundred dollars.

The first three nights, I only saw Dionne on the small stage. When I wasn't watching her, Sarita and I spent all our time in the tiny, opening act dressing room next to George Marienthal's office, to the right of the bar. There were two ordinary metal chairs, a two-person sofa, and a dirty-white makeup table with a large mirror. All three nights one of the chairs was occupied by a nice, eager, short young man with dark hair, and a forced smile. He seldom spoke. Toward the end of the third night, I said, "Pardon me, but why are you here every night?"

"Mr. Marienthal's orders. My boss. He likes his performers to be happy and taken care of. In case you want company or something. That's my job."

"Well, you can see, Sarita and I don't need anything, so you don't have to be here. You can go."

"I can't. Mr. Marienthal's orders. I have to keep an eye on you, in case you need something."

"How about some privacy?"

"I can wait outside the door."

"Why aren't you in Dionne's dressing room?" I asked.

"Oh, there's a bodyguard there."

"What's your name?"

"Jeff Wald."

"Your job must be a pain in the ass. Who were some of your toughest assignments?" I asked. He hesitated, then said, "A few weeks ago Woody Allen was here. It was brutal." Then he stopped. "What was so brutal?" He looked around to make sure it was just the three of us. Then spoke almost in a whisper. "Every night, every single night, he'd send me out to find some young girl for him. Every single night. Hell, I can't even find them for me; how was I going to find them for him? If I didn't come back with one, he'd have a fit."

"Did your boss know what you had to do?"

"Yes. He told me to do what I was told; by him or Woody."

A few years later, Jeff's job was to manage his new young wife, singer Helen Reddy. She deservedly became a huge star. Jeff became a major manager with a huge coke habit which eventually ended their marriage and his career.

There was a knock on the door. Jeff, doing his job, rushed to open it. Standing in the doorway was the handsomest black man I'd ever seen. He looked to be in his mid-thirties, almost six-feet tall, slight wavy black hair, an appealing, open face and dentist-made smile. The suit was obviously very expensive, perfectly tailored.

"My name's Bill. I'm Dionne's husband. Sorry we haven't met sooner. Lots going on. John, Dionne really likes your show. She sent me to see if you and Sarita would like to join us for a bit in our dressing room after her set."

"We'd love to."

Dionne's dressing room was one that was befitting a star. It was spacious, sumptuous, very colorful, and stocked with food, beverage and flowers. This wasn't so much Mr. Marienthal's doings, as it was Dionne's.

Dionne was standing in the middle of the room talking to a short, middle-aged man in a dark suit. Bill mentioned it was her manager. She continued talking to him, or rather telling him something. When she finished, she turned to us. Her invitation was pleasant, but not what you'd call warm.

"Sit down. Are you hungry or thirsty? There's plenty here," she said, now smiling."Bill, pour them a drink."

"Oh, no thanks. We don't drink," I said.

"It's nice to meet you. Finally. I wanted to meet you sooner. Do you wanna know the truth of why I didn't meet you opening night? I wanted to see if you were any good. And you are."

"Thank you."

"Who's your manager?"

"I don't have one."

"You'd better get one. You're funny. Smart, too. I like you."

"Johnny, she doesn't like many people," Bill said.

Dionne continued, "Next month I'm going to be at Bimbo's in San Francisco. I'd like you to open for me."

"Really? I'm honored. Thank you. When Sarita was a dancer, she sometimes worked there. That's her home. That would be wonderful."

"Well, get a manager first. A good one. And keep after him."

"Dionne, in some cases, a manager can make a career, but are they really that important?" I asked.

"John," she said, "my father worked as a Pullman porter for over thirty years. Hard. I loved him. He said, 'Honey, don't you ever be a porter for anyone. You be your own engineer.' I'm still working at it. Nobody can pull your train but you, and my manager knows if he don't help drive this thing called Dionne Warwick, I will throw him out and run him over."

I was impressed with her. There was more to her than what was on stage.

The phone next to her rang. Bill picked it up and said hello; he listened for a moment then gasped, "Jesus" and handed the phone to Dionne.

As she listened, she seemed to shrink, started to tremble. She handed the phone back to Bill. "Oh, God, oh, God, oh, God."

Sarita and I didn't know what to do. We looked at Bill who was trying to put his arms around his wife. Dionne bowed her head and sobbed. "God, I can't believe it. I can't believe it. Otis. Our Otis. He's dead. I can't believe it. A goddamned plane crash. In Canada."

"I'm so sorry. We'd better go." Sarita and I rose to leave.

"No. No," Dionne said through her choking. "Please stay. Please." She was a little quieter, sniffling now more than crying. "Stay. Just a bit. I'll ... I'll be all right soon."

Sarita and I sat. The room was quiet for a long time until I said, "Tell us about Otis. How you met him. What he was like, and tell us more about your dad."

Dionne sat down close to us and said very graciously, "John, Sarita, thank you for being here." Dionne talked for an hour. Her life. Her family. Her father. Otis. Her career. Even a little about Bill. There were moments she was so vulnerable, you didn't just want to hug her, but love her. For the remainder of the gig, she had us in her dressing room after every show just to talk. A month later, Sarita and I were in San Francisco, where I'd be opening for her.

Sarita and I saved money staying with her parents. Every morning at six I'd walk over the wooden bridge to Harding Park Golf Course, rent clubs and play in the fog. I did it because I loved it, and loved even more being away from Sarita's mother. Every morning going out the door, I could hear her admonishing her daughter for allowing me to do this, with her father trying to defend us both. Her father had desperately wanted a son, but his wife, twenty years his junior, certainly capable of producing more progeny, announced loudly following the birth of the second daughter, even before they named her, "That's enough. Two's enough." The doctors and nurses thought Sarita's name was 'Enough.'

From the beginning, I told her if her mother were candy she'd be peanut brittle; if she were a plant, she'd be poison ivy. How did she get to be a parent, let alone a wife? I even questioned why the father stayed with her. I said, "If she were not your mother, just a person you knew, you'd never want to know her."

Sarita listened patiently, and one day said, "When my grandmother was dying, I was the only one who took care of her on her death bed. She said she didn't worry about any of her children. Just my mother. She told me to look after her after she died. She knew, I guess, what you sense."

I wanted the father to finally see me perform in person, but I was leery about inviting them to the opening. Having someone sitting ringside not liking me could be very unnerving. They came anyway. Uninvited. And sat at the very front table not ten feet from me. After a very nice intro, I walked to the mike. The father was applauding, but not her mother. Sarita couldn't applaud because she had her left hand firmly on her mother's arm as though to stop her from tossing something. For my twenty-minute set, I never looked at them. But I could hear her father. It wasn't quite laughter, but grunting sounds at the end of a joke, as though he'd been punched.

The loudest grunts came during my bit about a Southern drill sergeant that Jim Nabors loved, instructing his troops in Vietnam. I didn't know of one comic on TV or in a club who was doing material about the very controversial questionable war. During the four-minute bit, it got frequent applause, huge laughs, accompanied by loud nervous, paternal grunts.

When Dionne's set was done, Sarita's parents and she came to the dressing room. The father was shaking his head. "Wow, Johnny, I never heard a comic do tough stuff like that, but they loved it."

Sarita's mother said only, "Dionne was marvelous. We've gotta go. Don't be late." At the door, she turned to me, and muttered, "Very nice, I guess."

Sarita said, "That means you were terrific."

After the scores of well-wishers and friends left Dionne's dressing room, Bill invited us to join them.·

"John," Dionne said, "that new material was wonderful. It was so fresh. Good for you. Sarita, your husband has guts! John, in a few days my agent from the Morris office in New York is coming out here. I'd like you to meet him. It's not about representation, even though he might be interested. Next month I'm going to The Copa, and I'd like you to still come with me."

"Dionne, I don't know what to say other than thank you and yes."

As promised, the very young, dark-haired agent from the William Morris office did show up. He sat in front in the same seat as Sarita's mother. This did not strike me as a very good omen; it turned out it wasn't. God, do I have good instincts for disasters! Unfortunately, I don't pay attention to them often enough. The truth is, even if you can sense it, you cannot change the inevitable.

My set, as it did every night, went well. The couple of times I glanced fleetingly at the agent there was no smile. His head was cocked as though he were studying me. When it was over, again to enthusiastic applause, I went straight to the dressing room, not to the bar. We heard the thunderous applause and bravos for Dionne, and waited for Bill's invitation to join them. It never came. I suggested to Sarita that we go home.

"Don't be silly, John. Say goodnight at least."

We walked to Dionne's dressing room and knocked. Bill opened the door. There was no motion to enter.

"We just popped by to say goodnight. See you tomorrow,"

Dionne looked at us. "Oh, goodnight. Drive safe."

Darkman, the agent, nodded a quick goodnight.

For the remainder of the booking, there were no more invites and gabfests. I was bursting to know what date I was supposed to open in New York so I could book a flight and a room, but didn't know how to ask her. Or Bill. My stomach was killing me. The last day Bill finally relieved the pain in my head, but not in my stomach.

While Dionne was still on, and probably on her instructions, Bill came to our dressing room.

"John, I hate to tell you this, but Dionne is going with someone else to The Copa."

"Who?" I asked.

"I don't know. Never heard of him. Some New York comic, I guess."

"What happened?"

"Truthfully, I don't know. But it seems her rep from the Morris office thought you weren't New York. Not right for a place like the Copa. He talked her out of it."

"Did it take much talking?"

"Oh, she wanted you, but he convinced her that you weren't right for her ... or The Copa with that Vietnam stuff. Too controversial, but we'll see each other a lot. In LA. We've got a real nice place there, and you guys'll come often." It was obvious Bill was hurt being the bearer of bad news. His invitation to visit them at home was heartfelt.

"Bill, we're going to leave now. Tell Dionne I understand and absolutely loved working with and talking to her." We shook hands.

As promised, in the mid-seventies, we got to see Dionne and Bill often in their mansion. The invites, though, only came from Bill. Soon there was no need to go to their place because Bill was coming to ours. Often. Each time, he looked and sounded sadder and sadder. That perfectly smooth skin was starting to wrinkle. The body was thinner; there was darkness under those once bright eyes. He was not a womanizer; a lot of men married to famous women are. Not Bill. Each visit became more painful, for him and us. He said living with her and her demands of everyone, her agent, and especially of him, were becoming increasingly unbearable. He said he'd consulted an attorney about divorcing her, but changed his mind. Twice. Suicide had also crossed his mind.

During these confessionals, I never spoke to him. It was Sarita, the peaceful comforting soul he had come to see. She had a way of soaking in his troubles, and washing them away. Watching her spiritually embracing him was like watching a faith healer getting a cripple to walk. When he left, it was always with a smile. But a few weeks later he was back. On one of those occasions, the last one, actually, from out of nowhere, he said, "Johnny, remember when Dionne didn't take you to New York 'cuz the agent said you weren't New York? Well, the real reason was, the agent's not dumb; he saw the kind of reaction ya got. The kind of stuff ya did. New Yorkers would've loved you, for God's sake. Who was doing what you were doing? He told her she's the star. She loves to hear that shit. He thought you and your material might be a distraction, not that you weren't good enough."

"It doesn't matter, Bill. It was all terrific, and I'm doing okay."

"I'll say you are. And you've got Sarita, too! The truth is I am only staying with her because I love our two boys. Well, I gotta go. Thanks again."

Bill never saw them grow up. Three months later, at forty, he died of a heart attack; a broken-heart attack.

Merv, Murray and Management Three

With Jack Paar retired, for me there was no longer a TV 'must watch' talk show host or personality. Johnny Carson was puckish, pleasant, and often funny during his monologues. His rare attempt at trying to converse with literate, witty intellectuals like Gore Vidal and William F. Buckley, though, was a disaster. His avoidance of commenting at all on the murder of Bobby Kennedy the day after it happened was pathetic cowardice. His later clumsy attempt to discredit New Orleans DA Jim Garrison was even more pathetic. My interest in Garrison was not keen at all at the time. I just loved talk shows. But no longer Johnny's. After that embarrassment with Garrison, nearly everyone on the couch came from showbiz. When they were comics, I watched.

The one I found myself turning to more and more though was Merv Griffin. Merv's was not an upscale network show like Carson's. It was a blue collar syndicated show for Westinghouse; it came on early evening in

Los Angeles. He was incapable of doing a monologue, didn't look nearly as sharp in a suit, sang fairly well, and, fortunately, not too often, but he was comfortable with himself and with some really unusual guests, not necessarily in showbiz, but the kind of outspoken, verbal guests Paar would frequently have on.

The other thing that Merv did, more so than Johnny, was have on new performers. I imagined myself being one of those performers. Of course, without an agent or manager, I didn't know how to go about it. I was afraid to send my appearance on the *Talent Scouts* for fear of losing it, never certain they'd even look at it. My first appearance was the result of yet another lucky accident.

A major national election was about a year away and the Democratic Party was in Los Angeles for another of their never-ending fundraisers. This new kind of fundraiser was to be held at The Palace Theater on Vine Street. It was to be a telethon. The head writer for the myriad famous politicians, power brokers and stars who would appear was Hal Kanter. He, next to Mort Lachman and Redd Foxx, became my biggest mentor. His wife and two daughters treated me as family. Hal's father, a southerner, had created the successful Classic Comics. Hal said his father realized that Americans would be more inclined to read Shakespeare, Dickens, Twain and Dostoyevsky, if they were in comic book form.

At the family gatherings of the famous I never spoke up. I didn't feel I'd earned the right to amongst those moguls, movers and shakers. The one person I did try to speak to briefly, because I couldn't stop myself, was Albert Maltz. He was introduced to me by Mahalia Jackson. I stared at him in disbelief. This was the blacklisted author whose book, *A Long Day in A Short Life,* I'd tried to turn into a screenplay for Haskell Wexler. All I could say was, "I love your writing." I didn't want to say more because if it brought back bad memories for me, it'd bring back worse for Albert.

Hal came over to my corner and sat down. He told me about the upcoming telethon. "How'd you like to do a spot?"

I was stunned. "Hal, what could I do? I'm not a Bob Hope or Carson. They don't even know me."

"I think you'd do terrific."

"Hal, that's the big leagues. The majors. I wouldn't know what to say to them."

"You could say whatever you want. Whatever suits the occasion. You'd certainly have a lot of stuff to work with."

"Could I think about it for a day or two?"

"Certainly, but I'd love to have you. I think you'd do well."

With Hal at my back, I almost instantly came up with something different from just one-liners. I called Hal the next morning. "Hal, thank you. I'd love to do it."

"Wonderful," he said. "We'll see you this weekend at the Palace. Around five-thirty."

"Is there a rehearsal?"

"No. Just some simple blocking. You won't have to worry about that."

"Don't you want to hear what I'm gonna do?"

"Absolutely."

"When?"

"When you do it. If you bomb, I'll tell them we'd just found out you were a Republican. See you then."

No appearance ever made me more frightened than this one. If I bombed in front of Hollywood and American Leaders, the Establishment, the Press, I'd be finished. It's comic harakiri! A couple of recognizable newsmakers, including John Lindsay, the towering good-looking, mayor of New York, came by to thank me and wish me well. The telethon was going well. The Palace was packed and receptive. About thirty minutes in, it was my turn. Hal motioned me forward to the wings while he walked to the microphone.

"Ladies and gentlemen, and those of you who are undecided, this young man is a very close Hollywood friend of mine...until after the show. (Chuckles.) He's not very famous, but I assure you, in a few years, you will all know... John Barbour!" Hal exited.

The band played *When Johnny comes Marching Home*. I thanked the audience, and told them with the elections coming up, the thing all politicians had to do was concentrate on selling themselves. Since this was difficult for a lot of them to do, they needed someone else to sell them: a salesman who could lie. (Loud laughter.) Especially the Republicans. (Applause.) In this town the best salesman is Cal Worthington, and his dog Spot. (They laughed and applauded again.) What I envision is Cal Worthington selling the five leading Republican candidates as used cars, (Chuckles.) which befits their used ideas. (More applause.) Here's how it would sound: Then, doing the best cowboy accent I could, which really wasn't that good, I did each one of their candidates, describing him like a used car. The audience absolutely loved it. When I got to the last one, I could hardly get through for the screams.

"And, finally, folks, here's the George Wallace white Mustang convertible. It only comes in white. White rims, White bumpers. White steerin' wheel, white exhaust, white wall tires. Not one black one!" (Some were standing and cheering.) And a white top that pulls down over your head ... with two eye holes!" Then during thunderous applause and laughter, I just walked off without even a thank you. I didn't want to break the mood. Everyone mobbed me backstage; even Jerry Brown, who'd stopped talking about himself for a moment and his plan to become the youngest Governor of California. Hal smiled. The whole evening was worth that smile.

At Hal's house a week later, he introduced me to a very popular and successful production executive, Marian Hooper. She'd worked on a number of shows in town. Everyone knew her. She was in her late thirties, energetic, with a quiet husband because she did all the talking.

"I saw you on *The Talent Scouts,*" she said. "It'd be terrific if you could've done on national TV what you did at The Palace last week."

"I don't know if I could get away with doing that" I said.

"You might on Merv's show," she answered.

"Maybe, but I don't know how to go about trying to do his show. I don't have an agent or manager."

"I may know someone at Merv's show. Would you like me to call them? Better still," she said, becoming more enthusiastic, "get me a copy of *Talent Scouts* and I'll send it to him."

"I only have the one copy."

"Well, make a couple more, and give me one."

"Who do you know there?

"Their accountant."

I looked at her quizzically, wondering how an accountant could book me on Merv's show.

"Believe me, honey," she said, "in this business you'll find they listen to their accountants more than their producers."

I did as she instructed; she sent off a copy to a fellow named Jim Geishheimer, the show's accountant. (I was bemused by the thought that an accountant might be helping, and not hurting me.)

Three weeks later, Marian called. "Write this down. His name is Bob Murphy. He's the producer. This is his number. Call him right away. He wants you on next week."

Merv's was a show and he the kind of person I felt I would be comfortable with. The cost of the airfare and hotel versus my modest upcoming paycheck meant I'd be losing money, but what I was about to experience and learn was priceless.

There was absolutely nothing elegant or upscale or even showbiz about the theater from which Merv did his show, beginning with the sidewalk and entrance where we had to step over sleeping derelicts. The entrance leading to the elevator was drab and grey. The elevator was right out of the twenties or thirties. The door was a sliding metal collapsible contraption that had to be slid in just a certain way. You felt like you were in a cage. If it hadn't been so small, it would have been a noisy freight elevator. Yet, I felt much more confident in those surroundings than I ever did around plush and elegance. That stuff always intimidated me because it all looked so pretentious. That place looked unpretentious. Happily, so was the staff.

The first to greet us was a slightly overweight middle-aged, spunky, loud woman with a gray head of hair covered by an elegant, floppy wide-brimmed black hat that looked like a too-large pizza. For the couple of years I did the show, I never saw her without it. I liked her immediately.

"Aw, finally a comic with a brain. Follow me." Sarita and I followed her. "Bobby," she announced, "here's that comic that's gonna make you look smart."

Bob Murphy said, "I see you've met our mad hatter. Thanks for coming. We loved your film. You'll do real well."

Bob made us feel even more at ease and at home answering all my questions about how he got this job and met Merv in San Francisco years earlier.

Merv's introduction was gracious and warm. Mort Lindsey's orchestra played a rousing short piece as I walked from behind the curtain to the mike stand at the front of a surprisingly small stage. (Everything looks larger on TV.) My set was almost the same as *The Talent Scouts*. Merv and his audience liked it as much as Linkletter's did. I was immediately booked for a second appearance the following month. Bob told me I would be on a show with a forty-one-year-old aluminum siding salesman who had tried stand-up for a few years, failed, went back to selling siding, and was trying to make a comeback. His name was Rodney Dangerfield.

When we got home, there were two things I had to do immediately. First was to develop material for my next appearance. Second, no matter how often I did Merv's show, the modest fees would never pay our rent. I had to find a steady gig where I could both perform and work out material. Three days after making the rounds of every possible club in LA, without luck, the phone rang. It was Murray Schwartz from the William Morris office in New York. He said, "I would like to represent you. I think you can go far in this business. Next month, before you do Merv again, why don't you come in a day early? I'll have you over to the apartment for dinner, and we'll get acquainted. You can make up your mind then. Sound okay?"

"Yes, thank you." I stammered. Wow, what a business. First the Morris Agency didn't want me at The Copa, then they wanted me as a client! I called Chris Haywards to hear if he'd ever heard of a Murray Schwartz at the Morris Agency. "There's a Murray Schwartz at every agency," he laughed. "I'll call you back." Within five minutes, he did. "Maybe you've hit the jackpot," he said. "The Morris Murray Schwartz is Merv's personal rep."

There were only a few clubs in Los Angeles that used a regular comic; they were strip clubs. I didn't, and couldn't, do that. The coffee houses like the Troubadour and The Ice House only booked for a week. The only place I could think of was a few doors up from The Slate Brothers Jazz Club on La Cienega. It was called The Losers. It was a topless club. Sarita and I had walked past it a few times after going to the Slate Brothers to see Redd Foxx or Mort Sahl. From the outside, it looked classy. On a hunch, and desperate, I asked Sarita if she'd mind going to The Losers one night. So we went.

The most astonishing thing about the place was the customers. There wasn't one man or woman who wasn't dressed as though they weren't going to Ciro's or The Biltmore. Surprisingly, there were almost no unaccompanied men in the place. They were all couples.

When the show was over, recorded music was piped in to cover the girls' twenty-minute break. I approached a tall slender fellow in a sharp dark brown suit who I noticed had been standing to the side, observing everything. Only the maître de could have that look. I introduced myself. He said his name was Pete. I then suggested that instead of having music piped in, did he think the owner would consider having a comic do a set during the break.

"I am the owner," Pete said, without smiling.

"Oh…oh…I'm sorry. You looked too young. I thought you were the maître de!"

"I thought you were a customer!" Again, that straight face.

I felt I was making a mistake. "That's funny. I'm sorry." I wanted to leave, but I blurted out, "I'm funny, too!"

"Where?" he retorted, the expression of grimness unchanged.

"On TV." I couldn't stop myself. I told him I was going back to do Merv's show and needed a place to develop material. More than that, I needed a job. How pathetic I thought I sounded.

"Come in tomorrow. At 7:30. Let's see what happens."

Sarita and I rushed out before he could change his mind. I never shook his hand. The following evening, I was there well before 7:30. Pete, not quite as grim, greeted me. The place was already filled with beautiful people. As I watched the audience watching those gorgeous topless dancers, one after the other seemingly more seductive, I thought this was gonna be tougher than being in Watts. Then the break came. Pete looked at me and gave me a "you're on" nod.

The room was awkwardly quiet. One of the musicians stepped forward, placed a mike stand in the middle of the stage and introduced me, surprisingly well. The applause was surprisingly full. All kinds of ad lib opening comments popped into my head. The strongest one made me uncomfortable. I do not do salacious material, but I could not stop it. "Thank you, Ladies and Gentlemen. The girls will be back in a few minutes, right after they shave."

They howled and applauded. That was as raunchy as I got. The rest of the clean topical set was easy. The audience looked pleased and surprised at hearing something here they did not expect. I was just as surprised.

When I walked off, Pete motioned me outside to the street."Very nice," he said, "but you pissed off a few of the girls."

"I'm sorry, Pete. Stuff like that sometimes just pops out of me."

He smiled for the first time. "It made me laugh. It might be a nice change. I'll give you three hundred a week and you're free to do any material you want."

So began my unexpected almost year-long gig at The Losers, for which I still have immensely fond memories. A couple of those memories are as fresh as when they happened.

The first of these is when I apologized to the dancers about my opening line. When I knocked on their door to tell them why I was there, they invited me in. Unembarrassed and actually at ease, half of them were naked, and a few were washing their crotches in the sink, and continued to do so while I attempted to not look. They laughed at me almost as much as the audience did. Their invitation to come back anytime went unanswered.

Another was the first appearance, and second appearance of Buddy Hackett sitting just a few feet from me in the front row. Buddy was a rotund, fat-faced comedian who was a major star, and hilarious. He gained fame on TV with his first routine called 'The Chinese Waiter' in which he placed a rubber band over his head and eyes so they'd appear slanted, then in a Chinese accent tried to take someone's order; a routine he could not get away with doing in today's politically correct climate. After the set he motioned me to his table.

"You're very good. You remind me a lot of Paar. Do you wanna be a comedian?"

I was perplexed by the question. Wasn't it obvious? Otherwise, what was I doing there? I said, "I don't quite follow."

"Think about it. If you have to be a comedian, nothing can stop you. If you just wanna be a comedian, you probably won't make it!" He stood up, letting it sink in. "I'll be back again," he said, and left.

For weeks I looked for this giant to return, but he didn't. Then one evening, for the second show, I noticed him again in the front row, this time accompanied by a couple of guys in shiny suits. Since it was the second show, I did different material.

When it was over, Buddy motioned me over, this time with a displeased look on his face. "What the fuck are you doing?"

"What do you mean?"

"What was with that stuff?" he said with an edge.

"I have to do two sets, so I have to do new stuff."

"Well, don't. I brought my buddies back because I loved the car and airline bits you do and you didn't do them. Look, when I go to hear Tony Bennett, I want to hear *I Left My Heart In San Francisco*, not some new shit!"

I tried to defend myself. "But it's a second set with some of the same people here."

"Fuck 'em. If you wanna be a star, just perfect eighteen minutes that are yours. That always works; and do nothing but that. Every successful comic on TV, including me, all had just eighteen good minutes. Some of us had only one routine. Do you understand?"

"I think so."

"Good. Then do it and fuck 'em! Keep it up, and we'll meet again."

We did meet again. A few years later I went to see him at the Desert Inn in Las Vegas. I didn't notify him I was there. I certainly wasn't one of his buddies. I was five rows from the stage. He spotted me, and stopped the show. He told the audience about this new comic that was in the front, then told me to come up. The audience also encouraged me. I did the airline routine he liked. It was a smash. I was to repeat it a few weeks later on Merv's show, and again a year after that on Dean Martin's.

Pete Rooney was the best boss I ever had. He had no interest in show business. Just business. Aside from the most popular classiest club of its kind in the city, he owned one of the best steak houses, Sneaky Pete's, on the Sunset Strip where we ate frequently as his guest. He seldom spoke, and when he did, always softly. Like Brando in *The Godfather*, listeners knew this young man was the boss. I pried every bit of information out of him I could over time. Unmarried. Born in the slums of Detroit. Friends of nearly every member of the infamous Purple Gang. Some of those friends came often to the club. Like I would ask Mickey Cohen on live TV a few years later if he ever killed anyone, I asked Pete if he was with the hoods.

He smiled. "No. Once you're in, you can't get out. I prefer out."

He never once questioned my material, even when it was sometimes questionable. You often hear people say, "I'll defend your freedom of speech." One night, he actually did.

Watts had almost broken out in another riot. A black man was shot and killed by an LAPD cop named Leonard Deadwiler after running red lights to get his pregnant wife to the hospital. I did a Bob Newhart-type routine where the Chief of Police is on the phone admonishing the guilty cop. It got a lot of nervous laughter, with a huge one at the last line, along with applause. Chief: "Deadwiler, how many times do we have to tell you the warning is: Stop or I'll shoot. Not stop AND I'll shoot!"

Two very large men in suits stood and hissed, calling me an asshole. Pete moved quickly from behind the bar. He was not their size, but he put his hand on the guy's arm. "You can leave now, please," he said.

"Fuck you!" one guy said, pulling Pete's arm away.

"We'll let you do that outside." Pete looked up at me. All this was not ten feet from me. "Finish your stuff."

The three vanished through the front door. I tried to continue as best I could. "I … I could have gotten those guys outside a lot faster than my boss could." They giggled at this improbability. "You know how? I'd have kicked them in the balls and run like hell out to the street." When I finished my routine, Pete had not returned. So, I went outside.

Nobody was in front. I could hear muttering from the alley. I turned to my left, looking down the side of the building. The guy who had mouthed off was doubled over leaning against the wall. The other had his hands up, protecting himself from Pete who was wielding a baseball bat. He spoke as quietly as he would to one of the girls. "Do you wanna fuck me again?" They left. Pete walked casually over to me. "Are you okay?"

"Whatta yah mean me?"

"How'd yah do?"

"Uh … like you. Almost killed them."

It was the loudest warmest laugh I'd ever heard from him. Nobody ever fought for me that hard. Except Sarita.

Murray Schwartz's apartment about twelve floors up in a posh apartment complex, complete with door man, was New York elegant, as was Murray's wife. She was five-feet-six, the same size as Sarita; like Sarita, a striking brunette, with a Mediterranean look. They bonded quickly.

Murray was open-faced and peaceful. He never gave any hint of his success with Merv or his sudden rise to prominence at the William Morris Agency. I loved his stories. My two favorites I retell fondly here: one about famed Italian pop singer, Katerina Valenti; the other about how Murray became Merv's agent.

A few years earlier Murray was just the lowly assistant to the second in charge of the Morris Office. Murray's boss's name escapes me, but not the name of his boss's boss. Everyone knew it. Frank Costello, New York's leading crime boss. Murray's boss had one special phone on his desk solely for Frank Costello. Murray said it was never used for an outgoing call. Always answered on the first ring by his boss. One day, after answering it, Murray said all he heard his boss say was, "Yes, yes, yes." a few times, then hung up shaking, and turning to Murray.

"Jesus Christ, you know what he wants me to do? He wants me to go to the Copa and talk to Katerina."

"About what?"

"Apparently, Jules is pissed at her." (Jules Podell was the mob connected owner of the city's most famous niterie.)

"Why?

"She's Italian. From Italy. Old country. The women still don't shave."

"Don't shave? Where?"

"Under their arms. She's rehearsing now for the opening tonight wearing this blouse she's gonna wear and all that hair is hangin' out. Mr. C ordered me to go down there and tell her to shave. Jesus Christ."

"Oh, My God," Murray exclaimed. "How do you do that?"

"I don't. You do."

"I can't do that. She doesn't even know me.'

"She will by the time you get there."

"But ... but ... I ... can't say something like that to a woman."

"If not, you'll see how easily my next assistant can say it!"

An hour later Murray was in Podell's office, scared jobless. He told Podell he thought telling a woman, especially a woman of Katerina's stature to shave, was an insult. In a voice that sounded as though he'd had his throat cut like comedian Joe E. Lewis, Podell croaked out, "Her fuckin' arm hair hangin' down, kid, is an insult to my customers. Now get in there an' tell that bitch to shave, an don't come out tills yah do. And she does!"

When Murray was greeted graciously by this beautiful superstar, and invited warmly into her lush dressing room, he started to sweat.

"Whatta you do ahere, young man?" she asked.

When he finally opened his mouth, all that came out was, "I just wanted to meet you. I am a big fan."

"That'sa sweet. Grazi."

Murray just stared at her. With lock jaw. Then left quickly to tell M. Podell he just could not do it. Podell exploded.

"You cowardly little piece of shit. You'll be outa the Morris office and outa this business in five fucking minutes. You useless ball-less little shit. I'll do it my fuckin' self."

He stormed out of his office straight to Katerina's dressing room, pushing the door open without knocking. Murray followed a safe ten steps behind. Jules Podell had a reputation as a very tough made man. Murray stayed safely outside, just peering in. Katerina was in no way disturbed by Podell barging in on her. Being beautiful and Italian she was probably used to it.

She rushed to Podell, hugging him and kissing his cheek.

"Oh a Mr. Podell. Hallo. Hallo. I lovea your place. Thank you again so much for have me."

Murray waited for Podell's instructions, to see how he would inform her of what he wanted. Nothing came. Murray saw Podell's jaw tighten, the vessels in his neck bulge.

"Oh My God," Murray thought. "He's gonna erupt." Finally, Podell opened his mouth, first waving his hand at her. "Tonight," he croaked. "Tonight, Katarina, I'd like you to wear a sweater."

Katerina's head tilted, like she was hearing something weird. Quickly Podell added, "I just bought the most beautiful Italian silk sweater for you."

Katerina hugged him again. "Oh, Mr. Podella. Anything for my bossa! Grazi. Grazi."

Podell quickly closed the door behind him, grabbed Murray by the arm, saying, "Get your cowardly fucking ass to Gimbels and get me a fucking sweater!"

Murray did. And Katerina wore it.

The other story, more interesting to me, though, was how Murray came to be chosen by Merv to become his sole agent. Murray was reluctant to brag about it, trying to just brush it off as luck, but his wife, truly proud of her quiet husband, helped tell it with him. They were like two happy kids.

After Merv lost his NBC morning show, the Morris office lost interest in him. The agency top dogs weren't convinced he had the personality or the ratings to have a future in television. Murray was just a minor assistant. He liked Merv. He also knew millions of middle-aged women in America liked Merv. On his own he called Merv and asked Merv how he would feel about working dinner theaters in the Midwest. Merv said it was better than not working in New York, and paid better than unemployment. On his own again, Murray booked Merv for a month of Midwest dinner theaters. Almost every show was sold out, every review a rave. New York and showbiz were again abuzz about the good press Merv was getting, thanks to well-planted stories by Murray.

Merv's contract with the Morris office was up for renewal. Management thoughts of terminating it were terminated by the sudden renewed interest in him. They hastily called a meeting of top level agents. In their best conference room at their best twenty-five-foot cherrywood conference table sat the agency's top dirty dozen suits. Six on each side. At the most important end sat Abe Lastfogel, the owner; at the other end, Merv. They all waited for Lastfogel to speak. But he did not speak long.

"Merv," Abe started, "you have definitely proved yourself a major talent and a–"

"Where's Murray?" Merv interrupted.

Everything got still. No one questioned Abe Lastfogel. "Where's Murray?" Merv repeated.

Lastfogel turned to his next in line. "Who's Murray?"

"He's my assistant. And–"

"Well, why isn't he here?" Lastfogel asked angrily.

"I'll get 'im."

Murray got the quick call to get up to the main conference room immediately. He had no idea why or what to expect. When he opened the door, he was cheered.

"There you are Murray," Lastfogel shouted. "Come on in." As he did, they applauded.

Merv got up and shook Murray's hand. Then, standing next to Murray, not taking a seat, he turned to the suits and said, "Gentlemen, this is the man responsible for this meeting." They stared back, bewildered. Merv continued. "On his own he booked me into those dinner theaters, which I loved by the way, and he got not a nickel's worth of commission. That went to you all. I want to more than give thanks to Murray. I want to give him my commissions. I would be happy to re-sign with your agency. After all, I know you all. but I will only sign if Murray is my sole agent, and with a few exceptions, I am his sole client."

The seated suits looked at Lastfogel, who rose, walking to Murray, extending his hand. "Young man, how does that sound to you."

Murray was stunned, but pleased. The room was filled with more cheers and applause.

Within weeks, Murray negotiated a talk-show deal for Merv at Westinghouse, which became the foundation for Merv's media empire of game shows, eventually bought by Coca Cola for one billion dollars.

Hearing this heartening showbiz story from this gracious young couple made me like Murray and Merv more. Murray deserved it. I was happy for him and his family with so much money for them to enjoy. A few years later, though, it was no more 'them.' It was just him. A few months after that wonderful evening, Murray committed his wife to an insane asylum.

Money changes people. A lot of money changes them a lot. Merv eventually forgot he owed much of his good fortune to Murray. He neglected to pay Murray a cent after the Coca Cola deal closed. Reluctantly, Murray, now living in Encino, hired a tough, successful showbiz lawsuit lawyer, Richard Ferko, to take on Merv. Richard got Murray his twelve-million-dollar commission, plus interest. (In a few years I would also have to hire Richard.)

Shortly after our delicious home-cooked dinner in his apartment, he signed me as a client and I became a regular on the Merv Griffin show. Before my second appearance, Merv pulled me aside.

"John, there's somebody I want you to meet or rather somebody who wants to meet you." Merv was guiding a very attractive woman in her mid-thirties toward me. "This is my wife. She came here just to meet you."

She clasped my hand tightly. "I'm very pleased to meet you. I like what you do!"

"Thank you, but maybe you should have waited till after my second set."

Merv laughed. "She's never wrong. She's the one who gave me the idea for *Jeopardy*."

During a commercial break, I asked Merv how much longer he thought he'd be doing the show. "You'd like my seat, would you?"

"Oh God! I'm just daydreaming out loud. With the hundreds of great talents I've seen in the movies and on TV, there are only two I'd like to be. You and Jack Paar."

"You'll get there. Just keep going. And keep coming here."

Mercifully, he broke the mood following the break by introducing a man who hadn't worked for five years, a comic making a comeback: Rodney Dangerfield. From behind the curtain shuffled this six-foot-two walking couch potato in an ill-fitting dark suit and loose tie. When he spoke, he constantly tugged at his tie, as though it was choking him. His hair was slightly wavy with touches of grey. His face was puffy and his eyes looked like they were trying to escape from their sockets. But what wonderful material. He had me from the first line: "I've been selling aluminum siding for five years. Five years ago, I retired from doin' comedy. I came back tonight 'cuz I'm the only one who knows I retired." I howled. God, did I know that feeling.

Then he went on to do line after line about getting no respect. Not even from his mother. "My mother told me as a kid never to take candy from a stranger, unless they offer me a ride."

When the show was over, I hurried backstage to tell him how well he'd done, that the world would be glad he came out of retirement.

He said thanks without slowing down on his way to the elevator. "I'd love to talk, but I gotta go to work."

"Selling siding at night?"

"I'm heading down to a comedy club near here. Ya wanna come? We can talk later."

"Sure." I followed him into the elevator, then into a cab, and a dozen blocks away, into this small, dark comedy club.

"Grab a seat and drink, and I'll see ya in about an hour." He left me sitting in the back. For a weekday night it was surprisingly full. When Rodney took the stage and the mike, I could see why. I could also see this was not the performer who was just on *The Merv Griffin Show* an hour earlier. He didn't just own the stage and audience, he dominated it. He was not this awkward, shuffling apologist for living that got no respect. He was Lenny Bruce and Shecky Greene and Don Rickles. The audience loved him. So, did I. I thought, this is a guy who should be doing a one-man show on Broadway. Or at Carnegie Hall. This I'd pay to see. It'd have to be a one-man show because nobody could follow him. It was evident, by some of the poor souls who tried to after he introduced them, the audience wanted only Rodney.

The show over, a mob of well-wishers rushed to encircle him. I decided to leave.

"Hey, kid, where ya goin? Come 'ere!" Rodney led me to his small, cluttered dressing room. "Well, whadda ya think?"

"Rodney, I'm just glad I get to work out my stuff at a topless club. Not here. I could not follow you. Those guys had a tough time."

"It's a tough business."

I proceeded to tell him that while I really liked the set he did on Merv's show, I loved his persona on stage and how he had somehow morphed into this prowling, howling powerhouse of righteous, funny, angry mix of Shecky Greene, Lenny Bruce, and Don Rickles. No question to me he could be bigger than all of them doing concerts and universities. I told him so, and added, "At this club, you are Superman; on Merv's show, Clark Kent."

He laughed. "Kid, I work out my anger and frustrations here, but let me tell you something. A performer should never appear superior to the audience. They'd resent you. The audience must always feel superior to the performer. That's why so many Jews were successful comedians. No matter how famous they are, audiences always feel superior to a Jew. I know I'm smarter than those idiots sitting out there, but I don't want them to know it or even sense it. So, from here on in, it's I get no respect. Those guys you mentioned don't do movies. I'm gonna. Don't forget that, kid."

I didn't.

I was making my third appearance on Merv. Murray was next to me on that 1920's elevator creaking its way to the second floor. He said, "There's a new company. Three agents just started it, and they're interested in you. They called me the other day. They're real hustlers. And Howard West of our West Coast office is going to be pitching you to Greg Garrison, the producer of *The Dean Martin Show*."

Before long, Murray was picking me up in a cab. We drove a few blocks to one of the numerous ordinary brick office buildings that surround Manhattan. The offices of Management 3, on a middle floor, were just as ordinary. Stenciled on the door were the names of this management trio: Marty Kummer, Jerry Weintraub, Bernie Brillstein. There was a small sparsely furnished waiting room with no plaques or trophies or even showbiz pictures on the wall, and three small, equally undecorated offices, one for each of the partners.

Murray opened the door; two of the trio were standing there to greet us. "Johnny, c'mon in. I'm Jerry Weintraub, and this is Bernie, one of my partners. Marty couldn't make it. But we're glad you could. We like your stuff. And your style." Jerry had a constant smile, and spoke faster than anyone I'd ever heard. Bernie, on the other hand, was very quiet, with a nice warm demeanor and voice. When he did speak it was to you, and not at you like his partner. They both looked to be in their mid-thirties.

"Grab a seat and let's talk." Jerry picked out where each should sit, then blurted, "Has Merv made a pass at you yet?" And laughed.

I looked at Murray, then to Jerry. "What?"

"Has Merv made a pass at you yet?"

I was stunned. "No, why should he?"

"You're kidding. He's fruitier than an apple orchid."

"He's married," I said.

"She's his beard."

"His what?"

"Beard. How long you been in this business. Since Tuesday?" He laughed again.

I kept glancing at Murray, who was shaking his head and smiling. ' "He's been awfully nice to me."

"Well, he should be. You're good. As good as he's had on in a while. That's why we'd like to represent you."

I said, "Do you mind if I ask a few questions?"

"Anything you want. Shoot!" Jerry said.

"The only manager I ever sought out was Jack Rollins."

"You got good taste," Jerry said.

"I sought him out because he knew what to do with Belafonte, Woody and Nichols and May, and probably what he'll do with Cavett, which is why he passed on me. So I'm not sure what a manager can do for me, and I don't know the kind of clients you represent."

"Perfect question," Jerry said. "We're just starting. We were all agents, but wanted to get more involved with the talent. Real talent. My main talent right now is Jane Morgan."

"The singer? She's good," I said,

"Damn right she is! She's my wife, too."

"We also represent Norm Crosby. Norm is the one that does all those malaprops."

"He is funny, but that's not the kind of stuff I do."

"That's why there'd be no conflict here," Jerry said.

"What about Marty, your other partner?" I asked.

They burst out laughing, like I'd sparked some inside joke. Jerry looked at Murray. "You tell him."

Murray was reluctant to, but he began. "There's kind of an inside industry joke that you never give Marty a choice between two things, because he'll always pick the worst. When he was at MCA, Lew Wasserman, who liked him, gave him a choice of heading up the new TV division or the big band division. Marty chose big bands."

"Well," I said, "he wouldn't be your partner, if he didn't have something to offer."

Bernie said, "That's right. For years he was Jack Paar's manager."

I lit up immediately. "Who does he manage now? Anybody like me?"

"Naw. He had Wayne and Shuster for a while."

Johnny Wayne and Frank Shuster I'd seen growing up in Toronto. They were Canada's top comedians and appeared on Ed Sullivan probably more than any act ever. "He doesn't have them anymore?" I asked.

Bernie began, "Wayne and Shuster were a huge hit on Sullivan; Universal was looking for a comedy team. Everybody was looking for a comedy team ever since Martin and Lewis. So, they called Marty. Marty made a good deal for them for a thirteen-week series. So, Marty, really pleased, called the boys and told them. Frank, who was always sort of the spokesperson for them, said no, they didn't want it. They were perfectly happy doing what they were doing with the CBC. Disappointed, Marty calls Universal, and tells them the boys pass."

Two days later, Universal calls back and says besides the thirteen-week guarantee for TV, they'll also guarantee a movie at a substantial fee. Marty's elated. He calls Frank and tells him the good news. Frank says he and Johnny are happy in Toronto and don't want to take that much time away from the CBC shows or their families. Marty can't believe it. He calls back Universal again, and tells them not to call back, that the boys are just flat out not interested. They're happy where they are.

Well, two days later, Universal *does* call back. They have upped the offer to a twenty-six-week TV guarantee and a two-movie guarantee. It's colossal! Marty's so excited, he can't believe it. They'll make a fortune. So will he. He calls Frank immediately and tells him the unbelievable windfall deal that Universal is offering. Frank doesn't even pause. He says that he and Johnny have kids in school in Toronto, all their family members and friends are there, and they're really happy with their coast to coast show even if it's just in Canada. Marty leaps up from his seat and screams into the phone, "Goddamn it, Frank, there's more to life than fucking happiness!" He doesn't represent them anymore.

"Johnny," Jerry said, "Bernie and I would like to represent you. We'd work night and day for you. At least I will. I've got insomnia. I never sleep. Can't sleep. So you'll be on my mind twenty-four hours. I promise. You have a huge future in this business."

Bernie said, "It'd be an honor to manage you. Jerry's right. You're perfect."

"Okay," I said. "Let's give it a try."

Jerry stood, shaking my hand. "The first thing we're gonna do is put you in The Sahara Tahoe with Jane."

So, with that wonderful job waiting, I signed with Management 3, or at least two of them.

There are few places in America more beautiful than Lake Tahoe, and for me, there was no place more beautiful to perform than the Sahara Tahoe. This was the place years earlier where I'd seen Sinatra strolling into the casino, his topcoat draped over his shoulders, with Sam Giancana, and three men in dark suits and fedoras. And now I was working there. With Jane Morgan. Amazing. America is just amazing. So is life.

Jane was a really nice lady, and terrific singer. Her big hit was, *Fascination*. Bernie said when Jerry started to make money he built a house in Palm Springs, where he designed her toilet seat to play that song every time it was raised.

On opening night, Jerry, the club's personable booker, Sarita between them, and Patty Andrews of The Andrew Sisters next to Jerry, sat in the last, middle cushioned booth in the center of the room. It gave them a perfect, unobstructed view.

Jerry motioned me over. "Patty wants to meet you."

Patty grabbed my hand. This was the lead vocalist in that wonderful trio of sisters that sang us, and America, through World War II films. I felt like I was six again, sitting in the Manor theater.

"Good luck, Johnny. I love you on Merv. You'll do terrific."

Then Jerry said, "You're gonna do eighteen minutes. At about seventeen minutes, a red light'll come on. That's your cue to wrap. And don't go a second over." I felt like Jerry was giving orders to a kid, a kid he wasn't too fond of. *Jesus, where were the encouraging words*? I stared at him, thinking that was no way to make a performer feel comfortable, or welcome. Or worse, secure.

The first seventeen minutes went great. Much, much better than I'd expected. Many of the lines were greeted with applause and laughter. Casino audiences can often be the easiest for a comic. They are out to have a good time; unlike today's casino crowds who dress like Walmart shoppers, in the 60's and 70's audiences people dressed like movie stars themselves. The red light flashed; I waited for the huge laugh to subside, finished my joke and thanked the audience to thunderous applause. It took all my willpower not to return for another bow. Jane was being introduced over the loudspeaker; as I exited, she gave me a huge hug and a round of applause herself.

I stood in the back wings to watch her. Thirty seconds hadn't passed when I heard a hiss. "What the fuck were you doing?"

I turned. It was Jerry, red-faced with rage. "Didn't you see the fucking light?"

"Yes, but I was in the middle–"

"Fuck the middle. You're to get off. They want these people back in the fucking casino!"

"I'm sorry," was all I could say. Jesus, wasn't there one compliment or atta boy?

"Now, Jane may have to cut out a song. Don't let it happen again."

Was that really all he had to say to me? Not a word about how I did, how the audience reacted. Nothing; just some shit about a red light. In spite of the fact Patty gave me a hug and kiss, and the booker saying how delighted he was, that he'd book me back, I felt depressed.

I told Sarita later in our room I didn't think Jerry was for me. He probably didn't think I was for him. Those thoughts got stronger when he came by to tell me he'd booked me into a club in Hollywood, Florida, and the biggest club in Puerto Rico with an outstanding lady impressionist, another of his clients, Marilyn Michaels.

"Thank you," I said without much enthusiasm. His 'red light' lecture was still hurting.

"And, I've booked you for a huge benefit at the Plaza the next time you do Merv."

"What kind of benefit?" I asked.

"Whatta you care? A bunch of millionaires, a bunch in the business. A thousand bucks a plate. It'll be great exposure for you!"

"How much will they pay us?"

Jerry laughed. "It's a fucking benefit. They pay nothing. You're gonna have to get used to doing a lot of these in this business. You'll meet and be seen by everybody! It'll be great for you."

"Jerry, I don't do benefits for millionaires." I couldn't believe what was coming out of my mouth. "I didn't even know any millionaires. How many are gonna be there?"

"About fifteen hundred? Why?"

"That's fifteen hundred times a thousand and how much to rent the room and the meals? How much does that leave for their so-called charity? They should all stay home and each write a check. The charity would get much more that way."

"Are you nuts? That's what the rich do. They go to these things to show off to each other and to advertise their good souls for helping the less fortunate. Do you think I like it? No. It's bullshit, but to get ahead, you've gotta do it in this business. Don't be an asshole."

"Or some of these people could convince the government to build one less nuclear sub and put the money toward a decent health system or whatever."

"Jesus Christ, I'm managing a radical," he grumbled.

"Jerry, if it's a benefit for an old folk's home or children's home or something like that, I'd be happy to do it, but if you want me at the Plaza, millionaires can afford to pay us."

"I don't do old folks homes," he stated flatly, turned and walked out.

I turned to Sarita. "Honey, I don't think Jerry and I are right for each other. I'll do those gigs, but I think I want to talk to Bernie. As you said, there's a warmth about him that Jerry just doesn't have. At least for me."

"I think you'd be more comfortable with Bernie," Sarita said, "but I think you'll find he has a lot of problems."

I couldn't help thinking how would she know? But her instincts, or forebodings, or whatever, were right. It was not the first time she'd demonstrated an uncanny, almost psychic, ability to read people. Moments after Jerry left, I was made even more uncomfortable by the unexpected appearance of someone who'd become a total, forgotten stranger.

A quiet knock on the door, and I opened it. A young uniformed bellman handed me a piece of paper. "Mr. Barbour?" he asked. "This is a note for you. A fellow downstairs in an Air Force uniform says he's your brother."

I took the note, shocked. "Could you wait a minute?" I left the door open and read the note. It said he'd read about my being there, and flew to see me, to see what I was up to, and to tell me about his son, whom he'd named John. I read it, shaking, to Sarita. "What do you think?"

"It's up to you," she said warmly.

I felt bad, bad because no feelings of warmth or even curiosity loomed in me. I should have felt something, but I didn't. I should have felt bad that he'd made that trip to see me, but I didn't. All I could remember was our terrible parting when I kept him from slashing my black friend with a broken beer bottle. I couldn't even bring myself to write 'No, sorry' on his note. I turned to the young man and said, "Tell him I'm sorry, but I can't see him. Not now," and gave him five dollars.

It may not be true of others; I've seen a few people who were avowed enemies somehow make up and continue a relationship that almost blossomed anew, as though no rupture had ever occurred. But I have never been able to build a scar over the cut of someone hurting, disappointing or cheating me. That emotional cut stays unhealed. I can't help it. That's just me. In those days, I hurt easily.

Fifteen years later I sat alone in a darkened room for hours contemplating the sadness and emptiness of it all. Was I wrong not to at least see my brother? This was prompted by a letter I had just received. Somehow, my long-deleted sister had gotten word to me. Her note said my brother's son, John, at twenty-one, had died of cancer.

Without even so much as a short conversation with Marty Kummer, the one I really wanted to talk to because he had managed Paar, Management 3 broke up. Bernie moved to Los Angeles. I asked him if I could go with him. He was delighted to have another client. Jerry's passion was success; Bernie's was talent. And loyalty to that talent. Even after Bernie became the most powerful manager in the business, and a mega-millionaire, he still did the best for his first client, Norm Crosby.

Jerry hustled, promoted and worked his way to a success he probably never imagined possible. For a year, he hounded Colonel Parker, Elvis' colorful manager, and the guy who sold America Hadicol, an alcohol-based, feel-good medicine; after a year, Jerry finally convinced the colonel to let him put together a year's personal appearance tour for The King. Parker relented, on one condition, that Jerry give him a million-dollar retainer. Jerry, amazingly, talked a banker friend into it. A year to the day later, the colonel showed up at Elvis's dressing room at the Hilton in Las Vegas, with two suitcases, each containing a few million. One suitcase for each of them. Jerry was on his way.

A few years later, he put together Sinatra's best public performance. It was called The Main Event, staged in Madison Square Garden, presented in a boxing ring. Sinatra, with his first aspirations of being a fighter, loved it.

He also guided the career of John Denver and a few others, and produced a dozen and a half films, notably the star-polluted remake of Sinatra's *Ocean's Eleven* and their dreadful sinking sequels. His best was probably the pleasantly entertaining *Karate Kid* films with my long-ago friend, Pat Morita.

Bernie's love of talent focused almost exclusively on comedy writers and comedians. With Lorne Michaels in tow, he convinced NBC to do a late-night weekend comedy show called *Saturday Night Live,* and ended up representing almost the entire cast, including John Belushi and Dan Aykroyd. He discovered Jim Henson and The Muppets, making it a permanent part of Americana. He managed Gary Shandling, Brad Pitt, and Adam Sandler, among others. His film *Ghostbusters,* which no company wanted to produce, became the highest grossing comedy in history. He went on to sell his company to Lorimar for twenty-six million dollars. It seemed for every million dollars he pocketed, he put on ten pounds. Richard Dreyfuss, a client, told him he looked like Shelly Winters with a beard. I saw and spoke to him often at the LA Kings hockey games. He still had that sweet simpatico, but looked like a Jewish Orson Welles.

Jerry made an enormous amount of money, but Bernie, who died in 2008, made a difference, and a contribution to the culture. He was a long, long way from that when he set up his first little office in Hollywood. I learned quickly that Sarita had indeed sensed something off kilter with him. He confided in me that he really didn't know what he was going to do with his life. He was an inveterate gambler, owing Las Vegas casinos eighty thousand dollars when we first met. He was also an alcoholic. He confessed this to me because he wanted people to know how much he owed to this bright young blonde who had come into his life, married him, and reformed him. Her name was Laura; I only knew her a few months. She became his secretary, counsellor, and constant companion. They were never apart. He got nervous if she was out of his sight. She wasn't just the female force behind Bernie, she was also the force in front of him. She got between him and the crap tables, and him and the bartenders. Soon he was sober and debt free and started to make money. Mega-millions.

Her hobby was frogs: ceramic frogs, painted frogs, knitted frogs, anything to do with frogs. His office and her desk were cluttered with them. He thought she deserved more than that so he constantly bought her very expensive diamond jewelry, rings, brooches, earrings, necklaces, bracelets. She loved to wear and show them off. One night two masked gunmen broke into their apartment and stripped her of every one of them. The next day Bernie replaced them all. He was crazy about her. So was I.

One morning, about three months into being with my new manager, with really nothing to do, I thought I'd stop by his office on my way home to chat. There was no Laura. Bernie was sitting at her desk, his head down, fiddling idly with a couple of the frogs. He didn't say hello when he looked up and saw me.

"Bernie, you OK?"

He didn't answer.

"Where's Laura?"

He looked up slowly. "She ... she ran off with some other guy. She ran off with her gynecologist."

After the initial shock, I hid my face to stifle the unexpected laughter. I couldn't contain it, and exploded. "Bernie ... Bernie, Jesus, forgive me, but that's so funny!"

Bernie started to chuckle. "Oh, shit. Maybe someday I'll put that scene in a fucking movie."

After he became more absorbed in his work, food took the place of alcohol. In our conversations about the direction of my career, he encouraged me to focus more on comedy. I told him my real interest was in having a talk show, that I only did standup because that's what Paar and Carson did at the top of their shows. People expected it. I'd love doing that, but I also had this intense curiosity about people and the choices and actions they make and take in their lives.

"Johnny," Bernie said in our last conversation as my manager, "that shit's a little too deep for me, but if you become a major comedian you could do what you want. Look at Woody. But whatever you do, we'll be friends, and I'll always be a fan."

With only Murray and Howard West at the Morris office interested in me, I'd have to pursue, on my own, something in television, where there were almost no job openings.

Remembering Lenny Bruce

While there are many comedians I enjoyed and made it a point to see them all in person, because being onstage alone doing comedy is such a hard, sometimes soul-crushing undertaking, the one I had total admiration for was Lenny Bruce.

There were the masters of one-liners from Henny Youngman to Bob Hope, the hilarious naughty ones from Moms Mabley to Redd Foxx, those who did masterfully structured bits utilizing a phone and an unseen listener like Shelley Berman and Bob Newhart, the political ones, Mort Sahl and Dick Gregory, the absolute masters of mayhem in their early days, Dean Martin and Jerry Lewis, the down on their luck ones, Rodney Dangerfield and George Gobel, the angry, articulate ones, George Carlin and Richard Pryor, the unpredictable eruptions of the comic geniuses, Jonathan Winters and Robin Williams. And those who roared on stage like Shecky Greene and Buddy Hackett. In my mind the list is much longer, and I smile as the names race by like the too-fast credits at the end of a TV movie. But there was only one Lenny Bruce. He was the only comic I ever saw, along with Bill Hicks, who had sex appeal. That may sound like a weird thing to say about a comedian, but it's true.

If you look at any of the names mentioned above, with the possible exception of Dean Martin, who was a handsome singer, you can't imagine any woman tossing their room keys or panties at them. But no matter how unattractive physically a singer is, nearly all of them elicit this kind of response from women. I've seen women race after Gene Simmons, whose face would have to improve to be ugly, and Rod Stewart, who looks and sounds like Carol Channing in drag. Perhaps that's because singers deal with emotions that get to people's hearts. Comedians don't get any deeper than the funny bone. Except Lenny.

Lenny died young, but not before he'd made his mark on America. And what a mark it was. With the stack of comedy records I'd gathered to see what was making the comedians successful, it was Lenny's I kept going back to, especially the early ones: *The Sick Humor of Lenny Bruce*, with him lying in a graveyard, smiling as he enjoys his picnic basket. The routines were more than classic comedy. They were insights into the human condition. Insights into the Catholic Church, and into the dark side of our culture and politics, all presented in an engaging voice with a hint of New York. He was about five-nine or ten, had deep, dark eyes, black wavy hair, a round tanned face, and always a hint of a smile, like he was going to be doing something a little risky or naughty. Which he did.

Once or twice he was on Hugh Heffner's *Playboy after Dark*, but the set was always too cluttered. The only one on television who gave him a real platform, even after his arrests, was Steve Allen. His movie take-offs were hilarious and his impressions spot on. It's no wonder, even after his numerous and much-publicized expensive trials, he sold out Carnegie Hall. He was arrested primarily for obscenity. But that's not why the political and church establishments were after him. They were after him because he pointed out the corruptions and hypocrisy of those sacred cows; cops in Chicago, New York and Los Angeles were ordered to shut him down. Even to get him on drugs, if they could. And they were successful in their underhandedness. He was denied a cabaret license in New York, and had a brutal time earning a living.

I met him at a low point in his life, in one of the few cities he could find work: San Francisco. I met him because through his mother Sally, he had asked to meet me. I had no idea why.

Sarita and I were to be his guests at The Jazz Club in North Beach. Sarita also knew the owner from her days as a dancer, so we got the best seats in the club. But, when you're watching Lenny on stage, any seat is a best seat.

The set I saw, one that the audience loved, was not a comedy set. It didn't have one of the great routines I'd memorized. It was a recounting of his trial in Chicago. It was immensely interesting, and sometimes funny, the idiocy of the actual quotes from the transcripts, the cops who were witnesses and the judge who was obviously a biased, legal idiot. It was like watching a Jewish Mark Twain and Clarence Darrow. I was enthralled by it, but it wasn't comedy. Sarita felt saddened by it all. She had seen him years earlier in a tiny hole in the wall, with her father, long before she met me, and couldn't wait to see him again. It was, for her, the same endearing, warm Lenny, but not the comedian she had seen. Not a comedian at all.

After the show, as instructed, we went to his dressing room. The audience had given him an ovation, but he looked pensive, like he'd never heard it. Knowing Lenny had asked to see me, Sarita excused herself, gave him a hug, and said she'd meet me later at her family's home.

"Do you mind going for a walk? I need to get a little air," he asked.

We walked out into the cool North Beach night and began to slowly walk the empty streets.

"I liked your comedy album," he said after a moment, chuckling. "That took some balls."

"Well, the truth is, the material is better than the performance. I was kinda nervous so my voice is a little high pitched."

"There's still funny stuff there. And Sally had me watch you on Merv's show. You have that good goyisha look for TV. You know, if I had it to do all over again, I'd do it all differently. I have no money, no savings, no car, and I live in a house I don't own. That's no way to live after all these years. I just wanted to be a comedian. I loved it. Stick to what you're doin'."

I felt awful. The man was a giant of a performer and personality compared to me.

"Sally says you were working at The Losers. I wish I'd seen you. I got started in strip clubs."

"I'm a huge fan. And know most of your stuff by heart."

He smiled. "You did two separate sets between shows."

"Yeah. A lot of people stayed over so I didn't want to repeat."

"You write some really good stuff. You know what I did when I found I had to do a different set? I'd take an old proven joke, from vaudeville or wherever, that had a great punchline, then I'd write a bunch of new stuff in front of that just to fill the time. And no matter how long it was, there was always that great payoff. That's how I learned to write. I never knew I could until I had to."

"Why didn't you do some of your early stuff, the cleaner stuff tonight?"

"They don't want to hear that. They want to hear the court shit."

"I didn't. For great court stuff I can watch *The Merchant of Venice*."

He laughed. "I'll be back in LA in a week. Would you and Sarita like to come by the house for a bit? I'm going into The Golden Bear in Huntington Beach in a few weeks, and I've put some stuff on a tape recorder. I'd like you to hear it."

Sarita and I arrived at his house half-way up the Hollywood Hills. The grounds were unattended and a little overgrown; some of the white stucco was peeling. The inside was in more disarray.

Lenny, in an open shirt, trousers and barefoot, greeted us warmly at the door, and apologized for the maze he was guiding us through, leading all the way from the hallway to the living room. There were stacks of unfiled court transcripts, newspapers and magazines strewn everyplace. Before we could sit on the sofa, he had to remove half a dozen crumpled cardboard boxes full of papers and audio tapes.

"Would you like anything to drink or eat?"

"Lenny," I said, "if this were a restaurant, would you order anything here?"

"John, stop it," Sarita said.

Lenny laughed. "No. I always order out. Sarita, your husband's funny. And honest."

"Well, he shouldn't be rude!" she said.

"Can I play you a couple of things?" He had this huge tape player on the coffee table, It was surrounded by loose papers and tapes, and was obviously now the center and most important thing in his life. He removed the tape that was in it, put a new one in, and pushed the play button. There was that beautiful, captivating, descriptive voice talking about some ideas he had for new bits, but every so often he'd slip into reading something again from the mountains of court transcripts. We listened for about ten minutes before he pressed the stop button. "What do you think?"

"Lenny," Sarita exclaimed, "it's wonderful. You're wonderful. Everything you do is terrific." She meant it. She never, ever has said something just to be nice. It's either the truth, or silence.

"John. How about you?"

"Lenny, I've been thinking a lot about our chat and I have to be honest with you. And mind you, these are just my feelings."

"That's why you're here."

"I think you are by far the most original, most creative, most daring, most appealing comic I've ever seen. But, you'll notice, I said comic. Some of the things you played, just hint at it. That's not comedy. As I said before, I fell in love with those original clean bits you did. If you're going into The Golden Bear, that's what you should be doing. That's just my opinion." Jesus, there I was, almost his same age, not a fraction of the talent as him, and feeling like his Father Confessor. I turned to Sarita. "What do you think, hon?"

"Whatever makes him happy."

"Lenny, did you hear what Sarita said? I don't think doing the court stuff makes you happy. It makes you angry, sad and frustrated, as it should. You said you loved comedy. Do comedy. That's what makes you happy. And the audience. You didn't become famous for doing this court shit. It was those great routines."

"Honey, stop it!" Sarita said.

Lenny said, "A lot of that is old stuff. I don't think they'd want to hear that again."

"I know I would. Your doing court stuff would be like Sinatra singing hillbilly. Nobody wants to hear that. They want to hear Gershwin and Cole Porter. Over and Over. And I guarantee you, those kids who go there now probably never heard you at your best. They just know you're famous from the newspaper reports. Please. Just try it."

"It's certainly easy enough. Will you two come opening night?"

"Are you kidding? We wouldn't miss it for free money!"

The Golden Bear in Long Beach at one time had to be a barn or a small airplane hangar. It was huge. The elevated stage was in the very far right-hand corner of the room. The room itself was filled with endless rows of round wooden tables and chairs. The floor was covered with sawdust. It was a folk club, but really looked more like Grand Ole Opry. The marquee said: "One week only: Lenny Bruce."

Sarita and I arrived early and were glad we did. There was standing room only. We went backstage to wish Lenny luck. He was with his mother, Sally, and a few friends. There was a charge in the room. We caught Lenny's eye, and just waved to let him know we were there.

There was no opening act. And no music. Just a simple announcement over the loudspeakers: "Ladies and Gentlemen, Lenny Bruce."

From such a youthful crowd, there was a surprisingly loud, warm reception, and a few whistles. Lenny walked confidently onto the stage. He never looked better. His dark eyes sparkled as the little grin kicked in. His first routine was 'The Lone Ranger,' which brought eruptions of applause and laughter from middle to the fabulous end, followed by all the bits I had memorized. They were more sparkling and fresh than when I first heard them. The audience began to cheer. His forty-five-minute set had turned into an hour and fifteen minutes. They didn't want him to leave. To the guys he was hilarious. To the women, God, did he have sex appeal.

After the show, it was impossible to get to him in the dressing room, so, once again, we waved, hollered, "Great show. See you later," and left.

On the way out we heard him holler, "Johnny, thank you!"

They were the last words we would hear from Lenny. Not too long after that the news reported the nude body of comedian Lenny Bruce was found in his bathroom, dead from an overdose with a needle stuck in his arm. To make sure the world got the picture, the *L.A. Times* printed it on the front page. His mother, Sally, was convinced that the LAPD had set him up by selling him treated cocaine, and that as a warning and an example to America, staged the gruesome death photo, sticking the needle in his arm. She also wondered aloud, when Bill Hicks, who reminded her of her son, started to fill auditoriums attacking the government, if maybe they, too, had something to do with his getting cancer at such a young age.

The Dean of Variety Shows

"We showed your Merv spot to Greg Garrison. He loved it and wants you to do the same thing on Dean's show in three weeks," said Howard West. He was a quiet, gentle agent, a rarity, who, along with his associate, George Shapiro, another equally down to earth man, were my West Coast 'Murray Schwartz's' doing their best to get me gigs. Being good at what they did, and concerned about talent, like many other agents, Howard and George eventually formed their own management company. Their main client was a struggling Jerry Seinfeld. That Dean Martin gig, though, was one I never could have thought possible. It was by far the most successful, engaging variety show in the country. Everybody wanted to be on it.

Whenever I was booked to do a show, I didn't just work on preparing my material, I researched the show and the personalities involved, curious about their backgrounds and how they got to be where they were. It made me feel as though I knew them better, even from a distance. It made me feel more comfortable performing with and for them. What I learned about Dean and Greg Garrison, his producer-director, made me want to be around them all the more.

When Dean's show first came on, it was not successful. Some programmer at NBC thought Dean should just be a host, a sort of Italian Ed Sullivan who would introduce guest stars and occasionally sing a song. It was a very flat show, with a very uninterested looking host. Dean didn't want to continue the show, at least not one like that. Plus, NBC was on the verge of justifiably canceling it.

Dean only knew of Greg Garrison and his limited work casually, but he liked what he knew and saw. So, he called him. He asked Greg to look at his show before it was terminated. Greg said he couldn't, it was too awful, especially to see one of his favorite personalities presented so badly. Dean asked Greg what he should do to make him watch it. Greg laughed and said: "Dean, you've got a reputation as a lady's man, a hard drinker, fun loving and an "I don't give a shit" kind of guy, and none of that is showing."

Dean said, "The network doesn't want that!"

"Dean, fuck the network. What do those assholes know? Your public wants that. I want that. I was your biggest fan until you did this."

Dean then asked if he should chuck the show and do movies.

"Shit, no!' Greg hollered. "More people will see one TV show than all your movies combined. Just do it right."

"What is right?"

"Look, you're a saloon singer. Be one on the air. Open the show at the piano, with you sitting on a bar stool with a drink. That's you. And you should be surrounded by beautiful broads. That definitely is you. Every guy watching will want to be you, and every gal, with you!"

Dean knew Greg was right. "Would you produce it, if I get to continue?"

"I'm too busy," Greg replied.

"Too busy to have lunch? Have a drink?" Dean asked.

At that casual meeting, Dean said, "Greg, not only am I gonna pick your brains, I'm gonna pay for the picking."

"Slim pickings, and slim chance, Dean."

Long after this luncheon, both recalled to me how quickly Greg became not only Dean's producer, but the man with the last word on the show. Shortly after more than one drink, they shook hands on what Dean had quickly offered. Half of the show in all forms in perpetuity. There was never a written contract or a piece of paper between them. Just a handshake. For a lifetime. It ran for nine years until 1974, making Dean Martin the largest single shareholder in General Electric, owner of NBC. After Dean died, his handshake with Greg held up. He continued to get his half.

In person, and privately, Dean Martin turned out to be an even nicer man than I could have imagined. Rehearsals were held in a vast, empty studio peopled by only the guest stars, a very small crew of technicians, musicians, and Greg and Dean. No more than a dozen and a half of us. The guest stars on my show were a quiet, distant Peggy Lee, a haughty more distant Lena Horne, and an engaging Van Johnson wearing what he called his lucky red socks. I was the mini-guest star.

During the rehearsals, nobody, but nobody, was allowed to talk or whisper or do anything that would distract the artist. That was Dean's doing. He insisted on quiet and focus for his performers. Greg implemented it. If someone so much as breathed too loudly, they heard about it instantly. While it was Dean's show, and Dean's ship, the captain steering it was solely Greg Garrison.

It was murder trying to do a comedy routine in a huge room with only a handful of people, but mercifully it went well, with the help of Dean's laughter. The only outsider in the room was Sarita. Greg had asked her to sit next to him. She did. Later that day, for the actual taping, he then asked her to join him in the booth to watch it. She did.

The broadcast show, with an audience that gave every indication they felt privileged to be there, went wonderfully. Afterward, Greg came on stage, shook my hand vigorously, and said, "Great job. I told Sarita you're coming back."

The second appearance, aside from doing a very well-received stand-up, I was elevated to doing some kind of small song and dance with Dean and other cast members. Not being musical, and unable to use my feet for anything except walking, skating or running, I had Sarita coaching me, which she did superbly, much to the delight of Greg. Again, he invited her to sit by him in the booth.

The third appearance started out a little oddly, and ended up even more so. One of the opening bits I did when first starting out was a couple of minutes on my father being Scotch and my mother Jewish, proving you could mix anything with Scotch, and that I had a hard time learning to play Hava Nagila on the bagpipes. I had decided to revive it for that show;

during rehearsal it got guffaws. During the actual taping of the show, though, in front of the audience, Greg stopped, leaving Sarita again in the booth and approached me on stage.

"John, I'm not sure I like that stuff. That Jew stuff. A little corny. A little easy. You've done some really good political stuff, that's generic, ya know, that might work in rerun ten years from now. Do you have anything new like that you could do?"

I was startled. Alone on stage, in front of an audience, confronted by this big, muscular force, all I could say was, "Can I have a few minutes?" I walked off to the side of the set and started to think about what was big in the news. The biggest story seemed to be about President Johnson's daughter, Linda. The White House had announced her engagement to an airman named Charles Robb, and that Chief Justice Earl Warren was to perform the ceremony. The joke came to me immediately. Having read excerpts of The Warren Commission out of curiosity, and, a few books critical of the government's findings about President Kennedy's murder, especially Mark Lane's *Rush to Judgment,* but forming no real opinions of my own, I was pleased and surprised when this funny thought popped into my head. I didn't even have to write it down. I motioned to Greg that I had something, and would he like to hear it.

"No. You say you got it. I believe you. Surprise me."

He returned to the booth; I returned to my mark. Dean and the guest stars were to my far right, out of camera view. We heard Greg over the intercom. "Okay, gang. Tape on Johnny. Roll 'em. You're on!"

The audience had been watching all this inside showbiz stuff with pleased curiosity and applauded louder than usual. I started. "Ladies and gentlemen, you've all seen the news about President Johnson's daughter being engaged to wed Airman Charles Robb, and that Chief Justice Earl Warren wants to perform the ceremony..." I paused. The audience was smiling and nodding. "Well, what the news won't tell you, is that LBJ does not want Earl Warren to perform the ceremony ... " I paused again, the audience grinning in anticipation. And casually said the punchline. "That's because, after The Warren Report, the President says he doesn't want to look back in twenty years and find out his daughter isn't really married." I paused a beat before continuing my spot, but I never got to continue. There wasn't just laughter, there was an absolute roar. Some even cheered. It was as though I had somehow struck an undercurrent nerve in the people; that I was joking about something they took very seriously, but couldn't express themselves. The roar filled the stage for what seemed like minutes. It was silenced and cut off by Greg bellowing into the intercom. "Cut! Cut!"

In a moment he was down on the stage, motioning angrily for me to come over to the bottom of the stairs that led to his booth. Next to him was a man in a dark blue suit and tie. "Wipe that goddamned smile off your face," he ordered.

I wasn't aware I was smiling, but if I had one it quickly evaporated in the heat. What could possibly be wrong?

"You can't do that!"

"But, Greg, you heard the reaction. They loved–"

"Not only can't you do it, you're not going to do it. Even if I liked it. It was clever, but I can't let you do it. This is Standards and Practices. When they say no, it's no."

I looked at the suit. He said, "Sorry. It's totally unacceptable."

I stood there wondering now if I was going to be doing a spot at all.

"Get back out," Greg ordered. "And do that Jew shit. And when you're done, come up to the booth. I wanna talk to you."

Later, in the booth, Greg and I were alone. He told me he had asked Sarita to leave, that he wanted to talk with me alone. His opening small-talk reeked of insincerity. He offered me a drink, which he knew I didn't do, and made an off-handed comment about how he appreciated the Earl Warren joke, but it wasn't right for Dean's show. I told him that was true and sorry I didn't think about that.

"Never mind," he said, leaning backward casually, like he was stretching his body to the fullest to let me know this was his domain. "That's not what I want to talk to you about. Remember when I told you all the women I've loved and been brokenhearted by were all Mexican brunettes?"

"Yes," I said. He'd said as much to me the first time I did the show after he'd met Sarita.

He paused, studying me then said, "How would you feel if I asked Sarita out?" He looked like someone used to getting yes for an answer. I didn't answer him right away. I was trying to absorb what he was saying, wondering if it was somehow an ultimatum about my future appearances, or nonappearances on his show.

"Well, what would you say? Would you mind if I asked her?"

I could feel show business slipping out of my near future. God, I thought, what arrogance. What nerve. And how bloody demeaning to me. What did he think I was? Some wimp? Some pimp? Somebody so desperate for fame, I'd sell my soul, and my wife's body? The rage in me, thankfully, subsided to absolutely calmness as I spoke. Quietly and deliberately.

"Greg, why are you asking me? If Sarita wants to go out with you, she will. It's not up to me, it's up to her. Ask her. You know this town is full of husbands and wives who cheat on each other. You've probably had a few dozen of those yourself. So, I have no doubt that you have no compunctions about asking her, even without my consent. And do I give my consent for you to ask her? Absolutely. I do not own my wife. She's her own person. But do you mind if I ask you a question?"

He looked stunned. "No, what?"

"Do you think you're more desirable than Frank Sinatra? Do you think you're more appealing to women than Frank Sinatra?" He just stared at me. I repeated calmly, "Do you?"

"Why are you asking that?" He was not sounding as confident.

"Well, Frank loved Earl Hines. Whenever he was in town in San Francisco he'd go and listen to him. So as not to disturb the crowd, Frank always sat quietly in the back. Sarita was Earl's band singer. After the show, Sinatra asked Earl to introduce him to her. Frank, of course, asked her out. She turned him down immediately. When I asked her how could she turn down America's biggest superstar, she said simply, he wasn't her type. So, if you think you are Sarita's type, go ahead and ask her." I got up and left.

At home, in our little second story apartment, across from Gelson's Market on Kling Street, Sarita and I sat on the balcony watching the evening traffic and shoppers.

"What did Greg want to talk to you about?" Sarita asked.

"You know damn well what he wanted to talk to me about."

"What did he say?" she asked.

"Jesus, Sarita, you know what he said. You know what I said. What I've always said to you. That I don't own you. You're your own person. If you want some other man or whatever, I can't stop you. That's up to you."

"John," she said, shaking her head, "you are absolutely the first man I've ever met who didn't have a jealous bone in his body. It's unbelievable."

"Sarita, it's not as if I don't. I do. It is meaningless and uncomfortable to show it and for others to see it."

"Well, I must say, honey, I do not understand how you can be so cool. But it does make me feel comfortable."

"I don't know why you're asking me this because he probably asked you out already."

"He did." She smiled. "I told him I was married."

"You've got to be kidding. In this town that is so corny."

She laughed. "He thought so, too. I told him that's why I was glad I was from San Francisco, and not from this town."

"Well," I said, "I guess I won't be doing Dean's show anymore."

"You don't need Dean, or anybody. You're better than you realize. Don't worry, you'll make it. They won't be able to keep you down."

I never did get to do Dean's show again, at least not his variety show, but when our close friend, Redd Foxx, became a megastar on *Sanford and Son,* Greg wanted him to be the subject of a Roast. Redd said only if Johnny Barbour is on it. When Greg said absolutely not, Redd said, "Then, Greg, find yo'self another nigger!"

Dis-Connections

"I'm glad I caught you. You gotta few minutes?" It was Murray calling from New York. "Call Merv right away. Then call me back."

I hung up, dialed right away. Merv answered before the first ring ended. "Johnny? I just got a call from the head of daytime TV for ABC. They asked if I would produce a talk show with you as the host."

"Are you kidding? My God, this is unbelievable."

"Yes. Just now. Evidently, they've seen you on the show. They liked you, and asked if I'd be interested. I told them definitely. It's more fun than doing another game show."

"Merv, I'm stunned. I don't know what to say."

"Just say yes and I'll have Murray meet with them tomorrow, and we'll put it all together."

"Merv, I don't know how to thank you."

"My fun and fees and seeing you doing this, which you are perfect for, will be plenty thanks enough. I'll call you tomorrow. Congratulations."

I hung up and rushed to tell Sarita, and then called Murray to thank him.

"You're a natural for this. Merv loves you. I have an eleven AM meeting at ABC tomorrow to work out the details. Merv and I will get right back to you. In the meantime, take Sarita out and celebrate." I did.

The next morning, I looked out the window at the sunrise, and wondered how high the sun was in the sky in New York. Was it shining on Murray and Merv? I spent the next five hours watching the clock, but no call. I was glad I hadn't eaten, because it would have had a very short visit to my stomach. Then the phone rang. The tone was somehow different from all the other times it rang. It sounded darker. I hated those negative forebodings. Somewhere inside me I have a very large antenna for picking up negative signals that are never wrong. Before Murray spoke, I knew it was negative because Merv wasn't on the line.

"What happened?" I asked.

"They signed Dick Cavett."

Oh, Jesus, I thought, feeling like I'd been punched in the gut. Rollins was right!

"It wasn't a total waste, though," Murray continued. "They asked me if you'd like to host a daytime game show that they think you'd be perfect for. I told them I'd ask you and get back to them. So, I'm asking you. Would you?"

"What kind of game show is it?"

"It's something called *Connections*. I'll get the details and send them to you. It'd be for thirteen weeks at twenty-five hundred a week. Plus paid for run-throughs and a pilot."

"Murray, I don't want to be a traffic cop. The shows I liked were *Who Do You Trust?* like Carson did. Or *You Bet Your Life* with Groucho where they talked to the guests first. That's what made those shows. Not the game or quiz. If it's like that, I'd be interested."

"I'll tell them that. They also want me to meet with the producer, so I'll pass that on to them. We'll see what they say, but I'm sorry."

After getting calls from Murray and the executive producer, I agreed to meet with them in New York. I don't recall much of the actual game itself, just that the contestants would be in pairs, a man and a woman. Somehow, they had to make some kind of connection, thus the name of the show.

The executive producer asked if I would mind doing a brief run-through in the studio, which had already been set up. He said there would be just a handful of people plus the daytime programming head. I suggested it might go better if there was an audience. He said they had made no plans to have an audience for the run-throughs or rehearsals. I told him I could understand that, so just ask the ABC exec to get his secretary and a few of the other employees to come down and watch. This way he would find out if the interview portion with me and the contestants worked.

They thought it was a great idea. Some phone calls were made, and bodies began to assemble. Happy to be out of their offices, they were an easy audience. They laughed easily at the brief interviews with the contestants. Step one was a hit. The next step was a full-blown run-through with a real audience and cameras.

I called Sarita to tell her I'd be a few more days, that it was going really well, and if it continued to, I might finally have a good steady job and a decent salary.

The following day, with a full house, before noon, it went even better. Everyone connected with *Connections* was ecstatic. They could feel they were part of a possible hit and that they, too, would have a job. I lost my ill feelings about how lucky Cavett was to have Jack Rollins. Doing the game show was turning out to be enjoyable, and word about how well it was going spread around ABC. Aside from the usual programming exec who was at every presentation, there were now half a dozen others. All in suits. Prior to all pilots and shows, there is a run-through, taped before a studio audience. This we did. With each one better. A lunch break was called, after which we'd do the real thing with a new audience.

My appetite for food is the same when I'm excited as when I'm depressed; it's nonexistent. How rewarding it was going to be to be on network television doing a fun show, doing my version of Johnny Carson, Groucho Marx or Jack Paar. And the money. I'd make more in a week than I made in some years. All the things I could finally buy for Sarita, that was happiness.

I was interrupted by the stage manager informing me I should get to makeup for a touch up. I did. While chatting with an equally happy makeup lady who would be assigned to the show, the executive producer walked in.

"Is our star all set?" he asked.

"Fine," I answered.

"A couple of small things to go over, John. We need you to cut down a bit on your interviews. We have a new Head of Programming, and he wants you to get right to the game."

I jumped out of the chair. "What do you mean? You heard the audience reaction."

"Look, I agree. I pointed that out. They think the game works well enough by itself. That's what they want to see."

"That's not what I agreed to. If I knew this a week ago, I'd be back in LA. I'm not a traffic cop. It's not me. Tape the interviews as promised, and if they don't like them, edit the fucking things."

"I'm sorry, John. I have no control over that. You'll just have to do the game."

"Well, I have control over me. If I weren't committed to this now, and you weren't all set up, I'd be leaving. I'll do it, but what is going to happen is that they'll see the game portion isn't all that good. And if it goes, it goes without me."

The taping started. The announcer announced the show and introduced me. I greeted the audience and introduced the first guests. They seemed startled when I didn't begin the interview with them as we did through the rehearsals. When I went straight to the first question, their smiles vanished, as it vanished from my insides. The show was flat. It was monumentally ordinary. Without the guests being recognized as people, charming or interesting or funny people, there was no reason to watch the show. Before it was over everyone knew it. I thanked no one when I was done. What for? For being idiots. For not telling those empty suits they had no idea what show business was? I just grunted to Murray that I'd see him later, and left for the airport.

The flight home was forever.The cab ride home seemed longer. I had not phoned from New York with the bad news. I didn't know what I was going to say to Sarita. I grabbed my bag, climbed the stairs, still thinking about what to tell her. Sarita, as always when I returned from a gig, greeted me in the same funny, endearing way, by tap-dancing and singing about Johnny marching home. Instead of my usual grin or laugh, I just stared at her. She stopped in mid-stride. "What's wrong?" she asked.

"They changed the format on me at the last moment. It wasn't for me. I'm not doing it."

Sarita's face flushed; she was trying to hold back tears. It didn't work. They began to trickle down her face. I had never seen her cry in the nearly five years we'd been together. Finally, she sputtered, "That means we can't have a baby."

"What?" I almost hollered.

She repeated, more softly this time, "That means we can't have a baby."

Before I could remind her of our conversations about no children, I stopped. It was one of the few times in my life I shut up at the right time. Instead of reminding her of her promise, I was drowning in those heartbreaking tears. Her sudden eruption of sadness, I thought, could have only been brought about by years of repressed hopes and dreams. I had my dreams and hopes. I talked about them all the time, and every moment was trying to live them. Suddenly, I understood; Sarita had had her own. All private, all kept quietly to herself, keeping them hers because they might interfere with mine.

I felt suddenly ashamed of myself. As gently as possible I placed my hands on her arms. "Sarita, I am so sorry. For five years or so, we've tried it my way and it really hasn't worked." I paused as she wiped away her tears. "If ... if ... you really want, we could try it your way for five years." She began to cry again. "If you really want a baby, let's go make one. Now." And we did. She must have conceived that afternoon.

Forty years later, she confessed that not wanting a child was the only lie she'd ever told in her life. And the child I never wanted for fear it would interfere with my life actually gave me a better one.

June 6, 1968

In June of 1968, Sarita was one month pregnant. A happier human I had never seen. She was an amniotic fluid junky. A smile never left her lips, even when she slept. Her voice was barely ever raised above a whisper. While she had been beautiful before, now she was stunning.

I didn't know what I felt. I didn't know if I was apprehensive or what; I was just delighted to see her happy. I still could not get over it; not once in the nearly five years together had she ever hinted at having a child. When she passed infants in a baby carriage, she never cooed or carried on. She'd just smile. She had also never asked for anything, any kind of gift. Nothing.

Knowing that she'd be spending a lot of time alone in the apartment, I bought our first TV set, which we put in the bedroom. She watched it very little. She was too wrapped up in reading books about baby's names. We were never curious about what the child's sex might be. We had plenty of names. From the beginning, I was convinced she'd have a boy. Very, very feminine, soft women like Sarita always seem to have boys. If she had been a fabric, it would have been silk or chiffon.

For some reason, the one name we wrote over and over was Christopher. Whether or not it had anything to do with the fact that Chris Hayward had asked to be the godfather, I don't know. So, the books became just something to look through in case there was another child, a thought that really terrified me. The middle name would be, of course, that of Sarita's father, Ernest. So, that was it. If a son, it would be Christopher Ernest Barbour.

A couple of our friends, older ladies, told us having a child, a first child, somehow, by some unwritten law of the universe, coaxes the gods to bestow good luck on the child and the parents. To me, of course, this was headshaking superstitious nonsense. When Sarita heard our neighborly soothsayers promising this, she'd just smile. I considered myself a realist. I trusted only my five senses, although my mind was always intellectually sidetracked by daydreams and omens. At first I blamed this malady on the endless youthful Hollywood films that misinformed me, but found I still did it when I had long outgrown them; but evidently, had never grown up!

Every day I took joy in watching Sarita glowing with that life inside her. I was like a tourist gazing at some great natural wonder. But, being this realist, things did seem to be changing for the better. I was not picking up one negative signal. Instead, every day seemed to bring good news about something. The best news came almost immediately: I was wanted on *The Tonight Show* in New York. I was booked for June 6th, and had two and a half weeks to prepare.

Like everyone, I enjoyed Johnny Carson's monologues. I'd been a fan of them from the time I watched his local CBS show in Los Angeles called *Carson's Cellar*, and later when he took over for Red Skelton on CBS for a summer show. However, as I said, I was not a fan of his interviews. I had been spoiled by Paar and Merv. They were as at home with intellectuals as with celebrities. Carson was at his best only with celebrities.

I had done well with Merv and Dean; however, to the industry, and to America, to really score on *The Tonight Show* was to board the launch pad to success. I had no doubts I'd do well.

Sarita was thrilled that one of the first things she'd get to watch on her new TV set would be her husband with Johnny Carson. I packed a small bag and left for New York. I checked into the downtown hotel near NBC, unpacked, called the booker to let him know I was there, and made an appointment to see him the following morning to go over the material, which we did.

The following day, back at the hotel, making notes and being my usual pacing self, I could barely eat and couldn't rest. I turned on the TV for distraction. I flipped through the channels and dozed off with the remote in my hand. I was awakened by the phone. For a moment, I didn't know where I was, just that I was in this fancy room with a lot of lights on. I picked it up, still groggy. I noticed the clock said it was just after three a.m. I panicked. Maybe something happened to Sarita. It was Sarita. And she did sound panicked.

"Honey. Honey, are you watching TV?"

"No. It's late."

"Turn it on. They've shot Bobby Kennedy."

I jumped up.

"At the Ambassador Hotel. He had just won, was giving a speech in the ballroom." She hesitated, "John, he's dead. He was shot in the head."

"Not again," I said.

"It's horrible. People are running all over the place."

"Honey, are you okay? Do you want me to come home?"

"No. No. I'm fine."

"Let me turn on the TV, and I'll call you back."

It was on every channel. I couldn't believe it. Not again. Not in America. Every channel had differing versions of the same thing. Shots ringing out in the pantry. People yelling and screaming, and some girl running out of the Ambassador Hotel in a polka dot dress who might be a suspect, or an accomplice.

In the morning, New York was as quiet as was San Francisco after JFK's murder. People were walking more slowly, talking more quietly, or not at all. Even the traffic seemed silent.

On the cab ride to NBC, the driver, in an East Indian accent asked me what was wrong with America. I had no answer. I just knew I had to cancel doing the show. It would be an impossibility. I was convinced the network was pre-empting it anyway to do a news special. But that wasn't the case, the booker telling me they were going ahead with the show.

"They've just murdered another Kennedy and NBC is still doing the show?" I almost yelled.

"They think it's best."

"What about Johnny? Is he taking the night off at least?"

"No. He asked about it, but they asked him to stay and do it. They said the audience would want something other than all this bad news."

"Jesus, there's nothing in the world that could distract people from this horror."

"Well, that's what we get paid for."

"Well, under the circumstances, I can't do the show. Not only is there nothing I can say to make people laugh, I don't want to even try. Have any of your other guests cancelled?"

He nodded. "A couple."

"They're smart," I said.

"They'll also never be back on the show again. And neither will you. Johnny feels if he has to do it, so does everybody else. For you, it's either now or never. It's up to you. I'll give you a moment to think about it."

Sitting alone trying to figure out what to do was physically painful. At times I bent over clutching my stomach to ease the cramps. It was hard enough thinking about the senseless horror of Bobby's killing, which never, ever left my mind, but debating with myself over whether or not to do the show, and what would happen if I did or didn't do it made me even sicker. Maybe people needing some kind of escape was nonsense. There was no escaping that; not for a long time. Even if there were an escape, I was no way capable of being the one to provide it. Johnny was doing the show, though. Maybe he needed some help. Maybe he'd be grateful I was there. I was there already. Maybe the staff would also appreciate the fact I stayed. I was leaning toward justifying why I should do it, but my heart and my negative gland, which I hadn't heard from since Sarita's pregnancy, told me no. Absolutely not! I wish, in retrospect, I had listened to them. My instincts are never wrong. Often, though, sadly, as in this case, my judgments were.

The booker walked briskly back into the room. "What have you decided?'

"I'll do it," I whispered.

"Good. I'll let everyone know."

I stood in the wings as the orchestra played the theme, which sounded horribly like taps, wondering if maybe I shouldn't do my monologue, just walk to the front of the stage and tell the audience that, like them, my heart was broken. Maybe, I thought, I'll make up my mind after I hear what Johnny has to say about Bobby.

Johnny came out and said nothing. Absolutely nothing. Was he kidding? How was that possible? The guy has the entire country at his feet, and ignores it. (He would demonstrate his total lack of humanity years later, again saying nothing about the 1972 Munich Olympic Massacre of Israeli athletes.) Jolted by his silence, I thought, *Jesus Christ, what am I going to do?*

Johnny introduced me. I walked to my spot in a fog. My lips felt like barbells as I tried to lift them into a smile. I did my act. It might as well have been a eulogy. Neither I nor the audience felt like laughing. When I was done, to polite applause, I tried to leave the stage, but Johnny called me over. Any other time, and for all aspiring comedians, to be invited by the king to sit next to him on the couch was akin to being placed on the throne. To me, it felt like the electric chair. And, watching close up, an uninterested and distant Johnny Carson was like having him pull the switch.

I cannot remember a word either of us spoke. The thing I remember most distinctly was the narrowness of his eyes that made them harder to see. He was clearly uncomfortable. Being physically that close to him, the last thought I had about him, when the show mercifully ended, was that he looked cruel.

I got no feedback from the show, which meant it probably never aired. Could that wonderful booking and the disastrous merciful cancelation still have been some sign of good fortune resulting from Sarita's pregnancy? In later years, it indeed turned out to be, but there was more good fortune in my immediate future.

Roger, Me and Merv... Again

Murray was still my primary agent, but with the talk show lost to Cavett at ABC, the dreadful game show pilot there also, and the disaster of *The Tonight Show*, his enthusiasm was obviously dampened; it all certainly soaked mine up a little. Merv was making him a great deal of money. I was barely making a living. Howard West told me word going around about my being difficult, made it difficult for him. I couldn't disagree.

The joy of watching Sarita singing to her stomach every night made me feel less fearful about my future, our future. Without a regular paycheck, or the expectations of one, I felt surprisingly confident. Again jobless, I made the rounds of the clubs, getting up with a bunch of other struggling comics. One of these comics was Murray Langston. Murray had a wonderfully relaxed, easygoing presence, unlike any comedian I'd ever met. He was so self-effacing, years later he put his face in a paper bag with eye-holes and became known as the unknown comic on *The Gong Show*.

Another was Bob Ridgely. He was a handsome, tall, constantly grinning hunk, as the ladies used to say, who played the guitar and sang the most hilarious parodies in a voice that any crooner would envy. He drifted away from that, though, which I was sorry to see, when his best friend and sometime roommate, a chunky comic, stuck his head in the gas oven. Robert became an actor instead, and a successful one, with a standout performance in *Philadelphia* as the boss who fires Tom Hanks.

Murray and Bob became my biggest boosters, introducing me to two talent managers named Artie Price and Alan Bernard. Alan managed singer, Andy Williams, and comedian, Bob Newhart. Artie was more into writers, comedy writers; one of his clients was James Brooks, who along with Alan Burns, my son's godfather's ex-partner, created *The Mary Tyler Moore Show.* It was Artie who, behind the scenes, saved the show from oblivion, and Grant Tinker. CBS was at best 'iffy' about the show, and told Tinker they might consider it if he replaced the writers. Tinker agreed.

Artie stormed the Black Eye, as the CBS building on Fairfax was called, and convinced them and Tinker that Brooks and Burns were the only two who could make the concept of a single working girl in Minnesota work. They backed off. Lucky for us; and lucky for television. And just like Artie, he never took any bows for it.

Both men took sort of a liking to me. I say, 'sort of' because if they had really liked me, they would have signed me. But, being liked by two very influential managers was good enough for me. They said they'd keep an eye open for anything I might be right for. If it worked out, they would go from there. Of course. I heard that a lot. Everyone starting in this business does. I gave it little thought, and even less hope. It was a nice gesture, and I let it go at that. So, it came as a total surprise when they called and said they'd lined up an audition for me for a solo spot on *The Roger Miller Show*. Roger wrote an irresistible catchy number and blockbuster called *King of The Road*. That monster hit and others led CBS to give him a summer replacement show for *The Smothers Brothers*.

His scratchy drawl when we met was as warm and appealing as when he sang. For someone who was three years younger than me, and not too much taller, the lines in his face and the paleness of his watery, squinting blue eyes, made him look forty-two instead of thirty-two.

"Ah hear yer funny," he said.

As in Dean's show, the audition was held in a large studio; this one, though, with a forty-foot high ceiling that made whispers echo. This was to be Roger's first show. The writers were there, about a dozen of the regular cast members, two singers, one country, one pop, no crew members and the two people who would audition for the one open spot, George Carlin and myself. Artie, as Roger's manager, was also there. And someone from CBS.

George was told that he'd be first. He got up and walked closer to the small audience, and I thought, my God, here I am again following George auditioning for a job. He looked good in his suit and tie, and launched easily into one of his better known early routines, The Hippy Dippy Weatherman. Except for me chuckling, the reaction was almost nonexistent. Perhaps they'd heard it too often; or perhaps it was just too tough an audience. I felt sorry for him. One could never imagine that he would morph into that brilliant cutting wordsmith that would later dominate HBO and fill university auditoriums and concert halls. I began to feel nervous for myself. He was well known. I wasn't. If he didn't get laughs, how could I?

I had decided that I didn't want to do my usual one-liners. I wanted to do something I didn't do often: a routine. The one I picked popped into my head, already written. It was how Ed Sullivan got his job.

This was CBS, Ed Sullivan's home, the network's number one show. Everybody in America knew who he was; nearly every performer in America did an imitation of him. No one in the world was easier to imitate. Even people who can't do imitations, like me, could do Ed Sullivan. He was a real-life Norm Crosby, someone who could never quite get the language or pronunciations right.

When I was motioned to get up and do my thing, I told the uninterested assemblage that I was going to tell them the inside story of how Ed Sullivan really got his job. They smiled, except for the guy from CBS. I said, "CBS wanted to do a Sunday Night variety show called *Toast of the Town*. They were initially looking for a star to host it, but someone said there's a columnist named Ed Sullivan who writes a column called that. Why don't we see if he'd like to do it?" It wasn't laughs, but the small audience was enjoying it, curious about where I was going. I continued, talking casually, not trying to get laughs, but just tell a story. But the laughs got bigger and bigger. I explained that the director told Ed just to say, "Welcome to the show." Ed, wanting to expand on it said, "Ladies and Gentlemen, welcome to a really big shoe!'" The small audience laughed. America knew Sullivan could not say 'show' without it coming out 'shoe!' I then described how one after another, the director would call executives to come down and listen to this guy, telling Ed just to say, "Welcome to the show," which Ed expanded on each time ending with "shoe!" This small group was laughing out loud. Even the executive. Then I did the punchline.

"The director got so excited about how much fun everybody was having with this bumbling columnist, he called Bill Paley, President of CBS, and said 'Mr. Paley, sir, you've got to come right down and see this!' And Mr. Paley said, (in my best Sullivan voice) 'Ah'll ah'll ... ah'll be right doon!"

The cast and crew not only screamed, they applauded. Again, even the exec! Roger rushed over. "Goddamn it, kiddo, you are a funny sonofabitch!"

Artie came over and shook my hand. "John, that was funny. Really funny. You've got it."

I thanked everyone from a distance and left. I glanced at Carlin who gave me a thumbs up. When I got home that afternoon, I was thrilled to tell Sarita all about it. However, there was surprisingly no expected phone call – not that day or the next. I waited a whole week. It was driving me nuts. What happened? It was impossible that they couldn't have booked me. They heard the reaction. Even the CBS guy applauded. I was head-shakingly baffled so I called Artie's office. He wasn't in; he was over at CBS. Hearing that made it worse. Then his secretary said, "Wait a minute. Alan wants to talk to you."

"Johnny, everybody's talkin' about it. Artie says you killed with that Sullivan bit. Way to go!"

"I thought they'd call that afternoon with the job," I said.

"They hired Carlin. Mason likes him. He's the producer."

"He was there. He was laughing too, and not once at George! Alan, something else is at work here."

"John, the truth is Mason Williams didn't like you. He said, he just doesn't like you. Personally."

"He doesn't even know me."

"I guess he doesn't want to. He thinks you're arrogant."

"What?" I yelled. "Arrogant?"

"Look, I don't know. He just said he didn't like you. I'm sorry, but cheer up. The word is out that you killed. Something will come up."

I was completely at a loss. I'd never been naturally funnier or more relaxed, but getting the gig came down to a personality contest. How does one compete with that? Jesus Christ. Jim Nabors was right: it is better to be liked.

I did not get to stew long, or wonder if I should reread Norman Vincent Peale's *How to Win Friends and Influence People,* when I discovered how much Merv Griffin liked me. He was speaking to me on the phone in a rushed whisper.

"John, this is just between you and me. You'll be getting a call in a couple of days from someone here at Westinghouse, in case I should leave the show. Westinghouse is preparing to sign a couple of backups. They have a couple in mind, and I recommended you."

"Are you leaving? Why?"

"No. It's a contingency. Good luck."

It was all so weird. I even wondered if it was really Merv. Why wouldn't Murray have called with such amazing news? Rather than making me feel elated, I felt down. I shared the contents of the call and my reserved feelings with Sarita, who had no doubt it was Merv.

"But why the secrecy?" I asked her.

"Because he likes you," she said. "So, just be patient."

As Merv had predicted, I got the call. It was from Jack Reeves from Westinghouse. He said he was coming to Los Angeles in two days and would I and Sarita meet him in the main dining room of the Ambassador Hotel? He would be staying there, and make the reservations.

"What are we meeting about?" I asked.

He chuckled. "Your future, young man. 7:30. Sharp."

Two days later, a gentleman approached the table. "How are you two? I'm Jack Reeves. John, I'm very familiar with your good work, but know nothing about this beautiful creature here. Sarita, tell me about yourself."

"There's nothing to tell. I was in show business, but now my husband is."

"Well, young lady, your husband may be about to become a star."

"He already is," Sarita said. "And in a few months, a father."

"Well, well, then I could not have popped up at a better time. This is wonderful." He motioned for the waiter, telling us he'd eaten there often and asked if we would mind if he ordered for us. He also ordered a bottle of wine, asking for a particular vintage and date. His conversation was about movie stars, the weather, everything but why he was there. His delaying chit-chatting was killing me.

I tried to steer him toward talking about Merv, or Westinghouse, but he waved me off saying, "In good time. First, we must have a get-acquainted conversation." He continued to converse, mostly to himself. The only thing I was listening for was hopefully his last sentence. After an uneaten meal by me, and a bottle of wine drunk by him, he finally said, "Mr. Barbour, my boy, we think someday you might be a really good replacement for Merv, if he decides to hang it up. No one knows when, but one must always be prepared. And to be prepared, we'd like to sign you for six months, just in case. An exclusive option. How does that sound?"

"That sounds absolutely wonderful. It'd sound better if I knew for how much."

His laughter eased me. "I was right about you. Funny and smart. Six hundred a week for six months. You can still do your stand up, variety and talk show appearances. You just can't accept any other job as a host,"

"Thank you," I said, "but can I ask you a question? Am I the only one you're signing? It seems to me, a big corporation wouldn't just buy one egg that might not hatch, and keep it in one basket."

He nodded. "Honestly, we're talking to two others. One you might know. Al Hamel. He's married to that blonde actress, Suzanne Somers, and the other fellow is from Detroit. Dennis Wholey. We're offering them the same deal. And the idea is, if Merv decides to leave or whatever, each one of you would get a shot at hosting for one night, and we'd evaluate from there. Sound fair?"

"It sounds fair. And smart."

"Wonderful. I'll get the paperwork to you immediately. When I get it back, we start sending checks."

More Things on Heaven and Earth

How and why one sperm in millions makes it up the fallopian tube, becomes a fetus, then nine months later, becomes a breathing baby, and twenty-nine years later a king or a killer, sometimes both, is beyond me. They are just facts of life and nature. Those who pontificate on how these facts came to be facts are on a wasted journey into mythmaking.

As a kid I discovered prayer didn't work, but I did not discard the Bible. I read it as literature or poetry. And to maybe discover something about human nature. However, there is more insight and truth into human conduct, and the human comedy in Shakespeare, Sholom Aleichem, Dostoyevsky, and especially Mark Twain.

I give no thought to the workings or origins of the universe. I just know it's there and marvel at its existence. But, like everyone, I am more interested in my existence, and marvel at how screwed up it can get even when I don't want it to. The Big Bang theory says there was this huge explosion, and up popped the origins of the universe into nothing. Nonsense. It had to pop into something. Even empty space, which had to be there to accommodate it. And if the Big Bang is the center of the universe, spraying planets and debris in all directions to the edges, the center would be easy to find. Just retrace the paths of these objects. What all agree on, though, is that we live in an electric universe. All life and objects give off electricity. It is entirely possible, therefore, to conclude in some small way, we are all senders and receivers of electrical impulses. Perhaps this is how and why some people are attracted to or repelled by others without even talking to them. Some of those impulses we send and receive may be thoughts. And a gifted few may be able to read them.

In other words, as much as I hate to say it, there may be honest to God psychics.

I would not be saying this if I had not been, as an unbeliever, an eyewitness to it – a few times with my wife, and once with a famous Dutch psychic, Peter Hurkos. In both instances, both were bumped on the head. In my wife's case, she was dropped on her head at four. Peter Hurkos fell off a ladder in Holland while painting the roof. I did not know my wife had this ability, gift, talent, or whatever you call it until just before her father's death. She had kept it from me thinking it was all too negative and weird. In the instance of her father's unexpected death, she had no choice. She was six months pregnant, and after a short visit to see her father in San Francisco, came home and this once happy, singing mother-to-be, did nothing but cry all day and night. I was helpless in comforting her. In desperation, fearing for her and our child, I suggested she see a psychiatrist. She declined. I got very loud, telling her she had to explain what was going on.

"I can't help it. It's silly."

"What is?" I yelled.

"My father is going to die."

"What?" I screamed. "What are you talking about. He's in fantastic shape. Look at him! He got a clean bill of health two months ago when he went in for his checkup."

"No, he's not," Sarita said. "He's going to die."

"Jesus Christ, Sarita, how can you say that?"

She stopped crying. "When I hugged him to say goodbye last week his body was cold. I could feel it."

"Jesus Christ, that is unbelievable. What a thing to say."

She had stopped crying. I looked at her differently. I truthfully thought there was something weird about her that I had not seen. There was a strained silence in our apartment and in our bed for two long awkward days. Then she got the phone call from her sister. Their father had died of a heart attack at sixty-three. He had gone to the hospital with a pain in his leg. It was a blood clot misdiagnosed by the hospital, so he was sent home. Having suspected it, Sarita did not cry. She had cried enough. I was devastated. I went on to miss his calling me Johnny.

I met Peter Hurkos through a wonderfully playful, handsome actor/singer named Jack Cassidy. He was a friend of Chris Hayward's, married to Shirley Jones. He was George Hamilton with talent. Jack was appearing in a sitcom filming at CBS studios in Studio City. I was the warm-up comic. I had already signed my agreement with Westinghouse, but this was a commitment I had made previously.

Peter, a large man, close to fifty, was a world-famous psychic, and the star attraction at a lot of Beverly Hills dinner parties. Jack and his wife asked Sarita and me if we would go in their place to one such gathering in the Hollywood Hills, just above the studio. Peter sat at the end of the table, his back to the kitchen. Sarita and I sat near the other end, across from us two attractive women in their late twenties. I recognized no one. It seemed we were a table of a dozen strangers. But not for long. Peter, encouraged by the diners, regaled us with countless interesting stories of his experiences and famous clients. Soon everyone was telling strange stories, and laughing.

One of the brunettes leaned toward me. "How long have you known Peter?"

"A few hours," I smiled. "And you?"

"Eight hours." She wasn't smiling.

"Eight hours? You're kidding."

"No, my friend and I are stewardesses on United. He was our passenger. When he got off at LAX, he handed us a card with his number and this address, and said we must show up."

"Why"

"I don't know."

From the far end of the table, Peter suddenly called the brunette stewardess by name. Guests became quiet, as though someone had told them to do so. Peter repeated her name, then added, "I want you to know, he is all right."

The girl gasped, then caught herself. Her friend reached over and touched her arm.

Peter continued, almost in a whisper, "You were engaged to be married three months ago." The brunette let out a hurtful yelp, like she'd been punched, clasping her hand quickly over her mouth. "He was a wonderful, vibrant, adventuresome young man. But what I see, I don't quite understand." He paused. A long time. The young woman started to sniffle.

"He is ... he is on a motorcycle ... and he crashes ... and ... and he drowns."

The brunette screamed, the throaty sounds of someone severely wounded. Tears poured out of her. *Was this some kind of dinner party act?* But the eeriness was too real.

"But ... but ... he ... he doesn't drown in water. He drowns in blood?" Peter finished the last sentence with a question mark. The girl sobbed, throwing herself back in the chair. She was gasping, deep and uncontrollably. Peter said, "I'm sorry, dear, but I saw that in you this afternoon on the plane. I just wanted to let you know, he was all right. I'm sorry."

We all stared at the girl. Helpless. She gasped for breath.

"Mr. Hurkos, I'm so sorry... I can't help it. I've been this way ever since it happened. My fiancé loved his motorcycle. I'd never get on it. One Sunday he went out riding, racing against this train. He was trying to beat a warning pole at a crossing, but crashed into it. The handle bars went through his chest." Everyone at the table was gasping and crying. Not me. It was just too horrifying and incomprehensible.

"The coroner said his lungs filled with blood. He drowned in his own blood." Peter rose. He looked fifteen years older than when he had sat down. His face was grey and creased. "I'm sorry, but I'm glad you came. I'm very tired. Had a long day, and a long trip. The evening is over for me. I thank you all for being here; you may continue to imbibe, but I'm off to bed."

Peter moved down our side of the long table, on his way to his bedroom, stopping by Sarita. He put his hand gently on her head. "You, my dear, are going to have a boy, a boy that will be a blessing."

"Thank you," Sarita said softly.

Then he said to me, "Young man, I expect to see you again. But maybe not in person. But I'll be seeing you. And watch out for foreigners." He went to his room.

We rose to leave, everyone saying their goodnights in hushed tones. Sarita said to the young woman, "Are you all right?"

"I'm fine, thank you. Actually, I feel as though I've been to a faith healer, and got healed."

Sitting in For Merv

I had signed my agreement with Westinghouse, as did Wholey and Hamel; however, I never heard or read anything about it in *Variety* or *The Reporter*. I also never heard a word from the Morris Agency. Or Murray. I thought that was weird since Murray, through Merv, had the very best "in" at Westinghouse. Since no reporter was putting out the story, I didn't have the foggiest notion as how to go about promoting myself and what I thought was pretty big showbiz news. I thought maybe a hired publicist would know. Since I had a good relationship with Alan Bernard, I asked him to help me put out a paid press release.

Alan said, "Don't bother, John. Save your money. Your wife's gonna have a baby soon, and you'll need that nest egg."

"But, Alan, this is a big deal. I want people to know that I was Merv's choice, and one of Westinghouse's choice to replace him."

"Don't worry," Alan assured me. 'It's a tiny town. Word'll get out soon." Against my better, burning instincts, I listened to him. After all, he was one of the biggest agents in town. Who would know better about this stuff than him? A few months later, in late November of 1968, rumors about Merv ditching Westinghouse to go to CBS were rampant. Word about my being signed as a possible replacement, along with Wholey and Hamel, was still nonexistent. What was wrong with Murray? Or the Morris office? Why hadn't I heard from them? Who I did hear from, though, was Jim Geishheimer, the accountant for Merv's show.

"John, I think you'll be getting a call shortly about setting a date for you to sit in for Merv and audition." Jim sounded more pleased than I felt. "Things are starting to stir a lot. Right now, Chet Collier is in serious negotiations with Newhart's people to get him."

"What?" I shouted.

"Yeah. They're after Newhart, but it looks like his price is too high."

"Jesus, Jim, have they been talking to Alan Bernard?"

"Yeah, that's the guy. How did you know?"

"He's been half-assed helping me, not managing, but helping. When you guys signed me, I went to him with the idea of hiring a publicist and he talked me out of it."

Jim laughed. "God, some business you're in."

"Jim, I'm not into it yet. Still on the fringes."

"In a few weeks you won't need a publicist. They'll see you on the show, and you'll be terrific. Believe me. Right now, even though you've only been on a few times, their research shows you're one of Merv's favorite guests."

"Why is it that I feel I'm operating in a vacuum?"

"You're going to be at The Fremont in Vegas in December through January, right?"

"How did you know that?"

"They've researched your schedule, and the other two guys, for the next few months. They're gonna send out a young producer to meet with you. To help them evaluate you. To see how he gets along with you. All that stuff."

"If I'm picked, couldn't I have anything to say about who and how my show is produced?"

He laughed heartily. "After five years when you're a star, you can kick ass; until then you have to kiss it. But you'll have some cute, successful ass to kiss. He's Westinghouse's new fair-haired, or rather dark-haired boy wonder, and they've assigned him to you, not those other guys."

"What's his name?"

"Roger Ailes. He used to do PR and media consulting for Nixon. Met Nixon producing *The Mike Douglas Show*."

"Westinghouse hired a guy who lost?" I cracked.

"He's really close with Pat. She loves him. And McGannon, Westinghouse's head honcho. You'll like him. He's very bright."

"Do you think I should get after the Morris office to push a little more for me?"

"John, this thing is potentially so big, unless you look like you're a lock, which could happen after your audition, they won't stick their necks out for you. Shit, they may also represent Newhart, for all you know. Call me from Vegas after you meet Ailes, and tell me how it goes."

The call came a week before I opened at The Fremont. It was from this Roger Ailes just as Jim had predicted.

"I'll be there opening night," he said. I know what you look like, and you'll be on stage, so I won't have any trouble finding you." He chuckled.

The act I was opening for at the Fremont Hotel was a singer named John Gary. He had a few number one hits, had appeared often on *The Danny Kaye Variety Show*, and even replaced him with his own summer show. It surprised me he would be appearing downtown and not on the strip. He had been extremely popular, and had an effortless beautiful baritone voice.

In 1968, downtown Las Vegas was no more than two or three blocks long, one street wide, with undeveloped desert on either side. A handful of gaudy, unappealing, neon lit clubs filled with penny and nickel slot machines filled those few blocks. It had not improved since I first saw it. John Gary was as pleasant as his voice. He was a year older than me, had a soft round Irish face with warm blue eyes. Some people mistook us for relatives. He wore a tuxedo on stage, and every night attracted an overflow crowd. Full, happy houses are the easiest for comedians. I was enormously happy: I was under contract to possibly replace Merv, Sarita was in her eighth month, and her condition provided me with material that brought screams from the audience, especially the women.

John's wife was an extremely attractive brunette-blonde in her early thirties. Looking at this very shapely lady, it was impossible to imagine, between her and John and a couple of marriages, they had nine kids. From the moment she saw Sarita, she became her guide and caretaker. We spent more time in John's dressing room than in our own. It was a feeling of friendship and fun that you want to last forever. But it never does. I never got used to it just disappearing.

John spent his days taking his motorcycle a few blocks off Fremont Street, racing for hours into the desert, often risking his life. Following his performance each night, he'd fill a shoebox with thousands of dollars in cash, rush to the Casino, and risk his life's savings. His wife never said a word. She was used to seeing large sums of money come and go all her life. She was the daughter of McDonnell of the McDonnell-Douglas Aircraft Company.

Following my show the second night, a very handsome, slender dark-haired young man, in his late twenties, intercepted me on my way to the dressing room, extending his hand. "Hi, John, I'm Roger Ailes."

I couldn't believe he was so young. Almost a kid. And so physically attractive. He could have been under contract to MGM. "Hi," I said, still evaluating him. "I was sort of expecting you last night, opening night."

"I was there, but I wanted to see if you could be that good a second night."

"Was I?"

"Better. Would you and your wife have breakfast with me in the morning? We should get acquainted."

At nine the next morning, the three of us were in a booth. I told Roger I was surprised he was behind the camera and not in front of it. He shrugged the compliment off as though he'd heard it often. He said emphatically it was not for him; he felt he could do so much more behind it. I asked him a lot about Nixon and Pat. He seemed pleased that I wasn't pushing him to talk about me and Westinghouse. I was curious because he was barely out of school when Nixon was debating Kennedy. How does one get that kind of job, to be advising a man just a few votes from the presidency? (When I saw Roger as the President of Fox News, where he said, "It's not what you put on the news that affects the world, it's what you don't put on," I recognized the mind, but not the body. He looked like he ate three of his former selves since that breakfast at The Fremont.)

"They've assigned me to produce your show. If you have any thoughts about the people you might want as guests, let me know. We'll see if we can get them."

"Roger, you were good enough for Nixon, you're good enough for me. Even though he lost!"

He laughed heartily. "Well, we'll see that you don't. I'm leaving this afternoon. Call me anytime for anything. I'll see you in New York." He then turned to Sarita. "I hope I see you, too, Sarita, but it's possible you may have to get a doctor's permission to fly, or you'll have to pay for a third ticket." He hugged her and left.

In the Eye of the Hurricane

The day I filled in for Merv I was focused and prepared. Being in that single-minded state, I was unaware of the wheeling, dealing and chicanery swirling around me. Even if I was aware of what was going on, I couldn't do anything about it anyway. I had to just do my job. It would not be the first time that possible success would be jeopardized by people and events beyond my control. Everyone I know in this business has a membership in this guild.

Merv was on hand to wish me luck. He posed happily for a picture with his son Tony and me and a very expectant Sarita. Roger did the perfect job putting the show together. The audience's reception was warm and welcoming, even more so after my opening monologue. I was where I felt I belonged. Usually when I feel that good, I can remember everything about a show – every guest, every question, every answer. In that case, though, I can remember only one guest, Jean Claude Killy. Jean was a dark-haired handsome heartthrob of the month, an Olympic Gold Medalist, the most famous Frenchman outside of Charles de Gaulle. Personality-wise, he was Burt Reynolds on skis. He was charming, playful, and outspoken. I was his perfect straight man.

After his appearance, the whole show was an upbeat breeze. When it was over, I had dozens of new back-slapping, hand-shaking friends, including a couple from William Morris. Roger approached me with a huge smile. "I think you're gonna outdo Nixon for me!" One fellow in a suit whose handshake and compliments were not quite as warm, was a fellow I'd never seen before. He introduced himself as Chet Collier, Head of Programming for Westinghouse. After saying, "Very nice job," he walked off.

The following day, back home, the overnight ratings were out, as was a very quick invitation to a major meeting of all the major domos in the main conference room of the Beverly Hills offices of The Morris Agency. My numbers, despite no star or headline names, except for Jean Claude, were as high as Merv's had ever been. Wholey's and Hamel's never came close. How could I not get it? Merv's personal choice, a success with the audience in studio and at home – what could possibly stop me?

I entered the Morris office with a chip on my shoulder the size of my head. I was pissed. They had done nothing to push for the job, but now wanted a percentage from me for doing nothing. It was the wrong attitude. And I gave my worst performance.

I entered to very loud applause. I was not impressed, and the fake affection pissed me off more. After the small talk and ebullient compliments, I asked why I was there since I'd had to do everything so far on my own. They were stunned.

The boss said, "John, there's little doubt in our minds that you'll get the job and deserve it. We apologize for not being more in your corner earlier, but we have a few major personalities who were pushing for that job."

"I understand," I said. "But it's not who wants the job, it's who would be best for it. Obviously, I wasn't on your list. So, you see, I have mixed feelings about this office, and what this office thinks of me."

The boss said, "We think you're fantastic. A major television personality. In case this thing with Westinghouse doesn't work out, there's a lot we can do for you."

"For example?"

Various agents spoke up. "We can send you to Mexico to be a judge for the Miss America contest."

"We have three game show pilots committed. You could have your choice," said another.

"We've got a movie of the week you'd be perfect for," from one more.

I said, "I didn't hear anything about maybe developing a talk show, which I keep telling you, is all I really want to do." They said nothing. So, I rose. "Thank you all very much, but right now, I have a lot to think about." I left.

The Morris office was now justifiably in no mood to campaign for me. Roger Ailes said he had no idea what was going on; the snippets of information I managed to get were still from Jim. To the best of his knowledge, Westinghouse, meaning Chet Collier, was pleased with me, especially my ratings. It seemed Alan Bernard had priced Newhart out of the job. Jim informed me Chet Collier would be on his way soon to England to meet with David Frost, his personal choice.

"Frost? They've got to be kidding. An Englishman can't host an American talk show, no matter how good he is."

"You know that, and I know that, but Collier doesn't."

"Is he still in town?"

"Yeah."

"In the building?"

"The main office. Downtown."

"Can you connect me, Jim?"

"Are you kidding?"

"No, I want to talk to him."

"What are you gonna say?"

"I haven't the foggiest idea, but he's making a mistake. Don't worry, I won't mention you. Can you transfer me?"

I waited for less than a minute, when Chet Collier picked up. After identifying myself, I said, "Mr. Collier, you remember when John Kennedy said, 'Ask not what your country can do for you, but what you can do for your country? Well, I'm here to tell you what I can do for my country, and for Westinghouse."

"John, what's your point, please? I'm rather busy."

"Mr. Collier, I know through a friend in London that you're planning on going there to see David Frost–"

"No, I'm not. I'm just on my way to London."

"Mr. Collier, I hope so, because no matter how charming David is on *That Was the Week That Was,* he couldn't make it hosting an American talk show."

"I don't think that's true," Chet snapped.

"Merv had on many guests who talked about government and corporate corruption, problems of all sorts in this country, including our foreign policy, and no foreigner should be an arbiter of that."

"John, I appreciate your concern, and you're still in the running–"

"I'm not calling because I'm in the running. I'm calling because I have a phenomenal idea for you."

"And what is that?"

"You could get more publicity than anything ever in show business since the search for Scarlet O'Hara if you made looking for your host a public popularity contest. Tell the public what you're doing, then have me, Alan, Dennis and whoever, guest host and have the audience vote! It'd be a smash."

"The public doesn't hire the talent. I do." (It wouldn't be the first time I heard this from those running the supposed public airways.)

"Of course you do, but they'd give you feedback on which to base your choice. It'd be huge. And honestly, even if I lose, I'd love the chance to go up against anybody."

"Well, I appreciate your concern and your call, and even your confidence, so, we'll see. Thank you." He hung up.

Two weeks later, Westinghouse announced signing David Frost and his clipboard. Jim called immediately with the news. I told him I couldn't believe it. I had relayed to him my short conversation with Collier before he left.

"Well, what did it, Johnny, had nothing to do with you or the show, which is really sad. When Collier went to England with McGannon, the president of this place, Frost was able to take him to Ten Downing Street and fucking Buckingham Palace. You can't beat that!"

"Jim, I don't know how to thank you for your support. I guess if this business was easy everybody would be doing it."

"What are you gonna do now?"

"Well, I've been on square one a number of times. It's probably pretty crowded now with newcomers, so I'll see if I can move up to square three."

If I was now back on square three, there were no callers. No friends. No agents. No managers. No club owners. If I owed money, I would have even welcomed a call from a creditor. The call I got after a very long week was as unlikely as it was exhilarating; not because it could have been a job offer, but because it came from someone in the business, in management, who knew what he was doing. It came from Chuck Young, the General Manager of the Metromedia station in Los Angeles. I had never met him, but I'd heard of him. I had enormous admiration for him based on one simple decision he'd made. He hired Joe Pyne, America's first angry man on TV, sight unseen. I cheer that rare kind of courage and independence.

"John, this is Chuck Young, channel eleven. Expect a call from a producer named Bill Walker. He's going to be talking to you about doing a Saturday night show for us. Westinghouse made a fucking mistake; that limey will die. I'm banking on you being a fallback when he does. Are you up for it?"

"Yes, sir!"

"Okay. Hang up and wait for the call. You won't be talking to me much anymore."

Within seconds, the phone rang. It was Bill Walker who'd done a number of local shows for Metromedia. He was also involved in Metromedia's failed attempt to mount a primetime talk show versus Merv with singer-dancer Donald O'Connor. It never got beyond Los Angeles.

Bill told me, in essence, that I'd be replacing O'Connor, not nightly, just on Saturdays. It would be for thirteen weeks at a reasonable salary. I told him my only concern was while he was the producer, I would have an equal say in the type of show we did, the guests we booked, and if he booked a guest I hated, I'd still have him or her on. He must do likewise for me. He agreed readily, saying, "This sounds like fun!"

Was it ever!

The John Barbour Show

For years, aside from writing material religiously every day on my legal pad, I often wrote over and over, The John Barbour Show. Those four words were what I lived to do, to be the next Jack Paar. It was the sole reason for doing stand-up, because that's what Jack did. Now, with Bill Walker, it was my turn. The John Barbour Show was just local, but that didn't matter. It had my name on it. Carson got started locally doing *Carson's Cellar*. I was pumped.

In spite of never having done a talk show, I had a crystal-clear picture of how one should be done, most of it infused by the years of watching Paar, both late night and later in prime time. After a short philosophical discussion of the show's content, we had an even shorter discussion about the set. Should we have a desk, or sofas? We decided on both.

I loved television. Everything about it. It was and is the country's electronic umbilical cord. As one of my first guests I wanted someone who was verbal, funny and knowledgeable about the medium, one who was as passionate about it as I was. I could only think of one person, but that person hated me. And said so in his column. His name was Harlan Ellison.

There was a widely read paper in LA at the time, *The Los Angeles Free Press*. It was widely read because LA is a movie and TV town. Everyone in or out of the business read Ellison's scathing, brilliant critiques in his column, appropriately called, *The Glass Teat*. I was drawn and quartered by Harlan the night I took over for Merv. It was the only negative review I got. And the only one I read. The nicest thing he said was that I was a faggot who fawned over and sucked up to the ultra-masculine, charming Olympic skier, Jean Claude Killy. Harlan wondered where in the hell I came from, and how could Westinghouse have ever let a fruit like me take over for Merv. Scathing, but funny. And, funny is funny!

Outside of that column, Harlan was an excellent, highly acclaimed, television and short story writer. He is best known for his uncannily prescient science fiction; however, if you tell him that, he will tell you what he's told many who've introduced him as such: "If you call me a science fiction writer again I'll rip your fucking head off and piss down your neck!" Paramount Pictures plagiarized his 'Terminator' story, turning it into one of Schwarzenegger's biggest hits. Harlan wanted to rip Paramount's heads off against the advice of everyone who told him he'd never work in that town again. He sued. And won. When he did so, he bought a huge billboard on Sunset Boulevard, on the most popular corner near Beverly Hills, and proclaimed: I beat the Bastards!

I knew none of this when I showed Bill the review. All I knew about Harlan was on that page.

"Jesus Christ," Bill said after reading it. "What'd you ever do to him?"

"I'd like to book him," I said.

"Are you nuts? He hates you."

"Bill, everybody in town knows it. So, if word gets out that he's going to be my first guest, there'll be a lot of folks tuning in."

"John, it might get really awkward and bloody."

"That sounds like great television to me. I mean, I don't know anything about him. He may be a good writer, but totally inarticulate. Do you know anyone who knows him?"

"No. But I could make some calls. Are you sure you wanna do this?"

"You know what, Bill, why don't I call him myself."

"Are you nuts? Do you have his number?"

"No. But we'll call the guild, or the Free Press, or let's just look in the phone book."

"Johnny, you're not serious."

"Bill, we haven't even done our first show, and already it sounds like fun. Got a phone book?"

Bill opened the white pages. "Jesus Christ. Here it is," he said, tapping his finger on the page. He pushed the phone book toward me. Halfway down, there it was. I dialed. The phone didn't ring more than twice, a sign the person on the other end is a no-nonsense kind of person. The gruff "Yeah!" verified it.

"Harlan Ellison?" I asked.

"Yeah!"

"This is John Barbour."

There was a long pause before he exclaimed, "Holy shit!"

"Have you got a minute?"

"Holy, holy shit! You don't sound mad."

"I'm not mad, but I must tell you, while it was a little unpleasant personally, it was well written."

"You're kidding?"

"Harlan, I don't know you, obviously. I've never heard of you 'til your column, but I like good writing. And I was curious to see if you could talk as well as you write?"

"What the fuck for?"

"I'm starting a Saturday night late night poor man's Johnny Carson show over here at channel eleven. I'd like you to be my first guest to talk about television."

"Christ, man, you have some balls. Why would you do that?"

"Is that a no?"

"No, man. But why me? After that review ... which I wouldn't change by the way–"

"I don't want you to change it. If you bring it up during the show, that's fine by me. I'll handle it."

"Is this a joke?"

"No. I'll give you our office number and you can call back."

"No, that's okay. I'm your first guest? And you want me to talk about ... ?"

"Television. I can't think of anyone who'd be more perfect. It doesn't pay much. If you're in a guild, minimum. If there's something you want to plug, besides me, you're welcome."

He laughed. "I wouldn't miss this for anything."

Our show played late, but it was pre-taped at seven p.m. to accommodate the audiences. At first, they were bussed in from retirement homes and tourist sites. With that, every show was a turn away crowd. Being local and low budget, we couldn't afford a band like the big boys, but we ended up with a more intimate musical sound than any of them, including Paar. We hired the Joe Pass Trio. Joe was one of jazz's most accomplished guitarists who often accompanied Ella Fitzgerald. Joe got scale, like everyone. How we got such an artist I do not know. He called out of the blue asking if we were going to have live music. When I said yes, he said he'd do it for nothing.

The set was the standard desk, a cushioned chair to my right, and a sofa to the right of that. The only thing that made it look any different was the floor. Instead of a rug or a plain wooden stage, we had two-and-a-half-foot alternating quarter inch white and black plastic squares. Like the floor at The Hungry i, it looked like a giant classy chessboard, a place where Fred Astaire and Ginger Rogers might dance. This led accidentally to one of the biggest laughs I got.

Harlan could not have been more wonderful. He was acerbic, engagingly angry, bashing television brilliantly. The audience applauded frequently during his tirades. The subject of me on Merv never came up. He was followed by a beautiful young health instructor who was going to show us how to use common items around the house to exercise. One of the items she used was a plunger. After she demonstrated to me how to use it to develop muscles and strength, I walked to center stage. As instructed, I started pumping up and down vigorously with it. One of the things plungers do, if pushed properly, is stick to a smooth service. This one did. I kept tugging and tugging, much to the delight of the audience, it finally popped up loudly. Attached to the bottom was one of the floors black plastic squares. The audience screamed. I bent down to look where it came from, as though I was staring into the basement, and hollered, "There's Donald O'Connor!" The audience, the crew, the cameramen, the guests erupted in a roar that seemed to continue through the whole show. It was a hit. A note from Chuck Young and the program director said, fantastic! The ratings were not great, but they were, as management said, very respectable. Bill said it was the most fun he'd ever had as a producer.

Harlan shook my hand as vigorously as it's ever been shaken. "Man, you're a natural. That was really cool."

"Thanks, but don't write about me in your next column," I said with a smile.

"I don't intend to. Once was enough."

The following Monday, back in the office preparing the next show, Bill read to me some of the nice calls we had received about the first show. Then he held up a piece of paper and said, laughing, "You're not going to believe this! It's from the program director." He stopped smiling.

"He says Harlan Ellison came in to see him first thing this morning. He wants to host it. He thinks you're shit and he'd be better."

I just shook my head. "Unbelievable." But, as far as I was concerned, it was still worth having Harlan on. He was and is a fabulously interesting, entertaining, opinionated guest. Perfect television. Every time I got another talk show, he was one of the first people I booked.

"You know who I want to book now? Redd Foxx."

"Redd Foxx?" Bill said. "You can't put him on television. He's filthy."

"I've known Redd for years. Aside from those party records, he's the funniest, wittiest person I know. He'd be terrific."

"I don't think management would be too thrilled."

"We tape early, so they'll have no concerns about anything getting out over the air. I saw him a couple of weeks ago on *The Today Show*. Hugh Downs said he loved him in a club he went to and interviewed him for a few minutes. Redd was fine."

"Yeah, but he's never been on a variety show–"

"That's because no one will book him. He's filthy *and* funny, but I know he can just be funny."

Bill said, "Maybe book him with other comedians so it looks like a comics' variety show."

"Bill, that's great. Let's do it."

That booking led to the biggest laugh I have ever heard in television. And, it was clean! Questionable, but clean!

For Redd Foxx's debut on a variety show we also booked three very different comics, along with a wonderfully engaging and attractive female, Charo, known to most of America as the "Goochy Goochy Girl;" known to Xavier Cugat as his ex-wife. We opened with Jack Carter, seen as frequently in The Catskills as matzo balls, and often on Ed Sullivan. The edgy brashness of his delivery made the material sound funnier than it actually was. He was followed by Rip Taylor, a performer known as the crying comedian, seen regularly on *Hollywood Squa*res. Like Carter, Rip delivered his stuff at the top of his cracking voice, accompanied by a flurry of tears. He was so endearing, it was difficult not to like and laugh at him.

The third comedian was a friend whom I tried to help often. He was a stranger to ambition. His name was Bill Morrison, the best man at my wedding. Bill owned the house where, years earlier, we held our comedy-acting workshops. He was quiet and very handsome. His greatest asset, though, was the peacefulness of his personality. The only other person with that quality was my wife. Like her, he could walk onstage, and no matter how noisy it was, people were magically attracted to his presence, stopping to hear what he had to say. The problem was, he had nothing to say, at least not anything funny; he also never made any effort to develop anything funny. He thought chatting was his act. Anyone else who just stood up there and chatted would be booed off the stage; folks somehow didn't mind listening.

Liking him, I wanted to give him a break, so I created a premise for him that would allow him to just chat and ad lib. The premise was he was a psychic and fortune teller who had accidentally discovered a way to read the inside of people's souls – how to predict their futures by having them blow the essence of their lungs into a balloon. He would then delicately fondle and caress the balloon, interpreting the mysteries of the balloon's contents. Doing this, he could say anything he wanted without making jokes; no matter what he said, it would get a laugh. Of course, it was announced that Bill, this new psychic, would read Charo's balloons. Since Charo looked like she was outfitted by Frederick's of Hollywood, this simple announcement by itself got huge laughs. When he actually did read her balloons with her huffing and puffing to fill one, the laughs got even bigger. Bill never went anywhere with this success. He later claimed 'his' balloon act was stolen by a young comic named Steve Martin who did it on *The Tonight Show*.

It was a colossal night for fun and frivolity. By the time I got around to introducing Redd, I was beginning to worry he might not be able to follow all that. Nobody could. Redd, however, ended up getting the biggest laugh I have ever heard in a television studio anywhere at any time, and I've heard them all. Redd got it on an unexpected ad lib.

I knew his act perfectly. After introducing him, I knew I could safely lead him to some smart clean topical laughs. With his entrance, he got a laugh just on his wardrobe. He came out wearing Scottish golf pants that stopped just below the knees. Before coming to sit next to me, he walked toward the audience and said, "I bet you didn't expect to see this on TV. Knickers!"

The audience howled and applauded, as did our fellow performers. But that's not the laugh I'm talking about.

He sat next to me. I asked Redd, since it was all over the news, about the Black Power movement, how he felt about it, knowing what he'd say. "I don't care about Black Power or White Power!"

"You don't?" I asked.

"No. I only believe in Green Power, because if you have the green you can buy the places where blacks 'n' whites hold their meetings."

While the audience laughed and applauded, a weird thought came out of nowhere. I did not want to throw Redd off. I had no idea how he'd respond, or even if he could respond at all, but I blurted, "Redd, why do you think money's colored green?"

Redd immediately puffed up his chest like he was an authority on everything, announcing knowingly, like it was common knowledge, "That's 'cuz Jews pick it before it gets ripe."

The reaction wasn't just laughter. It was roars and screams, people bending over, slapping one another. It was bedlam. Jack Carter, sitting on the sofa, tumbled onto the floor clutching his stomach. It lasted for minutes. When it died down, Jack would pull a twenty from his wallet, holding it up for the audience. He didn't have to say a word, and the hysteria started all over again.

Redd was a show-stopping hit. And deserved to be. I was pleased I could give him a platform, albeit a small one, after all he had done for me. Of the scores and scores of talents and stars, major or minor, whom I've known or been close to over the years, Redd is the only one who remained a friend until he died.

Redd did better than my little show did. The ratings were respectable enough to keep it on, but with *The David Frost Show* getting fair ratings, Chuck thought his station in that time slot was safe. He felt they could make more money airing a late-night movie. Chuck told me he was sorry, that he was a fan, but business was business. He smiled slightly. "Johnny, you're not in show business. You're just in business."

It was a terrific show, but I had no idea how to go about promoting it. I thought it would sell itself. We had great guests, great music, great singers, some newcomers, and every author who came on was stunned that I had read his or her book. We were the first to book Bob Guccione, who was starting a magazine to compete with *Playboy* called *Penthouse*. We booked a Mafiosi who had testified before congress, and subsequently had his tale told in a famous film. We even got away with booking two nudists. Not all socially redeeming, but must-watch TV; however, there just wasn't enough must-watching.

To me, self-promotion, then and now, is as difficult as shoveling smoke. They say, whoever 'they' are, that when something dies, something else is born. In my case, what was to be born was not a something, but a someone, a someone who wouldn't only change my life, but give me one. My son.

January 29, 1969

Of all the chapters I'm compiling for this book, this, with the simple heading of the date, had the most profound impact on me, the emotional impact, for which I was totally unprepared. It is the date of my son's birth. And mine as a person. A date that led to the happiest most fulfilling, rewarding, meaningful dozen and a half years of my life. The place was The First Presbyterian Hospital in the heart of The San Fernando Valley. This was not the hospital my wife and I picked; we would have picked the one just a few blocks from our apartment. As a matter of fact, we never ever relaxed enough to even think about any hospital. We spent our time thinking of names. Of the few names we came up with, not one was a girl. Just boys. Sarita's father told her she'd have a son. So did Mahalia Jackson; she even went so far as to buy Sarita our son's first blue outfit. So did my friend Chris Hayward, who asked to be, and became, his godfather. It was the hospital where my wife's doctor practiced. His name was Dr. Faust. His total calmness and professionalism made you feel, like Allstate, that you were in good hands.

Sarita began to feel strong contractions early in the morning, but never said anything about them. She would stop whatever it was she was doing, stay motionless for a moment, grimace slightly, then continue.

I noticed it. "Honey, are your contractions getting stronger?" She just looked at me. "I mean it looks like they're spreading all the way to your face. I think I'd better take you to the hospital."

Dr. Faust met us at the front, put Sarita in a wheelchair and wheeled her off to the maternity room. Her water broke on the way. Going through the doors she looked back at me with this ever so soft hint of a smile; she looked like a kid at Christmas awaiting a much longed for present. Me, I was lost. I was assigned, or rather quietly ordered, to the waiting room, which should be given another name: The anguish room. The nail-biting room. The can't sit down room. The throw-up room. The where's the bathroom room? For me it was the pacing room.

Watching Sarita go through those doors, trying to smile back at me, I felt like a stranger. I had never seen anyone under what must be tough circumstances so peaceful, so self-contained, so radiantly happy. Her demeanor left me in awe; I was a spectator watching a genius, a genius at just being alive. A genius I could never be like.

(Before continuing, a thought occurs to me, about money. We didn't have much, if any. During the few years leading up to that day I had a jaw broken in two places, having been hit in the face during a celebrity baseball game while running to first, by somebody who couldn't throw, or who didn't like me. During a make-up hockey game, I got a stick rammed into my mouth by someone on my team and was rushed to the hospital for stitches. There were other minor calamities and accidents that took me to doctors. And then a baby. I can't recall what any doctor or hospital charged. All I know is with few funds, we still somehow managed to pay everyone. Immediately. All in cash.)

Except for a nurse and receptionist at the desk, I was the only one in the waiting room. My head was cluttered with unsettling thoughts that zipped from one to the other so quickly. I couldn't focus. How was Sarita? Was she in pain? Will the baby be okay? A baby is a permanent stranger! What was I going to do with that helpless being? What if I dropped it? Those thoughts are not the thoughts of a father. Those are the thoughts of a scared kid. *I wasn't adult enough for this.*

I recalled when Sarita was in her seventh month, Mort Lachman, Bob Hope's head writer, friend, and one-time neighbor said to everybody, "Look, Johnny Barbour had to grow his own friend!"

I couldn't envision whatever was going to come out of my wife as a friend. What it was for me was a mountain of uncertainties and insecurities. Geez, what if I turned out like my father? Or some of my mother's uncles? I couldn't face being alone with myself or my thoughts another step. I asked the nurse if I could see my wife.

She spoke briefly on the phone, then hung up. "Dr. Faust will be right here."

Within seconds he came strolling down the hall. I rushed to meet him. He said, "We're going to be taking her into delivery soon, so I suggest you stay here. She'll be fine. John, your wife is amazing, unlike any patient I've ever had."

"Doctor, I'm not fine, and I'm not amazing. I'm a wreck. Could I just peek at her? I need to know she's all right!"

"She's more than all right. She is quiet, has refused any painkillers whatsoever, saying she wants to feel every moment and movement of her baby coming into the world. I've never had a woman ever say that to me."

"Look, I may need the painkillers. Please. Just a peek."

"Just a peek. I don't want her distracted."

I almost clung to him as he led me through the entrance to the maternity ward. Once inside, he immediately put up his arm, like some kind of school crossing guard, motioning me to stop. I could not believe what I was seeing or hearing. There were about twenty expectant mothers, but it didn't look like a maternity ward. It looked like an insane asylum. It looked like a scene out of *Snake Pit* with Olivia de Havilland. Most of the women were screaming, moaning or yelling profanities at their doctors, nurses, God, and even at their husbands. That they'd never let them touch them again.

He pointed to a bed in the left-hand corner. Lying there, serenely, was Sarita. "She'll be fine. You'd better go back now. I'll see you later."

Exhausted and mystified by it all, I walked back to the waiting room and forced myself to sit. A half hour later Dr. Faust reappeared wearing a huge smile. I jumped up. He took my hand to calm me. "Congratulations, John. In Sarita's own words, she told me to tell you, you are now the proud father of an eight-pound, nine-ounce host! Congratulations!"

Tears flooded my eyes. It wasn't that I was a father, which terrified me, that brought the sudden tears. It was what she told the doctor to tell me, revealing Sarita was not thinking of her new child, or herself; she was thinking about me, her husband. For months she would occasionally say to me that Westinghouse would realize they were making a mistake with Frost, that they'd be calling me back. In her most precious longed-for moment, she told the doctor to tell me she had given birth to a host. I could not stop crying thinking of her thinking of me. The more I tried to stop crying, the more helpless and stupid I felt. *Why*? I screamed in my head, *are you such a mess?*

The answer was immediate. Because for the first time in my life, I felt loved.

A Child Born; A Father Created

Sarita was discharged from the hospital after a day and a half. I stayed with her the whole time. I couldn't believe a little body had been added to our life. I was more than scared. In our cozy apartment on Kling Street, life was obviously now more about Christopher than me. Sarita and Christopher had won the mother-son lottery. They adored each other. It was difficult for me to adore that little alien creature. I was fearful of holding him for fear I'd drop him. In the beginning, that's how I fathered him, out of fear. Fear that I'd forget how neglectful my mother and father were. Fear of forgetting the few times when my mother did speak to me, it was either baby talk or screaming. I vowed that the moment I looked into his little red face and spoke, I would say the words as one human to another. From his first breath, that was how Sarita and I talked to him. It was three of us having a conversation; Sarita's baby talk to him didn't pop up until he was thirty!

Remembering the non-touching barrenness of my youth, I made it a point to hug him often. Soon, I didn't have to make it a point. I couldn't help myself. I just had to touch him all the time. To wrestle with him, fly him around as I twirled in a circle. Cuddle with him. The more I did this, the more the fear evaporated. The more love I gave him, the more he gave me. The more that vessel of love pours, the more it is replenished.

The first year, he was never out of the apartment, except onto the balcony. Friends called wondering when they were going to see the baby. A few of my fellow comics insisted on coming over just to prove we had a child. But not Sarita's mother or sister. Our two-bedroom apartment was our universe, and Christopher the sun!

The world is full of parents who've had children, who could delight us with endless anecdotes about how amazing their offspring are. But from none of them have I ever heard of the wonders I witnessed with Christopher. I'll recount just a few of them here, so I can get back to my tale. I recount them not as a pleased father, but more as a startled stranger in the presence of a natural wonder,

As a child, he never cried. Not once. On one occasion, when he was two, I was changing his diaper. After I had fastened the adhesive, I wanted to make sure they were secure, so I got this huge pin, forced it through the diaper, through the other side, pushing hard. I noticed the baby grimacing a little, but just ascribed it to my clumsiness. Finally, I fastened the pin. Pleased with my accomplishment, I decided to run my fingers under the diaper to make sure all was right. All wasn't right. I had pushed the huge pin through two inches of his skin. Horrified, I quickly unfastened the pin. For years my ineptness remained our little secret.

When he was two, I was watching the Masters Golf Tournament on television, casually swinging a wedge in front of the set. Soon, from behind me, I heard this clank clank sound. I turned; there he was. He had retrieved a wooden spoon from the kitchen and was bashing his little blocks across the room. I gave up the Masters to watch him. The next day I got a little plastic putter and a whiffle ball, handing it to him without any instructions. I mean, what instructions can you give an infant? He dropped the ball on the carpet, gripped the putter and swung. The ball moved only along the floor. I thought he'd be pleased, but he wasn't. It had not been airborne. For hours, he continued patiently trying to get it flying. Suddenly, he decided to lay the putter on its edge to flatten it, and tried again. The whiffle ball flew across the table into the kitchen. We both shrieked with delight. Me louder than him. He did this every day for a year until I got him sawed down real golf clubs.

He was the Caucasian Tiger Woods before there was a Tiger Woods. He appeared on NBC News and CBS. He shot his first competitive sixty-nine at thirteen against Bobby May, who decades later lost in a questionable PGA playoff to Tiger. Along with Craig Stadler, he was the only high schooler in Los Angeles to win back-to-back city championships. He won the Canadian National Juvenile at fifteen. He was recruited, on his grades, by Harvard, Princeton, Yale and Stanford. He chose Stanford; Tom Watson had gone there. But, back to the kid stuff:

Every night I read him to sleep with fairytales, even though I never really liked them. Maybe because I'd never heard them. He had a particular favorite. That's the one he wanted to hear. Every single night. One evening, shortly after his third birthday, he asked if he could read it to me. I smiled, thinking, *is he kidding,* and handed it to him. He turned it right side up, opened to the first page and began. Word for amazing word. Four pages in, though, I realized he wasn't reading it at all. He had memorized it so completely, he knew when to turn the page.

Because Sarita was musical, we thought without question, just from his intense interest in music and his mother, that he'd be a musician. His favorite singers were Buddy Holly and Tom Jones. We saw *The Buddy Holly Story* four times, had all his records, which were constantly playing in the car or at home, with Christopher singing along perfectly. What he did with Tom Jones, however, was phenomenal. Had we had cell phones then, he would have been an infant superstar. For some reason, he took a deep liking to that ribald Welshman. He never missed him on television. And he did more than memorize every single album and song; he memorized Tom's opening act, comedian Pat Henry, from one of the live albums at Caesars Palace. He was four. He had his own separate bedroom next to ours with bunk beds.

One evening he wandered purposely into our bedroom telling us to get dressed, to come and see the show. When we asked what show, he just said to get dressed and bring money.

We dressed and headed to his room. He was standing at the doorway, though, asking us for a nickel for admission. We paid him. Like a maître de, he then led us to our seats on the bottom bunk bed. In the middle of the room was his slide, about six feet high. He walked to it holding a rubber skip rope, which we soon discovered was his microphone. Satisfied we were seated and paying attention, he lifted the handle of the skip rope to his mouth, announcing, "Ladies and gentlemen, Caesars Palace is proud to present Pat Henry and the one and only Tom Jones!"

Of course, we dutifully applauded. Christopher clambered up the ladder, stood at the top, and not only did Pat's act, but every single Tom

Jones' song, topped off with the recorded banter with the women in the audience. It was his first standing ovation.

A few years later, with Christopher still belting out *It's Not Unusual*, we thought what a thrill if he could actually see Tom Jones in person. So, like eager happy-to-please parents, we took him to Caesars. We dressed him in a beautiful, fitted blue Levi suit. He looked like a little rock star. Luckily, we got the middle seats in the front row. At the spot in his act where Tom does his 'wives' in the audience bit, the first person Tom looked at was Sarita. Why not? She was gorgeous in blue chiffon. As Tom leaned into Sarita, doing material Christopher already knew, Christopher placed a protective hand on his mother's arm. Tom saw this and laughed. He quickly invited Christopher on stage. Without hesitating, as though he'd done it all his life, with Tom holding his hand, Christopher climbed up and stood next to him. The audience cheered. They chatted for a few moments. Tom and the audience were clearly bewildered because this handsome, bright child talked as naturally and casually with him as though he'd been a part of the act forever. There was an ovation when he returned to his seat, unaffected by it all. We were invited backstage afterwards, where Tom was somewhat hostile and verbally abusive to his assistant in front of people. On the way home to Los Angeles, Christopher never said a word. Neither did we, but Christopher never sang another Tom Jones song.

When Christopher was four we managed somehow to move into a small bungalow in Toluca Lake, just off the tenth fairway of Lakeside golf course. He had his own little front bedroom next to the kitchen. We knew he was bright, but when it was suggested we enroll him in a preschool called Rio Vista, known for having progressive teachers and bright students, we knew it wasn't just misplaced parental pride. We enrolled him. Two months later, we got a call from a young Chinese-American children's counsellor. She informed us it was her sole job to make the rounds of Los Angeles preschools to test students. That week she was testing children at Rio Vista, and calling to inform us, happily, that our son was a genius. She said in the last month she had tested hundreds of students, but amazingly encountered two in the same class who were geniuses, Christopher and a Chinese girl.

I asked, "How on earth do you test kids for being geniuses?"

She said, "Various ways. Pictures, images, arithmetic, and questions."

"What kind of questions? Could you give me a sample?"

"Yes. One was, what do laughter and tears have in common."

"I'm not sure I could answer that." I thanked her for calling.

I couldn't wait to get in the car to pick my son up after school. Having done so, something I looked forward to every afternoon, I said nothing in the car. At home, he rushed to his mother, as usual, leaping at her. Before we sat down to eat, I asked him what do laughter and tears have in common."

"They're both emotions," he said matter-of-factly.

"How would you know that?"

"Dad, *Star Trek*."

Star Trek, which he never missed, would also provide another answer for him. The only thing he did that came close to being not a bad, but a rather negative habit, was occasional thumb sucking. Sometimes when happy, peaceful or listening to music, he would stick his thumb in his mouth. My concern was it might affect how his front teeth grew. Neither Sarita nor I ever took his thumb out of his mouth, or said anything. However, since he was now identified as a genius, I felt I could use quiet reasoning with him. One evening, while the three of us were cuddled together on our bed, him in the middle, watching TV, I reached over and gently removed his right thumb from his mouth. The one he always used.

I said, "The reason I have good teeth, aside from having a good dentist, is that I never sucked my thumb. It could make them come in crooked." I just looked at him, still holding his right hand gently in mine.

He looked at me with a hint of a smile, then extended his left arm, his fist closed but thumb pointing straight up. "But I have an auxiliary thumb."

"*Star Trek*?" I asked.

"*Star Trek*," he answered. But never sucked it again.

When Christopher came into our lives, so did good luck. Especially with people we would encounter or need. One person we would need was a babysitter. For the first five years, when it was to my advantage to have Sarita attend a function, she never came. She stayed with Christopher. For her sake, I suggested she get out once in a while; first of all to prove we were still married. Second, while it was years off, but knowing her joy with him, I told her jokingly she'd better start preparing for when the house would be an empty nest. She agreed, but how does one find a babysitter? One to whom you could entrust your child, the most valuable thing in your life? I had no idea. And knew of no one to ask. So, I just opened the Yellow Pages, the only thing I could think of. And there it was, the first name we looked at: Margaret Schadler, retired nurse from Scotland. Amongst her previous clients was singer Neil Diamond. Neil, we found out later in references, had asked Margaret to go with them when they moved from Los Angeles. Margaret, in her late fifties, declined. She said she needed the sun.

She was frail and feisty with curly white hair, had a Scottish accent with a slight lisp from her false teeth, loved tea, playing cards, and sneaking a smoke. She adored Christopher. More important, he absolutely adored her. She became a very important part of our family, and Christopher's life – more than Sarita's mother or sister.

It was always early when Sarita and I got home from whatever we had to attend. No matter what show we saw, it was never as much fun as the show we would see when we got home. There the two of them would be sitting across from one another at a small table in the dining room, playing cards, checkers or chess, or reading or singing. Christopher often composed little songs and poems just for her; they were all about the things they did together. Many a time we'd hear him recite or sing them to her, tears running down our three faces.

I was convinced he would be a singer, but Margaret said, in a lisping brogue, "He's got that Scots blood in him, like Bobby Burns. He's gonna be a writer."

On one occasion when Christopher was six, Margaret was taken ill. It was imperative Sarita and I attend a very important dinner together. This was the night I changed my mind about the profession he was destined to follow. We had to find someone to sit with him. But who? Where? We talked to a few friends, but not one described their sitter with enough enthusiasm to convince Sarita. Our last call was made to a friend of Carol Burnett's. His name was Dick Patterson.

Dick was an enormously charming, funny fellow who was always on the verge of almost making it. He had co-starred in a movie, hosted a short-lived game show, sometimes a panelist on a few others. He always hoped, because of her genuine fondness for him, that Carol would somehow find a place for him on her show. She never did. But Carol always sought out his company. Dick had two little girls our son's age. His babysitter was in her early twenties. He assured a very nervous Sarita that she was wonderful, that Christopher would love her.

Interviewing her fiercely, like the girl was the enemy, Sarita succumbed, confident her son would be in good hands. We then told Christopher, because of Margaret's illness, someone would be taking her place that night for a few hours. He looked at us with a very straight face, then said, "Mom, did you always want me?"

"What do you mean?" Sarita asked.

"When you met Dad, did you want me right away?"

"Of course, I did. I wanted you all my life."

"So why didn't you have me right away?"

"Well, your father didn't have a loving father and mother like you, so he wanted to wait until things got a little better for us financially."

When he looked directly at me, I said, "Like your mother said, son, and I've mentioned this to you before, I wasn't sure I'd be a good father."

"How long before you changed your mind?"

"Well, your mother changed my mind. She wanted you so badly I thought it would be unfair of me not to let her have you; things were going better for me and I thought we could afford to bring you into the world."

"How long was that after you married?"

We both said in unison, "Five years."

"Well, if you waited for so long to have me, why would you leave me now with a stranger?"

I was stunned. How could any child, barely out of diapers, reason like that? Like Aristotle for God's sake! My body tingled at the sheer joy of having listened to and experiencing his mind. I rushed at him, calling his name repeatedly, putting my hands under his arms, lifting him as high as I could like a trophy. "My God, son, you're not going to be a musician. You're going to be a lawyer. You're our little Clarence Darrow. We won't be long, son. I promise!"

All night I couldn't help mumbling, "A lawyer. A lawyer. Another goddamn lawyer." But this time a good one.

AM Los Angeles

Christopher was a year old when the gods or guardians of newborn babies brought another lucky stranger briefly into our lives that changed it forever. His name was Mario Machado. He was not only one of the handsomest men I ever met, but had by far the most beautiful speaking voice of anyone I knew, except Sarita. Everyone, everywhere heard it. He did countless voiceovers for commercials; he was also the announcer for many local radio and TV shows. Mario was my age, had jet black hair with eyes to match. His father was Mexican; his mother Portuguese or Pilipino. He was born in China, spoke Mandarin and five other languages. He loved it when one evening at an awards dinner at which I spoke, I said, "The reason every station in town likes to hire Mario is because he's everybody's ethnic!"

He sought me out afterwards, introduced himself, and said, "John, you ought to go where I'm going tomorrow. KABC is holding auditions this week for the host of a new morning news show. They're dumping the morning cartoons. They want to make brownie points with the FCC because some Chicano groups have been challenging their license. They called me, because I'm everyone's ethnic!" He laughed a full hearty laugh.

"If they called you, they obviously must want you. So, why would you tell me?"

"There are about thirty guys. Not just me. I think Ralph Story already turned it down. He said that time slot on KABC is a career graveyard. You should do it." (Ralph Story was the successful host of an excellent local weekend show on the CBS affiliate called *Ralph Story's Los Angeles,* a wonderfully written and researched show.)

"Mario, that's nice. But, again, why would you suggest I audition? I'd be competition. Besides, I'm a comic."

"Simply, John, because you'd be better at it. I read well, but you think on your feet. I'm not sure I could do that. Here's who to call." He handed me a piece of paper with a phone number and the name Brad Lachman.

Mario's generosity was not as surprising as one might think. We were in that large group of sometimes working performers scrambling constantly to get a foothold on the second or third rung of that ladder to success. To this group, it wasn't a narrow ladder. It was a wide one. We all felt there was room for everyone. Today all that closeness and camaraderie is gone; it's as nonexistent now as the Fairness Doctrine.

The next day I called KABC, asking for Brad. He spoke so softly I could barely hear him. I told him I was calling at Mario's suggestion, asking if there was still an audition spot open. He told me there was and gave me the directions and time. As Mario had said there were over thirty guys in suits milling about in a large rehearsal hall.

There was a friendly pat on my back. It was Mario. "Glad you could make it." I repeated to Mario the impossibility of selecting a host. "Well, they have to pick somebody. It might as well be one of us."

At that point a tall young man accompanied by a young lady with a clipboard entered the room walking straight to Mario. "Glad you could make it." It was Brad. He could not have been more than twenty-six.

"Brad," Mario said, "this is John Barbour. I thought you should meet him. He's very funny."

"Funny's not what we're looking for," Brad said.

"Well, in that case, he's very bright."

"Are you ready?" Brad asked Mario.

The girl with the clipboard checked off his name. I wondered how kids that young got jobs like that, producing a live morning news show. Maybe he'd done something great I wasn't aware of. Like being born to somebody rich. One by one, I watched Brad select another suit. There were three of us left two hours later when they came to fetch me. They were clearly fatigued and bored. I followed them to the studio. There were five crew members, one camera, two monitors, an audio man, and a woman in her late thirties sitting in one of two seats behind a desk. She looked familiar. I had seen her in the movies. Brad led me straight to the seat on her left. He directed me to sit, talking as the engineer placed a mike on my tie.

"Phyllis, this is John..." He looked at the clipboard. "John Barbour. He's a friend of Mario's. John, this is Phyllis Kirk."

I said, "Miss Kirk, if you're as good at this as you are as an actress, you'll get the job." I smiled.

"I've already got the job," she said flatly.

I wanted to just get up and leave.

"Phyllis is the co-host of this new show. *AM, Los Angeles*. We're looking for her partner," Brad said. "I want you to talk to Phyllis for a minute or so, then I'm going to put someone in her place. I want you to interview him for a moment, then I'm going to ask you a few questions. Okay?"

I nodded.

"Okay. Roll tape." Brad pointed at me.

My questions to Phyllis were short and casual. I asked if acting was what she really wanted to do as a child. It wasn't. One question made her blossom: In a film I named, she had a steamy love scene, I asked how she felt, and how her husband felt when they sat in the theater together and saw it. Looking at her respond, I sensed she liked me. Brad stopped us suddenly, then asked a few questions I can't remember. He put some fellow in Phyllis's chair. I remember nothing about him or my interview.

In minutes, it was all over. I thanked Phyllis, the audio engineer as he removed the mike, and shook hands with Brad. It hadn't taken long, and I felt as though it had no content. How could a host be picked like that? I was happy to get back home, see Sarita and play with Christopher. But I didn't get much of a chance.

"Sandy called. He wants you to call him right away," Sarita said. Sandy Wernick was my new agent at the Agency for the Performing Arts, one of a number I'd have, without even knowing how I ended up with him.

"Why didn't you tell me you were auditioning at ABC today?" he asked.

"It was last minute. I didn't think it was important and don't think it went anywhere anyway. And what could you have done?"

"I know Larry Einhorn, the program director, and John McMahon, the GM. I could have set it up for you. Put in a good word."

"Mario Machado already did that."

"John, whenever stuff like that pops up, let me know. I can run interference for you. That's my job. What agents do. I'll call and tell them to keep an eye out for you."

"Sandy don't bother, please. But if you can find out anything, can you find out what this kid Brad Lachman did that gets him a job producing this thing?"

"His father's a big shot in Beverly Hills. Stocks 'n' stuff."

The audition early in the week was forgotten. When the phone rang the next Friday, the last person I expected to hear from was a soft-spoken boy producer.

"You got it. You're Phyllis's sidekick," Brad said simply.

"You're kidding." I chuckled.

"You were the best. You're a natural at this. You looked so at home. I want you to come in Monday to meet Larry Einhorn and John McMahan, and my assistant Robert Harris. Then you're going to meet his dad who is the best haberdasher in Beverly Hills. We're going to have to get you some suits."

Immediately after I hung up the phone rang again. It was Sandy. "Jesus Christ, Johnny. I just heard from Einhorn. It seems Brad was insistent that you were his only choice. It'll be twelve hundred a week to start for thirteen weeks. How about that, kiddo. Way to go."

I called Mario, thanking him profusely, and apologizing for stealing his job.

"Hey, John, are you kidding. It just proves I have good taste." He laughed. "If they don't have a staff announcer, you know how to reach me."

KABC did have a staff announcer, but a dozen years later I hired Mario as the announcer on an outrageous comedy quiz show.

How Do These People Get These Jobs?

Monday morning Brad and I were sitting in the General Manager's office, across the desk from John McMahon. John looked the part of a GM. He was nice looking, very clean cut, in his mid-forties. Larry Einhorn was just the opposite; maybe that's why John hired him, to look better by comparison. Einhorn was thirty pounds bulkier, a little taller, with darker hair, and a kind of swarthy complexion that gave one the impression soap didn't work, and no tailor could make a suit that would fit. His voice, always gruff, usually sarcastic, especially toward me, perfectly reflected his appearance. From the moment I sat down, especially after listening to them expound on their new show, I felt uncomfortable with them. And they evidently with me. It was a discomfort that grew over the months, paradoxically with the show's increasing success.

Following the casual formalities of welcoming me to the ABC family, talking about the show's importance, especially for the community and the FCC, John asked me what my thoughts were. I told him I was glad there was such a morning show like it in LA and that it would be a nice, informative, and sometimes entertaining way for people to start their day.

"How would you propose doing that?" John asked.

"You book the most interesting and meaningful people making news here and out of town."

"Out of town? How do you propose that?"

"By phone."

"It's a TV show." John smiled at his brilliance.

"You put a picture up, and hear the voice. More news is made in Washington these days than in New York and LA combined. Especially with the war and the draft."

"Then what?" Einhorn threw in.

"After we've interviewed these people, Phyllis and I, we open the phones so callers can ask them questions."

"Jesus, John, this isn't San Francisco. People here aren't smart enough to call in."

"Mr. McMahan, I think you will be pleasantly surprised how bright a lot of people actually are. I assure you, they will ask questions, good ones that Phyllis and I may never think of. Especially if the interviews are done well enough."

They both stared at me, then looked at Brad.

"I think he's right," Brad said. "It's worth a try. Nobody in town does it."

Now that Brad, surprisingly, supported it, they nodded in agreement. "What else?" Einhorn asked pointedly.

"This is the kind of show I've always wanted to do. I believe we can do things on this show that no one else does, anywhere, which will also help your six o'clock news. For instance–"

"How can this possibly help the six o'clock news?" Einhorn asked.

"What do people do in the morning as they get ready for work?" I asked them. "They watch the morning news. Right now, that's *The Today Show*. And what do they do when they go to work? They turn it off. And what do they do when they come home?" I waited a moment of silence out, before adding, "They turn it back on to the same station. I believe Phyllis, Brad and I will soon make AM the morning show to watch here."

"You started to say something else, before you mentioned the six o'clock news. You said 'for instance.'"

I was stunned, John was paying attention. "Oh, yes. For instance, this is the movie-making capital of the world. No one reviews movies on the news. I'd like to do that. Three times a week. Monday, Wednesday, and Friday.'

Now Einhorn openly laughed. "Jesus, John, that's intellectual crap. Nobody gives a shit anymore about movies. They don't even go to them. Now it's all TV."

"I could do that occasionally, too."

"No, you can't. Nobody cares," Einhorn added.

I leaned forward to emphasize my point. "They may not go to movies, but they talk about them. This is a celebrity based town. Soon the whole country will be. Since it's an industry town, if they hear us doing reviews, they will tune in to our show."

We all looked at Brad. "It's ... it's live," he said. "It is new. So is the show. It wouldn't hurt to try it."

McMahan and Einhorn shrugged as they rose, not looking convinced. John shook my hand, without enthusiasm. He said, "I'm having a special remote put into my car, so every morning on the way to work I'll be listening." It sounded more like a warning than a compliment.

"I'll take John now to the office to meet with Robert and Phyllis," Brad said.

I was glad to be out of there. They sounded more like authority figures than broadcasters. Robert Harris was Brad's age, much shorter, about my size, a whole lot warmer and enthusiastic. As was his assistant, a bright, outspoken women's libber, and sometimes writer for the *L.A. Times*, Diane Morang. This was our staff for an hour and a half live news show every weekday morning. Four people, including me. That was it. Phyllis, in her office, was extremely welcoming, even to the point of extending a dinner invitation to me and Sarita, to meet her husband. She said he was a fan, and he couldn't believe one of his favorite comics was going to be hosting a news show. She said he wouldn't miss it for the world.

"Phyllis, I've only hosted a show a few times. Once when I subbed for Merv and later over at KTTV. This'll be the first time I'll be doing it with a partner, so if it ever looks like when I'm interviewing, I get carried away, just give me a little kick under the table. I'll stop and you jump in."

She smiled. "I don't think I'll have to do that, but if I do, it won't be too hard."

Our first show was a week away. Assigned to be the anchor doing the half hourly news breaks was an engaging, laid back black reporter, Hugh Williams. The show would start at seven a.m. Live with a ten second delay in case something libelous or profane came from the callers. The ratings for the opening show were a dismal .03. The ratings for our fortieth show were five, just about even with NBC's *Today Show*. Reviewers caught this show. They were all universal in their unrestrained praise, especially *Variety* and *The Hollywood Reporter*:

The Hollywood Reporter, Friday, July 10th, 1970

Set the alarm. Turn on the set. Pour a cup of coffee. Watch, enjoy and most important of all, learn. Learn how provocative 90 minutes of daybreak can be. Learn how a host, John Barbour, can merge the best elements of any talk show on the air with a commitment to using the medium for both enlightenment and education.... Occasionally, telephone questions are solicited, and to pay the show the highest compliment, the responses are from bright, interested people ...

While this particular show, (with Tommy Smothers) showed the possibilities of 'AM' at its best, the program had the feeling it would be the same no matter what morning one tuned in. KABC is to be heartily congratulated. Brad Lachman is the Producer. Mark Massari the Director. John Barbour is the Man!' Tony Lawrence.

I was certain my predictions, especially about the phone calls, would please McMahan and Einhorn. They didn't.

There were countless requests for copies of the movie reviews I did. They became so popular and talked about, I got a call from Geoff Miller, the editor of *Los Angeles Magazine*, asking me if I would replace their departing, very popular movie critic Burt Prelutsky. Burt and I had become casual friends one morning after I'd told the audience my very favorite movie review line was written by Burt – the closing line of his review of Disney's *Chitty Chitty Bang Bang*: "It starts out with a bang and ends up chitty."

Burt was leaving the magazine to do a column at the *L.A. Times*. He felt I should be the one to replace him. So I did for ten years. One of the first reviews I did on the *AM Show,* which I always ran by Brad so he wouldn't be surprised or caught off guard, but who never changed a word, was a small anti-war film by Brian DePalma playing only at a small local art house. Fifteen minutes to seven, Einhorn walks unannounced into my office and asks abruptly to see my first review. I handed it to him. After glancing at it, and still holding it, like it was toilet paper, he said. "What is this shit?"

"It's a review!"

"I can see that. But what of it, for Christ's sake? Who cares? Review *The Ten Commandments*. It's gonna be on this week."

"Larry," I blurted, "everybody's seen it, and broken them."

Brad, standing in the doorway, whom I didn't see, laughed loudly. The only loud laugh I ever heard from him.

"Nobody cares about this crap."

"Larry, I do. And I wouldn't call the war crap, even though it is. It's just my opinion. If I find something I think is terrific, that people might like, I should tell them about it. If it really were crap, I wouldn't bother bashing it. I'd bash *The Ten Commandments* instead."

He turned and stomped out, mumbling.

Two months into the show, hearing about the public's response to the reviews, I got a call from Bob Irvine, the station's News Director. "John," he said, "the reviews are terrific. How'd you like to do the same thing on our six o'clock news, Monday, Wednesday, and Friday? The same ones you do in the morning? I'll give you a hundred bucks each. I love your writing and I hope you love mine. I'm sending you over a book. I'll get back to you right away." The paperback came by messenger. It was a crime novel. That was Bob's real passion. Not news, but writing. The crime was that none of them sold.

This newfound money would go into a college kitty for Christopher, if he decided to go to one. I even picked out a huge piggy bank for it, but it got no deposits. Bob called saying McMahan said no way. Bob said he was shocked, arguing in vain that my presence would increase the audience. Again, as I had predicted, KABC's six o'clock news had made Bill Bonds the number one newscaster-anchorman in LA, beating the perennial Jerry Dunphy at CBS.

The Fairness Doctrine

The airwaves, over which television and radio broadcast, are supposed to be owned by the public. That concept now is as remote as the Twin Towers rising from the dust. However, it was closer to reality and the FCC rules in 1970 when I began the *AM Show*. As late as 1983, ninety percent of all radio and television stations were owned by sixty companies. As of this writing, that ninety-five percent, plus all publishing and newspaper outlets, is now owned by only six corporations. This narrowing and narrow-minded funneling of our information and entertainment sources began first under Presidency Reagan. The final nail came under Clinton, (probably America's worst President) signing The Communications Act with his harmless, freedom-sounding word called 'deregulation.' This was the freedom given to six CEO's and their few hundred major stockholders to now own ninety-five percent of media and determine what over three hundred million of us would see and hear. This was not so in 1970. At that time a corporation, like ABC, NBC, or CBS, the major broadcasters, could only own seven radio or television stations across the entire country. Of course, these major corporations acquired their seven stations in the seven major cities and population centers, from New York to Chicago to Los Angeles. The seven stations were continually under government pressure to abide by what they called 'The Fairness Doctrine,' and 'The Equal Time Rule.' These weren't exactly laws; they were hard rules laid down by The Federal Communications Commission. They were strictly enforced in spite of stations continually trying to circumvent them. In 1963, when President Kennedy was murdered, a company could only own five tv stations. There were over 1,500 different owners compared to today's half dozen!

At the height of the Vietnam War, President Johnson was all over the air pushing for its escalation and continuance. Eugene McCarthy, also a Democrat, but an anti-war candidate for the presidency, was rejected three times by broadcasters when he demanded equal time. The networks claimed LBJ was not an announced candidate, therefore they didn't need to give Eugene equal time. The Supreme Court ruled otherwise and Johnson stepped down. The country then got to hear and make McCarthy a leading contender.

Even a lowly book author could get airtime, if hammered by a critic, if the FCC felt the author's work was of public import. The same for a film producer whose movie was savaged by a critic. In one Supreme Court case, I was the critic; the producer demanding equal time. The film was *Soylent Green,* starring Charlton Heston. I hammered it. But then feeling so bad about doing so, at the end of the review I said to the viewers, "I should really try to say something nice about this film. The sets are beautiful. But they'd be more beautiful if they were placed in front of the actors." For five years every court in California turned down the producer's request for equal time. He finally got his case to the Supreme Court, which also turned him down, stating, John Barbour's review was of no public importance.

During the tumultuous early seventies, hundreds of civic and private groups around the country were challenging local stations, claiming they were ignoring socially relevant public issues. These groups got meaningful hearings before the FCC. Sometimes winning. Station managers, such as John McMahon, had no interest in serving the public. His interest was in keeping his job and his station's license. But because of very strong petitioning, especially from Chicano leaders, often resulting in riots, *AM Los Angeles* was forced into existence, replacing cartoons. I was totally unaware of all of this when I started. A few weeks earlier I was just a reasonably successful sometimes working comic, who watched the news to write jokes. However, I learned quickly.

What happened to the laws limiting corporate multiple ownership and fairer broadcasting? What happened to the diversity in news, views, and programming? What happened is that the Titanic, loaded with talent and originality, and controversy and free speech ran into the American iceberg of big business and politics. And sank.

I give you this brief backdrop about the conditions under which we worked, to provide a clearer picture and fuller understanding of the stories I'm about to tell you. To also give you a deeper insight into how our show, which former FCC member Nicholas Johnson said publicly and to ABC President Leonard Goldenson, was "the best, most intelligent talk show on television," and how John McMahon killed it, and, years later, at NBC, tried to kill my career again.

There was no one on the planet as happy and as exhilarated about his life as I was. I had just won the dreams-come-true lottery. I was about to cash in on it, and more important, spread the wealth of imparting information and entertainment as I saw it. Not dictated by someone else. Just me. I was filled with loving being me. I was thirty-seven. Still not a citizen. Really not thinking about that a whole lot; having the Green Card was thrill enough. I didn't need to vote. I was too focused on what I was about to embark on. In spite of my love of movies, theater, and television, I had never given one thought to being famous or rich. I just wanted to be a part of it. It gave my life a purpose. Getting the *AM Show* gave me that feeling. I never thought of having a wife, but accidentally ended up winning the wife lottery and then, only to please her, stumbled into the child lottery. But, I had always wanted a talk show. Again, by accident, it came my way.

I would have a steady job to go to every day. No longer would I have to grind out hopefully funny material, looking for a place to try it out to try to get laughs. My focus would be on meaningful material. I read every book by everyone who ever appeared on the show, and one by an author who never appeared, New Orleans's D.A. Jim Garrison. That story soon.

In the fifties and sixties, there were two great interviewers on television, Jack Paar and David Susskind. They never regaled or tried to impress the audience with their knowledge of the subject; that was to come only from the guest. Not only has there not been a good interviewer for many years, there hasn't even been a decent one. On *AM Los Angeles,* not only was Phyllis Kirk sitting next to me, so were Paar and Susskind. Every guest who came on was treated like that, as a guest, made to feel comfortable, even if I didn't like him or her or their philosophies. We booked unpopular people, because they had something to say. We only booked a celebrity if we felt they had something to say. Bob Hope, one of my comedy heroes, as big a star as Hollywood produces, was stunned when we turned him down. He wanted to talk about his upcoming NBC special. We told him if he would also talk about his support of the Vietnam War, and field calls from viewers, we'd be happy to have him.

As I had predicted to the McMahon-Einhorn odd couple in the front office, the calls became an important, popular feature. Often the caller would be on for four or five minutes, almost becoming co-hosts or guests themselves. Sometimes those calls created the greatest drama or laughter.

Occasionally, we would not book a guest; we'd devote an entire segment or two to open phones. Folks flooded us with calls, talking about or sounding off about whatever was on their mind. This call came from an elderly lady near Laguna Beach. "I just called in to talk to you a bit. I like you. And to say goodbye."

"Where are you going, if you're saying goodbye?"

"Heaven, I hope. Hell, probably. It can't be worse than this."

"What do you mean?" I felt something eerie.

"I'm going to kill myself!"

Everyone stared in silence at the studio speaker

"Then why did you call me to say goodbye?" I was very matter-of-fact.

"I told you. Because I like you. I watch you every morning."

"Are there other shows you watch? I'm only on a short time. There must be other shows you watch."

"Not really," she said. "I can't find myself enjoying anything anymore. Young man, my life is totally empty. Especially my heart. You're the only one I feel I can talk to you. Like a friend."

"What's your name?"

"Alice."

"Alice, can we be friends for a few minutes? Talk like friends?"

"Yes."

"Okay, I'm going to be very brutal. I want you to answer this uncomfortable question honestly. Will you?"

"You're going to ask me how I'm going to kill myself, aren't you?" The studio was still.

"Absolutely not. That is your own business. It's depressing me enough knowing you're going to do it. Knowing how only makes it worse. I'm sure you don't want to depress me more. Your new friend. I want to know how old are you?"

"Seventy-four."

"Alice, I'm half your age. I haven't been around enough to know what to ask or say to a strange woman who just announced to all of Southern California from the mountains to the seas, (This phrase was the famous lead in announcement for Jerry Dunphy's highly rated news show on the CBS affiliate,) that you're going to commit suicide." When she and the crew heard this, they chuckled. I continued. "Alice, being lost on what to say to you makes me angry at myself. Even a little angry at you for causing it. I would like to feel sympathy for you, but I can't. I don't know you. If you do what you say you're going to do after calling me, you're going to make me feel like I failed a friend. So, will you talk to me a little bit about yourself so I can at least understand why you or anybody would do such a thing?"

"Have you ever thought of killing yourself?"

"Alice, you really know how to depress a person. Truthfully, in my three and a half decades I've known more people who've committed suicide than have died of natural causes. Not one was poor or homeless. They were all relatively comfortable or successful." I stopped there.

"So am I, very comfortable. I was once very successful, but I asked you if you ever thought of killing yourself."

"Boy, you're a pain as a friend. Alice, when I was sixteen, I was having problems with staying in this country. I was looking in the bathroom mirror. Really, really depressed. I remembered all the people I'd known who had done away with themselves. The thought crossed my mind. But just for a few seconds. Do you know what stopped me? The thought that no one would miss me. It made me angry. You can see a lot of things make me angry. I stared into the mirror, and decided I was going to become my own best friend. Now I have family and friends who would miss me. Would you miss me?"

"Of course, I would."

"Well, I'd miss you, too. Tell me what you did that made you successful."

"I was one of the best ballerinas in the world."

"A dancer? Really? So is my wife, Sarita. A tap dancer. The best. Better than Eleanor Powell or Ginger Rogers. She tells me being a ballerina is much, much tougher. Tell me about it."

She did. On the air for nearly twenty more minutes. The famous companies she was with. The famous lovers. Two of her longest, both dead. One a suicide. The other a famous sculptor who did a small white porcelain statue of her seated in costume on a fence. We decided, still on the air live, to meet shortly for lunch, her, Sarita and me. And we did.

She was frail, slender and still beautiful, now glowing with enthusiasm about her future. At the end of the meal, she told me I had given her the gift of hope, that I should have the most treasured gift she had. With that, she unwrapped from a large pink bag the sculpture of the sitting ballerina. It is in front of me as I type. We saw her a few more times over the months. The last time was when she and a few of her newfound lady friends confronted John McMahon on my behalf.

The first thirteen weeks flew by. When not going or preparing for the show, I was almost never out, except to review a movie or play, always with my wife and son. My agent at the time, Sandy Wernick, called, elated with the news I'd been renewed before the cycle ended, with an increase in salary. I was not surprised. Every week saw a bump in the ratings. I also got a call from Brad asking if I could stay after the show one day to chat with him. When I entered his office, he shook my hand and congratulated me. Then said, "How are your ankles?" And laughed. "You showed me them once after a show. They looked a little bruised from Phyllis's pointy toes!" He laughed again.

"Oh, that's okay. It doesn't bother me. I can get carried away sometimes when I get with a guest, but we've worked it out."

"Well," he said, "they'll heal very shortly. I'm not bringing her back."

"Why not? She's good."

"Frankly, I think you'd be better without her."

"Did McMahon and Einhorn have anything to do with this?"

"Actually, they like the show the way it is. I convinced them you'd be much better than you are. And right now, you're really good."

I was surprised by Brad's stand on my behalf. He almost never talked. Seldom laughed. Never got enthused about anything. As a plus, never got angry if something went wrong. He was extremely difficult to get to know. In the months we worked together, we never once had a social outing or casual get together. When someone asked me what his greatest asset was, I said, "His height."

Starting the fourteenth week, *AM Los Angeles* would be a one-man show, and I was the man!

Be My Guest

If there is something really fresh about a television show, any show for that matter, something different, original or smart, something that reaches people's guts and grey matter, if given a little time, it will reach a growing word-of-mouth audience. It happens as if by osmosis or telepathy. It never fails. It has happened to dozens of shows over the years. In Los Angeles, it happened with our show. It became must-watch morning television. Los Angeles, like America, was in a state of turmoil over Vietnam and Civil Rights, and, in our town, Chicanos' rights. It was an invigorating, challenging time to be an American, and an important, rewarding time to be on television. The kind of energy and unpredictability, and edginess and news-making ability our show had can be summed up in the telling of brief stories of five guests: Ronald Reagan, Mohammed Ali, Jane Fonda, Cesar Chavez, and Jim Garrison. And two phone calls.

The first call came from Tom Bradley. Also, the second one. Tom was the highly respected new Chief of Police. He was black. He asked me if I would meet with him privately. Privately wasn't in his office, or a restaurant. It was in my office. He came on his own, unescorted.

After introductions, he said, "You're doing a magnificent job on the show. My family loves it. Especially that interview with Joseph Wambaugh about his book. Terrific stuff."

"Do you want equal time?"

He laughed. "Do you still do comedy?"

"No. I don't have time. I get more of a rush doing this."

"You wrote some funny stuff. Do you still do that part of it, write?"

"Oh, once in a while. When something pops into my head, I write it down. But that's about as far as it goes. Why?"

"You've heard that I might be running for mayor. Would you be interested at all in writing some material for me?"

"Seriously?"

"No, funny." He smiled at his own joke. "Would it be conflicting in any way?"

"Only that I wouldn't want it public; just you and your secretary or whoever and your wife, I guess, should know."

"Mr. Bradley, if President Kennedy could have joke writers, it's certainly good enough for a Chief of Police."

"Well, I'm certainly not as glib. I never tell jokes because I'm so bad at it. Uncomfortable actually."

"In that case, sir, can I make a little suggestion? Don't tell jokes. Yorty or his staff are always attacking you. Use what they say as straight lines. Respond to their attacks hopefully with something that's funny. For instance, Yorty never says you're black, but he implies it to scare the people. How many times has he said, 'If Bradley becomes Mayor, there'll be crime in the streets?'"

Tom smiled. "That's his favorite line!"

"Then you just say, that's true. If I'm mayor, Sam Yorty will have to find some place other than City Hall to conduct his business."

"God, that's beautiful."

"Thanks. It's easy. Some of his staff have referred to you as Uncle Tom Bradley. Then you say, Yorty's staff has sadly called me Uncle Tom. I told my staff we're not going that low. You've told your staff they are not to call him Uncle Sambo."

"I'm not sure I can pull that off."

"I will keep an eye on what Yorty says, and just send my stuff to whomever. It'll be fun. I'm happy to do it."

A couple of months later, at his most important, last news conference before the election, the throng of reporters threw at him the barbs from Yorty quoted often in the *L.A. Times*. I was grinning in anticipation of their reactions to Tom's smart responses. They never came. He froze. He was quiet. And gentle. And dull. And lost. Yorty was barely re-elected.

An hour after the election, Tom made his second call to me. "I'm sorry, John. I just felt uncomfortable. I loved your material. But that wouldn't be me. I know I would have won had I used it. I'm sorry."

"The only thing you have to apologize for is inflicting Yorty on this town for another term."

"I promise, though. I'll run again, and will use it next time."

He did run again; the material now flowed out of him easily. He won handily. Sadly, I no longer had the show, but he continued to ask me to write material for him for his ever-increasing number of appearances as the city's first black mayor, many of which he invited me to.

Jane Fonda

She was one of Hollywood's most promising, versatile young actresses, the daughter of the iconic, all-American Henry Fonda, whose roles, along with James Stewart, made us believe in America. He was revered as a Depression dirt farmer in *Grapes of Wrath*, and as *Young Abe Lincoln*. His daughter, though, who was to appear on our show, was the most hated woman in America.

Jane Fonda was not just speaking out loudly against the U.S. war in Southeast Asia. She was campaigning against war, courageously and often recklessly putting her feet where her mouth was, gaining the wrath of the entire country. She didn't stop there. She made it worse by then going to North Vietnam, posing with the Vietcong. A tsunami of vitriol gushed out of the mainstream media calling for her arrest and even execution for treason. She was safer in Asia than America. One who vilified her the most, frothing at the mouth and typewriter because of an award being presented to Ms. Fonda was Barbara Walters. Now, of course, like all of those after the fact, Walters says she was always opposed to the war, but not once did she say one word against it when she was at the height of her media popularity. Not once did this hack ever put her foot on the pavement to march against it. Or use her airtime to speak against it. Today, now that it's safe, nearly the entire population thinks the war was a fraud, but the hangover of the media assault on Jane was so strong, thousands still hate her for trying to stop it. Including Barbara Wa Wa. They totally and conveniently ignore war criminals LBJ and McNamara and the other lying politicians who started it.

Ms. Fonda's actions by posing for that photo on an "enemy" anti-aircraft gun not only cost her making pictures in Hollywood, it so unnerved the town's leading liberals, they spoke only softly against the war. They and other leading activists moved to keep a distance from her. Mark Twain said: *Physical courage is easy; moral courage is hard*!

To me, Jane Fonda evidenced a courage, even then, a moral and physical courage, I had never seen. And could never do. There were scores of unreported heartbreaking stories of brave young people trying to physically stop the carnage, from a California student who lost her limbs lying down on railroad tracks trying to stop the delivery of munitions to a ship, to a young man setting himself on fire in DC. To halt the lie of the fake Gulf of Tonkin Resolution, the reason for the invasion, Jane Fonda, the country's most prominent activist, was not only risking her life, but her fairytale movie star career. I felt about Jane then, the same way I feel now. She was and is Nobel Prize material. One doesn't get much more courageous than that. It was Dr. Albert Schweitzer's reverence for life put to the ultimate test. I had only heard of one other woman in history, going against her own nation for her beliefs, and they burned Joan of Arc at the stake.

I was as strongly opposed to that war then as I am all these years later. I never spoke out or marched for a few reasons. I had neither the physical nor moral courage. I never join groups, even those I agreed with, but as a host of a news show, it wasn't my job, forced by long abandoned 'fairness' laws, to be impartial. And truthfully, demonstrating for anything is not in my nature.

My one concern about interviewing her was how to deal with her cold attitude. I was uncomfortable. I am not at ease with angry, loud people. The morning of her appearance, I arrived an hour and a half early, to view news clips of her. And to talk to Brad. Before a show, no matter how important a guest, I never talked to him or her. I did not want any spontaneity left in the dressing room. My fear of Ms. Fonda perhaps getting out of control compelled me to break my own rule. I had to talk to her beforehand. I asked Brad if he'd introduce me to her about fifteen minutes before we went on the air.

He was startled, but said, "Okay. She's coming with Mark Lane."

"Really. The *Rush to Judgment* Mark Lane about the Warren Report?"

"Thank God there's a ten second delay on the phones." He smiled and left. A few minutes later he opened the door. "She's here. With him. Whew, are they cold! I didn't tell her you wanted to see her. She looks like she just might walk out. I'll just take you over there."

That was the only time I saw Brad uncomfortable.

Standing near the exit, there she was. To her left, almost touching her, was Mark Lane. He was pleasant looking, a little taller than Jane, but looked as grim as she did. I told Brad he didn't have to introduce me. He could leave. I'd greet them myself. Brad rushed away.

I walked briskly to her, extending my hand. "Good morning, Ms. Fonda," I said. "Thank you for coming." She nodded. Her handshake was weak and quick. I turned to her escort, extending my hand again. "Mr. Lane, thank you, too. Thank you especially for *Rush to Judgment.* A terrific book. It's nice of both of you to be here." I was certain this would impress Mark or perk him up. It didn't. He remained as cool as his companion.

"We'll see how nice it is," Mark said.

I found out over the years, through long personal and professional contact, that Mark had a terrific talent for being sardonic. I had no small talk in me. I never have. In a desperately important situation like that, I just got to what was on my mind, and unloaded.

"Ms. Fonda," I said, "could we go back in the corner a bit to chat for a moment?"

"Chat about what? We'll do that on the air."

"No, you won't," I said, matter-of-factly. "Ms. Fonda, you don't chat."

"I don't what?"

"You don't chat. You preach."

She moved toward me, bristling. Lane leaned in, staring at me. I held up both hands, palms forward. "Ms. Fonda, please listen to me. I agree with you about your stance on the war. A hundred percent. I could never have the courage to do what you're doing and have done. So, please, listen."

"I'm listening."

"Ms. Fonda, as the host of this show, even though I do agree with you, I can never take that position. My position is to be the devil's advocate, to ask the guests, as politely as possible, the tough questions, to get guests to explain and defend their positions. I'm going to be brutally honest with you, as I hope you will be with me. About seventy percent of the country supports the war, no matter what you say. Maybe ten percent are opposed to it, no matter what the president says, but there's a twenty percent block out there that you could convince. But you can't do it by expressing yourself the way you do."

"How else do you express the truth, damn it?"

"Ms. Fonda, (I hated the sound of beginning every sentence with her name, but it just kept popping out.) people are never moved by facts, but the facts are on your side. They are only moved by emotions. Your yelling at them turns them off emotionally."

"What the hell are you talking about?"

"People are not reasoning creatures; they're emotional creatures. If we were reasoning creatures evaluating all the facts of history, we'd all be

Catholics or Jews or Protestants or Muslims or Republicans or Democrats, but we're not, because we're conditioned emotionally before we can even think, then we use our minds to justify our prejudices."

"Jesus Christ!" She shook her head.

"Let me prove it to you. It is not what you say that changes people's minds, but how you say it."

"Prove it."

I held up my left hand, holding aloft three fingers, and whispered, "Ms. Fonda, how many fingers?"

She shook her head slightly, as though this was all so meaningless, answering, "Three."

I then raised my right hand, raising two fingers in the 'V for victory' sign, and hissed and yelled, "All right, you goddamned stupid traitorous fucking hairy commie cunt, how many fingers do you see?"

She froze. Her eyes bulged in shock. Her jaw muscles tightened and trembled in rage.

I leaned forward and repeated: "Answer me, you cunt!" When we shook hands, I noticed how hairy her arms were. I knew she was probably more upset over pointing that out rather than my profanity.

She never answered me. She turned to Mark, stunned. Mark looked like he was going to punch me.

I then blurted, "Ms. Fonda, please, please forgive me. You see? You couldn't answer. It was impossible. That's what I mean. My repulsiveness didn't change the fact that there were two fingers there. Look, you will in no way be censored on the show. You can say whatever you wish. There will be calls from people, most of them probably who hate you, who will yell at you. Don't yell back. Chat with them. Please!"

Her demeanor suddenly relaxed. She said nothing for a while, before she said, "When do we go on?"

Her appearance and performance was magnificent, even elegant. She handled the expected many vicious calls with the calmness and ease of a pope. It was a major news-making moment for our show, another one that John McMahon refused to even show a clip from on the six o'clock news. But that didn't matter. What mattered was that this gutsy, committed young woman got her points across with ease and intelligence. From that moment on, I noticed her anti-war speeches got quieter, and as a result, more powerful.

Four days after the show, she called. "Johnny, would you and your wife like to come to the house for dinner? I'd like to talk to you about something."

I had turned down every invitation from guests up until then. That one I couldn't. I was just too curious. In attendance at her elegant, but not too large Beverly Hills house, or actually a small mansion, were a dozen people; Fred Weintraub, now a film producer, was the only one I recognized. Following a great casual buffet, Sarita and I wandered onto the spacious green front yard. We were marveling at how far we'd come even though we were still living in our two-room apartment.

"Johnny," Jane said warmly, "this is my Tom. Tom Hayden. We've heard that you write or wrote material for our friend Tom Bradley. Tom's running for office here in California. Could you, or would you, do the same for him?"

"I've heard your Tom many times; he certainly doesn't need any help!"

Tom extended his hand. "John, these days, we need all the help we can get!"

So, for two years, I did for this Tom as I had done for the other. Write jokes. He also won.

Mohammed Ali

In 1970, on the nation's hit list, the most vilified man in America was Mohammed Ali. Perhaps even more of a target than Jane. The mainstream media pounded Jane, as they did Ali. But Jane never had to suffer the slings and arrows of the government's legal and illegal machinery trying to run over her and ruin her. Ali did. He was the heavyweight champion of the world. After he won his title from Sonny Liston in 1964, he said he would fight anyone; however, when he changed his name from Cassius Clay, and his religion to Muslim, at the same time LBJ, the CIA, and Pentagon were ramping up the war and draft for Vietnam, he proclaimed loudly he'd fight anybody but the Vietnamese. The world's most prominent athlete was standing toe to toe with what he called the world's biggest bully: U.S Foreign Policy and The Pentagon. The gall of a black man making those remarks made the attacks on him more vicious. How dare he. He said he had often been degraded and abused by white Americans, never by one yellow Asian. To nearly every black, which made the government all the more nervous, he was a monumental hero. Some prominent blacks, though, as liberals did with Jane, kept their quiet distance.

When he was still Cassius Clay, his personality, his poems and his Olympic triumphs made him a media darling. Jack Paar had him on a few times. In one appearance in 1963, Liberace played background piano while he recited an entertaining poem about how he was going to thump the cowardly Liston. The audience loved him. Soon those same audiences wanted to lynch him when he said he wouldn't kill yellow people running around in black pajamas. How quickly cheers became jeers.

The one man in the media who did give Ali a voice was a man who was known as the Voice of Sports, a fixture on ABC's *Monday Night Football,* Howard Cosell. Howard was a former lawyer turned sportscaster, a very opinionated, outspoken renegade, with a deep edge to his voice, and a much-imitated singsong delivery. He sounded like a Jewish John Wayne doing unrhymed rap. He also wore an obvious dreadful toupee atop one of the best brains in broadcasting. It was only because of Howard that we saw the human side of Ali, the traitorous coward the government and media were trying to impale on the cross of National Security.

Without Howard, it was just quick, out-of-context news clips coupled with the reporter's cutting remarks.

In 1970, comedian Flip Wilson was hosting NBC's and TV's highest rated variety show. Flip fought to book Ali. And won. He had become a super comedy star, like Milton Berle before him, dressing in drag. Hollywood was abuzz with Flip's daring and NBC caving into him. It would be a monumental audience. The community perked up even more when they heard that Ali, on his own, called our show. He asked if he could do it on his way to Flip's show, the morning before. Brad and I were first stunned, then elated. I had no idea what Brad's feelings were about Ali, Fonda or the war. I didn't know what his feelings were about anything. We never talked outside the show. But he, too, knew Ali live with phone calls was a major coup. The world knew Ali was going to be on Flip's show in prime time, so there was no way McMahon could turn it down. Ali was the biggest showbiz/sports news story in the country. You could have run the entire network on the electricity in the air when Ali arrived, shockingly without an entourage. No bodyguards; not noticeably anyway. Just a couple of men in smart suits. They behaved more like friends than associates. I took my seat behind the wide desk. I glanced at a couple of notes about his introduction to make sure I had it right. He spotted me from a distance, in the darkness, and raised his hand slightly with a friendly wave. I returned it.

With five minutes to go before airtime, suddenly the doors opened and in came a flood of reporters. They had come from every newspaper, radio and TV station within a hundred miles. They rushed to Ali. His two friends held up their hands, pointed to their watches, and to me. They stopped.

Brad counted me down: five, four, three, two, one. The red camera light went on. Knowing, as everyone did, of Ali's obvious joy in writing poems and couplets about himself and his views of the world, I decided to do that as an introduction for the man who would be our only guest for an hour and a half. I don't remember the entirety of my little poem. Sadly, very sadly, even though this show is the show that won me my first Emmy, it was never saved, so I can't look it up. No show was ever saved. What was saved was ABC's money that management would not spend on new tapes; they were reused and reused until they were useless.

I do remember parts of one line. Ali sitting inches to my right beamed. "Mohammed Ali sings to every black American this very song, telling them not to go to Asia to fight the Vietcong; 'cuz unlike a bunch of whites, none of them has done him any wrong."

His friends applauded as Ali laughed, slapping me on the shoulder. When I felt his hand, I flinched like he'd hurt me. He had done the same on the Paar show when Liberace shook his hand; Ali grimaced in pain and sank to the floor. He smiled a real smile at me. It was an instant chemistry.

On the show, like an old friend, he told us about his life and views. Unexpectedly, there was not one negative or angry call. Not even from Orange County. The most startling thing to me, though, was the discovery of who his hero was. Whom he admired the most. The one he worked so hard and so consciously to emulate. His response came about when I asked him,

"Mohammed, you are perceived as a slightly loud showoff braggart–"

He interrupted me. "Not slightly. Fully. I am." He straightened up, haughty, proud and straight-faced.

"But even on the Paar show and before that, when you were Cassius Clay you were like that. Were you always like that, as a kid?"

"No, of course not. I was just a kid. Like every other kid. But I knew I wanted to be a fighter, especially when some other kid stole my bike. But I wanted to be a fighter that people would want to see. Even if they saw me beat, which they never would. You know who my hero was? Who I watched all the time? Gorgeous George," he said loudly.

"Gorgeous George?" I gasped.

"Yes, man. The flashiest white wrestler ever. He dressed up in them fancy duds, had that great mop of wavy white hair, and that wild silk cape, and he'd yell and brag and the folks would boo and hiss. They come to see him lose. And every single seat was sold out. All the time. Every fight."

"Gorgeous George? Your hero was a white man?"

"No, John, my fighting hero was a showman. Of course, I couldn't wear those duds in the ring, but I could talk like that outside the ring. And I did. That's how all that started. And it worked. Still does. Of course, I'm a better boxer than he was a wrestler."

Ali was the most compelling, moving, and stimulating interview I had ever done, until I met Jim Garrison. The show flew by. When he got up to leave, he took my right hand in both of his and pressed hard. "Thank you, sir. This was even more fun than talking to Howard Cosell." I was about to ask why he had called us in the first place, when he added, "Tomorrow, I'm doin' Flip's show. Do you mind giving me that piece of paper with your little intro on it? I'm going to ask Flip to use it."

I handed it to him eagerly.

The mob of newsmen trying to corner him early, now swarmed over him. His aides did not intervene. Ali was as gracious with them as he had been with me and the callers. He answered every question as they followed him outside, cameras whirring and pencils and microphones waving.

Bob Irving, our news director, called immediately, complimenting me and Brad for an outstanding news-making show. He asked what clip we thought would be best for their news. I told him you could pick any thirty seconds, but my favorite was the Gorgeous George story, which didn't fit into a news program. Brad suggested a few sound bites about the war and draft. Bob agreed.

We all gathered at six to watch Ali again, but he wasn't on. At least not from a clip on our show. The clip we saw was taped outside our studio with one of KABC's reporters asking questions I'd asked that morning. What was this? I didn't want to call Bob to ask him what happened. Brad was pissed, so he did.

Hanging up, he turned to me. "Evidently, McMahon won't use stuff from our show."

"Why not?"

"I'll talk to him, and see."

I wondered why McMahon had even bothered renewing me.

Ronald Reagan

Some folks seeing the heading of this chapter might be wondering why I'm not referring to him as President Reagan or Governor Reagan, which is what he was when he almost walked out of our show five minutes before airtime. For years my impression of him was simply as a star in movies, then for a while as a spokesperson on television, primarily for General Electric and Borax. His image and name were imbedded in me as Ronald Reagan. He was coming to our show because he was running for a second term as governor. Surprisingly, he picked our local show to make this announcement, and not NBC's *Today Show* with which we were bumping heads in the ratings.

Despite the constant nationally reported stories of turmoil in California under his tenure, his re-election seemed a slam dunk. To more liberal or progressive voters, he was considered heartless. One of his first acts as governor was to shut down the state's long established and lauded mental health facilities. This money-saving move started the continuing wave of homelessness in America. It put thousands of people onto the streets, some of them ill. Reagan kept saying calmly in his defense that the charitable nature of Americans and Christians would take care of them. It didn't.

The most disruptive and active anti-war campus in America, which was getting news coverage around the world, was UC Berkeley. Berkeley was not too far from Sacramento, but years away from Reagan and his views. Berkeley and the San Francisco Bay area for weeks found more angry students on the streets than in class rooms. They left the classrooms to listen to a brilliant, volatile, impassioned young man named Mario Savio regale against the system and the illegal war. He put Berkeley in the news and on the map as the founder of The Free Speech Movement. Mario became a favorite target for Reagan. Almost daily, Ronnie, almost as loudly and articulately, would denounce Savio, warning that his motley, threatening radicals should be in class learning something. To the left, Reagan was a bully. To the right, it was bully for him.

The governor's most quoted comment, which we heard dozens of times from him in impromptu speeches and news conferences was his favorite: "These longhaired, unwashed, undisciplined students who are disrespecting their teachers and their parents and their government remind me of similar students whose actions nearly 2,000 years ago brought down the Roman Empire."

Conservatives and others who just wanted a little more normalcy in society and their lives, loved him. He was going to save our country and our empire. To them, he was Braveheart.

Once again, management did nothing to publicize the governor's appearance. This meant that, once again, McMahon would decline to let our news director use a clip from our show. In self-defense, and partially out of anger, I had no choice but to hire a personal publicist. I lucked out on a recommendation from Sandy Wernick. I hired a friend of his, Joe Seigman. Joe was the perfect fit for the Hollywood phrase, tall, dark, and handsome. He was also a rarity, a gentleman. And witty. Like me, he doted on his son. Talking about our sons' higher education one day, he said, "I hope my boy goes up to Berkeley, 'cuz I'd get to see him every day in the news!"

Sarita and I had frequent but uncomfortable dinners with Joe and his 'Jewish Princess' blonde wife in their luxurious Beverly Hills apartment. The meals were always kosher and appetizing, but not the conversation. She was forever picking at him about being more ambitious. Two months after our first visit with them, it did not surprise me when Joe informed me they were divorcing.

"John, not only was there no communication, there was no copulation."

I smiled, uncomfortably. I did not want to hear about my friend's sex life, or lack of one, but I am glad he continued because it was the first time I'd heard the word prostate.

"My stomach and groin were starting to kill me," he continued. "I thought, geez, I'm too young to feel like this. The doctor I go to tells me I have a swollen prostate."

"A swollen what? What is that?" I asked.

"A guy's sex gland. In his rectum of all places. Anyway, I ask the doc why it would be swollen. He says not enough sex. Of course, I tell the princess, but it makes no difference. Two weeks I bug her. Finally, pissed at me, she calls the doctor and screams at him, how dare he tell her husband to have more sex. And the doctor says, 'Mrs. Seigman, I didn't say it had to be with you!'"

The next time I saw Joe, he was with a brunette. A few years after we parted, his renewed ambitions paid off; he created and produced two popular shows in syndication, *Bowling For Dollars,* and a half hour comedy show which introduced new comics. One of them was Jay Leno.

For me, Joe focused mostly on what they call the Trades, *The Hollywood Reporter,* and *Daily Variety* because, he said, that's what the people who could hire me read. There were snippets, quotes and comments in the trades almost daily. When 'Ronnie' was about to make his appearance, Joe made us the most talked about show in town.

The governor arrived, not surprisingly, as befits a governor, especially a very popular one, with a very large entourage. A dozen suits. A few advisors; the others, bodyguards. Upon entering, Reagan walked to the middle of the studio and stopped. His groupies hustled after him. He had stopped about twenty-five feet in front of me. I was seated. It was ten minutes to airtime. He nodded toward one of his aides, then made a slight motion toward me. The aide nodded back, made his way quickly past the cameras toward me. As usual, I had made no attempt to get up to greet my guest. Joe was standing off to the side, watching it all, giving me the thumbs up.

The aide reached me, saying, "The governor would like to see a list of the questions you wish to ask him."

"So would I. I don't have one."

"You must have a list of questions. Everybody does."

"I don't. I'm sorry."

"Then what are some of the things you're going to ask-him?"

"Honestly, I haven't the foggiest idea. It'll all be spontaneous. As all good conversations should be."

He stared at me coldly, then scurried back to his boss. They whispered. The aide looked at me and strutted back, a smirk on his face. "The governor says if you can't give him some idea of at least a few of the questions you are going to ask, he says he has no choice but to leave."

I stared at him calmly, waiting to see what would happen to that smirk, then said, "That's okay. Since we're going live in less than five minutes, I have no choice but to open the phones. I will tell the viewers exactly what has transpired between you and me, and explain why the governor is not here. I will then let them call in to express their opinions."

The blood and smirk drained from his face. He returned to his boss to relay the news of my lack of cooperation. Reagan listened intently. He then turned to me. I expected a stern stare. Instead, he smiled, and continued to smile as he walked briskly over, extending his hand, shaking mine vigorously. "Young man, I can't wait to hear what both of us have to say." (The photo of him shaking my hand, is in my office, and this book.)

It was a relaxed, quick moving, sometimes personal, but mostly topical, interview. No matter what questions came from me or the very informed viewers, if he didn't feel like responding, he'd just slide into only what he wanted to say, always with charm and purpose. One caller's mother had been forced out on the street by his closure of the mental health facilities. Reagan expressed his sympathy; feeling that was enough, he turned again to the war and our schools, announcing he was also considering closing Berkeley. Once more came the canned, oft-quoted observation, comparing longhaired disrespectful rioting students to their counterparts two thousand years earlier which led to the collapse of the Roman Empire. Truthfully, I had prepared one question. And now was the perfect time to ask it. I was so tired of hearing him hammering students protesting the war. I was going to nail him. If he were a fish, his tiresome remark provided me with the perfect bait with which to snag him.

"Governor," I said, "perhaps it wasn't the protesting long-haired students in Rome that led to their collapse."

"Believe me it was!" He was righteously emphatic, as only Ronnie could be.

"Governor, two thousand years ago those Roman students were protesting their leaders' expansionist, empire building, illegal war in Palestine, a country that wasn't theirs, against people who never attacked them. The same kind of war our leaders have led us into with the questionable Gulf of Tonkin Resolution. Perhaps those students in Berkeley are really trying to keep our leaders from collapsing our own empire. Have you thought about that?"

I was so pleased and proud of the logic of my observation and question. It was one of the best questions, I thought, I had ever asked anyone. It was such an important question asked of a very important politician. Gleefully, I thought I had nailed him. Not even the Gipper could avoid answering the obvious truth without fumbling. I waited for an answer, but it wasn't there. With a slight dismissive nod, he simply sidestepped it, earnestly and sincerely, without missing a beat, continuing with the platitudes and certitudes we heard on the six o'clock news. I was left holding a well-baited hook, looking at an empty suit. I experienced something I'd never felt with a guest, like I was talking to the Invisible Man.

At the end of the show, his handshake was firmer, his movie star smile broader. He was pleased with himself. His last on-air comment, aside from thanking me and the callers was, "It's been a very interesting, informative exchange, John. Democracy at its best."

"Thank you, Governor, and thanks also to our viewers. In a democracy, sir, it's not important for our leaders to always answer questions; it's just important that someone ask them. Thank you."

He waved goodbye as though he were boarding Air Force One. Joe was the first one at my side. "Geez, that was just terrific television. If McMahon doesn't use a clip of this, he's nuts! But, we'll get a lot of mileage out of this for you."

I was still ill at ease. His avoiding what I thought was a show-stopping, valid question, made me feel I was the one left hanging. To some, his not answering made me look like a bully; to others, even worse, a Lefty!

After every show, my staff and I gathered to discuss the following day's lineup. Not that day. Reagan, aside from Ali, had been our most important guest. Each of us was anxious to see it. By the next day the tape would be gone, reused for the next show.

We gathered in the editing booth to watch it. What I saw with Reagan, is exactly what I had witnessed with Cary Grant. On the set, there didn't seem to be much presence or vitality there, but on camera that was all you saw. The camera loved him. He sparkled. It didn't matter what he said. He was so likable.

Our staff was commenting at how good the show was. I was silent, waiting for the moment I nailed him. It wasn't there. It had been gobbled up by his charm. He had not avoided the brilliant question at all. It was just beneath him to answer it. He was no longer a guest sitting there. It was his show. He was Governor, the leader expounding on the goodness and peaceful purpose of America, informing us he was going to prove the nation's destiny was God's purpose, his purpose. What we had just witnessed was one of the worst things about TV, and one of the best. That empty suit, which an hour ago was inches from me, was suddenly filled with a man of conviction and charisma. Not even Nancy could have loved Ronnie more than the camera did.

Reagan was proof Marshall McLuhan was right, *the medium is the message.*

Cesar Chavez

In the long hot summer of 1970, it wasn't just draft resisters taking to the streets of Los Angeles. More than in any city in America, it was also Mexicans by the thousands. Their protests had little to do with Vietnam, and everything to do with America, about equality, about immigration reform. Bricklayers, gardeners, cooks, students, entrepreneurs, mothers, secretaries, nurses, and doctors, were building toward one impending mass demonstration called The Chicano Moratorium march. It loomed as a march feared by the citizenry and the authorities that would become uncontainable. They would prove to be right.

Since my wife is Mexican, and since it was the justified constant pressures from Chicano leaders to the FCC challenging KABC's license that brought about the *AM Show*, I took an intense interest in that movement. I, and anyone who read the *L.A. Times*, got the deepest insight and information about the growing, restless community from the paper's best columnist, Ruben Salazar, a Mexican-American, and wonderful writer.

Having the name Salazar gave his reporting deeper more powerful meaning. He was the Chicano voice. Their only voice. He was fast becoming a one-man force in the city. In one of his columns about the upcoming march, he mentioned two young organizers, young men under thirty, whom he felt were the soul of the movement, comparing them to Cesar Chavez and Martin Luther King. Their names: Rosalio Munoz and Gonzalo Javier. (As a sidebar, what surprises and I guess pleases me a little, is that it has been forty-five years since I read their names and interviewed them. Yet, the emotional impact of their brief appearance and the subsequent events were so profound, like every name in this book, I don't have to refer to notes or tapes to recall them. They are still deeply etched in my mind.)

We booked Gonzalo and Rosalio. On all stations and newspapers, there was reporting of mounting tension concerning the massive demonstration. Yet, we were the only show to give them a platform. As Ruben had discovered, they were wonderful. Both were in their twenties; both dark, handsome, and articulate. Casual in dress. Soft spoken, intense in delivery. They explained their purpose without anger. They pointed out the non-representation in the media, which led to challenging multiple broadcasters' licenses, discrimination in employment, in voting and mounting friction on the street with the Los Angeles Police Department. They believed in nonviolent change, but voiced a strong fear of the city's establishment, as evidenced by the Zoot Suit Riots after the Second World War was too resistant to change. They feared the city would use force like Selma and Montgomery. And the South against browns. Their warning of disruptions was picked up by every local news outlet. Even ours. Again, though, the appearance of important newsmakers was not allowed by McMahon to be excerpted from our show.

A week later the Chicano Moratorium March, with 20,000 bodies, flooded the streets from East Los Angeles to City Hall. The violence, as predicted, also came. Storefronts were smashed. Cars overturned. Skirmishes with the police. No one knew how it started. It just did. It grew like LA's hillside fires, until it was out of control. Hundreds of helmeted, shielded police fired a constant countless barrage of rubber bullets into the crowds, followed by hundreds of tear gas canisters. One of those canisters hit Ruben Salazar in the head. It killed him instantly.

Fearing an actual revolution, Reagan was on the verge of calling out the National Guard. But, it wasn't necessary. Word spread amongst the marchers, Ruben Salazar was dead on the sidewalk. Instead of becoming more outraged, they suddenly stopped. The streets got eerily quiet. What police clubs, rubber bullets, and tear gas could not do, the sight of Ruben Salazar's bloody body lying on the cement did.

There were countless arrests, but not of any policemen. Just protesters. Rosalio and Ganzalo were among them; also, a fellow named Corky Gonzalez. A day or two later my previous guests, along with most of the others, were released. Not Corky Gonzalez. Not even on bail. Evidently, he was the rabble rouser the attorney general was going to prosecute 'to the fullest limit of the law,' claiming proof he had initiated the riot that led to Salazar's death. The city attorney announced Gonzalez would go to trial within sixty days.

A few days later, the march and Ruben's death were no longer news. Only in the Latino papers. It was no longer news for us, either. We were busy preparing and doing our shows. Nearly a month had passed when we got a call from Cesar Chavez's assistant. He asked if we'd like to have Cesar as a guest. We were stunned. The most prominent voice for labour in America. The voice of the farmworkers. The most revered, nonviolent reformer in the country since Dr. King. The plight of underpaid, non-union farmers was first brought to us in the fifties by Edward E. Murrow on CBS in *Harvest of Shame*, ignored for twenty years until Cesar Chavez brought it to the fields, dusty roads and markets. Just taking one picture with Cesar Chavez a couple of years earlier, made Bobby Kennedy the leading candidate to become President of the United States. He brought out the growing compassion in Bobby, totally absent when he worked with Senator Joe McCarthy.

Cesar wasn't seeking high office, or any office. He was just seeking a livable, decent life for those who picked our food. After John Kennedy, Martin Luther King and Bobby Kennedy, Chavez was looked upon by millions, and by much of the media, as the last of The Four Horsemen, the last of the major movers and shakers with a soul.

"Why is he calling us?" I asked the aide.

"He will be in town for Corky Gonzalez's trial as a character witness. Cesar said he heard from Corky and a few others that you were the only person to give the cause time prior to the march. You're the only person on TV he wants to talk to."

"Wow. Will he mind if we open the phones to callers?"

"Cesar is a people person. He's familiar with your show. Certainly."

No guest ever got more pre-appearance coverage than did Cesar Chavez. Not Ali. Not Reagan. Not Fonda. No one. Everyone knew, like Santa at Christmas, he was coming to town. Only the president or pope could have gotten more press. Joe Seigman said he had never gotten so much attention for stories as a publicist. Joe said he never mailed any out; just answered the phone. From New York to LA!

Before our guest arrived, the press arrived. Six forty-five in the morning, three times the number of those wanting to talk to Ali or Reagan. Forty or fifty of them, along with everyone from the front office and newsroom. There was barely room to move in the studio. Watching them jostling for position near the door, and listening to the subdued but excited chattering, I was surprisingly calm. They weren't there for me. But Cesar was there for me. I felt at home. At peace. I was where I belonged, doing what I love. And what I loved was listening to and sharing my guests' stories. All this was zipping through my happy mind, when Cesar entered.

Unlike the entrance of Ali and Reagan, which created a surge of activity and purpose, when Cesar entered, they became quiet. They stared in silence at this dark-haired, brown, round-faced man wearing jeans and a plaid shirt. He was about my size, five-feet-eight. They were in awe, as if watching a Holy Man. It was the only time I ever saw or was around a prominent figure who was protected by a force field of decency. Cesar was accompanied by only two or three other men; all were dressed as casually as he was. Cesar made his way directly toward me, as though he knew me, smiled slightly, said "good morning," shook my hand and sat to my right, as though he'd done it often.

He had the gentlest demeanor, the sweetest face, the oldest soul, and the warmest voice I'd ever heard on a man, except for maybe my wife's father. On the air, we talked about his life, being raised and working on a farm, his difficulty in school because he couldn't speak English. Finding solace in religion, finding friends in his brothers and sisters. Like many of the poor, losing their home to a bank. Moving to San Jose. Joining the Navy. Marrying his childhood sweetheart. Working again in the fields. Driving sick and ill workers to the hospital. He laughed when I asked him what his favorite foods were, and did it include meat? It didn't. The change came about in his life when he accidentally met a man named Fred Ross, a community organizer who took a liking to him, asking him to help organize the workers. He spoke quietly, but brilliantly about the loss of John, Martin and Bobby, calling them only by their first names, as though they were the people's best friends. Not only was Cesar a natural organizer, he was also a compelling storyteller.

For the entire show he told his story, the farm workers' story. America's story. When the commercial breaks came, everyone was quiet and eager waiting for him to continue, and most of all, finish. I watched them making notes and fidgeting. In the background I saw an unsmiling, puffed up John McMahon. This was the last break. In ten minutes Cesar would step down, only to be mobbed by members of the Fifth Estate. I suddenly had the impulse to ask Cesar a question, a personal one, a selfish one, actually. The reporters were crowded behind the three cameras that were about fifteen feet away. I knew they couldn't hear me. Just to be sure, I put my hand over the microphone on my shirt, and turned to Cesar.

"Mr. Chavez, would you mind if I asked you a favor?" He turned to me, but didn't answer. "You see all these reporters here?" He looked at them, nodding slightly. "When we're finished here, they're going to drag you outside, and ask you a lot of questions, questions that I've asked you here." I paused, thinking I should stop, but instead continued, embarrassed at what I was about to say. "Mr. Chavez, I feel really awful asking you this. I mean it is so selfish and unimportant really. I mean what you have to say is important. You should go out and talk to them ... " I stopped again. He was looking at me without a word or expression. His silence made me feel I was digging a deeper more selfish showbiz hole! "See that man over there?" I looked at McMahon.

"Yes," he said quietly.

"For some reason he doesn't like me. We've had wonderful news-making guests on the show, but he will never, ever take a clip from the show and put it on his news. He just has his crew take the guest outside and ask them questions that I'd already asked. Please, please, forgive me. I mean it is selfish. And again, your story is what's important, and should be told to everyone–"

He interrupted me. "What is it, John?"

"Mr. Chavez, when the show is over, when they ask you to come outside for questions, could you tell them you have a bad back from picking grapes." I was finished. I had said it, but it was like he hadn't heard me. I wanted to hide.

The last ten minutes took forever. We continued a warm conversation, taking up where he'd left off, as though I hadn't uttered such an egomaniacal thing. And it was over. The red lights went off. The cameras were pushed aside as the throng rushed to surround him, ignoring me. I moved my chair back to separate myself, to give them and Mr. Chavez more room. I was sitting back, watching them groveling over Cesar, a man whose work and words were making a real difference to the world. My work felt suddenly meaningless.

In unison, they were imploring him to spend a few more minutes with them so they could talk to him. Cesar had not yet moved from his chair. He looked at them, listening calmly and patiently as they asked him if he'd mind stepping outside. After a few moments, Cesar raised his hand a little, like the pope. There was suddenly silence and expectation.

"Gentlemen, unfortunately I can't. I've gotten a really bad back recently from picking grapes. I'm off for treatments."

He got up slowly and left, never looking back. I could have cried with gratitude. Cesar and I were on the six o'clock KABC news. And again, on the morning news. Finally!

Jim Garrison

The two places I loved to linger, outside of our apartment or the office, were almost right across the street from one another on Hollywood Boulevard: Musso and Frank's Grill and Edmund's Used Books. One to nourish my stomach; the other to nourish my mind. One Saturday after a late breakfast, I sauntered across to Edmund's, looking for nothing in particular. I loved it there, even the smell.

In a section marked twenty-five percent off, I spotted what looked like a new light-grey hardcover titled, *Heritage of Stone.* It meant nothing to me until I noticed that it was by Jim Garrison. *Garrison,* I thought. *Isn't that the guy, the DA from New Orleans who tried unsuccessfully to prosecute a prominent businessman for conspiracy in the killing of John Kennedy?* I was about to pass it up when I asked myself, *if he lost the case, why bother writing a book about it*? That thought compelled me to pick it up, just to peek inside. I was immediately caught by the terrific writing of the first few sentences. This was the writing of a bright, articulate, extremely well-educated man, not some egomaniacal ambitious nutcase, as he was incessantly described by all the major media, the government, and by J. Edgar Hoover. All those pronouncements from the aforementioned, I, like everyone I knew, took for granted as gospel. I mean, who could doubt Hoover, the head of the FBI?

I stood, book in hand, reading for an hour, astonished at information I'd never heard about. It all had the ring of truth to it; four pieces of information, each one more jaw-dropping than the next. In order to get the famous or infamous Zapruder film of the headshot to the president, the most important piece of evidence, which the FBI declined saying it has no evidentiary value, Garrison not only had to sue *Time-Life*, he had to take it to the Supreme Court, where he won. A doctor testified at the trial of Clay Shaw that generals and admirals were preventing them from performing a proper autopsy. Over forty witnesses testified under oath they saw Shaw and Oswald together before the assassination. The jury had found Shaw guilty of perjury. For Garrison, this would have been a slam dunk conviction, but the federal government stepped in to stop that trial.

And there was Garrison's haunting chapter heading, translated from the Latin, *Let Justice Be Done Though the Heavens Fall.* Who had I ever heard of in America talk that passionately about justice since the Founding Fathers or Teddy and Franklin Roosevelt, or Edward R. Murrow or Clarence Darrow, whom Garrison named one of his three sons after? No one.

I purchased and finished the book before midnight at the dining room table, my dinner left untouched. I literally jumped out of bed the next morning. What a guest! What a story!

What news!

Like most Americans, even though I wasn't one yet, I believed The Warren Report's findings: Lee Harvey Oswald was the crazy commie loner who had done the dirty deed in Dallas.

I tried to bolster my belief in those conclusions by reading the one volume condensation of the twenty-six volumes; it was turgid, visual quicksand. I barely got halfway through it. Sadly, it wasn't until after the Shaw trial in sixty-nine that I stumbled upon Mark Lane's impeccably researched and beautifully written classic, *Rush to Judgment.* Like Garrison, Lane was later savaged by the press, telling the nation, "he's only in it for the money". Those crucifiers never mentioned that every publisher in America turned it down. It had to be published in England. Mark was paid $1,500.00. He brought up obvious mistakes, legal and otherwise, in The Warren Report, that screamed out to be answered; at the time, though, I was not interested in being one of those screamers. I had my show to do. Lane's book made great provable points about the commission's deliberate falsifications that would hold up in any courtroom. I was certain lawyers and judges around the country would see that and take action. It was their job. The law. The pursuit of justice. I had no real interest in the murder of President Kennedy beyond curiosity; that was the extent of it. Nobody I knew talked about it. It was over. A sad part of history.

All day that early Sunday, I reread certain passages pacing the room. I couldn't wait until Monday morning to call Garrison in New Orleans. I wasn't thinking about solving Kennedy's killing. I wasn't thinking of shocking anyone. I just wanted people to hear Jim Garrison's stunning story about being caught up in the crime of the century. The story of his life. His trial. His book. Even if I didn't have a show, I would want to sit down with him and listen to that story. With my popular show, though, thousands and thousands of others could sit and listen to him, and *talk* to him. I smiled as I pictured it.

Monday morning, I dialed long distance information for the New Orleans' District Attorney's office. My mind was spinning with nervous pleasure. Mr. Garrison, not a secretary, answered. I explained who I was and then added, "I just read *Heritage of Stone* and I was–"

His laugh interrupted me. "Oh, you must be the other one. I only sold two copies."

"Mr. Garrison, I know little about your case but–"

"Well, John, neither do two hundred million other Americans who watch or read the news."

"I am astonished, truly astonished, at what I learned from your book. We have as large a morning audience in LA as *The Today Show*. I know people would love to hear your story. Would you come on our show? We'll pay for your hotel and–"

"John, you'll never get away with it." He was very matter-of-fact. "How many times have you seen me as a guest on those news or interview shows?"

"I saw you once on Carson. A little bit. I say a little bit because he kept interrupting you."

"It wasn't so much he was interrupting me. He couldn't remember the questions the FBI and CIA had coached him with beforehand."

This sounded too deep for me, maybe a little too farfetched, so I said nothing. I made a quick note to explore this when he was on the show. "I saw you alone on NBC. I think they had to give you equal time or something. You were really good. I especially liked the opening reference to our trusting the honorable men of the Warren Commission. It sounded right out of *Julius Caesar*!"

"You do read!" He chuckled. "Unusual for people in your profession."

"Yes, I do, sir, a lot. If you do the show, I'll interview you for about half an hour, then we'll open the phones. I guarantee you the lines will be flooded. And your book will sell out as it deserves to."

"Well, young man, I'd be happy to do it, but–"

"Oh, thank you. Thank you. It'll be fantastic!"

"What will be fantastic is if you get away with it. But, again, I'd be happy to do it. Do you know that according to the Harris polls, eighty-one percent of Americans believe that Oswald either didn't do it or there was a conspiracy, but only twenty-three percent want a new commission to investigate it? What does that tell you?"

"Mr. Garrison, it tells me that I know what my mother and father did in the bedroom, or the car, or in an alley, but don't ever tell me my mother's not a virgin."

There was a full loud laugh! "John, if you don't mind, I may just use that. I look forward to meeting you."

We set the date. A little over two weeks away. For me, more than any of the fantastic guests I'd had, Jim Garrison, whom I didn't even know, or really know of, was the most exciting, important person on the planet to talk to. Thinking of all the truths we would be hearing in two weeks thrilled me.

I happily informed Brad of my conversation, apologizing for not running it by him first. I told him I was just too excited. It was the second time I saw him smile. This meant he was excited. Brad said he'd make the travel and hotel arrangements, assuring me they'd be first class, but we never got to interview Garrison. He was right. We wouldn't get away with it.

I vividly remember the day it happened. It was the Monday after I talked to Garrison. He was awaiting confirmation and travel arrangements from Brad. It was five minutes to seven in the morning. I was sitting at my desk feeling lucky to have the young family I had and to have, even though it was just local, the very best talk show in television. I wanted to say out loud that I was the happiest luckiest men in the world. The show's excellence wasn't just my opinion. It was the opinion of FCC Commissioner, Nicholas Johnson, who'd written a letter to the President of ABC, Leonard Goldenson, saying so, then copying me with a funny note that read: *Now that they have found they have someone intelligent on their network, I hope it doesn't cost you your job!*

I sought out Brad to ask about Garrison's arrangements, but he was very matter-of-fact. "He's not doing the show."

"Why not?" I was stunned.

"Neither are you," he continued. "McMahon is replacing you with Ralph Story. John, I swear I had nothing to do with it. I just found out."

"What do you mean, Ralph Story? He already turned it down."

"Well, now that it is a success, in a successful time slot, he wants it."

"McMahon did this? And didn't even consult you?" I asked.

"Only after the fact. I told him I didn't think he'd be as good as you. That it'd be a different show. But he agreed that you should at least be allowed to finish the next week."

"You mean, he's going to let me still go on the air, not knowing what I might say?"

"I told him you were a pro."

Brad said he was sorry, but didn't look or sound it. He was his usual low-key, passive self. How could McMahon be so fucking stupid? How? We were, an award-winning hit. I had gone from sky-scraping euphoria to sinkhole depression in a matter of seconds. Why? What made the horror worse was not only my fate determined by an asshole, but l was being punished for obvious excellence by that same asshole.

The following morning, I opened the show welcoming viewers to my last week. Ralph Story would soon be filling my chair, but not my boots. It would be his show. His boots are different. The kind that kick you from behind. I told them we'd continue to do the best show possible. I added that I did not want to hear any phone calls about how you might miss me.

"Management also took away my Kleenex," I said.

Even so, calls, as did letters, came in by the thousands. All of which I saved in a huge carton. I tried to read a few, but they broke my heart. Hundreds were typed. Hundreds had beautifully crafted handwriting. Some were scrawled. Some printed. Some with embossed letterhead. Some on scraps of paper. I stopped after reading one in particular, one I would read on the air on my last show. I told Brad I'd like five or ten minutes at the end of my last Friday's show to say goodbye. He agreed.

The crew was intense and somber. They had no idea of what I was about to say. I thanked them and staff publicly. I thanked the viewers for their cards and letters. I told them I was often asked what it was like to host an important show like that and to get to talk to so many famous and interesting people. Then I held up that one letter, and said, "Being on television or talking to all of these famous, interesting people over the months has nothing to do with why I loved being here. This letter says it all." I began to read:

Mr. Barbour, you have no idea how much I'll miss you. I cried for days. But I have to tell you why. For six months, you were my only friend. I never finished high school since I was pregnant. I dropped out and married. I was pregnant four more times. I am twenty-six and looking after my children. My husband never took me out. Then you came into my life. More than you can imagine. I began to learn things, things I might have never learned in school. When my husband would come home, I couldn't wait to tell him what I'd been learning. But he didn't care. He told me I'd always be stupid, pregnant and barefoot. When he wasn't verbally abusive, he was physically abusive. Then I learned from you and your guests that I didn't have to live like this. In fear. So, screwing up my courage, I did something I'd never thought I'd do. I left him. Today, except for knowing you're leaving, I don't know any woman happier. My kids, too. We are in a loving home with a caring man. I'm going to school again. It would have never happened, if I hadn't stumbled onto you. God bless you. And thank you from the bottom of my heart ... and reawakened brain, Sylvia

I put down the letter and looked into the camera. "Folks, Sylvia's letter says it all for me. I never got into this for the money or fame, all of which is fleeting, as you can see. I loved only the thought that I might somehow be making a difference. I'm the one who should be thanking Sylvia. And you. Thank you. Management, as you know, is now making a difference in my life. Good luck to all of us."

There was a spontaneous eruption of applause, whistles and cheers from the crew, the staff and a few employees who wandered in to see what was going on. Then it was over. After personally thanking everyone present, I left the studio.

Walking toward me was John McMahon. He didn't extend his hand. "You did a good job. I'm surprised you handled the last week as well as you did. It wasn't what I expected."

"Neither was my firing."

Larry Einhorn, accompanied by our ballerina dancer and two very well-dressed distinguished looking ladies, walked toward us. They were each carrying a box. "John," Einhorn said, "these ladies insist they see you."

The women introduced themselves. My ballerina spoke for them. "Mr. McMahon, John saved my life a few months ago. We're here to save his job. He is irreplaceable. For this past week scores of us every day from sun-up to sundown at malls all around the county have had people signing these petitions to save John Barbour on *AM*. There are over five thousand names. Surely this must mean something."

McMahon was stunned. As was I. But he was smooth, as executives usually are. It's a commodity more important to them than a soul. He said, "Ladies, it does mean something. I assure you, I am impressed by what you've done. I will look at them and see what I can do. Larry, here, will take you to my office where I'd like you to put them on my desk."

One of the other ladies spoke. "No matter what or who you get, they'll never be as good as John. If you are not fair to him and us, you'll hear from us again."

"As John said this morning, change is the nature of this business. Sometimes beyond even my control. I have heard you. I promise I'll do my best for you and him." He looked at them, then Larry, who got the message.

"Come with me, ladies," Larry said, walking away.

"Call me later, John, please," the ballerina said, as she held her box up.

I was pleased to see she had made a new life with new friends. She was, happily, not at all the same person.

McMahon had a smirk on his face. "There goes your audience."

His arrogance was repulsive. I said, "You shouldn't want them to go. Look, I know you don't care for me much. I'm not good in offices, but I am good on camera. Just so you don't lose an audience, even of little old ladies, give some thought to perhaps my doing something else."

"There's no room on the schedule," he said flatly.

"Bob has asked you a few times about my doing reviews on your news. I could do it three times a week. Then the public, the people who've liked us, won't think that you don't."

His face flushed with obvious anger. "Fuck the public," he hissed. "They don't hire you!"

I missed getting up at five in the morning, missed the late-night reading of books, missed the interviews and phone calls, but I wasn't depressed about it. Having been successful at it, I was certain it would be just a matter of time before I got a call to do another show, or even replace Story's fluffy style. Knowing how cost-conscious McMahon was, I felt I might be called back to bolster what was a dull show. Management was forced to spend a lot of money on new staff and new features which didn't work. I was even more optimistic about my return to it, when a few weeks later I won my first of five Emmys, for a show I was no longer on. Not once did I give any thought to the fact my departure was due to booking the controversial Jim Garrison. I thought it was just show business as usual.

Six more weeks went by. There wasn't a call from one of the people with whom I'd worked with for nearly a year. I read that Brad went to the

Griffin show and Robert got a job at CBS. I don't mean to be vain here. Just factual. I didn't understand how they got job offers and I didn't. They weren't the show. I was. I figured since Brad was with Merv's show, maybe I should call there. When Merv was on vacation, I could sit in. But I'd heard that I'd offended Merv when some lady called into my show and asked what I thought of his leaving New York to come to LA and his CBS show. I said, "The Queen Mary also came West when it was no longer useful as a ship." Apparently, that joke, and it was only a joke, implied he'd never make it on CBS, and using the Queen Mary reference suggested him being gay. In other words, I'd outed him unintentionally.

A call eventually came. It was another local station caving into the FCC. The station was KNXT, where Carson had done *Carson's Cellar* and Jack Owens his show. But, this was not to be an entertainment show. Just Public Service. I met immediately with the caller, a wonderful warm bright woman named Carmen, whom Joe Sands, the program director, had assigned to produce it.

"John," she said, "Management needs a Public Affairs show. You were absolutely the only one I wanted to host it. You may not be thanking me after a while. Management thinks public service, especially when it's forced on them, is money stolen from them. They won't look on you as a host but as a burden.

"Carmen, are you trying to talk me out of this?"

"No. I'm just warning you and giving you the facts of life here. But the upside is, it's a job, for at least thirteen weeks, and you'll be on the air, where you should be. Do you want to see the studio?"

"You mean, I have the job?"

"Yes. Now, let me show you the studio."

It wasn't just a studio; it was a beautiful small theater. "Wow, this is beautiful," I said. "It looks almost like the studio I saw Jack Owens in years ago. Will you have audiences?"

"Jesus, no. When Bob Crosby did his show here they couldn't get fifteen little old ladies, and when Johnny Carson did *Carson Cellar,* there was no one. For a public service show, they wouldn't show up for free money!"

"What if we tried to get an audience, though?"

"John, we'll be lucky to get guests."

We started *Barbour's People* weekday afternoons. I had boxes of letters and petitions in our apartment. I spent hours night and day for fourteen days answering them, thanking them. In longhand. I had no typewriter. I informed them of our new undertaking at CBS locally and hoped they would watch.

Not only did they watch. They showed up! There were just over a hundred seats in our studio. Every afternoon, for nearly a month, every seat was occupied by well-dressed women, and occasionally, men. It was astonishing; we had only asked that they watch, not attend! Word spread through the station that people, real live people, were coming to see our little half hour show. Employees popped in from everywhere just to peek.

Carmen was an energetic delight to work with. Our guests, authors, stars, and politicians, were all outstanding. Everyone liked the show, except management. As predicted or forewarned by Carmen thirteen weeks earlier, she was the one assigned to be Isis and chop my head off.

Aside from the people I met as staff or guests, what pleased me most was the way I ended the last show. I stood center stage, thanked the audience for watching, then did a monologue about the importance and purpose of television, how it could educate and ennoble, improve society and our lives. All the while, a crew of twelve workmen were making their way on and off the set behind me, removing the chairs, the table, then the lights, then the plants and walls of the set. And, finally, the cameras. It was funny. Sad, but funny.

Other than Carmen, the person I am most thankful for and to is Herb Nannas, one of the William Morris office's young agents. He asked me to put an hour composite tape together, and the day after I was fired brought some fellow agents down to view it. This is part of what he wrote: Wm Morris Agency Memo To: Howard West. From: Herb Nannas

> *This morning Fred Apollo, Bill Tannenbaum, Bill Haber, Mike Chandler and I went over to KNXT where we saw the 1 hr. composite of JOHN BARBOUR. I can now fully understand why Westinghouse was so excited about JOHN BARBOUR replacing MERV GRIFFIN! This man has the combination of wit, charm, and personality to compare with JOHNNY CARSON, MERV, and JACK PAAR. His monologues on each show were sensational and he handled each and every one of his guests with smooth professional assurance. I'm certain we can build him into one of the most important talk-personality hosts on the national market today. I strongly suggest that George Shapiro, Elliot Wax, Tony Fantozzi, Marty Dubow, etc. go down to KNXT to see this one-hour composite. The fellow is absolutely sensational!*

Sandy Wernick had disappeared along with the *AM Show*, so with Herb's memo in hand, I thought I'd go back to the Morris Agency, my tail between my legs. But Howard West and George Shapiro were gone, now managing Jerry Seinfeld. And Herb's memo excited no one.

Not being wanted by an agent or a station was like losing a limb. It made me sick feeling it would never grow back. I had gone from being one of the biggest things in town for a year, to being nonexistent, even though I was still writing reviews for *Los Angeles Magazine*. It was a feeling of abandonment, much worse than I'd ever felt as a kid. I may have been an unworthy kid, but by God, I was worthy as a performer. The emptiness and hopelessness killed me, but I never brought that feeling of loss home. Because home was the only place I never felt it. I loved being with my son and wife. I was a good host, but a greater father.

For extra money, I could go back to The Losers, where Pete Rooney said I'd be welcome. I couldn't, though. It would make me feel like a loser. From star on TV to strip club comic, I'd be better off unseen, but remembered. The only thing I could think of to stay on TV would be to maybe become a movie/tv critic.There were not any. Geoff Miller, the editor of *LA Magazine* said my reviews, for which I only got $150.00, were their most popular feature. And he loved to brag that Lucille Ball said publicly, "Aside from my writers, John Barbour is my favorite. The first thing I read every month." So, I started making a new round of calls. I didn't say I was John Barbour. I just said I was from *Los Angeles Magazine.*

Critic-At-Large

I called Chuck Young, General Manager of KTTV, the man who'd given me my first full talk show, if only for thirteen weeks.

"John, how are you? What are you up to?"

"Job hunting!"

Chuck laughed. "Is it not going too well?"

"I'll let you know after this brief conversation."

"Well, we're not looking to do any sort of show, unless you could convince us otherwise. What'd you have in mind?"

"I'd like to do movie and television reviews on your eleven o'clock news. They were really popular when I did them on the *AM Show* and my afternoon show. They're really popular in *LA Magazine.* There is no one on any news show doing them."

"I'm not sure there'd be room for something like that."

"I'm not talking about every night. I'm not sure I could do them every night. I'm just talking about three times a week, Monday, Wednesday, and Friday."

"John, you know this is not a company that likes to spend money."

"Reviews would be a lot more interesting and entertaining than the bloody weather. No one needs a weather girl. All they have to do is look out the window. The only interesting thing about your weather girl is that she does it in sign language that only eight people can understand."

"You do sound like a critic. Look, wait a day, then call Riley, our news director. I'll tell him to expect your call. I'll just tell him you have an interesting notion that I'd like him to hear."

Two days later I was in Riley's office with two copies of *LA Magazine*. Riley was in his late forties, a slender six feet or more, greying hair around the ears, and, thankfully, a face that was easy to look at. He always looked pleased about something.

After the introductions, he pointed at the magazines. "I see you brought your portfolio."

"Just in case you wanted to see how I write."

"I've already read them. And do so every month. My wife and I fight over who gets them first. Nobody's done anything like that on a news show yet. Do you think it'd work?"

"*AM* was a news show and they worked great there. Bob Irvine, the news director, will tell you he wanted them on the news, but McMahon, his boss, didn't think they'd work."

"Let's give it a shot, but we don't have extra money budgeted for another feature. You said you only wanted to do this thing three times a week. All I can give you is a hundred dollars a show. It's not much."

"I'd be glad to do it for that."

"We'll feature you as our Critic-At-Large. Next Monday you can start."

As predicted, I almost became as popular as the weather girl. Three months in, Riley asked if I'd like to anchor their new noon news.

"I'm not an anchorman. I'd rather comment on the news than report it. Besides, I don't have that kind of voice."

"Just read it the way you read your reviews. It's simple. It's an extra five hundred a week. You start Monday."

For a week, at noon, I sat in front of two cameras and a teleprompter reading copy I had no hand in writing. I felt like a robot, embarrassed about taking the extra money. Friday, my fifth day, Riley poked his head out of his office and motioned for me. "You know, John, you really are a wonderful, honest critic. You were right. You were awful. It's back to eleven o'clock."

"Thank you," I said, meaning it.

Arriving every evening to polish my copy, the one diversion the entire staff had was stopping to watch NBC's live feed of *The Tonight Show* from Burbank to New York. When that familiar theme song played, everyone would pause at his or her desk, lean back and listen to Johnny Carson's monologue. It was a ritual.

On September 6, 1972, though, when the music played, no one was seated. They had rushed to the monitors, not to hear jokes, but to hear what Johnny would have to say about the horror we and the world had been witnessing for a day. A hooded Palestinian terrorist group calling itself Black September had somehow stormed the Israeli athletes' Olympic compound, taking hostages. They were demanding Israel release 234 Palestinian prisoners. The Israeli government refused to negotiate. They said they never do. Ever.

For hours the world was held spellbound and horrified by the sickening reality of this barbaric intrusion into the world's celebration of amateur sports. Cameras with long-distance lenses followed the gunmen pacing on balconies, weapons held high, peering through eye-slits in their black woolen hoods, screaming at the Israelis. At the world. To Allah.

When this unfolding disaster suddenly interrupted the camaraderie of the world's togetherness, ABC, which was broadcasting the Olympics was fortunate, as were we, that their lead commentator was Jim McKay. This professional, polished commentator was abruptly forced from being a cheery sportscaster into a subdued, reasoned, calming journalist; listening to him and watching the pictures unfold, no one could move. It was television at its best. Humanity at its worst.

Israel repeated their stance on not dealing with terrorists. Black September shot their first victim. Gasps filled the room and the airways. Then they shot a second. And a third. Eleven in total. The world had gone mad!

Later, gathering around *The Tonight Show* live feed, everyone was silent. A few placed their palms together, raising them to their lips as in prayer. Doc Severinson played the theme. Ed McMahon's powerful, salesman's voice announced the always happy, "Heeere's Johnny!"

Johnny, as usual, pushed his way through the center of the billowy curtains moving with his quick gait toward the audience. He was smiling.

Jesus Christ, I thought. *Why is he smiling?* Jack Paar wouldn't be smiling. He wouldn't even have music or an announcer. He'd just come out cold and give you his thoughts on the massacre we'd had just witnessed. Johnny patted his jacket as he often did, then looked at Doc. Jesus Christ, it was a repeat of his saying not a word about Bobby Kennedy's murder the day after.! What a cold bastard.

"Have you seen that plaid jacket Doc is wearing?" The audience laughed. Then he made some feeble joke about it, about maybe looking like the inside of Ed's head. Then another weak joke about Ed's drinking. That was it. And a few jokes about meaningless news. We all stood and stared. Waiting. He had to say something. Anything. But not a word. Or a hint of one. As he went to commercial, one of the news writers muttered, "What the fuck was that?" We returned to our desks.

I sat staring at my review. It was about a movie I loved and was eager to tell the audience about. But on such a night and day, who wanted to talk about a movie or hear about a movie? I was repulsed by Carson's indifference. Maybe it wasn't his doing. Maybe he wanted to say something, but management told him not to. He was an entertainer. He was there to help people forget their troubles. Paar would have told them to screw off or quit.

Like a corny scene in a Hollywood movie out of the forties, I tore up the review and started to type. The following poured out of me in a matter of a few minutes. This would be my review, unseen and unapproved by Riley.

KTTV: Critic-At Large ... John Barbour ... September 6th, 1972. "Because of what has happened in Munich I've found it impossible to think about anything else. All of us are constantly bombarded by the horrors of death and brutality with which man infects his world, and in order to maintain a sense of sanity and purpose we each go about our business looking at that side of us which is optimistic and cheerful. But the horror and senselessness of Munich is so real there is no escape into optimism, because when you think of it, the whole world is Munich.

"Violent death of man at the hands of another man has become so acceptable and commonplace it may one day be listed as death by natural causes. And you think about the irony of how the Olympic Games, a celebration of life, are called off even temporarily by the death of those athletes, and yet a half a world away hundreds of thousands can die in Vietnam and no one calls off the war.

"There is something else, though, that bothers me about Munich. When you see a Vietnamese mother, it hurts, but you know at least there was somebody, some country on her side. When you see an American soldier die in Vietnam, it hurts, but, you also know there was someone on his side. However, when a Jew dies, in Munich, or in Auschwitz, it seems he dies alone, and when he fights, he fights alone. These killings took place not too many days before Yom Kippur, the holiest of Jewish holidays, the Day of Atonement, the day Jews ask forgiveness for their sins. Why is it in a world where historically the Jew has been more sinned against than sinner, would he ask forgiveness for his transgressions? Why, while his fellow man has been cruel, would a Jew talk about his fellow man's kindness? Why? Because a Jew is special. The Jew is different, a difference that all too often was used as an excuse by others to suppress him. And in spite of that suppression, the Jew has become the yeast in the bread of civilization that caused it to rise. Because they were so frequently near death themselves, they developed, as Dr. Albert Schweitzer said, a reverence for life. They became the healers, the philosophers, the scientists, and even if he became an unknown tailor in some small haberdashery, he invested it with dignity. And, most importantly, he invested it with hope. For the Jew knows without that hope there can be no survival, and if there is one thing the Jew has learned, it is the bitter art of survival. On his own, the Jew managed to maintain and strengthen his difference and his individuality. In the respect that we're all struggling to maintain individuality, and we are struggling to maintain hope. In that respect, regardless of our national origin or religious affiliation, we are all spiritually Jews.

"What happened in Munich must have brought home to Jews of every nationality, even to those that never thought about it, a sense of their own Jewishness. To the rest of the world, this horror should stir in them some reflections about their own Day of Atonement. Because in the long run, if a Jew is not safe in Munich or Tel Aviv or Moscow or anywhere, then none of us are safe."

There was a long silence in the newsroom. Everyone was standing or sitting still. Going to commercial, they rose and applauded. Hearing it, the tears flowed harder. Then, as almost never happened after the news, the phones began to ring. One of the calls was for me. It was from Riley, calling from his home.

"John, tomorrow you're on the noon news again. You're not going to anchor. You have to repeat what you just said. Get in before noon!" He hung up.

I was in before noon, copy in hand. "Sorry I didn't run it by you before going on the air, but it was a last-minute impulse."

"If I'd seen it, you know what I'd've changed?" he said straight faced.

"What?"

"I'd have had it taped. Today it will be. We have already received over 500 requests for copies, and when you're done, you need to call this guy in Century City. His name is Carter."

He handed me a piece of paper with the name and number.

"Why?"

"How would I know? He's a billionaire philanthropist, friend of Chuck's. He says he wants to talk to you."

On the air, I again choked up, barely getting through it. Immediately after I called the mysterious Mr. Carter.

"Young man," he, said, "you have no idea of the impact you've had on us with what you said." He paused.

"Who is *us*?" I asked.

"Jews. The Jews."

"Mr. Carter, that never, ever once occurred to me. I was just getting it out of my system. Really."

"Thousands of people in your business, and most of them Jews, and others, probably felt the same. But nobody said it. I would like permission to reprint it, and distribute it, to transfer it to film and make it this year's fundraising film for the United Jewish Appeal."

"Absolutely. I'm honored!"

"And I would like to make you an honorary member of The Guardians."

"What is that?"

"The leading group of Jewish philanthropists. And I'd like you to speak at our next function, where we'll honor you, and at a few other gatherings where they already want to hear you."

"Anything you want, sir, and anything I can do."

"Come and see me. I'm in Century City."

It was the busiest month I ever had. I met with Mr. Carter. He had 5,000 reprints and recordings made; they were the only non-Jewish items sold at a massive Israeli memorial fair held that year at the LA convention center. The proceeds went to the families of the athletes. As he said, it became the fundraising film for two consecutive years. It raised thirty-five million dollars.

At the Guardians' major annual function, I was embraced by Neil Simon. I was made an honorary Jew. I still have the statue. I told them that prior to the night I did my commentary, about once a month, as a former comic, I would do modest speaking gigs before one or two hundred people for three hundred dollars each. But since doing that piece, once every few nights, I'm speaking to thousands of Jews for nothing. They loved it! I told them also that I was making a five-thousand-dollar pledge to Israel, then added, "Paying it off, fifty dollars a year." They loved that. It was a heady month. What a wonderful feeling my work meant something. Another phone call indicated it might also mean something to someone else.

"John Barbour?" the edgy voice asked. "This is Irwin Safchik, KNBC New Director. We're thinking of doing something like you're doing on our six o'clock news with Tom Snyder. Tom Brokaw suggested I talk to you. Would you be interested in auditioning for us?"

"Auditioning? Can't you just watch me at eleven or I could tape it for you?"

"We prefer to see how you might look in our surroundings."

I mulled it over. Jesus. *Audition?* Again?

"Can you come by Tuesday, bring one or two reviews?" he asked.

"Yes. I'll be there." I was on my way to sitting next to NBC's Burbank Peacock, Tom Snyder.

One Foot in the Stirrup

An ancient Persian proverb says, *if you are going to tell the truth you better have one foot in the stirrup*. So, before I get into some of the tales of my stay at KNBC, I want to give you just a few thoughts on how I personally approached being a critic. I told the audience this when I began. If I tell them a movie, play, book or TV show is great or dreadful, it may not actually be the truth. What was the truth, was how I felt about it. I was never wrong about my feelings, therefore never changed my mind, regardless of what anyone else thought. I confessed I did not watch movies with my eyes or mind, but with the seat of my pants. If my pants moved or didn't, I used my mind to interpret what my pants were trying to tell me. I also told them movies were a lot like people; most were disappointing. But the one or two outstanding ones that came along, that enhance or change your life for the better, make all your previous disappointments worthwhile.

In 1973 when I started at KNBC, sitting next to Snyder, the most watched Dean of Critics was Gene Shalit on *The Today Show*. Gene had this Harpo Marx mop of black hair, and almost that much as a mustache. In 1967, I was not yet a paid critic; I was still doing stand-up. But I saw a lot of movies to talk about in my act. Of course, Warren Beatty, this generation's Errol Flynn, was the perfect source for material. Gene so thoroughly savaged *Bonnie and Clyde* the morning I was going to see it, I couldn't wait to also trash it, but with jokes. Shalit didn't just hate it. He loathed it. I rushed to the theater, but I never wrote one joke about the film – only about Shalit.

From the opening scenes, I wondered what film Gene had seen. It wasn't the movie I saw. Next to *The Godfather*, which came out five years later, *Bonnie and Clyde*, directed by Arthur Penn, written by David Newman and Robert Benton, starring Warren Beatty and Faye Dunaway, is the second-best Technicolor gangster film to ever come out of Hollywood. I said of Gene Shalit: "As a critic he has no equals; superiors yes, equals, no!" Audiences loved it. Scared off by the attacks on it, the box office started slowly; within weeks, however, word of mouth turned it into a monster hit. A month later, it was on the cover of *Time* magazine. After the enormous success of the film, Shalit was forced to revisit it on *The Today Show*. This time he gave it a rave review. Gene Shalit was for me no longer a critic. He was a shill for the industry. I had promised myself that if I ever became a critic, I would only listen to my pants and keep one foot in the stirrup.

For the five years I was at KNBC, I won three consecutive Emmys. For doing my reviews, I was also thrown out of the building physically three times by Irwin, our news director, once accompanied by armed security. Those brief encounters I will relate shortly. Now, though, my first awkward few hours on the new job:

I was sitting in Irwin's surprisingly small office. He said, "John, I think you'll do real well here. We're paying you a hundred and fifty dollars a review, but Sid Graw in Business Affairs tells me you don't want to sign a contract. You want more money? It's not gonna happen."

"No, it's got nothing to do with money. The contract, which is nice, says that NBC would own my material. I don't have a contract at *LA Magazine* either, for that same reason. I have been over there two years. I don't want anyone owning my material."

"That means you'd just be going day to day. We could get rid of you in a minute."

"That's true, but while my work is small, in the scale of things, it's big to me."

"Well, if that's how you like it, fine, let me show you your office." He led me through the newsroom. Pleasantly, many waved a greeting at me. One was Tom Brokaw.

"That's your benefactor," Irwin said, leading me down a narrow hall, to a small room where there was a typewriter and phone. It was perfect for me. Irwin left and I sat down on the flimsy fabric chair, staring at a brand new electric typewriter.

"Is this who I have to fuck next?"

Startled, I looked up. Leaning in the doorway was Kelly Lange. She was LA's most popular weather girl. If you did not know Kelly, she was quite attractive, but from the beginning, with her crude introduction, and for the five years I got to know her really well, her visual appeal vanished like *The Picture of Dorian Gray*.

"You're the new guy on the block?" she asked.

"I guess so. My name's John Barbour."

"I know who you are. They tell me you might be also cohosting *The Sunday Show*. I want you to know, I prefer to do it alone."

"No one has said anything to me about hosting or co-hosting anything. And … and … you are?" I, of course, knew who it was; it was just my way of trying to deflate her obvious hostility.

She was born Dorothy Scafard in New England. Moving to LA, she modeled bras for Frederick's of Hollywood, won a contest at a mall to become a helicopter weather girl for radio station KABC, where her popularity brought her to KNBC. She had a well-known long affair with a popular married game show host, Jim Lange. Not being able to steal Mrs. Lange's husband, who refused to leave his wife, Kelly stole his name.

I always thought when Paddy Cheyevsky wrote that brilliant, ball-busting, ambitious female executive Faye Dunaway portrayed in *Network*, he modeled her after Kelly. To Kelly's credit, though, in this killer business, she became one of the best, at a hundred thousand dollars year, the highest paid weather girl in the country. Decades later, when she retired as an anchor, she moved to Las Vegas where she became successful writing mystery novels about a female reporter.

"You know fucking well who I am!' she hissed. Her immediate hostility toward me was baffling. My couple of attempts later to befriend her failed. Her continual attempts to get me fired, also failed. We were thankfully interrupted.

"Welcome. I'm Bob Howard, the GM here. My wife and I are big fans. I'm glad you're here. By the way, John McMahon, your old boss at KABC, is now a network exec here."

"You're kidding."

"No. When he heard we'd hired you, he sort of gave you a bad review, which we ignored. You're a breath of fresh air. Give 'em hell." He shook my hand vigorously, nodding and smiling before he dashed out.

I should have been pleased that the GM had come over to personally welcome me. But I wasn't. I was seething. That pasty-faced, no nothing, incompetent sonofabitch McMahon. Why would he do that to me? My rage lifted me out of the chair, down the hall and the stairs, across the pavement into the network building, into an elevator, up to McMahon's office, stopping briefly at his secretary's desk.

"Is he in?" I asked sharply.

"Yes, but he's busy," she answered.

"I won't be long." I started toward the door.

"Let me announce–"

"He knows me."

I opened the door and stormed in. He was silhouetted behind his desk in front of a sunlit window. The shadowy dark sinister perfect picture of him. I closed the door, took two steps in, and stopped, trying to catch my breath. I fought to be as calm as l could. He looked up, startled at seeing me.

"Do, you have a minute?"

"Not exactly," he answered with indifference.

"Then I'll try to keep what I have to say under that. From the very beginning you never liked me. I never felt that way about you. Until now. I don't even know you personally; just professionally. Professionally, if you did your job in an office as well as I do mine on camera, you'd now be President at ABC, sitting in Elton Rule's chair instead of some assistant programmer's. And what did you ever program? Nothing. You deprogrammed. You ruined the best morning talk show in television. But you can't see that because you can't see past my lack of office etiquette. I am lousy in an office. But not on camera. Not knowing you are in show business you try to hurt me personally, and worse, professionally, you hurt the company you're now working for, telling them not to hire me. Jesus, John, that is awful. Look, I'm sorry for this intrusion, and I hope we can somehow restart. I'll try to view you as a person. If you finally try to view me as a performer, a professional performer."

I turned and stormed out, not waiting for a reply, returning to my cubbyhole relaxed and relieved, glad that I said what I said and did what I did. More than that, I no longer hated him. A wary smile curled my lips as I sat down once again in front of my typewriter. Jesus, there I was, not three hours into my new job, and already two people were out to fuck me!

The Not So Great Gatsby

There have been several films made of the F. Scott Fitzgerald classic novel of the rich in the twenties. All of them have been dreadful. The worst was the extremely expensive version produced by Paramount in 1974 starring Robert Redford, promoted heavily by Paramount's president, Barry Diller. Before its release, Barry was flitting all over the media heralding it as a society-changing epic. He got it on the covers of *Time* and *Newsweek*. The biggest change he said it would have on America was in the way we would dress after seeing it. He predicted a new line of Gatsby fashion that Paramount would cash in on. The other prediction he made was the box office bonanza. At the time, the average ticket price for movies in America was three dollars. Diller said that would have to be increased to six dollars. TV stations were swamped with "Gatsby" commercials. Billboards cluttered Hollywood and Sunset Boulevards. Every critic in town bowed to Jack Clayton's sumptuous brilliant direction and Robert Redford's perfect performance. Except yours truly. The town was abuzz with excitement and anticipation. Movie stars and ordinary folk all over town were hosting "Gatsby" parties.

The reason all the "Gatsby" films, even the most tolerable with Alan Ladd, were so unappealing is that the story was told on film the same way Fitzgerald told it in the book. Beginning to end. That was a mistake. As a film, it should have been the other way around. This would be one time the book should have been ignored and the film to begin where the novel ends, which reveals for us Gatsby's Oliver Twist-like, dreadfully poor childhood and struggles. The film, like the book, opens with this unbelievably handsome multimillionaire throwing an expensive in your face self-indulgent party attended by unpleasant people. Not even the one percenters like these kinds of characters. The ninety-nine percenters, us, do not just dislike them, we loathe them. By the too-long-getting-there end when we finally learn of his poor roots, it's too late. We don't care.

Irwin was the only one in the building who knew the content of my review. Every one had to be approved by him for grammar and libel. When he read it, his mouth twitched. He made a cautious humming sound to himself and handed it back.

The introduction to me was always made by Tom, who had a very puckish on camera quality about him. Feigning objectivity, he made it subtly clear with that twinkle he enjoyed my reviews; the harsher the better. It was his way, he told me off camera, of getting even for the things he could not say. With my opening sentence, it was clear I thought the film was awful. Fortunately, the sound engineers had learned to turn Tom's mike off when I was on; otherwise the audience would hear his moans and groans, like a boxer being punched. Then I hit the last line, which to Diller's horror, ended up in *Time* magazine. I concluded: *Paramount has announced it is thinking of charging a hard ticket price of six dollars to see this film. The only way Paramount could get six dollars would be to charge three to get in and three to get out.* As always, I threw the show back to Tom.

He had this serious, straight newsman's expression, as though he was above what I had just said. He was letting me know, if I was in trouble, he had nothing to do with it. Then, leading to commercial, he said to the camera, "Some of us will be right back!"

I was in my first major on-air trouble. The next day, those in the newsroom who had chuckled and had enjoyed my comments, avoided me. Word was out that Diller and his sales chief had called Bob Howard and KNBC, threatening to withdraw their ads if I continued on the air. That was the warning imparted to me by the two secretaries who did come near me. It was my in-between day off. On those days, I usually went in for a few hours to check my mail and calls. That day, Irwin advised me to stay home.

Home was now a very small bungalow near the corner of Forman Avenue and Valley Spring Lane in Toluca Lake. We were a block down from Bing Crosby's old magnificent red brick house, and a block and a half from Bob Hope's estate. I was certain being asked to stay home meant I was going to lose my job. With no contract, I also thought I was going to lose our house.

The next day, I snuck into my office, avoiding the people trying to avoid me. Having not been notified of my termination, I was writing that night's review. I heard that familiar warm voice.

"Wow. You really did it!" It was Bob Howard, standing in the doorway.

"Sorry if I caused you any problems."

He smiled. "Not as much as you caused Paramount. And our sales. John, part of my job is handling trouble here. And thankfully, you have given me more to do. Your job is to tell it as you see it. You do a very good job."

"Did they really cancel ads?" I asked weakly.

He laughed. "Of course not. They want to sell more of those six-dollar tickets!"

He was still chuckling when he walked away. It wouldn't be the only time Bob Howard would have to save my ass and console me. I loved that man!

Three Producers

Robert Evans

I caught *Alice Doesn't Live Here Anymore* by accident. It starred Ellyn Burstyn, Kris Kristofferson, Diane Ladd, Harvey Keitel, and a young Jodie Foster. I watched it from the back row in an almost empty theater, and loved it. Reviewing it the next night, I told the audience that I was taking my wife back to see this perfect woman's picture that very night. The theater was packed. At least a dozen people came up to me and asked if the lady next to me was indeed my wife, with mild threats on my life if the movie wasn't what I said it was. What I found out was that Warner Bros. hated the film. It had a weird opening similar to the opening of *The Wizard of Oz*. The studio demanded Scorsese change it. He refused. Seeing it as an artsy, unprofitable film, they decided to dump it, releasing it in just one theater in Westwood. It was Scorsese's fourth film. After he heard my review, he called the next day asking if I'd mind calling the powers that be, urging them to keep the opening. I did. And they did

Soon thereafter, in a Sunday *L.A. Times* interview, Scorsese publicly thanked me for saving his movie. Immediately I received a number of calls from producers asking if I would view a private screening of their film prior to release. I told them I thought it was unprofessional and a conflict of interest. I turned them down, except four: Ray Stark, Alan Pakula, Richard Brooks and Robert Evans. The invitations to meet with Stark and Pakula were easier to accept than Evans'. They wanted to talk to me about something other than their films. Not Bob Evans; he was insistent I come to his office at Paramount to view a film he had high hopes for. I felt Evans never received the credit he deserved for one of the world's great films, *The Godfather*. He saved Coppola and Pacino's jobs, and had a major hand in the flawless editing. I thought I'd tell him that in person, and decided reluctantly to look at his new movie.

We met in his sumptuous office at Paramount. He greeted me warmly, asking me to sit in his inner office while he tended to some personal business. I did so, but could see and hear the personal business he was unsuccessfully tending to. He was trying to get his loudly reluctant eight or nine-year-old son to go somewhere with the chauffeur. Eventually, Evans returned unflustered. "I'm sorry about that," he said casually.

Just as casually, I said, "You handled it well. Used to dealing with actors."

He chuckled. "I was hoping to sit with you, but as you can see, I have a lot of other stuff to tend to. The screening room is yours, with drinks and food or whatever you want. I appreciate this

"Oh, I don't need anything. What's it called?"

"*Black Sunday* with Robert Shaw and Bruce Dern."

"Good actors," I said.

"Great actors. My secretary will take you over; I'll be here when you're done."

"I don't feel comfortable doing this, as I said on the phone, so any comments I might have, I'd like to be just between us."

The secretary led me to the plush private screening room where I sat alone through nearly two hours of *Black Sunday*, one of the first terrorists-attacking-America films. It was inspired, if that's the right word, by the horrible events in Munich during the '72 Olympics. Simply put, the terrorists were planning on setting off a massive bomb at The Superbowl in New Orleans. It was Robert Shaw's job to stop them.

As promised, when it was over, Evans was waiting for me in his office, alone. 'Well, how was it?"

"Mr. Evans, I'm not going to say whether I like the film or don't like the film, but I will tell you how you can speed it up, if you care to hear."

"Speed it up? What do you mean, speed it up?"

"In the final climactic scene, Shaw realizes who the bad guy is and how to stop the attack. He starts running and jumping over fans for five minutes until he reaches the broadcasting truck outside. We, the audience, know he has a phone in his pocket. All he has to do is call the truck."

"Are you kidding? It's a really exciting action scene!"

I didn't want to dampen his enthusiasms, and thought of stopping, but I didn't. "Mr. Evans, the audience is going to think he's dumb ... or absent minded. Either insert a scene where the phone doesn't work, or that he's lost it. Or shorten it."

"Do you know how much that fucking scene alone cost? Fifty thousand fucking dollars. It's the high point of the movie. I can't cut it down!"

"That's just my opinion, which certainly isn't worth fifty thousand dollars."

There was tension now between us. He said, "Is that how you're going to review it?"

"I won't know until I write it."

"Other than that, didn't you like it?"

"Mr. Evans, you asked me to look at the film, not to review it. I looked at it. And gave you a thought."

The scene with Robert Shaw leaping over fans and seats remained. *Black Sunday* was not as well received as my Monday review.

Alan Pakula

Answering Alan Pakula's request to come by was easier. We had chatted earlier, a dozen years earlier. I was a mail boy at Paramount delivering mail to his office. He had no secretary, so I usually handed it right to him. Frequently he asked me to stick around to chat. I was completely baffled at how that soft-spoken, gentle, sweet twenty-something ever became a producer. In person, he had none of the presence or confidence of any of the producers I encountered. His films, though, did have that power, and his intellect and class. He consistently made some of the smartest films to come out of Hollywood. One of Jane Fonda's best, *Klute*. One of Meryl Streep's best, *Sophie's Choice*. Gregory Peck's best, *To Kill a Mockingbird*. *All the President's Men*, and dozens more.

Alan Pakula handed me an open script. "Here. Look at this. The part of the young senator. I want you to play it."

"Are you kidding?"

"No. You're perfect for it. It's just a small part, but I'd like you to do it."

"Alan, thank you, but I couldn't do that. I'm a critic. This would be a monumental conflict of interest. I'd lose credibility."

"But you might gain a new career. John, you don't have to answer now. Read it first. It's a terrific script."

I looked at the cover. *The Parallax View,* to star Warren Beatty.

"What's it about?"

"It's a political thriller about the assassination of a presidential contender. I'm really excited about it. I'd like to see you in it."

I handed the script back to him. "I can't. I just wouldn't feel comfortable."

The Parallax View is still one of my favorite films, one of only a handful of terrific political thrillers that have held up over the years, along with *Z, The Battle Of Algiers, Seven Days In May* and *The Manchurian Candidate.*

I bumped into Alan often over the years, usually in Trader Vic's, his favorite, or Scandia, one of mine. Every time he saw me with my wife and son, no matter with whom he was sitting, he always made his way to our table to shake hands and say hello. His sudden death, and the bizarreness of it, broke my heart. He was driving on the Long Island Expressway. Somehow a short piece of pipe came loose from the back of a plumbing truck in front of him. It hit the road and began to tumble and rocket toward Alan's car. He never saw it. It crashed through the windshield, right into his head. He died instantly.

Ray Stark

The phone rang in my little cubbyhole of an office."This is Ray Stark at Warner Bros. Thursday, if you have nothing planned, would you like to come by for lunch? I have something I'd like to chat with you about. Can we get together?"

"I'd be delighted," I said, not believing I was talking to *the* Ray Stark.

"Wonderful. There'll be a drive-on pass for you. Come right to my office, then we'll go to lunch. See you at noon."

I held the phone for a moment, wondering why a man of his stature, the most important A-group producer in Hollywood, would want to talk to me.

There was indeed a drive-on pass for me. I walked in. Ray was talking to his secretary.

"Oh, John. Terrific. Let's go." He turned to his secretary. "No calls for an hour. We'll be in the dining room."

We sat opposite one another in his elegant private dining room. He asked for his usual, whatever that was. Too curious to have an appetite, I ordered salmon and salad that I barely picked at. After some introductory small talk, he mentioned a few reviews he specifically enjoyed.

"You write that stuff very well. That's why I called you. Have you ever thought of writing a film?"

I was surprised by his question. "No. Not really. I tried it once, twice actually, and it didn't quite work out. I've had no interest since." I then told him briefly about the western I'd done for Angelo, then the story of the Albert Maltz adaptation for Haskell Wexler, plus the reason we parted company.

Ray laughed, nodding. "A terrific cinematographer."

"You could call him and he could review me for you," I said.

"I don't need to. I can see that you can write. I've also got good instincts. How would you feel about trying it again?"

"Mr. Stark, I'm a critic now, I think it'd just be another conflict of interest. You know, I've been offered parts, small parts in good movies, something I'd love to do, but I turned them down for the same reason."

"James Agee was the critic for *Time* and he had no problem doing *African Queen.*

"A wonderful movie!" I said.

"That it was. One of the few to come out of this town."

I was a little startled to hear him say that. "You've done a few terrific films yourself."

"John," he said, becoming serious, "as you know from having to review so many, and I know from making them, nearly everything that comes out of this town is shit. I've made a lot of shit myself, but I've gotten to the point in the business where I'm in a position to get offered the best shit first. This is an art form trapped in a business; it wouldn't exist without talent. And the most important talent is the ability to put words on a blank page."

"My favorite writer, next to Mark Twain, was Ben Hecht–"

He interrupted me with a look of pride. "I used to represent Ben. I was an agent. Represented him and Raymond Chandler and a few others. Ben hated writing movies. Most anyway. He did it for the money. If you were going to write a film, John, what would it be about?"

"Well, to me," I answered, loving to talk about movies, "European films are mostly about people. Our films are mostly about things or events. In American films, for the most part, nobody ever has a job. We have no idea what kind of society the characters live in. I'd write a love story. Everybody loves a love story. I'd have it begin at a New Year's Party where the couple meet for the first time and I'd end it a year later at the next New Year, but in between, in many scenes, I'd have television playing in the background. Game shows. Soaps, but especially newscasters and politicians talking about what's going on. Maybe I'd even make the lead a struggling journalist." I stopped. I had nothing left to say. And took my first bite of the salmon.

Ray leaned forward. "How'd you like to do that for me?"

"Do what?"

"The story you just outlined. I love the sound of it. It could be a small sleeper. I'd pay you fifty thousand dollars. Fifteen to start. Fifteen when you turn it in. And twenty when it goes into production."

"Mr. Stark, the thought of that much money, my salary for two and a half years, and the responsibility to do it right, to be honest, scares me a little."

"Good. It means you'll do a good job."

"The truth is, my heart wouldn't be in it. I'm just a movie watching person. Not a movie making person. I'm a TV person. That's where I'm most comfortable. In front of a camera, live, doing my own stuff, and, as I said, the conflict makes me uncomfortable."

He looked at me almost paternally. "Then what would you like to do? You must have something in mind."

"Well, next to my office are the wire service teletype machines. Reuters. AP, etc. I go in there all the time to read the stories. The best, most interesting ones are the ones they warn are not for broadcast. The other day I read one about something they call The Nub Club in rural Mississippi. It consists only of poor members, men, who in order to get insurance or workman's comp shoot off a finger or toe or foot. It sounds sick, but it's funny. Today, before coming here, I read one about a New York dancer, a stripper, who says she strips for God. Those stories would make an unbelievable show."

He smiled. "You think so?"

I nodded. "Television is the electronic umbilical cord that feeds America. It can only grow. There aren't enough actors and writers to fill the space. Besides, real people are much more interesting than actors. It's what I call, The Entertainment of Reality."

You know what, John, I've never done TV. I have no interest in it, but I like you. And it is funny. If my name is not involved, but I had some financial interest in your show, I might be able to help you."

"You would?" I was stunned.

"Let me talk to my agent at the Morris office. I'll have him set up a couple of appointments for us. Is that okay?"

We shook hands firmly, and parted. My salmon had only one bite out of it.

I said nothing to anyone about my meeting with Ray Stark. I didn't want to have bad Karma putting up roadblocks. For three days I gathered up all the stories from the wire services that I'd put in my drawer, and some new ones. I couldn't wait to tell Ray. Three days later I got a call from his agent from the William Morris office. When he mentioned his name, I had no idea if that was good or bad news. But I was certainly curious.

He said, "John, Ray is a filmmaker. One of the best in the world. That is what we want him to do. Not television. He thinks you have a terrific idea, but we don't want it for him. He and I wish you luck." That was it. The William Morris Agency was, for me, always more bad news than good.

Of course, I was let down. Thankfully, not as much as I thought I would be. After all, the show I was talking about had never been done; it might never be done. I had to accept it would be hard for anyone to buy something original. Things were easier to sell in that town if there'd been something like it seen and sold before. If it ever got on the air, it'd be just luck. Or an accident. Six years later, it was both.

Backlash from Biggies

Johnny Carson

The entertainment industry is no different from any other industry in America with a philosophy over five-thousand years old. If it's not good news, kill the messenger. Ralph Nader wrote *Unsafe at Any Speed* about General Motors' dangerous vehicles. Their CEO admitted before Congress that he'd hired hookers to try to entrap and shut Ralph up. Karen Silkwood blew the whistle on the leakage and danger at a Kerr-McGee nuclear facility, and died in a mysterious car crash. Ed Snowden spoke up about the illegal spying of NSA and our government on American citizens, and had to flee the country. As a lowly critic reviewing films, TV and the people who make them, I was not making nearly as major a contribution to society as the three aforementioned, but as a prominent critic, l was forever risking my job. And a couple of times, my life.

I will tell you, as briefly as possible, of three incidences involving three of America's most successful and beloved performers: Johnny Carson, Jerry Lewis, and Bob Hope. I'll start with Johnny Carson.

As mentioned previously, I was stunned when Carson didn't cancel *The Tonight Show* after Robert Kennedy's assassination, but maybe, he too, was forced to appear that night. However, when he failed to make the slightest reference to the slaughter of the eleven Israeli athletes during the Munich Olympics, there was no more doubt. To me, he was an insecure job-hugging establishment sycophant. When it comes to one of its own, Hollywood has a way of taking an ordinary mirror and turning it into a magnifying glass, making the object larger than life. They were doing that with Johnny. It was the recognition of his twelfth or thirteenth year on the job. The Trades were full of ads and hallelujahs. Every star was patting him on the back because there was too big a crowd kissing his ass. All that praise attracted my attention, so I decided to review the anniversary show.

As a forever outsider, I had this uncontrollable urge to prick the hot air balloons of the insiders; that is if I felt they deserved it. Johnny did. There's nothing more satisfying than pricking a prick! Of course, I started by comparing Carson to Jack Paar, his predecessor, unfavorably. It'd be like comparing Frank Sinatra Jr. to the father. I pointed out that I could remember lines from Paar's monologues, and not one from Johnny's. I reminded the audience that Paar had introduced dozens of unknown new performers, including Phyllis Diller, Jonathan Winters, and The Smothers Brothers. If they bombed, as did Nichols and May on their first appearance, Paar would still bring them back. If one bombed on Johnny's show, they'd be gone. Johnny only brought on a new act if it had succeeded elsewhere. He always bragged that he'd given comedian Flip Wilson his big break. The truth was the only reason he booked Flip was not because he was funny, but because he'd been on a plane that was hijacked to Cuba.

I pointed out the dozens of intellectuals and artists unseen by Americans that Paar interviewed. Carson tried once to bring on Gore Vidal and William F. Buckley; he was incapable of keeping up with them. Carson's most pathetic interview was his feeble, scurrilous attempt to sabotage and undermine D.A. Jim Garrison pointing out the CIA's involvement in murdering President Kennedy. I said Johnny was often funny, especially with guests who were also funny, but his greatest talent, in a brutal business, was his ability to last. When I was finished with my review, the studio was so quiet, you could hear my contract drop. Nobody on the set spoke to me. Snyder just pursed his lips. On camera, he said once again, "Some of us will be right back."

Walking back through the newsroom, people parted like the Red Sea. The phone in my office was ringing, louder than usual, it seemed. I didn't pick it up. The next day I also avoided answering it. I avoided contact with anyone. As they did me. The hate mail poured in. Not only did I read them to myself, in fairness to the audience, especially those who loved Johnny, I read them on the air, letting the audience criticize the critic. I also did that later with Jerry Lewis.

Three days later, Bob Howard once again appeared at my open door. "John," he said, then, in a playful pantomime, stopped to look to either side, as though he didn't want anyone to hear him, "I guess you're not getting much good mail, so I thought I'd drop by to console you." He paused, before adding, "His people are going nuts! I've been on the phone for three days. At this moment, you are not very popular."

"I'm sorry."

"Don't be. Johnny's psychiatrist isn't." He smiled. "Who else is going to tell the emperor?"

It no longer mattered everyone was avoiding me. Bob Howard, my station manager, unlike McMahon, was once again defending me. That was all I needed. For weeks I avoided going to make-up for fear of running into Johnny. A couple of years later, though, I ran into the revenge he was long seeking.

Jerry Lewis

I was sixteen when I first saw Jerry Lewis with Dean Martin in their film debut, *My Friend Irma.* After that I never missed his movies, until I got older and acquired a little taste. Aside from *Your Show of Shows* with Sid Caesar, when Martin and Lewis were on *The Colgate Comedy Hour,* it was the funniest, most undisciplined show on television. Like everyone, when that superstar team parted, I thought Dean was weeks away from being a showbiz memory. I felt sorry for him and wanted to see his act before he disappeared. His first solo appearance was at the huge Earl Carrol Theater on Sunset near Vine. The place was full. A lot of curious people were there to witness a disaster. I could tell because the entire crowd talked, ate and drank during the first five minutes of his act. What was astonishing, though, was that it didn't faze Dean. He began to improvise the lyrics to *That's Amore.* "Booze will flow, don't you know, pour me mo." The entire song was brilliantly and playfully about that unruly crowd. "Glasses refill, clink a clink a clink; some even spill. Oh shit!"

Suddenly, a few laughs from the audience. Dean was having fun. The quiet spread through the room like a wave in reverse. They started to applaud. Then cheer. All of them. It was a roar of approval. Dean could stand on his own anywhere. And he did.

Jerry continued to make a few successful films, honored more in France than here. His largest impact, though, was as the American-as-apple pie-and-the-flag hero as host of the annual Muscular Dystrophy Telethon. He was worshipped as the godfather and guardian angel of our country's stricken children.

It was my third year as NBC's critic-at-large. Jerry Lewis was celebrating his twentieth year as the solo host of what was now called, *The Jerry Lewis Telethon.* News people are a lot like police and doctors; because of all the negativity they see, to survive psychologically, they acquire a darker sense of humor. They see humor in things that make others uncomfortable. Even poke fun at it. That is what our entire newsroom did at the end of every telethon. Jerry closed his show with his trademark song, *You'll Never Walk Alone.* The first two years at KNBC, I was a stunned witness to that spontaneous, hilarious event. The second

Lewis began to sing, the entire newsroom staff would rise to their feet singing along as loudly as possible. It was like a mock national anthem. The song over, they'd applaud, whistle loudly, then return to their jobs as though it never happened. This particular day, I was looking forward once again to that very funny moment.

I wandered into the newsroom. While waiting, I watched the telethon. I was stunned when I saw Jerry lean into the camera and say very seriously: "I'm here to correct God's mistakes." What did he just say? He continued to pontificate on his importance to the cause, of being the savior of these sick children. I found his self-adulation offensive. I didn't hang around for our newsroom's Mormon Tabernacle Choir of a closing. I would not be doing the film review I had planned for that night. I was off to write a review of *The Jerry Lewis Telethon*.

It took ten minutes. Words and fingers fly faster when you're angry. Tom introduced me, with a sarcastic question mark in his voice, suggesting, what was there to review about that heralded hero and his telethon?

I began: "They now call this annual event *The Jerry Lewis Telethon*. They used to call it *The Muscular Dystrophy Telethon*. They changed the name to Jerry Lewis because one day they'll find a cure for muscular dystrophy, but there'll never be a cure for Jerry Lewis."

There was a loud groan from Tom as he ducked under the desk. I catalogued Lewis' own quotes, beginning with how he said he was there to fix God's mistakes, then listed half a dozen others. I closed saying, "It is commendable, that this year they raised thirty-four million dollars. Perhaps they could raise twice that amount, though, if every man, woman, and child who never wanted to see him again, sent in a quarter."

Tom stared expressionless at me for a very uncomfortable few seconds, then said to the audience: "The weather next. Very, very hot weather, for some of us."

I couldn't wait to go through the newsroom, to receive the plaudits of my co-workers. I had just said publicly what they were thinking or saying with their singing, but there was not one smiling face or thumbs up. I was this misfit *Walking Alone*. What was missing here? My phone began to ring, and never stopped. I was afraid to answer it.

The newscast over, Tom sauntered into my office, grinning. "I just got off the phone with my pal, Jerry Lewis. He screamed at me to fire you. I told him I would if I could, but I can't. That's up to the GM. He asked for his number. I told him I didn't have it handy. Boy, is he pissed."

I didn't know what to say, or how to respond.

"You'd better go home, in the dark. Everybody hates you." Tom laughed and left.

I did go home in the dark, in my classic Studebaker Gran Turismo. The next morning there were bullet holes through the windshield. All the next day, my day off, I stayed home, avoiding the nonstop ringing phone. When I went in reluctantly the following day, I was escorted to my office by a temporary security guard whom Bob Howard had hired just for me. There was a stack of mail, messages and telegrams on my desk. All hate mail. One was from The Synagogue for the Performing. Arts. It was a Beverly Hills Synagogue that didn't have rabbis speaking to their congregation; instead, they had Hollywood's famous performers, producers, and writers, from Neil Simon to Walter Matthau. It was the best attended synagogue in Los Angeles. I was scheduled to speak in three weeks. Their telegram uninvited me, saying if I showed up, half the congregation would walk out, and the other half would probably stone me.

My next review was obvious. I owed it to those who wrote and whom I offended. I would do for them what I had done for Carson's fans. I would read, by name, the hate mail, each one more vicious than the next. I thought it only fair to give enraged viewers a voice, which I did. Live. But I was determined to still have the last word. I closed by saying, "As you know, we have tours here at NBC. Yesterday one elderly lady rushed over to me screaming, 'You idiot, can you do what Jerry Lewis does?' I looked at her for a moment, then raised my crooked hand, and screamed in that nasty, nasally voice, "Hey, Dean!" Some chuckled. Then I added: "So I said to the lady, do you want to give me a quarter?"

The crew howled; something totally out of place on a newscast. I barely got my mike off when the studio door flew open. In flew Irwin Safchik, screaming, "This isn't a fucking nightclub. You fucking idiot. Get out of here. I mean it. You're out. Get out!"

At home, I told Sarita I was fired. She tried to calm me saying what I had said was true. The only thing I did feel bad about was not getting a call from Tom. The call I did get was from Sid Graw in business affairs.

"Johnny, tomorrow Irwin would like you to show him your review before three, and not late like you usually do."

"Sid, I thought he fired me."

"Well, just for the day. It seems you have some fans in and out of NBC. A lot of them sent you love notes to make up for your hate mail. Will you be in before three?"

I apologized to Irwin for upsetting him, saying that I didn't think the crew would laugh like they did. He told me in the future to please refrain from jokes as much as possible, and handed me a note. "Here, he wants you to call him. Now get out of my office."

Written on the paper was the name Bud Yorkin with his extension. Bud Yorkin was half of Tandem Productions. The other half was Norman Lear. Tandem was the company Bud and fellow writer Norman formed in the late fifties. They were often employed journeymen writers until the early seventies. That was the decade they became the most successful production team in the history of TV, creating three of the most controversial entertaining, society-changing shows on television: *All in the Family*, *Maude*, and *Sanford and Son*. I had seen Bud a few times when I visited the Sanford set to talk with Redd. Nearly every time I was there, he and Bud would be arguing about the interpretation of some line of dialogue. So, Redd never introduced me. Now, though, Bud wanted to meet me. I dialed his number.

"Thanks for callin' back," he said. "I understand the last few days haven't been too pleasant for you."

"No, sir. Not exactly."

"Come on down to my office for a minute. I'd like to talk with you."

Bud's office was not nearly as grand as those of lesser producers. It was rather ordinary. No big plaques on the wall. No ego-boosting pictures posing with stars. Just a family picture. From the size and decor, one would never guess that he and Norman were currently the most successful production team in America. He was seated alone in the inner office. He motioned me in, rising quickly to shake my hand.

"I told my secretary to take a long break. Come on in. I heard everybody's been knockin' the crap out of you. Are you holding up okay?"

"I'm used to it."

"You know, it was absolutely right-on what you said. Lots of folks wish we could say it. He's an asshole. I figured you'd want a little cheering up or a little company, that's why I called. I'm glad you're here. He tried to get you fired, right?"

"That's what Tom said."

"And he'll keep trying. He's a vengeful bastard."

"So far, I'm still here. I was canceled from speaking at the Performing Arts Synagogue, though."

"Fuck 'em," he said laughing. "You don't need them. Just keep doing what you're doing. The town needs it." He leaned forward. "John, I'm gonna tell you something very few people know outside of me and Norman. And you can do with this information whatever you like. Do you know that Jerry Lewis had no fucking idea what muscular dystrophy was? You've heard him countless times tell this bullshit story about his uncle having it?"

I nodded.

"Horseshit. You know how it started? Norman and I were two of the original writers on *The Colgate Comedy Hour*. One day, we get a call that someone wants to try and raise some money and awareness for something called muscular dystrophy. Jerry and Dean agreed to host it, provided it's just one hour. And just local. New York. We're asked to write it. Jerry is complaining he's never heard of the fucking thing, and tells us he has no idea what to say. Norman and I tell him to relax, that we'd do the necessary research and put it on the cue cards. All he has to do is read it. He says he doesn't like cue cards, but Dean calms him down. And they go on the air.

"Well, of course, these guys are big, and the money they ask for pours in. Tons of it. Just from around New York. We're all stunned. It's soon suggested something like this be done nationally, but Lewis isn't interested. This information is passed on to the man who wants to see it go nationwide, the President and CEO of Minnesota Mining and Manufacturing, now known as 3M. It seems this guy had MD, or someone in his family did. He informed Lewis that if they would do it, continue to do this telethon thing, he would sell them 3M shares at ten percent of market value. Jerry got more money from that than he did performing. And today gets ten percent off the top of all that comes in. His uncle, my ass!

"John, this is something I've never talked about, but thought you should know the real story. And you can do with it, whatever way you wish."

"Mr. Yorkin–"

He interrupted me. "It's Bud, and I hope we get to chat often."

"Bud, that is really interesting, but I see no reason for me to reveal it. I have no vendetta against him personally, even if he gets me fired. I was just offended by his performance, and I've already said my piece on that. But I really thank you for wanting to see me, to tell me this. I really appreciate it."

"Well, I'm just as glad you did what you did, and you came to see me. I've got it off my chest, and maybe someday, you'll get it off yours."

Outside of my wife, I've never repeated Bud's story to anyone. Until now. I hate to see a good story go to waste.

Bob Hope

If you compiled a top-ten list of the greatest most popular or most influential entertainers of the 20th Century, along with Charlie Chaplin, The Beatles, Elvis Presley, Paul Robeson, Enrico Caruso, Bing Crosby, and Frank Sinatra, you'd have to include Bob Hope. I loved him the first time I heard him on the radio. I was a kid and it was the Second World War: 'Hi, this is Bob broadcasting from Fort Ord Hope." It was his formula for opening every show. There was a sparkle and pitch to his voice that made the material funnier. I liked him even more when I saw him later with Bing Crosby in those engaging 'Road' pictures. They were so much fun, they almost looked ad libbed.

His early television shows were also fun for me. He was also the best host the Oscars ever had. He never walked onto the stage; he strutted. On his later TV shows, however, it was the youthful nostalgia I was watching and remembering. He got sloppy, not bothering to memorize his monologues. He read them off of cue cards. When the Vietnam War started, he began attacking those who opposed it. He no longer was funny, or even relevant. His ratings reduced him to doing a few specials, as opposed to a regular show. Those were sponsored by Texaco that originally had sponsored Uncle Miltie Berle. The last one I saw was unwatchable. With a heavy heart I knew I had to review it. It had been like watching a great pitcher like Satchel Page throw a fastball years past his elegant prime. You want to turn away.

Hope's specials, of course, were broadcast on NBC, where I worked. Walking around the building I'd seen him many times for an occasional nod or wave. Before my segment, Tom said, "Pal, I don't know what you're gonna say, but I wouldn't."

Tom introduced me saying, "Bob Hope's second special aired here on NBC last night. Here is John's take on one of the century's greatest entertainers."

I opened saying it was sponsored by Texaco, a company that hopes they don't end up like Bob Hope, running out of gas. I went on to recount what I've written above, how I loved him, his radio show, his movies, his early TV, but that I've grown up, the country's grown up, but he has grown tired. I pointed out the lazy, sloppy flaws in his performance and the writing, the once perfect ingredients that had made him a major star. I closed, saying, "He has become the J. Edgar Hoover of humor. If it is true in most businesses that it is compulsory one retire at sixty-five, then in this case, it should be compulsory in show business."

When finished, I was used to the stares and shaking heads and avoidance of those around me. These were my opinions. Knowing that was all the comfort I needed, I went home happy. I returned to my office a day and a half later. The newsroom was in an uproar. Evidently Hope had more influence and staff than Carson and Lewis combined.

"You'd better call Bob Howard," Irwin said briskly. "Right away."

Mr. Howard was the one who had hired me, who often came to give me verbal pats on the back. This time, though, he wasn't coming over. Oops! I'd probably have to go there. I called, as instructed.

"Jesus, John, I'm supposed to be the GM here; not an answering service."

"I'm sorry, sir.'

"Look, I'm tired of talking to Hope's people for two days." He paused. I was prepared for his next line telling me about how bad he felt about having to let me go. "Would you do me a favor? Would you take a call from Hope's lawyer for me? He wants to talk to you personally."

"Certainly. Whoever you wish me to talk to, I will."

"Good. I'm going to give him your number now, so wait for the call."

We hung up. I stared at the phone like it was some kind of beast that was going to get bigger and angrier, then attack me. It rang.

"John Barbour?" an angry voice asked.

"Yes?"

"This is Bob Hope."

"Oh, God," I uttered, startled and frightened. It wasn't the lawyer. It was the king!

"You're goddamn right. It's God!"

I chuckled. "Now that's funny, Mr. Hope."

"Well, it's not gonna be to you. What did I ever do to you?"

His tone was threatening. If anyone could get me fired, it was him. I figured what the hell, if that's my fate, I might as well be honest. "Bored me," was my fast firm answer.

There was silence. I continued, not wanting to hear what he'd say to that.

"Mr. Hope, if you really heard the parts of my review where I talked about how much I loved you, how much the world loved you, you could understand how disappointed and even angry I felt when I see someone with this monstrous talent not live up to it, or use it. Surely you must have seen some of the performers you loved get sloppy or lazy at their craft."

There was a harsh silence, then he said, just as brusquely, "You wanna know the truth? NBC doesn't want me."

"What do you mean?"

"I don't fit the demographics they want. Everybody's after a younger audience. Evidently, I don't deliver it anymore."

This wasn't the angry man I had just heard. He sounded now like he needed someone to talk to. The conversation which followed flowed easily.

"But they still put you on. Is that contractual?" I asked.

"Hell, no. The truth is they wish I wasn't on."

"Mr. Hope, I don't understand that. Are they still putting you on because you are Bob Hope?"

"They have no choice. I make them put me on. You know how? I pick up the phone and call the president of Texaco. I ask if he'd like to play a round of golf. During the game, I ask if he'd like to make more money than beating me in a skins game by sponsoring my next special. He then buys the hour. He keeps half the ad minutes. NBC gets the other half."

I was speechless. Why was Bob Hope, this legend, telling this to a local critic who just bashed him?

"It's called barter. That'll be getting bigger in this business, believe me."

"Well, it's a cinch Mr. Hope, you won't be playing golf with the President of Humble Oil!'

"Jesus Christ, kid, you've got some nerve."

"Mr. Hope, you are a legend, and you've earned that. You're known as one of the wealthiest men in show business. Why would you want to keep doing it? And, forgive me, and not do it right?"

"What else would I do? Play golf? No, kid, I have nothing else to do. It's all I know how to do. And I love it. As for being rich, I've done okay obviously, but I'm not as smart as some people think I am."

"What do you mean?"

"I started in vaudeville. I thought it'd last forever. I put some money in theaters and lost it. I was in radio. Thought that'd last forever. Bought a station. Did okay. Not what I thought. I thought movies would last forever. That's shrinking. As will TV. So, I wasn't that smart, kid. The thing I woke up to was that theaters and radio stations and TV stations had to be someplace. And that someplace was on land. So that's all I bought after that."

"My goodness, Mr. Hope, how interesting.'

"In the 50's there was a ninety-percent tax on people like me. On our salaries. It was tough. So, when I renegotiated my contract with NBC I told them I didn't want a raise or stock or anything. I just told them to buy a bunch of my land. Which they did. As capital gains. You're sitting on my land."

What Bob Hope was telling me was thrilling verbal gold, and I told him so. "Mr. Hope, this stuff is amazing. It should not be wasted. You should not be just telling *me* this; you should be telling the world. This is really interesting. You know, sir, I have never seen you in a serious interview. Even when you were on *Open End* talking about the war. But never in a serious interview about your life and work. Why don't you come on my show and continue this conversation? You'd be a smash."

"What show?"

"I have a half hour live show, on Channel 13, KCOP, Mondays through Fridays. It follows Vidal Sassoon."

"That's where Mayor Sam Yorty has his show. No. No. I don't think so. He's been bugging me for months to do his show. I don't want to. And I wouldn't want to run into him doing yours."

"Mr. Hope, if you do it, and you must, there will be absolutely no publicity or mention whatsoever of your appearance. You'd be like a surprise drop-in guest. I'm telling you, sir, right now you are as interesting as you ever were, and funny. You've got to tell your story."

He paused. "What night?"

"You pick it. It's up to you."

"I'll see you Wednesday next week. By myself. Make sure Yorty's not around."

"I will. Thank you and thank you and thank you. See you then."

I could not sit I was so excited. The more I realized I couldn't say a word about this unbelievable turn of events and his appearance on my show, the more excited I got. The phone rang again.

"Yes?"

"Bob Howard, John. Did Hope's lawyer call?"

"No, sir. Bob Hope did."

"What happened?"

"Well, I promised him I wouldn't say anything, so I can't, but you'll see next week."

"What'll I see next week?"

"I wish I could tell you, Mr. Howard, but I can't. But you'll be pleased. I promise."

"Johnny, being pleased by you would be a nice change. Unbelievable. The guy who keeps saving your ass has to wait. One day you'll either be this business's biggest star or a fond memory. Or not so fond memory."

My early evening live half hour show with call-ins on KCOP followed famed hair stylist Vidal Sassoon. Vidal had become the world's most renowned hair stylist on the strength of one haircut, that short stylish cut he gave Mia Farrow in *Rosemary's Baby*. It brought him from the slums of London to a mansion in Bel Air. He was about forty, movie star handsome himself, and soft spoken. Unlike many of the underprivileged I had met, the richer Vidal got, the nicer he got. His brunette wife, a dozen years his junior, was even more stunning. Vidal's gentle demeanor was unchanged when during a commercial break he found out his wife ran off to Acapulco with a Mexican.

Our little, live thirty-minute show surprisingly had the famous and infamous calling asking if they could be guests. The town's most famous gangster, Mickey Cohen, recently out of prison, after a beating, told his publicist ours was the only show he'd do to talk about his book. During his appearance, I asked him if he had ever really killed anyone.

He laughed. "Kid, you got balls. You are the first person to ask me that in public." Mickey then described how the guy he knifed deserved it.

Kirk Douglas, talking about one of his first books, confessed that in spite of success beyond his wildest dreams, he never took the time to be happy, fearing it was all going to slip away as mysteriously as it had come.

Charlie's Angels' co-star, Jaclyn Smith, was startled when a reporter called in with the first live announcement that kidnapped heiress turned Symbionese Liberation Army bank robber, Patty Hearst, had just been captured. She was startled because during a break, I asked her if she would like to comment on Patty Hearst. She said, "Who's that?"

Then I was stunned! Jesus, actresses!

The most notoriety the show got, along with the only Entertainment Emmy given out in Los Angeles that year, was when we turned the half hour into an hour special called *John Barbour's First Annual Telethon to Save New York City*. The Big Apple had been making headlines for weeks, bemoaning the economic disaster that might cause it to close down. As a tongue in cheek joke, we announced off-handedly that we were going to do this live telethon, with a pledge goal of a billion dollars, and a real cash goal of $300.00. To our astonishment, this dopey idea caught on. Dozens of stars called to contribute. Wolfman Jack called asking to co-host, which he did. Don Rickles gave us hockey pucks to sell. Freddy Prinze made one of his last appearances before blowing his brains out. He gave us hubcaps stolen by Puerto Ricans to sell. Peter Falk, the endearing star of *Columbo,* made news giving us his used trench coat from the show. A restaurant owner from Arizona bought it for $2,000.

We exceeded our $300 cash goal. The decision as what to do with the excess was solved when New York's Mayor Beame called asking if we would deliver it to him. So, we did. Spending nearly $1,000 of my own, money, I flew to New York. Never missing an opportunity for a photo-op, the mayor met us on City Hall steps. In front of a throng of press, I presented him with a check for $3,000. He smiled his photographer's smile.

"Young man, you have done our city a service. How come I've never heard of you?"

I said, "Mr. Mayor, I guess it's because I've been running my career the way you run your city."

It cost me money to do that special hour. My salary was scale to do the half hour; but the absolute joy of moments like that was priceless. It was a show surrounded by happy people, made even happier when Bob Hope showed up.

He arrived an hour early. No one was with him; not a publicist, not a lawyer, not even a friend. This was unheard of for a star, astonishing for a legend. He was carrying an old black case.

Looking around, he said, "Yorty's not near, is he?"

I smiled. "No, sir." I led him to the very small two-chair make-up room with fading mirrors and introduced him to our makeup lady.

"That's okay. I like to do my own," he said, opening this black case, taking out powders, paste, and sponges, which he placed neatly in front of him. He leaned into the mirror and began meticulously applying it.

"Mr. Hope, why don't you let her do that for you?"

He didn't take his eyes off his image in the mirror. "Kid, I've been doing this for over fifty years. I've always put on my own make-up. When I was in vaudeville, I did as many as five shows a day, sometimes in different theaters. It makes me feel like I'm still in showbiz I guess, and it got to be a bit of a superstition."

Watching him staring into that looking-glass turned my admiration for that man into affection.

Bob Hope was never better, never more interesting, never more appealing or wittier than he was in that too-short half hour just talking. The time flew by so quickly, we never got to all of his story, or never got to the flooded phone calls. We did take one totally unexpected call from Bing Crosby. Bing wanted to check out how well his buddy was doing without writers. Listening to them chat briefly and happily about their first radio show would give a careful listener a quick insight into what interested each the most as young performers. Bing could remember their first girl singer. Bob remembered their first sponsor.

Like KABC, KCOP was too cost conscious to buy new tapes for each show. In re-using them, we lost many great interviews. One was Jimmy Carter announcing from Georgia his candidacy for the presidency, but I wasn't about to lose that one with Bob Hope. I've saved and treasured it for years. It can be seen on my site: www.johnbarboursworld.com.

The next day at NBC, I was asked by a very surprised Bob Howard "How did that happen? You've now made me a fan of Bob Hope!"

Critical Tidbits

Although I won another Emmy for my KCOP NY Telethon, I had lost another talk show. I was never possessed with driving ambition, but just enough to keep me going. I had few social skills and no political skills. I never once tried to acquire a friend. So, I had few. Losing that show, I still was pleased with being a part-time critic at KNBC and *Los Angeles Magazine*. On the air and in print, I could express my thoughts and opinions on anything I wanted. Inform and entertain the public for a few minutes three nights a week, get paid enough to pay the mortgage and go home. That and spending more family time with a son and wife than anyone I knew, was the perfect life for me. It was the first time I felt contentment. I was a critic before I even knew what the word was. My first words were critical of my parenting, my teachers, my playmates, Santa Claus and God.

As a critic, I was paid for what I had seen. But as an incurable born critic, twice, even before I was a paid professional, I was compelled to be a critic of something I'd never seen. I was compelled to make two critical phone calls because in my gut I knew I was right. They were both to Elton Rule, President of ABC in the 60's.

ABC was always making a feeble attempt to mount a late-night show against Carson. Their first attempt was with comic Joey Bishop. It was my first call. Elton always took them, from the time I met him sitting in the sun having a sandwich, when he was just KABC's GM, and I was producing *Chucko The Clown*. He made me feel so comfortable, I always called him Elton.

"Elton, I just read you hired Joey bishop to go up against Johnny. Elton, Joey is a great entertainer, but a lousy host. He cannot conduct a conversation."

"John, he'll do just fine. He sat in often for Carson."

"Then that should have been his audition. He does not talk to people. He can't."

"John," he repeated my name like he was talking to a child, "we have programming people who get paid well to make these decisions."

"Then they are overpaid. You need new programming people."

"Right now we're happy with them and Joey."

"Elton, it's so simple. Let me show you how to prepare to replace him."

"We are not planning on replacing him."

"You will soon. Believe me. Look, you have seven stations you own. Use them as a farm system. Like baseball. Have each station do a late-night Saturday night show with a local host that in no way interferes with Joey during the week, and you might discover a great replacement. And give me the Saturday Night spot here in LA." (The call was prompted by my still-burning ambition to do a national talk show.)

Elton chuckled. "John, we do not groom people. We buy them. We bought Joey, but it's always nice to hear from you, John."

"The next time you hear from me in about six months, I promise not to say I told you so."

During Joey's ill-fated run against Carson, I surprisingly got a chance to appear on it. I called Elton a second time after reading they were replacing him with Dick Cavett. Cavett, like Letterman, had bombed badly doing a morning show. For some reason NBC hung on to Letterman, and ABC hung on to Cavett. That reason was Jack Rollins. He managed both. He had said Cavett did not have to appeal to Middle America, just the New York critics. Those critics deemed Dick an intellectual, and ABC deemed him therefore worthy of a late-night show.

Again, Elton took my call.

"I presume this is your 'I told you so' call!" he said flatly.

"No, sir." I chuckled. "I never break a promise. Elton, I don't mean to be a pest, but I am going to tell you why Cavett can never make it outside of New York."

"John, this is ABC. We're happy if we can get New York." His giggle was truly sincere.

"No question Dick is bright." I kept going. "Brighter than Joey. He can talk, but he is brittle. He just seems uncomfortable and ill at ease with himself. The audience senses it." I tried to repeat the business of using his stations as a farm system, but Elton cut me off.

"John, I am sure you will call again. But you'll have to wait a few years. Dick will be on a long time. Good luck." He hung up.

In spite of Cavett's low rating, he was on for five years. I could not watch him. He made me uncomfortable, but I did watch some of his fabulous guests who only did the show because of him. Especially John Lennon and Richard Burton. Decades later, Cavett confessed that during the time he did the show he had to be on anti-depressants.

As KNBC's critic-at large, there was no secretary to screen calls that came to me. One scary one came from director-writer, Sam Peckinpah. I had loved his TV series *The Westerner,* with Brian Keith, and a couple of his films, in spite of their brutality, but not *The Getaway* with Robert Redford and Faye Dunaway. I said, "The good news about this lifeless film is that it will make money. The bad news is it will make money. Which means maybe another one!"

In a shrill screaming drunken voice, Peckinpah identified himself. I had to hold the receiver three feet away. "You pasty-faced motherfucking moron. I'm gonna come down there and shove that fucking typewriter up your ass and wrap the chord around your fucking slimy neck and blow your fuckin' brains out." He was still dismembering me when I hung up.

I often got calls from Milton Berle, President of the Friars Club, to be part of some famous star's men-only roast. A few I accepted. Certainly, as Don Rickles pointed out, it is easier to get laughs attacking someone. I took no pleasure in doing that then, nor recalling it now. But I still loved the laughs. My greatest joy, though, was in finding shows and events or books I loved, and could share. Those included seeing Hal Holbrook three times, recreating with casual brilliance America's greatest writer and wit in *Mark Twain Tonight*; receiving an endearing note and a roomful of roses from legendary icon seventy-year-old Josephine Baker performing her last shows at The Dorothy Chandler Pavilion after reading an open love letter to her on the air: and, although my wife was a superb dancer, I had no interest in ballet until I saw Rudolph Nureyev with the Royal Canadian Ballet defying gravity by floating and spinning above the stage. I urged audiences to see that stunning Russian artist who was so sexy he should be billed as 'Deep Toes!'

Which brings me to *Deep Throat,* the first pornographic movie to go main stream. It starred a young woman with the perfect name playing herself, Linda Lovelace. If she were a man, she'd have been a sword swallower in the circus. The film's title would be immortalized in American politics and culture a few years later. The intelligence source who was giving secret information to the *Washington Posts'* reporters, Woodward and Bernstein, about the infamous Watergate break-in by President Nixon's 'plumbers' was identified as Deep Throat. The movie was the highest grossing gross film in history. It attracted even more mainstream attention after it was reported that Jackie Kennedy had been to see it. During its media-drenched success, Hugh Hefner hired Linda Lovelace frequently to demonstrate her talents for his celebrity guests at his Brentwood Playboy mansion.

With such notoriety, and word of mouth, as a critic, I could not ignore it. It was my responsibility to see it. If I did see it, I felt I could write about it fully in the magazine, but how could I possibly describe it on TV to an audience eating dinner? Before I could figure that out, I first had to see it. Sarita and I had no interest in pornography at all, but if folks wanted to see it, that was their private business.

When I asked Sarita if she would mind coming with me to the Paris Theater on Santa Monica to see it, she said yes as casually as if we would be going to the market. The line for the eight o'clock show was around the block. Oh, my God. How embarrassing. Walking to the end of that line people were going to recognize me. Many people did, but only the guys spoke up. "We'll be watching at six, Johnny!"

But there was no just buying a ticket and walking in. We had to sign a release which we did, and no one read, except Sarita. In the dim box-office light, it took nearly five minutes for her to read it. Even women started to holler, "For God's sake, sign it lady!" Finally, she did, unperturbed and unhurried.

The theater was packed and warm. I always watched a film from the back row. There were two seats in the middle. We squeezed in apologetically, and sat down. The atmosphere was extremely uncomfortable, made more so when the film started. Fifteen minutes into the film, I was not only uncomfortable, I was monumentally bored. I asked Sarita if she felt the same.

She did; we squeezed our way out.

On the air the next day, the set was full. Folks had heard I was about to review *Deep Throat.* Irwin, my news director, was the only one who read my review beforehand. I was stunned and surprised he let me do it, especially because of the last line. I did not review the film at all. I reviewed the experience of taking my wife. The crowds. The comments. The stickiness of the floor scrambling to our seats. When I got to the end, I told the viewers, "We walked out after the first fifteen inches." The crew, cast, and strangers exploded with laughter. Irwin exploded with rage. Again, he stormed onto the set yelling that it was not a goddamned burlesque comedy club. I told him he saw the review. He said it was so fucking boring, he never got to the last line. Everyone yelled at him that it was his fault and he stormed out.

The following week, I was in a courtroom in Orange County to repeat my review. Immediately after the six o'clock news I got a call from a fellow identifying himself as a lawyer. He said he represented a theater owner in Orange County on trial for showing *Deep Throat.*

"It's right here at The Paris and there's no problem," I said, surprised.

"That's Hollywood. This is Orange County."

"Why are you calling me?"

"To ask if you'd mind being a witness for the defense, my client, as a professional critic to tell the court what you just told your viewers."

"I don't quite understand."

"Mr. Barbour, we need professional testimony. We have first amendment experts. That helps. We'll pay your transportation and expenses whatever they are and a small fee for your time and–"

"Sir, I could not charge you a fee for something I just said. Couldn't you just get a transcript or I'll send the copy I'm sending to *LA Magazine.*"

"Mr. Barbour, no one could read it like you."

There was standing room only in the courthouse. When I took the stand, the prosecutor said he had no questions for me. The defense lawyer, the voice on the phone, asked about my professional background and how many Emmys and Golden Mikes I'd won as a critic and commentator, and the number of stars I'd worked with and performed and wrote for, including Mayor Bradley. Even I was impressed. He then asked me to read my review of *Deep Throat.*

"Sir, I do not need to read it. I remember it quite well." Word for word I recounted the experience of attending that film. When I got to the last sentence, I stopped, embarrassed to say in the important official surroundings what I had said on the air. The lawyer spotted it.

"And? And? Mr. Barbour?"

I turned to the judge. "Your Honor, I'm sorry. I'm a little embarrassed to repeat this in a courtroom.

"Mr. Barbour, I've been on the bench for twenty years, and I assure you I have heard more horrible things in here than you could ever say. Please continue."

I almost whispered. "Well, I told our viewers that my wife and I left after the first fifteen inches."

The laughter was an absolute explosion, even the prosecutor. Every man and woman was doubled over with clutching at themselves and others. It was hard to imagine that roar of hilarity in such a serious legal setting. I was the only one not smiling. I just soaked in the sound of it all.

The judge raised his gavel, but didn't bring it down. He was watching the people as was I, a huge grin on his face. Finally, he pounded and pounded it till the room got quieter, still filled with isolated giggles.

"Mr. Barbour. Mr. Barbour," he said with a smile, "you are dismissed, as is this case." As he left, he looked down. "Young man, that is the funniest thing I've heard here or anywhere."

Joyce Haber and the Oscars

"John, I need you to do me favor." It was Hal Kanter. "I can't do the Oscars warm-up tomorrow night. I'd like you to fill in for me."

"Hal, no one can fill in for you. You've been doing it for years. And they'd kill me. A critic. Are you kidding?"

He laughed.

"You might be surprised. You're the only one I think could handle it."

"Jesus. What'd the producers say?"

"It's only the warmup, not the show. It's my call. I think you'll do great."

"Hal, against my better judgment, I'll do it for you. No fee."

During the mid-70's, Americans were frequently amused or irritated by a wacky stunt that popped up periodically. It was called streaking. A young man or woman would disrobe and run naked through some popular gathering, mostly onto the field during baseball or football games, cheered on by the fans, and chased by security cops. The most notorious of these was during the previous year's Oscars. At the height of the show, a naked young man streaked across the stage while British actor David Niven was introducing Elizabeth Taylor. David's response about the streaker's "shortcomings," got a huge laugh. I wanted to somehow reference streaking during my monologue.

At the time, the most powerful and caustic Hollywood columnist was Joyce Haber. She had been anointed the heir to Hedda Hopper by the *L.A. Times*, but unlike Hedda, Joyce could write, as her best-selling novel *The Users*, shows. She once described Julie Andrews as having "a blossoming dullness." She was made more influential by being the wife of one of TV's most successful producers, Douglas Cramer.

Walking onto the stage, I was greeted with a mixture of boos and polite applause. as was most of my material. The theater overflowing with stars was not hostile; and at times, receptive. I was very comfortable delivering my last line.

"During the rehearsals this morning, there was an unconfirmed rumor that we were streaked by Joyce Haber." (The audience giggled.)."It is unconfirmed … because nobody wanted to look." I walked off to an ovation.

When the phone rang in my little office the next day, I thought it would be Hal. It wasn't. It was Joyce Haber.

"Well, Mr. critic-at-small, my friends called me last night to tell me how badly you bombed."

"Miss Haber, you do not have any friends."

"I have a ton of friends."

"Readers aren't friends. You have a ton of readers. A real friend, Miss Haber, would not be calling you to repeat my joke to you. Only people who do not like you would take delight in that. I do not know you. I read you sometimes, and you are a better writer than most. But, in general, I am no fan of any gossip columnist, folks making a living off celebrities."

"Jesus Christ, that's what you do!"

I howled. "You are so right, and that is really funny, and so was my joke."

She chuckled. "It was. So, you don't think I have any friends?"

"I am sure you do; those are the ones who did not call you."

"How would you like to have dinner together. Doug and I only live a few blocks from you. I'd love you to come by and meet him. I think you and I would get along well."

Over the next few months, Sarita and I spent three early evenings visiting Joyce. Her husband was never home. She said he was off again with one of the boys. She was smart and funny, a great story-teller, but seemingly never sober and one of the saddest women I had ever met. I did like talking to her, and listening to her, but that joy was diminished by being around a woman who drank. Shortly after we stopped visiting her, she divorced. She died in her early sixties of kidney failure.

More Kelly Lange and Bryant Gumbel

As management had promised, when I first started I would occasionally get to co-host the popular local live Sunday Show. As Kelly Lange had promised, she made it difficult for me. The first show I did, Kelly was given most of the interviews, which I did not mind. The producer thought, since I was their film critic, I should do the solo interview with the new James Bond, Roger Moore. I was more than pleased with that, but when the interview started, suddenly there was Kelly sitting next to him. Had this handsome Englishman not been so charming and glib, her fawning over him with shallow celebrity questions would have made this a waste of air time. I had said very little other than, it must be tough following Sean Connery. He surprisingly said, "Sean was the best."

The second time the producer asked me to do the show, I told him I wasn't comfortable. I did not want to tell him I loathed the co-host, so, I declined. But he didn't give up.

"John, the major guest is Allard Lowenstein, the New York Congressman; he occasionally speaks out about the assassination of Bobby Kennedy. I've heard you talking about it a few times. I think he'd be comfortable with you – talking to someone who knows something about it. I'd really appreciate it, if you'd do it."

"On one condition, I do the interview by myself. You can give the rest of the show to Kelly, I don't care. But this I do alone, or not at all."

"You've got it."

When it came time to introduce Lowenstein, there she was to my left, having ignored the producer's directions to stand down. Fortunately, Lowenstein was to my right. I was between Kelly and him. I introduced him immediately, turned quickly, and asked my first question. It was about Dr. Noguchi's autopsy, which indicated that the fatal shot came from behind the left ear, making it impossible for Sirhan Sirhan to have fired it. Lowenstein was at first stunned, then pleased. The two of us launched into an intense conversation about that horrifying night at The Ambassador Hotel. The crew was spellbound, Kelly seething. When we finished, with not one question from Kelly, Lowenstein thanked me profusely for giving him a chance to speak, especially to someone who obviously cared. He was the last guest. He left. The crew began to disassemble.

Kelly rushed at me. "You son-of-a-bitch piece of shit. You hog. I wanted to ask him some questions. You fucking pig."

Everyone stopped, shocked. I said, "Kelly, the only thing you know about the assassination of Robert Kennedy is that the day he was shot, it was seventy-two degrees." The crew howled, then caught themselves when she turned on them. I never got to do the show again. Two weeks later I was called into our local Program Director Phil Boyer's office.

"John, there's something I'd like to talk to you about," he said, before I could sit down. He started to shift uncomfortably. "It has come to my attention from a couple of sources that you have been spreading a rumor about my having an affair with Kelly."

"Phil, if you heard about that a couple of times, you heard it only from Kelly. Not from anyone else. You wanna know why it is bullshit, my saying that? Because I know Kelly Lange would never fuck you. You know why?'

Phil stared at me with a blank face. "Why?" he asked in a whisper.

"Because you're only local!"

He shook his head like a dog who had just come out of the water. Without looking at me, he raised his hand, motioning me to leave. "Get out of here."

On my days off I spent hours with Christopher playing golf or hitting balls at night at the Studio City Driving Range. His astonishing ability never failed to attract a crowd. Among them often were actors Peter Falk, Sheldon Leonard, and singer, Billy Eckstine. Word spread quickly about this prodigy, as it did a few years later with a young Tiger Woods. NBC eventually sent a crew, featuring him on the news.

When not with my son, I was playing hockey. In my mind, on the ice, I was back at the reformatory in Toronto. The duo I skated with were actors Bo Svenson of *Walking Tall* and *The Great Waldo Pepper* fame, and John Perry, father of the soon to be successful Matthew. Hockey was the only thing Bo would leave a bar or woman for. Those weekly pickup games soon grew into a legitimate incorporated celebrity hockey team. Dozens called to be added to our roster, including Alan Thicke, Alex Trebek, and Jerry Hauser. For the next half-dozen years, we travelled the southwest in a bus doing charity events. Jerry's hilarious ad lib songs filled the bus, fans filled the stadiums, and groupies filled the hotels.

Two months after being told to leave Phil's office, he called asking if I would like to do a ninety-minute talk-variety show on Saturday nights. What a wonderful surprise. I said of course I would, if I could pick a co-host or sidekick other than Kelly Lange. He didn't think that was very funny. He said it was my ninety minutes to do with as I wished. I called it *The Nineteen-Inch Variety Show*, that being the size of our TV set at home; picking my Ed McMahon was even easier.

There was a nice looking, bright young black man doing weekend sports on the station. His name was Bryant Gumbel. We had chatted amiably and often when we bumped into each other during work. He was sharp, with a major in Russian Literature. He approached me one day, asking to be a backup goalie on our team. I told him he'd be way back, since we had one, Stu Nahan, another sportscaster. I asked him instead if he'd like to be my sidekick on my new TV show.

"That's even better," he said.

It was also better for me. He was a natural. Also, wonderful for him, Bryant was as ambitious as he was attractive. Women flocked to him. He always found time for them, even though he had a beautiful wife, June, and two adorable kids. Infidelity in Hollywood is more common than large egos. His horny hobby was none of my business, as long as he was good on the show, which indeed he was.

During the weeks we did the show, almost every morning Bryant was on the phone calling New York, telling whoever was on the other end he wanted to come back and cohost *The Today Show*. He eventually got what he was after. His marriage barely lasted longer than our little show, but we did have some amazing moments on it.

Burt Reynolds was the hottest, highest paid actor in Hollywood and, like Bob Hope, after I bombed him and a number of his films, he called asking to be a guest. For scale. He was brilliant, witty and funny, as he demonstrated often later on *The Tonight Show*. When Kenny Rogers left the First Edition to go out on his own, ours was the first show he did as a solo artist.

The best moment, though, was a serious one; a very serious one.

The biggest news story of the week in LA., one that went national, was of a young Vietnam veteran named John Gabron. He had what was described by psychiatrists as a flashback. Unseen by anyone, he took a sniper rifle up into Griffith Park, a lush, hilly massive retreat three or four times the size of New York's Central Park, filled with golf courses, tennis courts, soccer fields, bike paths, horse trails, stable, a zoo, and thousands of trees and bushes. Perfect pickings and hiding places for someone with a rifle. John held two park rangers and a hiker hostage. Police and helicopters swarmed over the area, fortunately apprehending him before he harmed anyone or himself.

It was, to me, just another Vietnam horror story. I paid no attention to it until I called Producer Bob Rafelson. Bob, like Alan Pakula, was a tasteful filmmaker. Among others, he did two terrific films with Jack Nicholson, *Easy Rider,* and *Five Easy Pieces,* and the remake of *The Postman Always Rings Twice*. I was calling him about an unreleased, outstanding Vietnam documentary called *Hearts and Minds*. Columbia Pictures financed the film, but because of the film's controversial and truthful content, backed away from releasing it. In it was a memorable line from General Patton's son, himself a general, saying with a smile how proud he was of the nice boys he was turning into terrific killers. Not the kind of thing their American mothers would like to hear. I read about the film by glancing through the Congressional Record; some politician opposed to the war, wanted his review posted there. On the phone, I asked Rafelson, since he was at Columbia, and played a part in making the documentary, if he would be a guest and bring a few clips; that way we might create enough interest to encourage Columbia to finally release it.

"John," Bob said, "I'd love to. The film deserves to be out there. But for you, I have a better idea. John Gabron, the kid who's been in the news all week. The kid they arrested in Griffith Park. My lawyer is his lawyer. We bailed him out. He'd be a fabulous guest."

"Why do you think that'd be better than your doc?"

"Because it's a flesh and blood story. He says he was a CIA-Intelligence assassin who killed dozens on assignments from his superiors. They tried to silence him by sending him to Letterman Hospital in San Francisco and filled him full of drugs. The newspapers are saying his breakdown was drug induced. It wasn't. It was truth induced."

I love people who have a way with words. Bob's last few lines were all I needed to hear. "Are you sure you can get him?"

"Absolutely. You just tell me where and when."

"Bob, I would want this fellow to feel comfortable, so I wouldn't be inclined to bring him into a studio, an artificial surrounding full of lights. If he agrees to it, I'd like to interview him in Griffith Park, on the spot he was arrested."

"Let's do it."

I did not tell management, the news department, or even the program director. I didn't want anyone to tell me I should have security around, or that such a story shouldn't be on a variety show. I only told my director, George Paul, (who went on to the ABC Network long afterward where he became Barbara Walters' director.) George picked a cameraman. The three of us met Bob and John at the bottom of the hill on a very warm still afternoon. The five of us climbed to John's sniper's nest. No one seemed ill at ease or nervous. We were all relaxed. John began to tell his story in vivid detail. He described how his superiors would give him his assigned kills with a name, picture and location. He repeated some of the names and locations to us. They were village leaders, soldiers, farmers, and sometimes women. You cannot respond to a horror story like that. You can only listen. I kept my questions brief and to the point. After airing, more than any guest I had on the *AM Show,* it was the most talked about story I had ever done. The military rearrested John and returned him to the Letterman Hospital Psych Ward and to drugs. It created enough stir to get *Hearts and Minds* eventually released.

The Gong Show

"Johnny Barbour!"

I knew the distinctive happy voice immediately when I answered the phone on an early afternoon in 1976. "Chuck Barris," I said, flatly.

"I've got something I'd like to show you. A TV clip. It's only about ten minutes long. Do you think you could drop by my office on Vine Street later today? In a couple of hours?"

Chuck's office was in a large ABC studio complex south of Sunset Blvd. At the time, Chuck was the most popular and recognizable producer of game shows in television, two of them being *The Dating Game* and *The Newlywed Game.* They made a fortune for him and ABC. He wasn't well-known for being on the air himself, but for his amazing ability to get publicity promoting himself and his shows. In person you could see why people liked him. He greeted me with a huge grin and handshake, almost pulling me into his office. "I've been looking for weeks for someone, and you were it. Right under my nose. Oh, Johnny, this is Chris Bearde, he's the co-producer on this."

Chuck led me to a seat in front of a large TV screen so quickly I had no time to shake Chris's hand. His hello was a grunt and nod. Chuck picked up the TV remote. "This is an Australian talent show. Of sorts. It's a huge hit Down Under. I bought the rights and sold it to NBC. It's called *The Gong Show.*

He played the short tape. It was charming, and at times funny. The host, after a brief introduction, would bring on the performers, nearly all of whom were obviously untalented or unprofessional. A minute into their acts, a panel of three judges would grab a huge mallet and whack a big gong. (It reminded me of the opening of all those old J. Arthur Rank movies from England.)

Chuck laughed with delight, clapping his hands with each gong. When it was over, he turned to me. "Whadda yah think?"

"Well, it is kind of funny, but it's also a little cruel."

"That's the idea. Like a car wreck. You can't take your eyes off it. It's a natural."

"Well, Chuck, you would know, but why are you showing it to me?"

"I want you to host it. You'd be the perfect host."

"You're kidding?"

"No, I'm not. You're the only one I've even considered. What do you think?"

"I don't know."

"Whadda yah mean, you don't know?"

"There was no performer in that clip who had talent."

"So?"

"Well, to just bang one bad act after another, frankly is cruel and predictable."

"How would you tweak the show?"

"In what you showed me, Chuck, the host never talked to the contestants. He just introduced them. If he had chatted with them for just a minute, to find out a little about them, then the audience would have a little more empathy for them. As would the judges, making it maybe a little harder to gong them."

"Perfect. Agreed. And you're great with people. I have no problem with that. So, would you consider doing it?"

"Can I consider it for a bit?"

"Not too long. NBC's hot to trot!

I informed Chuck of my unpleasant experience with *Connections* at ABC, and why I turned it down.

"John, this is not a talk show. It's a talent show. Or rather a no-talent show. But I agree, learning a little about the people would make them people. Call me in the morning. If it's a yes, you'll be getting $3,500.00 a show, ten times what you make as a critic and you can keep your critic's job. I'll arrange for you to have lunch at The Beverly Hills Hotel with my business manager. You'll love him. Used to do PR for Sinatra. And sign the deal. Okay?"

"Thank you. I appreciate your interest in me. I'll call you one way or the other early."

The money had nothing to do with my saying yes to a delighted Chuck the next morning. I could keep my critic's job. The studio was downstairs, five minutes away. On a national level, it would give me a chance, even though a short one, to talk to people, real people, which I enjoyed.

At noon I was in the Polo Lounge of The Beverly Hills Hotel, sitting across from Chuck's business manager. He was almost fifty, with an appealing world-weariness about him, especially when I got him to talk about show business, He had seen it all, and been impressed by none of it, except by a brief meeting with a down-and-out Frank Sinatra.

"Yah. About twenty years ago. I was a kid myself." He started slowly, remembering. "But I was one of the town's PR hotshots. I got a call from Sinatra, whom I didn't know. He was almost out of the business. He asked if I would meet with him. I said sure. I mean he was on his ass. Ava had left him. MGM had dropped him. Even Columbia records. For a time, he even lost his voice. Couldn't use it for six months. There were rumors he was gonna stick his head in a gas oven. So, we met for lunch. He matter-of-factly told me how shitty things were for him, but now that his voice felt better, he wanted to try and start over. To do that, he said, more than ever, he needed a great PR guy. Me. And asked if I'd do it. Of course, I felt sorry for the guy. I mean what a star. And what a fall. I told him I would, and that I'd only charge him half my fee. He cussed me like I'd never been cussed at before. He got pissed. He said, 'I don't want charity. I am the best, and I want the best, and I will pay whatever your fee is! Full load.' And he did. Never missed a payment. And the rest, as they say, is history."

"Are you still friends with him?"

"No. Once in a while he drops me a note. In this town, success, like failure, makes people grow apart. I just send a thank you note."

"Why did you get out of the PR business?" I loved listening to him.

He smiled broadly. 'Movie stars! Egos! They are the worst. So, how do you feel about *The Gong Show*? Are you excited?"

"It's different. I'm pleased for the chance, but excited is not the right word."

"That's the perfect attitude. The only thing in this town that is definite is disappointment. Success is a surprise. No matter how it goes, though, with the show and Chuck, believe me, it'll be a great experience." He looked at me as though he wanted to tell me something else, but held back.

"Okay," he said, "sign this and let's go to work."

The three celebrity judges for the run-throughs, rehearsals, and the first pilot were Jaye P. Morgan, Jamie Farr, from *Mash*, and Arte

Johnson, from *Laugh-In*. They were perfect and supportive. For me, though, the run-throughs were uncomfortable. It was difficult for me to make any kind of real contact with the contestants asking just a few background questions. As I feared, as we went along, Chuck wanted my already brief questions cut down or eliminated, reducing me once again to a traffic cop. This time a traffic cop who enjoyed watching people crash. NBC was also feeling uncomfortable with me and the show. There was never a talent show on TV that was deliberately set up to bash and make fun of the untalented. In the days of radio, on *The Major Bowes Amateur Hour,* where Sinatra got his start as part of *The Hoboken Four,* in a rare instance, a hook was brought out and a gong banged to remove an act that shouldn't have been there in the first place. The audience always laughed, but it was a very rare occurrence. On this show, on TV, for the first time, they'd be gonged and gone every few minutes.

At the end of the awkward first pilot's taping, the very tough, attractive head of daytime programming stopped everything and called Chuck aside. She thrust a piece of paper at him. After looking at it, and a brief tense discussion, Chuck walked over and handed it to me.

"This is how she wants you to introduce the show before you introduce the guests. Go over it, and let's do it again."

I looked at it. It said something to the effect that the guests had been warned about what may happen to them as a result of their appearance. I was appalled and motioned to Chuck.

"Chuck, this is awful. What she wants you to do, in essence, is apologize beforehand for the show. There are better ways to say it. You can say something like, all of us have talent, some of us more than others, and they'd like that talent to be shared and seen. This is the show that provides them that stage, and as you'll see, some of us have more talent than others, or, a different kind of talent."

"John, we have to give the lady what she wants. Here." He took the paper from my hand, and as he did frequently, demonstrated how to perform it. He was doing something he wanted to do: be the Jewish Ed Sullivan.

In the final taping of that pilot, my discomfort saying those apologetic words, and not being able to get to know the guests, was evident. I was not right for the show. It came as no surprise, and maybe a little relief when a few hours later, the business manager handed me a check for $17,500.00, my fee for the first five shows.

"Chuck's gonna host the show," he said. "I liked what you had to say, but I have no say. Chuck has no hard feelings."

"Chuck has five shows to tape, right? Would he mind if I asked him something?"

Chuck appeared, smiling and bubbly as usual. He said, "I'm sorry it didn't work out, but I'm putting together a gift for you."

I held up the check. "Chuck, are you a betting man?"

"Sometimes. Depends. Why?"

"You have five shows to tape. I'll make you this bet. Let me host just one show my way; you do the other four your way and her way. I'll bet this $17,5000.00 that my way will be better. And you can be the judge."

He stared at me. The first time I saw him without a smile. "It's outa my hands. Too late. But you'll still get your gift."

The Gong Show went on to become an enormous hit, Chuck's way, proving as H.L. Mencken said, *No one over went broke underestimating the intelligence of the American people.* I only watched it a couple of times when my once-upon-a-time friend Murray Langston appeared as The Unknown Comic. It was funny. The gift Chuck gave me was a large trophy with a gong mounted on it, and a warm inscription from him indicating I was the first person gonged. I keep it on my desk.

A decade or so after the last episode aired, efforts were made to remount it. They all failed. Perhaps what really made it work, and what they now didn't have, was Chuck. Like a number of successful performers and producers in this business, success had gone early to Chuck Barris's nose. That was why he was always so bubbly when I saw him.

I was never, for an instant, sorry I didn't do *The Gong Show*, or adapt to it. Making $17,500.00 a week meant absolutely nothing to me. I was still doing my reviews. When I lost the *AM Show*, though, which was only local, and only paid just over a thousand, I was devastated. It was a meaningful show. The anger at the thoughtless incompetence of KABC's management still resonates after all these years. I see that incompetence spreading through the media and America like a tsunami, drowning us. I am often asked, still, what I think of Chuck's autobiographical book, *Confessions of a Dangerous Mind*, in which he claims to have been a hitman for the CIA. All I say is that I interviewed a soldier, John Gabron, who I believe was a hitman for the CIA, and after he went public on my show, the government dragged him off to a mental ward. They didn't drag Chuck off to one. He died of natural causes at the age of eighty-seven.

The *Laugh-In* Revival, Sinatra's Arrival, Redd's Departure, and a Small Dinner

The year was 1977. I was forty-four. My son was eight, and my wife wasn't showing anyone her driver's license. My only close friend in showbiz, Redd Foxx, was having difficulties with NBC and the show's creators, Norman Lear and Bud Yorkin. He was making $25,000.00 on each episode of *Sanford & Son*. He wanted a percentage from Lear and Yorkin. From NBC, he wanted a window in his dressing room. He wanted a window in a basement where there was no outside view. He got neither, so he walked out.

In a midnight moment, Redd, sounding very stoned, called and woke Sarita up, asking her to run away and marry him. Sarita chuckled and said, "Redd, don't be silly. That's not your heart talking. That's your nose."

Redd responded, "In that case, will you manage a hair salon I'm gonna open on Sunset opposite The Directors Guild?"

"Yes, I'll do that for you, for a while."

Redd opened the hair salon, the only side business of the half dozen he got involved in that was successful. It stayed that way until Sarita left.

One day, he came to tell us ABC had approached him about bringing his production company to their network. He could develop shows there and host his own variety show. He asked if I had any ideas for shows for him to develop that I'd like to get involved in, or any advice in general. Redd was one of only three stars or people I met in Hollywood who had kept his word to me. The other two were Sinatra and Neil Simon. Neil had told me if I ever did another album, he'd love to do the liner notes. I did. Made up of a lot of material from my reviews, it was called *I Met a Man I Didn't Like*. After it was out a few weeks, Neil called to tell me it was the least successful writing he'd ever done.

When Redd was to be in the hot seat on *The Dean Martin Celebrity Roast,* he called and asked if I'd like to do it. I told him Greg Garrison would never let me near Dean.

"Well, you're on. Expect a call."

To my delight and surprise, Dean was as happy to see me as he always was. Greg, on the other hand, was cool and distant. Redd had told him if Johnny Barbour wasn't on he'd have to find another nigger. Greg told me I had five minutes, that'd probably be cut down to two. He asked if I wanted help with my material. When I told him no, he said that was fine but that he wanted to see it.

"Certainly, you're the boss. But if you don't mind, I wouldn't like it on cue cards for everyone to see. I'll have it memorized."

"No problem," he said.

The Roasts were a major event at NBC. Everyone in the buildings wanted to be in attendance. There was also a line of civilians a block long. The studio was jammed, with a wonderful buzz in the air. On the dais, on either side of Dean and Redd, facing the audience, were a dozen major movie and television stars and powerhouse comics. Facing them, but out of view of the audience, were dozens of cue cards with huge black lettering with everyone's jokes on them. Everyone could see what everyone else was going to say. Except mine.

As planned and rehearsed awkwardly with only Greg, my set was timed at five minutes. With my very brief opening words, I got a huge laugh; the laughter with each following line built. My five minutes ran closer to seven or eight. I got a terrific hand from the audience, capped by a hug from Redd. (The two minutes that Greg cut it down to can be seen on www.johnbarboursword.com) What can't be seen is what followed. Dean, standing next me, smiling that charming playful smile, and saying, "Geez, we had to stand here and listen to eight minutes of that shit!"

The air exploded with laughter. The audience heard their idol, Dean, say "Shit!" Wait till they tell their friends. They couldn't contain themselves. Neither could I. As much as I liked Dean, I liked my material more. I was flushed. As the laughter trickled down to giggles, I moved a little closer to Dean, stared at him, then put my head back much like Redd did as Sanford, and said in a growly voice, imitating Redd, "Dean, in the words of our esteemed roastee tonight, fuuuck you!"

The dais exploded; some of the comics actually fell out of their chairs onto the floor. The studio audience was howling. Dean was speechless. Casually, I walked off. If there was applause, it couldn't be heard above the laughter.

So, when Redd showed up this particular day that he was hiding from the world, I felt I owed him a lot, but what I owed him the most was honesty.

"Can I give you the best thing first, the advice?" I said.

"What's that?"

"Don't leave Sanford–"

"Fuck 'em," he snorted.

"Redd, you're wonderful in it. It could go on forever as long as Norman and Bud are writing and running it. You don't know any writers like that. You can't make it on TV or anywhere but a nightclub unless you have them."

"Tight mother fuckin' Jews. They won't give me a piece of it."

"If you called me that, I wouldn't either. Be patient, they will. It'll run for a hundred years in syndication. You'd never have to work again. And remember, they gave you a break."

"I wanna do my own thing."

"Redd, your thing is standup and acting. You have no interest in producing anything, otherwise you'd have done so by now. Look, $25,000.00 an episode is a lot of money. It will keep you in all the joints you need."

"I'm goin' to ABC, and I'd like you to give me a couple of ideas I could pitch."

"Honey," Sarita said, putting her hand on my shoulder, restraining me, "Redd will do fine. He wants your help. Is there something he might do?"

It didn't take me long. It was an idea I often wondered about. "Redd, there's only one thing I think you could do as a producer. You're the only one I think who could sell it. And you are perfect for it."

"What's that?"

"The greatest, legendary showcase for black talent in the world. The Apollo. You could and should do amateur night or talent night at The Apollo. No one's ever done it before."

He rose and grabbed my hand. "Goddamn, that's great. If you get tired of doing reviews, come see me at ABC." Then he turned to Sarita. "You shouldn't uh left me. The salon went under. Why'd you leave?"

"You weren't paying me enough." Saria smiled.

"Then yah shoulda asked for more!" He drove off happily in his Roll Royce.

Redd's move to ABC was a disaster. He was funny in clubs, albeit filthy, but he was never better than when he was Fred Sanford. Sanford was his real name. Fred his dead older brother's. In that role, his humanity and real sweetness came through. Redd had more input into the show than even he realized. Or maybe he did, thus the hurt and anger. Redd's sweetness was only hinted at in a nightclub.

Redd was just short of his fiftieth birthday when he got Sanford. He was on it a wonderful five years. I was six years younger, and never got close to that kind of show or success. I may have blown *The Gong Show*, but what kind of creative satisfaction would I have had doing that? None. No wonder Chuck took to drugs! I was beginning to wonder why I was even in this business. Redd suggested to Carson a couple of times that I fill in for him on nights he was off. *That* I would have loved to have done. Of course, Johnny ignored him. There wasn't anything else I was excited about doing. I wasn't interested in writing movies. I wasn't interested in hosting game shows. I wasn't even really that interested anymore in doing standup.

Our six o'clock anchor, Tom Snyder, had long since left to do *Tomorrow* on the network following Carson. The day he left he did an astonishing and unexpected thing. Like some outraged kid in the ghetto or barrio, he bought a large spray can of black paint, and on the walls of the entire newsroom, and his glass encased office, plastered profanities you wouldn't see on buildings in Central Los Angeles. He did it in the middle of the night when no one was around. He left the empty can on my desk with a note. *See you on my show, kid*! Even though he was only three years older than me, he often called me kid. That was the second time he said I'd be on his show, and the second time I'd never hear from him.

I was pondering all this in my little cubicle when the phone rang. It was George Schlatter. "I love your reviews. Terrific stuff. This last issue of *L.A. Magazine* had a couple of gems. We're doing a couple of *Laugh-In* revival specials for NBC. I was wondering if you'd mind if I used a couple of your lines."

"Not at all, I'm flattered. Who's hosting it?"

"No one, guest hosts. I'd be happy to pay you for the lines."

"No, not at all. My pleasure." Then I stopped myself on impulse and surprised myself by saying, "Since the lines you want are about movies and actors, why not let me deliver them as your resident critic-at-large."

He laughed, a deep, edgy laugh. "That's not a bad idea. Would you mind also writing other material? We have a large staff already and you'd fit right in. The pay is scale."

"I'd love to."

"Terrific. Come by the office tomorrow before noon and I'll introduce you to Digby and the crew."

I was more interested in meeting Schlatter than writing and appearing briefly on a couple of *Laugh-Ins*. He was widely known for creating the original *Laugh-In,* a monster, ground-breaking entertaining hit in the sixties, hosted by Rowan and Martin. It instantly became a part of the culture. He was widely known as an independent outspoken Peck's bad boy. My kind of guy. I was anxious to meet someone of his stature who had made it on his own terms, without benefit of agents or publicists.

His offices were in a small two-story building he owned on Beverly Boulevard. His office was at the top of the stairs near the entrance. George rose to greet me. He was about five-feet-ten with the large barrel chest and a goatee that made him look like Mephistopheles. His most distinguishing feature was his voice, the perfect announcer's voice.

"John, this is Digby Wolfe. He is also a big fan and delighted you're coming aboard."

Digby was the exact opposite of George; soft spoken with soft blue eyes. I discovered later, he was a recovering alcoholic. I also learned later from Digby and Ernie Kovacs's widow, Edie Adams, about the real origins of *Laugh-In*. Schlatter, like Chuck Barris, had a genius for self-promotion. He claimed he got the idea for *Laugh-In* from a Broadway show called *Hellzapoppin*. Edie, on the other hand, proclaimed, in threats to sue him, that he plagiarized her husband, Ernie's material. The title itself came to Digby while shopping in the supermarket. It was the height of the Civil Rights Movement with their sit-ins. Why not a *Laugh-in*?

Sitting there chatting with George and Digby I knew none of that. I just knew what I read in the Trades. It was all George's idea and doing. I wanted to know all about George, how he'd managed to make it on his own in that town. I started asking meaningless questions; to him maybe, but not to me.

"George, how old are you?"

He smiled. "Fifty. And you?"

"Forty-four. And four is my lucky number." I smiled back. "I'm on channel four. I live at 4254 Forman Avenue. Born in the fourth month, and now doing something with you on four!'

"And we have an order for four specials." He chuckled that deep chuckle.

"And you did all that without an agent?"

"No. No. I've always been with the Morris Agency. Tony Fantozzi. The toughest Dago in the business."

Hearing he hadn't done it all by himself surprised me. That was definitely the impression I'd gotten from the press. "Do you have a publicist?"

"A necessary part of the business."

"Geez, I'm sorry. I feel like I'm doing a talk show, but I've always admired your outspokenness and work. How did you guys start and meet?"

For the next fifteen minutes he and Digby took delighted turns recounting George's career. They talked about his early days in St. Louis. Singing in musical theater. Moving to LA. Becoming a bouncer at Ciro's, and a body guard for Mae West. Then finally getting to produce his first variety show.

Here Digby laughed out loud. "And, Johnny, this is what you're in for if you screw up around him. When he got this first show, he took this famous director out in the hall, picked him up, slammed him against the wall and said, 'This is my first fucking show and if you fuck it up, I will kill you!'"

George laughed at the memory. "It was a good show!"

He then told stories about producing Judy Garland's show. He was a fabulous story-teller. I could and did listen to him often, enchanted by it all.

"Do you wanna start now?" George asked.

"Absolutely."

"Digby, show him that other office in front where he can work alone. Give him a typewriter and paper, put him in, then shut the door." He laughed, a loud hard laugh.

Knowing there'd be an outlet for my material, if not for me, but for a great cast and great guests, the jokes poured out. In less than an hour I had filled three pages. Hearing that Sinatra might be on one of the shows, I did a whole page for him. I also wrote a whole catalogue of visuals showing Chuck Barris striking the gong. Everything from the mallet sticking to it with no sound, to the mallet sinking into a custard pie.

Ten minutes after I'd turned in my three pages to a surprised George, he rushed back in, gave me a huge hug, plus the three pages with his scribbled glowing remarks. I still have a briefcase filled with almost every joke I wrote, including those first three marked sheets.

George had hired a dozen writers at scale. It reminded me of the old Bob Newhart joke about sitting a dozen monkeys at typewriters hoping that *to be or not to be* would pop out. Unfortunately for them, nothing much popped out of George's dirty dozen. There was one bright, funny young lady among them, though, who ended up dating and living with David Letterman for nearly fifteen years.

For the four specials, all the writing was done by George, Digby, a garrulous middle-aged writer for the *L.A. Times*, Kendis Rochlen, and myself. Some of the funniest lyrics and couplets and poems I'd ever heard poured out of Digby every day. George was extremely witty, but it seldom came out of him when he was sitting – only standing. Or walking around making comments about everything. Then he'd have to grab a pen and write it down. Patience and an attention span of more than ten seconds were not part of his character. Often Digby and I battled him constantly to keep him from ruining good verbal jokes. While a performer was mouthing one joke, George wanted to run another printed joke along the bottom of the screen, like a news report, making both meaningless.

"The news does it all the time," George would holler.

"George, that's the news," I would answer. "It's not supposed to get laughs. You cannot listen to a joke and look at another different one running across the screen at the same time."

Some fights we won. Some we didn't. But they were fun fights. Truly exhilarating. When it came time for me to do my one or two lines, though, I would stop if he tried to clutter the screen. George not only had a quick tongue, he had a quick eye, especially for unique talent. He somehow found half a dozen wonderful zanies for those specials, two who were beyond brilliant: Robin Williams and Wayland Flowers and Madame. George was frequently criticized for exploiting those talents, paying them only minimum, but talent struggling to be seen would have gladly paid him just for the opportunity to be on that historic show. Wayland, a brilliant ventriloquist, had created by far the most deliciously enjoyable outrageous dummy in showbiz history. He called her Madame, obviously direct from the whorehouse. She got away with saying the most salacious, censorable, funniest things I'd ever heard on the air. She gave questionable taste, taste.

Robin, in his twenties, was a vibrant volcano of ad lib comic eruptions; a gentle genius not seen since Jonathan Winters brought us to our feet and our knees on *The Jack Paar Show*. It was a joy to write for them and be around them.

It was the start of an amazing year. Made more amazing, memorable, and meaningful with a small gathering for dinner in the wine cellar at Scandia. We were to celebrate my becoming an American citizen. The handful of toasters included Chris Hayward, with his wife, Linda, elegant TV Producer Roland Young, married to stunning actress, Joan Fontaine, actor Ed Asner, producer and co-creator of *Barney Miller*, Danny Arnold, Charo, and Senator John Tunney, holding my citizenship papers. And Sarita. After popping the champagne, Senator Tunney rose, and gave a speech worthy of Jimmy Stewart in any Frank Capra movie. Amid cheers, whistles and tears from me, he handed them to me and said, "We're lucky and glad you made it!" More cheers and tears.

Suddenly, Charo said in her broken English, "Okey dokeys. Everybody up. Toda."

We all rose with smiles, wondering what was going on. What went on was Charo singing the most beautiful version of the National Anthem that I'd ever heard. My God, was I the luckiest, happiest man in the world!

"Clear the stage," our floor manager hollered. Everyone who was not absolutely essential to be on the closed *Laugh-In* set was told to leave. George held the material for the day's shoot in his hands. Since some were mine, I wanted to stay and watch. I sat in the very back against the wall, viewing from a distance. Every other seat was empty. The reason for the ordered exit soon appeared. It was Frank Sinatra. He was tailed closely by two men I didn't recognize. He stopped in the middle of the set, greeted George without a handshake, and took the few pages George handed to him. He looked at them quickly and impatiently.

Sinatra! My God, I couldn't believe it. I couldn't tell if he was giving off all this energy and electricity, or my memories of him and his work were infusing it into him. Hundreds of images and sounds fast-forwarded through my head. Listening to him on the radio in the mid-forties singing *Saturday Night Is the Loneliest Night of the Week.* Seeing him in a long-forgotten film playing a down-and-out singer when he was down and out, called, *Meet Danny Wilson.* Then singing what should really be the national anthem, *That's America To Me,* to a bunch of ruffian kids in an Academy Award winning short, written ironically by Albert Maltz. And how could I forget a beaten dying Maggio in *Fom Here to Eternity*. At his best in *Manchurian Candidate.* And many years ago, seeing him live in Lake Tahoe strutting in next to Sam Giancana. The dizzying images were brought to a sudden halt when he said sharply, "George, who wrote this shit?"

I sank down in my back seat, afraid he was looking at my stuff. I didn't want him looking at me. George handed him a few more sheets. Sinatra glanced at them, chuckling as he went down the page. "Who wrote this?" His tone was softer.

George took the page from him. He was looking around when Digby pointed at me. "Johnny Barbour. In the cheap seats."

"Hey, kid. Come 'ere," Sinatra said.

I walked down the stairs and over to him. He was slightly taller than me, but still seemed as big as if he were on the screen. It was like an out-of-body experience standing inches from him.

"You're *that* critic?"

"Yes, sir, I'm known as the heterosexual Rex Reed."

His grin lit up the stage; on cue, everyone around him laughed. "You're funny. You wrote this?"

"Yes, sir."

Digby spoke up. "He's got a very funny album called, *It's Tough to Be White*.

Sinatra looked at Digby, then me. "Never heard of it," he said.

"Neither has anyone else except Digby," I said.

"Send me a copy. Call my office at Formosa Studios. Tell Dorothy, my secretary, that you're sending it. I have a couple of things I'd like to talk to you about." He then turned to George. "Okay, let's finish this. And quickly."

As they moved away setting up the cameras, I stood alone in a paralyzing fog trying to make sense out of what had just happened. In a matter of minutes, Sinatra wanted to talk to me. That only happens in the movies.

On the phone, Dorothy suggested it would be easier for her to keep track of it if I delivered the album in person. Besides, she said, Mr. Sinatra wanted to hear it right away. Hearing that made me fearful the album was a flop. Only a handful of black DJ's and critics applauded it. It would certainly offend him.

Dorothy in her early 30's was quite attractive, wore almost no makeup, with long wavy brown hair. She was remarkably efficient, and at ease with herself. She immediately put me at ease. I handed her the album. She glanced at the title, then smiled broadly. As I stood now empty-handed, I felt even if I never heard from him, those few seconds I'd spent with him on that empty stage would expand into a lifetime of unbeatable memories. But I did hear from him. Almost immediately. And the memories would multiply.

My Friend, Francis

It wasn't a call I got from him. It was a letter. To my house. Dictated and typed by his secretary, signed simply, Francis Albert. It said, in part, he liked the saltiness and the delivery of material, that I wasn't Henny Youngman, but I was all his; when he got back to LA to appear at Wasserman's Universal Amphitheater, he'd call because he had some things in mind that he wanted to do with me, closing with love from him and Barbara. It is the only framed letter hanging on my office wall.

I was so in awe of what I was looking at, I told Sarita I didn't care if he ever called.

Having that brief note from the most influential singer in the world, the powerful entertainer who probably put John Kennedy in the White House, was enough for me. From where I had come from, it was beyond belief. No substance or liquid could equal the buzz I would get just looking at it. It was a visual drug that kept me high for a long time.

Then the call came. I was alone in the small office George had given me. There was no mistaking the voice. "Kid, this is Francis!"

"Oh, yes, Mr. Sinatra, and thank you for that nice note."

"Call me Francis. That's what I like my close friends to call me. I like you. I like your stuff. And we're gonna do a lot together. Beginning next week." I was speechless. "I'm being roasted on Dean's show, and I'm gonna tell Greg that I want you on the dais. How's that sound for starters?"

Hearing him mention Greg, all I could think of was how short my relationship was going to be with that icon. My mind was suddenly a disturbed hornets' nest of thoughts. Should I tell him of my ruptured history with Greg and that it wasn't likely he'd book me? Certainly, if the king wanted his jester, not even Greg would object. Besides, who was I to tell Sinatra a simple request from him might be turned down? I certainly wasn't going to. Thinking, once again, that would be the last I'd ever to talk to him, I said thank you in a voice that sounded more like goodbye.

"Terrific. I'll have them call you with the details."

It was around eleven in the morning. I didn't have to do a review that night, for which I was grateful. I'd be too depressed. I was daydreaming about how nice those last few days were, putting it in the past tense.

I was too depressed to eat, turning down an invitation from George and Digby to join them for lunch. For a couple of hours I tried to write jokes, but none appeared. My pages were blank. So were my hopes. I just wanted to go home and take a nap when the phone rang a little after two.

"Jesus Christ, kid. What did you do? Tell my favorite dago to go fuck himself?"

"Mr. Sinatra, it's a long--"

"He had a fit. Did you really say fuck you to Dean?"

"He called my material shit!" I said quite forcefully.

Francis laughed. "Geez, kid, you got balls!'

"It's a long story and begins and ends with Greg trying to have me pimp my wife."

"Jesus Christ!" He laughed. "Kid, Dean lets Greg run his show because, frankly, Greg saved it. They have a special relationship. I can understand that, so I didn't push the matter."

"Please," I said, "you don't know how good your letter made me feel. Please don't even try to do anything for me. Just knowing you think that much of me is applause and reward enough. You've made me unbelievably happy."

"Kid, I really like you. When I say we're gonna do something together, we are gonna do something together. So, don't give up."

Late that same afternoon, Digby, Kendis, George and I were in George's office going over the material we'd finally put together. After Sinatra's call, I was in blissful enough shape to fill a few of those previously blank pages. The door opened and George's secretary leaned in, whispering intensely, "Excuse me, folks, but John, it's Sinatra. Again."

Digby looked at me. "Again?"

George and Kendis stared at me in disbelief. I don't know why I said what I said when I picked up the phone, but often when I'm nervous I blurt out things. I said with mock anger, "Francis, how many times have I told you not to call me at work? We're trying to write some jokes here!"

There was a momentary silence, then that wonderful laughter, like singing, rang out. "Goddamn it, I hope you're this funny in two weeks. I'm hosting *The Tonight Show* and I want you to do a spot. That's even better than Dean's."

Oh, shit. My stomach got tighter. Carson hated me more than Greg. Should I say anything? I felt this time I had to say something. I didn't want him surprised again by what Carson or his producer might say. "Uh, Frank–"

"Francis, Johnny, Francis," he interrupted warmly.

"Francis. About Carson–"

"Don't tell me anything. This has nothing to do with Carson. You're on. Freddy will call you to go over your stuff. See you then. And save some of those great jokes for my show."

The trio was still staring at me. "Was that really Frank?" Kendis asked.

I nodded.

"What did he want?"

I answered as if in a daydream. "To be on *The Tonight Show* with him."

"Holy shit," Kendis and Digby chorused. George didn't say a word.

The next morning, Carson's producer, Freddy de Cordova, called. I took it privately. He complimented me for Sinatra picking me to be a guest, and asked how many days would I need to put together my five or six minutes. I told him one or two at the most.

"It's Tuesday. Could you come in Friday around eleven so we can go over it? It's about time we did something together. See you then."

Friday morning, early, I was in Freddy's office. He greeted me like a long-lost friend. "You know, John, you and I might be doing different things today if ABC had listened to me and given you the part of Manley. You were good. But I like what you're doing now more. Anyway, let's see what you have."

I did my five or six minutes again with an audience of one without looking at notes. Fred either smiled or nodded approval at each joke. "Very nice," he said.

"Thank you. Would you like my notes?"

"No. That's perfect. We'll see you the night of the show. There's no rehearsal. Glad to have you."

Everyone at *Laugh-In* wished me luck but George.

From the afternoon of the show until hours afterward, just walking into NBC there was the impression something new and exciting was afoot. Like a visit from the pope. Even more so because with the pope there wouldn't be so many stunning women around.

Hollywood's legendary hustler and best known literary agent, Irving 'Swifty' Lazar, showed up two hours early. The five-foot-two Hollywood giant was accompanied by a staggeringly beautiful six-foot French actress. Irving delighted in telling everyone that the night before in a Beverly Hills bar, his date punched out our weekend anchor-man John Shubek. He kept hitting on her not knowing she was a lesbian. Merriment and mayhem were in the air. I was there an hour and a half early, pacing a rut in the green room. Sinatra was already in his dressing room, where he stayed until show time.

"Frank would like to see you," Freddy said, poking his head in.

Sinatra's dressing room was filled with people, booze, flowers, and laughter.

"Here's your boy," Freddy said as we entered.

Sinatra turned away from the small crowd surrounding him, walked toward me as though I was the star, and grabbed my hand in one of the warmest, firmest handshakes I've ever felt. "Good luck, kid," he said. "You'll kill 'em."

He then introduced me to his wife, Barbara, a very attractive dirty blonde. "And this is my best friend, Jilly." Jilly was also well known as Frank's bodyguard. He was built like an in-shape Ernest Borgnine in *From*

Here to Eternity. Instead of taking my hand, Jilly put a warm tight grip on my shoulders. "Love your, stuff, kid. Can't wait to see it." Jilly had the hardest most solid body mass I had ever felt. The perfect container for a soft heart. Then it was show time!

Ed McMahan's loud, boisterous announcement of that night's stars, from Carol O'Connor on, brought an eruption of applause. With the mention of my name, it wasn't quite at that level, but there were two loud, distinctive girlish squeals. They had come from my two teenage sister fans who bicycled often from Long Beach to Burbank just to hear the reviews in person, the only people for whom I got tickets. Ed's introduction of the host, "Heere's Frank," brought bedlam.

Sinatra was surprisingly good, at ease interviewing, and in great voice when he sang. The first forty minutes flew by. Excitement seemed to build with each commercial break. During those breaks, Doc Severinsen's excellent band rocked the room. At the end of the fourth break, Sinatra announced that we'd be right back with me, but then something weird happened. The studio got deathly quiet. The band was not playing. They were just sitting there, chatting amongst themselves. The audience, getting restless, started to do the same. The noise got louder. I panicked. Was I supposed to follow that? Only two things kept me from throwing up. One was, I had no choice. The other was the thought that at least there were two young girls in the audience who would listen.

The break was over. The band played loudly to bring us back to Sinatra. As he raised the white card on which my introduction was written, the crowd was still chatting. The applause for me, at best, was pleasant, except for those two loud female squeals that made me smile as I made my way through the curtains. (The entire segment can be seen on my site: youtube/johnbarboursworld.com.)

During the first minute or so, the laughter was muted, then I did a line about the Watergate scandal, an event I said that put America on the brink of democracy. It got a hand. My planned and rehearsed five or six minutes expanded into nearly nine or ten. At the end, I had the playful nerve to thank Frank Sinatra for being my opening act.

In Sinatra's dressing room afterwards, Francis made me feel I was indeed the star. He looked proud of his pick. Invitations to lunches, dinners and speaking gigs flew at me. I was interested in none of them. I was just too filled with joy.

"John," Francis said, "I want you around a lot. We've got things to talk about."

He then joined his wife and cronies while Sarita and I backed out of the crowd into the hallway to savor what had just happened. We were interrupted by a stranger with a horn in his hand.

"John, I hate to interrupt, but could I talk to you a minute?"

"Certainly." I didn't know who he was, but I was feeling so high I would have talked to anyone. I excused myself from Sarita and walked down the hallway with him.

"I'm sorry we didn't play music in the break before you came on."

"That's okay. It worked out all right, but I must say for a moment I did panic."

"Carson ordered us not to play during the break before you came out."

"Why would he do that? I'm just a peanut in this business, for God's sake. He's the whole fucking plantation!"

"I'm sorry, but the guys love you. Great job. That'll piss him off!"

And it did. The very next night, in his opening monologue, Carson asked the audience if they saw this John Barbour try to do a monologue that should keep him in his critic's corner. I mentioned this the next night on the news, and added: "Carson's staff has a large bucket in the office, and every morning they drop a quarter in it. The first one Johnny says hello to gets the contents. It is now up to $46,000.50!" Another call from Sinatra made me forget all that.

He asked me to come to his offices in the Formosa Studios. One would never guess that those were the offices of one the world's most famous entertainers. They were simple and uncluttered; they looked more like the offices of a writer.

Francis was dressed smartly but casually with an open-neck colored shirt, sitting behind a neat but busy desk. "Kid, how do you feel about traveling?"

"I started out doing that. What kind of traveling?"

"With me. On the road."

"Wow, that'd be wonderful, but–"

"But what?"

"I enjoy doing the reviews on the news. Even more than that, in my spare time, I love taking my son to junior golf tournaments."

"How old is he?"

"Eight. He's a prodigy. He already has about twenty first place trophies, and he's a genius, a joy to be around."

"Good for you. Your boy's lucky. There's also something else you could do for me in the meantime, 'til we see what else pops up. I don't have the time or patience to write letters to the editor, to get things off my chest. Also, there are times at dinners or functions or whatever when I need to say something, and don't have the time to write it. I'd like you to do some of that for me, if that's okay."

"I'd be happy to."

"I'll be paying you."

"Mr. Sinatra, after what you've already done for me–"

"Kid, I always pay my way. I have your number. I'll call myself and give you enough time."

Feeling surprisingly at ease with him, I stunned myself with what popped out of me. "Francis, do you mind if I say something to you?"

"Not at all."

"You know, Bing Crosby died a short while ago. He was one of the greatest entertainers of the century, but frankly, I think before long he'll be totally forgotten."

"Be careful what you say about Bing. He was my idol. And buddy."

"But you wouldn't be forgotten. For two reasons. First, you're a better singer. Fifty years from now every Italian restaurant in the country will be piping in your music. Second, unlike Crosby or any other entertainer, except maybe Will Rogers, or even Mark Twain, you are a social and cultural force. You and your buddies doing *High Hopes* really put John Kennedy into The White House. You know what you should think of doing, that I think would be not only a first, but one of the biggest events in showbiz history?" I hesitated.

"And that is?"

"You should do an Italian *Roots*."

"A what?"

"Sorry, that's just my funny way of describing it because running five nights *Roots* was the biggest hit ABC ever had. What I think would be an important, monumentally entertaining event would be you on camera, for hours, telling us your life story. It would be the first visual autobiography of a major personality, augmented by visuals and comments from people you've influenced and worked with. Maybe some with whom you had differences."

"How would you go about it?"

"I'd come to your house in Palm Springs one or two days a week, where you're comfortable, for as many weeks as it took. I would sit you down and interview you for two or three hours at a time. In the show you'd never hear my voice. Only yours. All the tapes would be kept in your possession. And all the editing done there, so nothing gets out. You know when I first saw you? In person?"

"Performing?"

"No. Walking!" He laughed. "I was just sixteen. Had come down from Toronto, and was in the Casino at the Cal Neva Lodge. By a crap table. Suddenly everybody stopped gambling and looked toward the door. You had just come through it. A topcoat over your shoulder like a cape. Behind you were three tough-looking Italians. And next to you, on your left, was Sam Giancana."

"You remember that?"

"Vividly. And you know what one of my favorite Sinatra movies was, that nobody talks about? *Meet Danny Wilson*."

"Jesus, that was a piece of crap."

"No. *Kissing Bandit* was a piece of crap. I liked Danny Wilson because it seemed to be about your life, or what I thought might be your life. But what I'm suggesting *is* your life. You could call it, My Life. My Way. I might ask you some uncomfortable questions, some that might even annoy you, but the tapes and the final cut would all be in your hands. It could run one or two hours every night for a week. The whole country would stop and watch it. It'd be a treasure.

"I like it. I'd like to think about it. Could you put everything you said in a proposal and give it to Dorothy? And what would you want from it?"

"My goodness, I'd be honored just to be able to do it. Afterwards you could give me whatever you think it's worth."

"I don't work that way. You should have a piece of it. Twenty percent sound okay?"

"Golly, yes!"

"Then get to work, and I'll be in touch with you soon about some letters and stuff." Again, that wonderful firm handshake, and I was out the door.

The typed proposal was on Dorothy's desk the next day. My days as the critic-at-large on KNBC were numbered. Not by working with Sinatra, but by not getting a small asked-for raise from KNBC.

Chicago, My Kind of Town... Almost

As Thanksgiving approached in 1977, I had been at KNBC a little over five years, getting the same $150.00 a review. Three years in a row I won an Emmy for Outstanding Achievement for Commentary. I also won an Entertainment Emmy, the only one handed out that year for *John Barbour's First Annual Telethon to Save NY*. I had done *Laugh-In, The Tonight Show,* and *The Dean Martin Roast*. I was also the town's most popular critic in print at *LA Magazine*. I had brought a lot of positive attention to the news, aside from the fact I was responsible, according to research, for ten percent of the audience. Pretty good for someone on the air less than nine minutes a week. I felt I deserved at least a small raise, a token of appreciation, just fifty or a hundred dollars extra a show. That would have made me happy. Not having an agent or manager I didn't quite know how to go about it. I had never asked for a raise before. Truthfully, it wasn't the money I wanted, just the reassurance that they liked me and my work.

The one who was my biggest booster in our cast, was our eleven o'clock anchor, golfing buddy, and Tom Snyder look-alike, Paul Moyer. Like the old movie studios who protected themselves from stars' egos and agents by hiring look-alikes, KNBC did the same by bringing on Paul. Viewers could hardly tell them apart. But we could. Paul was a whole lot less full of himself, and not nearly as ambitious as Tom. He was content to stay in town, play golf and fly his plane.

When I answered in the negative, after Paul asked me on the golf course if I'd been given a raise after five years and three Emmys, he suggested I talk to his lawyer-manager, George Bain.

George and his partner had neat, contemporary offices on Beverly Drive. Aside from Paul, George represented a number of local news personalities. He was someone to whom news directors would listen, but not in my case. When he approached Irwin, our news director, about how deserving I was of an increase, even a slight one, Irwin said no. I was stunned. Jesus, I could have gotten that answer without his help. My pride wasn't so much damaged as my feelings. I was never good at handling rejection. If my word meant anything, I now had no choice but to give Irwin two weeks' notice. Reluctantly, I did. Irwin didn't seem to care, which hurt even more. Not once did he ask me to reconsider or stay.

The word I was leaving spread quickly throughout the building, then the town. I did not get one call asking me to stay, or suggesting that they'd miss me. Not one. But I did get a call to go to Chicago for two weeks. It came from Phil Mayer, Program Director, who was being transferred to Chicago as that station's new General Manager. He said that they needed a host for a couple of weeks over the Christmas holidays.

"Steve Edwards, their *AM* host is moving to LA to take over here. I need somebody I know can keep the show together for a couple of weeks till we find a replacement. Could you do it?"

"Just a couple of weeks?'

"Yeah. A piece of cake for you."

"Let me talk to my wife, and call you back."

"Don't take long. You're the only one I've asked. You'll get round-trip, first class airfare, a limo, hotel, all expenses, plus fifteen hundred a week."

Sarita said simply, "Why not. It'd be sort of a Christmas present, Christopher can see some snow."

I had nothing to look forward to in LA, and could write my stuff for Frank anywhere; so I called Phil and accepted, but if the Bible wanted to punish wrongdoers for their transgressions, it could have created for them a destination more punishing than a fiery hell; it could have sent them to Chicago in the winter. We were given a luxury suite in an elegant hotel on N. Michigan Avenue. WLS TV, the ABC affiliate, was a block to our left; Water Tower Place, an upscale shopping mall, was half a block to our right. For the first three days we could not use the revolving doors at the mall. They were frozen shut. Some women found they couldn't wear mascara outdoors. If they blinked, their eyes also froze shut. The zoo, which we tried to visit, had confined the polar bears to an indoor compound; it was too cold for them outside.

I declined the limo ride to the station every morning. I preferred the walk in the snow. It reminded me of Toronto when I'd trudge blocks in a blizzard to play hockey. I liked Chicago. A lot. It had been home to my second-favorite American writer, Ben Hecht, and was currently home to the wittiest columnist in America, Mike Royko, who once defended John Kennedy's hobby of fornication as being more satisfying and less time-consuming than Eisenhower's frustrating hobby of golf. On Chicago radio and in print was the most passionate voice and writer in the country for blue-collar Americans, Studs Terkel, author of *Working*. *The Tribune* boasted the brightest TV critic in the land, Gary Deeb. It was where legendary lawyer Clarence Darrow lived, practiced, and died. It was where poet Carl Sandburg painted word pictures about the city in his epic poem *Hog Butcher to the World*. It was also home to one of the original six teams in the NHL, The Chicago Blackhawks.

When the Los Angeles Kings came to town for a game, Sarita, Christopher and I were the only boosters in the stands in yellow sweaters amongst a sea of red. Chicagoans were as industrious and as busy as New

Yorkers, but could manage both while still being pleasant. They were almost as casual as Los Angelinos, and better dressed.

As was my habit, I arrived early, two days early. I wanted to meet everyone with whom I'd be working, beginning with Phil. Seated opposite him in his office was a tall twenty-six-year-old introduced to me as Howard Schultz, no relation to the Starbucks CEO.

Phil said, "Howard will help you produce the show, but how you run it is up to you. We had a co-host, Sonia Freeman, but I know you don't need a co-host so I'll have Howard dismiss her."

"Oh, don't do that. I'm only gonna be here a couple of weeks. I don't want to cost anybody their job."

"Well, she's not gonna be around for the next host. Why not do the show by yourself?"

"Then let the next host fire her. There are probably viewers who like her. I wouldn't want them to think she's gone because of me."

"That's nice. And would you do some reviews in the morning? I love them."

"Certainly. It'll be fun." And it was!

After my first show and first review, the news director asked if I would repeat them on his evening news. Phil readily agreed.

The shows were a joy to do. Sonia was very good at her job, grateful she still had one. She and Howard introduced us to the best restaurants in the city. We ate at a different one every night when we were not dining with Phil and his wife in their elegant apartment.

Happily, for everyone, positive audience reaction was almost immediate. There were calls within three days from Studs Terkel and Gary Deeb, with whom I became friends for years. There were also calls from the past. One was from Angelo, my twitchy Greek friend from Gower Street in Hollywood; his father had hounded him into leaving Hollywood to return and take over their successful bakery business. I chatted briefly with him on the phone. He said he was thrilled to see my success after leaving Paramount. His voice had volume, but there was a hollowness to it. I promised I'd come by to see him. It was a promise I had no intentions of keeping. It would hurt me to see he'd probably grown greyer, with even more twitches. I felt it might hurt him to see me living his dream.

The other call was for Sarita. Sarita had told me years earlier about this stunning dancer in their chorus line who, in her late teens, had mapped out her entire life. At the top of her list was marrying only the wealthiest of men. Sarita had no such blueprint. She took life as it came along. And

I came along, the only real poor person she'd ever met. When she ran off with me, her friend told Sarita she was nuts, that they'd probably never see each other again. Her friend married one of the richest men in Chicago. The fourth day I was on the air, Sarita got the excited call from Mrs. Money. She said she was thrilled to see Sarita's husband doing so well, and would Sarita please bring me with her to dinner at her estate? Sarita was never like me, or anyone else I knew, who would utter the simplest of white lies. She told her former friend we would be too busy the short two weeks doing the show.

On every show I had an author, as always. Of the dozen authors I interviewed, I remember only one. Amazingly, the entire hour was based on only two throw away lines in his book, a book about Richard Nixon by one of his speechwriters. He had written offhandedly, almost as an afterthought, that the 1972 Watergate break-in had nothing to do with Nixon trying to get dope on the democrats and George McGovern. He pointed out Nixon clearly had a huge lead in the polls. He felt the burglary had more to do with Nixon or the CIA wanting to get secret information Larry O'Brien might have in his files; information about the CIA's plot to kill Castro.

Larry O'Brien was the Democratic party's chairman. He had also been the lawyer who, on behalf of the CIA, assembled a small group of CIA assets and mafia members at the Desert Inn in Las Vegas to plot the killing of Cuba's leader. Among those attending and plotting were Howard Hughes' right hand man and CIA asset, Robert Mahue, and gangsters Johnny Roselli and Sam Giancana. The crew and staff were spellbound for the entire sixty minutes. The phones lit up, anxious to ask questions. Studs Terkel and the town were abuzz with the revelations. A group of lawyers sent a letter to Phil urging him to keep me on the air in Chicago, bringing up subjects needing to be heard. The author was thrilled with the attention. He said he wished he had explored the subject more than just the two lines. I was not then, or even now, any kind of conspiracy pursuer. What I like to think I am, at times, is a storyteller. Or someone who can find good storytellers. Then and now there is no better material for stories than those surrounding the murder of President Kennedy. Just as I had no inkling two weeks earlier I'd be spending two weeks in Chicago, I had no inkling that, later in life, I'd be spending weeks in Dallas or New Orleans, listening to Jim Garrison's story.

Five years I was at KNBC, and no one asked me to stay. Just two weeks in Chicago and everyone was asking me to stay. I began giving it serious thought. Encouraging me was Sarita. She thought it would be terrific. She said I could fly to Burbank on Friday mornings and return to Chicago Sunday nights. Sarita's biggest ally was Phil's wife.

A passing observation about Sarita's persona that I have marveled at and envied for fifty years that I have never seen in anyone else: Tibetan monks and Indian Swamis are legendary for looking for it. She was born with it. It is the essence of supreme peacefulness. It is almost magnetic. I have seen dozens of the world's best known performers walk on a stage, and capture an audience's attention because they are famous. Sarita is totally unknown, but I have seen her walk onto a stage numerous times, and the crowd is instantly hushed. After our first pleasant dinner, Phil's wife confided in Sarita that her husband was having an affair with his secretary. Every day she looked forward to talking more and more to her. Sarita mentioned I was thinking about staying in Chicago. She blurted out how terrific that would be, saving Phil and ABC the hassle of auditioning others. Hearing that, at our next dinner with them, I told Phil I really liked Chicago, and would love to stay as his host.

"I've already talked to my boss about it," Phil said. "They think you're too controversial."

Phil's wife said, "Controversial, how? You said yourself the audience loves him. Even the ratings show it."

"Honey, I'd love to have him. I brought him here. I know what he can do. But for whatever reason or where or who it came from, they said he was too controversial." He then looked at me. "John, I'm sorry. After the first week I wanted you."

"Thanks, Phil. Thanks to both of you. I'm used to hearing that."

Back at the hotel, with just two days remaining, Sarita decided to go home early, saying she missed the animals. And that she wanted to call Danny Arnold."

"Why Danny?" I asked.

"Remember at dinner one night, Chris Hayward said you should maybe talk to Danny about having him help you develop that show you talked to Ray Stark about?"

"Real people, yeah."

"Well, Chris has already put in a good word for you. You should be doing your own show, not waiting around for somebody to hire you, especially the somebodies in this business who've never done anything in this business. So, I'm going to call Danny."

Sarita and Christopher left on Wednesday. Suddenly Chicago was lonely as well as cold. She called on Friday. "You start a week after you get home."

"Start what?"

"With Danny. You take a week off to rest, then you start. A thousand dollars a week for three to six months to work on your show."

"You're kidding! How did you do that?"

"I called him and told him to hire you because you had a great idea for a show."

Now I didn't even want the hosting job. So, it was with a sincere smile and happy handshake I made the rounds. I mentioned the good news to no one. I didn't want to jinx it, or have someone make a phone call. Howard was the only one to whom I even hinted that something new was afoot.

"Howard," I said, "if you're not thrilled with staying in Chicago, I might be giving you a call to come west."

"I'd love to see Hollywood. And I don't think this new host from what I've seen is going to work out."

The new host was Charlie Rose. And he didn't work out. He ended up somewhere in the Midwest doing a show for nothing ... for a while. He was replaced in Chicago by what a local ABC executive called a necessary minority hire from Baltimore: Oprah Winfrey. Sonia Freeman was fired immediately, but ended up at CNN doing a noon talk show into the late eighties.

Without an inkling, just a blurred picture of where I was going, I was beginning the most exhilarating, rewarding, unpredictable, heartbreaking, roller-coaster ride of my haphazard, accidental career.

Oh, Boy, Oh, Danny Boy

There are dozens of very well-known talented producer-comedy writers in Hollywood for whom this was really a second choice for an occupation. I knew many of them. What they really wanted to be they had failed at; to be a famous comic or actor. Every one of those I knew, although eminently successful behind the camera, always thought they were the real stars of the shows they produced. The most egomaniacal, colorful, screwed up, and frustrating of these was the man with whom I'd be spending the next nine months, Danny Arnold. During those nine months, I was trying to give birth to television's first reality show while Danny 'segomania turned it into an abortion.

Danny was immensely charming, as his ilk of killers are. He was also an alcoholic, workaholic, womanizer, compulsive smoker, and an incorregible heavy gambler. And never wrong. About anything, except the outcome of football games and horse races. After a fling, or big loss, he'd buy his sweet wife, Donna, expensive jewelry she seldom wore. She'd get those about every six weeks. He had two wonderful, ignored teenage sons, Daniel and David, whom Sarita, Christopher and I took to every Kings Hockey game we attended. When we would drive the boys home afterwards, if Danny or Donna weren't in, we'd have to wait in the car until they showed up. Danny never trusted his sons with a house key.

Danny grew up a tough New York Jew. He was fifty-eight when I went to work with him. A little over six feet, about 240 pounds, a fun head of curly grayish hair, a great smile and a great storyteller. He had come to Hollywood wanting to be an actor, but only managed getting parts in two Martin and Lewis films at Paramount. Martin and Lewis liked him, so they hired him to help write their film *The Caddy*. He was good at it. Although it was successful, he found there weren't nearly enough movies being made looking for new writers, but plenty of television shows. He started in live TV with Tennessee Ernie Ford and Rosemary Clooney, then on to the sitcom *The Real McCoys*. He made a major contribution to the pilot of *Bewitched*, moving onto his own production, *That Girl* for ABC with Marlo Thomas. What later justifiably won him The Writers' Guild Lifetime Achievement Award, making him enormously rich, was the superbly written, performed and produced *Barney Miller*, one of only a handful of American sitcoms that could be considered groundbreaking. The show was at its peak in 1978 when I started with him. Much of the success of the show, though, was an accident, out of the hands of Danny. A number of searches as to who was the creator of *Barney Miller* show only the name Danny Arnold. The equal co-creator, however, was writer Ted Flicker. Both were represented as partners by the William Morris office. After the sale to ABC for a thirteen-week commitment, Danny somehow managed to get Ted removed from active participation in the show, ending the partnership.

In my week off prior to starting with Danny, I had lunch with Chris Hayward, along with a brief meeting with Morrie Gelman. Morrie was the widely read columnist in *Daily Variety;* he mentioned me favorably a few times over the years. On that casual occasion when he heard I had some kind of development deal with Danny, he asked me what I was up to. I told him confidently, "I'm going to change the face of American television."

"Doing what?" He laughed.

"I'm going to do what I call the entertainment of reality."

"What on earth is that?"

"It's stories about real people, people who have offbeat or unusual lifestyles."

"Who would want to see that?"

"Everybody. Because it's about everybody. When I was a kid, eight years old, our teacher would read to us, and have us read to the class stories by a guy named Gordon Sinclair. They were all about real people. I loved them. We all did. When I was at NBC, I started pulling these weird wonderful stories off the wire service and thought they would make a great show."

"It doesn't sound like much to me, but good luck with it. You're working with a powerful producer."

The next day my comment, which I thought was off the record, showed up in Morrie's column, prompting the call from Chris. He came down from his beautiful home halfway up the Hollywood Hills to have lunch with me. He got right to the point.

"Are you sure you want to get involved with Danny? Your show idea sounds kinda interesting. There must be other producers around, like David Wolper, who do decent documentaries. Have you talked to him?"

"No. I have to earn a living. Danny's paying me a thousand a week for the six months or so that I'm putting it together. You know, Chris, I've done what I thought was a lot of good work, but no one, I mean no one, is calling me. It's disheartening."

"You don't know what disheartening is until you work with Danny."

"You worked with him, it couldn't have been that bad."

Chris had a badly withered left hand, a childhood deformity. It made it difficult for him to hold a golf club, a game which he loved, a game we played often from Pebble Beach to San Diego. He held both his hands up in front of my face.

"Danny starts out like this." He raised his right hand, his good one. "Then ends up like this." He waved his deformed left hand.

"Jesus, Chris. But I have no place else to go. You still see him, and isn't he always calling you to come back?"

"Yeah. But I'm here with you. I don't like to tell stories about people. Especially in this business because you never know when you're gonna be working for or with them. But, I love you and your family, and I especially like your work, the things you say. It's no wonder no one is calling you. So, I'm gonna tell you a few stories about Danny, which I trust you'll never repeat. They'll prepare you for the worst, which will come, which will show you how totally self-absorbed he is."

No one was in a better position to know Danny Arnold professionally than Chris. Not only was he a principal writer-producer of the show, but the one who saved it from certain oblivion after the first thirteen weeks of weak ratings. Chris and Danny are dead. So, "for the rest of the story" as Paul Harvey used to intone on his radio show, I'll repeat as best I can the stories and forewarnings imparted to me that day by Chris. Listening to him, I was so proud he was my son's Godfather.

"John, he has no idea of what kind of show you are thinking about. Nobody does. Because it's never been done before. But if it works, believe me, no one will ever hear your name. It'll all be his doing. He takes credit for everything. And never the blame for screw ups. And there are plenty. I won't go into how he got rid of Ted Flicker. We had a good writing team. They'd think up various ideas and pitch them to Danny. Danny would pick one, tell them how he wanted it done, and they'd go and do it. A few days later they'd bring it to him and he'd tear it to pieces, screaming that if they were cops they couldn't even write traffic tickets. They'd show him the notes showing that's what he asked for. He'd scream bullshit. He never said that. This happened so often, instead of taking notes, they decided to record him. Once again, Danny told them how to do it right this time so he didn't have to rewrite their shit again. A couple of days later they brought it to him as he had instructed. Danny cursed them out again, threatening to fire their sorry asses. He needed younger writers who paid attention. They told him they had followed his exact instructions. He screamed that it wasn't like anything he wanted.

"With that, they opened their briefcase and placed the small tape recorder on his desk, and played it. Listening, Danny's face got all flushed. He smashed his fist on the recorder, and yelled, 'You guys've been here long enough. That may be what I said, but you should know what I meant!'"

I laughed out loud. "Did he fire them?"

"No. He needs punching bags. Also he didn't want to hire another hooker.'

"A hooker? To do what? Write?"

"No. To hump, but deducted it by getting her into the Writers Guild."

I laughed again. I had to hear this one. "What happened?"

"You'll find if you last long enough, that Danny only cares about three things: money, his cock, and his heart. He has a safe under his staircase half filled with gold coins. He is so concerned about having a heart attack, he has installed a buzzer on the headboard of his bed that leads directly to the fire department. You know, John, I am no one to talk about marriage or fidelity, having screwed up my life and marriage. So, telling you about Danny's flings is in no way passing some kind of moral judgment. But he could have paid a hooker five hundred bucks and had it over with. Instead, he picks this bimbo who wants to be a writer. Minimum is five thousand dollars. He pays her, writes the script, she gets in the Guild, and gets into his bed whenever Donna and the kids are in Palm Springs. One Sunday morning she wakes up and Danny's not there. He's in the bathroom. She gets hungry. She thinks the maid's in the kitchen. So, she sees this buzzer. Of course, she thinks it's a buzzer to the kitchen, and pushes it. Nothing happens. So, she keeps pushing it. When Danny comes out of the bathroom standing at the foot of the bed naked, she asks him why the maid didn't answer the buzzer. He asks, what buzzer? She points to it. Danny said he didn't have a chance to answer. There was a thunderous explosion at the front doors. They had been battered open by paramedics and firemen, four or five altogether..."

Chris could not finish the story I was laughing so hard. "Is ... is that true? Did Danny tell you that?"

Chris smiled. "She's in the Guild!"

"Chris, tell me, about when you worked on the first thirteen weeks, working with him. And why wasn't the show cancelled as everyone thought it would be?"

"Do you remember any of the first shows at all?" he asked.

"Not really. It just looked like another living room sitcom."

"At first it was. Exactly like the format for *That Girl* with Marlo Thomas. Half the show took place in Hal Linden's apartment, the other half in the precinct. I kept telling him to make it like *Detective Story,* the movie with Kirk Douglas. Danny said no one would watch a grubby police station for a half hour, and said no way. I told him no one was watching anyway, so why not try it? He kept putting me off. He gave up, though, when he thought the show was going to be cancelled anyway. He said 'What the hell, give it a shot Chris. Last show. What do you have in mind?' I said a snowstorm that forces them to stay in the precinct. They can't get home. That's what I wrote. Chris Shickel at *Time* happens to see the show, and writes about it. The next day it was renewed."

"That's amazing," I blurted.

"What is more amazing is, Danny never thought just being in the precinct would last, that they'd have to go home to the apartment. And for five years kept Barbara Barrie under contract as Hal's wife and only used her four times. She was even luckier than him. Got paid for five years and didn't have to work with him."

"Chris, I can't thank you enough for being interested, but I don't think I'll have any problems."

"As I said, John, nobody has any idea what you are talking about."

"I start Monday, so I hope you don't mind if I call you occasionally."

"That's what godfathers are for. But, whatever you do, make sure you register stuff immediately with the Guild before you show it to anyone. Good luck. I hope it works out."

Danny's offices and studio where *Barney Miller* was filmed were in the ABC complex on Vine Street. His production company was called Four D Productions, the first initial of his wife's, two boys and his name. My tiny enterprise would become Chrisita Corporation, for my wife and son.

At our first meeting, Sarita and I sat in rather small, ordinary chairs across from Danny, who sat behind a desk the size of a barge.

"John," Danny said, "this is a new venture for me. Sarita and Chris tell me that you have a great original idea for a show. Never been done before." He then held up *The Daily Variety* "That you're gonna change the face of American TV!" He laughed, a condescending laugh. Then added, "I don't think audiences give a shit about little people."

"Danny, they're not little people, they're real people. They just happen to live different lifestyles than most of us, or pursue different interests."

"For example?"

"Well, one you'd be interest in. There's a gorgeous brunette in New York, a burlesque star who bills herself as The Stripper for God. She says God told her to show her beautiful natural God-made body to the world."

"Do you have a picture of her?"

"A dozen of them. And her phone number. I've already interviewed her, knowing I'd be working here with you. She's wonderful."

"Can I see her?"

"See, there you go." I smiled. "See how interested you are. You can see her in the pilot, and I've got dozens of great stories to choose from."

"How do you write this stuff?"

"You don't. You just shape it. They tell their own stories."

"What are you calling it?"

"National Graffiti. A lot of the stories come out of *The National Enquirer*. I loved the movie *American Graffiti*. If there hadn't been that film, that's what I'd call it."

"I don't like the word graffiti."

Sarita said, "Danny, it's perfect. These are people who'd never otherwise be seen. They are sort of visual graffiti."

"I still don't like it," Danny said. "It can be the working title until we come up with something better. What time do you see this playing?"

"Early evening. It could be the perfect family show. There's something for everyone."

"Well, it's gonna have to be late night. I talked to Lew Ehrlich at ABC and told him we were trying this thing. He was intrigued, but said it sounded more like late night, and if the pilot is decent, he'll give us a week's run. Have you got enough material for five half hours?"

"Absolutely. Once on the air, the audience will become our researchers and sources, believe me."

"Can you get all this together in thirteen weeks?"

"I thought I was going to have six or nine months!"

"If you think you need it. Who's gonna host this thing?"

"I think there should be three hosts. Different personalities for different stories. I'd be one, then we'd get two unknowns."

"Why you? And why unknowns? You need stars. The audience wants to watch somebody they know."

Sarita said, "Why not John? There's no one better on camera, and he has a bunch of Emmys, Golden Mikes and reviews to prove it."

Danny softened quickly, as he often did around her. "Sarita, that's not what I meant. I meant, I thought he may just want to produce it. He'd be fine. Naturally, but you still need a couple of names."

I was beginning to feel uncomfortable, Ted Flicker uncomfortable. "Danny, you said yourself this is a new venture for you. It is a new venture for television. That you're giving me this opportunity is terrific, and I'm extremely grateful. If you leave me alone to put this together as I see it and write it, of course I'll run everything by you so nothing is a surprise, I will make you more famous and richer than you are now. It's your production company, Four D, in smaller print in association with Chrisita Corporation. You'll own sixty percent, I'll get forty. I'll get a small royalty as creator, and you get whatever fee for 'developed by.' I'll have a host fee, a writer's fee, a producer's fee. You get, deservedly so, the largest hunk as executive producer and a joint copyright. I think we should take a little time just to put a couple of paragraphs on paper so we all know where we stand."

I had never talked like that before. Because of my anxiety over Chris's warnings, I wanted to avoid upfront the conflict and interference I'd had with John McMahon and at KABC. I was surprised by Danny's sudden warmth.

"John, I love you, and your work. I love Sarita, and I love your son's godfather. Right now, there's no need to put anything on paper because right now we have nothing. The show is yours. You run it your way. I agree with everything you've said. If it doesn't work out, it doesn't work out, we'll still be friends, and it's yours."

"I only want thirteen weeks. Nothing more. I work better on a deadline, and if it doesn't work out the way I'm sure it will, and I go elsewhere, I'll refund the thirteen thousand."

"No, you won't. The money is yours. For the pleasure of your company. And so is whatever we end up calling this thing." He got up from his desk, shook my hand and hugged Sarita. "See Jordan Davis, my accountant, about your check, and try to keep costs down. I'll set up a meeting for you with Ehrlich. Let's have some fun."

"The only cost I see right now is as assistant producer. I met this fellow in Chicago, Howard Schultz. He's terrific. Can I hire him, four or five hundred a week?"

"If he's paying his own way out."

At the end of the week, Howard was in my office.

The first thing l had to do, and quickly, considering I only had thirteen weeks and reservations about Danny, was put together not just a pilot script, but all five shows. I did this in one day. I also added two small departments at the suggestion of Sergio Aragonés, a close friend, and one of the country's quickest and brightest cartoonists with a popular running feature, *I Spy*, in *National Lampoon*. One of those he suggested was right out of *National Lampoon*, a one-page feature, *Signs of the Times*: a page of photographs of funny real signs found on highways, store windows, and billboards; the other was a short feature about newspaper and magazine misprints, doctors or lawyers with weird names and similar items. Those two short segments would allow our cast, whoever it was, to have some playful byplay, plus encourage viewers to send in material.

America is a nation of consumers. Every major store has a Department of Consumer Complaints. We would have one, too. For our consumer advocate, I engaged an enthusiastic and funny Jackie Mason. Having all the stories and material, putting the scripts and intros together, was simple. On the third day, I registered all five scripts with the Writers Guild as Chris had suggested. The following day I walked into Danny's office and put them on his desk.

"What's this?"

"The first five shows."

He opened the top one. His eyes bulged at seeing The Writers Guild stamp; then he closed it. "I'll send these over to Ehrlich. I don't need to read them; just give me a quick overview."

"There are four stories I'll shoot, and we'll pick the three best. The Stripper for God, Roy Reep, the unluckiest man in the world according to *The Guinness Book of Records,* a lawyer in New York, Kaplan, who claims he's the only professional vampire hunter in America, and the King of Oyutunji–"

"What the fuck is that?" Danny blurted.

"A black guy who bought acreage in South Carolina and declared it a separate country from the U.S. He has already notified the State Department and UN, and has thirty-five converted Oyutunji citizens living in African huts."

"That's fuckin' nuts!"

"But it's true! He's articulate and dresses like a king." I then told Danny of the two little departments our cast would present and our occasional Consumer Advocate, Jackie Mason.

"What makes you think you can get Jackie Mason?"

"I've already talked to him. He said he'd do it for fifteen hundred."

He stared at me. I couldn't tell if he was impressed or pissed. "I'll tell Lew to see you as soon as possible, then you can put together a schedule and crew."

Two days later I got the call from Danny to see Lew Ehrlich. It would be the most uncomfortable, unpleasant meeting I had to date – until a worse one a year later with Freddy Silverman. ABC seemed to hire executives based on how much they hated me.

Fred Silverman was the boy-wonder programmer first at CBS; one would wonder how the boy kept his job after canceling *Hollywood Squares,* pontificating that it would never work. It became one of NBC's and America's favorite shows. He had told my agent years earlier, in front of me, but not to my face, that I'd never make it in television because I was "too soft." If Fred Silverman was stranded in the Sahara Desert and an original thought would create Niagara Falls, he would die of thirst.

Silverman was hired away from ABC by a desperate NBC to become their Head of Prime time. He signed a huge contract with a couple of stiff restrictions. First, he had to leave ABC immediately. Second, he was to have no contact for six months with anyone at NBC or ABC. It would be a long vacation for Freddy, a better one than he could ever have imagined. Most of it was spent at Danny Arnold's home in Hawaii, all paid for by Danny. That tidbit of information meant nothing to me when Danny gleefully told me about it. But accidentally, within a year, it would change my life, and television forever.

Lew Ehrlich's dark, unsmiling countenance and let's-get-this-over-in-a-hurry greeting made me feel like an intruder. He held up the five scripts, waving them as if he were looking for a trash can. After plopping them on his desk, he said, "We're only doing this because of Danny."

"I'm well aware of that. But, believe me, it'll work."

"You're gonna be one of the hosts, along with Steve Landesburg?"

I was stunned. "Steve Landesburg, no. This is not–"

"Danny told me he was. I like Steve. Everybody does."

"This is not a show to be hosted by stars. The stars are the people profiled. I told Danny that. Landesburg is news to me. Let me pick some hosts, then you–"

"Who would you pick? Besides yourself?"

"Well, if you think one of them should have marquee value, I'd like to have Richard Pryor."

His face flushed with anger, as did his voice. "Are you kidding? Richard Pryor? That nigger's never getting on this network, and no other. He's facing assault charges for punching out an executive at NBC, and the IRS is going to put him in prison. Are you crazy?"

"I know he's had some problems, but I've seen him on stage. He puts five thousand people into auditoriums all around the country. He's going to be huge."

"Black auditoriums. The chitlin circuit and jail is where he'll end up. Landesburg is Danny's pick for a host, so it's Landesburg."

"Mr. Ehrlich, he isn't right for this kind of show!"

"What kind of show? We don't even know what it is. I've got five scripts here, and I don't even know what I'm looking at. Just a little chit chat then film clips."

"That's it. The film clips are the stars. They will make the hosts stars, but it's better if they're unknown.'

"Pryor's not unknown."

"That's true," I conceded.

"And I'll tell you what else is true. As I said before, we're only doing this, whatever this is, because of Danny. Danny Arnold is king in television. And you mean shit to television."

I couldn't believe that asshole would say something so blunt to me. Or anyone. "I wouldn't call five Emmys and a Golden Mike shit. And let me tell you something that is also true. There are thousands of Xerox machines in this town, but only half a dozen original typewriters, and I own one of them. I am sorry that this meeting didn't go better for us, but I assure you that the show will. Thank you."

I rose deliberately, walking out without extending a hand he wouldn't take anyway. I went immediately back to Danny's office to tell him what had transpired. Ehrlich's phone call beat my car.

"Wow, what did you say to him? Jesus!"

"It's not so much what I said to him; it's what he said to me. He said you were king in television, and that I was shit."

Danny howled with laughter. "Don't worry about it. Just remember, in Hollywood, first you sell 'em, then you fuck 'em!" He laughed again.

I wanted to tell Danny that Landesburg was not right, that he should have at least consulted me, but I figured Landesburg couldn't screw up short introductions, so I let it pass. I also didn't want to challenge him when he suggested the female co-host be an actress he was interested in. What I didn't let pass, though, was the thought that now Danny had sold ABC, he was he about to fuck me. It wasn't a co-host I thought about, it was a lawyer. Danny was a Goliath in town. I was no David. I put a call in to Chris Hayward. Each day, more and more, I felt I was traveling a road with Danny filling with sinkholes. I had no control over what was happening.

What kept me focused was that I had the opportunity to go across the country with a crew, camera and microphone, and put on film stories of real people, stories of the human comedy I long wanted to tell. I was confident they'd be so good, all the intrigue and politics would disappear. And the potholes would become highways.

Before shooting those stories, I got a call from Sinatra. I hadn't heard from him in months. I had his home phone number in Palm Springs and his private office number. He told me to call whenever I felt like it. I never felt like it. He was not the kind of person you have as a friend. He anoints you. Our chats were always upbeat and warm; he always referred to me as a friend, but I never considered him one. Dean and Sammy were his friends. I was nowhere in that league. His calls to me were always an unexpected bonus.

"Do you think you'd have the time to help me with a couple of things? I'm at a Friars' Roast in a few days. I'd like you on the dais, and maybe help with some jokes."

"That'd be wonderful. Thank you."

"Also, I'm pissed at *People* magazine. Dorothy'll send over the details. I want to send them a nasty letter." He chuckled. "Would you mind?"

"Not at all. I've wanted to send them a few myself."

"Well, this one you'll sign my name to."

"I'd be delighted."

"Good. In a few months, I'll be takin' some time off. Maybe you could come down to the Springs and we could chat about my Italian Roots. I'm interested."

Ninety minutes later a messenger arrived from Sinatra's office with a copy of *People*, a couple of notes on the piece Francis wanted to respond to, and ten crisp one hundred-dollar bills.

My brief response to *People*, which was forwarded to him and then to the editor, is referenced briefly in Kitty Kelly's unauthorized biography of Sinatra, *His Way*. That same week myself and a crew of four, including a director, Don Davis, whom I didn't know, but who was recommended by Danny's accountant, headed out on the road. Danny and everyone who heard the stories of the people I was profiling could not restrain themselves from commenting how weird or bizarre they were. I planned on doing the same in the editing room. Intermittently, I was going to intercut brief comments I'd gather from people on the street; the same kinds of comments I knew viewers would have while watching them.

In Chicago, I accidentally stumbled upon gold: Richard Pryor. We were on Michigan Avenue shooting our third man in the street when he just walked over to say hello.

"Johnny, is this the thing you said you wanted me for?"

"Yes, I'm sorry it didn't work out. They picked Landesburg over my objections."

"The dude's funny."

"I didn't want funny. I wanted real. But the stories are great." Then it hit me. Who could be a better man on the street, commenting on these unusual people and lifestyles than Richard Pryor? Especially getting his comments on the King of Oyutunji? Ehrlich would be pissed, but fuck Ehrlich. It was my show. I mentioned this to Richard.

He grinned. "Roll the cameras!"

He gave us twenty minutes of opinions, observations and comments about every story, which ended up in the final pieces. (They are still in my archives.)

Ten days later we were all packed, stories in the can, on a plane back to LAX. There was never a happier, more boisterous, laugh-filled trip on an airliner. It was long before the days of Homeland Security. Our crew was in the tail end. Even without the numerous cocktails some had, we were screaming with laughter. Each one of us took turns telling the stories of the people we had just put on film. One weird incident would remind someone of another weird one, and off we'd go. The kicker was when we catalogued the endless calamity that had befallen poor Roy Reep, the Unluckiest Man in The World. Each disaster to befall him led to more hilarity. It ended with the final indignity. His ex-wife, jealous over this sixty-seven-year old's affair with a twenty-year-old hooker, broke into his motor home and shot him in the mouth. The bullet bounced off his partials and out his cheek. He needed repairs to his palate. The doctors screwed up, creating an even bigger hole. When Roy tried to eat, food squirted out his nose.

I couldn't wait to tell Danny how fabulous the shoots were, how they would be shaped into riveting hilarious stories. But others were also anxious to tell him. At first, I was pleased to hear how everyone was running to him about how good the material was. There was something about this "too many cooks" business, though, that made me uncomfortable. I was made even more uncomfortable when I was summoned to a private meeting with Danny. When I walked in, he was on the phone, all smiles. He was telling somebody on the phone the Roy Reep story in its entirety.

"Yeah. Real people. Then we've got this stripper for God! Unbelievable stuff. I'm gonna change the face of America television!"

I stiffened. What did he mean, "*He's* going to change the face of American television?" What was he saying? And to whom? Jesus Christ, Chris was right. I was feeling helpless.

He hung up, all puffed up and pleased. I stared at him in disbelief. He either didn't notice my displeasure or ignored it. I didn't have to ask to whom he was talking. Bragging was part of his persona.

"That was Freddy Silverman!"

"I thought he wasn't supposed to talk to–"

"Danny laughed. "He's staying at my place in Hawaii."

"I thought he wasn't supposed to have-–"

Danny ignored my comment. "I hear it went great. I can't wait to see the stuff."

"I should have the first couple of stories for you to look at in a couple of days.

"I've got Don down in editing working on them now."

I was seething. "Danny, he's not editing my stories. I'm doing that."

"John, he's in the Director's Guild. They're required to get the first cut."

"*After* the writer has finished with them. I am the writer." I got up to leave.

"Let him have a pass at it!"

"No. After the pilot is taped in the studio and the show is finished, then he can have his director's pass. Danny, you arbitrarily picked Steve for my show. *My* show. You didn't even ask me. He is totally all wrong for it, which you'll see when we finally get on stage. Just leave me alone, as you promised, and if it's not perfect, you can fix it."

I rushed to the editing room and told Don as calmly as I could I was going to begin editing. He told me he was editing, that he wasn't finished, that as the director, he had first cut.

"Don, I'll tell you what I just told Danny. This is not a movie. Not a director's show. This is a writer's show. I am not only the writer, I am as you can see on the credits, the creator. I'm going to edit now, which is part of the writing process. SO GET OUT TILL I AM FINISHED!"

He rose, pushing the chair back. "Fuck you." And slammed the door.

The need for a lawyer, or a hit man, was looming larger. Chris informed me most of the lawyers he knew were friends of Danny Arnold's and that consulting one of them would not be a good idea. In desperation, I called my friend, my first publicist, to whom I hadn't spoken in seven years, Joe Seigman. Joe was a bright, struggling publicist in 1970 who out of nowhere called and volunteered to do publicity for me for nothing for my *AM Show.* For a few months he got my name in the papers when McMahon wouldn't. We had little contact when the show ended. If anyone deserved success, it was Joe. Over the years I was delighted to see him grow. He was now producing a couple of syndicated shows, one about bowling and the other showcasing new comics, one of whom was Jay Leno. Among his client list as a publicist was America's biggest TV star, Carroll O'Connor of *All in the Family*. I was reluctant to make the call, but too panicked not to. He could not have been nicer.

After hearing me out, he chuckled. "Jesus, John. Danny Arnold is not just God, he is Godzilla. My guy wouldn't be right for you, but I know of one who might be. Nathan Markowitz. I don't know the guy personally," Joe said, "but I know his partner, a nice guy. Howard Abelese. He's the stepfather of Melissa Gilbert, the girl on *Little House on the Prairie*. His partner he says is one tough sonofabitch. Sort of a Jewish James Bond. They're on Wilshire near LaCienega. Keep me posted."

I met with Markowitz and Abelese the next day, offering them whatever fee they wanted for a half-hour consultation. They declined the fee. As Joe said, Abelese, the older one, in his early fifties, was laid back and dignified. Nathan, in his mid-forties, was quiet, firm, unsmiling and confident. Like a lot of good partnerships, they were exact opposites. I recounted my brief turbulent experiences asking what I could do legally, to further protect myself.

"You've already done that by registering your stuff with the guild," Nathan said. "You don't have a written contract with Danny, just a verbal contract, which often holds up in court. Any witnesses to it?"

"Just my wife and Chris Hayward."

"So far you're on safe ground. You're just dealing with pricks whose word you hope they keep. Just keep going and let us know what happens. It sounds interesting. Different, anyway. We'd be glad to help. Money's not an issue."

I made up my mind then and there, that if and when I needed a lawyer, it'd be Markowitz. I did need him.

There's No Business...

I told Nathan I was not in immediate need of hiring him, but certain I would be calling him.

"John, knowing this business and these people you might be calling sooner than you think. Even if you don't need our services, my wife and I are fans. Would you and your wife be up for a dinner out?"

Sarita and I had a few pleasant dinners with them at Trader Vics, the Polo Lounge, and later at their expansive beautiful single-story home on Mulholland Drive near Laurel Canyon. I learned why Joe called him the Jewish James Bond. He told us of the escapades of his unnamed gun-running clients. About bank accounts on the Cayman Islands, where he put one of his lady client's half a million dollars, suggesting we do the same when the show was a hit. One client had old news footage of Pancho Villa in Mexico. Because of Sarita, he had his client give it to me. I still have a copy. Nathan's wife never joined in those conversations. When at home, she listened bemused, stroking the little white poodle on her lap.

One night leaving Trader Vics, Sarita asked me if I noticed a couple of men in suits staring at us from a nearby table. I told her it was probably two guys who thought she was a movie star. The same thing happened again, though, when leaving their home. Parked just in front of our car was another with two men in suits sitting in the front in the dark.

"What's that?" Sarita whispered.

Trying to be funny, I said, "I don't know. Either fairies or feds." Two years later I found out they weren't fairies. And it wasn't funny.

Finally, the evening came at KCOP to shoot our pilot, still called *National Grafitti*. The first piece of bad news, though, was that Sarita and Christopher could not make it. I was devastated. I always considered my wife and son my good luck charms. She called saying Christopher had such a bad cold she would not even leave him with Margaret, our babysitting retired nurse.

"That's all right," Sarita said, "Edna and all her friends will be there. You'll have a lot of support."

Edna was our 300-pound part-time cook and full-time friend. When she died a few years later, she left her home in Compton to Sarita. Sarita turned it back over to her family in Detroit. Edna, true to her word, gathered up thirty of her cooking, cleaning, sewing circle, and choir-singing friends and filled the seats. And fill the seats they did.

As in *Barney Miller*, Steve Landesburg delivered his lines in a slow sing-song voice. The actress Danny had picked was just as bad. Jackie Mason was worse. He was not even there. He had called in the morning to say he had a five-thousand-dollar gig in Palm springs, and could he do it another day? I told him that would be fine; I'd introduce it and we would tape and insert him another day. All that negative stuff wasn't just bad omens – it was a train full of tragedy bearing down on me, and I was tied to the tracks.

The three finished stories, though, were wonderful. As out of place and as bad as Steve and the girl were, the stories got howls and applause. Even more when they saw a sparkling Richard Pryor commenting on the King of Oyutunji. The clapping and laughter grew with the next two stories: Roy Reep and the Stripper for God. Edna's people were talking back to the screen. "Oh, pray for her. Oh, Jesus and Mary!" This created more laughter among the crew and cameramen.

I was thrilled with what I had done. But I had the sinking feeling I was also done. Within minutes, I was.

When the show ended, Ehrlich signaled Danny that he wanted to talk to him. I tried to follow. Ehrlich turned and said, "Nice what you did with Pryor," then led Danny away.

I called after him. "I told you I could make Pryor work and I told you the stories were the stars. Did you hear the reaction to the stories?" Everybody was staring at me.

"Probably your friends," Ehrlich said.

I stepped closer and got louder. "You can't fake laughter. Even you laughed. It's the hosts you guys picked that are the disaster."

Danny said, "We'll talk later."

"No, Danny, we'll talk now. It's my show."

"It's Danny's show," Ehrlich hissed.

"It is *my* show, and why don't you two guys who have no idea what it is about just get out of my way and let me do it my way. It's the stories. The stories!" I was in such a rage I knew if I didn't leave immediately, I'd end up like Richard Pryor punching a network executive.

I don't remember the drive home in the dark. Thankfully, Christopher was feeling better and asleep. I told Sarita how horribly it had all gone, that Edna and her friends were wonderful, that the stories went fantastic, but that there was no question Chris had warned me accurately; Danny was going to squeeze me out. If he did, not only would the show be destroyed, so would the idea. What network would want a show about real people after a star producer like Arnold could not make it work? No one. How could I stop him?

"Call Nathan," Sarita said calmly.

It was late. I woke him up. I apologized, recounting quickly the events, and ended by telling Nathan I did not think Danny would be keeping his word to me and Sarita that the show was mine and I would be free to take it elsewhere if ABC passes.

"John," Nathan said calmly. "ABC may not pass. They may just pass on you."

"But it's my show. It's all registered at the Guild."

"That may be a legal battle you cannot afford. If they go ahead, we can sue them"

"But he'll destroy the show and the concept."

There was a long pause. "Then, John, beat him to it."

"What do you mean?"

"Do you have tape copies of your stories?"

"No."

"The scripts and content of the tapes are yours. The physical tapes are his. See if you can get them. Make copies. And call me tomorrow."

I hung up and told Sarita I'd be right back. Within minutes I was back at Vine Street rushing to the fortunately still unlocked editing rooms. The solo editor's greeting was cooler than usual. He was rewinding a one-inch tape. The box had 'Grafitti Master' on it.

"When you're done, could I borrow it for an hour?"

"No. Danny said not to give it to you. Sorry."

That did not surprise me. I just needed the individual stories. "That's okay. Thanks anyway. See you tomorrow."

Casually, I rushed to where the originals were on the shelf. All four of them. I felt like a kid stealing money out of milk bottles in the dead of winter. In an all-night editing facility on Burbank Boulevard, I copied them to three-quarter inch. At nine in the morning with no sleep, I returned the tapes unseen, then made my way to Danny's office, adrenaline pumping, not knowing whether to be calm or confrontational. Danny made up my mind with his first comment.

"Well, that was a pile of shit!"

"Danny, that was your pile of shit. Mine was the gold that you buried it in. If you'd left me alone as promised, you'd have had a hit. If you're not going to let me redo it right, my way, then just give me my material, as you also promised. Or is that another promise you're not keeping?"

"No, I'm going to redo it."

"You haven't the foggiest fucking idea of how to do anything real, let alone this show."

"Howard's going to redo it. He said all along he could do it better than you, so I'm going to give him a shot."

Howard? *My Howard*. The guy I brought out from Chicago? Hearing that was almost as much of a painful blow as trying to make Danny live up to his word. "Jesus, Danny, he knows less than you. It'll be a disaster. Just give me my tapes and I'll be on my way."

"The tapes are mine."

"The content is mine."

He smirked a smirk of someone who knows he has you by the balls. I let him think he was crushing them and me, as powerful people like him like to do. Control. It's their orgasm. "The tapes are locked in your editing bays."

"That's right!"

"And my tapes, with my content, are locked in my house."

His face contorted. "I am going to be redoing it with Howard. Ehrlich said the sooner the better."

"No, you won't, you lying sack of shit. For three reasons. First, you are incapable of keeping your word. You are incapable of doing a show you don't understand, and once you announce it, I will sue your unfaithful ass!" (I was thinking of the buzzer on the bed board story when I said that.) His face and neck flushed. He looked like he was going to have a heart attack.

No announcements were ever made by his company.

Again, I had no job. No income. Very little savings. But I was still enthused by what I had proven at KCOP. The stories were the stars. Surely, somewhere in that town there was someone who could see just a little of what l saw.

Two weeks later, Chris called. He said Danny had called him, told him he was sorry about what happened with me; that he felt bad and was not going to redo the pilot, and if he saw me to wish me luck.

"Chris, Danny is full of shit."

"John, that's what he said."

"He didn't say it to me!"

"What are you gonna do now?"

"Well, you once mentioned David Wolper, so I guess I'll start there."

Giving Up

"Giving Up" seems like a rather depressing heading for this brief chapter, but that's what it was. A giving up. It happened on the tenth of January,1979, the month of my son's tenth birthday. In preparation for his party, I felt the greatest gift I could give him was the constant secure presence of a loving father; not the uncertainty of a performer father struggling in a haphazard, cruel business to make a living, let alone a difference. I had decided to quit being a performer of any kind. I wasn't even going to call Francis. I was just going to be a fulltime father, and hopefully, a part-time joke writer. I remember everything about that moment. Where I was. The feel of the day and the sunlight. I was standing on the corner of Forman and Valley Spring Lane, across from Lakeside Country Club and our little bungalow, the smallest house in Toluca Lake. It is as clear to me today as is the keyboard on which I write this. This is why I was standing there and giving up:

A couple of weeks earlier I had taken the pilot tapes to David Wolper, who was delighted to sit with me and look at them. David was a respected and intelligent producer, documentary and filmmaker in Hollywood. He made scores of award winning documentaries about everything and everyone. Reality and history were the sources for his material. He also produced two successful sitcoms, *Chico and the Man* and *Welcome Back, Kotter,* as well as one of TV's most successful mini-series, *Roots.* One would assume those accolades would create in him an ego all pumped and postured, but bragging was as alien to him as truth-telling was to Danny Arnold. He was one of the most accessible and gracious people I ever met. To have him readily agree to see me, someone he'd never met, on one quick phone call, was a compliment in itself.

Before screening the clips, I filled him in on the entire history of my little project, from Ray Stark to Danny Arnold. He chuckled frequently during the screenings. "You edited this? It is funny! I do like it. And I like the idea of real people stories in television. My problem is this…" My stomach tightened. "With a sitcom you can sometimes replace the stars, and certainly replace the writers, and still have a show that works. The problem is this is obviously put together as you write it, your view of the human comedy. How would I replace you, if something happened to you?"

I wasn't sure how to answer that, but said, "All I know, Mr. Wolper, is it would be huge and you'd never run out of material."

"That's not what I'm saying. Where is the show if it runs out of you?"

"I don't know. Maybe we could just do it for five years then retire."

He laughed, a warm laugh. "I don't feel it's quite right for me. No question I like it and no question it'll succeed. Can I think about it for a while? What I'd actually be doing, like impresario Sol Hurok presenting violinist Isaac Stern, is being David Wolper presenting John Barbour. It's an alien feeling, so can I think about it a bit?"

While waiting for that call, I met with one of the most applauded producers in town. He worked hard to promote that image, almost more than he worked to promote his show, *The Mary Tyler Moore Show*. And it was an image. Over the next ten years, trying to work with him, I was to learn I was talking to a very charming empty suit. Or in his case, an empty sweater. His name was Grant Tinker, husband of Mary Tyler Moore. I say empty sweater because in an effort to create a posture of down to earth, everyman casualness, he always wore a sweater. Then he insisted all his important male employees from writers to directors do the same. Which they dutifully did. It became the fashion uniform of mediocrity.

The meeting in Grant's office had been set by Artie Price. At the time, I was much more in awe of Tinker than I was of Wolper. I had read his endless press releases. I believed them, like those about Schlatter. The amazing thing is, I was in awe in spite of the fact Wolper had scores of great shows behind him. Tinker was involved with only one. Such is the power of the Press. And the depth of my gullibility.

As with Wolper, I was quick to inform Tinker of the project's troubled history. As did all who saw the stories, Grant and Artie chuckled and smiled. They watched two of the tapes.

"It's interesting and amusing in a weird way," Grant said. "But it's not for me. I wouldn't know what to do with it. And with your problems at ABC."

There was only one name left in town to call, Pierre Cossette. Pierre was a fan whom I'd met casually over the years. He was primarily a fan because he was also from Canada. He was born in Quebec, became quite a successful Broadway producer, then more famous for initiating and producing The Grammys. Mine was certainly not his kind of show, but because he was successful and accessible, and my last chance, I called. To my surprise, he loved it. His reaction was not just pleasant, but enthusiastic.

"John, it is wonderful stuff. You have more?"

"Yes, much more. On tape already, and dozens of great stories on file."

"It's like nothing I've ever seen. I will be tied up for six weeks or so, but l can get us facilities at KTLA. We can get together to talk about maybe doing a pilot. Maybe a half hour. Maybe an hour. What's to lose? I'll be in touch. If not, you call me."

He didn't call, for weeks. His silence pulled the plug on my enthusiasm.

So, there I was, a warm sunny day, standing at the corner of Forman and Valley Spring saying out loud that I wasn't going to do this any longer. I had gone for a walk to be by myself. What was in my heart was transparent in my face. Had I stayed in the house, Sarita and Christopher would be asking me what was wrong. I had stopped across from my house, staring at it, imagining Christopher and Sarita inside. I had stopped walking because I had stopped daydreaming.

All the meetings I mentioned above, I relived during that stroll. I relived the images and people and the work I'd done over the years. Most of it good. Multiple awards, great reviews. What good had it done? Where did it get me? How could I have been so goddamned impressionable, believing all that Hollywood crap I saw as a kid? Wasn't I smarter than that? Evidently not. I was forty-six years old.

I loved where we lived. Our first little house. Large lush lawns fronted all the gorgeous houses. The leaves of the tall trees lining the golf course fluttered in a soft breeze. People played golf. Ladies walked their dogs. I looked at our house number, 4254 Forman Avenue. Four was my lucky number. A lot of fours in that address. I was out of work much to the delight of many folks whose work I hammered. My modest income from *Los Angeles Magazine* would not pay my mortgage.

Unlike showbiz success, a great child, and great wife and mother came to me easily. The stuff I had planned and worked for fell apart. Every time. Christopher would be ten in nineteen days. He would need me more than he did when he was five, six, or seven. Every ounce of ambition in every cell in my body just drained out of me. Astonishingly, though, my whole being was filled with a contentment and peace I would never feel again. With that simple decision, I became what I now wanted to be, somebody to my son. I was floating as I crossed the street to go home, smiling with wet eyes when I opened the door. I was Judy coming back to Kansas. There's no place like home.

Indeed, four was my lucky number. I had a one of a kind child, a one of a kind wife, in a house full of hugs. From where I had begun, no one could get any luckier than me. But, from out of nowhere, I got even luckier.

The Best Things Happen by Accident

If you look back on your life and the good things that happened to improve it, you'd probably find most of them happened by accident; while most of the things that went wrong, were well planned. That has been, and still is, the case with me. As was the next phone call I got within hours of deciding never to perform again. That call resulted in another accidental encounter that changed my life and television.

I was in a perfect place mentally when the call came. Digby Wolf said, "John, how are yah? What are you doing? This is Digby. What are yah doing workwise?"

"I've got a great job."

"What's that?"

"Parenting. It's a full-time job."

He laughed. "With that kid, it's a pleasure. Miss workin' with you on *Laugh-In*. That was a ball. Now I've just gotten this deal with Westinghouse. They've asked me to come up with some show ideas and I immediately thought of you."

"Me? Why me?"

"I was hearing about this thing you were working on with Danny Arnold and was curious to see where it was."

"Under my desk, where it'll probably stay."

"Well, would you care to show it to me, and maybe show it to Westinghouse?"

"Digby, I'm not sure I want to go through this selling process again. I'm not a salesman."

"You don't have to sell me. If I like it, I don't have to sell Westinghouse. Just come by for a few minutes. Tomorrow, if you can. Around eleven. I'm across the hall from Schlatter."

"I'll be there."

"What'll you be bringing

"A script and a couple of three-quarter inch tapes. You won't need to see more than that."

The following morning I drove to Schlatter's familiar office. Digby had not arrived yet. I sat on the small sofa in the waiting area on the second floor between Digby's and George's offices, and waited. I was seated about fifteen minutes when George's door opened. He was surprised to see me.

"What are you doing here?"' he asked

"Waiting for Digby."

"Digby? What for?"

I chuckled. "He says he has a deal with Westinghouse, and wants to talk to me."

"Wanna come inside for a while? Wait in there?"

George sat behind his large clean desk, which he was constantly tidying. He kept meticulous records. Nothing was out of place. He was constantly unfurling the tangled telephone wires. We used to tease him that it was the German in him.

"Things didn't go well with Arnold?" he asked.

"How'd you know that?

He grinned. "There are no secrets in this town. Especially when shit goes wrong. So, what are you going to do with *National Graffiti*?"

"You know the name?"

George handed me a couple of *Daily Varietys* with articles circled.

"I'll be darned," I said after reading about my quote and my show.

"It's your show, though? No ties to Danny?"

"Absolutely mine. Why?"

"I got a call from Silverman the other day asking me if I could do a show about real people."

"What? Why would he call you?"

"I have a deal for four specials. Country versus city. Comedy and music. He wanted to know if I could do something about real people in their place."

"Jesus Christ, that hack. Do you know all the time he was not supposed to have contact with anybody at NBC or ABC when he was at Danny's place in Hawaii? Every day Danny'd be calling him, telling him about the stories we shot. What a fucking thief."

"At Danny's place? No wonder Danny's richer than me!" He chuckled. "How'd you like to do your show here? Work together again?"

"With you?"

"Yeah. Four specials."

I stared at him. It couldn't be this easy. Not after all the horrifying difficulties. It just couldn't be. "I'm here to see Digby."

"You can see him, but look at this." He pushed a slip of paper he'd been doodling on across the table. Circled was $5,000.00.

"What's this mean?"

"Your per-show fee."

"As what?"

"One of the hosts."

"What about the writer's fee?"

"You'll get that, too. Minimum plus a royalty. $1,500.00 per show."

"I don't have or want an agent."

He smiled. "Then you just saved yourself some commission."

Jesus, it just could not be this easy. "I'd like a 'Created By' credit."

He looked both impressed and stunned. "I'll give you the fifteen-hundred-dollar royalty, but I can't give you a credit. I don't want Danny's lawyers up my ass. And I want Silverman to think it was his idea."

I was mulling this when he added: " Your paycheck and I and the Writers Guild will know you created it. Does it make sense? Sound good?"

"What would we call it? *National Graffiti*?'"

"Fuck, no. It's Freddy's idea. *Real People*." He was obviously pleased with himself.

I was impressed at how smart he was. "George, I loved working with you and would love to again. Especially on my show. But, I promised Digby I'd let him look at it."

Within seconds Digby opened the door. "Digby," George said grandly, "John says he'd like to do his show here, four specials, but says he was here to see you first."

Digby tried to smile. "Johnny, I could never offer you what George can offer you, even if Westinghouse likes it. You've got a slam-dunk network deal with George. And a lot more money."

"You wouldn't mind?"

"Are you kidding? Not at all. Maybe I could even work on it!"

I stared at Digby, wondering if he'd been in his office all the time.

George leaned forward. "Is that the script?"

"Just one. I have five. All half hours. But the total concept is all there."

"Could I see it? How many stories did you shoot, which we'll have to reshoot with our people?"

"Half a dozen, but I have a file of about twenty or thirty."

"Terrific. We air in a few months."

I put up my hand to halt the conversation. "George, I have just two things I'd like to talk to you about first in private."

George glanced at Digby who left quickly.

"Just two things, George. Since I'm not getting an on air created by credit, I'd like a producer credit, and ten-percent ownership."

George laughed that deep, hard sarcastic laugh that was one of his trademarks, along with his tantrums. "I can't give you a producer's credit. It cannot appear as though it's your show. So, that's out. And I'm never partners with anyone, even on a minor level. Besides, this isn't going to go beyond the specials. NBC is in the toilet. They've lost the Olympics. They've got nothing. This shit is something no one's ever seen before. So, a piece is out. That's just the reality of your reality show."

"George, this is not shit, and if you and Silverman think it is, I'll turn it into TV fertilizer. It is going to surprise everyone. I'll do the four specials, but with no options for my services beyond that."

He studied me with a slight smile. "Good deal. I'll send the figures over to Tony Fantozzi. We'll have him draw up a contract for you." He grabbed my hand firmly. "See you first thing Monday. Digby'll be here. And Kendis. We'll get started, first on the other hosts. I have some ideas I think you'll like."

I left stupefied. How easy that happened. I didn't have to sell. I was being sold. Amazing. Like it was ordained. I had only two thoughts. One: to be patient. I would make it work and eventually become the producer of it. Two: If George was at all like Danny, the first casting meeting would be our first minor confrontation.

Not Heavenly Hosts

George, Digby, and Kendis were seated around the television set in George's office. With each story they leaned closer to the set howling and, like Edna and her friends, clapping their hands. I showed three: The Stripper for God, The Vampire Hunter, and The World's Unluckiest Man.

"Wow, are they weird," Kendis exclaimed.

I said, "They may be weird or a little off kilter to us, but not to them. On the show we never, ever describe them that way. We are just helping them tell their own stories."

George spoke up. "It is funny. Unbelievable, but all those stories were about eight minutes long. That's a little too long."

Digby laughed. "John, watch out for the axman. You know George has the attention span of an erection."

"George," I said, "*60 Minutes* is an hour long. They only tell three stories. Over fifteen minutes each. *The Godfather* was three hours long. If it's done right, there is no time limit on a story. I watched you all closely; not once did one of you look bored."

George said, "I noticed you didn't have any voiceover narration, just a few comments from people on the street. Hilarious. Especially Pryor. I think to make it a little different from what you did with Danny Arnold, we should do voiceovers."

"Piece of cake," I said. "Even easier and funnier."

"I've picked out some music you'll like. Having a set built, and hired a director."

"Why wouldn't you direct?" I asked George. "It's easy enough with this format."

"I prefer to be on the set. And, like I said, I have the perfect pair to host with John. Susan Anton and David Steinberg." George looked for our approval. He got it from Digby and Kendis.

"She's beautiful and David's smart," they said.

George noticed my silence. He did not miss much. "Whadda yah think, John?"

"George, I don't want to be the odd man out here. You're the executive producer and you have the final say, but if you want my two cents worth, my gut feeling, it's just my deep belief in what this show could be."

"You're the creator and the critic, so let's have it," Digby chimed in.

"First, I don't think any known celebrity should be a host. I think they should all be unknowns."

"You're not unknown," Kendis said.

"I'm only known, barely, in LA. David is smart, and funny, but he's a walking political commentary. A liberal commentary, which I'm not opposed to on *Meet the Press*. I just think viewers would be distracted by that image of him on a show about real people. The show and the stories will make the hosts stars."

George said, "He's coming in tomorrow for an interview."

"George, if he doesn't strike you as right, or if he turns it down because he has no idea what it's all about, it'll be no loss. Together we can think of some good people."

"Everybody like Susan?" George looked directly at me. "You don't think she's right? Too famous for you?"

"Not for being a good singer, or even six-feet-tall. She's more famous for sleeping with Dudley Moore."

"What's so funny about that? Wouldn't we all like to sleep with her?" George smiled.

"That's just it. If I'm sitting in the audience looking at her, I'm not listening to her introducing some real person I've never heard of. I'm thinking what on earth has Dudley Moore got that gets him into bed with this stunning blonde who towers over him?"

George said, "You guys come up with some names. Tomorrow I'm talking to David. John, I'd like you to sit in."

That night at dinner, I replayed the whole day for Sarita and Christopher, without rancor or frustration. I was pleased with the day and George. At the end of the meal, Christopher surprised me by mentioning a song he liked that Susan had sung on a show, then he astonished his mother and me when he asked if he could make a suggestion.

"Dad, you've seen the morning show on ABC with Regis?"

"Occasionally."

"You've seen the lady with him?"

"I never paid much attention. Why?"

"The lady on it with him is very nice. Sarah Purcell. Mommy, you've seen her."

I turned to Sarita. "Is she any good?"

"Yes," Sarita said. "And if your son says she is, she is."

The following morning, I got up to watch Sarah Purcell. She was at ease, articulate, engaging and rather attractive. A decent, comfortable interviewer. She was someone I could tell George about.

David Steinberg was sitting across from George. I sat on the far side of the room on a sofa. George didn't bother introducing David to me. David didn't evidence any need to know who I was or why I was in the room. I could have been just another piece of furniture. They chatted and chuckled quietly for about fifteen minutes; I caught very little of it. All I noticed was David's body language. He seemed ill at ease; towards the end he shook his head a couple of times in the negative. After he left, George looked across the room at me, asking what I thought.

"I could barely hear you, but even if I had, it was the same as yesterday."

"He turned it down."

"Why? Not enough money?"

"No. Not any stars."

"Are you kidding?"

"He doesn't know from real people. He's Jewish." George laughed.

"You're not displeased?"

"Naw. The Morris office has this kid Rafferty from San Francisco; and Kendis saw this skinny white comic she saw on *Dinah* she thought was pretty good."

"A comic? What's his name? Maybe I know him."

George looked a piece of paper. "Skip. Skip Stephenson. Know him?"

"No. But we need to get someone soon. We're short on time."

George smiled. "Speaking of short, you talked me out of Dudley's girlfriend."

"Well, maybe I can talk you into meeting a girl Christopher watches every morning."

"On Sesame Street?' George was quick.

I chuckled. "No. She's with Regis in the morning on KABC. Her name's Sarah Purcell. I saw her this morning, George, and she is perfect. If she's available. Have you seen her?"

"No."

"Watch her tomorrow morning, or have her agent send you a tape. Another guy you might want to talk to as a host is Freddy Willard. He's a comic, but he's really low key and a very nice guy."

"I'm not a fan of Freddy's. A little weird. But, I'll think about it. Are there any production people you'd like to bring aboard and work with? And I've got a couple of writers. David Panitch and his partner."

"George, you don't need writers. I'll be doing the stories, and the intros are simple. Kendis and Digby and you and I can do those in our sleep."

Four of the people I brought in were not people I'd hang around with, with the exception of Donna Kanter. I was indebted to her father, producer-writer Hal Kanter, and his wife, who fed me food and jokes often. I had no problem working with unusual characters as long as they had talent that suited the show. One of my editors I brought over from KNBC News was a giant six-foot-two bearded Harley Davidson rider and kleptomaniac, Keith Burns. George nicknamed him Sasquatch. I brought over Robert Long whom I'd met at *Barbour's People*, a bright verbal field producer, womanizer and alcoholic who seldom paid a bar bill. He and George got along like gangbusters. I also brought in Fred Willard.

As with David, George asked me to be present the following morning, just before noon, when Sarah showed up for her interview. Instead of sitting in the chair by George's desk, she sat on the sofa next to me, but mostly she stood. As did George. She was even more refreshing in person. I thought George would be nuts if he didn't hire her. When it comes to showbiz, George is not nuts, even though his personalized license plate read: Crazy George! They shook hands within minutes. She also gave me a little hug.

After she left, George said with a very big grin, "If your show is as good as her, it'll be a hit."

"George, you have no idea how big it will be."

"Oh, tomorrow, if you get a chance, could you bring Sarita and Christopher in for a minute. I'd like to really meet them."

Late the following day, after picking Christopher up at school, I drove him and Sarita to the office. The instant George saw Christopher, he jumped up from his desk, reached down for something and rushed to him.

"Christopher, just the young man I wanted to see. And thank. The lady you found for me is super. Thank you. I understand you're a fan, so this is for you." He unfurled a very large poster of Superman.

"Thank you, sir," Christopher said.

"George, that is really thoughtful of you," I said, with Sarita adding, "It's one of his favorites."

"And you guys are one of mine. This time around, John, we're going to get to know one another much, much better." After a long look at us, George added, "John, does anybody give you any trouble?"

"Trouble? What do you mean?"

"You know, from what you do and say as a critic, there are a lot of people who might give you some trouble. Some real grief."

I smiled. "That's the price I pay. It's my job. I don't mind."

He turned to Sarita. "If anybody causes any of you trouble, you must tell me. I have friends. Anyway, Christopher, thank you again. You take your mom and dad to dinner on me at Trader Vic's. It's all set up. I know it's one of your favorites. Then your dad and I are going to make a show."

We went to Trader Vic's; indeed, everything had been taken care of. Over their famous lamb with peach and peanut butter sauce, Sarita said, "Friends? Honey, George isn't Italian. What kind of *friends* could he mean?"

I shrugged "I don't know. Politicians maybe."

Real People

It started with only four specials, but I was about to begin the most exhilarating, creative, confrontational, happiest three years of my professional life. Actually, two and a half years! Being a performer or actor is really the occupation of a grownup child. Being a producer-writer-director is that of an adult. At forty-six, that was the first time I felt like an adult.

George, like Danny, had no concept of how to do a show like *Real People*. He had only worked with stars, comedians and comedy writers. But he knew I knew what I was talking about. He saw it in the tapes. In the beginning, he gave me complete control of writing and editing. He was the Jerry Jones or George Steinbrenner of television. He owned the stadium and team, but didn't play the game. I was the quarterback and the coach. For the first two years, he was my biggest cheerleader. He would smile bemused when I told him, which I did frequently, that within a year it would be the biggest show in television. Number one. My enthusiasm was as unshakable as my confidence. I felt I was predestined to do that show.

The confidence I expressed is not bragging. Just absolute and total confidence. Most people don't take kindly to braggarts, even though what they say might be true. The only profession in which Americans not only accept braggarts, but encourage it, is in politicians. Particularly presidential candidates. They only vote for the ones who speak the loudest about how well they can run the country or lead the army or build the economy. They would shun a candidate who says he thinks he would do an all-right job. *Hamlet* was a four-hundred-year-old tale, told often, but forgotten until Shakespeare penned his version. *The Celebrated Jumping Frog of Calaveras County* written by Mark Twain was a competition written about every year in the local California newspaper. It did not become a national comic classic event until Mark Twain penned his version. It isn't always the story that matters as much as the storyteller. I was the storyteller for the three years of *Real People*'s ground-breaking success and impact. I am the only one on the planet in a position to tell you the true stories, the exhilarating, heartbreaking, revealing, newsmaking, behind the scenes tales of how it was born, how it grew, and how it died. And who killed it. As Bette Davis said to her guests as she ascended the stairs in her apartment in the classic *All About Eve*, "Fasten your seat belts everybody. It's going to be a bumpy ride."

APRIL 18TH, 1979, #101

It was six days before my forty-sixth birthday. Our first special was to air live to the Eastern and Central time zones on Wednesday night at seven p.m. NBC, as Schlatter pointed out, probably wouldn't do too well, stuck at a distant third in the ratings. NBC was to go even deeper into the cellar when tensions between Russia and the United States forced America to withdraw from the 1980 Moscow Olympics. NBC had placed all its peacock eggs in one broadcasting basket, which were now all scrambled.

With or without the Olympics, nobody had any high hopes for *Real People*. It was ignored, but around the show there was an aura of excitement during preproduction, shooting, and editing. Everyone was having a good time doing something different.

To give the show a little touch of class, we hired Washington's best-known satirist, Mark Russell. He would do brief bits about the 'real' inside of government. We also hired iconic columnist Jimmy Breslin to comment on the real cost of trying to live in New York. The opening of the first show, and every one thereafter, was a delightful, delicious surprise to everyone. Especially for prime time. Today, and ever since *Real People* set the trend, *Good Morning, America* and the other so-called morning news shows open with crowds of people on the street eager for the chance to be on camera. That did not exist in 1979. Everything was structured and controlled. Not *Real People*; it was crafted to appear spontaneous.

The first thing viewers saw and heard was a handful of Americans of all shapes and sizes and ethnicities making a comment or observation about anything from politics to religion to celebrities' sex lives. Each engaging montage closed with the same seventy-year-old, blue eyed round-faced lady with a voice like Louis 'Satchmo' Armstrong saying, "*Welcome to Real People*." It was impossible not to be amused seconds into the show. Except for billboarding the stories with a voiceover, there was no announcer. Every commercial break was a real person on the street or in the audience announcing, "We'll be right back with more *Real People*." We did that for the first year until the Guild forced us into using real actors.

The first story for Fred Willard proved he had the perfect laid-back personality to be one of our hosts. He visited the smallest television station in America, in Iowa, a mom and pop, three-person enterprise. They often interrupted the network news to air the more important news of a local farmer who had a puppy for sale.

Skip Stephenson's engaging puckishness captured us in his first story. It was the funniest consumer concept piece anyone had ever seen. I had done it originally on my local show on KNBC, courtesy of our consumer advocate, David Horowitz. It was called Sweet Thing. We made a foul-tasting red liquid concoction out of sauerkraut, limes and a bunch of other bitters and placed it in a beautiful soft drink bottle labelled 'Sweet Thing.' We then set up a table in the busiest supermarket we could find, and put Skip in a white coat. He asked customers if they would mind sampling the new drink. Everyone obliged, spitting it out quickly, commenting on how disgusting it was. After about a dozen of those taste tests, we then mounted a large camera in front of the table. Skip asked the now-increasing number of customers if they would mind tasting this new, sweet drink, plus would they mind if the company used their comments about it in a new national commercial. Of course, everyone downed it with joy and gusto.

The entire cast helped present another piece I'd also done on my local show: Outtakes from our crack field reporters. When it comes to getting honest laughs, few things can compete with serious, intense journalists screwing up. Repeatedly.

Sarah Purcell revealed there was probably no other young woman as appealing as she was for that kind of show. She visited the largest truck-stop in the south and rode in a big-rig driven by a shapely, stunning twenty-two-year-old brunette who had just won a big race against the big boys with their bigger rigs and big tattoos. Those two ladies could have been Thelma and Louise.

A likable smiling Bill Rafferty profiled a young man in San Francisco known by a book he published as *Sherlock Bones,* the finder of lost pets. My story also took place in San Francisco. I went to do a story on a middle-aged, plump, plucky Irish-American named McNulty, who had recently won the Irish Sweepstakes. When he brought his $130,000.00 of winnings into the country, he failed to give the IRS their share. They threw him in jail. McNulty kept asking the judge and Mr. Cardosa, the local IRS head, to show him the law that says he has to pay them taxes. They could not. They could only show him the regulations. Mr. Cardosa told me on camera that the 1040 guidelines and regulations were written to be understandable by any eight-year-old, therefore they should be easy for Mr. McNulty. I took his guidelines to a classroom of eight-year-olds. Their readings were hilarious, as were the numerous people-on-the-street comments about the IRS we intercut into the story.

Like things that are meant to happen, the show was blessed. The day we arrived in San Francisco was the day they released Mr. McNulty, taxes still unpaid. In closing, I asked Mr. Cardosa if he'd ever been audited. He informed me that it was a prerequisite of being hired by the IRS that every new employee had to be. He then asked me if I'd ever been audited.

I said, "No. But if you plan on it, remember, my name is Tom Snyder." The final shot was of a lonely, quiet me behind bars.

Mark Russell did a fun informative bit about the government's new Department of Fraud. Jimmy Breslin railed against the high cost of sneakers for his kids in New York. Fred and I did separate short solo features on funny traffic signs and misprinted ads, telling folks if they sent in any items we used on the show, we'd send them a *Real People* properly-spelled T-shirt. (These T-shirts later would become so popular they bought stuff that cash could not).

Our entire cast signoff and good night was a witty round of couplets, brilliantly written by Digby. When the show ended, there was huge applause from the audience and the crew. There was a glow of pleasure from happy people.

A few weeks earlier, as we were preparing for the show, editing and writing, Fred Silverman popped in unannounced. George's editing facilities were across the street from his office building. Silverman arrived with George, asking to see a couple of the opening show's pieces. George showed him Skip's piece, mine, and Sarah's. Silverman didn't crack a smile and said nothing. Just stared.

"I don't quite know what I'm looking at, but somehow I like it," he finally said. Everyone cheered and applauded, except me. He and George left without a word, full of smiles.

As expected, the first special did not do well in the ratings. It ranked around number forty. Not even promising. NBC conducted extensive research at a few locations. Their conclusions were cautiously upbeat based on the fact so many of those surveyed said it was different, refreshing. The biggest boost and surprise, though, came three days later in the mail. We had received over 8,000 letters for a show that almost no one had seen. This was as much mail as any show in the top ten.

George called me in the middle of the night, as he often did, to tell me the news. He then added, "Silverman wants us to do two more shows, two more specials. Do you have enough stuff?"

"Tons. When you open some of that mail, you'll probably find dozens and dozens of great leads and stories."

"Jesus, you've struck gold. And you knew it!"

"Not until we're number one, George. Not till we're number one!"

A House Call

It was just before eight a.m. when I walked in to say good morning to George. Digby was waving *Daily Variety* at him and laughing. "George, why would you ever say something like that?" He continued. "Johnny, listen to this." He started to read: "When asked in the courtroom why he lied, George Schlatter said everybody in this town does it. It is how they conduct business. Jesus, George." Digby shook his head.

"In a courtroom, George?" I asked. "Why were you in a court room?"

George chuckled, but didn't speak. Digby did. "He claimed he had Robin Williams under personal contract. When it was announced Robin was gonna start *Mork and Mindy* a year ago, he sued. Two days ago, he lost."

"Did you have him under contract, George?" I asked.

George shrugged. "Thought I did."

"But, Jesus, George, why did you say you lied in court?"

George laughed. "Well, so I told the truth outside it. Oh, John, a couple of things for you. One you'll like, one you won't."

"What's that?"

"I got a call from Kelly Lange. She wants to be one of the hosts. Would you like the pleasure of telling her to fuck off or do you want me to?"

"You know I can't stand her, George, but I don't want to be the one to tell her no."

"Good boy. I already did. I told her we only have room for the one girl, courtesy of John Barbour's son. John, remember this, you're way above her now, so … only hate up. Not down."

George often said a lot of very bright things. "Oh, and the thing you might not like, but I need you to try it. I don't want to be hearing from Danny Arnold."

"George, it wouldn't matter anyway. You've seen the material is already registered to me at the Guild. He knew we were doing this with you. We would've heard from him by now. He knows it'd be thrown out of court."

"You don't know these people. I do!"

"That's 'cuz George's one of them." Digby laughed.

"You said he told Chris Hayward he wished you luck," George asked. "Did he tell you? In front of anyone? Did he send you a note?"

"No."

"I'd like you to do us all a favor. I'd like you to get a note from him somehow, saying as much. Shouldn't be hard."

"I haven't spoken to him since then. We don't need it. I can prove a million ways it's mine alone."

"John, I'd feel a whole lot better if we had such a note. Believe me. Would you please try? If your show gets to be as big as you say it will be, he and his lawyers will be on me like flies on shit! We don't need that."

"Okay, but it's a waste of time. I'll take one of the original scripts with the Guild's stamp on it. Maybe he can't refuse then."

Danny came immediately to the phone, and was quite pleasant. He thanked me for still taking his boys to a hockey game. I told him l had some private business to discuss with him. Would he mind if I came by the office?

He said, "Better still, come by the house tonight. Donna and the boys would love to see you. Bring Sarita."

I didn't take Sarita, in case there was some kind of confrontation. Donna and the boys did greet me warmly, giving me the hope that perhaps I'd have no problem with Danny.

Donna said, "Danny wanted me to send you into the living room. He's there with someone. Just for a few more minutes. The boys and I will be in the kitchen. If you want anything, holler."

I walked into the living room, and stopped. On the far side sat Danny. He was waving his arms, shaking his head, mumbling with anguish to a middle-aged man with grey hair wearing a conservative suit and tie. The man spoke softly to Danny, as though he was consoling him. I thought it was a Rabbi. I tried not to watch or listen. It was so private. But I was curious. After about fifteen minutes of this exchange, Danny abruptly stopped, rose, and shook the man's hand, thanking him for coming by. It had to be a Rabbi. I was even more convinced when he passed by me, saying "Good night" and waving his hand as if in blessing me.

"Johnny, great to see you. Come on over here and sit down." Danny was suddenly his grandiose self.

I couldn't contain my curiosity. "Danny, why was the Rabbi here?" Danny howled. "That's not my Rabbi. I don't have one. That's my psychiatrist!"

"A psychiatrist? Making house calls?"

"Every Wednesday night if I can. Woody Allen talks to his every day."

"Jesus Christ, Danny. To cure you of what? Your success?"

"He helps."

"Danny, he probably wishes he was you for cryin' out loud. If you're trying to cure yourself of whatever, it'll not happen like this."

"Whatta you mean?"

"If you were serious, not just pampering or humoring yourself, you'd be going to his office. He's coming here like a mental manicurist. Just catering to you, your whims. You do not need a psychiatrist, especially one who doesn't have the balls or professionalism to tell you he doesn't make house calls."

"If I got what I'm paying him, I'd make midnight house calls." He chuckled. "OK. What can I do for you?"

"Chris told me you'd called him a while ago and said you wished me luck with my show."

"That's true. I did. And do."

"Danny, this may sound shitty, but could you just give me a little note to that effect?"

"Why?"

"So, I have it." I handed him the script. Would you mind just writing that on the front?"

He handed it back to me. "You're making this sound like it's something legal." He no longer looked pleasant.

"In a way it is. It'd make me feel a whole lot more comfortable going forward, feeling I still had a supportive, encouraging friend."

"My word is good enough."

"What about all those good words last year, that I'd get to run the show. That if it didn't work out, it was mine to take elsewhere, or that you didn't want the money back? What about those words?"

He stared at me, then said, "I am not going to fuck anything up for you. I like you. The boys like you. And Donna. I just don't like to feel cornered or told what to do."

"Jesus, Danny, who am I to corner you or tell you what to do? I was just asking for a good faith favor. If it's not forthcoming, then I'll have to believe you mean it. This time."

"Johnny, I do wish you well. And thanks for coming by. It was good to see you."

I rose and shook his hand. "I'll tell Chris I saw you. Say goodnight to Donna and the boys."

The next day, George was totally unconcerned when I recounted the previous evening to him.

"No problem, John. I've gone over it with my boys. We're fine. So, as they say in the movies, let's make a show!"

This Shit's Not Going Anywhere

Another of the bright talents I met at KNXT doing *Barbour's People* was Dan Gingold. He was the writer mostly responsible for the scripts that made *Ralph Story's Los Angeles,* the town's highest rated local show. In our second show, Dan was the field producer on a story I did that made the town talk. It was called *The Dirt Eater*. I accidentally met him while Sarita, Christopher and I were having one of our favorite meals at Charley's Fish 'n' Chip restaurant. This nice-looking fellow, in his early thirties, in a suit, recognized me, came over, introduced himself, and asked if we'd mind if he gave a little lecture on nutrition. We smiled and told him not at all. He proceeded to explain how potatoes, carrots, beets and whatever food grows from the earth recycle the nutrients. He said, rather than have them recycled, he takes them directly from the soil. Like a glass of wine at dinner, he always eats a small portion of dirt. We asked if he would mind if I filmed his little secret. He said he felt he would be contributing to the nation's health. A few days later Dan and I filmed him.

At the end of the piece, he took me out to his garden, asking if I had the courage to sample what he had just eaten. Reluctantly, I scooped up a small portion and ingested it. It was sandy and bitter, but I swallowed it, then looked up at him and asked, "What's your cat's name?"

The word was spreading quickly that this show was funny, and different. I did not gain friends in Hollywood or the Writers Guild, though, when I said, "The reason it is so good is because we don't need actors or writers."

The story we told on our fifth special, though, was the one that really made the show. It was called, *Walking George*. This story came to us from a columnist at the *L.A. Times,* Chuck Hellinger, one of our researchers. A fellow named George lived literally in a hole in the ground. He had given up on most of society and its downward spiral into tastelessness. He also rebelled against the cost of living, so he dug a thirty-square-foot, six-foot-deep home for himself in the middle of the Mojave Desert, a few miles from the nearest town. He divided it into four different living areas, separated by boards. On imbedded two by fours he built a raggedy roof of corrugated steel. His outhouse was cactus bushes.

George lived in this hole in the ground every day and night of the month, except two. The second to last day, he placed his one good navy suit in his ratty little suitcase, walked to town, and boarded a bus to LA, sitting in the back alone so as not to offend people by his smell. In LA, he went immediately to a decent hotel, to the same room he reserved every month for just that occasion. There he would take his monthly shower, shave, put on his suit and tie, and sprinkle himself with cologne. He then called a cab to a very nice apartment complex downtown. Scrubbed and clean, George then took the elevator, got off at the usual floor, and walked directly to a familiar apartment, where he knocked gently. There to greet him was a stunning, tall blonde in her late twenties, dressed for a night on the town. She greeted George with a smile and hug, invited him in and closed the door. Shortly, it would open, George grinning. Arm in arm they'd descend to the taxi that took them to the opera. Following the opera, they went to a fine restaurant for wine and a late-night dinner, then back to her place. The closing shot of George walking happily down the desert highway to his home was accompanied by a thrilling piano concerto. The audience not only laughed, they applauded and cheered. It was like a small Frank Capra movie.

The story ran over eight minutes. Schlatter objected, stating it was too long for comedy. I reminded him that *Some Like It Hot* was nearly two hours, and that the best sitcoms were half an hour. Funny is funny.

We got the same reaction to a story I did on our sixth and final special. It was called Omar the Beggar. 1979 was not a good year for a lot of Americans. The interest rate was around twenty percent and unemployment was high. Trickledown economics evidently wasn't trickling down; it was sucking up. There were often lines around the block for gasoline. An enterprising fellow in New York named Omar had become semi-wealthy by begging. As a public service, Omar wanted to share his skill and knowledge with his fellow underprivileged Americans; for them he opened the low-cost School for Beggars. I attended the class, interviewed some nice people forced to try to survive, and filmed some of them being successful. I, on the other hand, on the street as a recent graduate, didn't look that needy. What few dollars some nice people gave me, I gave to real beggars.

People's joy in telling their stories, and the enjoyment of those who watched, made me happier than all of them. Working with George, and occasionally having differences with him, (which actually made the work better) and sharing my meager spare time with my family made my life complete. I was finally a full-blown success. I had made my point. And I was an American making a contribution. I could not want for more, at least money; but felt I deserved more credit.

In the beginning, not a day went by George didn't give me a massive bear hug or compliment me or run interference for me. He was like a big, older, protective brother. He always stood by me, encouraging me to do my thing. I would occasionally wander into his office just to visit, but he was always on the phone. I told him if he'd been a woman his clitoris would have been in his ear. For George the phone wasn't just for conversing; it was for conquering. And no one wielded it better.

Most of the time when I walked in on him he was regaling columnists or critics or executives with some showbiz anecdote. No one told them better. One afternoon I walked in on him, though, and immediately got very uncomfortable. He was repeating to someone things I had told him often about our show and our stories. He was telling the listener that Walking George was eight minutes, but it was like a Frank Capra movie. Funny is funny. Sitcoms are a half hour. And on another occasion, I heard him saying, "This show is going to change the face of television."

Sometimes George did not talk on the phone; sometimes he would bellow and scream. The first time I heard it was from my office across the hall. The building was vibrating with his rage. I rushed over to see who was the object of such wrath, expecting to have to save his or her life. He was verbally disemboweling someone at NBC. Hearing him screaming the names of our cast members, what I gathered was that someone at NBC had passed a commercial job offer to one or all of the cast, without clearing it with George. I listened, frightened.

He was yelling, "These people are mine. I own them. It's my show. I am the only one who will tell them what fucking shows or commercials or interviews or publicity or shit they can do. Not you. Not anybody. You send all that shit to me. Not them. Immediately. If not, you will not be hearing from me again, or anyone in this business." He smashed down the phone, and looked up at me with a calm impish smile. His rage was over. Like an orgasm.

"Johnny," he said, grinning, "that is chapter five on how to talk to network executives."

During one of our live shows, I discovered his rage was not just confined to the phone. George was always at his producer's podium left of the audience, separated only by a decorative cardboard wall. Neatly, on the podium, was his script, pencils, and the phone to the director. Just before the half hour commercial break, a cue card holder fumbled his cards. The cast had nothing to say. Skip, Sarah and Rafferty fumbled a few words, while the cameramen did not know which one to focus on. It was mercifully only a brief screw up before the break. But at the break, there was a sudden roar and crash. The roar was George screaming, "YOU IDIOTS!" The crash was him tearing the phone right out of its socket and heaving it against the partition, screaming profanities. The audience, like the crew was dumbfounded or terrified.

I rushed to George as fast as I could. "George. George, what's wrong?" I was as calm as I could manage.

"They're fucking up my show." Everyone could hear him.

I put my hand on his arm gently. "George, no one is screwing up your show. Stuff like that happens. It just proves we are live. Audiences love screw ups. It makes us human."

He did calm down; not because of me. The break was over. Back live, Skip and Bill joked about the foul up. The audience cheered while George retrieved the phone without a word, untangled the wire, and plugged it back in.

While all this gave me pause, George was interesting and fascinating to listen to and observe. And hopefully to learn from; a piece of work, as they say in Hollywood. I was lucky to be working with such a smart, successful, witty pro. Without him, the show, even just those six specials, would not be on the air. I liked him. With those hugs and backslaps, he daily gave me physical and verbal credit for *Real People*.

At the end of the show with his tirade, he asked me to come to his office. It was night. I had no idea what to expect, especially that late. But I did not expect what I heard. He said nothing about what had happened. There was a big warm smile on his face.

"John, I want you to go home and give Sarita and Christopher the good news. We've been picked up for the fall."

"Honestly?" Although I had always felt it would happen, I was stunned. "Really? Thirteen weeks?"

His smile was bigger. "No twenty-two."

"George, nobody gets twenty-two. Just thirteen."

"NBC's in the toilet. We're their only plumber." God, sometimes he said the cleverest things.

"John, you're gonna make a lot of money. More than you've ever made, and I can help you make it into more."

"How?"

"I come across a lot of great deals. Investments. Hotels, buildings. Stuff. Right now, I have a Mouton Cadet dealership here in LA."

"What's that?"

"Wine. I'll send you a case. To celebrate. And when you run out, I'll send more. You happy?"

"Yes. George. Thank you."

"No. thank you. You did it."

Hearing him say that, I felt brave. "George, you know what would make me happy? I understand why you don't want to give me a created-by credit; the fifteen hundred royalty is fine. I would be happy if I could get the credit for what I am doing anyway, which is producing the show. A producer credit." He stared at me. Without a smile. "And, I'd like at least ten percent of the show."

At this, he suddenly burst out laughing. Actually, it was more of a harsh, derisive cackle. "John, as I said before, I don't partner with anyone. Give pieces to anyone. This is a live show. It has no syndication value. So, this shit's not going anyplace. So, again, that's a no."

I was unable to focus on what to say or do next. But unlike talking to Danny, I was at ease talking to George.

"And, l can't give you a producer credit. We'd hear from Danny for sure."

Now, hearing that, all the joy of a moment ago evaporated. I got up calmly and extended my hand. Seeing no more smile, George wasn't sure whether to shake it or not.

"In that case, George, I'm done. I proved my point. If I stayed without getting what I know in my gut is what I deserve, I'd make myself sick. I'd probably grow to resent you for being so greedy as to not give me just a little piece of my own show. Do you want me to leave? Or stay? As your producer?"

"I guess you'd better go."

I did.

Crazy George

I had gambled and lost – to a better gambler. George wasn't so Crazy George after all. His only interest in being in television was money. And fame, which can get you more money. He knew I was the goose that laid the golden egg. He knew, as I did, without me the goose would be cooked, laying a rotten egg, which it did three years later when he fired me on my son's thirteenth birthday. But at that point, he had the quick easy money of twenty-two pay or play shows.Offering me thirty times my critic's salary, George was certain I'd fold my hand. Indeed, I thought about it. That was a lot of guaranteed money for a year, fees for performing, writing, and a royalty. I had a family. I could pay off the mortgage in two months. If I didn't accept, I had no job. If I did accept, I knew in my gut, I would get sick, physically and emotionally. So what, that I was forty-six? I'd quit the business half a year earlier anyway, happy and contented. I'd just be back where I peacefully was, and able to live on the weekly fifteen-hundred-dollar royalty. That was good enough for me. Almost.

For the next three weeks I heard from no one. Not Sarah. Not Skip. Not Willard. Not even Digby. The disappointment in their silence, or even ingratitude, was something I never quite got used to. It happened with every show. The closest of sworn lifelong friendships ended with a show's cancellation. I might have gone on with my life if I had not kept reading George's puffy self-aggrandizing press releases. Daily there were stories about Sarah and Skip traveling the country to tell the tales of weird, funny people. They were not weird, I told George and Danny a hundred times. They were different. There was no question George would exploit those people, not explain them. He would destroy them and my show. I had to stop him. When I had called Elton Rule to warn him that ABC's choices for late night hosts were a disaster, there was nothing I could do about it. I had no influence. But maybe I did have a little, just a little, at NBC.

Through a few friends, I had access to when and where NBC executives would be holding conferences or affiliate meetings. One happened almost immediately at Freddy Silverman's favorite hotel, The Century Plaza. He was alone by the bar after his luncheon speech, in which he lauded the exciting new show, *Real People*.

I wandered over casually. "Fred. Mr. Silverman." He was younger than me, but because of his position, not his age, I didn't quite know how to address him. He looked bugged to see me.

"What is it?"

"Do you know that I'm not coming back with *Real People*?"

"Yes. What about it?"

"Didn't you think the cast made a terrific family? And why would you want that family broken up?"

"It's George's family. And George's business."

"You don't think I am an important enough member of the family to stick up for?"

"What are you getting at? It's not up to me."

"You're the head of programming. It's your business to give the audience the best show possible, your business to know how it got to be such a good show. It got that way because of me."

His nose crinkled, like there was a foul odor. "What?"

"That *Real People* show you ordered after hearing tales about it from Danny Arnold while you were in Hawaii was, and is, my show. I created it. I write and edit the stories. If I'm not behind the cameras to do that, it will disappear like a turd down the NBC toilet."

"This show will go on forever with or without you. The stories are endless, thousands of them every week."

"Fred, there's only one storyteller. Me. I am more important to this show than Norman Lear is to *All in the Family*. Or Carol O'Connor. There are dozens more sitcom writers, but the real stories you liked were written and edited by me." I was so angry, I may have overstated my case, but in my marrow, I knew it would die without me. His face distorted in disdain. I wanted to punch him.

"George Schlatter is a very successful producer."

I retaliated. "He's more successful at destroying hits like he did *Laugh-In*. You don't work with him. I do. He has no fucking taste. He just likes quick jokes! Without me, this won't last eight weeks."

"Neither will this conversation." He walked away without another word.

That arrogant know-nothing bastard. If I uttered another word, I'd even hate myself for groveling.

The next day, my concern was Silverman relaying to George my bragging encounter. I thought of calling George. Instead, I called Fantozzi.

"Johnny, how are you? We miss you."

"Evidently not that much, Tony. I'm calling to see if I could come by for a little chat."

"I'm free right after lunch. One o'clock. Come right up."

Fantozzi had been Tom Brokaw and Schlatter's agent for years. He was one of the agency's biggies. I liked him. He seemed to like me. He motioned for me to sit. "What's on your mind?"

"Tony, you know what's on my mind. George. I cannot believe he thinks he can go ahead with this show without me. You of all people know this is not George's kind of show. He has no concept of what it is. It is not showbiz. You obviously weren't around behind the scenes while we were putting it together; you know I created it, and now I'm telling you, I put it together. I'm stunned he wouldn't give me a producer credit."

He smiled a broad smile. "John, George can go ahead with the show because he has a bird in hand. An order. That's how."

"Tony, in just one show that bird will be a turkey. Dead before eight weeks are up. You've known him better than anyone for years. Comedy and music are his bag. Not reality. Certainly not real people. I was not and am not asking for money. I am asking only for what I deserve, credit. I don't care about the money."

He leaned back. "If it'll make you feel any better, when I asked him why you weren't there, he told me what you wanted, I said, 'Why not?'"

"What'd he say?"

"Nothing. That's George."

"Tony, if he won't listen to you, his best friend, he won't listen to anybody. I don't know what to do."

"Call 'im. You went to see Freddy and me. You obviously care a lot. But he's the only one you should be talkin' to, so call him. Better still, just go visit him. His door is always open. You know that. He'd like to see you, I'm sure. He does like you a lot. You've got nothing to lose."

"When?"

"Right now. You might be surprised." He paused.

"You'll do better with him than Freddy. George likes to win. Money and winning is all he cares about. That's all this town cares about. If you go back, he'll think he's won."

I thanked Tony and hurried out of his office, wondering how he knew I confronted Silverman. The small town was getting smaller.

Arriving at George's building, I didn't think I'd be with him long, if at all. I parked in front in a loading zone on Beverly. His door, as usual, was open. He was on the phone. When he saw me, he hung up. "John, come on in. Sit down. How've yah been holding up?"

"Honestly, not too well. I just came from talking with Tony."

"I know."

"And yesterday I talked with Silverman."

"I know." He smiled.

"I much prefer talking to Tony."

"Me too."

"George, I'll be honest with you. I love working with you. You know how much I love the show. If it's money you're worried about, give me the minimum, or nothing as a producer, if you can. That's not what I'm after. I just want the justifiable credit for what I am contributing. That's all."

He twirled a pencil nervously like Humphrey Bogart with his marbles in *The Caine Mutiny*.

I continued, "The reason you called this a piece of shit is because it's live and has no syndication value. I understand that, but the first six pieces of shit, I turned into fertilizer. If you let me continue to do that, just the way we did the first six, I will give you an entertainment show that will last longer than *Sixty Minutes*. If you still believe it is shit and not going anyplace you have nothing to lose by giving me ten per cent of nothing. It just makes me feel that you value my work and maybe my friendship.'

It was at least ten seconds of staring before he answered. "You must be a great card player. A great gambler."

"Neither, George. Neither."

"You've got a deal." He reached over and shook my hand.

"Really? Really? Thank you!" I gushed, astonished.

"I am glad you came in. I am glad you're back. I would have never called you. Can you start right away?"

"Now? I'm in a loading zone."

He laughed. "Put it in back. I'll have a permanent spot for you."

A Show for All Seasons

This chapter title is prompted by a wonderful 1960's multi-Academy award-winning British film, *A Man for All Seasons*, starring Robert Shaw as Henry VIII and Paul Scofield as Sir Thomas More. Henry, looking to bed and wed someone else, wants a divorce or annulment from his present wife, Catherine. Because of his intense belief and faith, Sir Thomas, England's Lord Chancellor, refuses to assist his best friend in violating the Church's laws. So, Henry cuts off his head. In describing More, a contemporary said he possessed wit, charm and intelligence, a man for all seasons. That perfectly describes *Real People* for three years. It possessed wit, charm, and intelligence.

In the back, next to George, I had a permanent spot, with my name. George called me into his office, saying he wanted to show me something. He also had someone he wanted me to meet.

"John, this is Bob Wynn. He's your new co-producer." I didn't extend my hand. George knew what I was thinking. It was all over my face. He sputtered, "Oh, Bob's not going to be writing or editing any of the stories. You'll still be doing that. He'll be helping me mostly with production problems. He was with me on *The Judy Garland Show* and he's done a lot of Perry Como's shows. The Christmas Specials."

"Pleased to meet you," was all I managed.

"Glad to be your partner," he said, extending his hand.

George then grabbed a tape and stuck it in the monitor. "While you were gone, I put together a few pieces. This is the one about the women boxers we talked about."

The film he showed me consisted mostly of fairly attractive women working out in sweaty T-shirts, then getting into the ring with lots of punches to the breasts. Wynn laughed a lot. George watched, smiling with pride. When it was over, he turned to me. "Whadda yah think?"

I didn't hesitate. "George, it's awful. Who are these women? What do they do? Why are they fighting? We know nothing about them. Do they have kids? Husbands?"

"We know they got nice tits!" Wynn cackled.

"People'll watch," George said.

"Not next week," I replied. "George, give me a day. Let me re-edit and rewrite it. You still have the select reel, all the material?"

"Yeah."

"Give me six hours. Then look at it, okay?"

"You got it. I guess you won't be too anxious to do a story Bob Long wants to do. He's found this really funny, interesting Madam in Nevada."

"At a whorehouse?"

"It's legal in Nevada." George smiled while Wynn again chimed in another supporting cackle.

"George," I snapped, "so is fucking sheep, but nobody wants to see it. She probably is a great story. What Madam wouldn't be? But let's wait three or four years until we're a hit. Then we can do it."

George surprisingly nodded. "Okay. Let's see what you can do with the girls."

At nine p.m. I was back in his office. He was still chatting with Wynn. (Many times after midnight editing sessions, I would drop by George's office when I saw a light. Often, he'd be at his desk, pensive and preoccupied. He was somewhere other than with the show, but I never asked.) I inserted the tape. It was three minutes longer, but twice as fast. We now knew who the young women were, single mothers, teachers, laborers, battered women, who, because of the economy or life, decided to or were forced to get into a ring and fight for their life and families. We could identify with them. Like them. Cheer for them. A lot of the T-shirt shots were still there, but they had a different impact.

George stared at the dark screen for a moment, then looked over at me. "You're a genius. That is terrific."

"Looks the same to me," Wynn said. Bob Wynn was George's age. Around fifty. He was the only person I ever met who had no sense of humor. A human black hole. At production meetings and read-throughs, he'd often try to joke; each was either sexual or racist, never funny, always met with silence or stares. He was incapable of holding one's attention with a story that told by others would be interesting. I had no affection or interest whatsoever in Bob. George, as promised, kept him away from any real input into the show.

Before setting out over the summer to shoot the stories, there were a few things I had to do first to prepare, in a business-like way, for the expected show's success – at least as much as possible, never having been in a position of being successful. Nathan Markowitz incorporated me as Chrisita Corporation, the company George would contract for my services. Nathan put me in touch with a brilliant accountant, Bob Mages. Bob then introduced me to one of his best friends, Tony Trattner, one of the managers of major accounts at Shearson Lehman Brothers in Century City, also on the Board of Directors of Cedars Sinai Hospital. This chain reaction of personal events flowed as easily as did the chain of events that led *Real People* to getting on NBC. It felt like it was all meant to be. At Shearson, Tony Trattner set up an amazing retirement account called the Cronkite Plan.

On CBS for years, news anchor Walter Cronkite was considered the Voice of America. He grumbled that in spite of his massive network paychecks, he wasn't able to keep what he felt he deserved. So, the IRS set up a plan whereby Cronkite could deposit all his checks into a special retirement account, and would not have to pay taxes on those deposits until he retired. That plan, over the years, could be invested, grow, earn interest, and, finally, upon retirement, he would only have to pay ten percent on what he withdrew. Fortunately, this is what Tony set up for Sarita and me. Sarita became our small company's creative consultant, with her own paycheck and plan. We maxed out both plans well before the IRS figured out they had screwed up, and cancelled them.

I also figured it was about time I had a strong agent. I didn't know any biggies, but I knew Chris Hayward knew some.

"Roland Perkins at Creative Artists," Chris suggested. "An ex-Morris agent. One of the cofounders of CAA." Not being a Morris agent, George's agency was good enough for me.

Roland was close to my age. Tall, thin, quiet. I remember nothing of our first conversation except the gold necklace he was wearing. On the end of a glistening chain hung this large solitary solid gold number four. That was my lucky number! I was curious to ask him the significance of it, but didn't. I wish I had asked, then maybe I could remember something he'd said that might have impressed me.

Believe it or not, I thought my lucky number around a very important agent's neck was a good omen. I asked if he'd like to represent me. Since I'd already made the deal with George on my own, I told him the first year I'd give him five percent of my earnings. The following years, he'd get his usual ten percent. He agreed. It was found money.

When Chris and George and everyone heard I was represented by Roland Perkins at Creative Artists they were impressed. The only other person I felt I'd need in my little camp was a publicist. I wasn't looking for one to pump my ego or to glorify me. I didn't need that. I was looking for one more for self-defense. NBC publicity was pumping out stories constantly about George Schlatter's original new show, the only one moving up in the network's ratings. Some of the stories mentioned Sarah. Not one mentioned me. Once again, I was on the phone to Joe Seigman. I thanked him for finding my lawyer; now I wanted Joe as my publicist again.

"John, except for Carol O'Connor I don't do that anymore. The perfect guy for you is Henri Bollinger, George Schlatter's first publicist."

"You're kidding?"

"No." He laughed. "You'll like him. A really sweet competent fellow. President of our guild."

Joe was right. Henri Bollinger could be described in one all-encompassing word: decent. He was close to fifty, slender, and as devoid of hair as he was anger, hostility or gossip. I never heard him once raise his voice. Or badmouth anyone. If he was telling you a well-known, unpleasant story about someone in the business, he sounded almost apologetic. His working partner was his wife, both of whom doted on their two teenage children, a boy and a girl. Having nothing negative to say about anyone in the business, no one had anything to say negative about Henri. He told me he watched the *AM Show* every morning, loved the reviews, and especially what little he saw of *Real People*.

"John, that'll be a huge hit since it is also the only thing on NBC. You'll have no trouble getting all kinds of press."

I interrupted him. "Henri, I don't want celebrity press. I hate that stuff. The only thing I want is for people, especially in the industry, to know not only did I create the show but that it's my writing and editing that make it work. You or anyone not actually there could possibly know that. I don't want to sound like an egomaniac at our first meeting, but–"

He interrupted me. "John, I've known and worked for George for years. I know what he does and does well. *Real People* is not in George's nature or interest. From what I've seen of your work, it is not a far stretch to believe that you are responsible."

I took even more of a liking to him. "You said you worked for George. Doing publicity?"

"Yes. For a while. He fired me."

"Fired you? What'd you do?"

"It's not what I did, it's what I didn't do." He paused. I could tell he was searching for a way to say it without sounding negative. "He was in New York doing a show and asked me to get Jolene's picture and a little story about her in *Women's Wear Daily,* and I couldn't."

"Why would he want his wife's picture in *Women's Wear Daily*?"

"He didn't. She did."

"She was beautiful, and a big producer's wife. Why'd they say no?"

"They didn't say."

"And he wanted to fire you over that?"

He smiled. "No, she did."

"Wow. Unbelievable," I muttered. "Since you know George so well maybe you'd be the perfect person to help me."

"It has nothing to do with George, but I'd love to be a part of it."

We shook hands. My little camp was now complete.

Jolene

Jolene was a smart, bright, attractive brunette in her mid-forties. You could see why Ernie Kovacs would pick her as a regular on his show. She seldom came into the office, but when she did, the staff was more at attention than when George was around. She had a reputation of verbally assaulting shopkeepers, clerks, workers, maids, and any other underling who did not immediately meet her demands. Since I was never a witness to those tongue lashings, I cannot vouch for the many I heard about. When I returned as producer, however, she was the only one, other than Skip, who made a point of coming in, finding me, welcoming me back.

"John, I am so glad you are back. This show needs you." She sat next to me on George's sofa, patting my lap. Without my asking, she began to recount her amazing life with George. At one time, she said they were so poor in their little bungalow in the valley, the only way they could get warm water was by laying their hose out in the sun. Seeing what television was becoming she pushed George, who had showbiz talents, into the medium, not as a performer, but as a producer, the force behind the camera. She never stopped pushing until she herself became a force among the rich and famous. She pushed or dragged him into getting involved in attending or producing every major charity event in town, especially the largest charity fashion show in Beverly Hills, in which she could model. (I thought I was listening to Jerry Weintraub.)

With the sudden growing success of *Real People*, Sarita and I were invited to everything imaginable by everyone imaginable. But never attended. We stayed home because I was planning on building a new one. The invitation from Jolene for us to join her and George at The Beverly Wilshire Celebrity $1,000 a plate fashion show was the only one we did not turn down because she had welcomed me as the new producer.

Our table of ten was right next to Sinatra's table. He wasn't five feet behind me. Although I'd had half a dozen calls over the years from him or Dorothy to write jokes or a letter or tribute, which always resulted in ten brand-new hundred-dollar bills, I never saw him. I had almost forgotten about the 'Italian Roots.' I was pleasantly shocked, as were Jolene and George, when he turned around, saw me, leaned backwards, and raised his thumb. "Soon, kid. soon!"

The show's second year we were nominated for an Emmy. The broadcast originated from The Ambassador Hotel. The Hollywood establishment and Emmy producers still thought so little of that 'reality' thing they did not know how to categorize it. If we won, which we didn't, it would be shown later in a recap. Our huge table was right in the center of the room, elevated a little so I could see everything around us. And what a sight I could see. We were surrounded by an army of the stars and talents I'd seen all my life. My head was on a swivel, like a bobble doll. My mouth must have been as wide as my eyes.

Jolene grabbed my arm, whispering, "John, what are you doing?"

"Look at all these people. I've watched many of them since I was a kid."

"Well, stop watching right now. Make them look at you. You're number one now."

It is impossible to say anything negative about a woman that says that to you, or a woman who is still hustling to keep her man on top.

Real People … Stories, Stories, Stories

As I was preparing to recount a few of the stories we told on *Real People*, I stumbled upon *Vanity Fair's* cover story on Bruce Jenner becoming Caitlyn Jenner. For months it dominated the media *ad nauseam*. I was waiting for him/her to be on *Time* as Man *and* Woman of The Year!) The Jenner story elicited an enormous amount of sympathy from viewers and readers about transgenders, which continues to this day. That was not the case when I told the first most outrageous story about transsexuals.

We profiled a Midwest Arizona couple married five years. On their honeymoon, the six-foot-tall husband realized he wished he was the five-foot wife. And the five-foot wife wished she was the husband, So, for five years they saved until they had their successful operations, returning home to a town that totally shunned them, and ran from the crew of our famous show. Absolutely no one would talk or look at me when I approached to ask questions about the new neighbors. The day after airing, the whole country was talking about them and our show.

As everyone knows, television shows live or die by the Neilson ratings. I found a family named Neilson in Utah that was having a long-delayed summer family reunion. Five hundred related Neilson cousins, aunts, uncles, nieces, nephews, grandparents and grandkids from nearly every state showed up for this massive gathering. I sat them on a field on a hill. We mounted a podium with a microphone, and with a list of TV shows, took our Neilson survey. It was hilarious and informative. It turned out their favorite show was *I, Claudius* on PBS.

We profiled an electrical engineer in Chicago who built the first house in the country run entirely by electronics and computer. He had made the money to do so at the racetrack. When betting he would sneakily insert an antenna in a horse's anus, and from the stands, when needed, give it a remote charge. He retired to just focus on his house when approached by the Mafia to become partners.

In a wonderful feel-good story, we profiled John and Greg Rice, identical twin little people in their late twenties who had become millionaires as two of Florida's most successful real estate salesmen, then sought-after public speakers and TV pitchmen.

We found a lively, loquacious, engaging gay physical fitness guru who gave part-time exercise classes. His full-time job was as a waiter in a Beverly Hills restaurant. He was Richard Simmons.

We profiled a garbologist, a New York businessman, A.J. Weberman, whose hobby was learning about people by stealing and analyzing their garbage. For me, he pointed out President Nixon's ground floor apartment with two large green garbage bags in front. Who wouldn't want to learn more about Tricky Dick! With cameras rolling, I grabbed them and took off. Instantly, a Secret Service agent was out the door chasing me, hollering, "John, what are you doing?" I returned the bags sheepishly to this laughing Secret Service agent. Probably the first laugh he'd had in years.

In Los Angeles, we watched a man in his thirties putting the finishing touches on his backyard dream of twenty years: a massive handmade wooden pirate ship similar to the one in Errol Flynn's *Captain Blood*. It was being completed and about to be towed onto the street and down to the ocean. It was another mini Frank Capra movie.

A nudist colony in Illinois called Naked City had a successful restaurant with excellently reviewed food open to the general, clothed public. Amongst those I profiled was the attractive nude young waitress who took my lunch order, with me trying to keep my eye on the menu. That piece closed with me standing behind the hood of our car, wearing a smart jacket and expensive shirt and tie. I was commenting tolerantly on the lifestyle those real people had chosen, though it might not be for everybody. I hate to say this, but with my very last words, I emerged from behind the car sans trousers. Seeing my bare legs, the studio audience erupted with screams and applause.

These were some of the stories I shot over the summer. The other cast members were filming others, just as interesting and entertaining. Their last stop before returning to Los Angeles was Las Vegas. We booked rooms on the same floor in one of the Strip's better hotels, and were to meet in Sarah's suite. Cast and crew were laughing and toasting when I walked in.

I had not seen Sarah since I had walked off after the specials. As I reached out to embrace her with a hug, she pushed me away. I was shocked and hurt. Close at her side was Bob Long, who I soon discovered had become her designated 'hugger.'

"Johnny you've got gold to mine when you get back," he said. "The stuff is great."

Back in LA, I couldn't wait to tell George how wonderful the shoots had been. In his office were his appendages, Bob Wynn and Digby. It was also the first time I'd also seen Digby since returning.

"Digby, how terrific to see you. Wait'll you see the stuff we've got."

"Well, Johnny, I guess I'll have to watch it when it airs. I'm not staying with the show."

I looked at George. "Why not?"

"He doesn't think it's for him," George said.

"It's a terrific show, Johnny. I really like it, but it's not what I do. It's what *you* do. I've got other things I'm workin' on."

I then turned to George and asked if Sarah was okay. "When I tried to hug her in Vegas, she shoved me away."

Bob Wynn laughed. "Why wouldn't she be happy? She's fucking Bob Long. Unless he cums quicker than her husband! She's dumping him, but keeping his name. Bob is her new shag." Wynn loved gossip.

"Well, George, That's none of my business. The show is. I think I'll go and look at the stuff."

Digby followed me out of the room. "John," he said softly, "a parting word of advice and a caution sign for you, if I may. The show is going to be a hit. I can smell it. But awful things can happen when it does, especially with people. They change. I was around for the terrific success of *Laugh-In* and the bloody personality battlefield it became. I know you won't change, but they will. Believe me. Don't let them change your show. Their egos will convince them it is theirs. I've seen it dozens of times. George went nuts when they called it *Rowan and Martin's Laugh-In.*" And killed it after three years. Don't let them fuck with you, because, believe me, they'll all be getting in line to do so."

I didn't know what to say. He looked so sad. My mind was on the wonderful stories waiting to be told. Digby's words never quite sank in. A barrier of happiness was blocking them.

I never saw or heard from Digby again. He became a writing professor at a university in New Mexico. In 2012, he died of lung cancer. He was 82. My age as I write this.

While the traveling and the performing were enormous fun, the real joy and satisfaction was in the editing room. That is where the show was made. That is where I lived sixteen hours a day for three years. And loved every minute of it. As I said, this was the first time in my life I felt like an adult. One morning I had to unexpectedly think and give advice like one.

"Johnny?" the soft voice asked.

I looked up from my desk. Peeking in at the door was George's lovely, tall, bright sixteen-year-old daughter, asking if she could come in, and if I would do her a favor. I told her I would try. Plaintively, she explained her desire to quit school. She'd just graduated from the best high school in California which the kids of the rich and famous attend, which she said she hated, pointing out most of them were on dope. She told her parents she did not want to encounter any more of this in college, where there was nothing she wanted to learn anyway. She wanted to work for her dad. She said even when she begged them to let her quit, they screamed that she was going to college. That was it.

"John," she said, "you're the only one my dad listens to. Would you talk to him?"

"Love, that truly is none of my business. I can't. Even if I agree with you that college isn't necessary."

"My dad loves you. Loves talking to you. You're one of the few people he doesn't joke about. Please. You're the only one I can talk to and you're the only one who can talk to my dad."

It was impossible not to be moved by this very together, very intelligent young woman staring at me. "OK."

"Oh, thank you. Thank you," she gushed.

"Hold it. I will not make a special point to talk to your father about this, but when the time is right, I will bring it up casually."

"Oh, thank you. Thank you," she repeated.

Unexpectedly, the right time came later that afternoon. After showing George a video he loved, I said offhandedly, "Your daughter came by to say 'hello' earlier."

"I think she wants to work for me this summer." George smiled.

"No, George, she wants to work for you full time."

"I already told her a hundred times, just for the summer. She's going to UCLA. Her mother's more adamant than I am."

"George, she is none of my business. You are. Can I just make an observation?"

"Like what?"

"The two most successful people I know and admire never went to college. You and me."

"John, my daughter already pointed that out to her mother. It didn't work."

"Okay. This is the last thing I'll say, then I'll go edit. You are the best negotiator I know. Negotiate with mother and daughter. Give her her way for one year. Let her work for you one year. If it doesn't work out for her and you, she goes back to school."

George glanced around his office, thinking. "She's been hounding us for months. I guess better here than having her play hookie. I'll try to run that one past the gatekeeper. I'll let you know."

But it was the daughter who let me know. The next morning she rushed into my office, followed by George. "Oh, thank you. Thank you, John." She then embraced her father. "Daddy, Daddy, thank you too." Then she was off and down the hall. Like a happy teenager.

George watched her, obviously touched. "Beautiful, isn't she?" "That she is, George. That she is."

"If she weren't my daughter, I'd fuck her!"

My mind hollered, *what did he just say*? But all I could manage was, "Jesus Christ, George." Her summer job became permanent.

All About the T-Shirt

Hal Parets wanted to be a part of the show. Twenty years earlier, Hal was one of the most influential producers in live talk TV. He was the guiding hand behind the powerful *Joe Pyne Show*. He was also one of the few people who booked me to plug *It's Tough to Be White*. At sixty, grey and tired, nobody would hire him. I hadn't talk to him since the day I did Pyne's show, but I took his call. He told me he'd spent years trying to find a job, how tough the business was getting, especially for older people. He asked if there was something he could do on the show. I recalled my grandfather, the retired baker, who couldn't get a job even as a janitor working for my mother, then went home and hanged himself.

"Let me talk to George," I said.

"What the fuck?" George said with a touch of mirth. "What are you doing, running a rescue mission? First for teenagers, and now the infirm!"

"George, he has an eye for the kind of people who are perfect for this show. That's what he did for years."

George threw up his hands in mock surrender. "He's not getting more than three-fifty a week, but he's your guy and keep him away from me!"

Within months, George begrudgingly acknowledged that the "old man" was the best prospector we had for mining real people. Hal was also involved in one of our weirdest, offbeat, scariest incidents. Around town it became known as the *Real People* T-shirt story.

It will be impossible for you to imagine the impact or importance of a *Real People* T-shirt had beginning in 1979-80. It was worth more than money to folks; one could be bartered for almost anything. We were receiving 18 to 20,000 pieces of mail a week. Nearly all were show ideas with the hope of getting a *Real People* T-shirt in return.

One shoot I had was in Wisconsin in the dead of one of their worst winters. I was doing a story about a religious lawyer who claimed he was filling scores and scores of bushel baskets with shrunken four-inch real people. He and they were to be picked up on a frozen field by flying saucers to be saved from the impending apocalypse and end times. I wanted our toughest and best field producer, Bob Long, originally trained as a volcanologist, to film it. Bob was stranded in a snowstorm in Detroit. He got George's okay to hire a private jet for a few thousand dollars. The pilot refused to fly in that weather...unless he also got a large *Real People* T-shirt. Bob arrived on time.

The Smithsonian called at the height of the show's enormous success. They asked for T-shirts and memorabilia. They were planning on setting up a display to reflect the impact of the revolutionary show.

Early one Monday morning Hal, who usually showed up slightly grumpy holding a cup of coffee, instead, was humming *Love for Sale,* an unlit cigar in his mouth. "Johnny, you'll never guess what a great weekend I had," he announced. "So, thank you." He waved the cigar as a salute.

"What are you talking about?"

"You know I live alone. This little apartment on Highland. I have a hard time sleeping sometimes, so Friday nights after dinner I usually walk down to Hollywood Boulevard. Just stroll around. Watch the people. Anyway, around nine o'clock, this gorgeous young girl walks over to me. I mean gorgeous. A hooker. She says it's a slow night and I'd get a quickie for a discount. I told her I was out of quickies and out of cash. As I started to walk away, I put my hand inside my coat jacket to reach for my cigarettes, and she says, "Is that a *Real People* T-shirt?" She pulls open my coat to look at it and asks how I got it. I told her I worked on the show. She went berserk, saying she'd take the shirt, instead of money. She wore it during the quickie."

"So, thank you for the T-shirt." He laughed. "She wants another one."

"Take all you want, Hal."

"Thanks. And I got an idea for you."

"What's that?"

"Ya know how Wynn is always talkin' about who Sarah is scewin'? So, why not get 'im laid!"

I smiled. "I'm not in the procurement business."

"I am," he said pleased. "I've got her number. I'll set it up."

"No, Hal. Besides I don't think Bob'd be interested in a hooker."

"She won't be a hooker. She'll be my niece. I'll invite her to lunch at Luigi's to meet you all."

"Hal, you do whatever you want, but I don't want to be a part of it."

"All you have to do is come over to meet her … with Wynn. I'll do the rest."

Four days later just before lunch, Hal called. "I'm at Luigi's with my niece. C'mon over quick. Wynn's on his way. And she just said she wants a hundred bucks. It's a work day."

"Jesus, Hal. I'll be right there."

I rushed down the stairs, across the street to Luigi's on the corner. Sitting at a middle booth was Hal with, as he described her, a very shapely brunette in her late twenties. I was relieved to see she was dressed quite conservatively. Hal introduced her as Michelle.

"Wow," she said. "John Barbour. Where's your vest? I love you in that vest."

"Michelle …" I did not know where to begin. "Michelle … this … this is not my idea."

"To fuck this asshole Bob you work with."

"Jesus, Hal, Michelle … this is all a mistake. I gotta get back to work,"

"And I gotta get paid for my time." Very businesslike.

"Look, Hal will take care of it. I'm sorry. Obviously, he didn't explain."

"Well, what's this?" It was the loud voice of Bob Wynn strutting toward us, grandly taking a seat next to Hal. "What's the special occasion? Are we all having lunch just to meet Hal's *niece*?"

He said 'niece' like he knew she wasn't a niece; at least, not Hal's. Michelle spotted his disdain immediately. It was hate at first sight. She said matter-of-factly, "If I'm gonna fuck him, I want another hundred!"

Wynn gasped, then howled with laughter. Diners in nearby booths suspended their forks in midair, staring at us. My face was flushed and hot from embarrassment. I squirmed in my seat.

Hal turned on his 'niece.' "Goddamn it, Michelle. Yer supposed to fuck, not fuck up."

She turned back to him. "Fuck you too. Just give me my money."

Wynn glared at me and Hal. "What the fuck is this? You trying to set me up with a hooker?" He got up laughing and left. I knew he'd be running to George to inform him of the screwup setup. I got up to follow him.

"Look, Hal, you work this out with Michelle. Michelle I'm so sorry about all this, but I have to go." I left with her telling the room she wanted her money.

Within an hour the whole building was rocking with laughter. I hid in my office. Hal came in to try to apologize, but I sent him away, telling him not to worry. Soon, though, I had to worry. The phone rang. A very low angry voice said, "Yo betta git yer ass downstairs."

"Who is this?"

"Michelle's manager. Git yer ass down heuh. We has some unfinished business tuh tend huh!"

"I don't think so," I said firmly.

"If yo likes huh sees that old man who works fo' yah come in every day, you'd bettuh."

It was a threat I believed. I had to go. I went to my closet and pulled out a large bag, and descended the stairs quickly and out to the sidewalk. Parked in front was a shiny new Cadillac.

Behind the wheel sat the largest most colorfully dressed black man I'd ever seen. He was right out of *Shaft*. I stood a few feet from the rolled-down window.

"Friend," he said, "you owes me two hundred bucks'"

"Wrong on two counts, sir. I am not your friend. And second, it was only supposed to be a hundred, but your talent screwed up. Nothing happened. So we're even."

He stared without blinking. "I went tuh a lot of trouble huh drive ova here. If yah ain't payin' for man girl's' time, you'll pay for mine!"

"How much?"

"Two hundred bucks."

I smiled. He was smart. "Sir, I am sorry you wasted your time, but if I had a bunch of money I could not pay you. I don't know who you are. You could be undercover for all I know. Soliciting is a crime. This could be a setup. I don't know who you are, and don't want to know."

I raised the bag. "But I will give you something better than money. Better than any dope you may have in that glove compartment." I handed him the bag that I had planned on giving Hal to subsidize his love life.

"What the fuck is this? Laundry?"

"There's even a couple of triple xxx large in there."

He opened the bag, pulling a handful of T-shirts out, holding one up to read it. *Real People*. "Goddamn." He grinned at me. "Goddamn, man. That's cool." The Caddy roared off.

The T-shirts were so popular and so in demand, George began selling them on the side. A young man in his late teens pushed open the door to my office, sticking in his head. "Mr. Barbour, I just wanted to say hello and tell you how much I love your show." I looked up. His arms were full of merchandise.

"Thank you very much. What is all that?"

"Oh, T-shirts, jackets, travel bags, even a phone. *Real People* stuff. I'm taking them to George. He wanted them."

"Where'd they come from?"

"Your warehouse."

"I don't have a warehouse."

"The one we keep all the stuff we sell."

"You mean, you sell it?"

"Thousands of them. I'm just one of half-a-dozen people out there that answer the mail and ship these things."

I'd never heard of this. "Tell me about it."

"It's huge. We have a table with trays and trays of letters we read. The story ideas we send here, others are responding to the catalogue we've sent, telling us what they want. It's amazing!"

"Thanks for stopping by. I appreciate it."

"Thank you, Mr. Barbour. It was a pleasure meeting you."

I walked casually into George's office. "George," I said offhandedly, "can I ask you a question?"

"Shoot."

"You know, I'm not greedy. Not once have I ever mentioned money or questioned the fees I'm getting. Right?"

"So that must mean you're gonna mention it now."

"Sort of. You said this *shit* wasn't going anywhere, but clearly it is. You gave me ten percent of what you thought was nothing. Now, though, it is clearly something. Soon it's going to number one. That ten percent will pay for Christopher's college. So, I appreciate it. I'll obviously have to wait a while to see how that pays off, but it seems the merchandising is paying off now. Huge. I know it's not in my contract. I'm not as smart about these things as you. I was just wondering if you had any plans on giving me ten percent of the merchandising."

He did not look pleased. He looked like an embarrassed Danny Arnold. "Most of that money is going into new editing equipment and facilities, so, right now, the answer is no."

I stared at him, feeling hurt. "George, it's not as though I want any more money. I'm doing fine. It's just that I thought you might offer it to me as a token of appreciation and even friendship. Forget I asked. I hope you sell millions for years. That'll mean we'll still be on the air." I walked out.

The next day a delivery was made to our house. It was a case of Mouton Cadet with a note from George. It said how much he really loved working with me and valued my friendship. He said he would continue to provide me with that red wine if I continued to provide him with a hit.

The Ides of March

Of all the chapters in this book this will be the most difficult to write, trying to describe the enormous joy I was experiencing along with the creeping, mounting frustration of fighting to keep the show's focus and integrity. I do not believe in a higher being, karma, predestination, or any of the crutches that help most people limp through life. If we are made in God's image, the majority of the folks I was meeting once success was upon me would disincline me from wanting to meet the maker of such people.

I have to admit, though, there were inexplicable metaphysical happenings afoot in the universe that led to bringing *Real People* to life that I cannot explain. That said, as Digby had forewarned, through ego, greed, ignorance and arrogance, human forces were rising to begin gnawing *Real People* to death. In a matter of months, it had become a major part of the culture. *Mad Magazine* did an entire issue spoofing it. Sitcoms like *WKRP in Cincinnati* were doing likewise. *Saturday Night Live* joked about it. Our cast, over my objections, and with the exception of me, appeared on game shows like *Family Feud* and series like *Love Boat*. I had tried to convince George not to allow our cast to do that; doing so diminished the specialness of our show, but the publicity magazines and newspapers were lauding him for his new show about weird people. Gary Deeb of *The Chicago Sun Times* was the only critic whose articles pointed out my role as the godfather and nursemaid.

As happens in this business, when a show is successful, the networks, in this case Freddy Silverman, rushes not to the creator of the show, but the owner, George Schlatter. Silverman asked George if he could do a show called *Real Kids*. Of course, George said yes. I rushed into George's office. He was sitting with a smiling Tony Fantozzi. Tony was drinking his usual beer, George a glass of wine. They were toasting their new sale to Silverman.

"Join us, John," Tony said.

George added, lifting his wine, "We fooled the Jews again." They smiled at each other in a ritual that they'd obviously performed before.

"George, is it true?" I asked. "Are you doing a show about kids?" When he nodded, I asked why.

"Because they asked me to and I can."

"John," Tony interjected, "if you play your cards right, and go along with us, you could become a force in this business."

"Tony, *Real People* is already a force. That's all I care about. I don't need any more money or TV exposure on meaningless shows."

"George just signed the cutest kid to be one of the hosts. Peter Billingsley. That kid'll be gold."

George raised his glass. "I've got the white Gary Coleman. When Silverman sees him, he'll be running to give us a sitcom deal."

"George," I pleaded, "he could be better showcased if once in a while we did a short feature in our show called *Real Kids*. He'd come across better."

"Too late," George said. "And speaking of hosts, Silverman called the other day telling me he wanted Sarah to be the host of *The Today Show*, I told him to fuck off, and to keep away from her. The same thing I told Tony about his client Billy Friedkin. (Friedkin had directed one of the great horror movies, *The Exorcist*, as well as *The French Connection*.) He's in love with her and wants to put her in his next film. I told Tony the bitch is mine."

"George, Sarah is adorable, and does come across as the star, but I am telling you, if Skip were the one male and the other hosts were female, he'd be the star. It's the show that makes them. They don't make the show."

"John," Tony said, "we're on our way, and we'd like you aboard."

"George, could I pose something to you since you obviously want to do more shows?"

"Go ahead."

"It has occurred to me that we could make whole shows, half hour shows just out of some of the segments we've done already. Real Outtakes. Real Home videos. Some of the stories would even make great movies of the week. Like the boat builder. Why don't you give me ten percent of your company and I will help you find the people to write and produce these other George Schlatter Productions?"

George snapped, "I told you before, I don't take partners. I just turned down an offer from MGM to sell my company. I do it alone. My way."

"It was just a suggestion. I thought it could help you because *Real Kids* will die, and it will diminish our show."

"Not if you help us," Tony said.

"Tony, I'm working twenty hours a day, seven days a week right now. I have no time."

Indeed, *Real Kids* died a quick embarrassing death, cancelled after the second show. As predicted, other production companies began successfully producing *Real Homes, Out-Takes,* and *America's Funniest Home Videos.*

Alan Landesburg, producer of *In Search Of,* called Bob Wynn, asking if he'd like to be the sole producer of a new show ABC had just ordered from him, to challenge *Real People,* called *That's Incredible.*

The worst thing about the death of *Real Kids* was that it wasn't the death of George's contract with Peter Billingsley. This resulted in my first loud, angry confrontation with George in front of others. We had gone toe-to-toe often in private, primarily over his tastelessness, which he playfully acknowledged. A few times he won the arguments; mostly I did. I admitted to him my work was frequently improved with those encounters. He once announced at a large dinner that he never had so much fun fighting with someone, but not on the occasion of Peter Billingsley.

A dozen of us, the cast, the director, some staff, and Wynn, were seated in our usual spots around the large rectangular production table going over the next show. George was at one end, I at the other. Those gatherings were usually full of laughs and warmth. The show was a hit. Everyone was happy. On this occasion, the merriment was interrupted by George announcing beginning soon we'd have a twelve-year-old co-host, Peter Billingsley.

"You're kidding?" I blurted.

"I am not. Starting next week."

"Jesus Christ, George, you can't do that!"

"I can and I did."

"George, he just died on that piece of shit show."

"He's starting next week. And that's it."

"Jesus Christ, George. You cannot have a kid telling life stories of real people. It's stupid and demeaning."

Everyone got quiet, pushing back a little from the table. George was flushed. "He is now a co-host and you will work with him!"

"I'll sit on the stage with him, but I will not be writing or editing any of his stories. Someone else can do that. And, hopefully, you don't bring over any of the people who did that crap for him on *Real Kids*.

George was seething. Skip broke the tension. "Well, that's settled. I guess we'll have to start making smaller T-shirts."

Peter came aboard. No offer ever came for George to do a sitcom with the Caucasian Gary Coleman. *Real People* was too good to be sunk by a kid, or the next host George brought aboard: Byron Allen.

Byron Allen was an aspiring twenty-year-old black comic and senior at USC. Managed or pushed by his mother, a secretary at NBC, he was signed to the Morris office and brought to George by Fantozzi. Tony thought the show should have a little color. Byron was pleasant, but I'm sad to say he was the dumbest, least informed person I had ever met. I did a story for him about a man who created and made his own Madame Tussauds Wax Museum, which filled every room in the house. At the dining room table were The Beatles. When given the voice-over copy to read, Byron asked, "Who are The Beatles?"

I did a story about great street performers and musicians in New Orleans. In the introduction I referenced and compared some to Satchmo. Byron didn't know who that was.

Someone sent us a clip from Cincinnati's Five O'clock News. A field reporter, excited to see someone from *Real People,* asked what he was doing in Cincinnati and Byron answered, "I'm on my way to Ohio!"

The second year on the show, George was enraged that this kid asked for a raise, so he threatened to air the clip from the Cincinnati News. I urged George not to; we couldn't embarrass the show by pointing out how dumb some of us were. Today, Byron Allen is financially, the most successful of all the ex-hosts, the mega-millionaire founder of Entertainment Studios, which, like a sausage factory, grinds out filler shows profiling endless celebrities and comics. If Byron learned one thing from George, it was how to profit and pander to an undiscerning public. His shows, like most TV, provide neither real entertainment nor real information. Just a lot of jobs.

As a co-host-producer and writer of a hit, I had something I'd never dreamt of having: a secretary. Out of habit, though, because I don't like to feel like a boss, I continued to do my own typing and filing. What Dolores did primarily was answer the phone. One early morning, when she said,

"It's the FBI," I picked up the phone. The polite voice identified himself as an agent from the main office. He asked if I would mind if he and his partner came over to chat with me.

"What about?" I asked, thinking it was something related to immigration.

"It's not something we can discuss on the phone."

"I'd be happy to talk to you, but there'd be too much gossip if you came by here. How about I buy you lunch at Lakeside Golf Club?"

I met them by myself in the dining room the following day. They were already seated, both younger than me. After my nervous greeting, I told them they could be my guests. They informed me the government was footing the bill. The slightly older one with the deep-set blue eyes, whose voice I recognized from the call, did all the talking.

"How long have you known Nathan Markowitz?"

"Nathan Markowitz? Why?"

"How long have you known him?"

"A couple of years. Why?"

"What kind of business do you do with him?"

"I don't do any kind of business with him. He's just my attorney. He put together my company for me. Helped with my pension plan. Lawyer stuff. Why?"

"You do any banking with him?"

"He's not a banker. What kind of banking?"

"Off-shore."

I laughed. "No. Are you kidding? He asked us about the Cayman Islands or some place to put our money, but my wife said she wouldn't even put our money in a bank in Chicago let alone some island."

"You see him a lot?"

"Not that much. Socially, a couple of dinners. Not much."

He reached into his inside pocket and pulled out an envelope. He opened it, spreading the contents in front of me. There were eight or ten pictures of me and Sarita with Nathan at his house on Mulholland, at Trader Vic's, the Beverly Hills Hotel, and Musso Frank's. I was flabbergasted.

"What are these for?" I asked, incredulously. "Why were you following me and my wife?"

"We follow everyone associated with him."

"What for? What's he done?"

"That's what we're trying to find out. Has he mentioned anything about his activities to you?"

"Not a word. About anything. Just what he likes to eat. What do you think he's doing that would compel the FBI to follow him?"

"Do you know he stole a half-a-million-dollar inheritance from his girlfriend?"

"He has a girlfriend?"

"Had. It's in his account in the Caymans."

"I didn't know he had a girlfriend, so why would I know anything else? Did she file charges against him or something?"

"No."

"Then how do you know it was stolen?"

He didn't answer; but asked, "Has he ever mentioned anything to you about guns?"

"Just that I should get one for home protection."

"Nothing about selling them?"

"If you've gone to the trouble of taking these pictures, you've obviously gone to the trouble to tap our phones, so you obviously know my wife and I know nothing about selling guns or banking. Just good places to eat."

"Well, thank you Mr. Barbour, for your time. If you can think of anything, or hear anything, please call us." He handed me his card. They left, their lunch untouched.

When I mentioned it to Sarita, she said, "I told you it felt like somebody was following us. What do you think we should we do about Nathan?"

"Nothing. He's been a good attorney, but I will tell him I'd like all of our files returned to us, just in case of fire or something, that I'll make copies and send them back."

I got so busy, I forgot to make that call until months later. When it was almost too late.

Within eleven months from the airing of the first special, *Real People* was the number-one show in the country. In Chicago and most of the Midwest it got an overwhelming fifty share. This was higher than any of the highest-rated sitcoms. Ever. Higher than *Mash, All in the Family, I Love Lucy,* all of them.

Sarita called the morning the staff heard the good news and asked if she could come by for a minute just before lunch. She wanted to see George, but wouldn't tell me why. Upon arrival, she was led into George's office where he and I were waiting. George never sat when Sarita came into the room. This time he almost sprinted across the room, giving her a huge hug.

"I have something for you," she said. "For the both of you."

She handed George and me identical, beautifully wrapped small boxes. We tore off the paper, undid the little catch on the box inside, and opened them. Inside each one was a solid twenty-four carat gold chain. Attached to the end was a fairly large solid gold pendant that said #1. We hugged her as she fastened them around our necks.

"When did you get these done?" George asked.

"A couple of months ago."

"You are amazing. So is your husband." George suddenly got quiet, almost wistful. "You know, I've never said this to anyone, but I've been thinking about it for the last few months. I'm not the kind of person who's really capable of loving someone, but I told your husband if I loved anybody, it is you guys."

I walked her to the car. "Honey, you're amazing. How did you know? When did you know?"

"Honey, Christopher and I attend every show. It was impossible not to know months ago that this was going to be a huge hit."

The following day, another carton of Mouton Cadet arrived with a note dated March 28, 1980, from George. In part it said, *Sarita, I wear it every day. It reminds me of what your husband said when we first started: We'll be number #1! That was last year. Look where we are now. I love you both … . George.*

As often happens when a show becomes an unexpected hit, (in TV any hit is unexpected) the performers, actors or hosts begin to think they are the ones responsible for that success. In the case of *Real People,* Sarah Purcell lived up, or rather down, to Digby's parting warning. Fortunately, for us, she was the only one. She had gone in just over a year from a sweet, natural unknown local TV personality to what she considered the solo star. Not just a star, but worse, one who thought she had talent. Sarah began to demand she write, edit, direct, produce and select her own stories.

Bill Rafferty, who travelled with her on a few shoots to New York, informed us that this star trip was drummed into her head by her new boyfriend, turned fiancé; a tall self-styled mysterious unseen investment banker from New York. She breezed into George's office one afternoon wearing a large smile and huge diamond engagement ring. She flashed it proudly, announcing her engagement, and her desire to be in charge of her stories. George and Bob seemed to happily agree. I said nothing. She hugged them, but not me, and left humming.

I turned to George. "Is she kidding? "

George smiled. "About the ring or the stories?"

"Both." I said. "I thought she was having a fling with Bob Long."

"That's just her cross-country bang, "Wynn chortled. "This guy's the New York LA lay. She probably bought her own ring. Rafferty said he went to the guy's apartment to pick her up and saw the guy had only one suit in his closet. He's a hustler, filling her head and pants. It won't last long. She'll probably marry a dentist."

"George, you're not gonna let her do her own stories, are you?"

"Yes, then you can fix them."

"I hear these horror stories about stars thinking they're the show. George, you had it on *Laugh-In* with Rowan and Martin. Destroyed a cultural hit in three years. You don't want that here. There are only three types of performers in front of a camera: those who are just personalities, famous for just being famous. There are talents, those who really do have talent. Then there are the rare, exceptional ones who are stars beyond talent, which they may or may not even have. There is an un-manufacturable charisma about them. Cary Grant had it. Sarah Purcell does not. She also does not have talent. She is only a personality, and only because of this show, without which she'd be back at Channel 7!"

"Are you finished?" George smiled.

"Jesus, George. Please say something to her before she gets out of hand. Maybe even warn her about this guy."

"Do you wanna fuck her?" George asked bluntly.

"I beg your pardon?"

Wynn laughed like he knew what was coming.

George repeated. "I'm serious. Do you wanna fuck her?"

"No. Of course not," I answered firmly.

George turned to Bob. "Do you wanna fuck her?"

"Not me. I'm tired."

"Johnny," George continued, "I would pay this guy, this fiancé, to continue fucking her because I don't wanna fuck her, Bob doesn't wanna fuck her, and you don't wanna fuck her. She's happy. That's all I care about. Believe me. At CBS, Bob and I got tired taking turns fucking Judy Garland. We had to go with her when she went to Vegas. We got so tired we went out on the strip asking guys if they'd like to fuck Judy Garland. Free. They thought we were drunks." Both began laughing.

"John," George said, "don't worry. As they always say in this town, we'll fix it in post. Or rather, you'll fix it in post."

They were still giggling when I closed the door behind me.

In the three years I was with the show, I only had three brief conversations or work encounters with Sarah. The first was unpleasant, the second awkward, the third, a favor for her. The first was in New York. One of the stories we were shooting there, one that I'd done previously for *National Graffiti,* was of America's only professional, registered vampire hunter. We assigned it to Sarah. To ensure it would go easily for her, I took the crew well in advance to Mr. Kaplan's house in the Bronx. We set everything up for the interview and waited. And waited. And waited. Over an hour. And no Sarah. Embarrassed, I apologized for the delay. Since our subject was miked, I put one on myself, and did a fifty-minute interview. When we were done, the front door swung open and in glides Sarah like Loretta Young in her TV show.

"Hi, everybody," she announced with no apology. She then ordered to be miked right away so she could start her interview. I informed her the interview was over and handed her a slip of paper with six questions on it.

"What is this?" she asked.

"Your questions. All you need is to ask those six questions"

"Are you fucking kidding?"

"That's all we need. The interview is done. We'll insert your questions in editing."

"Wait a minute, I didn't fly all the way from LA to the Plaza to drive all the way out here to ask just six fucking questions. I'm doing an interview."

"You were late. He's not here. He's gone for location shoots. So, we need the six questions. Please."

She stared at me, then the sheet, then with an angry edge, read the first question. I had to have her repeat it since she sounded so cold. She was no better the second time. Or the third. Finally, I had to tell her to be her warm charming self like she is in the studio. She rolled her eyes, calmed down, then did it right.

She was there no more than fifteen minutes and bolted out to her limousine. In editing the story, I needed to find a reaction shot to one of our vampire hunter's more outrageous comments about the living dead; there before me on the monitor was our star rolling her eyes at me. That was the cutaway. When the audience saw Sarah's reaction to the living dead question, they howled and applauded with glee at her comedic timing! Of course, Sarah believed she'd planned it that way.

The second encounter was backstage after a dress rehearsal in front of a live audience. It was about a question I had in the story about John and Greg Rice, the millionaire midget real estate twins from Florida. The question was simply, "Do you guys date normal size women?"

With the rehearsal over, Sarah rushed to me backstage. "Where's George?"

"Across the hall I think. Why?"

"I told him I didn't think that question you have is appropriate for a family audience."

"What question?"

"About who these guys are sleeping with."

"I didn't ask who they're sleeping with. I asked if they dated normal size women."

"Everybody knows what you mean."

"I hope they do! Because I know everybody wants to know if they do."

"I don't. It's too graphic."

"You're kidding! It will answer what's on everybody's mind. It is harmless."

She got quiet, then began talking, almost as if to herself. Or a priest. Or psychiatrist.

"I ... I ... unbelievable ... married all those years ... never knew what an orgasm was. Just something I read or heard about. Bob ... Bob ... was ... was the man to make me ... feel something. For some reason that question to them brings up some really awful pictures in my head."

"I hope so. I don't know much about sex myself, certainly not about anything you've gone through, but I do know about telling stories. I do not tell these stories to the audience, Sarah. I tell them to myself, and just hope people like them. As your very large check you cash every week tells you, they obviously do. Don't even bother going to George. I've already told him, if the question is not in the piece, I am not in the piece.

"I'm sorry," she said, and walked away.

The third unexpected exchange occurred in an editing room. As promised, George let her shoot and assemble her own stories. One of those was about the monumental Crazy Horse memorial carved into the Black Hills of Dakota. A Lakota Chief commissioned a Polish-American sculptor, Korczak Ziolkowski, from New England, to carve it as memorial to all of Native Americans. He set off the first dynamite in 1947 in the presence of five survivors of Little Big Horn. It is and was a magnificent, moving story. I got a phone call.

"John, this is Sarah. Could you come down to editing for a minute and do me a favor?"

"Certainly," I said, surprised at her pleasantness. When I entered, she was standing next to a monitor, her bright young editor, Beverly, seated in front of it.

"Thank you," Sarah said. "Would you mind looking at this?"

"Not at all. Play it."

As a story, it was awful, but with wonderful visuals. The story was not only nonexistent, it was lugubrious, with endless shots of Sarah crying or tearing up. When it was over, she asked what I thought.

"Sarah, I'll answer your question with a question. Why did you call me?"

"George won't let me air it. He hates it. Says it's maudlin. A downer. He told me to show it to you."

My first thought was about George. He never, ever had any reluctance trying to insert something into the show of questionable taste, nearly all of which I prevented. But he abhorred excessive sentiment in any story. Sarah must have had to swallow her 'I am the star' pride to call me. I was touched by her honesty.

"Sarah, first of all, I don't know what your focus is, the Indians, the sculptor, the tourists, or you. There's no story. That's not the worst of it, pardon me, but it is those endless shots of you crying."

"But it moved me. I wanted the audience to see that."

"It is too much. In a long-ago *Life* magazine interview about acting, Laurence Olivier gave the perfect advice. 'If you want the audience to cry, the actor should not, otherwise, they'll be watching him.' Does Bev have the select reel and out-takes?"

"Yes."

"Then let me work on it."

When the piece aired, with the story focusing on the Indians, we never saw Sarah sobbing. All we saw was her holding back. The audience cried for her.

Sarah never spoke to me again, but, Beverly, her editor did. "John, that was so nice of you." She had tears in her eyes. "It's not what I expected. What I was told about you."

"What do you mean?"

"Bob Long warned us that if you ever got to be the sole producer, you'd fire us all."

I was stunned. Then, with more than Bob to worry about, I said, "Bev, long ago I read the greatest line in the book *Citizen Hearst*. Hearst wanted to partner with a young genius he'd just heard about. He sent his aide from San Simeon to meet him over a couple of days in LA to talk a proposal. The next day the aide came back and said, 'Mr. Hearst, the young man does not even want to talk about it. He hates you.' William

Randolph Hearst said, 'Why would he hate me? I never did him a favor!' Beverly, it cannot be said better than that. Thank you."

The Power and the Glory

Pardon me for the title of this little chapter. It sounds a little overboard and inflated, but it is not. No show in television had the social or legislative impact that *Real People* did. The possible exception might have been Ed Murrow exposing Senator Joe McCarthy's witch hunt and, in another special, exposing Coca Cola's exploitation of migrant workers in *Harvest of Shame*; impossible to imagine with today's gutless fare. Murrow's were news shows, but mine was an entertainment show.

In the three years writing and editing most of the hours myself in their entirety, *Real People* contributed more to influence legislation and improving society than did *Sixty Minutes* in forty-seven years. I could have never imagined sitting as a deportee in the law library in Toronto rummaging through books, reading that one final way to become a citizen would be to make a major contribution to the country. That show did. I'll begin with a minor fun-fact about its influence.

While in New York shooting our hour special about The Big Apple, I felt it would be incomplete if we didn't film fans in the bleachers at Yankee Stadium. I wanted them hollering, "Welcome to *Real People*." We didn't even buy a ticket. My cameraman and I headed for the house that Ruth built. We walked straight to the ticket taker. He called my name happily. I asked him to look into the camera, saying, "From Yankee Stadium, welcome to *Real People*." He was thrilled. Delighted, he let us through unquestioned. On our way to the bleachers, we stopped ushers and vendors, and had them do the same. We were almost through the tunnels to the stands, when a guard intercepted us. "Hey, John, whatta yah think yer doin?"

"Just getting some bumpers for our show. Would you like to do one?"

"No. Follow me. Both of you." He led us up an elevator to an office marked Security Director. "Here they are," the guard said to a tall broad-shouldered, mean-looking man. His name was Kelly, the stadium's security chief.

"John, what do you think you're doing?" He sounded like he was talking to a child.

"Our being in New York wouldn't be complete, sir, if we didn't get your fans to be the announcers on our special about New York."

"Did you get permission? Did you even buy a ticket?"

"No, sir."

"This stadium has never had and never will have any cameras of any sort filming the stands, except those used to televise the games. Do you understand that? Never!"

"I didn't know that."

"Even with those cameras during the game, we are very cautious about what we show of the fans. You never quite know who or what's out there. Understand?"

"Does that mean we have to give you what we've already shot?"

"No. Where were you off to when we stopped you?"

"To the bleachers. We thought those fans would be the most fun. And the loudest."

"Don't you know a game is going on?'"

I smiled. "That's why we and the fans are here."

He put his hands in his pocket and pulled out his card. "Try not to disrupt things too much. Get your shots between innings. Some staff and broadcast folk'll be pissed. Just show them my card. And make it quick, if you can."

We stood at the end of the tunnel to the bleachers, waiting for the inning to end. When it did, we turned on the camera, and headed up. As we did, fans began to recognize us. At first there was isolated yelling, then cheering, then a massive roar that began to envelop the whole stadium. It was like the crowd's vocal wave at a major sporting event. It was deafening. Even players looked up.

I waved my hands above my head, motioning for quiet. They were suddenly silent. I then asked if they would holler, "From the bleachers at Yankee Stadium, welcome to *Real People*." I waved my hand again for them to begin. Hundreds and hundreds of them roared lustily, waving their arms and cheering. They were so happy. But not nearly as happy as I was. To this day, we are the only ones who filmed in Yankee Stadium without a permit!

You know the name John Walsh, the host of *America's Most Wanted*. He was not that host in 1981. In 1981 he was the grieving father of a murdered six-year-old son, Adam. The boy's decapitated body was found shortly after he was abducted from in front of a Hollywood, Florida department store. John was enraged by the law's delay and lack of cooperation between state and federal police agencies in the search for his son and his killer. They were too late to save Adam. John channeled his grief and disgust into traveling the country, encouraging a federal law be put in place to help future parents avoid such heartbreak. In 1981, a missing child was just that particular state's issue. He campaigned for it to be a national issue, one involving even the FBI. Alone, he lobbied Congress, urging the passage of a Missing Childrens' Act with no success. I saw him on a national talk show and was moved by his story. I handed George an article about the case. "I want to do this story."

He glanced at it, then handed it back. "We're not doing any story about some kid who had his head cut off, for God's sake. And the father's been all over the place. It's old hat."

"But *we* haven't told it."

"And we're not going to."

"George, with a show as entertaining as ours, with an audience this big, when we come across a story this important, and this human, it's a must that we tell them once in a while. To give the show balance and heart. I want to do it. On my own time, even if you don't air it."

After a moment, he said, "Just don't mention they cut off his head."

Within ninety days of airing our version, The Missing Children's Act became law.

John Walsh thanked us publicly. In 1983, *Adam* was the movie of the week to thirty-five million viewers. A few less than us! We, meaning the entire cast, were suddenly on the cover of *TV Guide*. For a week everyone strutted around waving the magazine above their heads, everyone except perhaps George and me. George was rather cool about it. He was after a bigger bang. Something the world would notice. I was moderately pleased, but I was after a bigger magazine: *Time*; something the industry would notice.

I sat in Bollinger's office. "Henry, the *TV Guide* cover is nice, but the story is absolute fluff. If I were a stranger reading it, I'd think that the guy on the top of that pyramid picture of us was being held up by the other hosts. The article says nothing about my input behind the camera, that I'm even a producer and writer, for crying out loud."

"John, it's a good start. Not many get a *TV Guide* cover."

"Only one writer in this whole industry, Gary Deeb, has pointed out what I do. Look, I may even retire when this thing is over. I don't care to be famous and I don't care if anyone else knows it, but I want the people who run this business to know it. The only magazine they'll believe is *Time*. What happens when you talk to them?"

"Frankly, I don't get any reaction. They sound as if they don't believe me. I know them well. I don't know what it is."

"Then call one of your friends there and ask him how he'd like to spend a month with me while we put together a show. Then he'll know. Tell him he'll see the inside of the show that is changing television."

He did call. *Time* declined.

In the meantime, for his bigger bang, George was talking to the Pentagon and Navy Department. At the next read-through he announced, "Gang, if Bob Hope can do it, so can we. We're going to entertain the troops. We're going to do a show from an aircraft carrier in San Diego. Of course, there was applause and cheers, but not from me. Not wanting to embarrass George by confronting him as I usually did when he had questionable notions, I said nothing until everybody left.

"George, why do you need a stunt to make the show bigger? It's already the biggest thing on TV."

"This'll cap it off! It'll be huge. Canons going off, planes flying overhead. Doesn't that stir you?"

"It is frankly Barnum & Bailey hokum pandering. I'll give you a thought, though. If you want to salute the military in some way, let me do an entire Veterans Day show. Do nothing but stories about every aspect of the military. I'll pick the stories with you. I'll write and edit them. If it's what you like, you do that show from the aircraft carrier on Veterans Day, but I won't appear on deck or on shore. Just in the stories."

"You get paid to appear." He glared at me.

"Not to do stunts," I shot back. "Oh, another thing, if you're interested in getting some great publicity, I've been toying with a couple of ideas I wanted to run by you. You know the mail department brings us pictures from people who look exactly like us? I've seen three of me that could fool Sarita. And some of Sarah, Skip and Bill. I mean amazing."

He smiled. "So?"

"So, let's hold a look-alike contest over the year. At the end pick those who look most like us, introduce them at the last show, and actually let them host while we sit in the audience." He chuckled. I continued. "First, it proves anyone could host this show, and if Sarah's agent or whoever gets greedy, just show them the show."

"I like it. Actually, I do. What's the other notion?"

"This is more serious and more meaningful, but could be great. Reagan's economic trickledown economics has defied gravity and stays up there. The economy is lousy. I'd like to pick a wealthy family, a middle-class family, and a poor family and assign a crew to follow each for a year, with maybe an update on them every three months or so. It could be really interesting."

"That's good, John. That's good. I'll think about it. And do me a favor, think about the carrier."

Everyone loved the idea of the look-alike contest, especially Skip, Rafferty and Willard. But, we never got to do it. Sarah went berserk! We also didn't get to profile the families we had already selected to follow. However, George did cancel the aircraft carrier because of what he saw in the Veterans' Day special. This leads me to two more stories on a parallel with John Walsh's.

On previous shows, we had already done stories about the military, stories unknown to the general public. We were the first to profile the Tuskegee Airmen, the first black air squadron to fly and fight in the Second World War. Segregated in their own country, then segregated again in the military, we heard heart-wrenching and uplifting personal accounts from men who still believed enough in America to fight for her. In our Veterans' Day special, we told an hour of those tales.

Two I am proudest of still move me. They seem even more relevant today. The first is about the Navajo Code Talkers.

Early in the war in the Pacific, the Pentagon discovered the Japanese had broken all of our codes. While scrambling to try to come up with an unbreakable one, a minister with military connections recalled while preaching to the Navajo, it was an unwritten language. Following Pearl Harbor, a number of Navajo had already volunteered to fight either the Germans or the Japanese. Rather than giving them guns, the Pentagon gave them their battle plan secrets and shipped them to the far Pacific, mostly into enemy territory. There were about forty young and old in foxholes and trenches with radios talking their language, the language they were forbidden to speak at home. When the war ended, they were totally unheralded or recognized. They remained a secret government asset. Our Pentagon wanted them again in case we went to war with Russia or China. They were unknown until 1981. Sons and nephews, proud of their fathers' or uncles' service, decided to follow in their boots and join the Marines. Their graduation as Marines suddenly appeared briefly on the news and the morning shows. Again, like John Walsh, it was a story aired and forgotten. But what a story. I took a crew to San Diego to tell it.

In the studio, when it ended, the audience rose to their feet, cheering. We introduced by name, on stage, over a dozen of the original Code

Talkers. Looking into the camera, I asked those who thought it was time our country recognize them for their sacrifice to write or call the president. The following morning, we received a call from an aide to President Reagan. He told us there were so many calls they had to add phone banks. The following program we presented a tape of President Reagan awarding the Navajo Code Talkers a Presidential Citation. President Reagan, for the three years I was the producer, was the only famous politician, actor or personality to ever appear on our show.

This next story was never on any newscast or talk show. But should have been. This year and every year, and in years to come, hundreds of thousands of Americans, and others, will journey to Washington to the Vietnam Veterans' War Memorial. They will gaze at, photograph, and touch some of the 58,300 names inscribed on it. It is the most visited and revered monument in Washington, but was almost never built. That may come as a surprise. Most Americans take it for granted. Of course, it should be there. It deserves to be, but in 1981Congress and scores of senators and media did not want the U.S. to fund a memorial to a socially disruptive, unpopular war. Families who had lost loved ones in that war and the few senators who were pushing for it, fought over the ordinariness of the design. And the designer – a young Asian-American architect, Maya Lin.

That was the backdrop to David Westfall's story, a story Hal Parets had found for me. David Westfall was a teacher at a small school near Val Verde, New Mexico. His wife was also a teacher. They were both in their late fifties. In the late seventies they lost their son, also named David, in Vietnam. He was killed within the week he arrived in Asia. He was twenty-one. The parents were shattered. For months they did nothing but grieve. Not being religious, there were no churches or preachers to comfort them. No prayers to be said. No place to go, except into memories. Inspired by those memories, the father decided he would work his grief off. When his son was a boy he loved to explore a certain mountain not far from their home. Father and son climbed, trekked and explored every inch of it. It was there atop that hill with a view of the valley, the father built his own memorial. First, he spent his salary. Then his wife's salary. Then their savings. Then their pension. With the help of his surviving son, Doug, they found the more they built, the more they had to build. They did it alone with no help. Townsfolk thought they were nuts.

But somehow, as if by some metaphysical wireless word, what the father was doing began to spread. First around New Mexico, then the

Southwest, then the whole country. Hundreds and hundreds of mothers and fathers somehow hearing about that lone persistent griever got onto planes and buses or into cars, and brought their pictures to the hilltop. For thirteen years, David Westfall greeted them, building a larger and larger cement cathedral to house the pictures. When that was full, he began building concrete walkways, scores of them around the hill leading to the top; each was lined every few feet with a plaque and a picture, illuminated at night.

Sitting quietly next to him, surrounded by those plaques, with his mute bowed wife sitting by herself in the distance, I asked if he had wished his son had done what many had done, gone to Canada. He answered very compassionately.

"Going to Canada, a country that's not yours, or going to a questionable war, each is a painful decision. And each is understandable. It is not for me to judge."

I never intruded on his wife's silence and closed the piece with a long, slow montage of David working, his wife in distant silhouette, individual faces of the thirty or forty other parents pointing at their child's picture, talking or wiping their eyes, close-ups of the faces on the wall and the plaques, black faces, white faces, yellow faces, all young faces. Over this I played Roberta Flack singing her haunting version of *The First Time Ever I Saw Your Face,* made more haunting by the images. In the studio, when it was over, people were sobbing.

The first call I got the next morning was from a senator from Utah. He was one of the few actively pushing for Maya Lin's memorial to be built. He asked if it would be possible for me to send him fifty copies of David's story so that he could send it to all fifty senatorial offices. I sent them that afternoon.

And there was a lighter side. If Walt Disney was the most famous cartoonist in the movies, the most famous cartoonist in the war, in which he fought, was Bill Mauldin. While in the infantry, Bill told us, as well as fighting, he was asked to also draw for *The Stars and Stripes*. There he created his beloved, edgy, wisecracking G.I's, Willie and Joe. They became more popular and beloved than Eisenhower and Patton. Mauldin's success in newspaper syndication continued long after the war, winning him two Pulitzer Prizes and a cover on *Time* magazine.

Tom Shales, the heralded critic for the *Washington Post,* gave the show a rave review, except for his last line. He said the Roberta Flack's song I chose was out of place. He said he did not understand it. It did not make sense to him. The reason I mention this seemingly minor tidbit is because we discovered, as you will, that Schlatter was in constant touch with him, using him to help pave the way for my departure.

Kill All the Lawyers – Henry VI

Making an undreamt amount of money, and having maxed out my Shearson Lehman pension plan, I had the happy quandary of what to do with the leftovers. Lawyers, accountants and idea men of all sorts, like termites, came crawling out of the woodwork. Two who found me were prominent Beverly Hills lawyers. They were heavily invested in acquiring two large hotels in downtown skid row. Sitting in their lush office, they gleefully outlined how much money Sarita and I would make immediately, if we joined them. And, of course, how the value of those maintenance-free buildings would increase. Sarita and I said that we did not want to be in the business of collecting rent from the poor. That ended my search for investments. Instead, I went searching for the contractor who had built a beautiful home I liked, two blocks from our bungalow. It was all cedar, nearly three stories high, with lots of natural red bricks and skylights. I wanted one like that for Sarita and Christopher.

The architect was in his thirties, trim, musclebound from his daily gym visits, and pleasant. I liked him immediately; so much so I didn't even ask to see his license. We made a deal on a handshake. He said he could build it in less than nine months for two-hundred-thousand. From *Mr. Blandings Builds His Dream House* with Cary Grant, to anyone who has gone through this, everyone knows getting involved in such an undertaking is akin to *Rosemary's Baby*, an unwanted fetus grows!

The last thing I saw on TV before vacating our soon to be demolished bungalow, and our move to a rented house a block away, was the stirring *Miracle on Ice*, the US vs the USSR, February 2nd, 1980. A collection of amateur college kids under coach Herb Brooks captured America and the world and an Olympic Gold Medal with their phenomenal win over the professional Red Russian juggernaut. Cheers echoed up and down the street, even from neighbors who never watched hockey. Like everything wonderful that was happening so quickly, who could dream within a year, I'd be working with Herb Brooks!

I will not write further about the emotional and financially draining ordeal of housebuilding, except for these few sentences on how it was surprisingly resolved. The contractor, seeing the nine months approaching, began to slow down; often he did not show up. Nine months became a year. Two-hundred-thousand was nearly three. Then one day he just walked off. Our young contractor, in an attempt to hold us hostage, refused to get a completion permit from the city in order for us to move in. Knowing I couldn't shoot him, I was at a loss. But Sarita wasn't.

All the subcontractors were Mexican. Every day they came to work, Sarita fed them, gave them drinks and talked to them in Spanish. When the lead sub showed up one workless day to see what was going on, Sarita told him. An hour later, the place was swarming with Mexicans. Like a scene out of a feel-good movie, they all showed up with their tools. Within ten days, they completed the fabulous house and pool. With their help, the city gave us our permit. The sound of construction, negotiating and arguing that was going on about the house was nothing compared to the noise that was going on at the office.

Once again, Freddy Silverman had made the mistake of giving George another show about to be a bigger disaster than *Real Kids*. This was a show dealing with real news, where George had even less experience than with real people. It was to be called *Speak up America*! It was based loosely on and inspired by Paddy Chayefsky's superbly written *Network*. In that glowing classic, Peter Finch plays an enraged anchorman assigned to host a prime-time show where he regales the audience with brilliant diatribes about society, politics, the economy, and why he's "mad as hell and won't take it anymore." What Silverman failed to notice in the movie was Finch's show dies so badly, the network brass decide he has to die; so, they have him assassinated on live TV. Assigning such a television show to George was like the network committing suicide; unfortunately for *Real People*, Schlatter lived.

He once again invited me into his office to celebrate, and once again, he and Fantozzi toasted their triumph over the Hebrews. George asked if I would like to be a part of what he said was perfect for me.

I said, "You know I don't have the time. But George, I suggest since you have no background in news you hire some real news people to help you."

He smiled. "Way ahead of you. We're bringing in Andy Friendly, Fred Friendly's son from Murrow and Friendly. And your friend Hal Kanter."

"Andy Friendly is a great idea. If you're gonna have jokes about the news, nobody writes them better than Hal. His daughter, Donna, is already working in news. You should hire her, too."

"John," Tony said, holding up his Schlitz, "you wouldn't have to do much, and you'd make a lot of money."

"Tony, thanks, even having trouble and expenses building a house, I don't need money. I just need to keep focusing on not letting our show get nibbled to death."

The day after declining their generous offer, Skip sent me this note: "John, please keep our show on the air. I too am building a new house!'

To Host *Speak Up*, George immediately hired a once-famous child evangelist turned actor, Marjoe Gortner. The female host was a beautiful, bright black actress-personality, Jayne Kennedy. Very surprisingly, the other male host was to be the US Olympic hockey team's coach, Herb Brooks. To welcome the cast, George asked if Sarita and I would attend a dinner at an exclusive Beverly Hills upstairs eatery. The reason George had to ask me was because I had begun distancing myself from the crew and cast. I avoided the company picnics and social gatherings. Some thought I was a snob, but I just wanted to spend my spare time at home. More than doing the show, my major joy was taking my son to junior golf tournaments. We accepted the dinner invitation on the condition we could bring Christopher. George was glad we did. So was Herb Brooks' wife.

Herb was as down to earth and pleasant as you'd expect a hockey player from Minnesota to be. I wanted to talk about Lake Placid. He wanted to talk about the celebrity hockey team. We were instant friends. He was unfazed by what might be bigger celebrity hood as the co-host of a network TV Show. For him, Hollywood for the short or long haul, would be an interesting adventure. His wife, as pleasant as she tried to be, felt out of place at dinner; even more out of place in Hollywood. She was happier talking to our son than any in the cast. Soon she was talking to her divorce lawyer.

The first episode of *Speak Up America* was summed up by one critic in three words as "Throw up America." It was godawful. The next morning, Andy Friendly burst into my office unannounced. He introduced himself, then asked how I managed to work with George, someone who kept interfering. I told him battling George, whom I actually liked, kept me more focused. I told him we often had differences, loud ones, which people ran from, but they were differences which improved the show. I explained it was obviously not the case with *Speak up America*, which was an artificial contrivance. It was nobody's point of view. Not so with *Real People,* which was my point of view. I was staunchly guarding and nursing it. I assured Andy I would talk to George about his backing off a little so Andy could run it. Andy had a point of view and could articulate it.

As promised, I passed on my opinion to George. "Would you do a few stories for me too?" was his answer.

"George, I can't. You know I'm swamped. I can't even get to most of Christopher's golf tournaments."

Early one morning shortly thereafter, George burst into my office, growling. "Well, your friend finally got around to it!"

"What friend?"

"Danny Arnold. He's suing us."

"Terrific. He'll fall on his ass in a courtroom."

"It's a disrupting pain in the ass."

"To you maybe. Not to me. I can't wait to see a judge toss him and the case out."

"I have errors and omissions insurance, which means we cover your legal costs, too. We can assign you a good lawyer."

"I've got one."

"Have I ever heard of him?"

"Probably not. But he's well established. And tough."

"Okay. My guys'll be in touch. Jesus Christ." He stormed out.

I was delighted. I couldn't wait to get into a court against Danny. Whoever said forgive your enemies in the Bible never got falsely sued. Whoever said, revenge is sweet, should have added Ben Hecht's observation about revenge: It's sweeter when you see your victim. I was pumped.

I alerted Nathan. He was thrilled. He'd be going up against the Century City big boys. I called the Writers Guild to get confirmation letters about my registering the first five scripts. I began calling all the people, including producers, who were exposed to my undertaking before I ended up with George: Gary Deeb, Ray Stark, David Wolper, Pierre Cossette, Digby Wolf and others. All agreed to give a statement or deposition under oath. The only person to refuse me was Grant Tinker. This was surprising because Tinker was now President of NBC and we were his biggest most lucrative show.

"But, Grant," I said, "why wouldn't you?"

"That's a problem between you and Schlatter. It has nothing to do with me."

"I have no problems with George. It's a problem with Danny Arnold."

"Well, I hear George is having problems with you, and you and he should just go out in an alley and punch it out."

"I don't know what you're talking about, but Artie was present when I was pitching this show to you. I just need a simple statement like that."

"I can't do it.'

"What if you're subpoenaed?"

"I won't remember. Besides they'd expect me to say something like that as the guy whose network it's on."

Mark Twain could have been talking about Tinker when he said: *It is curious how common is physical courage in the world, and moral courage so rare.*

Chris Hayward called. "The pig actually did it. He's suing you. Hasn't he got enough money? He's got a safe full of gold coins under his stairs."

"Chris, he's not suing for money. He's suing because everyone in town is aware of how dumb he was. He's suing to get even. Believe me, he'll feel worse once he gets into court."

"Don't be surprised if it doesn't go to court. These things get settled out of court."

"You and Alan Burns went to court over *The Munsters*."

"Eight years. That is a rarity. To save costs and embarrassment they eventually settle. And if Schlatter's ego is like Danny's, he'll wanna settle quickly so they won't know he's lying again. He doesn't want another Robin Williams court case. Believe me."

A week later, Nathan and I were called for our get-acquainted meeting at George's lawyers' offices in Century City. The lead lawyer, whose name I cannot recall, did not want to be a lawyer. One could see immediately from entering his sumptuous glass-encased corner office, he wanted to be a musician. Or conductor. There were two large music stands in the middle of his office with classical sheet music and a baton. He was the kind of gentle misplaced soul who would not like Nathan Markowitz. Neither would his associates. Or George.

There were ten lawyers seated around the conference table. The conductor was at the head. They motioned me to sit at the other end. I asked Nathan to sit there. After introductions, someone identified as George's lawyer began to talk in obscure legalese about the difficulties we would have with Danny's lawyers, who they warned us were legal heavyweights. The costliest in town.

"That is all bullshit," Nathan announced.

"How so?" one asked with a hint of arrogance.

"It is absolutely and totally simple. An open and shut case of harassment, which we should move to get tossed out tomorrow."

"It is not that simple," another chimed.

"Yes, it is." Nathan opened his briefcase. "Here I have the five scripts registered at the Guild as John's before doing business with Danny, who on a witnessed handshake with Danny told John he was free to take it elsewhere. And statements from some of the biggest in the business who considered the material long before John gave it to George. Move to get Danny's shit tossed out."

"Danny has witnesses to the contrary. There are people who will testify your client didn't run the show, that–"

I jumped up. "Jesus Christ, whose side are you on? Are you Danny's fucking attorney or ours? Not one of you was there. Not one of you went through what I went through. How Danny and ABC screwed it up. Not one of you knows what goes on in the editing rooms at *Real People.* You haven't the foggiest fucking idea. I created this show. Nathan has the proof of that. When we get into court, we'll prove that. I am the one keeping it on the fucking air. Pardon me for yelling. I assure you in court I won't raise my voice. I'll leave that to Nathan."

The conductor said,"We'd better make a list of those to be deposed, and set another, quieter meeting."

Nathan stood up. "There does not have to be another meeting. Just take this material to a judge and have it summarily tossed out as frivolous harassment."

The conductor repeated, "We'll have a second quieter meeting. We'll let you know." He left to retrieve his baton.

Nathan and I left, stopping a few minutes later at Nathan's deli in Beverly Hills.

"Oh, God, Nathan. I'm sorry I flew off the handle." I thought about the FBI and the pictures they showed me, but felt uncomfortable mentioning it to him under the circumstances. "By the way. You have all our records in your office. I'd like to pick them up and make copies of them, and get them back to you."

"Fine. You don't have to come by. I'll have my assistant bring them to you."

The following morning, George barged into my office, much angrier than when delivering the news about the lawsuit. "Who is this fucking loudmouth attorney you have?" he bellowed.

"Nathan Martkowitz"

."I don't know who the fuck he is, but he's not going to be paid by my insurance to represent you. He's an asshole. Nobody wants to work with him."

"Nathan gave them sufficient material and cause to have a judge summarily throw Danny's suit out as a nuisance, harassment suit."

"I have the best lawyers in town. He is not going to be among them."

"Evidently, your best lawyers think Danny has the best lawyers. If they go about taking depositions and all that lawyer shit they do, they are just stretching it out to milk your insurance company."

"Get rid of him. We'll get you someone else."

"I am not getting rid of him. He is the only one who helped in the beginning. Not only am I not dumping him, I am going to have him sue ABC over *That's Incredible*! Fuck them, too!"

"John, you are not making this easy for me."

"Showing what a fraud Danny is, is easy. Nathan showed them. Have your guys follow his advice. If it's not tossed out, I'll talk to him and consider what you're saying."

He slammed the door behind him.

For a week, Nathan and I heard nothing from Century City. And I had not received my files from his office. Late one night, he called us at our rented house. Sarita answered.

"Nathan, why are you whispering? Where are you? What motel? What's the number? What do you mean, you can't tell us? What if we have to get in touch with you! Wait a minute." She cupped her hand over the receiver."Honey, Nathan says he can't tell us where he is. He thinks his phone is tapped"

"Certainly, it is. Give it to me." I took the phone. "Nathan, you don't have to tell us where you are, but give us a number in case of an emergency." He did. "And please don't forget our files." He said he wouldn't, and hung up. It was the last time I spoke to him.

Two days later, the front page of *the Los Angeles Times* and every newscast carried the story of the murder of a Beverly Hills lawyer, Nathan Markowitz. He had been gunned down in broad daylight in the parking garage of the Century City Broadway Department store. There was twenty-thousand dollars in his pocket. Detectives on the scene said it was not a robbery, more like a hit for hire.

Sarita and I were staggered in total disbelief. Stuff like that just didn't happen. It was a nightmare. Why? Who could have done such a thing? We called his wife. She could barely speak. Through her tears she said he was just on his way to buy a new suit, and they shot him in the back as he was walking up the stairs to the store.

At the office a couple of days later, George was indifferent to the news. He had no interest whatsoever in my mutterings about how weird and mysterious it all was. He just asked me if I had another attorney in mind. I was in no state to think clearly. Even when I wasn't distraught, I never thought too clearly about business or career moves. I obviously didn't think too clearly when I called George Bane to take Nathan's place to represent me. George had been the Beverly Hills attorney recommended by his principal client, newscaster Paul Moyer, when I was at KNBC. He had been unable to get me, a multiple Emmy winning critic for them, a measly fifty dollar a week raise! I was in no mood to try to find someone else. Sadly, it never occurred to me to call Chris Hayward, who had a lot of expert experience with lawsuits.

George Bane was introduced to the barrage of barristers. They loved him. But not as much as he loved them. As we walked toward the elevator after the introductory meeting he said, "John, thank you very much for bringing me aboard, introducing me to them. They are the best, the best in town, and I'm going to be working as part of their team."

"Jesus Christ, George, I don't want you to be their fan or on their team. You're my lawyer, not one of Schlatter's. I need you to kick their ass and Danny Arnold's."

"I can do it!" But he didn't.

That night, another late call. It was a hoarse whisper I did not recognize. "Mr. Barbour? Mr. Barbour? This is Lenny. Nathan's assistant."

"Oh, yes, Lenny. How are you holding up?"

"Not well. I need to see you right away? I've got your files."

"Can't I get them in the morning?"

"No, I'm leaving in the morning. If you want them, I gotta bring them now. Where can I meet you?"

"Where you coming from?"

"The Valley."

"Meet me at Vineland and Ventura. Charlie's Restaurant."

He was standing at the back of a ten-year-old grey Chevy when I got there. The trunk was open. In the dim light, I could see he was sweating and trembling. As I walked over to shake his hand, he opened the trunk higher. Inside were two large cardboard boxes.

"This one's yours," he said, still whispering. "I thought you might want this one, too. It's got a lot of Nathan's private stuff in it."

"Don't you think you'd want to give that to his wife?"

"I don't think she'd wanna see it. I'll just leave it. The Feds have been all over the place the last couple of days. A lot of shit going on. This was my first job outta law school. Not what I expected."

"Have you got a job lined up?"

"No. Just a flight to Denmark. Tomorrow."

I placed the cartons in my front seat. When I turned to thank him, he was already backing out and was off.

That was just all bad B-movie intrigue, made even weirder by a call from my accountant, Bob Mages. He shared the new office near the beach with Nathan.

"The office burned down. It burned down last night. After the Feds left. They've been here all week."

"Bob, did they talk to you?"

"A couple of times. Jesus, what's going on?"

"I don't know. You must know something, Bob. You shared the office with him. Was he up to gunrunning or money laundering or shit like that?"

"I don't know. Honestly. He was very secretive. And the Feds have been up my ass. I'm scared as hell!"

The word 'Feds' kept going around in my head. I remembered the card from the FBI agent. Shortly after daybreak, I called him.

"There hasn't been anything in the paper about a suspect or motive or what the killer looks like or anything."

"True. So, why are you calling me?"

"Just that you guys must know what the killer looks like."

He laughed. "Why would we know that?"

"You showed me that he never went anywhere without one of your guys tailing him. Nathan couldn't have ditched your guys in broad daylight in a parking garage."

His tone darkened. "John, you just stick to doing your show." The phone went dead.

Speak Up, Jim Garrison

As Chris Hayward predicted, the lawsuit was settled out of court. The very substantial amount paid to Danny Arnold was secret. I attended no one else's deposition but my own. I was curious about attending George's, but didn't. I felt if I did so, he might feel I was being confrontational. I did instruct George Bane to press Schlatter for answers to just two questions; one being, who writes and edits all of John's stories? And, did John show you the five scripts from *National Graffiti* at your first accidental meeting? In sworn deposition, George's answers were, "I don't know," or "can't remember." I ordered George Bane to sue ABC over *That's Incredible.*

Bane suggested I refrain from doing so; as did Henri Bollinger, both saying I already had a reputation for being difficult and uncontrollable. Suing a major network would make finding future work difficult.

Bob Long called. He wanted to commiserate with me over cocktails at Luigi's. I joined him, reluctantly, thinking about his comments to Sarah and Beverly. He was on his third luncheon boilermaker, which brought his unpaid bar bill to over $900.00. He was now a field producer on both shows. Bob was a heavy drinker who never sounded drunk. Liquor actually made him more literate. And funny. His deep pleasant almost flowery voice describing the inanities of humanity was a delight to listen to. He raised his glass as if in a toast.

"Well, sir, here is to your success in our corrupt courts of injustice. That lady statuette put the blindfold on herself because she couldn't stand to look." His chuckle filled the room. "You know, my leader, you are embarking on a slippery slope, which I am afraid a few envious folks are greasing for you."

"Bob, I have no control over that."

"And, dear man, the same seems to be happening to your show."

That hurt, because it was becoming more obvious to even the crew, many of whom were avoiding me.

"If it goes off, a light of intelligence and joy will be gone from this moronic tube." He raised his glass again. "Here's to its staying on so I can continue to bask in the glow and add to my bar bill."

Hearing his openness, I finally asked him what I had long thought about. "Bob, it's none of my business, but are you still involved in any way with Sarah? You know, a year ago she said you were the first man to ever please her."

He laughed. "Thank you, sir. She is currently tenuously engaged to this shadowy banker. On the road we don't copulate quite as frequently as we used to. Just a few pumps and a squirt. Oh, speaking of copulating, did you know that apes and gorillas copulate more than humans. Even Warren Beatty."

I smiled. "I hadn't noticed."

"Have you ever noticed that gorillas have no asses?"

"Maybe I noticed when I saw Cheetah in a Tarzan movie."

"Darwin says we were descended from apes. Wrong. Only some of us were. Not you. Not I. You know why? Because we have asses. You know who has no ass. Absolutely no ass?"

"Who?"

"George Schlatter. He's as devoid of ass as he is of taste."

I chuckled. "Bob, how on earth could you know he has no ass?"

"I saw it. Or rather the absence of it. Rather close up. At a whorehouse. Yah know that Madam story you wouldn't let him do the first year. Well, he finally did. And the Madam. And a few more for *Speak Up*."

"Jesus Christ," I gasped.

"He's a lusty sonofabitch."

A few years later, Bob ended up where I had once started out – at KNBC, as their news director. When he retired, he moved to Europe where he got a university job teaching. I am sure he was wonderful at it until he dropped dead of a heart attack.

And Sarah, his 'few pumps and a squirt' girlfriend as he called her, did not marry her banker; she married a dentist. After George fired me, he had the *Real People* hour-ceremony aboard a cruise ship in one of the most embarrassing hours ever broadcast. NBC's wedding present was notice that the show would be cancelled.

Up until then, in spite of the sickening silences, I had to somehow try to keep the show and myself from falling apart. Stories by the thousands poured in daily. We had a great research staff. In spite of that, I still went through every paper and magazine I could find looking for my own.

One morning, in the middle pages of the *L.A. Times,* I caught a small headline: The House Select Committee on Assassinations Concluded Four Shots Had Been Fired in Dealey Plaza. Therefore, *a conspiracy to kill President Kennedy had to exist.*

The body of the short paragraph stated a TV newsman in Dallas, Gary Mack, had discovered the dictabelt of a motorcycle officer in the motorcade that had been accidentally left open during the motorcade in Dealey Plaza. Analysis of that recording revealed four or more gunshots. I leafed through the pages of the other three papers, looking for confirmation, but it wasn't there. Suddenly, I thought I could get confirmation from Jim Garrison. I hadn't spoken to him since I was at KNBC.

Just like the first time, eleven years earlier when I called New Orleans to book him on *AM,* that same deep warm voice answered.

"Mr. Garrison, this is John Barbour. Do you feel vindicated?"

"In what way?"

"I've got the *L.A. Times* in front of me. It says the House Select Committee concluded four shots were fired, therefore a conspiracy existed."

"John, I feel like a blind man in a dark room who has gotten a small trophy. Only I know I got it."

"Did you testify? Or provide material?"

"I refused to testify once they got rid of Sprague, who said he wasn't hiring any FBI or CIA, and brought in that shill Blakey. I knew it was another whitewash. But, yes, I did supply documents which you won't see for fifty years."

"You must be swamped with requests for interviews."

"From whom?"

"Everybody. Huntley, Brinkley, Brokaw, Jennings, Cronkite … all of them."

He laughed softly. "You are the only one I've heard from."

"You're kidding!"

"John, I'm not very good at kidding, but it's nice to talk to you again. My family loves your show."

"Mr. Garrison, I have a thought. What if I bring my cameras to you and do an interview? I don't think it suits *Real People*, but they're doing another one here, sort of a news show that might be a perfect platform for you."

"John, I have declined to do any interviews for the past ten years, but if you're up to it, bring your cameras. I'd love to finally meet and talk with you."

"Thank you, sir. I'll call you right back." I hung up, grabbed the *L.A. Times* and rushed into George's office. Fortunately, he was alone. Garrison's story would be fantastic, but uppermost in mind was the thought that George and I seldom spoke; maybe we could begin again if he felt I would help him with *Speak Up*. I spoke up immediately.

"George, if you like, there is something I'd like to do on *Speak Up*. Years ago, I tried to book Jim Garrison on–"

"That DA from New Orleans?"

"Yes. Tried to book him on *AM*, but I was fired and he was cancelled. He hasn't spoken to any press since then, but he'll speak to us. It's an exclusive. Look at this." I handed George the article. He glanced at it, then looked up. He shrugged.

"George, the government is agreeing there was a conspiracy to kill Kennedy, vindicating Garrison. It's the biggest murder mystery in American history. Garrison may have solved it. And he'll only talk to us. Can you imagine the number of people who will tune in? He's never been on network prime time."

"I'm not comfortable with it."

"Look, I will do it for nothing. You don't have to pay me any sort of fee. I'll find some *Real People* stories to do down there. It'll be huge."

He shrugged. "All right. Take Marjoe; it's not for Herb."

"The story is so big, it's probably a two-parter, which will only increase your audience. I only want two things."

"Money isn't one of them?"

"No. Complete control over the writing and editing, subject to approval from legal, plus a copy of the entire taped interview to make a real documentary."

"When do you plan on doing that?"

"When this is all over."

"You said it would outlast *Sixty Minutes.*

"It should."

"Fine." He paused. "I'm glad you're doing this."

I called Mr. Garrison back, telling him the name of the show, that Marjoe Gortner would be the host who would be seen interviewing him on air, but I'd actually be doing the interview in his office. He suggested he'd be more at ease if we came to his home. We set a date less than ten days away. To help with the logistics, the crew, the travel, everything, to be around someone I already liked and trusted, I engaged Donna Kanter as our field producer. I was delighted to give her such an important assignment, a small repayment for her father's generosity to me.

We first did a few *Real People* stories in New Orleans about street performers. Twenty-four hours later we were in Jim Garrison's downstairs front office in his home. It looked more like a library. Hundreds and hundreds of books were stacked in floor to ceiling bookcases against three walls. On the other wall were half a dozen pictures, mostly family, except for one, a picture of a young Jim Garrison in uniform, in the military in 1945, sitting on a short cement wall at Dachau. In the background allied soldiers were tending to survivors of one of the scores of Germany's labor-death camps. On the bottom of the photo, Mr. Garrison had written: 'Lest we forget'

On camera we talked for almost three hours. I couldn't stop. I wanted to do this in 1970. I read the first two of his books, *Heritage of Stone* and *The Star Spangled Contract.* Made more curious by these, I read dozens of others beginning with Mark Lane's *Rush to Judgment.* I was in no way an assassination conspiracy theorist, as the government and media maligned those who questioned the veracity of the Warren Report; I just loved a great story. President Kennedy's murder was the world's greatest mystery story. Jim Garrison's attempt to investigate and challenge the government was as truly an American story as I'd ever heard. I wanted to give him a chance to tell that story.

He talked passionately about his accidentally getting involved in starting his own investigation. For me this was the most compelling, informative, frightening and thrilling three hours I'd ever spent. Names, dates and facts poured out of him. All had the gut wrenching, mind-blowing unmistakable ring of truth. The real bell ringer to me was not the verifiable material and documents he laid out before us. It was an off-handed comment he made about himself. He had been an FBI agent, served in the military, still an officer in the reserve, was politically unaligned with any party, relatively conservative, a proud southerner, who at first believed the Warren Report.

I asked, "Mr. Garrison, with such a background, when you started your own investigation, what made you think you could take on the federal government?"

Without missing a beat, he smiled warmly, and said, "John, I guess as a kid, I saw one too many Frank Capra movies."

Wow. Did that ring a bell! As a kid I devoured Frank Capra movies. My favorite was *Mr. Smith Goes to Washington*. That wasn't Jimmy Stewart up there on screen losing his voice filibustering for truth, that was seven-year-old me.

One of the questions to him was, "How many shooters do you think there were in Dealy Plaza?"

"It was triangulation. A military style operation. Three shooters. One at the Grassy Knoll, another in front. One behind, but not in that book depository. Likely the Dal-Tex building. There'd be a second with each shooter to pick up the shells, and since this was such a big kill, probably a radio man with each."

"How many people do you think actually knew Kennedy would be killed in Dallas?"

He paused to reflect. "Well, it began when he stopped the planes at the Bay of Pigs. It's on a-need-to-know basis. Aside from the three shooting teams, and those in the Dallas Police Department and city government who changed the route and called off security, those agents by the picket fence with fake Secret Service ID's, one or two assets in the press, and a handful in Washington and Arlington, I'd say about thirty-two."

When I was finished, I sat Marjoe in my chair, miked him up, and gave him eight questions to ask, including the two mentioned above. The flight back to Los Angeles had our crew abuzz, thrilled being present and an exclusive part of the most important news story in a hundred years.

Donna Kanter hugged me. "Oh, John, thank you for making me a part of this. It's going to be a blockbuster. I can't wait to tell my dad. To have him see it."

As expected, it would be a two-parter. I rushed to put together part one. George's office was packed with people waiting to see it. I put the tape in. No one moved; they were spellbound, leaning forward in silence. When it was over, there were hushed "wows," and "Jesus," and "Oh, my Gods," and pats on the back. I went home happier than I had been in a year. I was getting no money for it. No recognition. Nothing but satisfaction.

I previously attended only one broadcast of *Speak up America*. That was to watch Herb's debut. I was too embarrassed by its artificial outrage to go again. But this night I was in the wings. More than watching the story, I wanted to watch the audience. Like the small crowd in George's office, they, too, were transfixed. No one had ever heard someone like Jim Garrison on network television in prime time, passionately and convincingly arguing his case about Oswald's innocence and the government's guilt. His voice and facts he chronicled were like gunshots of truth. The audience's applause was huge. It also had a ring of thankful people having their suspicions rewarded. I couldn't wait for Part Two.

I almost became religious, so grateful to the fates for the job I had lucked into. Two days before the airing, I delivered it and screened it for George. The reaction from those in his packed office was even more intense. Content knowing Mr. Garrison finally had a primetime platform to tell his story, I decided to stay home, in our huge rented house, and experience watching it like a viewer. Sarita, Christopher, and I huddled excitedly on our sofa, and turned on the set. We applauded the opening billboarding. And waited. Soon it came on. We couldn't help lean forward to watch. Then the close up of Marjo asking: "Mr. Garrison, how many shooters do you think there were in Dealy Plaza?" Then the full face close shot of Garrison. "Thirty two."

There was a gasp from the audience. I screamed. "What? What is that?"

The phone rang immediately. Certain it was Garrison, I rushed to it. It was Schlatter. His voice, which was already sharp, had an edge to it. "What did you think?"

I screamed, "What did you do, George? What was that?"

"Garrison's a nut!"

"No, George, you are the nut. How could you do such a thing?"

"He's a nut case," he repeated more firmly.

"How could you do that, deliberately destroy someone? I hope he sues your fucking ass and NBC. He'll fucking own you. I'll be his chief witness with the recording. You evil bastard!" I slammed down the phone. I had accidentally recorded it. Thank god! (In pre-cellphone days, we had answering machines. Mine accidentally and luckily recorded Schlatter.) I then called Garrison at home. It rang once and he picked it up.

I began to cry. "Mr. Garrison, Mr. Garrison, I don't know what happened. How it happened. That's not what I turned in. I swear. I'm so sorry." Tears were streaming down my face. Sarita and Christopher were rubbing my back to console me.

"John ... John." Garrison's voice was calm and assuring. "Calm down. Calm down. I believe you. I'm used to this."

"I'm not. Mr. Garrison, I don't understand why he would do such a thing. George Schlatter just called gloating over what he had done, saying you were a nut, and did that to prove it. I recorded him. He libeled you. Intentionally. He slandered you deliberately–"

"John–" He tried to stop me, but my outrage and tears were unstoppable.

"Mr. Garrison, sue him. Please. Sue him. And NBC. You'll own them. I'll be your principal witness, and the editors he had re-edit it. Subpoena them. Please. It is recorded. You can't lose."

"But, John, you can. Your show. If I spent all my time suing all the libelous, slandering winnable cases thrown at me over this case, I'd never see my office or my family. You've just experienced a little of what I've been subjected to. It happened to you once on your morning show, which you lost. I don't want you to lose this wonderful show." He stopped briefly. "And, if you like, if you still have the stomach to try to tell the story of President Kennedy's murder, I'll give you the name of a fake Oswald who's serving time in an Eastern federal prison. He'll probably tell you his whole story for a *Real People* T-shirt."

I couldn't believe anyone who had just been so callously and deliberately maligned on national television, made to look like a kook, was not in a murderous rage. How could he be so calm when as a lawyer he knew he had a slam-dunk win? I did not sleep that night. I did not even undress. I sat with Sarita on the sofa waiting until morning, waiting to confront Schlatter. At eight a.m., I stormed into his office. Three staff people were present. I never saw who they were. I only saw Schlatter sitting behind his desk. I was in a rage.

"When and why did you do that? What is wrong with you? This isn't fucking *Laugh-In* where you can deliberately re-edit shit to ridicule someone who has something meaningful to say!"

He jumped up, pushing the heavy desk toward me. "I did what was necessary. He's a fraud."

"You're the fucking fraud. And I hope he sues your fucking ass and NBC's. He'll own you. Again, asshole, I recorded your snide fucking voice bragging about how you did it deliberately."

His neck and face were crimson with rage. This was the bouncer from Ciro's. This was the new producer who threatened to kill his director. He moved toward me; the three people in the room ran toward the exit.

"You're the one who's gonna lose," he hissed. "You'll be outa this business so fast you'll never know what hit you. And I can do it. Believe me, I can do it. If you're so upset, go see a fucking psychiatrist, thinking you're the one who made my show, *my show,* work. You're fucking nuts, too. You are never gonna work again in this town. Or anywhere. I will see to it!"'

I suddenly got calm. "George, what chapter in your book is this threat from? The chapter on how to talk to the folks with the real talent? I used to think you were smart and witty and greedy. Now there's nothing in there but evil." I walked out and down the hall looking for Donna Kanter. George was still bellowing threats from his office. Having heard the screaming, like the others, Donna had rushed out of her office, and down the hall. Tears were rolling down her cheeks.

"Donna, what happened?" I was angry, but not yelling.

"John, I'm so sorry. George called me just before midnight and told me to come over to re-edit something. He ordered me not to call you."

"Donna, you saw what he was doing. He was deliberately maligning Garrison. Didn't you say something? Didn't you ask him what he was doing? And why? Did you say anything?"

She couldn't answer. She just bowed her head, sobbing.

"Shame on you. And I got you this job. Jesus Christ. What awful fucking people!"

The exquisite joy of a few days earlier, doing something meaningful, had just been reduced to an empty rage. I was trying not to cry and scream, struggling to stay in touch with reality. Driving home, tears bubbled up again. I mumbled to a God I didn't believe in: "How can people be so evil? How can they be so cruel?" Like every word since childhood directed skyward, they are still unanswered.

January 29, 1982

I was still under contract in that third year, but after our confrontation over Garrison, I didn't want to be there. Neither did George. Everyone avoided me as though I wasn't even there. I made it known I was only going to write and edit my stories, no one else's. At the production meetings my chair made more noise than I did. I was mute. George or Wynn never asked an opinion or for a suggestion, and I never offered one. But at the last production meeting I attended, I could not hold back. George had just finished announcing grandly and proudly that he was going to close the season with the greatest PR event in the history of television: a *Real People* train ride across country from New York to LA, with huge stops and celebrations along the way. I was the only one not cheering and applauding and 'ooing' and 'awing.'

There was no reason any longer for me to be diplomatic, or even try; so I just blurted out, bringing a silent chill to the room, "George, that is so fucking corny."

George looked at me. He had to show he was the boss. "We're doing it, and you'll be on it."

"You don't like corn. You wouldn't air Sarah's Crazy Horse piece till I took the corn out. The train is corn."

"You'll be on it."

"I'll do my story for it, but I will definitely not be on it."

"Then you might not be on the air."

"George, after a few more of your tasteless shows, you won't be on the air. It's not a train you're on. It's the Titanic."

Often, when I am that verbally truthful, I wish maybe I had not said it. Not that time. That time I wish I had added: "And you and Wynn will be the icebergs that sink it!"

Then there was my contract. It had been on my desk unsigned for two and a half years. Something always told me to hold off on signing it. Nothing specific; just an uneasy feeling. Neither George's agent nor George ever asked for it during all those months. Neither did Roland Perkins. So, it just sat there.

However, late in 1981, the Morris office was calling a couple of times a week. Why would they want to talk to me when George wouldn't? Something had to be up, something I wasn't aware of. I called George Bane. First, to push him harder with my lawsuit with ABC over *That's Incredible*, then about what I should do about my unsigned contract.

He said, "ABC has been served. I wouldn't be surprised if they want to settle right away."

"George, I'd rather have my day in court. And the Morris office is hounding me now every other day about signing my contract. Something must be up."

"It's fine. Straightforward. I saw nothing wrong with it."

I then called Roland Perkins, my super-agent at Creative Artists. I told him of my unease at sending the Morris office my signed contract. "Roland, is there something going on I don't know about?"

"There's a rumor that Telepictures has bought your show for syndication; they say for thirty-five million. You'll have a nice payday!"

"Roland, I only get ten percent of net. Who knows what'll be left. Are they syndicating it in its hour form?"

"No. I hear they're gonna cut them into half-hours and strip them five days a week. I think it's gonna be called *More Real People*.

"Jesus, Roland, they'll butcher it."

"Butchered or not, they still have to pay you."

"I feel uncomfortable about signing this."

"You'll have to, to get paid."

"I'll get back to you. Thanks."

I began to worry about how George or whoever was going to slice up those amazing hours. What would be left of them? I struggled with the urge to go in to talk to him. I knew he did not care to talk to me. Or even see me. Instead I sent a brief note:

> *George, I am happy for you that this wonderful show you said was shit that's going nowhere has suddenly turned into a fertilizer fortune for you. The only slight blight in that pleasure is the fear of what Telepictures might do in hacking these wonderful stories and hours into half hours. They are perfectly complete as they are. You can't take three-minute Cole Porter or George Gershwin songs, cut them to ninety seconds and have the same pleasurable impact. I'd be happy in any way to help assemble those half hours for you. Let me know. John.*

He never replied.

If there is one thing that surprises me about myself, even pleases me, something over which I have no control, is unlike a number of people I knew, I never succumbed to drugs or alcohol, or even suicide. I have never been seriously depressed. Down, yes. Quite often. I reasoned those dark moments were the result of something that happened beyond my control. I never fought that darkness. I accepted it as a natural emotional and chemical reaction. After a while, those chemicals would just as naturally abate. They always did. I was not depressed over the impending loss of my job, or the quandary about signing the contract. I was pissed I wasn't getting better advice from supposed professionals to whom I had been paying a small fortune.

Two more urgent calls came requesting the signed contract. I called Bane and Perkins back.

"If I don't sign this thing, Telepictures and George would not legally be in a position to syndicate this, right?" I asked.

They both said it wouldn't matter. Telepictures could still syndicate it. My signing just helps get their accounting together, so I should go ahead.

The following day, I got a call from Bane. He was bragging, as he predicted, that ABC wanted to settle my lawsuit for fifty thousand dollars. As much as I wanted to get into a courtroom, to kick Danny Arnold's ass, Schlatter's, ass, Silverman's ass, everybody's ass, my mind and heart were exhausted. I had enough to pay off the house and send Christopher to Stanford or on the PGA tour if that's what he wanted. I had proven my point, even if just to myself. That was good enough. If I continued against ABC, I would have to be pushing Bane, who was obviously too timid and in awe of the opposition to do the job. I gave in. I signed and sent my contract to the Morris office. The trades reported ABC's settlement with me.

"Jesus Christ, John, what did you just do?" It was Chris Hayward on the phone. "How much did you settle for from ABC?"

"Fifty thousand."

"You idiot. Danny got a million and a half plus legal fees. You had a better case than him. You could have retired. Why didn't you call me?"

"Chris, I just never thought of it. I have so much going on. Since you called, let me ask you, I never signed my contract until a couple of days ago. Could they have syndicated it without my signature?"

"No way. Are you kidding?"

"Perkins and my lawyer told me otherwise."

"Jesus, you may have to sue them for incompetence."

"Oh, God, Chris, it's getting so complicated. You know I was never in this for the money. That's not how I think."

"Speaking of that, are you signed for the next two years?"

"No, why?"

"Because NBC just signed a two-year deal with Schlatter."

"Are you sure?"

"That's the word. You and I better get together soon. You need to talk to someone."

"Chris, I'll call you soon."

I didn't call him. It was too late. I screwed up again not trusting my instincts; the instincts that left the contract in my drawer for two and a half years.

January 29th, 1982 was my son's thirteenth birthday. We all awoke to an exceptionally happy day. Christopher grew to be more of one every day. He was, and is, one of the three brightest human beings I'd ever met. The other two were scientist Buckminster Fuller with whom I spent an hour on the *AM Show,* and New Orleans's DA, Jim Garrison. As a critic, I often took him to movies or plays, even R rated ones. Seeing *Superman,* a comic strip for kids, but characters he loved as a child, I let him write and read his own review. He was a bigger hit than I was.

On this birthday, the one where a boy becomes a young man, I wanted to play golf with him, even though he always beat me. Some junior tournaments would not allow parents to walk or follow their kids. Nobody was going to stop this little league father. Once, on a private course in Palos Verdes, I gave a Mexican worker $100.00 for his hardhat and rake and scratched my way through nine holes watching Christopher ... until some outraged parents called security. Three carts full of the law came out and removed me.

We were finally in our fabulous Architectural Digest three-story home. Christopher was preparing for his special birthday when the phone rang. It was Roland Perkins. He blurted, "George is not picking up your contract."

I didn't respond. I couldn't believe it. Despite his new millions, I believed his need to have a hit would compel him to make peace with me.

"Are you there?" Roland asked, adding, "What do you think?"

"I'm a little too shocked to think. Whatever I have been thinking these past months has never worked out."

"Well, it's not entirely all bad news."

"Schlatter has cancer?"

"No, but he did say he'd welcome your appearance on it."

"Are you kidding? Did he tell you this, or his agent?"

"Fantozzi."

"Roland, like most rich egomaniacs, his orgasm is control. He wants me there for two reasons: to save face and to see me crawl."

"Well, you would still get a terrific fee, which Tony added would probably help with paying for your new home."

"Roland, there you go. That's the crawling part. He thinks I need his fucking money. In his hands that show will be dead in a month."

"He's got a two-year, forty-four show deal."

"Believe me, when the ratings start plummeting, and Silverman and Tartikoff find out how Schlatter and Fantozi fooled the Jews, as they always brag about, he'll be out on his ass."

"Is there anything I can do for you?'"

"As a matter of fact, there is. The reason I got into TV was to do a late-night show like Paar. Now that I'm still in the number one show during the reruns, I'd like you to call ABC nighttime and set up an appointment for me."

"Don't you think you'd get an appointment faster, if you did it?"

"Roland, I don't even know who to call. You're Creative Artists, the biggest agency in town. You're my agent. You should do it."

"I don't think I should do it."

"Why? You don't think I could do a late-night show?"

"I think they'd rather hear from you directly."

"For the past two and a half years I've been sending you over $2,000.00 a week for a contract I negotiated. Now earn it. Call them." He didn't reply. "Roland, you still there?"

"Yes."

"Good." I then hung up.

When Christopher appeared, I told him as matter-of-factly as I could, he wouldn't have to come to the studio once a week anymore to see the show.

"Dad, we didn't come much at all this last year."

That was true. I had been so embroiled and embattled constantly, I barely noticed their absence. I turned to Sarita. "That's true. How come?"

"I didn't like seeing you stressed. There were bad vibrations all over. So, we stayed home to watch it."

I am not superstitious. At least I don't think I am. But you've seen me admit I have this weird belief number four was my lucky number. Now I had this creepy thought: could Sarita's absence have been a negative omen? My mind wandered back to the night at KCOP when we were to tape the pilot for *National Graffiti,* when Christopher suddenly took ill and Sarita stayed home with him. The show died that night. Bad news does bad things to the mind. It makes it worse.

Christopher said he didn't want any kind of special event, or any friends around. He just wanted to have dinner with us at The Smoke House. The three of us celebrated his thirteenth birthday, laughing over great roast beef and the best garlic bread in California.

No more *Real People* was a loss in my life. A very big one. So was the loss of the *AM Show*. I felt horrible. Yet, there I was, in rerun, on the number one show in the country, running nationally for two years longer than the *AM Show*. Ten years earlier how could I have ever predicted that? Every loss had mysteriously led to a step up. After that monumental loss, how big would the next step up be?

At dinner, I told Sarita and Christopher my Terminal Island story, zipping down a laundry chute at Terminal Island decades ago, ending up in chains in the Cook County Jail. They chuckled.

I said, "If the King of Karma had appeared to me and said, 'John, one day you are going to have the greatest child a father could know, and the greatest wife a husband could have and you're going to create the greatest most original show in television and you're going to live in the greatest house on your block and after three years you are going to get fired, would you want it?' I'd leap up and scream, Fire me. Fire me!"

Christopher leaned over and kissed me. "I love you, Dad."

Sarita put her hand on mine. "Don't worry. It was a wonderful show. But you will do something even better. If you were still doing *Real People,* you wouldn't do what you were meant to do."

I hadn't the slightest idea of what I was meant to do. What possibly could be better than *Real People*? The next page in front of me was another blank. I had not the foggiest notion. But Sarita and the King of Karma did. It was the best birthday party I ever attended.

That Awful Quiz Show

If I was startled by the absence of phone calls from producers or stations, or even from people with whom I'd worked, showing interest in me after being fired from the number one show in Los Angeles, I was even more staggered by the total absence of even one call after being fired from the number one show in the country! Not even a call from my super-agent. The first one without me the ratings plummeted. Still no call from those to whom I had predicted it. George had indeed screamed he would end my career in this town, but I gave no more time to thinking about his threats than I did in writing this sentence. What I needed was to just have some fun. And I was going to get it by lampooning the country's growing interest in and preoccupation with celebrity-hood. I had gotten the idea years earlier, watching my friend Rona Barrett dominate the ratings with her gossip show about nothing but celebrities, the first of its kind. People, especially in Hollywood, hated her, but never missed her.

The completed concept popped out of my head full blown in the form of a quiz show. We would have the kind of contestants that we profiled on *Real People*. Nothing new about that, but the quiz would be monumentally different. It would not only be different from anything ever seen on television, it would be absolutely outrageous. And funny. The questions would be multiple choice, all designed around gossip, but supported by facts. This is how it would work: A pair of contestants would be given $500.00. There would be four questions from various categories on which they could bet up to $200.00. At the end of the show, the pair with the most money would get a question suggested by a viewer for $1,000.00 and a first-class round trip to Puerto Vallarta, Mexico. Here are a few examples from actual questions asked during the broadcast shows, and the reaction to them:

Host: Your category is presidents. How much do you bet?

Contestant : $200.00.

Host: How old was President John Kennedy when he lost his virginity: 13, 19, 23, or 42?

After their answer, they were given the next category, which was education. Then they'd bet.

Host: What school was President Kennedy attending when he lost his virginity? Dexter preschool, Choate Academy, Exeter, or Harvard?

After answering, they were given a third category: finance and banking. After their bet, they were given this question: How much did President Kennedy pay for this hooker brought in by a friend: $50.00, $60.00 $79.00, or a Hershey Bar? Audiences were screaming and ducking in embarrassment. Their final category was geography. Making their final bet, this was the question: What country were President Kennedy's virginity-ending hooker's parents from: China, England, Poland, or New Jersey? (New Jersey became a funny running joke in the shows. The answer was China.)

In every case, every question, right or wrong, the host would read the source facts. In the case of these questions about JFK, they came from a biography by one of his roommates, later a Whitehouse advisor. (Many excerpts from these hilarious shows are on youtube/johnbarboursworld.com.)

Each half-hour was a constant chuckle, interrupted by applause. When the questions were asked, a rear screen was filled with a distinctive photograph or graphic, accompanied often by funny sound effects. In the pilot episode, the winning couple, the world's female Frisbee champion, a stunning shapely young brunette, Laura Engel, partnered with the President of the Flat Earth Society, had this bonus question sent in by a viewer in New Jersey: When David Begelman was President of Columbia Pictures and was arrested for theft, how much did he admit in court to stealing: $30,000.00, $60,000,00, or $130,000? The answer was $60,000.00, but when they missed it, saying $130,000.00, Laura brought down the house when she said, "I heard he was a bigger crook?"

Everyone in town watched the show. But, there is only one Hollywood. Getting a title for this thing was just as easy as the concept. Every time I thought of a question, I said to myself, *God, that's awful.* So, that was it: *That Awful Quiz Show*. That was the easy part, getting a host was a little more difficult. Getting a sale, usually the hardest part, was the first phone call. For the host, I wanted somebody waspy and witty. The first person I chose was Bill Rafferty. He had a quick blue-eyed infectious smile and easy wit. I had worked with him for three years, had been to his home for dinner a few times in San Francisco. I called him. He was still on *Real People.*

He talked in a hushed tone, afraid he'd be overheard talking to me. After explaining it to him, he said, "Geez, John, that is really funny. I'd love to do it, but you know George would have a fit if I did it with you. That'd be the end of me on the show. As it is, I get calls for other things I often don't even hear about that he turns down. I don't know why he hates me."

"Bill, you're still there. He can't hate you that much!"

"The mood around here is shit. So is the show. When it's done, I'm just gonna stay here in San Francisco and do some easy game show. This is too much. Miss you, man. Good luck."

We never spoke again. He got to host a couple of game shows, *Card Sharks* being one of them. Later, he also hosted a show about retirement living. Bill died in 2012 from congestive heart failure.

I thought fleetingly of hosting it myself. I had bombed out on *The Gong Show*, but here I could interview the contestants as long as I wanted. What stood in my way, though, was the immediate memory of how classy and intelligent *Real People* had been. I didn't want my appearance on such a totally different and outrageous show to diminish that. So, I decided to make the hosting job even more outrageous and hire John and Greg Rice, the millionaire real estate little people from Florida. They had become so successful after appearing on *Real People* they were traveling the country as two of the highest paid motivational speakers. They were in LA on one such engagement. When I called, they came right over. They loved it, committing to do it before I was halfway through. They never asked about a fee.

"Fellas," I said, "the budget to do this five nights a week, taping five in one day, is about $20,000.00. I'll give you each $1500.00 a show and ten percent of the show. That's of the gross, not the net. If it's successful your ownership will increase another ten percent a year for three more years, ending up 60-40.

"That's awfully generous. We would have settled for less," John said.

"If it succeeds, even though the material and the guests are funny and interesting, it'll be because the audience likes you. So, it's only fair you get a big part of it."

"We're in.'

"Okay, I don't want a twenty-page contract. A simple two paragraph letter of agreement and a handshake."

"Write it up now, John, and we'll sign it." I did; and they did. "Now," Greg said, "who's gonna buy this thing?"

"I have no idea. But there is one person I can call who'll give us an audience."

The following morning, I called Chuck Young at KTTV. As tough as he was, and as totally different in personality, we were somehow always simpatico.

"Chuck, you recall how I was running around a few years ago saying how I'd change the face of TV?"

"Yes. And now you're no longer on it," he said, without laughing.

I laughed for him. "That's funny, and true. Well, now I have a concept that is gonna change the face of game shows."

"You want to do a game show?"

"Produce and write it. Chuck, it's hilarious. I'd like to do a five or ten-minute presentations for you."

"Are you gonna host it as well?"

"No. I have the perfect two hosts."

"Whatta yah mean hosts? No game show has two hosts."

"That's one of the original things about it."

There was a pause, then: "Okay. Thursday at eleven. You got a half hour. But, before you bring in your hosts, give me five minutes of your time."

I called John and Greg with the date and time. They cancelled two weeks of engagements that cost them more than our show's budget. Thursday the three of us were sitting in Chuck's outer corner office. The boys, as their friends referred to them, looked fabulous in their smart suits and ties. I explained I'd be spending a few minutes with Chuck first before bringing them in.

The secretary opened the door, announcing me. Chuck rose to shake my hand. "Great to see you," he said. "You've come a long way and done a lot of good things since you did reviews for us. Before we get to your game show thing, though, that's what I'd like to talk to you about. The toughest thing for independent stations like us after the early news is to hold the audience over two or three minutes for the programming. We've been struggling with this for a long time. When you called, I thought you'd be perfect. Nobody writes or wrote better reviews in this town or did better commentaries than you. Frankly, I miss them. So do some of my friends. They loved to hate you. I'd like to give you two or three minutes at seven, following the early news, to say anything you wish to say, short of profanity and slander. You'll never be censored. You'd be totally on your own. If it works, as I think it will, we could syndicate it to other stations. You'd start out making two or three thousand a week."

"Wow, Chuck, I almost don't know what to say. I love doing that stuff and having a platform, and God knows there's plenty to talk about, but it would give me the feeling of going a little backwards. I've already done that."

"Is that a no?"

"Yes, sir, it is. And it wouldn't be fair to what I'm working on now."

"Okay," he said, slapping his hand on his desk, "let's get to your game show thing."

I went to the door, motioning for John and Greg. They came in, straight toward Chuck, announcing loudly, "Mr. Young, glad to meet you, sir. Heard a lot of wonderful things about you. And not just from John."

At that moment I felt like Alan Funt of *Candid Camera*. For the briefest of moments, the fleeting frozen expression of Chuck Young's face was worth the Mona Lisa. Here was this six-foot-three, crewcut ex-Marine officer who had seen everything, except identical twin midgets gazing up at him, wanting to host a game show on television.

Chuck shook their hands. "John, Greg, pleased to meet you."

I played the first two guests, whom we'd already contacted and interviewed in case we got a pilot. John and Greg, as hosts, welcomed the invisible audience to the show, interviewed me briefly, and then asked the questions. They sparkled, but Chuck did not crack a smile. He just watched us, his head cocked slightly. I had the feeling it was not going well. When we were done, he thanked us, saying he'd think about it. As I walked to the door with the boys, he called out, "John, could you stay for just a minute?"

In his chair behind his desk, he bent over almost touching the top of his desk with his forehead, then looked up at me. "Jesus Christ, John. What was that?"

I was too embarrassed to answer. Was it *that* godawful?

"I think there is something wrong with me," he said. "Fucking weird. I liked it. Jesus Christ. There must be something wrong with me."

"Did … did you say you liked it?"

"God help me, yes. The questions are funny. I mean really funny. And John and Greg, a delight."

"What happens now?"

"My people are gonna think I've lost it. It is definitely not an after the news show, family show, which I hoped for. It's only late night. After the ten o'clock news. Give me a few days to talk to my people. Get me a budget. You may have to come back and do your dog and pony show again. Nobody will believe me."

I had the budget in my pocket. "Here. We'll wait for your call and would be happy to come back." I shook his hand.

"Are you sure you wouldn't rather do commentaries?" he asked weakly.

The following week we were in production. I hired Hal Parets, who'd been fired by George, as our announcer. His years of drinking and smoking gave him an edgy, raspy speaking voice that sounded like Louis Armstrong. The director of *Real People* became our director. Doing that show for thirteen hilarious weeks was more fun than any MGM musical with Judy and Mickey. Our entire tiny staff, including John and Greg, would sit with me in our production room for hours every afternoon putting together the questions. We could have done them in half an hour, they were so easy, but trying to refrain from rolling around with laughter took up the rest of the time. Often, we were so loud, casts and staff from other shows filming there wandered down the hall to see what all the hilarity was about. Ralph Edwards and Bob Barker were frequent visitors.

In the middle of production, I got an unexpected phone call from Roland. NBC had recently debuted a live afternoon network hour, with two hosts, male and female, who would interview people via satellite, and sometimes in studio, about helping make their dreams come true. It was every critic's dream to see it go away. It was on the verge of it when Roland called.

He said, "Brandon would like to know if you'd consider producing it."

"Tartikoff?" I almost screamed. "You've got to be kidding me."

"I'm serious."

"Roland, in three years he never spoke to me."

"Well, since *Real People* died when you did, he figured he made a mistake. Would you consider it?"

"Roland, I cannot lie to you. That concept is too cumbersome and unmanageable."

"He knows that. That's why he thinks you could fix it."

"The only way I could fix it, is dump it. Just turn it into a good afternoon talk show. He'd save a ton of money on hosts and production costs. And I would host and produce it."

There was a long pause. I had no qualms about spouting all this out so bluntly. After all, it was no secret that's all I ever wanted.

"What should I tell him, then?"

"Just what I told you. That's the only way I would consider it."

"I'll call you back this afternoon."

I hung up and forgot about it, certain Brandon would never go for it. But he did.

"Can you come in tomorrow for a meeting?" Roland was pleased, and as surprised as I was.

I also felt trapped. I was in the middle of this fun little show, with a commitment to John and Greg and Chuck Young.

"Roland, you know personally, I'd love more than anything to be able to do this. But I just cannot. Please, please thank Brandon for thinking about me. Finally. But I have this previous commitment."

The reviews when *That Awful Quiz Show* debuted were mixed, but leaned toward liking its outrageousness. One critic, at first, thought it was an extended *Saturday Night Live* skit. It only got into five markets, one of them being Las Vegas where it was a hit, as well as in Los Angeles where studio audiences were turned away for every taping. Unfortunately, though, viewers in the other three cities either turned away or didn't tune in.

Over the thirteen weeks we did sixty-five funny, way ahead of its time shows. Watching a few while putting this chapter together still brought out loud laughter. At that time, all we needed was a few more markets to stay in production. Our very highly respected distributor, D. L. Taffner, who bravely tarnished his respectability by taking it on, was unable to sell more cities. Word had only been out an hour that we'd been cancelled when Nell Carter, the celebrated, boisterous star of her own sitcom, burst in the office hollering, "John, who do I gotta fuck in this building to keep my boys on the air?"

With its demise, I got more condolences for that little piece of nonsense from more people than I did for losing *Real People*. That might have been a precursor of how taste in America was receding to low tides. I would like to say, as with reality television, that I was also first in bad taste. But funny is funny. And that was funny truth-telling about the rich and famous, a club that I would now never be a member of.

Chuck came to see me. "John, I'm really sorry. I loved it. So did my wife. I hate to say, I thought she had better taste." He smiled. "You know what, my sales guys say they could sell fifty cities, if you hosted it. You're still relatively famous. Would you consider that?"

I didn't give it a thought. "No. I discounted that in the beginning. John and Greg are perfect."

I instructed our staff and John and Greg to meet me and Christopher and Sarita at Musso and Frank's. It would be our version of The Last Supper, eating a great meal with great company. The show had obviously not been a step up. Or what Sarita said what I was meant to do, but, my God, was it fun.

Shakespeare said about sleep: "It knits up the raveled sleeve of care… balm of hurt minds. Chief nourisher in life."

He was wrong. It is laughter.

The Little Engine and Ernie Kovacs

Three quarters of a million dollars in a pension plan. A stunning, unique, fully paid-for home in prestigious Toluca Lake worth almost as much. Almost fifty years old. Married to a beautiful, supportive brunette. Father to a gentle genius. A phenomenal resume of co-hosting and creating for the three years I was there, the number one, trend-setting *Real People*. All nothing I ever looked or planned for or expected. All wonderfully mysterious gifted rewards of doggedly pursuing a job where only three were available in America, hosting a late-night talk show. The seventh inning stretch was the quiz show. Its rollicking relief from the stress of the last couple of years did not diminish that dream. But past middle age, I was once again unemployed. I had to face the reality that my chances of getting such a show were getting slimmer than seeing a male Olympic Gold-winning athlete turn into a woman. You just never know.

I never worked or dreamt of having that bank account and fabulous family. As I said, they just happened. They were just there. Lucky me. What I had been chasing and not achieving, what was always churning in my head, I couldn't turnoff. It was the little engine that kept that dream of having that late-night show.

To avoid the lingering disappointment of never realizing my prime goal, the vision that got me into this business in the first place, I had to put the brakes on that engine in my head. I would have to take another track to another goal. What it was, I had no idea. That is where my head was when I got a call from Henri Bollinger.

"John, would you have time to have a luncheon meeting tomorrow with Edie Adams, Ernie Kovacs' widow? The London Grill. Next door to my office. Noon."

"Is it all right if I bring Sarita?"

"Absolutely."

Aside from Jack Paar and Ed Murrow, and perhaps Sid Ceasar and Alistair Cook, the one other person I tried never to miss was Ernie Kovacs. He was to television what Chaplin was to film. A visual clown, the only one, even to this day, to use this new medium as such. His great wide face, thick moustache, wavy dark hair, and playfully appealing personality, made the genius of his visuals all the more arresting. He was also the first to make commercials an art form in themselves. His commercials made Murrieta cigars as famous as he was. They are still classics.

His widowed wife, Edie, whom I was about to meet with Henri, had been a singer on his daytime show early in his career. A few pounds heavier, but with no discernible age lines, she was still attractive. After the greetings and lunch orders, she got right to the point.

"I've told Henri a number of times that I'd like to meet you, especially since your unfortunate parting with Schlatter, but he said you were wrapped up in that adorable little show."

"Thank you," I said. "I was and still am a huge fan of your husband's."

"I'm glad, because that's what I want to talk to you about." She paused. "I could kill Schlatter. He is the only one I've ever met in the business whom I really hate. A despicable thieving, perverted bastard. Wouldn't you agree?"

"Edie, I don't hate George. I never did. I hated some of what he did to the show and especially to Jim Garrison. We had some screaming arguments, true. But hate is too heavy a load for me to carry. I became more fascinated by him, sort of like a scientist watching a deadly virus under a microscope. But I have a lovely home, family, will be able to pay cash if my son goes to Stanford or Harvard. It wouldn't have happened if he hadn't had that deal at NBC to fill."

"Well, you got some money out of it. I didn't. That son of a bitch stole my husband's material, out of which he built *Laugh-In*. I got nothing but promises. When Ernie was alive, George used to suck around our house all the time, him and Jolene. When we had pool parties, every time he showed up it was in drag, in a dress and heels for God's sake. Like a fat German Milton Berle. I really could kill the son of a bitch."

"Maybe you should be having lunch with someone from the CIA. That's their job."

"Oh, I'm sorry. I'm getting off the point. You're the only one other than my daughter, Kippie, and Henri I felt I could vent to. Sorry. Let me get to the point. I have all of Ernie's old shows, the ones I could save. Once in a while, PBS will air something for which they pay almost nothing. I have had a dozen producers calling me, asking if they could do a documentary about Ernie. I turned them all down. They either wanted total creative control, or I just didn't trust them. Then I thought of you."

"To do what?" I asked.

"To tell my husband's story."

"Edie, I've never done a documentary."

"But your stories are fantastic. Nobody tells a story on tape like you. Doing Ernie's story would be a version of what you did on your show. Just longer. Would you do it? Please?"

"I don't want any dead air here, so let me think out loud for you, so you'll know where I'm coming from. Doing a documentary is not what I'm thinking about. It's not what I want to do, although on a very back burner I have this tentative on-again off-again thing with Sinatra, his visual autobiography. That's been on a long hold. I've had no offers to do another show, and I'm not quite sure where I want to go from here, so I would consider it."

"Wonderful," she interjected.

"If I do it, you must leave me totally alone to do it as I see fit. If you have objections to anything I've done, he's your husband, it's your material, you are free to change it in any way you see fit. If I don't like your changes, my name is off it and the show is yours. To make you feel more comfortable, since you've mentioned money a few times, I will take no fees whatsoever. Writing, hosting, co-execing with you, none whatsoever."

"Wonderful," she repeated.

"I will do it as reasonably as possible, Henri will get his ten percent for bringing us together. What is left we'll split sixty-forty. The sixty for you. My company will own the copyright, but I will not be able to sell it for, let's say seven years without your permission, and if I sell it after that, it's still sixty-forty."

Tears slid down her cheek. "Oh, John, thank you. Thank you."

"Edie, for me it will be only a one-page deal, a handshake and a hug. I don't want to see a lawyer."

"You sound like Ernie." She smiled.

The brief paperwork done, and a warm hug, it was now about trying to sell it, plus screening and transferring her hours of material. The first place I considered approaching was Showtime's head of programming, Greg Nathanson, who I had met years earlier in the programming department at KTTV. He had always been gracious, encouraging, and accessible. Again, it was a happy accident he was now heading up Showtime's programming. I didn't know that when I decided to call Showtime. I approached them because of Gallagher.

Gallagher appeared intermittently on Showtime, in his wickedly funny, often sharply intelligent hours of prop comedy. His most notable routine being the Sledge-O-Matic. He would distribute clear plastic covering to the front rows of giggling, nervous patrons, take center stage, and with a sledge hammer bash watermelons. But that is not how he started.

I met him while at NBC. He would occasionally drop by just to listen to a review, and did the same later when I was doing *Real People*. He had majored in English. When he came to Los Angeles from Florida to begin his quest as a standup, his first routines were about language. The English language. How difficult and senseless it was. He pointed out the backwardness of it with observations like, why is it we park in a driveway, but drive on a parkway? They were brilliant, true, and funny. Somehow or other, his words morphed into the props that made him an irresistible star. His being on Showtime made it the perfect venue for Ernie Kovacs, who invented hilarious props for this visual medium. Nathanson's being there made it happen.

The meeting was surprisingly short. There were the three of us, myself, Greg, and his assistant, Peter Chernin. Their offer: $80,000.00 for a six-month continuous multiple run, reverting to me. Edie was thrilled. As was Henri. Then began the nuts and bolts task of screening and recording Ernie's shows, hiring a crew, setting up a travel schedule that would take us around the country, setting up interviews. All the practical stuff I would be doing to make my first documentary.

Everything about doing it was new, informing, and stimulating. I felt I was performing a public service, recording for posterity the work and untold story of this one-of-a kind entertainer-personality. It would be for those who remembered him, and for those who would discover him. When enterprises like that are meant to be, they move ahead effortlessly. That was the case here, as it was in the beginning year and a half of *Real People*. The only cinder in the eye came from Roland Perkins. He sent me a bill for Creative Artist's commission marked, FYI: $8,000.00 due. My response was the shortest letter I ever sent: Roland: FY and Creative Artists. You were not there. Neither will the $8,000.00 be.

Everyone who was part of Ernie's life and work called to be in it. Steve Allen and Chevy Chase were a delight, Jack Lemmon maybe even more so. He had been one of the apes in Ernie's memorable Nairobi Trio. Jack confessed that was the happiest time he ever spent in showbiz.

It aired as *Ernie Kovacs, TV's Original Genius.*

It was not only one of Showtime's highest-rated specials, it was the one that received from across the country and on the networks that network's most ecstatic reviews. One said that it was the best documentary ever made of a performer. (To date, for me, it may now be in second place following the Academy Award winner, *Searching for Superman*. Mine can be seen free at my site: youtube/www.johnbarboursworld.com.)

The review which shocked and made my head snap, though, was that of Tom Shales of *The Washington Post*. His entire review was a long rave, well thought out and articulated, except for his last stunning line: He wrote: 'It is a shame that Edie Adams put her material in the hands of such a Hollywood sleaze.'

What? What was that? The man didn't even know me. It was outright libel. How could he have done such a thing? Then it hit me. His unknowing comment about The Vietnam Memorial piece, not understanding the choice of Roberta Flack's *The First Time Ever I Saw Your Face*, replaced later by Schlatter in the butchered syndicated version with the trite *Where Have All the Flowers Gone*? And the sound still ringing in my ears of Schlatter screaming, "I'll see you never work again!"

I grabbed the phone and called Tom Shales at *The Washington Post.* "Tom, this is John Barbour."

"Oh," he blurted.

"I appreciate, in spite of your uninformed bias, obviously, the first ninety-nine percent of your review. But why that last libelous comment? Have you ever met me?"

"No."

"Have we ever talked?"

"No."

"Did you like my work before this one?"

"I don't know. What work?"

"How about the first three years of *Real People,* and especially the Veterans Day show, which you praised except for my choice of Roberta Flack's song?"

"That was you?" he said, tentatively.

"Not just that show, but the entire concept, with lawsuits to prove it. For the first three years of *Real People,* I wrote, edited or supervised the editing of nearly every one of the hours."

"I was under the impression it was George Schlatter's show."

"He only owned it. Like Steinbrenner owns Yankee stadium, but he doesn't play the game. Pardon me, I was the team. Now that I'm gone, how does his fucking show look?"

He didn't answer.

"It's a piece of crap, which he turns everything into. Including you. How on earth could a respected journalist on the paper uncovering Watergate fall for such a libelous fraud as Schlatter? How could you? Didn't you ask for proof of my sleaziness? Pictures? Whatever? I'm sure he didn't bribe you. How on earth could you have been suckered in like that? How?"

Still no reply.

"He got you only with words? What could he have said? And how often? Tom, I hope someday you publicly acknowledge your very hurtful mistake!"

After a long pause, he said, "George is a very charming man."

I hung up. I never heard or read any such apology.

I then called Henri, my publicist, who was more in shock than me. Then Chris Hayward.

I was looking for some advice on whether or not to file not just one but two slander lawsuits. The other one would be against our local

Emmy Magazine. As an industry periodical, it just informed its readers about trends in the business, puff pieces. It never engaged in an attack on anyone. Except me.

Months after I left *Real People* came a devastating long piece. It was a vicious assault on "my limited talents, my personality, my ideas." What made it more head-shaking was that one of the so-called sources, Dan Gingold, had been another one I had hired. It was easy to draft a quick four-page factual response to everything in the article, which I hand-delivered, in a rage, to the editor who refused to run it.

I didn't call George Bane. I had no confidence in his having the required barrister balls for such an undertaking against the *Washington Post*, America's second most respected newspaper, and *Emmy*, a company-town magazine. I thought briefly of calling Harlan Ellison, a good friend now and the most publicly successful litigant in Hollywood, but settled on just speaking to Chris and Henri.

Henri's insistent soft-spoken advice was a resounding "No."He said if I persisted, I would be viewed across the country as I was viewed in Hollywood, as an angry, uncontrollable sour grapes troublemaker, that I should keep that reputation local. Chris, on the other hand, was all for me "bashing the bastards" as he called them, that it would be something I'd undoubtedly win. How happy would I be, though, never working again?

I knew of no retired writers in Hollywood who made more money from lawsuits than they ever did from work. My reputation was out of my hands. My work was in my hands. That was all I wanted to do. Just work. Not sue. So I dropped it.

For Edie, that special was a deserved gift. The reason it played so well, is in the beginning we got to see Ernie's wondrous work, the pixyish glee with which he performed it. By the second half, though, we are captured by the story of the man himself; a heavy drinker, an incorrigible losing gambler, paying ninety percent income tax, spending two years tracking down his two daughters kidnapped by his first wife, discovering he was the first man in America to be awarded custody of his children in a divorce settlement. And all the time trying to make America laugh; his becoming a star in movies, then his sudden, untimely death. His Corvair, with the engine in the rear, spun out of control, killing him.

It was the kind of story that becomes a Movie of the Week, which is just what happened for Edie. ABC bought the rights from Edie for a very large sum, plus additional payment as a consultant. I was happy for her. It didn't bother me that she never called to inform me of her good news and good fortune, or even to thank me. For two years, we let PBS air it as a fundraising special. For reasons that bewilder me still, while it is perfect for the Biography channel, Comedy Central, and dozens of other cable outlets, they still decline to air it.

A few years later, Henri called me to tell me Edie had made some kind of deal with George Schlatter for a lot of money. She died a millionaire in 2008 of cancer.

Aside from the thrill of getting to know more about Ernie Kovacs and his never-duplicated work, the most wonderful, accidental reward I got from knowing Edie Adams was the gift of getting to know George Burns.

A Late-Night Dinner with George Burns

Because of the sudden attention brought to Edie by our film, a promoter thought it'd be a great idea to put on a one-night show at The Pantages Theater, starring half a dozen once famous singing stars. It sold out immediately. One of the stars was Edie. Another, Frankie Lane, one of my childhood favorites. I couldn't wait to hear again, *That's My Desire, Cry of The Wildgoose,* and *Rawhide*. Christopher, now thirteen, came with me and Sarita. Henri Bollinger sat next to Edie's date, George Burns.

As a critic, whenever with Sarita, after seeing a play or film we enjoyed, which was not too often, we always wanted to extend that pleasure, to savor it just a little more by going to the best late-night dinners in town at Scandia's. This was one of those nights. It was filled with good vibes and great memories, which would get even better.

We arrived at ten, the same time they started the late-night menu. Greeting George Burns like an old friend, the manager led the seven of us to a large special round table in the middle of the dining room. I was surprised we weren't led to the downstairs wine cellar, but the manager knew George relished the center of the room, to be the center of attention. This attention from the diners and staff with any other star would have puffed them up, as though they were on stage. Not George. It made him look at home and relaxed doing what he loved: to talk. I don't know how it all began, but I never wanted it to stop. He started casually and was still going at 12:30 when we were the only customers left, and all but one waiter and the manager had gone, and the restaurant closed.

Knowing Christopher played golf, George told him how his friends at Brentwood Country Club refused to play with him anymore because he never shut up. He said he only liked sports where you get to yell. He enchanted us with tales about his childhood, his family, his friends, his wife, his work, about his likes and his dislikes. One of his biggest dislikes was sick people. He said, like Richard Burton and Dean Martin, he couldn't be around sick people until they died.

"I once went to see my sister in the hospital," came that sweet growly voice. "I asked her if she was feeling better. She said she wasn't, so I said I'll come back when you do." He was not trying to be funny, just honest. But he was hilarious.

The filet mignons went uneaten while we dined on his every word. At 1:30 a.m. the manager still made no move to ask us to leave. George noticed the time himself. He pulled out another cigar and lit it. Good. That meant he wasn't finished. I will try to recount it, just as he told it. You'll have to imagine the voice.

"They say there's no business like show business. There is no business as dumb and lucky as show business. Lucy told me this. Love that lady. One tough broad. She had this really successful radio show, *I Love Lucy*. Her costar a semi-successful B-actor. Very pleasant nice lookin' Wasp. Richard Denning. Women loved him. Tall, blue eyes better than Newman. Blonde. Good voice. What's not to like? Lucy liked him. She'd picked him. One day, CBS comes to Lucy and says they'd like to do a pilot. TV was getting big. They needed shows. Lucy says she will on one condition, that her real husband Desi play the husband. CBS tells her she must be crazy. A Hispanic. Not even Mexican. Worse, a Cuban. America isn't ready for that. Lucy says the whole world knows Desi is her real husband, it helps make the show real. If not, as much as she likes Richard, the people know it's fake. They tell her TV is make-believe, that folks already know that and still love her radio show. Denning is gorgeous. Women will kvell when they see him.

"She says no Desi, no her. She'll stick with the radio show till it's over. A couple of days later, CBS comes back with a proposition. They tell her they will do a pilot with her husband Dizzy, they called him 'Dizzy.' And if it didn't come out to her satisfaction, not theirs, that she would redo the pilot with Denning. She agrees.

"They do the pilot. So, here comes Desi, this babaloo bongo player. All of a sudden, he starts telling all these production pros what he wants. Lucy lets him. He wants a live audience and three cameras and a bunch of stuff that's never been done. They finish it and ship it to New York. Nobody at CBS is impressed. Somehow it is seen in the sales department by the President of Old Gold cigarettes. He loves it. He immediately orders thirteen episodes, which CBS immediately sells him. CBS calls Lucy at home with the great news. One of TV biggest sponsors. Thirteen weeks. Lucy says nothing. They tell her it's a go for the fall. She tells them, no it isn't.

"'What yah mean,'" they yell all happy. 'We've signed the contract.' Lucy says, 'Not with Desi you haven't.' Thinking he'd bomb they'd neglected to sign him. She says on the other end she was waiting for a heart attack. She says they scramble to tell her they'll sign Desi, immediately, at a great price. She stops them and says 'No you won't. What you'll do is sign the show over to our new company, Desilu, and we'll deliver it. They scream 'Lucy you cannot do that. Not to us. Your family. 'I can and will,' she says. 'Otherwise you can tell your boss and Old Gold to blow smoke up their ass!'

George paused savoring his last puff, but more for the looks of awe and admiration on our faces. What a story. What a storyteller. The best I would ever hear.

"That, lady and gentlemen, is how Lucy got her show, bought RKO, and built an empire. I love that broad. And with that, as with Gracie, it's time to say, goodnight, George."

My son is now in his late forties. On his own he has become one of the writers and co-executive producers of *Criminal Minds*. To this day, he says, that long-ago dinner as a thirteen-year-old was the most memorable dinner he has ever had, and that George's story is still his favorite showbiz tale.

Mine too.

John Barbour's World vs. the Real World

I had dozens of wonderful unfinished stories on my desk, stories I would have done the fourth and fifth years on *Real People*. I didn't want them to go untold. So, it was a natural to call Greg Nathanson again, since he'd said Showtime was considering submitting my Kovacs special for Peabody consideration.

In his office once again, Greg Nathanson, with Peter Chernin, his silent assistant at his side, he said yes to at least one episode. Greg gave me an air date for 'John Barbour's World' four months away. That was fortunate because suddenly a couple of incidents popped up, one of which would detour my career path forever. The first incident I welcomed; the second was a stranger, which got me involved in events that got even stranger.

Our house was like a Swiss chalet, the most beautiful house on a street full of beautiful houses. We repeatedly turned down *Architectural Digest* that wished to do a picture feature about it. It was not uncommon for neighbors or strangers to buzz the front door asking to see it.

Two days after making the deal with Greg, it was a friendly neighbor who showed up. His name was Alan, a successful musician and arranger. With him was Jilly, Sinatra's bodyguard, whom I hadn't seen in three years. They wanted a tour, which we happily gave them.

"Johnny, you know, you gotta give Francis a call. Or Dorothy. He talks about ya all the time, and once in a while brings up that thing you wanna do with him."

"Jilly, I never wanted to bug Francis. I figured he'd call when he was ready."

"I think he's ready. And since you're not doing your show any more, I'm sure you're ready." He chuckled. "I'll tell him I saw you, but call Dorothy."

They left and I called Dorothy. She said Francis would be delighted to meet to work out some kind of schedule, but it'd probably be a few weeks before he could do so. I told her I was in no hurry.

Then came a call from someone I'd never heard of. He identified himself as a writer. His name was Robert Blair Kaiser. His book, he said, was becoming a bestseller. It was called *RFK Must Die*. The title he said came from the notes supposedly written repeatedly on a notepad by Sirhan Sirhan before he shot Robert Kennedy. I asked why he was calling me. He said he had long been a fan from the days of my morning show, and added, "I remember you announced booking Jim Garrison on your morning show, then you were gone. I just started thinking about you and thought I'd like to meet you. Especially after that disaster on *Speak up America.*

I told Robert to come to my house. He showed up with an autographed copy of his book. During the next few weeks, he showed up three times for dinner. I was sorry I didn't have a regular show; he was a fabulous storyteller. Maybe there's a segment about him l could do for *John Barbour's World*. He was a former priest, quit to become a writer, and quite by accident got involved in not only writing about Sirhan, but also interviewing him.

"Do you know Dr. Noguchi?" he asked one evening.

"I've never met him, but I heard of him a lot during the morning show. The City Council was trying to get rid of him because, as I remember, they said he was a ghoul who couldn't wait for a plane crash so he could forage among the bodies."

"That's not why they were getting rid of him," he said flatly. "They wanted to get rid of him because he wouldn't alter his autopsy report on Bobby."

"What do you mean?"

"Have you seen it?"

"No."

"It's part of the public record. It says the gun that fired the fatal shot that killed Bobby was no more than two to two and a half inches from behind his left ear because of the extensive powder burns to the hair and skull."

"Meaning?"

"Meaning that Sirhan, who was standing six feet in front of Bobby, even with his arm extended, could not have fired the killing shot. Now they're trying to get rid of him because of his autopsy of William Holden."

"Holden! Why Holden?"

"When Holden fell down in his apartment in Santa Monica, it was reported that he somehow tripped, hit his head on a coffee table, and bled to death. Maybe a heart attack. What they didn't report, and Noguchi revealed in his autopsy, was that Holden was stone drunk when he fell; his autopsy pissed off not only the media for their incompetence, but especially Hollywood because Noguchi is denigrating one of their own. They are all out to get him."

"If he's telling the truth, how can they get rid of him?"

"They get rid of him because he is telling the truth. I know Godfrey Isaacs, his lawyer. Would you like to meet him?"

"Why would I want to meet him?"

"Because it's an important story, not just in LA but all over. One I thought would interest you."

"Right now," I said, "I'm trying to tell my own stories."

"Okay, I understand." He paused, then added, "I'm going to a small gathering in Beverly Hills to listen to Godfrey speak. Would you like to come? Just out of curiosity?"

I went. The auditorium was packed. Isaacs pointed out they were attacking Dr. Noguchi for telling the truth. I was moved. Afterward, Robert introduced me.

Without actually meaning it, I said, "If there's anything I can do to help you and Dr. Noguchi, Mr. Isaacs, here's my number. Thank you. It was really informative."

One night later, Robert called, asking if he could see me right away. When he arrived, he didn't sit. He was agitated; actually frightened. He handed me a few pages with some notes, saying he did not feel safe, that he was going to disappear for a while. And was gone. I never saw him again.

Then Godfrey called. After expressing his concern over Robert, he asked if I would like to meet Dr. Noguchi. I couldn't say no, since I had offered my help. But what kind of help could I give?

Aside from Sarita's father, Dr. Thomas Noguchi was the quietest, gentlest man I ever met. My question to him at our first dinner meeting was not about his plight or his famous cases. Instead, I asked, "In all the autopsies you've done, what was the one condition in their bodies that you noticed most?"

Immediately, he answered in a slight soft Japanese accent, "Dehydrated. Americans do not drink enough water."

During that engaging chat we did not touch on his job, or his fight to keep it. He told me his story, his childhood, coming to America, his hobbies, which were cooking, painting and watercolors. Over the next few weeks we dined once a week at his favorite Japanese restaurant on Ventura Boulevard, near Laurel Canyon. We attended many crowded gatherings in fancy homes and estates from Studio City to Beverly Hills where Godfrey spoke.

The more I heard of his unfair fight, the angrier I got. I hate bullies; I had just gone through five years of dealing with bullies. Seeing so much public support for him, I said to Godfrey, "Why don't we form a committee, a public committee to retain Dr. Noguchi as the independent coroner of Los Angeles with you as the chairman?"

"That's a wonderful idea, John, and you'll be co-chair."

"I don't want any titles. I'll speak or lick envelopes or whatever is needed, but I'm not built to be a joiner or co-chair of anything."

"You are an extremely popular public personality, very well respected for your integrity and truth telling, albeit maybe not to everyone's liking, so your presence on the letterhead would mean a lot. Okay?"

I agreed.

The public was developing a growing interest in the Robert Kennedy killing because of the city's establishment's front-page attempts to silence

Dr. Noguchi. The first place I got to speak was the Sportsman's Lodge. There was an overflow standing crowd of 1500. Tom Bradley spoke, as did scores of police officers whom I had met playing for years in The Police Celebrity Golf Tournament. Dr. Noguchi was finally given another hearing before the City Council which I attended.

More support poured in. Firemen. Doctors. Lawyers. His chances of retaining his job looked assured. Even predicted by the Press. The opposition of the City Fathers and the Press began to crank out its fake fear-mongering. They were joined now by a growing contingent of Hollywood elite, repulsed by Dr. Noguchi's honest autopsies of Natalie Wood, but especially his revealing William Holden's drunken end. It was announced loudly that this fact-avoiding tsunami of celebrities was now to be headed up by one of Bill Holden's best friends, The Chairman of the Board, the Founding Father of the Rat Pack, Frank Sinatra! I was staggered. I could see what was coming ... and going.

Considering Dr. Noguchi's broad public and professional support, and the endorsement of some smaller newspapers, his firing came as a total surprise. Gracious even in defeat, Dr. Noguchi called, inviting me, Sarita and Christopher to dinner. Aside from picking up the check, he gifted us with a beautiful autographed watercolor painting. It hangs in our bedroom.

It was no surprise, though, when Dorothy called me. "John, I am so sorry to tell you this."

I interrupted her, laughing to myself. "Dorothy, I can hear it coming!"

"John, I am so sorry, but Mr. Sinatra is making other plans and right now he says they don't include your project."

It was time I got my mind back on my special for Greg. I decided not to do a segment on Robert Kaiser. That would mean we'd have to bring up Robert Kennedy. God, no. This assassination stuff is a killer!

Showtime on Showtime

Roland was still sending notes about CAA's $ 8,000.00 commission, which went unanswered.

He was the last agent I would ever want. And the last one to ever want me, even though I knew I handled my career with the finesse of a blackjack dealer wearing boxing gloves.

I began work for *John Barbour's World.* The first week into it, my wife and I ran into Skip Stephenson at Charlie's Fish 'n' Chips. It was shortly after *Real People* had been cancelled. He was at the counter by himself. He looked tired. We asked him to join us at a booth. For the five years on the air, he had been the delightfully salacious sidekick to Sarah. Privately, he was a pushover to everyone wanting a handout, especially to the comics he had passed on the way up. He lent thousands. A lot of it to his ex-wife with whom he had a lingering intense love-hate relationship; she hated him, loved his money. The house he had asked me to help save was gone.

"Johnny, my only friend now is my dog." He tried to smile. He said he'd heard about my problems with City Hall over Noguchi, wondering why I would ever get involved in such nonsense.

"Skip," I said, "I've had a number of people ask me how I ever got involved with Schlatter."

"I meant to call ya," he said. "I'm embarrassed I didn't. I was having too many problems of my own. Geez, you did better than all of us, except maybe Sarah. Why don't you just retire? Why do you keep bashing your head against the wall?"

"Because I love it, and I think my head is harder than any wall. And one small one I just broke down. I am doing an hour special on Showtime."

When the check came, Sarita picked it up. "Skip, it was wonderful seeing you again. Dinner's on us." She patted his hand.

He got halfway to the door, and turned. "Ya know why that damn dog is still with me?" he hollered. "'Cuz it's the only bitch I never gave money to!"

He was delighted at the laughter from his small audience of diners. Sadly, he died of a heart attack in 1992.

The first person I hired was once again Sergio Aragone who had designed the set for the *Quiz Show*. America had great newspaper cartoonists like Conrad in the *L.A. Times* and Herblock in DC, but no one was faster than Sergio. At lunch at Musso's, as I lifted my glass of cabernet, he grabbed the napkin. Before I'd finished a sip, he put it back.

"I thought you might like a Christmas card." He smiled.

In front of me was this cartoon piece of art, me, my wife, my son swinging a golf club, our cat, our dog, our TV camera with *Real People* on it. Working with this kind of unique talent, is one of the joys that make the pain of getting into and staying in this business worth it, as was the delight of doing the stories. Finally, we'd get to tell Roy Reep's, the unluckiest man in the world.

Then one about a retired middle-aged government employee who decided upon retiring to change her life and residence. She moved from DC to LA where she became a nude model for Larry Flint's *Hustler Magazine*.

While these were hilarious, this story should have been a movie of the week. It was about a beautiful young brunette who became one of UCLA's first heart transplant recipients, and the tale that led up to it. Her father was German. During the Second World War he was a policeman. His job was to arrest Jews. One he arrested was a brilliant doctor. He was sent to Auschwitz, and never came out. The deceased doctor had a daughter. She hid for five years, eventually rescued by American soldiers. An American family adopted her. Like her father, she became a doctor, and a renowned surgeon.

After the war, the policeman also moved to America, to St. Louis, where he married and had a daughter. His daughter, however, had a defective heart. In her early twenties, she needed a transplant. The procedure was relatively new in America; one of the few and best places for her to go would be UCLA. She got her transplant, survived magnificently, got a job and a boyfriend. Her surgeon was the daughter of the man whom her father had murdered.

On Showtime our hour did well, well enough to get a call from Peter Chernin, Greg's assistant, inviting me to a lunch meeting.

"John, congratulations," Peter said. 'It was a really nice show. We have something in mind for you. Greg and I think you'd be the perfect one for it. Interstitials."

"Interstitials?" I stammered. "What is that?"

"It's in the cable world. They are short three or four-minute pieces that would air at the end or beginning of a show to keep the audience around. You'd be perfect to do that. Do or say or film what you want. We've already made up a list of some of the things we'd like to see you do."

I couldn't believe it. It sounded like what I'd turned down for Chuck Young.

"I can say or do what I want? As long as it's your list? Peter, my hope was to do what I did in *Real People* with the added touch of news pieces. A series of monthly specials."

"Reality is dead," Peter said emphatically.

"No, it's not! It is just beginning."

"Reality is not what we want. *Real People* is dead and gone."

"It's dead and gone because I'm no longer there to do it. If they had called me back, it would still be alive and well."

"I do not think so."

"Certainly, you wouldn't think so. You weren't there to know."

"It's not that I don't believe you, but reality is going nowhere. Cable is. And while it is only a few minutes on a growing network, it'd give you a great platform and resumé."

"Interstitials? Honestly; you know what I feel like? Woody Allen. Like he's just made *Annie Hall,* and the studio wants him to start doing Pete Smith specialties. I would feel like I was going backwards. Thanks, but no thanks. The best of luck."

And indeed, Peter Chernin went on to have the best of luck. In this brutal business, Chernin went on to become the industry's most successful assistant!

If at First You Succeed, It's Harder to Do It Again

When Peter Chernin informed me reality TV was dead, along with my chances to do it, my mind and upset stomach went back to the offer I'd turned down from Tartikoff. I screwed up my courage, and placed a call to Brandon. And another. Then a letter. And another letter. All unanswered. In comedy, as in careers, timing is everything. My time with him had come and gone. I began to think I'd worn out mv welcome in Hollywood. Maybe even America. My standup career had started as this guy from the NAACP, the National Association for The Advancement of Canadian People. Maybe now that I was a successful transplant, I could return to Toronto as a star and host of a late-night show. After all, I was featured in a huge hardcover book called *Entertaining Canadians.*

Excited about Johnny coming marching home, I made a long-distance phone call to the CBC, asking to speak directly to the head of programming. In seconds, this happy voice with a French-Canadian accent said, "Well, hallo Jean!" (Sadly, I don't remember his name.) "What can I do for you, Jean?"

"I would like to come back to Toronto, and do what Canada has never had, a good, live late-night talk show."

"I don't think so." His instant negative comment stunned me.

"Why not? I'm well established. I can send you half a dozen great interviews and standup. It would be terrific."

"I don't think so."

"You don't think it'd be terrific, or you don't think you're interested?"

"I heard all about you. I was Tartikoff's assistant for three years."

"What does that mean, you heard all about me? You can't believe what you hear. In your position, you have to believe what you see. My work. And it was number one when I was doing it."

"Your work?"

"Yes. *Real People.*"

"That's not what I hear. You have a bad reputation."

"*Real People* went into the toilet under Schlatter. Doesn't that tell you something? And Brandon wouldn't have offered me that producing job while you were there, to shape up that dumb make a wish show." He didn't answer, so I continued. "Look, I'll make it easy for you to see what I can do. At no cost. Give me ninety minutes one Saturday night, live. I'll pay for it. That's how confident I am. Let the show and the reaction determine whether or not you'll do it."

"I don't think so."

"Didn't Tartikoff ever teach you to say, I think so? If you're being so negative why on earth did you answer the phone?"

"I couldn't believe it was the real John Barbour."

"Jesus Christ, are you kidding? In Canada, too. How do you fucking people get your jobs?" I slammed down the phone. Goddamn it. Incompetence has no borders! Within a few months, though, I was in Canada. Not doing my own talk show, but being one of three panelists on someone else's game show.

I got a phone call from a fellow Canuck, Alan Thicke's brother, himself a writer asking if I'd be interested in a job he turned down, but recommended me. And I'd never met him.

"John, it's to be shot in Vancouver. I don't know if you remember *The Liars' Club*, but Blair Murdoch bought it. He's shooting it there. I can't do it. They need what they call Canadian content, so I recommended you. Should I have him call you?"

"Will I be billed as writer-panelist or Canadian content?"

He laughed. "It should be fun."

"Sure, have Blair call. And thank you very much. I truly appreciate it."

Vancouver is one of the most beautiful cities in North America. With their greenbelt laws, there are magnificent parks and lawns between buildings, stunning public gardens, a spotless downtown with what look like scrubbed skyscrapers, a breathtaking view of the ocean, tour quality golf courses, and one street that is turned over to the most gorgeous hookers on the continent.

Blair himself was the nicest producer I ever worked for. He was a successful independent, without agent or manager, doing everything on his own. What he did, he never considered work. It was all like a fun hobby to him. Previously, he'd been one of Canada's top computer gurus.

Blair, plus my two co-panelists and the audience's reaction, made it enjoyable. So much so, that not once did I miss being on a major network. My two co-panelists were Pete Barbutti, a successful Italian-American comedian-trumpet player. He had appeared on almost every variety show, and was a regular in the lounges of Las Vegas where he lived. The other had the most physically attractive body I have ever seen on a woman, which also contained one of the brightest minds. Shannon Tweed was as breathtaking to look at as she was to listen to, especially her story about how her twin became Bill Cosby's mistress after meeting him at Hefner's mansion. Shannon, herself, had been a Playmate of the Year, and had become Gene Simmons' live-in. She and her twin sister were born in Canada's Maritime Provinces. Following this nearly half-a-year stint with *The Liars' Club*, Shannon went on to become one of America's most successful semi-porn stars in films which she produced. At the time, though, her main ambition was to make her young son, Chris, legitimate, by marrying a very reluctant Gene. Decades, and another child later, she succeeded in wearing him down on their own reality show.

As said so often in this business, the friends you think are going to last a lifetime only last as long as the enterprise on which you are working. The only one I chat with occasionally now is Blair. Every so often I get a nice piece of fan mail from someone near the Arctic who loves the reruns.

Almost Above Being Local Again

Maybe word was out that I wasn't such a troublemaker; the phone started to ring.

"John, this is Walt Baker. I have an opening on Friday nights for an hour. Would you be interested in doing a local talk show again?"

"Could it be live with call-ins?"

"Absolutely."

"I'd be very interested."

"Let's have lunch tomorrow."

Walt Baker was the long-time, well-respected program director of KHJ Channel Nine, a large man, almost the size of Orson Welles, with the voice to match. Over the years he had presented many good daytime talk shows, my favorite being the one hosted by Nat King Cole's smart, attractive widow. Regis Philbin also did one. KHJ's studios were on Melrose Avenue, a few blocks east of Vine Street, adjacent to Desilu Studios, formerly RKO. We met at the Mexican restaurant across the street, famous as the eatery where Jerry Brown and Linda Rondstadt frequently dined.

"John, we're an independently-owned station, as you know. My boss is a fan of yours. He brought up your name. You have carte blanche to do or book whoever you want. It'll be live with a ten-second delay, just in case. I personally would like to see you do some reviews again. You may not want to–"

"I'd be happy to."

"My only admonition is this is a company town. You have been known to bash people. Just try not to be cruel. And speaking of cruelty, I can only give you fifteen hundred a week, with increases, small ones, every few weeks."

"Walt, I don't need money. I need to work. That and taking Christopher to golf tournaments are all I need"

"Wonderful. Okay if we call it *John Barbour Live*? Either that or, *John Barbour Still Alive*?"

It was called the former. Once again, I hired Hal Parets, who was well known to Walt. Hal became my booker and producer. Sarita became our creative consultant. That was the staff. Just the three of us. We booked nearly everyone of interest in town, as well as national newsmakers. Actors and directors I had previously blasted called to be guests. Ricardo Montalban was the first to call; astonishing, because I had been cruel about his performance at The Dorothy Chandler Pavilion in *The King and I*. I'd said, *Montalban's stilted performance was a perfect match for that stage, wood on wood*. I did not know he actually had a wooden leg, and on camera, I apologized profusely. He hugged me, saying, "We love you. Who else says such things? And good to see you again on TV. You're like grass in the sidewalk, always popping up."

We had the country's greatest comics, including Phyllis Diller and Shelly Berman, regaling us with hilarious anecdotes about their lives and the business; an outstanding hour with the town's most prolific writer-producer, Stephan Cannell, creator of *The Rockford Files* and *The*

A Team, recalling his troubling early years because of his dyslexia. And an unbelievably interesting, mind-expanding hour with the Nicholas Testa of music, Frank Zappa. I opened every show either with a review accompanied by visuals, or a hopefully humorous social or political commentary at a blackboard. The ratings were very respectful. Enough to keep us going. I loved my little creative cocoon, cheered on by Walt.

The third week into the show Hal came into my office. "There's some kid it sounds like, who says he's from CNN, and he wants to talk to you. Should I ask him what's it about?"

"No. I'll talk to him." I picked up the phone.

The young voice gave me his name. He said he was the producer of *Sonya Live* on CNN, asking if I was familiar with it. I told him no, but the name sounded familiar, like the name of the lady whose co-hosting job I had saved in Chicago, Steve Edwards's co-host.

"Well, if it is, she'd be delighted to return the favor. She's going on vacation for two weeks. We're looking for someone good enough to take over for her. Would they let you do it? And would you like to?"

"I'm sure management here would love for me to get that kind of exposure again."

"What do you mean again?"

"On a network."

"You were on the network?"

"NBC. Three years. *Real People*. Then a bunch of shows doing standup. Dean Martin. Griffin. *Tonight* with Sinatra."

"Sounds great. Never saw them."

"The *AM Show* locally. Did you see that?"

"No. I'm from back East."

"You mean, you've never seen me before?"

"No. Just the last three weeks. I caught you by accident channel surfing and stuck with it."

"On that alone, you feel confident in putting Ted Turner's noon hour in my hands?"

"You are as good as I've seen, network or otherwise."

"For somebody like you, who trusts what he sees, I'd do it for nothing."

"Have your agent call. Could you come by tomorrow, noonish, to meet Sonya? The CNN building Sunset and Vine. Not far."

"I no longer have an agent, but I still have a car. I'll be there."

Although I filled in as host for just two weeks, it was the most at ease feeling I'd had since the morning show. It was expensively produced, live, with phone calls, and on a classy, (at the time) cable network. This may not say much for me, but I always felt more alive, more me, and more at peace in front of a camera than I ever did off camera.

One of my first interviews was with the Judd girls, mother and daughter. Everywhere they went after that they played brief clips, saying it was the best interview they ever did. Gallagher, the reigning king of comedy with his breakthrough specials on Showtime, displayed his inventive genius. Actors, newsmakers, filmmakers all filled the quick hours, as did lit-up phone lines.

One day, a caller faked a question for a guest, got through onto the air, and complimented me. It was innocent enough, but my producer went berserk. After the show he told me he had instructions to not let these kinds of calls go through. No personal calls. Just news," he said loudly. "This is a news network, not *This Is Your Life*."

I replied that I had no control over what calls came through, they were not any voice I recognized, so obviously not a friend. While this was a news network, my show, I added, or rather Sonya's show, was not a news show. It was primarily a talk show.

The next day, a calmer, smiling producer handed me a sealed letter from Atlanta. It was a fan letter from the head of programming for CNN. Two days later, after the show, he called.

"John, you've been an absolute and pleasant surprise. Thoroughly professional, totally at ease with performers or politicians. In other words, terrific."

"Thank you, sir, Thanks for the opportunity. It's obvious I love doing this stuff. Even on my little local show."

There was a bit of a pause, then he said, "Don't give up on us. We're not giving up on you. As a matter of fact, and this is not for publication, Larry King may be going into the hospital shortly for heart surgery. You'd be perfect to fill in for him."

"Wow!" I gasped. I was torn, being sad for him and happy for me.

As pumped as I was, I only told Sarita. But word got out around town, originating from a few of the CNN staff. People I barely knew were asking me about it. This was not a good sign. Another not so good sign was the announcement Disney was buying KHJ. I was definitely not a Disney kind of guy.

Three weeks after the purchase, Walt called me into his office. I knew what was coming. I didn't want him to feel uncomfortable telling me that *John Barbour Live* was dead.

"Walt, I only came to cheer you up. I know you hate to tell me Mickey Mouse is replacing me, but I still am so thankful to you. Cheer up. I'm used to it. It is the business."

"I was always a fan of your work, John, but I'm now a bigger fan of you personally. Thank you. Do you think anything will come of the CNN thing? If you want, I'll call Atlanta for you. I may do it anyway. I've already made a half-dozen calls on your behalf."

"Where? Why?"

"When we first announced your show, within two days I got six phone calls from people, some prominent people in this town, warning me not to hire you. Frankly, I was stunned. First, by how prominent some of them were, then by their numbers, then by their vitriol. Jesus, what did you do to them? It made me nervous. They were telling me shit about you that frankly scared me. Ten days later I called them all back, telling them they were absolutely mistaken, they must have been talking about another John Barbour."

"Who were they?"

"I can't tell you, John. It was all private. I'm sorry."

"Walt, I wouldn't call them. I'd just like to know."

"John, I am not going to tell you. I don't want to start a pissing contest. If it's not those people trying to destroy you or anyone jealous of or pissed off at you, there's a bunch more in this fucking town. Just keep hanging in there."

"I try. Will you still be doing your job now that Disney's taking over?"

"Not me. I'm retiring. I could hack it out a few more years here, but I haven't the stomach for it anymore. We're comfortable, so, that's it."

Walt retired a few months later to a farm in Idaho. He wrote one brief note saying he was much happier growing potatoes, and wanted to know how my possible thing at CNN was working out.

I wrote back saying, *Walt, if you need help growing your potatoes, I can supply you with great fertilizer. Nearly every promise I've gotten from biggies in this town has been absolute bullshit. If only I could bag it for you. I never did hear from CNN. Evidently your 'friends' must have called Ted Turner, too!*

Really ... News?

Once again, I was left with the worst company possible: myself and spare time, tough time to fill and kill while thinking of people I couldn't kill. During those interludes, I tried to think about

Joseph Campbell's oft-quoted formula for success, follow your joy. That's easy for him to say. He was never in such a soul-destroying business.

Following *Real People,* the work I did was just 'jobs.' But I did not want another 'job.' I wanted what we all want, a purpose. To do something important. It sounds a little grandiose, but that's what daydreams are supposed to be. Then the idea hit me that quickly. What is bigger than the news? What is more important and more of a sacred cow in American TV? The news!

The concept, like Tesla said often of his inventions, blossomed in my mind full-blown and complete. The seed had been planted years earlier in the middle of my monologue with Frank Sinatra on *The Tonight Show*. It was a casual throwaway line. I said, "You know, comics no longer have to write jokes about politicians to get laughs. All you have to do is quote them." It got a huge laugh.

Over the years, I had scrapbooked news stories that struck me as funny or ridiculous. One in particular stayed with me. It appeared as a small paragraph in the *L.A. Times;* it was obvious it was a story that needed to be looked into, but wasn't. The story revealed when Bechtel originally built the nuclear reactor at San Onofre, California, they had accidentally installed all the pipes backwards; they were still installed that way. Flipping through my folios of folly, I had enough material, not just for a pilot, but for a series. This was my joyful purpose, to put together a show devoted entirely to real news from all reliable sources on every imaginable subject, true news that reflected and revealed every aspect of the human comedy. And that's what I'd call it, *Reliable Sources*. Isn't this what every news anchor says as an introduction to every unverified story, "Reliable sources tell us ... " Writing the pilot took less than an hour. Investigating the *L.A. Times* San Onofre story took two days.

I could not try to sell the show without showing a network how we would handle such a story. I had the money, and I certainly had the time, so I got on the phone immediately. I called everyone quoted in the *L.A. Times* piece, and many who weren't; first, the public relations department, the plant manager and, finally, the builder, Bechtel, who had recently been in the news. They had just lost a multimillion-dollar lawsuit brought by a plant in the northeast for faulty construction there. With each person, I identified myself. Fortunately, some recognized the name. Before questioning them about that long-ago *Times* story, of which they were aware, I informed each I was recording them. They agreed. Their answers were unintentionally hilarious. The San Onofre plant engineer said, "The Japanese screw up like this all the time." (Fukushima was a horrifying reminder.)

Last came the spokesman for Bechtel. After admitting, awkwardly, "Yes, the pipes that were supposed to be installed on the north were installed on the south, and vice versa, but they are still working fine."

My final question was, "Is Bechtel the company building the new nuclear power plant in the Philippines next to an active volcano?"

He said, "No. We're just building the hotel."

Oh, my God, the idiocy of those in charge of the world is gold! You cannot write this stuff. Just report it. Who to sell it to? Certainly not NBC. Certainly not ABC. That left CBS with its good memories of *Talent Scouts,* and current President, Bob Wood.

A few days after the announced firing of me by Schlatter, Sarita and I were having lunch at Musso and Franks. We were interrupted by a pleasant man who identified himself as Bob Wood, from CBS. He said he had just gotten off the phone with Schlatter. He said he called Schlatter, scolding him for screwing up two of the best shows in television. And now a bigger blunder by firing John Barbour, whose show it obviously was. "So, John, I just wanted you to know, a lot of us know."

Recalling that, I took a chance and called CBS. Immediately, at his request, I got a meeting with one of their heads of programming. He was the only attendee. Why? I would find out shortly. The rapport and receptiveness were immediate. I did the whole pitch. He smiled, chuckled, twice applauded and kept repeating, "You're kidding me. John, that's an absolutely terrific idea, but you're not the first to pitch such a show."

I was stunned. "I wasn't?"

"No. Don Hewitt was, about five months ago." Don Hewitt was Executive Producer of *60 Minutes.* "He wants to do an entertainment show just like yours. But not as funny."

"You're kidding? How could you say no to Don Hewitt?"

"*60 Minutes* is the flagship show of the network. Our Rock of Gibraltar for integrity and straight talk. To let him do what you're talking about would make it look like he was doing a satirical version of his own show. One that could only denigrate it. To allow anyone else to do such a show, like you, no matter how good, would have the same effect on audiences and piss off everyone at *60 Minutes,* as well as the whole news division. It's a show I'd like to see. But not here."

"But why did you see me?"

"We all like you and your work, thought maybe you'd like to know your idea is in the wind and may show up somewhere. I certainly wish you luck."

I thanked him and went home to think about my next step, and to pack. Christopher was about to play in the Canadian National Junior Golf Tournament in Winnipeg, Manitoba, the country I had struggled to get out of. Now I couldn't wait to go back and be his caddy. He was fifteen. I was fifty.

The golf course, the surrounding terrain, gave the impression that early scientists who said the earth was flat must have been from Manitoba. The practice rounds were an easy walk for me. The next day, making me even happier, Christopher won the Canadian National Junior Championship.

With no agent or manager to help peddle *Reliable Sources,* my only sources for possible leads were *The Reporter* and *Daily Variety.* They carried a brief blurb about Dick Clark Productions signing a development deal with NBC. Dick was quoted as saying, "I want to develop something different, something out of the ordinary."

This was a bold statement for Dick Clark. He was King of the Ordinary. He'd built an empire on it from *American Bandstand* to his perennial New Year's show from Times Square. He was the perfect host; great smile, great voice, easy manner, and a face that never aged. It was rumored he had a painting in his attic. He was Hollywood's Dorian Gray! But Dick was in no way evil. He was eminently approachable and as down to earth as any of the rich and famous. I met him numerous times while at NBC. He told me there were three things he loved: an easy sale, easy money, and Krispy Kreme donuts. His offices were just ten blocks from my house. Even if he said no, it was a short drive. I called him.

"Dick, did you mean what you said when you said you wanted to develop something out of the ordinary?"

"Johnny, is there any such beast in television?" He chuckled.

"I might have something."

"What is it in ten words?"

"I want to do with real news what I did with *Real People.*"

"That's twelve words. Have you got anything put together?"

"Yes, actually. Great tapes and a great pilot script. I almost got a deal at CBS, but news over there is sacrosanct."

"Do you wanna come by tomorrow, say ten a.m., meet the crew and pitch us?"

"I'd be delighted."

I did my pitch, standing to introduce two videos, then reading, as both hosts, the hilarious news items. There was much laughter and applause.

"John, that is wonderful." Dick turned to his staff. "Gang, do you mind if John and I chat."

The lady and one of the men left. The business manager stayed. A good sign.

"John, can you do this stuff every week?"

"Certainly. It's only a half hour."

"Right now, could I option it from you, and give you a fifteen-hundred dollar royalty?"

I was stunned. Actually insulted.

"What? Option it? No. Why would I do that?"

"What did you have in mind? You know this would be a Dick Clark Production."

"That's what I'm hoping, rather than a Dick Clark stickup!"

"Meaning?'

"Certainly, it'd be yours in association with mine. You're executive producer. I'm the producer and one of the co-hosts and head writer."

"Okay. That's open for discussion. I like it, John. Truthfully, all the stuff I produce is a bucket of worms. None of it I am really proud of. I am proud of the money it has made me, but it is nothing to brag about. Bubble gum for the eyes. I like your thing, but it'd be a hard sell."

As he talked, my mind slipped back to a luncheon meeting at Warner Bros. with Ray Stark, the premiere producer of pictures in Hollywood, listening to him describing his films as shit. But the best shit in town. If those two enormously successful men were not proud of what they were doing, how do the less successful feel? No wonder the town was filled with so many dysfunctional, frustrated souls, talented and otherwise, who seek comfort in booze, pills, and other people's bedrooms.

"Jesus Christ, Dick, it's not a hard sell. It's a cinch. You're Dick Clark. One of the biggies. All you have to say to them is that it's something different. Something you really like. That you believe in. I wouldn't even have to be there. You just tell them you'd like to do a pilot that they'd air."

"That doesn't sound like selling. It sounds like begging. When I go into any one of these meetings with these outfits, I wanna shoot a silver bullet. I don't wanna shoot blanks. I'm sure the idea is a silver bullet. I'm not sure about you."

"What do you mean?"

"Oh, I'm dead sure about your work. I think when I mention your name, their faces might go blank. You don't have any fans at NBC. In fact, a bunch of enemies."

"Dick, I told Tinker and wrote Tartikoff that without me *Real People* would die. Just remind them of that."

"You mean you want me to make the same mistake you did. Telling them the fucking truth. Remind them that they were too stupid to know who was responsible for that show. I don't think so."

"I hate even mentioning that show anymore. It's like I'm talking to myself."

He paused, tapping his fingertips together. "Look, John, let me sleep on it. Maybe I can figure this out. And I'll call you tomorrow." He rose, shook my hand firmly, put a comforting hand on my shoulder and led me to the door. "You know what, you're the kind of person that makes this business fun."

"Well, Dick, call me tomorrow and maybe let me in on some of that fun."

I knew we wouldn't be having any fun. Regardless, I still liked him. I doubt Dick had ever been that candid with anyone, except maybe his wife. The next day Dick did not call. His business manager did.

"John, Dick is still trying to figure out how to approach NBC about this, but until he figures it out he'd like to buy a three or six-month option from you for fifteen hundred dollars."

"I said it to him yesterday, and I'll repeat it for you today. No. And thank Dick again for me." I hung up.

"John, Marvin wants to talk to you." It was Henri Bollinger. Henri's office was right next door to Marvin Moss,' Ernie Kovacs' former agent, featured prominently in the film.

"Put him on," I told Henri.

"I have a client, an executive with D.L. Taffner's company you know from your quiz show. He's going on his own and he already has a deal at CBS for a pilot, but he doesn't have a pilot in mind, and wants to know if you have something. He wants to strike before the ink gets dry. Have you got something?"

"I have, but CBS has passed on it. Twice. They wouldn't want to look at again. Besides they turned down a similar idea from Don Hewitt, their God."

"Well, they have some new faces over there. Their head of entertainment is a guy named Harvey Shepherd and he's my client's benefactor. Would you meet with my client?"

I always chose to have meetings at Musso's. Even if the deal didn't work out, the meal and atmosphere always did. Sarita and I met with him. I have long since forgotten his name because there was no more room in that large memory bank marked 'assholes.' He guaranteed me, at worst, that he could get at least twenty G's toward what networks called a pilot presentation, a short video of what a half-hour or hour would look like. He also guaranteed me I would be present at the meeting.

"And what would you like?" I asked.

"To own at least twenty-five percent of it in perpetuity. To get top executive producer credit, and a fee equal to yours, excluding what you get as talent, which should not be exorbitant."

"I'll go you one better. I'll give you a third of all gross profits in perpetuity, plus what you asked as exec producer, but only I will own the copyright and have creative control, subject to CBS's approval."

"That's wonderful, John. Thank you. He shook my hand. We raised our wine glasses and clinked a toast. I took the little paper napkin from under his glass, handed him a pen, and asked him to write our deal on it. He scribbled it and signed his name. I then signed mine. Two days later, I found myself with him sitting in plush offices at CBS TV. Within moments of describing the show, just from notes in my hand, without even screening a video, we had a deal. Twenty thousand dollars to tape a presentation to be delivered in two weeks. The deal would be drawn up right away by their business affairs people and my new partner.

I read in *The Wall Street Journal* the largest consumers of wine in America were the very rich and the very poor. I decided to set up a bar in a chic shop on Rodeo Drive in Beverly Hills, and to set up a card table on skid row. In the chic shop, the bartender was French. On skid row, the bartender was me. I got a hundred and fifty-dollar bottle of Lafitte Rothschild and a bottle of cheap California cabernet, and began challenging drinkers to tell the difference. Unknown to the tester, the French wine was in glass A, the cheap California wine in glass B. It was a riot and mayhem on skid row. Cops arrested some of our testers. A trio of well-dressed women, obviously slumming, yelled at us for doing such a terrible thing to those people, and screamed that we should be doing that in Beverly Hills. The honest upshot of all of this was that the 'bums' without fail, knew the plush vintage from the poor one while the shoppers in Beverly Hills did not. It is, to this day, a classic clip of the human comedy that can be seen easily in its entirety on my YouTube channel, youtube/johnbarboursworld.com, as well as the reactor piece.

While deciding what other gems I'd put in the presentation, I got a call from Marvin. "John, we need to talk about my client. He saw your wine piece. He thinks the show is going to be a smash." He paused. "He wants half."

"I beg your pardon?"

"He wants fifty percent. He said he deserves it because he got you the deal."

I didn't answer. I couldn't. Rather than yelling, I thought I'd get my point across like Brando in *The Godfather*. I whispered, "Marvin, you're my friend as well as his agent. What is more important to you? Friendship or clients?"

"John, I have to defend my client's interests."

"In that case, Marvin, you can consider whatever friendship we have over. As for your client, he can go fuck himself."

"What are you saying?"

"You heard me. Both of you can go fuck yourselves. You know what he already agreed to. I've got it written down right here in front of me. On my napkin. It seems his fucking word isn't worth the flimsy paper it's written on. So fuck you all."

"Hold it, John. Hold it. Don't hang up. If he leaves, there's no show. No deal."

"That's right. So now, call CBS and tell them to fuck off. I've got great pieces of video I paid for. I'll see what I can do on my own." I banged down the phone. Five minutes later, Marvin called back. "John, my client apologizes, says he's sorry, and says you were right to be upset. He'd like back in."

"Too late, Marvin. I wouldn't have him around, if he worked for nothing. I hate pigs who can't keep their word." I banged down the phone again. Three minutes later it was Marvin once more.

"Look, John, he doesn't think you should blow the deal with CBS. It'd make him look questionable, and–"

"He's a prick!"

"Granted, but you should go ahead with the deal. Just give him half of the ten thousand, and he'll keep his mouth shut and pull out."

"Where do I send the check, to you?"

"Yeah."

"I'll send it tomorrow along with a release, which I'll write. Sign that and the check is his. If not, piss on him!"

"It'll be done. I promise."

I slammed the phone down for the last time. I got the release, went to the bank, and back to KCOP.

My two co-hosts were perfect, a winning young man with dark full hair, Maurice LaMarche, and a beautiful young Asian reporter, Anna

Marie Poon. The opening music was Huey Lewis and the News, over a collage of quick clips of almost every human activity. When the announcer was finished with the billboarding of the stories and the hosts, we came to a close shot of a beautiful brunette with a beautiful smile announcing the name of the show: *That's the American Way*. That was Sarita.

The audience and crew reaction were every bit as wonderful as for any *Real People* episode. I felt confident when I delivered it to the fellow we'd met at CBS. Without my ex-partner with me, he was not as at ease as before. He told me if they'd liked it, they send it to Harvey. I went home and waited.

A week later, it came. The programming exec said he liked it enough to forward it to Harvey Shepherd, but that Harvey, to his surprise, passed on it.

A month later I was eating at a posh Beverly Hills outdoor restaurant, and spotted Harvey. He was sitting with a young blonde whose breasts were as fake as Harvey's hair. Harvey Shepherd had absolutely the ugliest, ill-fitting toupee I had ever seen. I stopped just short of his table. "Mr. Shepherd, excuse me, I'm John Barbour."

He looked up, displeased. "I know who you are."

"Do you mind if I ask why you passed on *That's the American Way*?"

He surprised me with the quickness of his response. "It was good, especially that wine thing, but I thought it was a funny fluke, something that couldn't be repeated every week."

"But I had done that previously for three years."

"How would I know that? Now, if you'll excuse me."

I nodded to the blonde, and returned to my table. I was losing my appetite, for food and showbiz.

At a Friars' Roast three weeks later, I was on the dais. I spotted him and got one of the biggest laughs when I said, "Harvey Shepherd, in spite of his station and salary, never spends much for his toupees. They are roadkill. Just a few cents for bullets. He is the only man in town whose hairdo has four sideburns and a tail."

The Barbour Report and Reliable Sources

Television is not in show business. It's no longer even in the news business; it's in the advertising business. Television needs shows and personalities in entertainment, news or reality that will attract viewers, potential consumers, whose numbers are sold to advertisers. Advertisers, of course, don't want potential customers upset. Controversial material, which can often be translated as truthful material, is rigorously avoided. It's television's no smoking zone. A show as outspoken as the 1970's *All in the Family* appearing in 2018, talking as candidly about race and politics, would be as welcome on a network today as an abortionist at a Right-To-Life rally.

Cable television, from HBO to Netflix, is a little edgier because they don't sell to advertisers; they sell to subscribers. Cable does do better documentaries, from *Gasland* to *Citizenfour*, and much more believable, realistic, grittier programming, from *House of Cards* to *Breaking Bad*. The three original networks are in freefall, as is the influence of advertisers. This was not so in the mid-eighties.

Some advertisers not only advertised, they financed and produced their own shows, many of which became quite successful. One of the most successful of these companies was Procter & Gamble. On daytime TV, they had numerous soap operas, most notably, *As the World Turns*. In prime time they had, amongst others, *In Search Of*. Their head of programming, based in Los Angeles, was Jim McGinn. I had met Jim at various roasts or charity events where I performed or he spoke. He called frequently asking for material or jokes. I happily obliged. He was six-feet tall and, befitting a man who represented America's largest companies, was always impeccably dressed in a suit and tie. Meeting him casually, you would never imagine he could be holding such a prominent position. He had the twinkly personality you'd expect of someone named McGinn, playfully Irish to the core. I never saw him frown or angry. Not once did I hear him raise his voice above the level of polite conversation. Even when things weren't going his way, there was always a hint of a smile, and a posture of "everything's going to be fine." The night our working together started accidentally, we were at an Alzheimer's charity event of which he was chairman. Before being called to speak, he asked, "John, should I tell them I have written this important speech about new research developments, but I forgot where I put it?" Then he chuckled. It was nice to see this puckishness in a man his age and stature. He gave a nice speech, which did not include the comment. He came back to our table admonishing himself for his cowardice. "I know you would have said it," he said to me.

"Probably Jim, that's my business."

"Speaking of business, what are you up to?"

For the next fifteen minutes I regaled him with the adventures and misadventures of my new concept. I tried to cut it short, but he loved hearing every gruesome detail.

"I love it. Maybe we can do something with it."

"Jim, when you say 'we', do you mean Procter & Gamble?"

"Absolutely."

"I don't know. It doesn't sound like something your company would be interested in."

"I'm interested in it. That's what matters. Shit, more controversial stuff has been done on *In Search Of*. Bring it by my office tomorrow before noon. We'll watch it and go to lunch."

In his office, near the Pacific, his reaction wasn't that of an executive. It was like a kid in a movie theater. He laughed and applauded, talking to the screen. After, he said he would call Fred Pierce, President of ABC, that afternoon to set up a meeting he wanted to attend alone in case the conversation got around to me.

"Jim, you make it sound as if my name comes up, it might be in a rather negative way."

He laughed. "That's right. You sued the bastards and won. Why would they think nice thoughts about you? But I can. You want to know how much I like this show, and how much I want our company involved? I'm in the Writers' Guild. I don't write for any of our shows, but I'd love to work with you as a writer on this."

The following Friday he had his meeting with Fred Pierce and his associates. He had predicted their reaction as if he'd been a psychic.

"John," he said when he called, "I only played a few minutes. They laughed. Out loud, but their concern mostly was you, as I expected."

"Jim, can't they just judge the work? They don't have to ever see me or even talk to me."

"That's what I told them. Dealing with you was my job. I and our company believe in you and the show. They kept saying, "Barbour's too controversial." When I asked them how, all they could say was that was the word going around town."

"In other words, they said no to Procter & Gamble, who would be paying for the special. It wouldn't cost them a nickel."

"Yeah, but don't worry about it. They have to be sold, and I can sell them. I'm meeting again with Fred alone next week."

The following Wednesday Jim called, sort of excited, inviting me to Musso's. "Fred won't go for a special, but he says he's leaving the job in a few weeks. He's not opposed, though, to the idea of giving you a couple of weeks to audition a late-night talk show."

"How on earth did that come up?"

"He just brought it up. He'd give you two weeks."

"But, Jim, that's meaningless. It's just a sop to you. He'll be gone in a couple of weeks and so will we. But a one hour special, is a special. That means something."

"That's true. But this is a half hour every night that we're paying for; and if it does half way decent, which it will, we will continue to pay for it. It is a no-lose situation for them. And didn't you always want to go against Carson?"

"My dream job, but as Bob Dylan said, I think it'll be just blowin' in the wind."

"Do you want me to take a shot at CBS or NBC for a special?"

"Geez, CBS'll get worn out passing on me. And I think NBC stands for No Barbour Crap!'

Jim laughed. "Do you want me to tell Fred we'll take it?"

"You might as well."

"Good, I already did!" He laughed louder.

"You did?"

"I have faith in you. In those two weeks, I'll think we'll do great stuff; I can't wait to be a part of it."

We shook hands and toasted what we'd call *The Barbour Report*. Not once did we get into a discussion about ownership, copyright or fees. Naturally, it would be owned by Procter & Gamble. I had no qualms about that because it was just a talk show. I trusted Jim to work it all out. I would be delighted just getting a fair salary as producer-host-writer.

When ABC and Procter & Gamble announced they were giving a two-week, late-night tryout to *The Barbour Report,* I asked to do it live, but they said no.

"Letterman's live. Carson's live," I argued. "Except I want to use being live to do live phone calls to stars or newsmakers around the world."

"Definitely not. You'll be taped a few hours before air."

"Why?"

"Mr. Barbour, you are not Letterman or Carson, and frankly you have a reputation for being too controversial to trust live."

"You've got to be kidding!"

"That's our position. You'll pre-tape by a few hours, and that's it."

There was another minor problem with ABC that Jim pointed out. "Remember I mentioned they were in the toilet? Well, it has been flushing fast. They are losing affiliates. A number of them probably wouldn't carry our show for those two weeks."

"Jim, get me a list of all of their affiliates and the general managers. I'm going to write each one a letter, and let's see what happens. I'll copy you."

The next day I had the list. I wrote over a hundred letters to the general manager of each station. I identified myself as the creator of *Real People*, and that I wanted to bring some of that difference to a late-night talk show. I also asked them to forward the letter to their news directors, saying if we aired any of their stories, we would credit the station and the reporters. I asked them if they would gamble on carrying us for ten days. Twenty stations, which otherwise would not have carried the show, signed on. Jim told me ABC was stunned.

To let the town know *The Barbour Report* would be 'Almost Live From Van Nuys,' we staged a big parade up Van Nuys Boulevard. We hired a couple of large busses with open upper decks. Banners hung from all sides. As many friends and fans as we could find stood on the top waving similar placards, shouting and screaming our arrival. We had an announcer on a loudspeaker, a musician and singer, without a permit, with cops following us. There was almost no one on the street. This absence of fans made it funnier to me. After all, I was the underdog. How better to depict it than this? Suddenly, a man in a suit, appearing to be in his late fifties, stepped off the curb, waving for us to stop. He motioned he wanted to come aboard. Why not? He ascended the steps and shook my hand.

"This looks like fun. I'm a big fan!"

He had one of the most beautiful male voices I'd ever heard. Then I recognized him. It was screen legend Dana Andrews. My God. I couldn't believe it. I'd seen him dozens of times; *The Best Years of Our Lives, Laura* with Gene Tierney. I forgot all about the parade. We chatted the rest of the ride. I loved listening to that voice talking about how much fun he was having. He said he had driven to Van Nuys after reading a blurb about my mounting the silly parade. He said he was a fan of silly.

My only regret about those two weeks was that I was so overwhelmed by everything, I neglected to extend an invitation to Dana Andrews to be on the show. But we did have amazing guests: Danny Glover, Jon Voight, Harlan Ellison, Frank Zappa and others. The monologues and openings were different every night, imaginative and funny. We aired a couple of terrific stories sent in by affiliates. We had a fantastic people-on-the-street segment every show hosted by a beautiful 6' 3" slender, shapely blonde from the Ozarks with the most engaging Southern accent. Even though we were in an obscure studio in Van Nuys, we turned away audiences every night.

There was never a squawk from Standards and Practices. The reviews were surprisingly upbeat. What was astonishing, though, was because some of the affiliates hung in there in the second week in many markets, the Nielsen ratings showed us bumping heads with Letterman. That thrilled Jim. Just before the last show, he burst into my office waving the ratings.

"They have got to be blown away with this. I'm going to call Fred right away. If it works out, do you think you could get this back up and running in a few months?"

"Certainly."

The second Friday was our last show. No one connected with it thought it would be. We were all positive, especially with Procter & Gamble's backing. Sunday, Jim called, asking me to meet him first thing Monday morning.

Jim was pacing when I entered his office.

"Fred's gone. He parted on Friday. They haven't even replaced him yet. So, the show is out."

"What?" I exclaimed. "Why out? You said they'd be thrilled about the ratings."

"John, it has nothing to do with the show. They had to admit it was better than they expected." He paused, then added, "They just simply don't like you."

"I don't even know them. Never met any of them."

"Who knows? The one guy I spoke to who did seem to like you, and liked the show, said it was too bad you weren't ten years younger."

"Oh, Jesus Christ, Jim."

"I am truly sorry. I may have done you wrong."

"Jim, for God's sake, without you we wouldn't have gotten this far."

"No. I accepted the late-night thing too easily. I should have forced them to do it as a special. I accepted the bone they threw; it had no meat on it. You were right. I am so sorry."

"Jim, that's showbiz. I just wish it was like your Ivory soap, 99% pure; instead of 99% bullshit."

Jim had other commitments. He said it was the best two weeks he ever spent in the business. He handed me the sheet with the Nielsen ratings. "For your scrap book."

Certainly, I was down. Really down. To have gotten that close; but knowing we had done well, I was not discouraged. When not even Don

Hewitt could get a presentation at CBS for a real news humor magazine show, I had. Against all odds and predictions, I had just finished two weeks, almost live, on ABC that bumped heads with Letterman. At least I was failing upwards.

Rupert Murdoch's growing media empire octopus had just wrapped their tentacles around Twentieth Century Fox, and then gobbled up the Metromedia stations to start their so called independent Fox TV. To head it up, Rupert appointed Barry Diller, former Paramount President who lost his job over *The Great Gatsby*, and who had tried to get me fired. Barry picked his number two, Hollywood's perennial assistant, Peter Chernin. Murdoch's acquisition included my old two-time alma mater, KTTV, channel eleven. Peter picked Peter's old boss, and a sort of friend of mine, Greg Nathanson, who ditched Showtime.

I gave no thought to who ran the new network. I was only focused on who was running the local station, Greg. He had barely taken his new seat when I called him. He took the call and invited me to do my pitch.

I first congratulated him and then handed him the sheet with the Nielsen ratings. "Look at these. Where I underlined in red."

He looked at them closely. "Pretty good. What's that?"

"The two weeks I did against Letterman."

"John, we're not looking to do late night."

"Neither am I."

"Then why are you showing me this?"

"To prove I can get viewers. It was truthfully better than any late-night show, except maybe Paar, but it was not what we approached ABC about doing. We approached them about an original concept special. They wanted the late-night thing. It was what we first showed them that they liked."

"What did you show them?"

I showed him the first ten minutes of *That's the American Way,* and he said, "That's pretty good. What did you have in mind?"

"I'd like to do half an hour once a week on your seven stations."

"You know stations like ours are looking for strip shows. Something we can just block out five nights a week."

"I understand that, Greg, but in prime time to become the network that Murdoch says he wants it to be with major sports and original programming, you are going to need some original programming. Nothing is more original than this. It has never been done before."

"What's never been done before?"

"An entertainment show based on actual news events. I'm doing with real news what I did with real people, except that with this concept there is much more material to choose from."

He looked again at the ratings sheet."Could you do it on a budget that seven stations could support?"

"Less actually. And any sales beyond that we'd just split."

"How much could you do a pilot for?"

"I already have a lot of unseen material. I could add some new stuff. Recast it. Rename it. You have facilities here. Just give me those facilities and office space and ten or fifteen thousand dollars, and I'll give you a gangbuster show."

He looked at me, thinking. "Four weeks," he said. "I'll get you together with business affairs so we can draw up some sort of preliminary agreement. You'll have the facilities for two days of shooting. Prior to that a week for set construction, and four weeks of office space. Let's see what you can come up with."

I finally had the feeling I was going to be back on television with a show that would have some impact. Everything flowed easily, as it does when things are meant to be. The new title was to be my original title, *Reliable Sources*. Next were the auditions for the other two hosts. Both were cast immediately, even before being put on camera. They were so charming, bright, and natural. The female was Patti Yasutake, an attractive Japanese-American actress in her early thirties whose father owned the best Japanese restaurant on the Sunset Strip. Her co-host was an even easier pick. I had seen him hosting some celebrity gossip show called *Talk Soup*. He had blondish curly hair, a puckish, constant grin, as if he knew the celebrity gossip he was delivering was totally meaningless. His name was Greg Kinnear.

Once again, I contacted stations around the country and in Canada asking for offbeat amusing stories they felt deserved a larger audience. I was swamped. Three ended up in the show. One from Canada was about a farmer in British Columbia who built his own private golf course. Instead of having the usual heavy mowers to clip his grass, he had it clipped by his large herd of sheep.

Another came from a station in Baltimore. A family with a lovely large home and front yard had adorned the lawn with a large plastic wooden rabbit. One day it was missing. Stolen. They reported this theft to the police who grinned and forgot about it. A little more than two weeks later, the owners of the home began to receive postcards every few days from all around the world. Posed in those was their plastic bunny. In Europe. In Australia, and Mexico. Evidently, this was someone's idea of a very cute harmless practical joke. He showed up one day stuck back in the owner's grass.

And there was a short story from Georgia. An aspiring politician with not much money or hope, running for a high local office, hired a hypnotist to do his campaign TV ads. We ran them. They were hilarious. He went unelected. The four weeks flew by, as did the completed half hour pilot. There were hugs, handshakes and backslapping all around. Patti was so pleased to have what she said was an important part in an important yet entertaining show, she bought me a beautiful clock with the inscription: Reliable Sources. It sits on my bathtub.

When I delivered the tape to Nathanson, I included a note: *When you see this, you'll see that within a very short time Greg Kinnear could become the most appealing male in American television.*

Nine days later, Greg Nathanson's secretary called, asking if I could come in the following morning to see Mr. Nathanson. He got right to the point. "John, I liked it. It is slick and funny, and I'd put it on, but Diller and Peter don't like it."

"You're kidding? Why not?"

"They didn't think it could be replicated at that level every week."

"Horseshit. You saw the material sent in by the stations, and we're not even on the air. After that there'd be tons from viewers, not to mention what our staff finds."

"I'm sorry. I'm just relaying what they said. They frankly surprised me. It was my first effort."

"Could you arrange for me to meet with them to explain all this, why it is so good, and why it'll work for them?"

"I don't think that's a possibility. They had no enthusiasm for it at all. I'm sorry. I'm disappointed, too. I liked it. And I like you."

I sank into the chair. All the air was out of me.

It was obvious Nathanson felt bad for me, then he said something from out of nowhere that made me perk up. "John, you know Schlatter is a major member of this town's A group."

"Greg, what has that got to do with anything?"

He shrugged. "I'm just saying we gave it a shot, but don't worry. You and I will do something together again."

"I'm sorry you didn't have better luck your first time out here." We shook hands and parted. Not long after that Nathanson became the GM of the Tribune Company's new acquisition, KTLA.

Greg Kinnear had been spotted by director Sydney Pollack. He was doing a remake of *Sabrina* and wanted Greg for the Bill Holden part. Sydney, ordinarily an excellent director and filmmaker, did not make a good remake, but Greg was a very bright young man, and worked his way into becoming a very believable, successful actor. Peter Chernin also moved on up to become an even bigger assistant, this time to Rupert Murdoch.

It was 1990. I was fifty-seven. God, what now?

The Garrison Tapes

Sarita has a severe allergy to alloys, metal and chemicals. She can only wear jewelry of pure gold, silver or platinum, and breathe fresh air. Beverly Hills and Toluca Lake were great places for shopping for such things, but by 1990 Toluca Lake was not a great city for breathing. We lived a short distance from Forest Lawn Cemetery. From our third floor, most days we could not see the hills above it. Every afternoon she had to take a two-hour nap or get sick. Her eyes began to water so frequently, we took her to an ophthalmologist. He discovered she had grown a protective film over her eyes, much like frogs do in polluted water. She refused to move, though, until I had exhausted all possibilities to get *Reliable Sources* on the air. My last shot was with my first manager, now a major force in Hollywood, Jerry Weintraub.

My involvement with Jerry Weintraub as a producer was shorter than my involvement with him as a comic. His company went belly up just after they opened their doors. He had moved into a new six-story building in Westwood with much fanfare, as only Jerry could generate. There were full-page ads about making bunches of movies and TV shows, all of it funded by a very rich Australian. Jerry never spent his own money. It was a shiny new building inside and out. I got to meet his head of programming, Andrew Susskind, before Jerry got to meet with his bankruptcy attorneys.

Andrew was the son of legendary talk show host and producer, David Susskind. Andrew was one of the sincerest people I'd ever met in Hollywood. He was only twenty-eight, but like Irving Thalberg, the young production genius behind MGM in the thirties, he knew what he was doing. He was a wonderful story teller.

"I love your idea, and I love this business. My dad had a partner named Levy. They were just starting. One day he runs into the office waving

Variety at my dad. He shows my Dad this article about MGM doing this movie with Charlton Heston, *Quo Vadis*. "So what," my dad says. Levy says, 'It's public domain.' My dad repeats, 'So what?' 'So tomorrow,' Levy says, 'We're gonna announce a Susskind-Levy live TV production of 'Quo Vadis.' My dad says we can't because it's too expensive. Levy says, 'No. No. We're not makin' the show, just the announcement.' My dad says, 'Why would we do that?'

"Levy says, 'You'll see.' And he was right. The next day within an hour of their press release the phone rings. It's Louis B. Mayer's office asking to speak to one of them. The secretary is told they're too busy. In production meetings. The next day another story about their live production. This time Mayer calls directly. He tells Levy if he and his partner ever want to work in this business again, they better get their asses into his office. Levy says they are tied up for two days and they'll be in New York. Mayer says, 'So will I. Be there.' They were.

"Mayer started yelling, 'OK, how much do you bastards want to call this crap off?' Levy tells Mayer it's not crap. They've already hired actors, a writer, and are training horses and– 'Bullshit,' Mayer screams. 'How much money to knock this shit off? How much?' Then my dad speaks up, and tells Mr. Mayer that they don't want any money. 'No money,' Mayer says. 'Then whadda yah want?' My dad says, 'Sir, we do not want any money. What we would like, and would accept, is just the TV rights to some of your movies.' 'That's it? You're shittin' me,' Mayer says. My dad tells him they aren't. Mayer instantly extends his hand. 'OK, that's it. Yah got a deal. Now knock that crap off.'

"And that," Andrew continued with a grin, "is how my father became a successful producer, doing some of the great MGM classics, beginning with *Ninotchka.*" I was so enamored of this story, I had Andrew retell it on camera.

A week later Jerry Weintraub Productions filed for Chapter Seven bankruptcy. Now, with no hope for me and no clean air for Sarita, it was time to leave LA. We picked three cities in order of preference: First: Vancouver, the most beautiful city in North America with great air and golf courses. However, with Christopher now at Stanford, that was just too far from him. Second: Pebble Beach, with greater air and even greater golf courses. For two weeks we scouted homes, and found a great bungalow on a seventeen-mile drive, but the fog never lifted. We couldn't see the sea. That left Las Vegas. With no state taxes. That was it. Worth close to a million dollars, to save commission, I put up a for-sale-by-owner sign.

Reading the Trades out of habit, while packing, was a press release announcing Oliver Stone starting a movie about the Kennedy assassination based on Jim Garrison's book, *On the Trail of the Assassins*. He's got to be kidding. Who could have the balls in Hollywood to make such a movie? I thought he showed balls years earlier when he made *Salvador* with James Woods, still among the best political movies ever made in America; in order to make it, he mortgaged his house. To show how the CIA murders presidents in other countries is one thing; to show them doing it in our own country is suicide; professionally and physically.

I was right. The professional attacks began immediately. The *Washington Post's*, George Lardner Jr., began that week trying to kill Stone's film in an article called, "Dallas In Wonderland." The media was doing in a smaller way to Oliver what they had done to Garrison in a monstrous way, trying to discredit and destroy him. And Oliver had not yet exposed one frame of film. For weeks, Americans were caught up reading almost daily verbal food-for-thought fights between a suddenly embattled Oliver and lackey Lardner. On impulse, I thought maybe I could help Oliver, so I called his office.

"lxtlan Productions," a woman's voice said.

I explained who I was and said that I had the only three-hour interview Mr. Garrison ever gave about his investigation. "A year after Oliver's film is out, I'd like him to be a part of executive producing my documentary, which will totally vindicate Oliver's film."

"One moment, please." I waited another moment. "Mr. Barbour, Mr. Stone would like you to send over your tapes."

"Tell him I will bring them there, or he can come here to see them."

"He would prefer you send them."

"No, thank you." I hung up. Why on earth would he pass on such an opportunity? I mean, even if he didn't want to get involved, out of curiosity alone I thought he'd want to see what was on the tapes. Fleetingly, I had given some thought over the past couple of years of doing a full *Real People* documentary about Garrison, but could never find the time or the desire. When I called Oliver, I had no intention of talking documentary. It just popped out because it was such a natural follow-up to his film. It was such a natural, I was now developing the desire. I had enough money in the pension plan to cover expenses until the house sold. And mine was certainly worth more than Oliver's when he made *Salvador*.

A few days later, after talking it over with Sarita, I called Mr. Garrison at home. His daughter Elizabeth answered. I replayed for her my non-conversation with Oliver Stone, and my desire to finally tell her father's story, and could I speak to him?

"John, Dad has been ill for months. He's bedridden. He doesn't talk to or see anyone. I'm sure if there someone he'd speak to, it would be you, but he can't. Oh, by the way, do you know anyone named Rose in Oliver Stone's office?"

"No. Why?"

"A couple of days ago this woman called saying it wouldn't be a good idea having John Barbour make a documentary about my father because he has no credibility in this town. A very bad reputation."

"Jesus Christ, Liz. You're kidding."

"I told her I wasn't sure you were making a documentary. I mentioned it to my dad, and he said if John is, whatever he wants, give it to him."

"Oh, Liz, I feel awful. Would you and your family mind doing interviews with me when I start?"

"Not at all. And we'll help with some of dad's friends."

I was adrift in a choppy ocean in a small raft, but as shark-infested as it might be, it was an ocean of opportunity. Oliver Stone would be getting publicity for a year in every magazine and newspaper, probably negative, but free publicity. That would mean an enormous box office hit for *JFK,* an historic film. But, after that, who would not want to see the real Jim Garrison, instead of Kevin Costner. Everybody. It could become the biggest money-making documentary ever, even outliving the movie. The thought of how big it could be, scared me.

I never did anything just to make money. But, if my musings turned out to be true, our family would make a fortune. Money to finance my own films. Maybe an actual movie. Money to finance other people's films. And most of all, money to fund a law scholarship at Tulane University in Jim Garrison's name. Just as I had given up on *Real People,* I had just given up on living in LA, and Oliver Stone, and now suddenly by accident I was about to make another documentary, about the most controversial man in America. I took out the three hours of tape, which I had re-transferred every few months to preserve them, and began re-watching them on my huge living room screen. Again, just as suddenly, fate or luck or whatever got instantly better. Joseph Campbell said, "Following your joy opens doors in the Universe you did not know were there." The door was our front door.

The buzzer at the front gate rang. I looked up at the security camera and saw three young men in suits standing there. I thought they were

FBI, but they looked too young. I put the tape on pause, and went to the intercom.

"Mr. Barbour, we'd like to see your house. We see it's for sale."

They were brothers and their last name was Brunson. The older one, around twenty-eight, turned out to be the spokesperson. He handed me their card. They were from Salt Lake City. Mormons. In that community, they were successful musicians, known as The Brunson Brothers. Their instrument was the trumpet, and they were every bit as good as anyone who ever played it. They never got to tour the house. Paused on the TV screen was a huge full-face close-up of Jim Garrison. The spokesperson said, "Who's that?"

"Jim Garrison, the DA of New Orleans," I said.

He perked up. "The guy that lost that trial with that businessman?"

"Yeah. Clay Shaw. You seem a little young to know about that."

"I was a kid. My brothers weren't even born, but next to music that Kennedy thing really interests me."

"Well, I'll be darned," I said. "It's surprising the number of young people who are fascinated by his murder."

"Do you think Garrison was right?"

"Nobody so far has challenged his evidence. They just malign him."

"Do you mind if we watch it?"

"There's only about twenty minutes left, but you're welcome to, then we'll show you the house."

His brothers, Sarita and I sat in a semi-circle around the set. When it was over, the older Brunson leaned into me. "What are you gonna do with this? It's unbelievable."

"I had offered it to Oliver Stone as a follow-up documentary to the film he's planning, but he passed, so I guess I'll be making it myself."

"How terrific. When are you gonna start."

"As soon as I can raise the rest of the money."

"How much do you need?"

"Probably 150 or 200 thousand."

"Do you think you can get it?"

"Well, I'm starting by selling the house. Are you guys paying cash?"

"No. But maybe we can help."

"You mean you'd put money in this?"

"No. We're broke. We're not even in the market for a house. We're just sightseeing among the rich and famous. But we might know someone. We just met him this morning. We were looking at a house in the Hollywood

Hills that this producer was looking at. We got real friendly. It seems his dad is real rich. He gave his kid a bunch of money to come out to Hollywood to try and make movies."

I laughed. "You got so friendly you think he'd lend you money?"

"No. No. Not me. You."

"Fellas, that is not very likely."

"Hey, you never know. Do you mind if I call him and tell him what you've got, and see what he says? His name is Lamar Card."

"You can call him, but before you do, let me make you feel comfortable. I think this is going nowhere. It doesn't happen like this. Except in shitty movies. But, if something does come of it, I will give you ten percent of any money I make as producer, writer, narrator or whatever ... for seven years. Is that okay?" Even though I said it, I didn't believe anything would come of it.

"That is extremely generous for just making a phone call. Sure. But why seven years?"

"Its real earning power is in the first year and a half following Oliver's film."

"I'll let you know." He got up, heading for the door, followed by the two brothers who spoke not a word, just grunts during the screening.

They left waving and smiling. "Great house," he shouted, closing the door behind them.

I shook my head. *They were nice, but my God, were they naive.*

The next morning, Brunson the elder was on the phone laughing. Lamar Card wants to meet you."

"Are you kidding?"

"No. At his office at eleven-thirty. Can you make it? His company is called Blue Ridge." He gave me the address.

I met Lamar Card at eleven-thirty, introduced by the older brother who was there by himself. Before the meeting I handed him an agreement I'd written up signed by me. He glanced at it, then put it in his coat pocket.

"That is very generous Mr. Barbour. It wasn't necessary. I am glad to help with such a thing."

"I am glad you're pleased, but I don't want anybody doing anything for me for nothing."

Lamar was in his mid-thirties. A handsome man with dark wavy hair and a soft southern accent. We hit it off immediately. I stuck in the tape of Garrison. Lamar was spellbound by the impassioned, sincere look and sound of the man on the screen.

"My word, John. That is unbelievable. How much of this do you have?"

"Just over three hours."

"Goodness, you know how historical this is?"

"Lamar, I am sure. It is a story I tried on and off for years to tell."

"Well, now sir, ah am gonna help you tell it. How much do yah think it'd cost?"

"I imagine it could all be done for around $200,000, which includes travel, editing, hotels, buying the rights to the Zapruder film, and no fees for me."

"Why no fees for you?"

"Following Oliver's film, this should be a blockbuster. There'll be plenty of money. Lamar, I love what I do. Sometimes a lot of money is the by-product. Sometimes it even costs me."

"You're right. It will be a blockbuster, and a piece of history. You are to be congratulated. What are you going to call it?"

"Just the Jim Garrison Story. I don't know."

Lamar said, "One of my favorite movies was *Sex, Lies, and Videotapes*. Do you mind calling it *The Garrison Tapes*?"

"Lamar, what a great title. Certainly. *The Garrison Tapes* it is." That is how the title came about. This is how the film came about:

Driving home, knowing by some weird metaphysical intervention I was going to make that movie, I was fearful again of how huge it could be. The fame or notoriety didn't scare me. I had plenty of that. It was the size of the production, and size of the worldwide attention that was inevitable. I needed a partner who could handle that. My first thought was David Wolper, the biggest and brightest, someone who already knew and liked me, but I'd only met him once. I didn't really know him, spend time with him, but I did know and spend a lot of time with another biggie, Fred Weintraub.

I had met Fred through Jack Rollins, spent many evenings and weekends at his home on Mullholland, and dinners with him, Jane Fonda and her husband. And sat with him often watching his films. He had discovered Bruce Lee, and co-produced *Enter the Dragon*. He also brought *Woodstock* to Warner Bros.

Fred's enthusiasms for anything he was involved in were as large as he was. He spoke like he was always on the verge of laughter. His new partner, Tom Kuhn, was the exact opposite. Early forties, five-nine, quiet, cultured, effete and walked as though he was afraid to crush his socks. They could have been Neil Simon's *Odd Couple*, making odd movies. The upscale new offices of Weintraub-Kuhn Productions occupied an upper floor in one of those intimidating towers on The Avenue of The Stars in Century City. Every wall was covered with posters of their films shot in Hungary and Czechoslovakia. The posters were the only thing seen in America.

Having mentioned the purpose of the meeting, and his quick scheduling of it for later that day, I felt encouraged. His intense interest and excitement greeted me the moment I opened the door. He didn't sit for the next twenty minutes. He stood transfixed, leaning into the set, watching and listening to Garrison.

"Stop it." He held up his hand. "How much of that have yah got?"

"Just over three hours."

"Who else has it?"

"No one. The only interview he did in ten years after he lost the case. Oh, maybe Schlatter. When we shot it for *Speak Up*.

"Would he do anything with it?"

I laughed. "Probably burn it."

"And Garrison will help you still?"

"He's ill. But his family and most of his staff have already agreed to do interviews, and give me some of his documents."

A big grin crossed Freddy's face. "John, even if Stone's film bombs, it's already gotten more press than Gone with the Fucking Wind. What you have is a political *Woodstock*. Let's do it."

Meetings were arranged with Lamar and agreements signed. The first moneys were to go, of course, to Lamar's Blue Ridge Film Company until his 200 g's was paid off. Any profits thereafter would be split between the three entities, Fred's company, Lamar's, and mine. I was to retain the copyright.

An account was opened in the name of the project at a Beverly Hills bank where three signatures would be required to write checks. I pre-signed a bunch of them at Fred's request, delighted and relieved at his involvement. He arranged everything; the travel plans, paying of the bills, my crew, and negotiations with the Zapruder heirs. Except for a few harsh encounters in the editing room, he gave me uninterrupted free reign to hire the crew, select those to be interviewed, and to write, edit, and direct it as I saw it, and how I knew Garrison would like it. My main cameraman was a sharp young man with whom I had worked before, George Elkins. I mention it now because, like the very bizarre, unbelievable way the project came to be, his side story, which I will relate briefly later, was even more bizarre. And scarier.

Only two people we called turned down our requests for interviews: Bill Moyers, former Press Secretary to President Johnson, and Dan Rather, formerly CBS anchorman, the street reporter CBS assigned to describe the Zapruder film on live TV – falsely. I did not consider Moyers much of a loss, but I did consider Rather one. He was the one telling the world he had just seen the Zapruder film, describing in detail exactly what Jackie was wearing, what Governor Connelly was wearing, what JFK was wearing, then stops the film, informing us it is too brutal to show, informing us he will just tell us the gruesome details. He describes the third fatal shot with the head being thrown violently forward. And at this, he leans his head forward. The head being thrown violently forward is what the world and we all thought until Dick Gregory, Robert Gordon, and Geraldo Rivera showed it on his late-night show on ABC a dozen years later.That screening led to hundreds of thousands of outraged letters, calls and telegrams to Congress, which had no choice but to set up The House Select Committee on Assassinations. From the beginning, Garrison said to me that committee, like The Warren Committee, was a sham, made obvious after they ousted the original chairman, Richard Sprague, replacing him with G. Robert Blakey.

Richard Sprague, at his first staff meeting of six, told them there would be no CIA or FBI agents on his staff. They were to be investigated. As the CIA had done to Garrison, the CIA would now do to Sprague – try to discredit him. Sadly, they succeeded, using all their media and Senataorial and Congressional assets, unknown at the time. He was replaced by G. Robert Blakey, who turned the entire 'investigation' over to the CIA, and later dedicated his shabby book blaming the Mafia, to the CIA.

It was obvious Dan Rather had lied; it was highly unlikely a lowly street reporter would lie unless told to. In his autobiography, *The Camera Never Blinks,* Rather says it was a momentary lapse of memory. That is total bullshit. As is George H.W. Bush's comment about not remembering exactly where he was on Nov. 22nd, 1963. Any idiot over ten years of age knows exactly where they were when they heard about those shots ringing out in Dallas.

The questions for Dan were: Who was with you when you first saw the Zapruder film? Anyone from the government? Or in uniform? What brass from CBS were present? Were you told to lie for national security purposes? If so, by whom? How did you feel knowing you were lying? How long after that were you promoted to anchorman? And why did they pick you, and not Walter Cronkite, their anchorman, to tell us? Our $25,000 offer for five minutes was declined.

Everyone else we contacted was anxious to help and participate, even Nicholas Katzenbach, formerly with the Attorney General's office. He hated Garrison, but graciously appeared anyway. And Clay Shaw's attorney, Diamond, wanted to be heard. Elizabeth helped us gather up her father's former assistants and investigators whose interviews and revelations were heartbreaking and newsworthy. Mark Lane, next to Garrison, the most informed original voice in the questioning of the Warren Report with *Rush to Judgment*, a book he had to first publish in England, was never better than in this film. And Jim Marrs, the tough, intelligent, persistent investigative journalist from Texas whose book *Crossfire* was used along with Garrison's, as the foundation for Oliver's film, was also an articulate eye and mind opener.

To help me with research I could not have been luckier. I had one of the three brightest people I had ever met. He was quickly learning as much about the case in two months as I had in ten years. He was someone I totally loved and trusted – my son, Christopher. He had just graduated from Stanford as an honor athlete; his first job was on my project. There could be no better introduction for him to showbiz and the real America than that film.

The first day of editing, at Sunset Post, Fred rushed in. "Johnny, boy, we got a deal with Turner. They want an exclusive for 400 g's."

"Is that good?" I asked. "What about a theatrical release?"

"We're still free to do that. This pays Lamar back, and leaves a bunch for us. Aren't you thrilled? CNN, Turner, that's a huge audience."

"That's great."

I spoke to neither Freddy nor Tom until it was finished. Freddy got our first public screening at a Major Studio Festival of Films in Santa Monica. Seeing it on a TV monitor was totally arresting, but blown up on an actual movie screen, its impact was overwhelming. The audience reacted with "bravos!" I was so pleased, until Fred pulled me aside.

"Johnny, great reaction, but Turner passed. They changed their mind."

"Wasn't there some kind of contract?"

"They said there would be. When I kept calling they said they were working on it. It never came. I'm sorry."

"Freddy, it's not your fault. We wouldn't have even had that bite without you. But you saw and heard the reaction here. This is natural for a theatrical release. Did you see how strong it was on the big screen? Amazing."

"I've already alerted a few of my buddies, so I'll get right on it."

Meanwhile, Sarita, Christopher and I flew to New Orleans to screen the film with and for the Garrison family. It was the longest and loudest reception to date. Afterward, speaking to the jammed large room, I said that the first moneys made would go to a law scholarship at Tulane University for a needy student in the name of Jim Garrison. The cheering and applause must have been heard by Oliver Stone because word got back to me to include him in.

Sadly, Jim was still bedridden. In the film, he says at one reflective moment, about the crushing illegal persistent government and media attacks, "I guess I was becoming aware that I wasn't living in the country in which I was born." His daughter, Elizabeth, screened it for him in his room and said her father, with tears in his eyes, told her to thank me. She did, with a wet kiss and a hug.

In spite of the buzz the film had generated, Fred was perplexed by his inability to get his friends and former partners at Warner and other studios to sign on to distribute it. There were no takers. He did get a DVD deal with a fairly large distributor, Vestron. They put together a colorful promotional package that included the DVD, brilliant artwork and a copy of the entire *New York Times* edition of their Nov 22nd, 1963 paper, a collectors' item. Lamar got us a supportive quote from Oliver Stone, saying the film was "the perfect companion piece to *JFK*."

As a former critic, even though I had made it, there was no doubt in my mind it would be nominated for an Oscar, and could probably walk away with it. In order to qualify, however, it first had to be in a theater. Fred assured me he would get somebody to distribute it in time. I knew nothing about film distribution, but I did know what some theaters liked, especially art houses. The best art houses in Los Angeles were The Laemmle Theaters. They had an upscale one in a multiplex at Sunset and Laurel Canyon. I called the manager. He said he was staggered by the possibility of the film's importance and totally enthused about doing whatever I wished with his theater.

I said, "It only needs to be screened one day. You pick the day. Preferably a Saturday. We'll put a poster or two in your lobby promoting it a few weeks in advance. I will try to get some radio interviews plugging it, and announce I will be live at each screening to introduce it, then afterwards take questions from the audience. I would suggest about ten or fifteen dollars a ticket, which you can keep. I just need it in a theater."

"John, it's done. Anything you wish."

I called Fred and Tom to inform them, asking they get every distributor in town there to see it for themselves. They said they would. The theater was standing room only half an hour before the screening. When it was over, nearly everyone in a seat was standing. I did a Q&A for over an hour, which the audience did not want to end. I rushed to the lobby looking for Freddy and his distributor friends. They were not there, but an uninvited critic from *The Los Angeles Times,* Michael Wilmington, was. I did not know this until his front-page review in the entertainment section came out. It was an unexpected rave from an establishment paper. Things seemed to be going our way for the film.

Fred said he hadn't been there because he had been finalizing the deal with Cinemax. Cinemax wanted to run it in tandem with *JFK,* which was a smart idea. They did so almost immediately to the largest audience they'd ever had. I was pumped.

In the meantime, I repeated my Q&A film screening in one of San Francisco's major art houses with the same overwhelming response. I asked two or three times if Fred had submitted the film yet to the Academy for entry and consideration. He said he had. Hearing nothing from· the Academy after a week, I called myself. The fellow to whom I spoke said, "John, we love your film. It certainly deserves to be an entry, but we can't. It's the rules."

"What rules?" I gasped.

"The film has to have had at least one theatrical screening in the year before–"

"It did. Here at The Laemmle, and in San Francisco."

"But that has to be before a sale to television. You had sold it to Cinemax. And it wasn't like an actual release."

I couldn't speak. I could barely breathe. What happened? I didn't want to call Fred. I was too pissed. I had to confront him in person.

"Fred, this is your business. Movies. You know all about it. The rules and everything. How could you fuck up a chance for an Academy Award by selling it to Cinemax? Jesus Christ!"

"John, it was the only sale we got."

"Who gives a shit? With an Academy Award, it would have had a hundred fucking sales. Even I know that. You should know it better! And why weren't any of your Warner friends at the screening?"

"Warners is just interested in Oliver's film."

"Well, Fred," I said, "I hope you and Tom are still interested in this film." I left with a cluttered mind. What to do next with the film? And how to do that while moving into our new house in a new town, Las Vegas?

In the midst of packing, I got a call from George Elkins, our excellent cinematographer. "John, can I come by to talk to you?"

"If you don't mind that your chair is a Bekins' box."

He was there within five minutes, seated on a barstool by the kitchen. He looked as serious as he had sounded. "I've got some weird shit to tell you. You know I never, ever really told you much or anything about my personal life, but I had a fucked-up father. We never saw him. He didn't run away or anything like that, we just never saw him. He was in the army or something he said, but was all over the fuckin' world. We haven't talked for years. I made no attempt to have contact with him. Fuck him. If he didn't want to see me that was his loss. Anyway, a few weeks ago or so, the phone rings and it's him. He congratulates me on the film. Then he says would you talk to him? Meet with him. He says he has something important to tell you. So I say, I'm sure he would, but what could you have to tell John that would mean anything at this point? He says, 'Son, for thirty years I've been with military intelligence in Viet Nam. Second in command. And retired two months ago.' I almost shit. He would like to meet you at Patty's at nine tomorrow for coffee for a few minutes. Would you meet him? He said you alone."

How weird, I thought, but agreed to do it.

Patty's on Riverside Drive was within walking distance. I was looking around for a table when a smart-looking man, seated, perhaps in his late fifties, raised his hand. He didn't wave it, just raised it. Even out of uniform, he looked like he was military. Short hair, stern blue eyes, perfect erect posture, solid broad shoulders, and no smile. I approached the table; he extended his hand. He had a cup of coffee in front of him.

"Mr. Barbour, thanks for coming. You made an excellent film. I'm glad George was a part of it."

A waitress appeared. I ordered only a coffee, too nervous to eat; too anxious to hear his story.

"Mr. Barbour," he began. Another indication he was military. It is always 'Mr.' or 'Sir.' "Thank you again for coming. I did tell George I wanted to talk to you, but, unfortunately, I've changed my mind. I hope you don't mind. I'm sorry if I wasted your time. As I said, I did want to talk to you, but I've decided not to. I retired a while ago, and I just want to forget all that stuff."

"I don't know what kind of stuff you're trying to forget, but I think I understand."

He stared at me. Hard. Then spoke, casually. "Since you're here, though, I will tell you two things." He looked at his cup, twirling it. "I was with military intelligence for nearly thirty years. Six of them in Vietnam, second in command in my division. After 1963. In 1962, for days before the Bay of Pigs, and during it, we, and every agency in the country, the FBI, Navy Intelligence, the CIA, the works, were holed up in a war room in Miami. We had detailed maps of every building in Havana. You know what we were doing? We were picking out where our offices would be located once we'd ousted Castro." He stopped and stared again. Not once blinking or lowering his eyes. Then continued.

"When Kennedy cancelled the air support and Castro's troops captured our guys, when we lost, there wasn't one officer in our war room who wasn't jumping up screaming, 'That mother fucker!' And they didn't mean Castro." He stopped, waiting for a response from me. I had none. "And this is the last thing I'll say." He paused again. "You've heard of Soldier Field in Chicago?"

I nodded.

"They have a huge officer's club there. Go in there anytime and it's almost empty. On Nov. 22nd, 1963, it was almost full. Check it out."

With that he rose, and placed a five-dollar bill on the table. Without extending his hand, he left, saying, "Thanks for coming. Good luck."

I sat there, cold coffee in hand, thinking about how much that man must really know, and how many others like him all around the country probably know more. I thought, Kennedy never had a chance. Neither did Garrison. It was hours before I called George to relay the conversation. George kept repeating, "Jesus Christ. You're kidding. Holy shit!" He never heard from his father again.

The City of Second Chances

The move to Las Vegas was quick and haphazard; I was preoccupied with the film. After the $900,000 sale of our house, we had over $600,000 left. Not wanting to pay a huge hunk in taxes, the government made us put it into a home. The one we found in 'The Fountains,' a walled-in elite enclave in Henderson was 6500 square feet. It had rooms we never visited. Each of the two dogs had a room. Our garage was a yacht garage. It became the home of our outdoor cat, Samantha. I had rescued her one night on my way to a movie. She and her litter had been dumped into the sewer in front of my house. I heard the cries of the last survivor and never got to the movies. Almost every morning for her twenty-two years she brought her kill to the back door to share with us. She died in her new cat castle, a dead mouse beside her.

In an effort to get attention for the film, I scurried around looking for festivals. Everyone we approached in North America turned it down. Only San Sebastian in Spain accepted it.

With all the justifiable monumental attention to Stone's film, no one in America would broadcast or distribute, or even screen T*he Garrison Tapes*. Even at universities. Cinemax screened it in tandem with *JFK* to their biggest audience ever, and refused to rescreen it. PBS and Frontline were offered it free. They passed on it without comment. I called my old friend and colleague, Tom Brokaw, a major longtime news personality at NBC. He was preparing his own documentary on the assassination. I asked if I could include five minutes of Jim in his film. He politely passed, adding it was nice hearing from me.

Fred was stunned by the total lack of interest in it, wondering aloud how it could not be making money. He said there was nothing else he could do. He had run out of ideas. He bowed out, turning it over to me to try and continue, wishing me well.

I saw not one cent from the Cinemax or DVD sales. I was left with the film, Freddy with the receipts. I was falling down Alice in Wonderland's rabbit hole where reality doesn't exist. I was the world's worst salesperson. The only little light I could see atop the rabbit hole was Spain.

Surprisingly, the organizers treated me like Oliver Stone's bankers must have treated him, like a hero. My picture was all over the place. Browsing around in little shops just passing time, owners wanted to talk to me about John Kennedy and Jim Garrison.

It won. I tried to thank them in Spanish. I spoke haltingly, not because my Spanish was broken, my heart was, choked up thinking about Jim and the barricades he and the film could not overcome. The ovation brought real tears, also, to scores in the audience. Sarita and I celebrated with the festival directors at what was the greatest, tastiest most elaborate twelve-course, three-hour meal we ever had. The chef gave us an autographed menu, which we have in our pantry.

A group of Russian filmmakers gifted me with a silver goblet and invited me to Moscow to screen the film. I reluctantly turned them down. Werner Herzog, the brilliant, passionate German film and documentary maker, invited me to Vienna. Sarita flew home to tend to the animals. I flew to Austria. I spent half a day with Werner and his students. Werner gave me a plaque, posed for a picture, gave a speech to the crowd about the importance of what I had done, and said he hoped I'd make more documentaries. Maybe a part two.

That trip was followed by one to Sydney, Australia. A woman film distributor had seen it at our first public screening in Santa Monica, and brought me to Australia first class. That is where it got its greatest reception. I was getting as much positive press there as Oliver was getting negative back home. Following its screening on national television, Australia's leading newspaper wrote a front-page review in which the critic said, 'John's film should have been three hours and Oliver's ninety minutes.'

All those international plaudits and awards did not make a dent in America. It had been like a stone thrown on an ice-covered lake; it gave off not one ripple. On the flight home, I heard worse news.

We were halfway over the Pacific. It was dark. I was one of the few on a full flight with a light on. I could not sleep. It was October 21st, 1992. Thirty-three days short of thirty years since Dallas. I was 59. The cockpit door opened; a man in uniform emerged. He stopped briefly to chat with a flight attendant, then began to walk down the aisle, looking in my direction. He stopped, leaned over and asked softly, "Mr. Barbour?"

"Yes, sir."

"Your wife called the airlines. She called the main office from Las Vegas and asked us to relay this message to you. Jim Garrison died today. I am sorry."

I couldn't answer him. He left. I closed my eyes. I had to. To stop the tears.

When I opened the door almost a half a day later, Sarita was crying. She told me Mark Lane had just called. I called Elizabeth, who answered immediately.

"Thank you for calling, John. But more important, thank you for making my father's last days happy. He was very pleased his story was out there. Now we can get on with our lives."

"We would like to come to his funeral."

"No. No, John. We'd love to see you all, but it will be just family. I am glad you called. It has been a hectic month. You know what my dad did before he died? He remarried mom. He found out that she was struggling after the divorce. He called her to come see him. We thought it was his wanting to say goodbye and apologize for how tough living with him had been with all the Kennedy stuff. Anyway, she comes over and he's lying in bed. His best friend and a minister is in the room. Dad tells Mom he wants to marry her again. She said no at first, but when he said that being our mother, he didn't want to leave her poor. Her new ex-husband had bankrupted her. Right there on his death bed, they got remarried. Now she'll get his pension."

"What a sweet man," I said.

"Oh," she added, with an edge to her voice, "we have to sue Warner Brothers and Oliver for the share of the profits they promised. Did they think they were making a deal with a bunch of hicks? That thing is making millions. Would you believe that? They say there are no profits."

"Liz, I am so sorry to hear that, too. But, it's Hollywood. Accountants are their most creative people."

"John, thank you. again. For everything. Please, please don't lose touch."

The city of second chances is how I described Las Vegas when I moved here. (*Time* magazine even did a colorful cover story on Sin City's growth.) But after the 2008 recession, it became just another ordinary troubled American city where second chances went the way of many people's homes. When we moved here, 8,000 others were doing the same every month. Only 2,000 a month were leaving. 72,000 people a year! That's a small town. Even with that massive influx for ten years, Las Vegas remained a small town. What we call great culture, Broadway plays, classical music, and concerts, were as hard to find here as suits and ties and evening dresses on the folks who attended the casinos' major shows. The great headliners were part of the past, from the Rat Pack, with Frank Sinatra, Dean Martin, Joey Bishop, Robert Goulet, Bobby Darin, (At The Sands, Bobby and I were the last main showroom act before they demolished it.) Sheckey Greene, Buddy Hacket, and scores more. In their place, the hotels themselves have become the stars. More people watch the water show in front of The Bellagio than attend the shows inside. Any events passing as culture were housed in auditoriums at UNLV. When a great speaker or lecturer came to appear at UNLV, people were admitted free.

As I write this, it's 2018, and there is a magnificently designed complex, just as beautiful as the Lincoln Theatre in D.C., called The Smith Center, a few short blocks from downtown. I am happy to report that it is strongly supported and well attended by what are called 'the locals,' who pay unhappy high prices. Other than that, the pervading primary culture is still the four 'C's: Casinos, Cowboys, Country, and Cash. It has no classical music station. There was one oldies AM station called The Jewel, (KJUL).

It switched to country. There was such a clamoring and rattling of canes and walkers at the retirement homes, the station owners brought it back, but stuck it on FM. All talk radio is 'doomsday is coming' conservative. Calling these guys 'talk' radio is like calling a twenty-car freeway crash a mishap. It is 'shout' radio. The last remotely quiet, semi-liberal host, Don Imus, was put out to pasture ten years ago, along with his hat.

When the mob ran the town, gambling was eighty-four percent of the revenue, even after the 'boys' skimmed it. Now that the hotels are run by major corporations, as is Congess, that percentage is down to forty-seven. Rooms, restaurants, shops, and shows now account for most of the profits. I enjoy living here, though. Probably because I don't go out too much, except to play golf. It has many good public golf courses, with a merciful absence of bugs to dive bomb, harass, bite and sting you. A claim that cannot be made by many courses on the continent.

Happiest days were spent taking my son for years to junior golf tournaments. I couldn't get enough of it. I wasn't a 'Little League dad' who stood behind him cheering him or instructing him. I just enjoyed him. In one major junior, he was allowed to have a caddy. I was thrilled to volunteer. He was twelve. He turned me down.

"Dad, you're too emotional."

I burst out laughing at his honesty. "Can I audition? A practice round?"

I got the job. If I had been that quiet and peaceful in my professional life as I was that day on a golf course in sunny Southern California, I might have had a much more successful career.

In Las Vegas, it was ten years later. Christopher was out of Stanford with ambitions to get on the PGA or Nike tour. He asked if I would caddy. Without auditioning. I was thrilled. At this late point in my life, I was relieved to be changing careers. I was going to be a caddy. A professional caddy for my son!

54 Pine Isle Court

Our house was ten blocks from the Legacy Golf Course. Its overwhelming space was too uncomfortable. It was the kind of place where you would shoot a great horror film or a bad porno. We moved, finding a beautiful 4200 square-foot corner house at 54 Pine Isle Court. It was in a four-house cul-de-sac, just off the fourth green of The Legacy Golf Course within walking distance. That made it easier for Christopher to practice and play; also, easier on our pocketbook. Christopher got a job as an outside bag boy. That gave him playing privileges, tip money, and an education he did not get at Stanford. I joined the Men's Club and played every day. Sometimes twice a day. I would have had to cut back to be a junkie. I was not as good as I was in other sports, or as good as I thought I was. I never got better than an eight handicap. But I do have seven holes-in-one!

I had always encouraged Christopher to play golf; it is the only endeavor I know of where your future is in your own hands. No matter how nice a guy you are, if you cannot put the ball in the hole, find another line of work. But if you can, you can earn a living.

Golf is also the only sport where the greatest in the world, from Jack Nicklaus and Arnold Palmer to Tiger and Jordan Spieth, have to pay to play. In baseball you have players batting .163, basketball players missing free throws, and hockey players missing empty nets making millions of dollars a year. All sports should be like golf, based solely on achievement, or a base salary with incentives.

Christopher worked and practiced hard. He was always diligent, conscientious and smart. Whenever he could get time off, we'd pack up and head for a Monday qualifier or to the Golden State Tour or some State Open. I was a kid again; he was the man. We did this for five years. He missed a couple of Monday qualifiers by just a couple of shots. They weren't shots, actually; they were putts. Christopher, without ever having a lesson, has as good a golf swing as anyone on the tour, as good a ball striker as anyone. Somehow, the simplest of moves, physically, did not translate to his putting.

In a major event in New Mexico, in the Wednesday pro am in the rain, he shot sixty-seven, tying for first. The next day in perfect sunny weather he hit eighteen greens and shot even par. Justin Leonard could hit only five greens and shot sixty-seven. Putting is to a golfer what a high note is to a tenor. If Pavarotti went flat on the last note of *Nussan Dorma,* the beauty that preceded it would have been totally destroyed.

Christopher didn't anguish over it as much as I did. Perhaps golf wasn't really in his heart. What he did do, though, was put all his experiences in his journal. Writing was his hobby. Golf was his profession. Unable to sink the putts he needed, he decided to switch them. He packed up and moved to a small apartment in Hollywood, knowing only one or two people.

I had left the business. Seeing him moving off to try and get into that often soul-destroying profession on his own pained me more than losing

Real People or meeting the resistance to *The Garrison Tapes*. They had happened to me. I didn't want those things to happen to him. Being no longer famous, or even employed, I felt as helpless as he must have felt trying to sink a three-footer.

Much like his mother, he has a quality about him that is peaceful. He could be as comfortable with himself as a bag boy as he could as a writer-co-executive producer of a hit show like *CSI Vegas*, which is exactly what he became – on his own. Starting as that show's version of a bag boy, he worked and earned his way over seven years to that lofty position. Within days of the demise of that long running, trendsetting hit, he was hired as a writer at *Criminal Minds, Beyond Borders*, starring Gary Sinise. He is now a writer and co-executive producer on the original *Criminal Minds*, as I write alone here, happier for his success than I ever was for mine.

About this time, I had two medical calamities. Both my fault. Over a relatively long life of physical activity, I had my ordinary share of mishaps and broken bones, but getting diabetes was totally stupid.

My son never eats sweets or candy. Neither does my wife. The reason: they had great childhoods. If you look around at your friends or family and find one not into sweets, get closer to them; they are probably happy, stable people. With my son and career gone, my appetite for sugary comforting carbohydrates grew. Watching a movie, a game or an author on C-Span, my dinner consisted of Godiva dark chocolates, strawberry ice cream you couldn't see through the Hershey's syrup, all washed down with a Coke. One day I looked down and saw my body was not only falling apart, it was leaking. The skin on my hands cracked so badly I was bleeding. I thought it was the dry heat and everyday golf. Then blood started pouring out of my backside. It was a healthy looking red, so I dismissed the thought of cancer, and ignored it. I had to urinate constantly. My vision got blurry. I kept it from my wife. One day, though, she saw the blood in the bathtub, and suggested very firmly that I see a doctor. To please her I did.

"Mr. Barbour, do you have any idea how sky-high your blood sugar is? You are a full-blown diabetic. What are you eating?"

"Well, doc, I wouldn't call it food."

"Well, you keep it up, you won't have too many more days. You must stop eating sugar. It is a poison. It should be labeled, like nicotine."

"Do you know what, doc," I said. "I know that. In 1970, I had a guest on my show who wrote a book called, *Sugar, Sugar, Sugar*, but it never bothered me."

"Well, it caught up to you. Do you have any willpower?"

"No."

"Well, you had better get some quickly, along with this medicine I am going to prescribe right away."

The next day, I stopped ingesting anything with sugar or corn syrup. Within two weeks every symptom cleared up. Even my vision. That was fifteen years ago. The medicines he prescribed I cut in half. I never check my blood-sugar level. I go to the doctor maybe three times a year.

The other medical mishap was my lifelong tendency to overdo anything athletic. In this case, it was golf. Golf was my Godiva chocolates.

One afternoon on a par five hole, I hit my three wood second shot. There was a mighty 'whack' sound. Not the ball; my back. My fifth vertebrae had snapped into my sciatic nerve. I collapsed like the Twin Towers. I awoke to find my two buddies staring down at me certain I had a heart attack.

I groaned, "Don't drag me. Don't drag me. Just go finish!" They laughed, familiar with the old joke.

For six months I could barely crawl. I could not sit. Four hours every day I would float in the bathtub to defy gravity. I have read about how the CIA tortures by waterboarding. Those who suffer it, do not know what torture is. All the CIA inquisitors have to do is take a hammer to the fifth vertebrae, and thump it into the sciatic nerve. In three minutes they'd be confessing to everything from shooting Lincoln to bringing nails to the crucifixion! My insurance plan was with Southwest Medical. Their doctors refused to operate, claiming my blood sugar was too high. They told me this after I lay in their waiting room writhing around and screaming in agony for an hour, unattended. People walked over me like I was homeless. I was worse. I was doctor-less. I fired them.

Eventually, I lucked out. I found a doctor named Kaplan, (the same name as my immigration lawyer in LA.) He was partnered with the surgeon who tended Siegfried, of Siegfried and Roy, after one their pet tigers put his head in his mouth and dragged him offstage.

In his perfect bedside manner, because I couldn't stand, he told me my blood sugar was too high. He was hesitant to operate, and asked what else he could do. I handed him a box of matches.

He looked befuddled. "What's this?"

"Matches, doc. You're either going to operate or cremate because I am not going to live with this pain."

He operated. My back is better than it ever was. As is my golf swing. Every Christmas, I'd send him a box of Godiva chocolates.

A Brief Break About Money

Everyone is interested in money. It is like air; you can't live without it. But breathing air is not the purpose of your life. The purpose is to live. My purpose was not to make money or acquire it. My purpose was to live; to enjoy what I loved doing, which was show business. A few times money arrived in bundles. Most of the time it did not. It did not matter to me. Only my work mattered.

I never bought things, cars or rings or buildings. I saw too many people owned by the stuff they bought. All I did that was extravagant was build a beautiful house in Toluca Lake for my small family. Sarita, cared even less about money than I did. So, the money not spent was put into our pension plan at Morgan Stanley. When we moved into 54 Pine Isle Court, it was well over $600,000. During the years I received very large pay checks, I just deposited them. I never looked at or commented or complained about the amount of taxes taken out or what went to Social Security or to The Writers' Guild Pension or the AFTRA pension plan. Then, nearing 60, I started getting notes from all these places asking how I would like my retirement checks sent, by mail or direct deposit. You mean I've got all this coming in and I didn't even plan it? Jesus Christ, how lucky was I! I also got a notice from Morgan Stanley, that it was compulsory for me to take a minimum monthly payment; the taxes all those years that were deferred, the government could now collect on. The total was over $10,000 a month. Interest from Morgan Stanley was paying the $2,000 mortgage on the house that cost $350,000. It was appraised in early 2008 at $840,000. Wow! According to *Forbes* magazine, I was in the top five percent income bracket in America. For doing nothing. Just opening my mail and playing golf. In that mail came bushels of credit cards. I have never wanted a credit card, but the system forces them on you. If you are calling a hotel for a reservation, you cannot read them the serial number off a hundred-dollar bill. So we had a couple.

Then, in 2008, after Bill Clinton repealed Glass-Steagall, passed during the Depression by FDR to protect us from Wall Street predators, the market collapsed. The bottom fell out of America, and the middle class went crashing through. What we all saw was that the whole system was a Bernie Madoff. To hide the obvious massive corruption, the government bailed out the causers and the criminal corporations. In a true capitalist free enterprise system, if you fail to make a product or deliver a service people will buy, you go out of business. But that is not what we have.

What have corporate socialism. Trillions went to those perpetrators, and none went to prison.

An economist calculated that if all the monies going for corporate bailouts had been divided amongst every voting American over twenty-one, we'd each have close to half a million dollars! That would have certainly avoided the millions of foreclosures and the economic quicksand which we still struggle to move out of.

My Morgan Stanley pension plan lost half its value overnight. The extra interest would no longer cover our monthly mortgage. But we continued to pay it. After six months, I called the manager of our Bank of America asking if we could have a short meeting with him. It was very short. I asked him if we could reduce our mortgage payments by half, that when the economy improved, we would not only return to the existing rate, but pay off the break they would give us. He said it was not their policy.

"You mean," I said, "it is not Bank of America's policy to help their long-lasting customers?"

"The only time we could help you, is if you foreclosed on us."

"But, that is what we're trying to avoid. What kind of logic is that?"

I stopped paying them. Six months later came the warnings of pending foreclosure. We moved out and found a perfect almost-new home, sadly another foreclosure victim. Shortly, Bank of America completed their Pine Isle foreclosure, and put it up for auction. Six days a week those auctions are held downtown in a parking lot, because there are too many to fit in the building. I went with a golfing real estate friend the day mine was to be sold. The lot was packed with buyers sitting on small wooden chairs or standing waiting to buy. Soon, mine, with its number; was announced. A bunch of hands went up. The bidding began. For five minutes there were shouts and figures. The bidding stopped at $240,000.00. What? A house a year ago appraised at $840,000.00 could be had for $240,000.00?

I rushed to my friend. "I'll buy it. I'll buy for $245,000.00."

"You can't," he said. "You don't have the cash here. You have to pay cash. Now."

"But I can prove I have it."

"Johnny, even if you had the cash, the bank wouldn't sell it to you."

"Why not? Then you buy it for me and I'll give you an extra $5,000.00 commission!"

"I don't have that much cash on me either. The reason the bank wouldn't let the owner buy it back is because the 400-thousand-dollar balance on your mortgage, the government still pays to your bank. If Bank of America lets you buy it, they lose all that government money. They and the government fuck you coming and going! With our tax money!"

I was in a rage at the cruel, inhuman, unpunished venality of it all. And expressed it in the only small way I could. On the internet, summed up in a satirical song called *Walkaway*. You can find it on my website.

This brings me to that point again when not the fickle finger of fate, but the fickle feet of fate walk into your life, and sends you on a path you were really meant to travel all along.

The Last Word on the Assassination

It was the spring of 2003. I was seventy. My weekend golfing buddy was David Schulman, a portly mid-forties, ex-Philadelphian, selling used steel to China. With his business growing, he told me he was getting a new computer, and was giving me the old one. I declined, telling him I had barely mastered the typewriter and had no interest in what they called the 'internet.' He sent it anyway, delivered by a younger more muscular looking fellow also named David. David Lispi.

He stood at the front door, this huge computer tucked under his arm like an empty box. "Hey," he said with a smile after studying my face for a moment, "You're John Barbour."

"Yeah," I said, stunned anybody would recognize me from *Real People* after all the years. But it wasn't *Real People* he remembered me from. It was from a film I did not even appear in, which made it more astonishing, *The Garrison Tapes*. I asked, "How can you know me from that?"

"We had a history teacher in high school who made your film our assignment for a week. We watched parts of it every day. He told us it was all we'd need to know about the assassination. He knew everything about you."

Sarita served us snacks, and he asked endless questions about the history of the film and my long involvement with Garrison. He, too, was perplexed and angry to hear the film, like Jim, had died with no afterlife anywhere in America.

"Maybe we can fix that," he said. "I'll build you a website, and you can show it. Preferably in segments like we saw it. People don't have any attention span anymore, especially with the internet, so that would be the best way."

"David, that is nice of you, but I know nothing about computers or internets. My mind would be incapable of absorbing anything technical. I hear building a good site is quite expensive, and I'd never use it."

"Yes, you will, Mr. Barbour. And I will help you. I will teach you. I don't care how lousy a student you are, I will teach you. Please, can I start?"

It was impossible to say no to that kind of sincerity.

For the next few weeks, that is what he did. He uploaded parts of *The Garrison Tapes* and *Ernie Kovacs: Television's Original Genius,* plus scores of clips from some of my shows. All free on www.johnbarboursworld.com. Within days, it began getting hits, thousands of them. Half the time after that, David was sending copyright infringement notices to numbers of folks who stuck *The Garrison Tapes* on their sites. It was one of the internets most stolen films; on my site and the plagiarized ones, it got over a million hits. David thought with that kind of traffic, we might get advertisers. We were told it was not 'advertiser friendly.' No matter. It was out there being seen.

With November 22nd rolling around again, I got to send my first emails. They were to every tv outlet in the country offering the film free. Having gotten not one reply from any media outlet anywhere in America, I was reduced to just trying locally. I sent one to George Knapp on the local CBS outlet. He is deservedly a multiple award winner, even nationally, and on Sunday nights is by far the best host of *Coast to Coast AM*. The next day I heard my first 'bing' and a voice that said, you have mail. George asked me to call him, saying he remembered my work. He booked me on his radio show. The immediate reaction was astonishing – hits on the film surged.

To hopefully expand the viewing, I then emailed the ten major JFK assassination sites, sending each a link. They could screen the Garrison film for their followers for nothing. I anticipated a quick flood of positive remarks. With their participation, it could go viral. Shockingly, not one response. They all turned down Jim Garrison, the most important voice on the planet to the investigation into the death of President Kennedy. Why would those sites do that? Then I recalled the Senator Frank Church hearings in the 70's into the CIA. He uncovered, through the CIA's 'Project Mockingbird,' that they had over 400 'assets' in every major media outlet in America writing 'fake news' in support of their warmongering foreign policy. It seemed the CIA was the only branch of government doing its job well, keeping America misinformed. If infiltrating the big birds of American Media was easy, then infiltrating the canaries in the coal mines, the so-called 'assassination sites,' would be easier.

The JFK assassination is the second most Googled subject in the world next to UFOs! I applauded this internet with its word of mouth underground guerrilla democracy at work, wondering how long they'd let it last. I recall a quote that has been attributed to Mark Twain: "It is easier to fool people, than to convince them they have been fooled."

The growing views of *The Garrison Tapes,* rapidly expanding free exposure, was letting people know they had been fooled. Encouraged by this, I began to think of what I might be able to do to bring it to a larger, more mainstream audience.

November 22, 2013 would mark the fiftieth anniversary of the assassination of President John F. Kennedy. The further away our media was getting from the day that changed America and the world, the further away they got from reporting any stories, no matter how well researched or documented, which reasonably questioned the Warren Report. Two of TV's most prominent news personalities and performers, no longer journalists, Bill O'Reilly and Geraldo Rivera, were now among the cheerleaders, trumpeting obvious trash. Long, long ago, when trying to make names for themselves, they were two strong young voices demanding more truth. It was Geraldo on ABC late night in 1975 with activist comedian Dick Gregory and photo analyst Robert Gordon who showed the public for the first time the real horror of the Zapruder film, which led to the sabotaged Select Committee on Assassinations. Gone along with the postured seriousness were his outrage and questions. The same with O'Reilly, also now beating the Warren Report's dead horse with his *Killing Kennedy*. That draft-dodging, military-avoiding mouthpiece for the American empire builders, has further been building his bank balance with other abysmal books like, *Killing Lincoln, Killing Christ.* (The one I wait for with relish is his very last one: Killing Myself.) Eventually Fox killed his show, not for his lying propagandizing for the empire, but for sexually harassing female employees.

On the other hand, the internet was alive and awash with a tsunami of theories, opinions, speculations, and facts about that dreadful day in Dallas. Most of the material is dreadful and distracting. Some is brilliant, new, and important.

I needed to think of a way other than the internet to bring the film to a mainstream audience. Sitting in a local Regal theater one afternoon, I saw a promo for The Metropolitan Opera presented by Fathom Events. My God, that was perfect. I didn't stay for the film. I rushed home, turned on my computer and Googled everything about Fathom Events, headquartered in Colorado, and whom to contact. For three intense weeks, I talked to or emailed links and letters to the very nice lady who booked the events. She expressed her interest. It would be a live screening of the documentary, doing a live email Q & A, and perhaps with a special guest. I suggested maybe Oliver Stone. I wanted to present it nationally in 1,000 theaters on Nov. 22nd. If we only got 200 into each theater at fifteen dollars a head, it would more than cover the costs. More important, there'd be enough money left over for maybe a part two of *The Garrison Tapes*. In 1963, there were over 1500 owners of TV stations in America; now, thanks again to Bill Clinton, signing The Communications Act, 95% of all Media is owned by six corporations.

This Fathom event could bypass the media. But this nice lady's bosses shot it down. Too controversial, they said. They preferred *The Wizard of Oz*.

What next? Browsing the internet for ideas, I stumbled on an obscure post. At an opera house in Dallas, this post said in an interview with Charlie Rose, Bobby Kennedy Jr., said his father publicly supported the Warren Report, but privately did not. I couldn't believe a Kennedy had finally spoken out! Rose refused to post it on his site, as did Bobby. It was being suppressed, even by the man who spoke it.

Maybe I could do it as a live webcast! I would bring in George Knapp as host and interviewer. I would bring in three of the best researchers in the crowded field of anti-Warren Reporters. These would be balanced with three who still support the Warren Report. Hopefully, finally, Dan Rather. I would pay everyone involved, plus give them a small piece of any DVD sales. My first call went to Joan Mellen, author of *A Farewell to Justice: Jim Garrison, JFK's Assassination, and the Case That Should Have Changed History*. Right off the bat, she said, "Jesus, John, why do you need people on the other side? That side's had the microphone for fifty years. Screw them. It's time to give a larger voice to the truth."

"Well, Joan, unlike Fox, I'd like to be fair and balanced."

"They aren't. Why should you be? But it's your show and I'll be glad to do it. Even for nothing. These things don't pay anyway."

"I do, Joan. I do. And thanks."

I next called Dick Russell, author of another excellent book, *The Man Who Knew Too Much*. I explained to him what I was trying to mount, and that Joan had already agreed.

"It sounds like a great idea; and Joan is wonderful," he said.

"Dick, just off the top of my head, I saw what he said to Charlie Rose. What do you think of my maybe approaching Bobby Kennedy as the third in your group?"

"I know Bobby very well," Dick said with a little spark in his voice. "We were in Mexico recently together with Jesse Ventura. Bobby and I write some articles about the environment together. But, frankly he and I have never had any real conversation about the subject of the assassinations. I never bring it up, and he never offers."

"Do you think I should maybe try to contact him and see if he'd join you and Joan?"

"I'll be talking to him tomorrow. I'd be happy to mention that you called me, and I was going to do it, and his name came up."

"Wow, Dick, that is fantastic. Thank you."

My God, I thought, this is serendipity. Dick knows Bobby Jr.! The next day Dick called.

"John, Bobby was surprisingly interested, but that you should be in touch with his agent at Keppler. That's his speaker's agency in Virginia. His personal agent is Sean Lawton. Call and mention you are calling at Bobby's suggestion. Tell them what you're up to. Keep me posted. You never know; this might work out."

Within fifteen minutes, Sean and I were chatting like old friends.

"My God, John, my mother will be thrilled," he said. "She just loved *Real People*. You and Sarah and Skip. Just loved it. I was just a kid, but it was a habit in our house. What can I do for you?"

As quickly and as concisely as possible, I explained it to Sean.

"Could you send me a copy of your Garrison film so I could look at it? If all goes well, I will be in LA in a month for a speakers' conference. Perhaps we could get together for a lunch."

"I would love to."

"Now my mother's gonna be even more impressed. Her boy is meeting John Barbour! I will get back to you within the week."

My God, this was serendipity! I called Dick immediately.

"Dick, you know, if Bobby decides to do this, and I can afford him, I think Joan is right, I don't need a panel of any sort. I'd like you to co-produce this thing with me. And act as a consultant. For that I'll pay you more than the $1,500.00 panel fee, maybe up to $5,000.00, plus five percent of the DVD sales. Because if Bobby does it, besides his fee, I'd give him a third of the DVD sales. With you on board, it will make him feel a lot more comfortable. What do you think?"

"That is generous and much more than fair. I'm happy to do it."

For someone as important, prominent and deeply involved in informing the world about the environment, and someone whose family has borne grief beyond belief, I thought the only venue for Robert Kennedy, Jr. was a university. In Nevada, the only campus with facilities as good as any Ivy League school, was UNLV. There I might have a slight in.

Fifteen years earlier, on the thirty-fifth anniversary, I offered the film free. The young lady producing the event for the school was named Laurel Fruth. Following the live screening, much to Laurel's astonishment, I answered viewers questions for over an hour and a half; we had to hang up still with a full switchboard. Luckily not only was Laurel still there, she was now in charge of the prestigious Greenspan School of Communications. She was thrilled, offering the theater and facilities free. With every phone call, things were rolling as if meant was meant to be.

George Knapp refused a $5,000 fee, saying it was a monumental public service he was honored to be a part of. Three and a half months before November 22nd, 2015, Dick, Sean, and I met at Musso's. Also present was actor-comedian-activist Richard Belzer, offering to assist in the enterprise in any way he could. Sean told us Bobby never talks about the assassinations. However, he said, an unnamed major corporation called him asking if Bobby would speak at a nonpublic, non-recorded private event for $100,000. Sean said, surprisingly, Bobby accepted, along with a female member of the family. Sean said people who attended still call him to talk about it. He added that he was impressed by the documentary, and was awaiting Bobby's feedback. He also speculated Bobby might consider doing it because he had spoken about it at this one private event, and with Charlie Rose, and that he may need the money.

I turned to Dick in amazement. "Jesus, Dick, how can a Kennedy need money?"

"John, the very rich spend at a lot higher rate than the rest of us, and like the rest of us, he probably needs money."

I turned back to Sean. "I will find out from UNLV what the best dates would be near November 22nd. Bobby and you can select one or two. I will give you a ten-thousand-dollar deposit upon request and acceptance, the balance the night he shows up. I will also outline his one-third participation in any and all sales, DVD, or whatever, in perpetuity. Sound okay?"

"I will do the best as I can to move this forward. The thing that will also appeal to Bobby is that it is being done at a University."

We all shook hands, elated and confident. We picked three days in November and sent them to Sean. The school was so thrilled to have the monumentally worldwide, newsmaking event on their campus, they wanted it presented as part of The Barrick Lecture Series. This amazing program set up Marjorie Barrick pays speakers like Michael Eisner, CEO of Disney $100,000 (as if he needed it) to speak in a fabulous 1200 seat theater, where patrons are admitted free. That's where we would be. The first cautionary note we got from Sean was that Bobby was tied up the three dates in November, and could we give him two in December. He also said he was nervous about the evening being focused on the Garrison film, and could that be just a sidebar; that he'd like the evening to be more about the Kennedy legacy.

I sent two dates for December, and agreed about the Kennedy legacy. Awaiting to fill in the date, we then had programs printed with pictures of Bobby to talk about his family's legacy and, at the bottom, pictures of George and myself, and a small mention of *The Garrison Tapes*. The school brass was elated. As was Sean.

The latter part of August, all of September and October were filled with daily endless emails and phone calls between me and Dick and me and Sean and Dick and Bobby. We wanted all to be to Bobby's liking, from the food in the dressing room to the all-important publicity. Going through the endless back and forth negotiations with Bobby was like Chinese water torture, one dreadful drop at a time until I wanted to scream. Bobby had turned down the first week in December. Laurel called me.

"John, I only have one date left for you. December 12th. That's it. We committed a year ago to renovations on the theater. They start on the 13th."

We were now in the middle of November. We were drifting past the 50th anniversary date. And its impact. We also had to print the date in the programs. I made a quick call to Sean to tell of him of our deadline. He called me back within minutes confirming Bobby for December 12th. I was so excited I couldn't sit or even stand. I ran around the room, my phone in my hand calling Dick.

"Dick, do you think I should call Bobby's office myself and thank him, since I'm the one writing the check?"

"It wouldn't hurt."

Five minutes later I was on the phone with Bobby's private secretary. Identifying myself as a friend of Dick's and Sean's, and as the producer of this event at UNLV, I asked if perhaps I might thank Bobby personally for his participation.

"He's not doing that," she said in a huff.

"Excuse me?"

"He's not doing your event."

"But, Sean, his agent, says he is."

"It's not on his schedule."

"Well, would you please pass along a message thanking him for considering it, and my phone number?"

After she hung up, I called Dick, relating my encounter with the shark in Bobby's moat.

"Well, she can be tough. But the last I talked to Bobby he did say the date was perfect. I have to talk to him again on another matter we're working on, so let me get back to you."

Three unbearable days later, Dick called. "He says he's still considering it, saying he is inclined to do it, if all his stipulations are met."

"Christ, Dick, we're doing everything we can to accommodate him, George and the school. What else does he want? And what did he think of *The Garrison Tapes*?

"He said he hasn't seen it yet."

"What?" I yelled. "He's had it three fucking months. The only law enforcement officer in America to truly investigate the murder of his uncle and he hasn't even watched the fucking thing? I don't believe it."

"Actually, John, he said he thought Garrison was a kook."

"Are you kidding me? How would he know unless he looked at the film or read Joan Mellen's book?"

"I cannot press him on that stuff. I have to be very casual about all this. Even if he opened up to me, which is unlikely, I'd still have to tiptoe around the subject."

I called Laurel, who set up another meeting with the Dean to appraise them of where we were with Bobby. Laurel's boss said, "John, perhaps we can help you further with this. As you know, Bobby has turned down our offers to have him come here and speak about the environment, but here is what we could do. Atop the $25,000 fee you are offering, we'll chip in another ten or fifteen thousand dollars, if he stays over a day, and does his lecture about the environment in another theater."

"My goodness, what a great idea. Let me get hold of Sean and Dick and get back to you."

November 22nd, the much-touted anniversary came and went. What came was more myth about Oswald, the lone assassin, but not one piece anywhere that questioned the government's stance. Then word came the last week of November from Sean that Bobby's decision was now in the hands of Sean's boss at Keppler, and of course Bobby himself. But that as far as he knew from his last conversations with everyone, it was a go for December 12th.

My emotional roller coast ride was at an apex. Finally, we would have the most perfect man on the planet, Robert Kennedy Jr., to bring massive attention to Jim's investigation and story. A director was picked. Crews were picked. Publicity prepared. Catering and limos put on standby. Word was already filtering out and there were hundreds of calls wanting reservations. George Knapp was primed.

December 7th, Pearl Harbor Day, the Day of Infamy, we got word from Sean's boss through Dick that Bobby had canceled again. The president of Keppler told him if he got involved with talking about the assassination, Keppler would have a hard time booking him for $25,000 to talk about his love, the environment.

"Jesus Christ," I yelled at Dick, "how fucking stupid are they? If Bobby was out talking only about the assassination, every university on the planet would be paying him $100,000! Bobby and these folks screaming about a polluted planet must know they can never clear that shit up unless they first clear up polluted politics. And it begins with his uncle's murder. Goddamn it. Tell him that! I'll put it in an email to you and you can forward it to him."

"John, I am not so sure I would send that to him. I am sorry. I don't know what else to tell you."

"Well, Dick, here is something you should tell him. And I'll send photos to prove it. Dr. Thomas Noguchi's autopsy proves Sirhan did not fire the shot that killed his father. And who was there trying to save his job when the city and CIA were working overtime to get him fired for not changing that autopsy? Me! Not Jr. In other words, I have done more to look into his father's death than even he did. Tell him that, and maybe he'll change his mind again. I can't believe this."

"John, as I said, I did my best."

"Dick, I have two things to say. One is, between you and me, if John Kennedy is in whatever heaven there is writing a sequel to *Profiles in Courage,* his fucking nephew won't be in it. He should be running around the country for free saying to us what he sneakily said to Charlie Rose. And secondly, I was saving this as a surprise bonus for him when he showed for the event. The school was going to give him an additional $15,000 to stay over a day to talk about the environment. Dick, I am so exhausted and down. I'll call the school. They've hung onto the theater for as long as they could. Thanks for everything. I'll get back to you. I just can't let all this go away."

I called Laurel and everyone to whom I had spoken at the school or hired, apologizing once again for Robert Kennedy, Jr.'s change of heart. Laurel said it was both bad news and good news. The bad news was losing the truly important event. The good news was that the contractors could get into the theater early to start the refurbishing.

On December 9th, Dick called, all excited, which he usually isn't. "John. John. Bobby's changed his mind again. He said he'd do it."

"Did he say this to you, or you heard it someplace else?"

"No. Him. I just got off the phone with him."

"Dick, this has happened too often. I need to hear if myself from his lips. I'll get right back to you." In less than a minute I had his secretary on the phone again. The bitch sounded the same. "Mr. Kennedy is not available, and he will not be doing your event."

I hung up and called Dick. "I don't know who this Marybeth is, but she seems to be running his life. She said he is not doing our event. And was very emphatic about it. So, I do not know what to say. I don't even know at this late date, if we have a theater. Let me call Laurel.

A call to Laurel confirmed my nervousness; the theater was unavailable. There would be nothing available until after the first of the year. January. I made my last call to Dick that would have the name Bobby in the conversation.

"Dick, I don't know why he said that to you and something else to Marybeth, or if she is just talking for him, but the theater is gone until after the first of the year. But, even if he is available, fuck your friend. Let him keep talking about acid rain until the shit in government is first cleaned up. I don't mean to denigrate your friend, but by calling Garrison a kook, he denigrated not only my friend, but the friend of anyone who wants the truth. If you're still interested in maybe doing something after the first, you'll be the first I call."

It was not a Merry Christmas or a happy New Year. Laurel called me very early in January 2014, asking if I was still interested in doing something with the film. If so, she said she had the perfect three-hundred seat small theater in her journalism building that we could still have free.

Getting off the phone, I turned to Sarita. "Sarita, the $25,000. I would have spent on Bobby would have come back a hundred-fold; not spending it now may not return a nickel. What do you think?"

"You've never worked or worried about money before. Why worry now? It is something that has to be done. I think Jim Garrison is looking down on you. So, do it. You have no choice. I'll go without a few manicures and you'll go without a few golf games."

$25,000 out of our pension plan went to the project. $8,000.in penalty taxes to the IRS. I was back on the phone with Joan and Dick, and this time Jim Marrs, author of *Crossfire*, who had made an enormous contribution with his appearance on *The Garrison Tapes,* and whose book was a major part of Stone's *JFK*. On Friday, January 31st, 2014, in a crowded theater in the UNLV School of Journalism, we presented a webcast of what we called *The Last Word on the Assassination*. We opened with the film, which is so powerful, I thought no one could ever follow it, but I was wrong. Joan, Dick and Jim were so lively and interesting, expanding on great questions from the audience, they could have taken their act off-Broadway. With the help of David Lispi, we showed a new clip of film showing how easy it was for Jim Garrison to track down the man who ordered Ruby to shoot Oswald, something the Warren Commission could have done in a day had they wanted the truth. Afterwards, to further thank them, we treated them and a few friends to a late farewell dinner at the Palm at Caesars.

In toasting them, I said, "You all know, especially Dick, that we struggled for months to get Bobby Kennedy, Jr. I wish we had. It would have gotten enormous press and millions of viewers on the web, which we didn't get. And he would have sold us a million DVDs. His being there would have had monetary value. But the truth is, he could have added no information to the story. His would have been just an emotional face to look at. But, from a historical standpoint, his appearance is meaningless. You three have improved Jim's story with your presence and your knowledge and your contributions. A hundred years from now, people will know who you are and the truths you were trying to tell, long after Bobby Kennedy, Jr. is a forgotten footnote. Thank you."

The American Media and the 2nd Assassination of President John F. Kennedy

Within weeks of putting it up on Amazon, *The Last Word on the Assassination* became one of their top-selling documentaries for over three years. So that everyone could see it free, I moved it to my site, youtube/johnbarboursworld.com. Viewers 'friended' me on Facebook, asking if they could send money for me to do a part two about the media. They had heard me talk about it on Black Op Radio with Len Osanic, and a few others. I mentioned that when Trump began talking about 'fake news,' it all sounded familiar. Then I remembered where I'd heard it – from Jim Garrison. I scurried back to look at that long-ago interview. And there it was, sounding as contemporary as today's headlines. Knowing that, I had no choice but to tell the rest of Mr. Garrison's very American story. When word got out, as Joseph Campbell said, doors again opened as if by magic, doors pouring out money, talent and help. Serendipity at its peak.

Myra Bronstein, an unknown corporate-employed computer whiz and self-confessed assassination junkie, offered to help open a Gofund Me account. Brian Lloyd, a successful D.C. lawyer of fifty who'd had three heart operations messaged me. He had mountains of media material he had saved since he was a kid. I could have it all. Gary Fannin, the author of *The Innocence of Oswald,* called from Georgia. He wanted to do research. As did Joe Sottile, from Oakland. Joe is an award-winning journalist and author of *Newsvandal,* one of the best most objective daily news letters in the country. Irina Clark, a bilingual Russian immigrant and mother of two, a news junkie, called from Boston. She wanted to contribute. All worked and contributed to the film, (with credit) sight unseen by me. John Haddad, owner of U-Edit provided me with low-cost editing space.

Within three hours of opening the Gofund Me account, a $500.00 deposit was made to it by a Geno Munari from Las Vegas. Two weeks later, this local unknown benefactor drop-boxed me sixty-seven boxes of Jim Garrison's records. I had to meet him in person to thank him. At what turned into a three-hour luncheon at Maggiano's on the Strip, I discovered he knew more about the assassination than I did. He was in his late sixties, my height, a few pounds heavier around the middle, and one of the sweetest and most successful business men I ever met. Multiple businesses at that. All of which he put on hold for over half a year helping me make the film, and without whom I could have never finished it.

In his main office building, he built a Mac editing bay, where we spent hours night and day together. Not once a harsh word between us. No working experience was ever more gratifying, or meant to be. The movie was blessed. Len Osanic, of Black Op Radio, on his own, gave us a fabulous visual opening, and contributed to the editing.

Dan Jacobs, known as 'Mr. Camera' in Las Vegas, once again came to my rescue. He had been the director on *The Last Word on the Assassination.*

He contacted the Motion Picture Academy, which sadly had rejected part one because it had been sold to TV before a legitimate theatrical release. The Academy put us in touch with a Gregory Gardner in LA who got us that release, again at a Laemmle theater. A week at The Music Hall in Beverly Hills, followed by a week at Cinema Village in New York. David Lispi, who had moved to Thailand with his wife and new daughter, designed our brilliant arresting posters that said it all. Dan put the finishing visual, audio and music touches, making it acceptable to the Academy for Oscar consideration. It was not nominated, but I didn't care. At least it is being seen. That was not the case of all twenty film festivals which rejected it, including San Sebastian. Even The Moscow Film Festival turned it down; I was hoping Putin would do for me what he did for Trump. The *L.A. Times* savaged my continuing Garrison story, dismissing it as 'conspiracy porn,' not once trying to refute one of the film's fountain of facts or the new CIA documents, and calling me "an angry curmudgeon," which I am. Those who attended, by the score, savaged the *L.A. Times.* The New York critic writing for *Rotten Tomatoes,* called it "a must-see movie by every American."

Not even wanting to pursue more theaters, which are vanishing faster than politicians for peace, and wanting everyone to be able to see it, we put it on Vimeo for $4.00 and Amazon for $1.99 where it is still going gangbusters. If you go to Amazon, there are scores of unsolicited reviews that brought tears to my eyes. My Jim Garrison story is done. So is mine.

Epilogue

It is May 2018. America seems more divided than ever. Once it was Civil Rights, voting rights, women's rights, abortion, and Vietnam. This time it is over the winner of the last presidential election. MSNBC devoted an hour with a psychiatrist and the ugliest pictures they could find trying to prove Donald Trump is insane. The internet is full of folks with guns warning us they'll keep him in office. The last election with Hilary and Donald proved if baseball's World Series were run like American politics, the two worst teams would be playing. In America, we, the 99%, get to elect who the 1% percent select. Donald Trump's victory shook up the 1%, the Establishment; he was not the one they selected.

Voting in our national elections is as useless as voting your one share of General Motors stock. You cast your vote at their annual meeting, but you have no say as to how they build the carburetor or design the car.

Likewise, you have no say over how to reconstitute or halt our growing perpetual-war machine. We are at war with phantoms with no Air force, no Navy, and no chance!

We have resigned ourselves to the fact all politicians lie. Perhaps, sadly, the biggest liar might have been our much-revered Abraham Lincoln when he said we had "government of the people, by the people, and for the people." The CEOs who really run the country since John F. Kennedy's murder must piss their pants with laughter when they hear that. Fortunately, though, in a few embattled corners of the Republic, the First Amendment is still struggling to stay alive. Freedom of speech is still allowed. It has been reduced to a privilege and no longer a right. And is only tolerated if the speaker has a small audience. Remember, throughout history, no group every made one contribution to improving society. All growth in science, music, art, politics, medicine or education came about because of the passion of only one black sheep and a few strays. Galileo, Copernicus, Tesla, Washington and Thomas Jefferson's and Thomas Paine's American Revolution had few on their side. Castro only had twelve in a rowboat. Jesus only had his dirty dozen at the Last Supper. The masses of white sheep continue to allow themselves to be led by only one shepherd, usually a dog.

All my life I wanted to fit in. To a family. To friends. To my work. To society. But never could. It wasn't from lack of trying. I guess it just wasn't meant to be. So, I ended up being called one of those black sheep. What a compliment. I thought my story and work were finished when I typed the last chapter. As you've seen, though, stuff pops up from out of nowhere when I think I'm happily done. Chronologically, I am at 85, what Hollywood and society say is 'over the hill.' Spiritually, though, I am still a kid, starting up another hill. And the next one after that. Until I run out of hills, or life runs out of me.

A few months ago, after appearing as a guest on a BBS radio show produced by a voice that belongs to a Mike Kim, he called asking if I would consider hosting my own show on their network. I told him I had no interest in either doing a daily show or even a weekly show. He asked if I would consider doing every other Monday at five p.m. Pacific time, before my bed time. I mulled his offer over for a couple of weeks and decided to do it for two reasons. The first, because there are so many interesting, involved Americans trying to inform and improve us, I'd like to give them a platform, albeit a small one, and interview them.

The second reason being, I would have a place other than Facebook on which to vent my comments, jokes, observations or whatever. With the immensely professional Mike Kim producing, whom I have still not met, we now do what is called *John Barbour's World* every other Monday on BBS Radio. We have interviewed and archived a free-thinking army of fabulous guests, from Chris Hedges, one of America's brightest men, Cynthia McKinney, the country's bravest smartest ex-Congresswoman-turned activist, Dr. Judy Wood, whose spectacular scientific research in *Where Did The Towers Go,* remains unchallenged, Gallagher, the genius comic who saved Showtime and invented stand-up TV comedy specials, Norman Lear, whose brilliant sitcoms entertained and informed a nation, unequalled today; Jeff Rense, the popular renegade internet host on whose show I appear the last Friday of every month, Richard Belzer, Ed Asner, and dozens of other great voices, especially my one regular, Joe Sotille, the most articulate, informed journalist I know, creator-author of America's best daily newsletter called *Newsvandal.*

I got more than my fifteen minutes of fame that, in 1968, artist Andy Warhol predicted we'd all have. I had undreamt years of it. That was never what I dreamt of, though. Doing good meaningful work for which I would get recognition for was my dream. I had that, too. And when my platforms were gone, I got up and tried to build another one. My current one is small, but the pleasure is large, albeit not quite as large as *Real People,* when half of America was watching.

Frequently people, of course, ask, "Don't you regret what you lost? The *AM Show, Real People,* $22,000 an hour in 1981 with another $11,000 per hour in reruns, your friendship and project with Sinatra?"

My answer is that I never lost anything. I gained everything. I gained more than everyone I know. I gained a purpose for my life. Many presidents cannot make that claim. Prior to my son, I had a life and ambition. Having him, gave that life and ambition meaning. Telling Mr. Garrison's story about the murder that changed America and the world, gave it even more meaning. How lucky could I be? Although I am, as you know, nonreligious, I am not above plagiarizing and admiring others' thoughts about God. One of my favorites is a quote attributed to an unknown dying civil war soldier who said, "I never got anything in life that I prayed for; but I got everything I needed." I say amen to that! I also say Lenny's ancient superstition turned out to be true!

In summing up one's life, one wonders if some things were meant to be. Predestiny. I don't know. My two most successful bids to be a star were struck down by my just wanting to tell a little of Jim Garrison's story. When I finally got to tell it in *The Garrison Tapes,* that was struck down by not knowing the Academy's rules. Yet, I got back up to tell it in Part Two. Was that my destiny? Or better still, was my destiny to be father to my son?

The only thing I remotely miss from once being rich and famous is getting great seats at good restaurants, and a platform on which to present talented people on a platform from which to entertain and inform. In other words, to make folks happy.

I have often said that if there is such a thing as reincarnation, I want to come back as my son. He has had the greatest parents on the planet. I have been lucky in a different way; in writing this book, looking back at all that has happened, I am experiencing sort of a reincarnation by reliving it all a second glorious, magical time. Emotionally and physically my stomach tells me I live in the present. In my head, though, like all of us I guess, I live all jumbled in the past, present, and future. The past is gone and unchanging. The present is fleeting. In my unknown future I do not see for me any more stardom, celebrities; maybe some great stories. I see a young me years ago sitting alone trying to write jokes, getting into a car, driving miles to get up to try them out at The Troubadour on Santa Monica or The Ice House in Pasadena, or The Golden Bear in Huntington Beach. I loved that. How it all started. I have that feeling again.

Las Vegas is now a very major metropolitan city of well over a million and a half people. No longer the desert country community of 25,000 with casinos when I opened for Robert Goulet or Bobby Darin. There are no longer the major talents and personalities, but it does have a number of upscale comedy clubs. I think I will put together five or ten minutes, get into my car once a week, and drive to one.

Good evening, ladies and gentlemen. My name is John Barbour. My wife and I have lived in this area for twenty years. I live in Henderson. She lives in Fashion Mall.

THE END (of the book only!)

POSTSCRIPT

Is it possible that the destiny of our lives is not in our hands alone?
Rather that the paths we take are in other hands unknown.
In my life, my perfect plans for perfect dreams often fell apart;
Next would appear an opened door that would accidentally touch my heart.
And through it I would go anxious to see where it would lead
Curiously, this path gave me not what I wanted, it gave me what I need.
Love magically came along, as did fame and riches, which went away.
And I became richer because more doors opened and the love did stay.
Reason does not answer this; our struggles the gods they amuse.
Knowing this, I thank them for my magic life, and more for my magic Muse!

...

Jane Fonda | **Ronald Reagan**

A shrill outspoken anti-war activist learned to be more softly outspoken.

The Governor was reluctant to sit for an interview; then sat and disappeared.

Mohammed Ali | **Cesar Chavez**

Pointing to his heavenly hero..Gorgeous George!

This amazing man used his bad back to cover my back against management.

Johnny Carson

'Here's the real Johnny!'

Bob Hope

In his only serious tv interview he was never wittier, warmer, or wiser.

Frank Sinatra.

The rarest of major Stars: one who kept his promise. For a while.

Celebrity Hockey.

Founded by Bo Swenson, John Perry and me, the team scored more with groupies.

George Burns.

By far the greatest verbal storyteller ever. His Lucy one is classic.

Dean Martin & Redd Foxx.

I roast my mentor Redd egged on by Dean who took my son golfing at 6.

Tom Snyder.

Our anchorman who thought the News was there to bring you him.

Lenny Bruce.

He and Bill Hicks were the only two comics who had sex appeal.

Rodney Dangerfield.

A superior talent getting rich pretending to be inferior.

Pat Morita.

A reluctant IBM operator learns how to tell Japanese jokes instead of Jew jokes!

Tee Shirt 3.

The tee shirts became priceless, as were my wife, Sarita, & our son, Christopher.

Chuck Barris.

He gonged me to become the perfect Host for a non talent show.

Our House.

I built a house to make a family; together we sold it to make a movie.

Susan Anton.

George Schlatter's 1st choice to Host 'Real People,' until my 10 year old son found Sarah Purcell.

The Nat'l Enquirer Choir.

Singing the praises of our tabloid celebrity society's leading journal.

Citizenship Cert.

No. 10677201

Petition No. 394928

-ORIGINAL-

April 24, 1933

Male

Married

Canada

UNITED STATES OF AMERICA
CENTRAL DIST. OF CALIFORNIA

The United States

Los Angeles

November 21, 1977

4234 Forman Avenue, Toluca Lake, California

November

Seal

U.S. District Court

My rebirth certificate!

Fred Silverman.

The Perfect proof of the Peter Principal.

George Carlin.

From ordinary comic to extraordinary humorist.

Merv & Me

Merv recommending a Canadian as his replacement; Westinghouse preferred an Englishman.

Neilsen Family.

Taking a Neilsen family tv survey in Utah.

TV guide Cover.

TV
GUIDE
40¢ Local Programs
June 20-26, 1981
Why Big Oil Gushes
Over Public Television
Page 4
The hosts of
'Real People'

Sarah Purcell, the perfect personality for our show until she mistook it for 'talent.' Skip Stephenson, a sweet generous soul who couldn't cope with success..or failure. Bill Rafferty, had the sparkle and gift of gab of the Irish; but not the luck. Byron Allen, The dumbest person I ever met who became one of tv's richest Producers.

John & Emmy.

Getting 5 of these didn't get me one job or one dollar.

Robert F. Kennedy Jr.

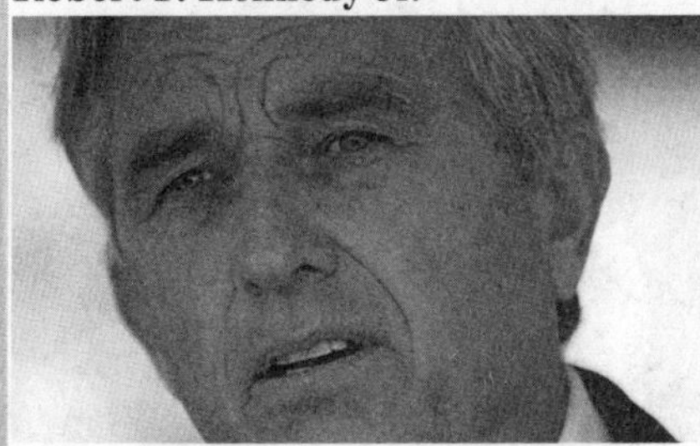

Not to be found in 'Profiles In courage.'

Garrison & LBJ.

One of America's greatest men, Jim Garrison, looking at one of the worst.

Murdoch & Chernin.

Here with Murdoch, Peter went on to become Hollywood's most successful assistant.

The Viet Nam Memorial.

'Real People' played a major role in getting this memorial for the 1,000's who died..when LBJ lied!

Kelly Lange

LA's hottest weather girl loved snowing on my parade.

Jack Nicholson.

Quit acting class to become a Movie Star.

Jack Rollins & Woody.

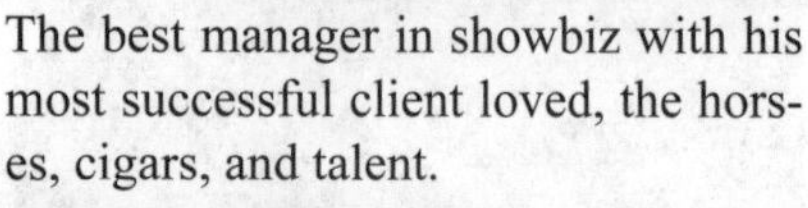

The best manager in showbiz with his most successful client loved, the horses, cigars, and talent.

Christopher Barbour

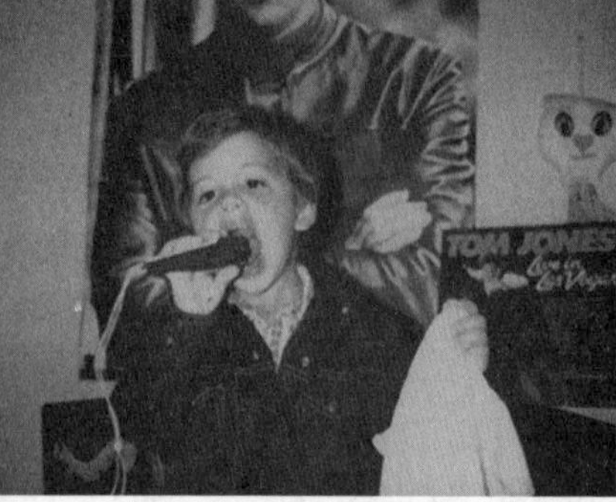

As a child our son had the talent of Tom Jones,and the golf swing of Bobby Jones; as an adult he's a gentle genius who is way ahead of any Joneses!

David Lipsi

My computer and graphics genius who brings my work to life … and you!

TELEVISION

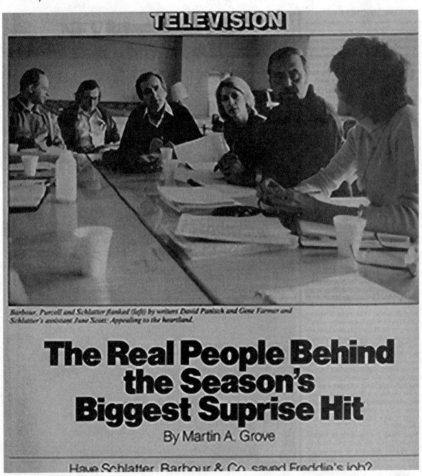

Barbour, Purcell and Schlatter flanked (left) by writers David Panich and Gene Farmer and Schlatter's assistant June Scott: Appealing to the heartland.

The Real People Behind the Season's Biggest Suprise Hit

By Martin A. Grove

Have Schlatter, Barbour & Co. saved Freddie's job?

LA Magazine pic.

George Schlatter, like a Hitchcock villain, used his wit and charm to get closer to his victims.

F R A N K   S I N A T R A

July 26, 1978

Dear John:

Because of preparing for the week in Wasserman's backyard, I just got around to hearing the LP... I liked most of the material and particularly the tenor of your delivery.

1) I can understand every single word. (Thank God)

2) It's nice and salty.

You ain't a Henny Youngman, but you're all mine.

I will be in touch during the two weeks I'm in L.A., I have a thought regarding you and me.

Barbara sends you love and so do I.

Francis Albert

FS:d

Mr. John Barbour
4254 Forman Avenue
Toluca Lake, Calif. 91602

Sinatra's Letter.
Just getting his letter was enough for me, but not for him.

GEORGE SCHLATTER PRODUCTIONS ©

8321 BEVERLY BOULEVARD
LOS ANGELES, CALIFORNIA 90048
(213) 655-1400

March 28, 1980

Sarita Barbour
4254 Forman Ave.
Toluca Lake, Ca.
91602

Dear Sarita,

You were so very sweet to think of me and present me with the beautiful "#1" necklace, and I want you to know that I wear it every day. Not only do I wear it because I like it (make that "love it"), but it reminds me of what your husband said when we first started this show: "We'll be number one!" That was last year...and look where we are now!

He's terrific, and so are you, and I love you both. Thanks again so very much for the necklace.

Love,

George

Schlatter's Thank you note.

George thanked Sarita for the '#1' necklace, and me for 'Real People.'

Postscript poem.

Is it possible that the destiny of our lives is not in our hands alone?
Rather that the paths we take are in other hands totally unknown.
In my life my perfect plans for perfect dreams often fell totally apart;
Next would appear an opened door that would accidentally touch my heart.
And through it I would go anxious to see where it would eventually lead.
Curiously this path gave me not what I wanted, but what I did need.
Love magically came along, as did fame and riches which went away.
And I became richer because more doors opened and the Love did stay.
Reason does not answer this; our struggles the Gods they totally amuse.
Knowing this I thank them for my magic life, and more for my magic Muse!

John Barbour

THE AMERICAN MEDIA

The 2nd Assassination of President John F. Kennedy

The Jim Garrison Tapes: Part 2

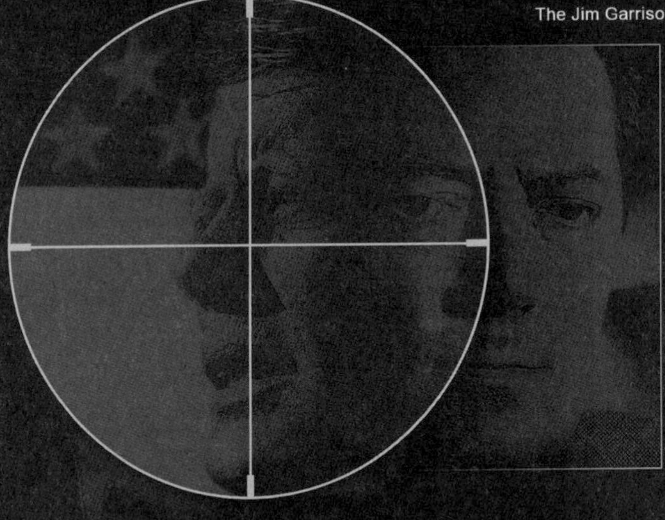

the

NEW YORK POST

Reader's Digest

The Washington Post

CBS NEWS

USA TODAY

Google

The New York Times

AP Associated Press

Newsweek

The Boston Globe

Los Angeles Times

- A John Barbour Film -

John Barbour's World | The "Godfa

JOHN BARBOUR'S WORLD

Home About John EPK  

About John

John Barbour changed the face of American television as the creator, producer, principal writer, and co-host of Real People, television's first reality show. He is a five-time Emmy award winner, a storied actor and performer, a joke and script writer, and entertainment professional across genres.

Read more...

The American Media & the 2nd Assassination of President John F. Kennedy

Tracing the history of mainstream media corruption how, where, and when it began. Revolving around the investigation by New Orleans District Attorney, Jim Garrison into the assassination of President John F. Kennedy, the film exposes how some in the media aided the killers before Dallas and how all protected them after Dallas. Directed, produced and narrated by John Barbour the godfather of reality TV, actor, comedian, television host, producer, director, writer and the only performer in television to win Emmys for both entertainment and news shows!

Available on iTunes, Amazon, & Vimeo

Johns Autobiogrraphy

YOUR MOTHER'S NOT A VIRGIN!
The bumpy life and times of the Canadian dropout who changed the face of American TV!

In his highly entertaining deeply informative autobiography you will indeed discover..what a storyteller. And what amazing stories!

Available at Trine Day, Book Depository, and Amazon.

John's YouTube Podcast

John's YouTube Channel

Files Release page

Watch Free On YouTube

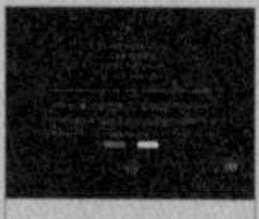

American Media... Trailer

Dr. Mary's Monkey

How the Unsolved Murder of a Doctor, a Secret Laboratory in New Orleans and Cancer-Causing Monkey Viruses are Linked to Lee Harvey Oswald, the JFK Assassination and Emerging Global Epidemics

BY EDWARD T. HASLAM, FOREWORD BY JIM MARRS

Evidence of top-secret medical experiments and cover-ups of clinical blunders

The 1964 murder of a nationally known cancer researcher sets the stage for this gripping exposé of medical professionals enmeshed in covert government operations over the course of three decades. Following a trail of police records, FBI files, cancer statistics, and medical journals, thisscontaminated polio vaccine, the genesis of the AIDS virus, and biological weapon research using infected monkeys.

Softcover: **$19.95** (ISBN: 9781634240307) • 432 pages • Size: 5 1/2 x 8 1/2

Hardcover: **$24.95** (ISBN: 9781937584597)

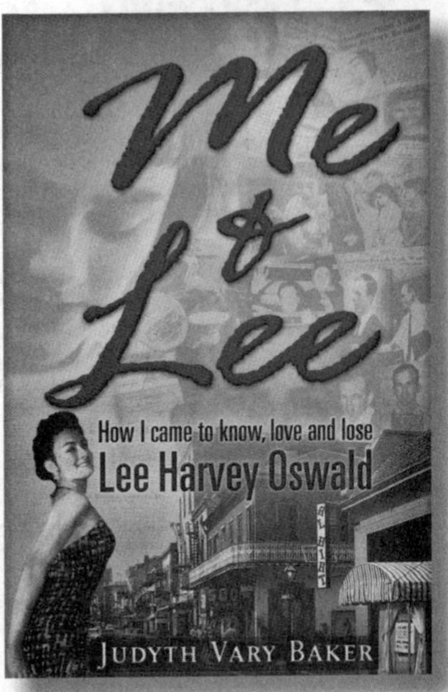

Me & Lee

How I Came to Know, Love and Lose Lee Harvey Oswald

BY JUDYTH VARY BAKER

FOREWORD BY EDWARD T. HASLAM

JUDYTH VARY WAS ONCE A PROMISING science student who dreamed of finding a cure for cancer; this exposé is her account of how she strayed from a path of mainstream scholarship at the University of Florida to a life of espionage in New Orleans with Lee Harvey Oswald. In her narrative she offers extensive documentation on how she came to be a cancer expert at such a young age, the personalities who urged her to relocate to New Orleans, and what lead to her involvement in the development of a biological weapon that Oswald was to smuggle into Cuba to eliminate Fidel Castro. Details on what she knew of Kennedy's impending assassination, her conversations with Oswald as late as two days before the killing, and her belief that Oswald was a deep-cover intelligence agent who was framed for an assassination he was actually trying to prevent, are also revealed.

JUDYTH VARY BAKER is a teacher, and artist. Edward T. Haslam is the author of *Dr. Mary's Monkey*.

Hardcover • $24.95 • Softrcover • $21.95 ISBN 9780979988677 / 978-1936296378 • 608 Pages

The Inheritance

Poisoned Fruit of JFK's Assassination

by Christopher & Michelle Fulton

How One Man's Custody of Bobby Kennedy's Hidden Evidence Changed Our Past and Continues to Shape Our Future...

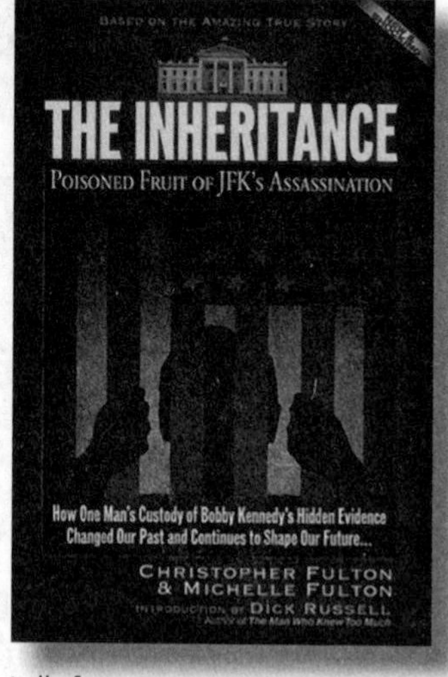

Bobby Kennedy quietly fought with the United States Government to keep control over key evidence in his brother's murder. He then used that secret evidence to prevent World War III. In the mid-1990s following the death of Evelyn Lincoln, President Kennedy's personal secretary, that evidence transferred into the hands of Christopher Fulton.

The incredible weight of Christopher's bequest crossed his fate with the Russian Government, President Ronald Reagan, the Clinton White House, future President Donald Trump, the U.S. Justice Department, the Secret Service, and the Kennedy family themselves. Christopher was obligated to expose a deeply hidden past to the world, which made him a threat to the national security state and their plans for America's future.

Christopher's roller coaster ride of discovery intertwines the JFK legacy and tragedy with his own ... and indeed with the fate of America itself. *The Inheritance* reveals the true intentions of Bobby Kennedy and Evelyn Lincoln, as well as Christopher's secret pact with John F. Kennedy Jr. This history must be uncovered in order for us to understand what is happening today.

Although this is Christopher Fulton's story, it is really about all of us.

CHRISTOPHER FULTON was born in 1965, just outside Washington, D.C., into a family with rich military history. Christopher rose to the top of the high-rise construction industry in Vancouver, British Columbia where, at age 33, during the height of his success, he was extradited and spent years in prison for his refusal to turn over possession of physical evidence in JFK's assassination. MICHELLE FULTON was born in Vancouver, Canada.

Softcover • **$24.95** • ISBN 9781634242172 • 528 Pages

Survivor's Guilt

The Secret Service and the Failure to Protect President Kennedy

by Vincent Michael Palamara

The actions and inactions of the Secret Service before, during, and after the Kennedy assassination

Painstakingly researched by an authority on the history of the Secret Service and based on primary, firsthand accounts from more than 80 former agents, White House aides, and family members, this is the definitive account of what went wrong with John F. Kennedy's security detail on the day he was assassinated.

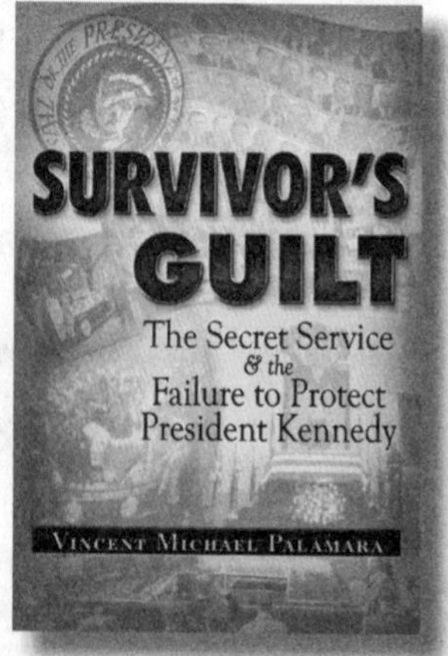

The work provides a detailed look at how JFK could and should have been protected and debunks numerous fraudulent notions that persist about the day in question, including that JFK ordered agents off the rear of his limousine; demanded the removal of the bubble top that covered the vehicle; and was difficult to protect and somehow, directly or indirectly, made his own tragic death easier for an assassin or assassins. This book also thoroughly investigates the threats on the president's life before traveling to Texas; the presence of unauthorized Secret Service agents in Dealey Plaza, the site of the assassination; the failure of the Secret Service in monitoring and securing the surrounding buildings, overhangs, and rooftops; and the surprising conspiratorial beliefs of several former agents.

Vincent Michael Palamara is an expert on the history of the Secret Service. He has appeared on the History Channel, C-SPAN, and numerous newspapers and journals, and his original research materials are stored in the National Archives. He lives in Pittsburgh, Pennsylvania.

Softcover • **$24.95** • ISBN 9781937584603 • 492 Pages

In the Eye of History

Disclosures in the JFK Assassination Medical Evidence

Second Edition

by William Matson Law

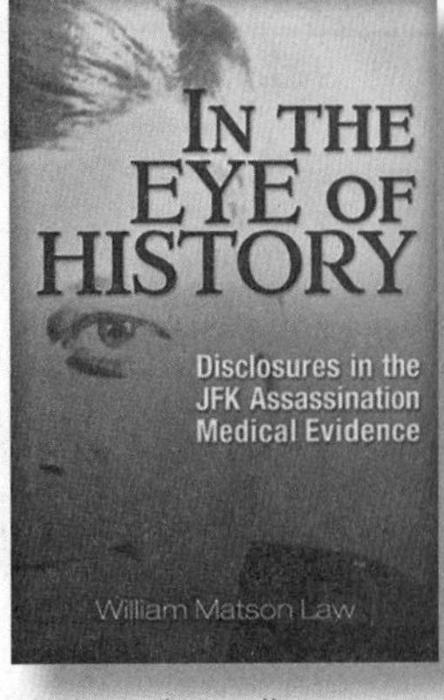

An oral history of the JFK autopsy

Anyone interested in the greatest mystery of the 20th century will benefit from the historic perspective of the attendees of President Kennedy's autopsy. For the first time in their own words these witnesses to history give firsthand accounts of what took place in the autopsy morgue at Bethesda, Maryland, on the night on November 22, 1963. Author William Matson Law set out on a personal quest to reach an understanding of the circumstances underpinning the assassination of John F. Kennedy. His investigation led him to the autopsy on the president's body at the National Naval Medical Center. In the Eye of History comprises conversations with eight individuals who agreed to talk: Dennis David, Paul O'Connor, James Jenkins, Jerrol Custer, Harold Rydberg, Saundra Spencer, and ex-FBI Special Agents James Sibert and Frances O'Neill. These eyewitnesses relate their stories comprehensively, and Law allows them to tell it as they remember it without attempting to fit any pro- or anticonspiracy agenda. The book also features a DVD featuring these firsthand interviews. Comes with DVD.

Softcover: **$29.95** (ISBN: 9781634240468) • 514 pages • Size: 6 x 9

JFK from Parkland to Bethesda

The Ultimate Kennedy Assassination Compendium

by Vincent Palamara

An all-in-one resource containing more than 15 years of research on the JFK assassination

A map through the jungle of statements, testimony, allegations, and theories relating to the assassination of John F. Kennedy, this compendium gives readers an all-in-one resource for facts from this intriguing slice of history. The book, which took more than 15 years to research and write, includes details on all of the most important aspects of the case, including old and new medical evidence from primary and secondary sources. JFK: From Parkland to Bethesda tackles the hard evidence of conspiracy and cover-up and presents a mass of sources and materials, making it an invaluable reference for anyone with interest in the President Kennedy and his assassination in 1963.

Softcover: **$19.95** (ISBN: 9781634240277) • 242 pages • Size: 6 x 9

The Polka Dot File on the Robert F. Kennedy Killing

Paris Peace Talks connection

by Fernando Faura

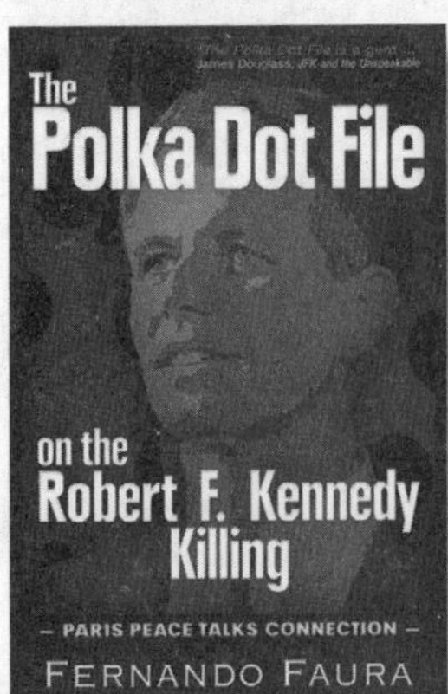

"The Polka Dot File is a gem in the field of RFK assassination research. Read it and learn."

—Jim Douglass, author, *JFK and the Unspeakable*

The Polka Dot File on the Robert F. Kennedy Killing describes the day-to-day chase for the mystery woman in the polka-dot dress. The book comments on but does not dwell on the police investigation, and reads like a detective thriller instead of an academic analysis of the investigation. It incorporates actual tapes made by an important witness, and introduces the testimony of witnesses not covered in other books and it is a new take on the assassination and the motives for it introduces a new theory for the reasons behind the assassination. Original and highly personal, it reaches a startling and different conclusion not exposed by other books.

Fernando Faura graduated cum laude with a degree in journalism from the California State University. In 1967 he joined *The Hollywood Citizens News.* Fernando has won awards from the Press Club, the National Newspaper Publishers Association, and was nominated for a Pulitzer Prize.

Softcover: **$24.95** (ISBN: 9781634240598) • 248 pages • Size: 6 x 9

From an Office Building with a High-Powered Rifle

A report to the public from an FBI agent involved in the official JFK assassination investigation

by Don Adams

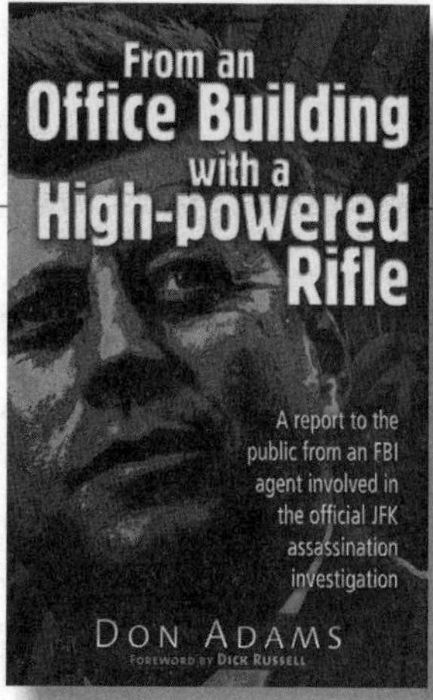

An insider's look at the mysteries behind the death of President Kennedy

The personal and professional story of a former FBI agent, this is the journey Don Adams has taken over the past 50 years that has connected him to the assassination of the 35th president of the United States. On November 13, 1963, Adams was given a priority assignment to investigate Joseph Milteer, a man who had made threats to assassinate the president. Two weeks later John F. Kennedy was dead, and Agent Adams was instructed to locate and question Milteer. Adams, however, was only allowed to ask the suspect five specific questions before being told to release him. He was puzzled by the bizarre orders but thought nothing more of it until years later when he read a report that stated that not only had Joseph Milteer made threats against the president, but also that he claimed Kennedy would be killed from an office building with a high-powered rifle. Since that time, Adams has compiled evidence and research from every avenue available to him, including his experiences in Georgia and Dallas FBI offices, to produce this compelling investigation that may just raise more questions than answers.

Don Adams is a former FBI agent who participated in the investigation of the assassination of John F. Kennedy. He is the author of numerous articles on the subject and is considered a respected authority on the topic. He lives in Akron, Ohio.

Softcover • **$24.95** • ISBN 9781936296866 • 236 Pages

Betrayal

A JFK Honor Guard Speaks

by Hugh Clark

with William Matson Law

The amazing story that William Law has documented with his historical interviews helps us to understanding our true history. This compelling information shreds the official narrative.In 2015, Law and fellow researcher Phil Singer got together the medical corpsman, who had been present at Bethesda Naval Hospital for President Kennedy's autopsy with some of the official honor guard, who had delivered the president's coffin. What happened next was extraordinary. The medical corpsmen told the honor guards that they had actually received the president's body almost a half-hour before the honor guard got there. The honor guard couldn't believe this. They had met the president's plane at Andrews, taken possession of his casket and shadowed it all the way to Bethesda. The two sides almost broke into fisticuffs, accusing the other of untruths. Once it was sifted out, and both sides came to the understanding that each was telling their own truths of their experience that fateful day, the feelings of betrayal experienced by the honor guards was deep and profound.

Hugh Clark was a member of the honor guard that took President Kennedy's body to Arlington Cemetery for burial. He was an investigator for the United Nations. After Hugh left the service he became a New York City detective and held that position for 22 years.

William Matson Law has been researching the Kennedy assassination for over 25 years. Results of that research have appeared in more than 30 books, including Douglas Horne's magnum opus Inside the Assassination Records Review Board. Law is the author of In the Eye of History and is working on a book about the murder of Robert F. Kennedy with the working title: Shadows and Light. He lives with his family in Central Oregon.

Softcover • **$19.95** • ISBN 9781634240932 • 144 Pages

Silent Coup

The Removal of a President

by Len Colodny & Robert Gettlin

25th Anniversay Edition – Includes Updates

Foreword by Roger Morris

This is the true story of betrayal at the nation's highest level. Unfolding with the suspenseful pace of a le Carre spy thriller, it reveals the personal motives and secret political goals that combined to cause the Watergate break-in and destroy Richard Nixon. Investigator Len Colodny and journalist Robert Gettlin relentlessly pursued the people who brought down the president. Their revelations shocked the world and forever changed our understanding of politics, of journalism, and of Washington behind closed doors. Dismantling decades of lies, *Silent Coup* tells the truth.

Len Colodny is a journalist. In 1992 he co-wrote with Robert Gettlin: *Silent Coup: The Removal Of Richard Nixon*. In the book the authors claim that John Dean ordered the Watergate break-in because he knew that a call-girl ring was operating out of the Democratic headquarters. The authors also argued that Alexander Haig was not Deep Throat but was a key source for Bob Woodward, who had briefed Haig at theWhite House in 1969 and 1970.

Softcover • **$24.95** • ISBN 9781634240536 • 520 Pages

Bond of Secrecy

My Life with CIA Spy and Watergate Conspirator E. Howard Hunt

by St. John Hunt

Foreword by Jesse Ventura

A father's last confession to his son about the CIA, Watergate, and the plot to assassinate President John F. Kennedy, this is the remarkable true story of St. John Hunt and his father E. Howard Hunt, the infamous Watergate burglar and CIA spymaster. In Howard Hunt's near-death confession to his son St. John, he revealed that key figures in the CIA were responsible for the plot to assassinate JFK in Dallas, and that Hunt himself was approached by the plotters, among whom included the CIA's David Atlee Phillips, Cord Meyer, Jr., and William Harvey, as well as future Watergate burglar Frank Sturgis. An incredible true story told from an inside, authoritative source, this is also a personal account of a uniquely dysfunctional American family caught up in two of the biggest political scandals of the 20th century.

Softcover • **$24.95** • ISBN 978-1936296835 • 192 Pages

Dorothy

The Murder of E. Howard Hunt's Wife – watergate's Darkest Secret

by St. John Hunt

Foreword by Roger Stone

Dorothy Hunt, "An Amoral and Dangerous Woman" tells the life story of ex-CIA agent Dorothy Hunt, who married Watergate mastermind and confessed contributor to the assassination of JFK. The book chronicles her rise in the intelligence field after World War II, as well as her experiences in Shanghai, Calcutta, Mexico, and Washington, DC. It reveals her war with President Nixon and asserts that she was killed by the CIA in the crash of Flight 553. Written by the only person who was privy to the behind-the-scenes details of the Hunt family during Watergate, this book sheds light on a dark secret of the scandal.

Softcover • **$24.95** • ISBN 978-1634240376 • 192 Pages

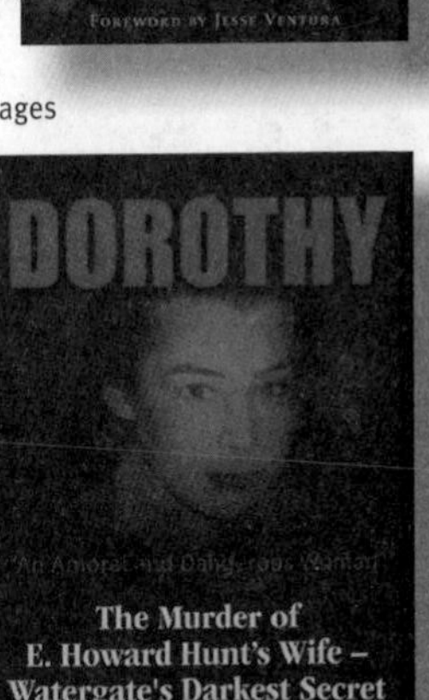

Saint John Hunt is an author, a musician, and the son of the infamous and legendary CIA covert operative and author, E. Howard Hunt. Saint John spent more than ten years searching for the truth about his father's involvement in JFK's death, resulting in his first book Bond of Secrecy. In his second book, Dorothy, he explored his mother's life as a CIA spy and her war with Nixon, which resulted in her murder. He lives in south Florida.